MANDATE FOR LEADERSHIP IV

Turning Ideas Into Actions

Edited by
Stuart M. Butler
and
Kim R. Holmes

The Heritage Foundation

VISIT THE HERITAGE FOUNDATION'S INTERNET SITE AT
http://www.heritage.org

The Heritage Foundation's World Wide Web site offers a library of public policy information for policymakers, students of government, and activists alike. Visitors will find the most recent Heritage publications—including excerpts from *Mandate for Leadership IV*; *Issues '96*, the handbook for conservative candidates of all parties seeking national office; and *Why America Needs a Tax Cut*, a compilation of Heritage analyses on tax reform—as well as hundreds of other publications on current issues. Samples of current articles in The Heritage Foundation's flagship publication, *Policy Review: The Journal of American Citizenship*, are available on line, and subscription information is readily available. By bookmarking the Heritage Web site and visiting it daily for updates, those who seek more responsible government will stay informed about policies that work on the federal, state, and local level.

ISBN 0-89195-064-8 (cloth)
ISBN 0-89195-065-6 (paper)
Copyright © 1997 by The Heritage Foundation
214 Massachusetts Avenue, N.E.
Washington, D.C. 20002-4999
(202) 546-4400
http://www.heritage.org

TABLE
OF CONTENTS

Putting U.S. Foreign and Defense Policies into Practice

ACKNOWLEDGMENTS

Mandate for Leadership IV: Turning Ideas Into Actions is the product not only of the authors of its chapters, but also of dozens of other individuals who helped to refine its ideas and turn them into a polished product. In addition to these authors, and the many experts who participated in task forces and working groups to assist them, the editors wish to thank the Heritage team that polished the manuscript and prepared it for publication. In the Research Department, we thank managing editor Janice A. Smith, who worked closely with each author—and with us—to edit each chapter, and Daniel Hickey, Melinda Schriver, Sarah Ross, Yvette Campos, Katherine A. Lawson, James H. St. Jean, and John T. Nixon who assisted her in various capacities. In the Heritage Production Department, we thank the team under production manager Ann Klucsarits: William T. Poole and James V. Rutherford, who were responsible for the copyediting; Michelle Fulton Smith, who handled chapter layout and design; and Thomas J. Timmons, who designed and prepared the charts, tables, and maps. We would also like to thank senior editor Richard Odermatt for his review and oversight. The cover for *Mandate for Leadership IV: Turning Ideas Into Actions* was designed by The Great American Art Co.

—*Stuart M. Butler and*
Kim R. Holmes

ABOUT
THE AUTHORS

Angela M. Antonelli is Deputy Director of the Roe Institute for Economic Policy Studies at The Heritage Foundation. She coordinates research on budget, tax, regulatory, labor, and environmental policy. A former adviser to Vice President Dan Quayle's Council on Competitiveness, Antonelli served as an analyst and Assistant Branch Chief in the White House Office of Management and Budget from 1989 to 1993, with responsibility for reviewing regulations developed by the U.S. Departments of Health and Human Services, Labor, Treasury, and Housing and Urban Development. She also has experience as a health care industry consultant. Antonelli holds a B.A. degree in political economy from Cornell University and earned an M.P.A. degree in public affairs from Princeton University.

John S. Barry is Policy Analyst at The Heritage Foundation for issues relating to federal fiscal and regulatory policies affecting the economy at the national, community, and household levels. He specializes in financial sector regulatory policy, determining the effect regulation has on the efficient delivery of financial products to American consumers and businesses. A former Heritage Research Assistant, Barry also has written on federal tax and budget issues. He holds a B.A. degree with honors in economics and government from the University of Notre Dame and is pursuing graduate studies in economics at George Mason University.

Stuart M. Butler is Vice President and Director of Domestic Policy Studies and the Roe Institute for Economic Policy Studies at The Heritage Foundation. A nationally recognized specialist on social and economic issues, Butler has co-authored the Heritage Consumer Choice Health Plan and *Out of the Poverty Trap: A Conservative Strategy for Welfare Reform.* He authored *Enterprise Zones: Greenlining the Inner Cities* and *Privatizing Federal Spending.* He also serves as an Adjunct Fellow at the National Center for Neighborhood Enterprise. Dr. Butler earned a B.A. degree in physics and mathematics, an M.A. degree in economics, and a Ph.D. degree in American economic history from St. Andrews University in Scotland.

Rhett DeHart is Special Counsel to Edwin Meese III at The Heritage Foundation. His areas of specialty include federalism, the federal judiciary, criminal law and procedure, and constitutional law. DeHart has extensive experience in the state legislative process, having served as a clerk of court in South Carolina and a law clerk to the South Carolina House Judiciary Committee, where he specialized in criminal and constitutional law issues. DeHart earned his B.A. degree in international studies and his J.D. degree from the University of South Carolina.

Donald J. Devine is an Adjunct Scholar at The Heritage Foundation and a former Director of the U.S. Office of Personnel Management from 1981 to 1985. Devine authored *Reagan's Terrible Swift Sword: Reforming and Controlling the Federal Bureaucracy* and the recently released *Restoring the Tenth Amendment.* He is a columnist for *The Washington Times*, an adjunct scholar at the American Conservative Union, and a Washington policy and management consultant.

John Hillen is Policy Analyst for Defense and National Security Policy at The Heritage Foundation. An expert on U.S. military operations and international peacekeeping missions, he specializes in threat assessment, alliance structure, conventional force planning, and combat readiness issues. He is a decorated veteran of the Persian Gulf War, a former Regular Army Officer who is active in the U.S. Army Reserve. He has served as a Research Scholar at the University of Oxford in England, where he is pursuing a doctorate in international relations. Hillen holds an M.A. degree in War Studies from Kings College in London. He authored *Blue Helmets in War and Peace* and has published numerous articles on military affairs and international security.

Kim R. Holmes is Vice President and Director of Foreign Policy and Defense Studies at The Heritage Foundation. Holmes is one of Washington's foremost authorities on foreign policy and the challenges facing the United States in what he calls the Age of Chaos. He is the principal architect of The Heritage Foundation's influential foreign policy publication, *Restoring American Leadership: A U.S. Foreign and Defense Policy Blueprint*, which addresses the country's changing strategic global interests in the post–Cold War world. Dr. Holmes earned his B.A. degree from Florida Technological University (now the University of South Florida) and his M.A. and Ph.D. degrees in history from Georgetown University.

Bryan T. Johnson is Policy Analyst for International Economic Affairs at The Heritage Foundation and an expert on U.S. foreign aid and trade policy. He is co-author of The Heritage Foundation's annual *Index of Economic Freedom*, an influential comparative survey measuring the level of economic freedom in 150 countries. Johnson previously served as Senior Editor and Writer at The Whalen Co., and conducted research at Smick Medley International, Inc. He holds a B.A. degree from the University of Tampa.

David Mason is Vice President for Government Relations at The Heritage Foundation and a leading authority on national politics and congressional reform. He is the former Director of The Heritage Foundation's U.S. Congress Assessment Project, which studied institutional problems facing Congress. Mason was an adviser to House Republicans during the framing of the Contract With America. He directed publication of the Heritage book, *The Ruling Class: Inside the Imperial Congress*. A former Deputy Assistant Secretary of Defense, Mason also served as Staff Director to then-House Minority Whip Representative Trent Lott (R-MS) and in a variety of positions for national, state, and local political campaigns. He holds a B.A. degree from Claremont McKenna College.

Edwin Meese III is the Ronald Reagan Fellow in Public Policy at The Heritage Foundation and a former U.S. Attorney General. Meese was an adviser to President Reagan; as Chairman of the Domestic Policy Council and the National Drug Policy Board and as a member of the National Security Council, he played a key role in the development and execution of domestic and foreign policy. During the 1970s, Meese was Director of the Center for Criminal Justice Policy and Management and Professor of Law at the University of San Diego. He had served as Chief of Staff for then-Governor Reagan and was a local prosecutor in California. Meese is a Distinguished Visiting Fellow at the Hoover Institution, Stanford

University, and a Distinguished Senior Fellow at The Institute of United States Studies, University of London. Meese earned his B.A. degree from Yale University and his J.D. degree from the University of California at Berkeley.

Adam Meyerson is Vice President for Educational Affairs and Editor of *Policy Review: The Journal of American Citizenship* at The Heritage Foundation. Meyerson supervises Heritage's academic programs, including the Bradley Fellows program, the Henry Salvatori Center for the Appreciation of the Founding Fathers, and Heritage lectures and seminars. Meyerson is a former editorial writer with *The Wall Street Journal* and managing editor of *The American Spectator*. He is co-editor of *The Wall Street Journal on Management* (Dow Jones: Irwin). He earned his B.A. degree from Yale University and has undertaken doctoral studies at the Harvard University Graduate School of Business.

Daniel J. Mitchell is the McKenna Senior Fellow in Political Economy and chief expert on tax policy and related economic issues at The Heritage Foundation. In 1995, Mitchell served as a Staff Economist for the National Commission on Tax Reform and Economic Growth. A former Director of Tax and Budget Policy at Citizens for a Sound Economy, Mitchell served on President Bush's Independent Agencies Transition Team in 1989, analyzing the Federal Reserve System. Mitchell and his wife, Nancy, co-host the popular public affairs show, "Mitchells in the Morning," on NET–The Political News Talk Network. He has served as an economist examining budgetary and tax matters for former Senator Robert Packwood (R-OR), the ranking minority member of the Senate Finance Committee. Mitchell holds an M.A. degree in economics from the University of Georgia and is a Ph.D. candidate in economics at George Mason University.

Robert E. Moffit is Deputy Director for Domestic Policy Studies at The Heritage Foundation. He specializes in health care policy and coordinates Heritage's research on poverty, welfare, crime, education, and family issues. Moffit is a 17-year veteran of Washington policymaking—he is a former Deputy Assistant Secretary at the U.S. Department of Health and Human Services, and senior official at the Office of Personnel Management. Dr. Moffit earned his B.A. degree from LaSalle University and his M.A. and Ph.D. degrees in political science from the University of Arizona.

Thomas Moore is Deputy Director for Foreign and Defense Policy Studies at The Heritage Foundation. He is a former professional staff member on the Senate Armed Services Committee and is well versed in all areas of U.S. foreign and defense policy, including U.S. global alliances, ballistic missile defense, arms control, defense spending, and the appropriate use of the military. Moore served two years in the Department of Defense and as legislative assistant for defense and foreign policy to former Senator Malcolm Wallop (R-WY). An officer in the U.S. Army Reserve, Armor Branch, Moore received an honorable discharge as a Major in 1993. A graduate of The Citadel, Moore studied in France and earned an M.A. degree in national security affairs from Georgetown University.

Robert P. O'Quinn is Policy Analyst for trade and Asian economies at The Heritage Foundation, and specializes in international trade and investment issues, the World Trade Organization, and the Asia–Pacific Economic Cooperation forum. He is one of Washington's foremost authorities on the economies of Japan, Australia, New Zealand, and Singapore. O'Quinn has served as an economist for the Federal Reserve System's Board of Governors and the Federal Trade Commission. He received his B.A. and M.B.A. degrees from the University of Georgia.

James Phillips is Senior Policy Analyst for Middle Eastern Affairs at The Heritage Foundation. He has nearly two decades of experience examining political and security issues in the Middle East and Persian Gulf region and serves on the Board of Editors of the *Middle East Quarterly*. A former Research Fellow at the Congressional Research Service and the East–West Center, Phillips earned a B.A. from Brown University and M.A. and M.A.L.D. degrees in international security studies from the Fletcher School of Law and Diplomacy at Tufts University.

James Przystup is Director of the Asian Studies Center at The Heritage Foundation and a specialist on U.S.–Japan and U.S.–China relations. He is a former Director of Planning for Asia-Pacific Security Strategy for the Department of Defense. Przystup has served on the State Department's policy planning staff and as Deputy Director of the Presidential Commission on U.S.–Japan Relations. He was also IBM's Manager for Governmental Programs for the Asia-Pacific region. Dr. Przystup holds an M.A. degree in international relations and a Ph.D. degree in diplomatic history from the University of Chicago. He also has served on the law faculty of Keio University in Tokyo, Japan.

Brett D. Schaefer is Jay Kingham Fellow in International Regulatory Affairs at The Heritage Foundation. His work examines such issues as intellectual property rights, international economic treaties and agreements, foreign aid, and the proper role of international organizations like the United Nations and the U.S. role within them. He previously served as a Research Assistant in The Heritage Foundation's Foreign and Defense Policy Studies department. Schaefer received a bachelor's degree in anthropology and archeology from Florida State University and earned his M.A. degree in international development and economics from American University.

Douglas Seay is Director of the Project on Federalism and the States at The Heritage Foundation. He is an authority on federalism, the 10th Amendment, and state–federal relations. Seay coordinates Heritage's efforts to help states take back power and responsibility from the federal government. He works closely with the country's governors to ensure their voices are heard on public policy matters affecting the states. A former Deputy Director of Foreign and Defense Policy Studies for Heritage, he previously held a fellowship at Harvard University's Center for Science and International Affairs and taught international relations at Brown University. Seay is a graduate of Georgetown University's School of Foreign Service and a former Foreign Service Officer at the U.S. Department of State.

Thomas P. Sheehy is currently Legislative Director for Representative Edward Royce (R-CA). As The Heritage Foundation's former Jay Kingham Fellow in International Regulatory Affairs, Sheehy's expertise covered issues relating to the regulatory aspects of international trade, intellectual property rights, the United Nations, Africa, and development aid. Sheehy co-authored the 1995 and 1996 editions of Heritage's *Index of Economic Freedom*. Sheehy earned his M.A. degree in foreign affairs at the University of Virginia.

Baker Spring is Senior Defense Policy Analyst at The Heritage Foundation. He is a former adviser on defense and foreign policy issues to two U.S. Senators. Spring is an expert on defense policy and budget issues as well as arms control, with special expertise on missile defense and chemical and biological warfare policy. A graduate of Washington and Lee

University, Spring received his M.A. degree in national security studies from Georgetown University.

John Sweeney is Policy Analyst on Latin America and Trade Policy at The Heritage Foundation. His work examines trade issues throughout the Americas, with special emphasis on Mexico, Brazil, Argentina, Chile, Venezuela, Colombia, and Peru. His specialty covers such international issues as NAFTA, drug trafficking, transnational organized crime, intellectual property, international finance, energy, and technology. A resident of Latin America for 33 years, Sweeney has been a newsletter publisher, political speechwriter, and business consultant in that region. He has reported on Latin American affairs for the *Journal of Commerce, Business Week, Newsweek,* and *The Toronto Globe and Mail.* Sweeney holds a B.A. degree in Latin American studies from Kent State University in Ohio.

Adam Thierer is the Alex C. Walker Fellow in Economic Policy at The Heritage Foundation. A leading advocate of telecommunications deregulation, Thierer's research examines how government regulations hinder American business and global competitiveness. His work focuses on communications policy, electricity regulation, antitrust law, tort reform, risk assessment of environmental regulation, and land privatization issues. He holds a B.A. degree in journalism and political science from Indiana University and an M.A. in international business management from the University of Maryland.

Ronald D. Utt is Senior Fellow in Economics at The Heritage Foundation. His research focuses on housing, transportation, federal budgetary matters, government waste and fraud, and privatization issues. The former "Privatization Czar" in the Reagan Administration's Office of Management and Budget, Utt has been a consultant on economic, trade, and privatization issues to government officials in such countries as Russia, Bulgaria, and Estonia. He has served as Executive Vice President of the National Chamber Foundation—the research and education division of the U.S. Chamber of Commerce. Dr. Utt holds a B.A. degree in business administration from Penn State University and a Ph.D. degree in economics from Indiana University.

INTRODUCTION

Stuart M. Butler and Kim R. Holmes

As Americans contemplate a new millennium, their government must take the steps needed to ensure that the country enters this new era on the soundest possible footing: Its deep-seated problems must be tackled and opportunities for improvement exploited. For America to be secure, its role in the world must be clarified and its defenses organized accordingly. For the nation's economy to perform at its peak, the tax and regulatory systems must be overhauled. For younger generations of Americans to be confident about their security in retirement in the next century, the Medicare and Social Security systems must be modernized and strengthened.

These and other tasks will require urgent and decisive action by the nation's leaders. For Congress and conservative policymakers to take such action, however, they must first understand the verdict delivered in the last election and then study the lessons learned thus far about the workings of the political system.

While the results of the November 1996 election seem to signify another period of divided government for America, they more importantly underscore the deeply conservative mood of the country. President Clinton won re-election not just because he was able to capitalize on the apparent soundness of the economy, but because he was able to project his Administration as the guardian of an ethereal and uncomplicated conservatism. In the last two years, he advocated such things as "ending welfare as we know it," moving toward a balanced budget, cracking down on crime, a seeming toughness and resolve abroad, a tax cut for the middle class, the strengthening of the family, and a strong national defense. He even declared that the "era of big government is over." All of these are conservative themes, of course, but Clinton's comfortable conservatism involves no hard choices and no determined recognition of the limits and proper role of the federal government.

Control of Congress also remained unchanged following the election. Americans re-elected a House and Senate led by a group of men and women who are strongly and very visibly committed to taking the country in a conservative direction. But the Hill's version of conservatism, which formed the core themes of the last two years' legislative program, differs sharply from that of the Clinton Administration. In the last Congress, the agenda included real and decisive steps to redefine the role of the federal government. Congress passed legislation that would devolve the welfare system to the states and end the entitlement to welfare. It ended 60 years of central planning in agriculture. It ended 200 obsolete and wasteful programs. And, among other decisive steps, it sent President Clinton legislation to cut taxes on middle-class families and to modernize the Medicare program.

President Clinton was able to veto key parts of this legislative program—such as the tax cut and Medicare reform—and to win public support for these vetoes for two related reasons. First, he recognized, better than Congress did, the crucial importance of defining the terms of public debate: In each case, he cast himself as the prudent conservative protecting America from "radicals" and "extremists." And second, he meticulously and relentlessly appealed to crucial constituencies in building united opposition to the conservative agenda of the 104th Congress.

Clinton displayed counterfeit conservatism in foreign and defense policy as well—and with equally positive political results. By appearing to be in favor of a whole host of conservative foreign policy causes — from maintaining a strong national defense to being tough on Fidel Castro—the President not only neutralized any conservative criticism of his efforts in this area, but also helped to buttress the comfortable feeling that many Americans have about him as President and Commander in Chief. At the same time, however, Clinton was able to stop a number of very important conservative defense initiatives in Congress. He blocked a decision to begin deploying ballistic missile defenses; he slashed defense spending; he sent U.S. troops off to Bosnia despite strong congressional and conservative reservations; and he blocked foreign aid reform and the elimination of obsolete foreign policy agencies, such as the Agency for International Development and the Arms Control and Disarmament Agency.

But while Clinton was successful in thwarting parts of the mandate given to Congress in the 1994 election, the American people elected a Congress in 1996 that remains committed to the uncompleted agenda of the 104th Congress. For the new Congress, with its reaffirmed mandate, the task will be not so much to identify a brand new agenda as to develop a more effective strategy to implement the legislative mandate already endorsed by the American people in two elections. The strategy must include legislative initiatives designed carefully to build support for the conservative agenda, as well as tactics to explain more effectively to the American people why these legislative steps are needed.

In the tradition of previous studies in The Heritage Foundation's *Mandate for Leadership* series,[1] **Mandate for Leadership IV: Turning Ideas Into Actions** lays out a framework for implementing this strategy. Other Heritage Foundation publications, such as *Issues '96: The Candidate's Briefing Book* and *Restoring American Leadership: A U.S. Foreign and Defense Policy Blueprint*, have developed the case for the conservative domestic and foreign policy agenda. *Turning Ideas Into Actions* complements that case with the strategy for turning this agenda into reality.

Turning Ideas Into Actions assumes that the primary impetus for conservative legislative action, at least on the domestic front, will come from Capitol Hill rather than from the White House. President Clinton most likely will send Congress limited proposals with a conservative tone—such as a modest tax cut adorned with a multitude of requirements as to how families must spend the money returned to them. But the assumption is that the initiative for true tax reform and reduction must and will come from Congress. The same is true of genuine entitlement reform, or a true end to the era of big government, or the strengthening of the roles that individual states, families, and community institutions will play in reshaping America.

As always, the initiative in developing foreign and defense policy is more likely to come from the President and executive branch. But here, too, the 105th Congress—and *Turning Ideas Into Actions*—have an important role to

---

1 The three previous studies in this series are *Mandate for Leadership: Policy Management in a Conservative Administration* (1981), *Mandate for Leadership II: Continuing the Conservative Revolution* (1984), and *Mandate for Leadership III: Policy Strategies for the 1990s* (1989).

play. Through its "power of the purse," not only can this Congress ensure adequate funding for America's armed forces, but it also can cut off funding for unwise overseas peacekeeping operations that are not genuinely in the national interest. Through its oversight responsibilities, the 105th Congress can ensure that America's armed forces are respected and well-trained. In addition, Congress can hold Clinton's foreign and defense policies up to scrutiny while serving as a national forum for an alternative viewpoint. Finally, through its treaty powers, Congress has the duty to ensure that all treaties and international agreements serve the national interest. Those that do not, like the Chemical Weapons Convention or the Anti-Ballistic Missile Treaty, should be questioned. By the same token, treaties or agreements that expand free trade or enhance American security should be embraced.

For Congress to be successful in completing its agenda, it must focus on the core structural elements of conservative reform. Congress also must weigh carefully the often painful lessons of the past in seeking these reforms. That is why the chapters of *Turning Ideas Into Actions* cover the structural elements of the conservative vision of governance and reform. Reflecting the need for policymakers to understand fully the experience of the past— not just the last two years, but the last 20 years—each chapter discusses the key lessons to be learned from previous attempts at reform. The chapters then build on these lessons to lay out specific strategies to achieve the goal of government reform in 1997 and beyond, doing so in a way that will build public understanding of the need for specific changes.

In the domestic policy section, the chapters are grouped according to strategic themes. Chapter 1 addresses the legislative process itself: how best to move a legislative agenda through Congress. It presents the successes and failures not only of the last Congress, but also of earlier attempts to achieve a conservative legislative program, and draws on these lessons, which cover such issues as the budget process and the committee system, to suggest a more successful approach.

Chapter 2 through Chapter 5 explore ways to reduce the size and scope of the federal government and return the role of government to its proper level. Included in these chapters are strategies, based on the experience of almost two decades, by which Congress can successfully close or privatize agencies and programs, devolve programs to the states, and strengthen the community institutions of civil society. In each case, the lessons are used to propose new ways to achieve these objectives.

Chapters 6 and 7 deal with two federal institutions—the civil service and the judiciary—which must be reformed if legislative accomplishments are not later to be undermined. The authors explain how these institutions have thwarted change in the past and then discuss the legislative and other steps that can be taken to return them to their proper functions.

The final three domestic policy chapters address three issues that are key to achieving the conservative agenda and that have frustrated conservatives in recent years. Chapter 8 deals with the political and economic problem of middle-class entitlements and how to reform and limit these programs. Chapter 9 deals with regulation, and in particular with the steps needed to explain deregulation to the American people. Chapter 10 examines the checkered experience of the campaign to develop a fairer tax system and provides guidelines for reviving the political momentum to achieve it.

These first ten chapters are designed to provide practical advice and steps for Members of Congress and other policymakers. For example:

- Chapter 8 examines, among other things, the proposal to create a commission to resolve the crisis in Medicare. It looks back at the track record of commissions over the last 15 years, and the lessons learned about their use and effectiveness, and provides a "dos" and "don'ts" commission checklist for Medicare reform.

- Chapter 7 includes a review of past legislative actions to curb judicial activism, including recently enacted curbs on the power of federal judges to order the early release of dangerous prisoners. It then suggests specific legislative actions that could be taken to place appropriate limits in other areas where judges have overstepped their constitutional role.

The foreign and defense policy section of *Mandate for Leadership IV: Turning Ideas Into Actions* begins with three chapters describing America's proper role in the world and establishing the conservative themes and overall objectives of U.S. foreign policy for which strategies are developed in the remaining chapters. These thematic chapters describe the conservative philosophy behind the book's foreign policy strategy because where conservatives will stand on foreign and defense policy issues is not as self-evident as where they will stand on domestic policy issues. They also explain the rationale behind the positions and strategies taken in subsequent chapters.

Chapter 11 describes the proper role for America in promoting freedom around the world. It calls for the U.S. to champion free trade, free markets, and free political institutions abroad, but also discusses the limits that must be imposed on America's attempts to change the social and political systems of foreign nations, particularly when it comes to using U.S. military power. Chapter 12 examines the proper U.S. role in maintaining global security, as well as how to devise an effective strategy of "selective engagement" that avoids the extremes of isolationism or excessive foreign military intervention. Chapter 13 makes the case for an aggressive U.S. strategy to promote free trade and free market institutions around the word which not only will strengthen the American economy, but also will promote global democracy and international stability.

A second group of chapters turns the ideas or principles of national security in Chapters 11, 12, and 13 into specific actions. Chapter 14 describes how to maintain a strong national defense in a budget straitjacket. It examines some of the mistakes conservatives have made in the defense debate—such as treating national security as a budget issue—and proposes the concrete steps Congress can take to reverse the declining strength, character, and morale of U.S. armed forces. Completing the theme of national defense is Chapter 15, which examines how to plan a sound military strategy—something America has not had since the end of the Cold War. This chapter outlines in detail the steps that the Pentagon and Congress should take to devise a strategy that matches means to ends, which the Clinton Administration has not done. Topping off the national security section is Chapter 16, which is devoted to the important issue of ballistic missile defense. This chapter outlines specific measures Congress can take to defeat, once and for all, the liberal opposition to defending America from nuclear attack.

The final set of chapters covers general foreign policy issues. Chapter 17 describes strategies Congress and the Administration can implement to protect America's interests in vital regions of the world—in Europe, Russia and Eurasia, Asia, the Middle East, and Latin America. Chapter 18 examines practical steps Congress can take to bolster America's free trade agenda, to restore American leadership in international trade policy, and to get the expansion of NAFTA and other trade agreements back on track. It is followed by Chapter 19, which examines how Congress can reduce and reform the ineffective and costly foreign aid program, and by Chapter 20, which specifies how the United States should deal with and reform the United Nations.

The foreign and defense policy chapters of *Mandate for Leadership IV: Turning Ideas Into Actions* are designed to provide practical steps, based on learned experience, for Members of Congress and other policymakers to achieve these strategic objectives. For example:

- Chapter 16 examines why Congress, even with a conservative majority, has been unable to achieve a long-standing conservative goal in national defense — a decision to begin deploying an active defense against ballistic missiles. It describes how proponents of missile defense have been outmaneuvered by opponents, allowing the opposition to define the terms of the debate. The chapter explains why, instead of trying to force an unwilling Administration to deploy missile defenses, Congress should target the Anti-Ballistic Missile Treaty, the chief obstacle to deployment. The strategy suggests that Congress could first demand that the Clinton Administration submit any agreements with the Russians on the ABM Treaty to the Senate for ratification and then vote down these agreements. In this way, the ABM Treaty would become effectively "null and void."

- Chapter 19 examines why Congress failed in its efforts last year to close down the Agency for International Development, the federal government's chief bureaucracy for dispensing foreign aid. The main reason for this failure was that Congress could not get a veto-proof majority for the authorization bills that called for AID's closing. The chapter recommends that rather than target AID directly in the authorization process, Congress should seek to "starve" it by cutting its funding in appropriations bills, which are less prone to presidential veto.

Mandate for Leadership IV: Turning Ideas Into Actions has been designed uniquely for the 105th Congress. By studying these 20 chapters, policymakers will find significant ways to target their efforts more specifically and to turn the goal of reform into fruitful reality. If these strategies are put into action, America will be better for the efforts of the 105th Congress. The government of the United States will have returned to its constitutional foundation, and its proper role in defending freedom and democracy at home and abroad will have been restored.

PART I:
DOMESTIC POLICY
ISSUES

Chapter I

MOVING AN AGENDA THROUGH CONGRESS

David M. Mason

Following the 1980 elections, Ronald Reagan swept into Washington, scoring major legislative victories. He did so despite a House of Representatives formally controlled by the opposition party and with the narrowest of conservative operating majorities on key floor votes. The Senate, though nominally Republican, was on balance indifferent to Reagan's overall philosophy. Reagan's program was a huge political success despite the fact that many of his major initiatives were rejected by Congress, others were subject to substantial compromise, and still others were wholly abandoned by his own Administration.

Twelve years later, Bill Clinton forged unified partisan control of the federal government, promising to transform government in significant, even fundamental, ways. Clinton scored several early successes but lost an important portion of his economic plan (the stimulus package) and then saw the centerpiece of his legislative program, a national health care plan, crash spectacularly, ushering in the first Republican Congress in 44 years with the 1994 elections.

Speaker Newt Gingrich and his freshmen promised a revolution, and the Contract With America arguably dominated the nation's political agenda more completely than the Reagan program had. The accomplishments of the 104th Congress in spending restraint, privatization, regulatory reform,

The author would like to thank Margo Carlisle, John Cogan, Edwin Meese III, and James L. Payne for their suggestions and contributions to this chapter. The views and opinions expressed, however, are solely the responsibility of the author.

and welfare[1] exceeded those of the Reagan Administration. GOP leaders identified two-thirds of the Contract's provisions that had been signed into law by the end of the congressional session. Yet after two years, Republicans were on the political defensive, the Contract was unmentionable, and the freshman class in particular was under assault. At the same time, Clinton had accomplished a political resurrection nearly as dramatic as the 1994 rebuke of his health care agenda, a reversal accomplished in part by accepting and then claiming credit for congressional initiatives on health care, welfare, deficit reduction, and (though not enacted) tax policy.

GENERAL PRINCIPLES OF POLICY PROCESS MANAGEMENT

While the experience of politicians who come to Washington with big ideas may feel like a roller coaster ride, some discernible lessons and useful guidelines can be derived from these experiences. The most important is that a successful policy campaign involves several discrete elements: designing a policy, advancing it through the governmental process, and marketing it. These elements must be managed in coordination to make the overall effort a success. How well leaders make these various elements work together will determine the overall success of a policy program. Significant weakness at any critical point can spell disaster for the entire effort.

The first element of the policy process is conceptual: designing a program by starting with a broad vision that has been enunciated by a candidate or leader, developing the details, and coming up with the legislative language of transition rules or statutory references. This chapter will not comment extensively on the mechanics of policy development, but will comment on how and when policy development must intersect with procedural and marketing efforts. Good marketing, for instance, requires that political allies be consulted during the policy development process. The governmental process requires that good policy ideas be transformed into detailed legislative proposals, often sooner and with more difficulty than sponsors realize.

---

1 For excellent discussions of these topics, see Chapters 2, 3, 4, 8, and 9, *infra*.

The second element of the policy process involves governmental mechanics: moving a proposal through the legislative process. This element is the principal topic of this chapter with some comments on the related administrative and judicial processes. The third policy element, the marketing effort necessary for a policy to succeed, will be addressed principally in relation to the governmental process. Building public support often starts in a campaign, but too often ends there as well. Continuing efforts to build public support are essential to success in the legislative arena. They also can have a marked effect on administrative and judicial actions and, most important, will determine public acceptance of and credit for a particular political proposal.

The Need for Management of the Policy Process

While the elements of the policy process overlap in practice, they are conceptually separate, involve different skills and activities, and often are conducted by different staffs and officials. If each of the elements of the policy process is not conducted adequately and is not coordinated, the overall policy effort is likely to fail. Thus, the key test of political leadership is often the ability to manage these separate components.

Designing the perfect legislative proposal is not enough. The Clinton health care team labored mightily to create a perfect plan which failed in part because it was handled poorly in Congress and was not marketed well. Republicans fell prey to a similar mistake with their 1995 balanced budget proposal, which they believed would be successful because it included "honest" numbers from the Congressional Budget Office (CBO) and aimed at a broadly supported goal. But as with the Clinton health plan, legislative strategy and marketing efforts on behalf of the GOP budget were insufficient, allowing opponents to rally opposition and defeat the plan.

Marketing alone cannot deliver policy victories, even in the case of a dramatic election victory dominated by a single issue or set of concerns. Victors in such cases sometimes wrongly assume that the opposition will disappear simply because a candidate won a presidential race or a party won a majority in Congress. In fact, the defeated faction is likely to learn something from an election and to adapt, either by altering their counterproposals, by changing their tactics, or both. Given the lack of parliamentary-style party discipline in the U.S. Congress, minorities can transform themselves into majorities on any given issue, or may be able to block action in other ways. In 1981, for instance, Ronald Reagan's tax cut package[2] was nearly defeated in the House of Representatives because liberals, who had belittled his proposals as "voodoo economics" during the campaign, changed course and offered a competing tax cut plan of their own. The liberal plan was drawn to attract particular interest groups in a way that was difficult for the Reagan plan to match, given its emphasis on overall tax relief. In addition to a decisive election victory, a well-crafted plan, and a sound legislative strategy, the President's outstanding skills as a communicator were essential to rescuing his tax plan from political defeat.

Political marketing cannot end with an election victory, even a decisive one. Reagan and his Administration had to mount a continuing public campaign on behalf of his program to get it passed. In later years, supporters had to continue a vigorous effort to defend the tax cut against charges that it swelled the deficit and resulted in the rich getting richer and the poor poorer. The war of ideas is never over, and the advocate who flags in repeatedly outlining objectives and defending specifics will see public support evaporate or turn hostile.

Procedural competence or legislative skill certainly is not enough to guarantee policy success, and not only for the ideologically committed. The Ford Administration was praised for effective congressional relations, and the Bush Administration was marked by its pragmatism and success with vetoes. But neither Administration is remembered for significant policy successes. The 104th Congress's 100 days was a legislative tour de force on behalf of an impressive policy agenda, a brilliant legislative strategy which led to substantial achievements. But the effort lacked the public understanding and support necessary to move it smoothly through the rest of the governmental process or to assure public enthusiasm for the portion that did succeed. Even delivering directly on campaign promises produces little political support if the public cannot perceive the delivery (partly due to the sheer volume of activity in the case of the Contract) or does not understand why the policies delivered can make a difference.

Comparing Reagan and Clinton

The Reagan Administration excelled at the overall policy management process, with every element in place. The President himself consistently

---

2 See Chapter 10, "Winning the Battle for a Fairer Tax System."

enunciated a compelling vision. By inauguration, the Administration had most of the elements of a broad legislative program assembled and had made key decisions about which items were top priorities. Managerially, during the first term, the senior White House team was organized around a legislative strategy group that included policy, political, and public relations elements working in a concentrated and integrated fashion toward the President's major goals. A staff highly loyal to the President and his goals was readily directed to work toward the orderly accomplishment of those goals.

The Reagan legislative group monitored legislative and political progress on a daily basis. It would marshal a variety of resources to advance the program and overcome obstacles in Congress, in the media, among interest groups, and with the public. Because the President and his senior team set goals and objectives clearly, White House and agency staff and supporters on the Hill understood what was important and were able to feed critical information back to the legislative team. Decisions were made on a daily basis about what issues to push and whether to rally core supporters and seek allies, to wage a media campaign, or to compromise (and with whom).

In short, Reagan and his team knew what they wanted, knew how to get as much of it as the political circumstances allowed, and knew how to sell the program to the public to maximize their political leverage and to ensure public support (and credit) for the resulting laws and policies. The Reagan program was a success because the most important elements as defined and explained to the public (tax cuts, budget restraint, and the defense buildup) were approved. The Administration won key votes on Capitol Hill which clarified differences, and the sales effort led to public enthusiasm and acclaim for the program.

The Clinton political team also has scored successes. But in comparison to the Reagan team, Clinton's politicos appear to lack a consistent vision which might inform and direct their activities. Clinton's visionary advisors appear not to communicate with his effective marketing team. As a result, Clinton's successes have been largely opportunistic and tactical. Early in his Administration, Clinton signed a number of relatively significant pieces of legislation (such as the Family Leave Act) which largely had been worked out by congressional Democrats and stymied by Republican Presidents. These bills did not relate in any discernible way to Clinton's campaign themes — for instance, to promote economic growth, end welfare, and provide a middle-class tax cut—and they certainly did not represent "New Democrat" theories. Clinton passed a tax increase, but that could hardly be rated a political success due to a lack of public support, and he lost a stimulus (spending) program through a lack of public support and a unified partisan opposition.

Health care, the one area in which the Clinton Administration had a bold and clear goal, failed primarily because of poor governmental mechanics and a flawed sales effort. Clinton's health plan was late in introduction, out of line with public opinion or any electoral mandate, and not well-supported politically. Few major stakeholders in the health care industry were strongly in favor of the Clinton plan, leaving it with insufficient allies in the public and legislative process. It was the lack of coordination among essential policy, political, and public relations elements (and the absence of some parts altogether) which doomed the Clinton health plan. Better (or better attended to) legislative strategists, for instance, would have insisted on getting such a major plan moving early in the legislative session, and on bringing key Hill players into early discussions. An aggressive public liaison effort might have reached out to secure major additional allies among interest groups and might have provided early warning about aspects of the plan which might engender opposition unnecessarily. And a better integrated overall operation might have limited the policy overreach endemic to the plan.

In the wake of the 1994 elections, Clinton initially abandoned the field, playing essentially no part in the policy process. He re-emerged only in opposition to Republican proposals from Congress and, in fact, gave much policy ground on discretionary spending issues. After the budget showdown, Clinton returned to his early term pattern of responding to congressional initiatives, this time from a Republican Congress. In this process, Clinton was able to shape some congressional actions, as he did, for instance, with the minimum wage. In light of Clinton's failure to propose a minimum wage increase during the first two years of his Administration when his party controlled Congress, that effort only underscored the degree to which he was responding to a tactical situation in Congress rather than driving a coherent policy agenda.

While Clinton's repetitive sales effort ("Medicare, Medicaid, education, and the environment") was effective in contrast to weaker opposition responses, it gives him little policy support, since his formula led nowhere.

Clinton's tactical approach to governing may have been good enough to re-elect an incumbent President in a non-recessionary economy, but it is not good enough for leaders interested in changing the course of public policy in a particular, definite direction.

Congress and Policy Leadership

In reviewing recent successes and failures on broad public policy initiatives, it is critical to note some fundamental differences between the executive and legislative branches of government. The institutions are so different that one must contrast more than compare. Political scholarship regarding the presidency itself discusses, preponderantly, executive power. Congressional scholars discuss process, and even those figures in Congress noted for their power tend to be oriented toward a process for its exercise. This is clearly a result of the nature of the organs, and even specifically of the intent of the framers of the Constitution, who valued "energy" in the Executive and deliberation in Congress.

One of the most obvious resulting differences is that congressional power tends to be exercised slowly and often incrementally, in comparison to the possibility — at least in the executive branch — of rapid and relatively dramatic action. Between 1981 and 1992, liberals in Congress achieved significant progress in parts of their agenda, notably in civil rights and entitlements. A number of civil rights statutes were passed (most notably the Civil Rights Restoration Act and the Americans With Disabilities Act), but generally they followed efforts over the course of several Congresses which wore down executive branch opposition, built public support, and refined the proposals themselves. In a related fashion, some notable expansions of entitlements were achieved, but on a piecemeal basis, largely by focusing on sympathy-generating targets including pregnant women, children, and the mentally ill.

Like successful efforts of the Reagan Administration during the same period, these congressional initiatives included design, marketing, and procedural elements. Liberals often came up with innovative responses to Reagan's priorities: the nuclear freeze, for example. Vigorous public campaigns often were led by nongovernmental groups rather than by legislative leaders. Liberal congressional leaders pursued multiple strategies, including oversight and omnibus legislation in addition to direct statutory approaches, to maneuver or bypass a hostile executive branch.

Clearly, leaders in Congress need to think more in incremental and multi-year terms rather than attempt a policy blitzkrieg more suited to the executive branch. Conservative policy initiatives can be advanced this way as well. In the mid-1980s, then-Representative Jack Kemp (R-NY) and Senator William Roth (R-DE) began pushing a significant across-the-board income tax cut. The proposal became a major issue in the 1978 elections, leading to conservative gains in Congress, which then came close to approving a major tax cut in 1980. Ronald Reagan adopted and campaigned on the Kemp-Roth proposal, but it was the congressional efforts in preceding years which made it possible for Reagan to promote the issue and far easier to move a plan through Congress after the election.

Significant changes in the governmental process can also occur on an evolutionary basis. In the late 1970s and early 1980s, Congress increasingly attached legislative veto provisions to regulatory statutes, a practice which might shortly have created a government-wide policy had the Supreme Court not intervened. Congress essentially has replaced the Administrative Procedures Act (APA), the basic law governing how the executive branch creates regulations, by specifying more detailed requirements in each individual regulatory statute. A wholesale rewrite of the APA at any one time might have been impossible to achieve. The congressional budget process, created in 1974, was significantly amended in 1986, 1988, and 1990, and less significantly altered in other years, amounting to a wide-ranging overhaul, which also would never have been achievable in a single package. Among these incremental budget reforms, Congress:

- **Established** discretionary spending caps limiting total spending in defense and non-defense categories;

- **Imposed** a pay-as-you-go (or "pay-go") rule requiring that entitlement expansions or tax cuts be offset by changes in other mandatory (entitlement or tax) programs;

- **Created** a "sequester" system to impose across-the-board budget cuts if Congress failed to live within established caps (1990 budget process changes made the sequester operative only in very narrow circumstances);

- **Substantially changed** the budget calendar, including eliminating the second budget resolution;

- **Changed** some "scoring" procedures to require House committees to compare spending totals to actual previous spending amounts rather than to inflated "baseline" figures; and

- **Restricted** subject matter in reconciliation bills in the Senate to items with a direct deficit affect (the Byrd Rule).

As compared with the powers of the executive branch, congressional power is far more dispersed and difficult to coordinate. While the dispersal can be varied somewhat — committees may be more or less independent, party discipline more or less rigorous — some significant dispersal is guaranteed by the size of Congress and the reliance of its members on individual electorates. Successful congressional leaders must centrally manage Congress and find ways by which to deploy dispersed powers to their advantage.

Finally, legislative power is, in many ways, indirect. Unlike some executive and most judicial functions, Congress generally does not deal with individuals and, compared to the other branches, deals less in particulars. Legislation is, or should be, addressed to general principles. While Congress may feel forced to resort to very specific legislation due to disputes with the executive branch or differences with the courts, it often exercises effective influence over particulars in a less direct fashion through inquiries, investigations, hearings, budget limitations, or simple publicity. Congressional leaders who have significant differences with the President must deploy the full range of these legislative powers and not simply rely on direct legislative efforts which, even when successful, might be vetoed, undermined by regulatory interpretations, or overturned by the courts.

Conservative leaders in Congress might also take lessons from the archives of the liberal Congresses which faced conservative Presidents in the 1980s. The relentlessness, volume, and breadth of oversight efforts slowed or stopped Administration initiatives which Congress could not defeat head-on while uncovering arguable weaknesses in policies and management and identifying areas in which liberals might counterattack. Tales of $600 toilet seats and $200 hammers did far more to reverse gains in defense spending than reasoned arguments about declining military threats or the affordability of a buildup. In a like manner, evidence of nonsensical regulations and obtuse bureaucrats may do more to advance the cause of regulatory relief than the finest imaginable cost-benefit analysis.

There are significant tactical and even strategic differences in the policy process, depending on where an agenda originates. For legislative leaders, defining a core agenda is a critical task which is far more difficult that it will be for a President. Agenda definition in the legislature will normally be through a party-centered but broad-based effort. The critical task for leaders is to forge a consensus that includes significant initiatives and a limited number of top priorities. Although the Contract With America was sufficiently broad-based and bold, it failed to define priorities or to take adequate account of factors outside the House of Representatives.

Legislative leaders also face more complex challenges in dealing with executive branch opposition, in part because the entire executive branch works for the President while the legislative branch is naturally divided. Legislative relations receive concentrated and ongoing attention from the executive branch, largely through a network of legislative affairs offices. In contrast, Congress has devoted far less organized and ongoing attention to managing its relations with the executive branch. Congressional leaders should take full advantage of the multiplicity of means available to the legislature in influencing, leading, and directing the executive branch, with enhanced attention to coordination of this function.

Using liberal legislative initiatives as a model, it is apparent that some of the most useful marketing efforts for Congress are conducted by nongovernmental groups. Congressional leaders lack the presidency's megaphone and have far greater difficulty in imposing message discipline on the many independent spokesmen addressing the public and the media.

Many of the successes of the 104th Congress have come through a process in which Congress maneuvered the President into agreeing, in areas including welfare, medical savings accounts, and discretionary budget cuts, to policies which he initially had opposed. In the last Congress, most of those efforts were almost exclusively legislative. Relying more on outside help and coordination in public outreach would greatly magnify congressional efforts to influence the executive branch through public opinion. Re-emphasizing oversight, which congressional leaders now intend to do, can be tremendously productive in influencing executive actions, especially if it is in addition to, rather than in place of, direct legislative efforts.

In order to manage policy initiatives from Congress successfully, legislative leaders must impose a greater degree of centralization, which is more natural to the executive branch. This does not mean that congressional leaders should themselves devise or dictate policies, but that they should review proposals, establish priorities, and assign responsibilities, taking advantage of the multiplicity of means naturally available to the legislature.

LESSONS LEARNED

Beyond these general principles, the experiences of conservatives in Washington have led to specific lessons which might now be applied by congressional leaders facing an unsupportive executive branch.

Assembling and Managing a Legislative Program

No matter how compelling a program may be, if it is unachievable within a definable time frame, the effort involved will prove disappointing, perhaps especially to enthusiastic supporters. Leaders should set incremental goals or make their time frame clear to avoid the perception of losing the war when the opposition has not been routed completely in the first battle. At the opposite extreme, a program that can be moved through the legislature and past the President easily is likely to be uncompelling politically.

Lesson #1: A political program needs the right balance of vision and practicality (political coherence, popular support, and achievability). A successful program will provide a vision, which may well go beyond the details immediately achievable and push the limits of practicality in terms of what can be achieved right away. In the 104th Congress, for instance, it was clear that a term limits amendment could not pass. House leaders acknowledged this by stating a goal of securing a vote on the amendment, but a weak follow-up effort combined with a setback from the Supreme Court (which declared that state-imposed limits were unconstitutional) left many advocates disillusioned. Term limit advocates and congressional leaders should devise a strategy in the 105th Congress which displays demonstrable progress toward the ultimate goal.

In another case, unfunded mandates legislation was approved early in the 104th Congress, but its specific provisions were so watered down that the law may be ineffective in practice. Backers of the legislation almost certainly could have secured a stronger law if they had taken a more aggressive approach, testing the limits through debate rather than accepting the lowest common denominator in order to avoid a fight.

LESSONS LEARNED
Assembling and Managing a Legislative Program

- A political program needs the right balance of vision and practicality.

- A successful political program must be conceptually clear and consistent, no matter how complex the details.

- A successful political program needs only a few consistent themes.

- A successful political program requires priorities.

- A political program should leave room for secondary initiatives.

- For conservatives, taxes matter most.

- Central management is essential to a broad-based legislative program.

- Detailed plans should be available early but open to change.

- Process does not sell.

Lesson #2: A successful political program must be conceptually clear and consistent, no matter how complex the details. Ronald Reagan's domestic program was to get the government "off our backs and out of our pockets." The reconciliation bill that implemented the first parts of that program was hundreds of pages long. The details were critical in Washington but largely unimportant to citizens, yet Reagan's overall formulation carried him through many subsequent spending and regulatory battles. Reagan's success in details was aided greatly by the simplicity and clarity of his fundamental concepts. The Contract With America, on the other hand, was relatively simple in its details but politically ineffective because the concepts behind it were not clear to the public. Among the pending policies, the flat tax has the virtue of conceptual clarity but some necessary complexity in details.

Lesson #3: A successful political program needs a few, and only a few, consistent themes. Typically, three points are as many as can be remembered and grasped easily. The central part of a political agenda might be limited to three elements, or its more various parts assembled into two or three strong themes. For many years, every active conservative repeated the mantra of "limited government, individual liberty, and a strong national defense." It was clear, concise, and simple. And every official in Reagan's Administration knew that he or she had the goal of devising policies to reduce the growth in domestic spending, reduce tax rates, deregulate the economy, and rebuild America's defenses. A successful political program should not need more than a sentence or two of description, at least at the vision level. Ten points are clearly too many; any multi-point program necessarily overwhelms its own elements.

The end of the Cold War, the rise of social issues, and the obeisance paid fiscal conservatism by nearly every politician have made it more difficult for conservatives to summarize and differentiate their political program. Conservative leaders and strategists must continue to strive for a better overall encapsulation of their current program, and to package their specific initiatives into understandable packages.

Lesson #4: A successful political program requires priorities. Big items matter more than small items. The Reagan agenda, while comprehensively broad, was focused legislatively on taxes, budget, and defense matters, with an additional emphasis within the Administration on regulation. Reagan was successful because he passed the big items. Clinton failed with the centerpiece of his legislative program.

Priorities not only allow policymakers to distinguish among more and less important tasks, but also help them avoid being overwhelmed by or tripped up by details. The beginning of the end for the congressional budget package in 1995 was the elevation of a small item — a single adjustment in Medicare Part B premiums—to a position which displaced the overall tax and budget goals.

A special danger in assembling a legislative package in Congress is the multiplication of agenda items without appropriate priorities. Every committee, sometimes nearly every Member, will have a pet project or two. In a necessarily consensus-based system, the temptation is to list every requested item and, even when setting priorities, to attempt to give "priority" status to at least one item from each of several critical groups. To be successful, legislative leaders must look outside their own chamber, assess public support and interest, determine achievability within the whole Congress and with the Executive, and then focus on a few (but only a few) significant, broadly supported, and achievable priorities.

Lesson #5: A political program should leave room for secondary initiatives. One way to ease the priority-setting process is to make clear that secondary initiatives are welcome. Strictly limiting top priorities can help make it clear that there will be room for second-tier initiatives. Issues may be placed in the second rank because they are not ripe for action or because they are of interest only to significant groups, not to the general public. Empowering committee chairmen (in Congress) or Cabinet secretaries (in the executive branch) to pursue their own initiatives consistent with an overall program can broaden the reach without diluting attention to central objectives.

Two of the most far-reaching proposals passed by the 104th Congress — telecommunications and agriculture reform — were not part of the Contract With America or the budget debate. The conservative majority might have benefited by fostering even more such initiatives, and the congressional committee structure is well suited to doing so.

Lesson #6: For conservatives, taxes matter most. The electoral evidence of the past two decades is overwhelming: Citizens support tax cuts; they believe that taxes are too high. Conservatives thrive when they address this conviction and often flounder when they fail to do so. Tax cuts represent far more than an economic or financial calculation; they are important symbolic statements about the role and control of government. Pursued properly, tax cuts and tax limitation are among the most effective limits on government. While tax cut proposals often are criticized as irresponsible, tax-cutting governors in states like Massachusetts, Michigan, and New Jersey have shown that they are as compatible with progressive government as with popular politics. George Bush's abandonment of his "no new taxes" pledge was the beginning of the end of his Administration. Bill Clinton's conversion to tax cutting has made it difficult for Republicans to rally support based on their economic program. Policymakers who support tax cuts must not abandon or ignore this issue, but must consider the opportunities that Clinton's position presents and how they might push the policy consensus further in a conservative direction.

Lesson #7: Central management is essential to a broad-based legislative program. It is possible for committee leaders to score significant successes on their own; but if congressional leaders aim for a broadly appealing comprehensive program, central management is essential. The lack of central management led to the political failure of Democratic Congresses. Even though they held their own, policywise, with Republican Presidents, congressional liberals slowly lost public support because they lacked a coherent political message. If conservatives are to thrive in Congress under a non-conservative President, they must restore strength to committees without losing central coordination. The obvious solution is for party leaders to formulate and manage an agenda while leaving committees with clear responsibility for developing and moving those ideas. Committee chairmen and members, for their parts, should adhere to that agenda, and especially should refrain from using their positions to oppose it.

Lesson #8: Detailed plans should be available early but open to change. Legislative details should be developed early in the policy process, with an understanding that they are subject to change. A major problem with the Clinton health plan was the long delay in producing a bill, which prevented legislative progress early in the Administration. While it may seem appealing to try to advance a concept while avoiding criticism over details, such strategies usually backfire. Failing to provide details until just before legislative action can allow opponents to raise doubts about particulars, implying broader faults. An early review of details allows supporters to dismiss ill-founded criticisms and avoid unnecessary surprises. An overinsistence on details can be particularly damaging, however, when a proposal passes, almost inevitably with some details altered. Advocates who have staked their case on every detail will be perceived to have suffered a defeat at the very moment their policies are adopted. Perhaps worse, their opponents may well be able to claim credit for popular policies which they in fact opposed, arguing that their alterations in details even improved the proposal.

In general, the Contract With America's elements were broadly supported by the public and in most cases received strong bipartisan support in the House of Representatives. But an insistence on specificity, understandably aimed at addressing public suspicion of politicians' promises, undid the program when details were necessarily altered. Even when the alterations were insignificant, such as simply breaking a single plank into multiple pieces of legislation, the program suffered. The Contract was a remarkable success in establishing a new political agenda, but its sponsors failed to get much credit — even though most of its elements were adopted—because every alteration or delay was seen as a defeat.

Lesson #9: Process does not sell. The Contract With America was essentially a process. The process itself overwhelmed the potentially popular and appealing elements within the Contract, turning it into an exercise that appeared meaningless to most voters. Changes in the political process — term limits, a balanced budget, tax limitation, or establishing an initiative and referendum process—can be compelling to voters. But to be attractive, process changes must be linked directly to a compelling substantive goal, usually of limiting government. Even when process issues are of high potential interest, they can be of little political effect if, as is the case with campaign finance reform, specific process proposals are not linked to definable outcomes.

Refining the Legislative Process

> *If you let me write the procedure, and I let you*
> *write the substance, I'll [beat] you every time.*

—John D. Dingell[3]

The public policy process, within Congress, the executive branch, and the judiciary and among the various branches, often has a decisive impact on policy outcomes. The Reagan economic package was maneuvered through Congress in 1981 with innovative use of the reconciliation process. At the time, some legislators who had been involved in creating the budget process which included reconciliation in 1974 objected that the process had never been intended to be used in that way. Without reconciliation, Reagan might never have been able to get his tax program through the Senate. Successful leaders often are those who best manipulate and change the policy process, and policy breakthroughs often are related to or enabled by process innovations.

While he is not associated with high-profile legislation as a sponsor, Senator Robert C. Byrd (D-WV) has been a hugely successful legislative leader in no small part because of his aggressiveness in managing and

---

3 The Honorable John D. Dingell (D-MI), former Chairman of the House Energy and Commerce Committee, quoted in *National Review*, February 27, 1987, p. 24.

LESSONS LEARNED
Refining the Legislative Process

- "Hostage-taking" does not work.
- Government shutdowns rarely force real change.
- Showdowns can produce notable process reforms.
- Centralization produces budget discipline.
- Excluding or ignoring the executive branch does not work.
- Successful congressionally led policies must have a bipartisan element.
- Incremental strategies can make great strides toward broad policy goals.

---

improvising Senate procedures. Conservative challenges to liberal domination in the House of Representatives were fought on procedural grounds, with conservatives making use of previously ignored procedures such as special orders. The fight by then-Representative James Inhofe (R-OK) to open up the House discharge petition process was a rare instance in which process did sell because it was linked to liberal leaders' moves to stifle a variety of popular causes. Speaker Newt Gingrich, rightly calculating that the congressional procedures he would need to roll back regulations would have to be different from the system which had created them, devised the House Corrections Day process.

Political failures often are linked to problems in the governmental process. The divided congressional committee process obviously was one factor in the eventual defeat of the Clinton health plan. Even generally sympathetic congressional leaders were unable to move that legislation through a diverse set of committees quickly, and leaders were unable or unwilling to take steps to bypass or short-circuit the committee process. The delays and division endemic in the then-practiced congressional committee system allowed opponents to rally opposition to the plan, even as the committees themselves exacerbated differences within the potentially supportive coalition.

Similarly, the federal deficit swelled dramatically after Congress radically altered the budget process in 1974. Congress began to make progress against the deficit only after the Gramm-Rudman law significantly revised the budget process in 1986. Changes made in the budget process in 1990 by Leon Panetta and Richard Darman (the "pay-go" rule) were the principal reasons that congressional Republicans in 1995 tied tax cuts and entitlement restraints together, producing a legislative combination which Bill Clinton was able to resist and even turn against the Republican sponsors. Had the budget process not demanded the combination, Republicans probably would have offered their tax and entitlement packages separately, forcing Clinton to choose between a balanced budget and tax relief, and between a balanced budget and spending restraint, instead of allowing him to pose as the champion of the elderly against the rich. Clinton still might have been able to mount effective opposition to the GOP program, but the Darman-Panetta budget process made it unnecessarily easy.

Because the budget process dominates internal congressional activity even more completely than it shapes relations with the President, it is in the budget area that the most critical procedural lessons are found. The budget showdown of the winter of 1995–1996 dominated the 104th Congress and, at least temporarily, reshaped national politics. Leaders of the 105th Congress will be eager to avoid last year's mistakes and determine how to make the budget process work in behalf of a conservative agenda. Specific recommendations for reforming the budget process are included below, but several principles are worth reviewing.

Lesson #1: "Hostage-taking" does not work. It was generally assumed in 1995 that President Clinton would back down in the face of a government shutdown. Republicans found themselves without a response when the President was able to blame Congress for government closures, even though it was Clinton himself who had vetoed legislation that would have kept the government open. Though media sympathies may have played a role in assigning blame, a more useful conclusion is that government shutdowns generally strengthen backers of the status quo—i.e., of big government. When the government is shut down, one party effectively is holding relatively innocent parties (government benefit recipients or federal employees) hostage to a relatively unrelated goal (closing or cutting a few specific programs). Whatever their opinion of the merits of the particular issues in dispute, many people eventually sympathize with the innocent parties and turn on the political faction insisting on change.

While deadline-dodging government shutdowns seem to be a perennial feature of the federal budget process, they are in fact only a recent relic of the Carter Administration. Prior to 1980, government agencies whose funding had temporarily lapsed were considered to have lost spending authority, but routine functions (and employment) generally continued. After several such experiences, President Carter asked Attorney General Benjamin Civiletti for a legal memorandum clarifying the status of agencies with lapsed appropriations. Civiletti replied with a finding that there was no authority for agencies to continue operating in such circumstances, that the Anti-Deficiency Act even prohibited government employees from volunteering their time, and that only emergency and shutdown activities could be carried on when appropriations lapse. There now is every reason for Congress to pass a general continuing appropriation statute to provide interim authority for agencies when funds lapse temporarily. Such a law would not eliminate end-of-fiscal-year confrontations between Congress and the White House, but it would remove the hostages who lend an advantage to the status quo.

Lesson #2: Government shutdowns rarely force real change. So convinced were congressional Republicans that large-scale confrontations tended to produce victories for big government that they vowed to avoid a summit in 1995, which led to the politically disastrous government shutdown. Even without hostages, it appears that the tendency in such situations is to favor the status quo, in part because it is difficult to marshal a predominantly conservative public opinion to influence a fast-moving, insider-dominated negotiation. To the extent that summits and similar negotiations produce split-the-difference compromises, committed conservatives are going to be disappointed by them. In fact, the experience of Reagan-era and Bush-era shutdowns showed that those interested in cutting domestic spending got far less than half a loaf.

Lesson #3: Showdowns can produce notable process reforms. The Gramm-Rudman deficit reduction plan was the fruit of an impasse over a debt limit increase in 1985. A second version of Gramm-Rudman was devised during a 1987 budget impasse. The 1990 budget summit between the Bush Administration and Congress produced a major revision of the budget process which has proven effective in limiting discretionary spending and blocking significant tax cuts. (While the latter reform would not generally be considered conservative, it has been effective in accomplishing the intent of its designers.)

If conservatives are caught in another budget showdown under current fiscal procedures, they should be willing (though not necessarily too ready) to make the inevitable short-term substantive compromises; but they should also insist, as the price, on permanent reforms that make spending and tax restraint easier to achieve. Committed parties, liberal or conservative, can also make significant progress during global budget negotiations on the lower priority agenda items which enjoy broad popular support. In the fall of 1996, for instance, a politically popular proposal requiring insurers to cover 48-hour hospital stays following childbirth was approved during negotiations over a broad continuing resolution. In the same period, legislative efforts to repeal a Clinton Administration policy effectively exempting the District of Columbia from workfare requirements prompted the Clinton Administration to reverse the policy.

In addition to their broad budget and process goals, conservatives should keep in mind that end-of-year budget packages can present opportunities for lower priority agenda items as well. Rather than decry the practice of attaching riders to bills, conservatives should take advantage of the opportunity to put their own passengers on such legislative vehicles.

Lesson #4: Centralization produces budget discipline. Hoover Institution scholar John Cogan has reviewed the history of congressional appropriations policy, arguing persuasively that spending control by a single committee in each house (traditionally the appropriations committees) produces spending restraint while divided spending authority produces higher spending and deficit totals.[4] While centralization-decentralization battles in Congress traditionally were over direct spending, the advent of entitlement programs has resulted in a

---

4 John F. Cogan, *Federal Budget Deficits: What's Wrong with the Congressional Budget Process* (Stanford: Hoover Institution, 1992).

radical decentralization of spending authority within Congress, with disastrous fiscal results. While 19th century battles were over whether three or four committees or just one would control spending, today at least 15 House and Senate committees share some degree of direct spending authority.

While conservatives are reflexively suspicious of the Appropriations Committee, due in large part to many notable examples of unjustifiable pork-barrel spending, the actual track record of this committee, in comparison to others, is excellent on spending matters. During the 104th Congress, the Appropriations Committee rescinded $16.3 billion in 1995 funding, cut an additional $20 billion in FY 1996, and allowed spending to recover by $16.5 billion for FY 1997. For the entire Congress, the Appropriations Committee held spending growth below the level of an absolute freeze, even after making substantial concessions to President Clinton's spending demands. In contrast, entitlement spending, which now represents a substantially larger portion of the budget than appropriated funding, was subject to virtually no restraint, growing by 17 percent over the same period.

While abolishing entitlements and returning related spending authority to the Appropriations Committee may not be possible, budget reforms should focus on restoring centralized control to government spending. One method for imposing such discipline on the budget process which has been shown to work is budget caps. The Gramm-Rudman system was based on a cap for various spending categories, enforced by an across-the-board sequester. Even though the Gramm-Rudman process was revised and later replaced, Congress did begin to exercise spending restraint in response to the Gramm-Rudman caps. The 1990 budget revisions worked more smoothly because caps have been restricted largely to discretionary spending, with sequesters (never yet used under the 1990 process) applying only to changes in entitlement law. GAO Associate Director Susan J. Irving attributes the 1990 system's effectiveness to its emphasis on behavior (legislative actions) rather than results which, in the case of entitlement programs, are sometimes difficult to predict.[5] Reimposing budget caps on entitlements could be effective in

---

5 U.S. General Accounting Office, "Budget Process: Evolution and Challenges," Statement of Susan J. Irving, Associate Director, Budget Issues, Accounting and

forcing Congress to address entitlement spending, but enforcement procedures should be based on the reasonably predictable results of legislative actions rather than on economic performance. Though such a system would be less precise in hitting budget targets, it would produce more effective budget discipline by defining legislative options during rather than after the normal budget process.

Lesson #5: Excluding or ignoring the executive branch does not work. The repeated budget crises under the 1974 Budget Act are in part a result of the fact that the process was designed to severely limit the President's authority over the budget, almost to the point of excluding him from the process. Congress's most important budget policy document, the annual budget resolution, is an internal resolution; the President plays no official part in its development. As a result, budget disputes typically are postponed until the end of the process, often with undesirable results. One byproduct is that Appropriations Committee subcommittees often are tempted to delay action, knowing that major budget compromises will be made at the last minute. Including an appropriations bill in the (probably inevitable) continuing resolution enhances the influence of subcommittee members over specific spending decisions by shielding them from scrutiny on the House floor and providing greater protection against a presidential veto. Bringing the President back into the process and forcing early decisions on aggregate budget totals would promote the general interest in spending restraints at the expense of specific spending appeals and make it easier for Congress to resolve competing spending claims by providing firm limits. Forcing the President to "ante up" with a credible budget proposal at the beginning of the process would enhance rather than dilute the ability of a conservative Congress to impose spending restraint on a non-conservative President.

Lesson #6: Successful congressionally led policies must have a bipartisan element. Two significant elements of Bill Clinton's initial legislative program — his health plan and his stimulus package — were defeated in a Democratic Congress due to unified opposition from the minority party. His tax and crime packages squeaked through with few or no Republican votes only to became political liabilities in the 1994

Information Management Division, before the Committee on the Budget, U.S. House of Representatives, July 11, 1996.

elections. If a President has trouble moving a partisan legislative package through a Congress with narrow majorities, it is certain that congressional leaders commanding narrow majorities and lacking presidential support will be frustrated in efforts to advance policy initiatives on partisan strength alone. Even when an idea or program is partisan in its conception, it is possible to build bipartisan support. Most elements of the Contract With America enjoyed significant support among Democrats, aiding their eventual adoption. Republican budget plans, on the other hand, had almost no Democratic support, making it impossible to win a battle with the President.

Within Congress, building bipartisan support forces opponents of a policy to play offense and defense at the same time. Even minimal bipartisanship can ease party discipline and help defuse tensions within the majority party by making it less critical when majority members dissent from one particular bill or issue for ideological or constituency reasons. Because it is easier to block than to advance legislation, it is more important for the majority than the minority party in a closely divided legislature to build bipartisan support for its positions. The committee process often provides the best opportunity to attract bipartisan support for a proposal which may have been partisan in its conception, especially if committees have the freedom to adjust details of a proposal to respond to reasonable criticisms.

Lesson #7: Incremental strategies can make great strides toward broad policy goals. The introductory section of this chapter outlined how congressional liberals were able to achieve significant expansions of entitlements and federal civil rights law with incremental changes in law over several decades. Budget and regulatory processes have been revised significantly in a similar step-by-step fashion. In the 104th Congress, conservatives were largely unsuccessful in bold and broad deregulatory efforts. They were successful, however, in achieving significant deregulation of the communications and agriculture sectors, and made some progress more broadly with a congressional review statute. Prospects are bright for deregulation of electricity and financial services in the 105th Congress.

Conservatives should identify additional areas in which incremental legislation might move notably toward visionary reforms which may be impossible to achieve in the short run. Tax policy may be one such area.

While fundamental tax reform may be impossible with the current political alignment, it may be possible to make major reforms in taxation of families and capital (both capital gains and the estate tax). Conservatives may make larger gains in these areas by restricting their efforts to family and capital taxation, and in so doing make more progress toward fundamental tax reform than would be possible with broader legislation.

Similar progress may be possible on federal mandates. While efforts to repeal, or even to review, all existing federal mandates were unsuccessful, conservatives might require, through House and Senate rules, that committees review mandates on a statute-by-statute basis whenever they consider reauthorization of existing laws and programs.

Marketing Legislation

If Congress cuts a tax but no one hears about it, it has not made a political noise. Ronald Reagan's skills in this area and their contribution to his overall policy success are widely recognized. Not only was Reagan able to sway public opinion to influence political and legislative battles, but his Administration's efforts continued, even after legislative successes, to build public acceptance of his policies.

Lesson #1: A vigorous and ongoing public campaign is essential to overall policy success. Celebrating victories, and claiming credit by doing so, is a key component of policy marketing. Congress faces a disadvantage in this regard in comparison to the President, who generally has the last word, assuming he signs a piece of legislation. Even if the President has fought a policy in Congress, he can adopt it by signing the final bill, and even seek credit from both sides by claiming to have moderated problematic but specific aspects of a proposal. This ability to claim a victory and then continue to campaign on it (as he has done, for example, with welfare reform) is a key element of Clinton's political success.

Inadequate marketing is one explanation for the political failure of the 104th Congress, despite its significant policy successes. During the budget showdown, for instance, congressional leaders focused too much on "CBO numbers," failing (perhaps because it was impossible) to make this abstraction into a legitimate public test of the President's commitment to a balanced budget. When the President opened a second front (claiming

---

| LESSONS LEARNED |
| Marketing Legislation |

- A vigorous and ongoing public campaign is essential to overall policy success.
- Focus and repetition are critical in public relations efforts.
- The media should not be treated as the enemy.
- Coalitions of interested nongovernmental groups are critical in policy battles.

that he wanted to balance the budget too, but criticizing nearly every significant element of the Republicans' plan), the GOP was slow to respond, staying focused for too long on the original argument alone.

When they do score successes, which often involve significant compromises, conservative leaders should recognize the need to claim credit and to continue to explain the principles and benefits involved. In addition to an after-action review of legislative battles, they need an after-action plan to explain what was done and to continue to build support for the policy involved. The sheer volume of activity during the first 100 days of the 104th Congress made it impossible to explain, and for the public to digest, the policies involved.

Lesson #2: Focus and repetition are critical in public relations efforts. Congressional leaders may never match the degree of focus possible within the executive branch. During the 104th Congress, conservative leaders did improve their efforts to coordinate public and media activities, and these efforts should continue. These legislative efforts, however, have largely concerned tactical questions: setting a message of the week or coordinating a series of town meetings. If the message is changing from week to week, it is likely that its creators are not in control of the agenda discussion. Congressional leaders should plan marketing efforts not merely around legislative events or presidential initiatives, but around their own long-term objectives. The "spin" may change from week to week, but themes should remain consistent, and marketing efforts should focus on efforts to direct rather than react to public and media attention.

Lesson #3: The media should not be treated as the enemy. It is widely known that most reporters are liberal, and the public has seen many instances in which reporters' views have produced bias in news reporting and commentary. While conservatives should point out this bias, that effort should be separated from issue advocacy, and conservatives' media efforts should remain focused principally on their own ideas. Treating the media as the enemy in an interview changes the focus from a policy question to a spat between a reporter and a politician. Even if a politician could win that fight (and he rarely can), he has lost the war, because the ideas at stake are no longer the focus of the discussion. Responses to media bias should be left largely to staff rather than to political principals, and politicians facing overt bias during an interview should merely note the fact and immediately shift the discussion back to their ideas and policies.

Few politicians were more reviled by the media than Ronald Reagan, yet he never attacked reporters (though he did sometimes indict "the media"); in fact, he became known as the Great Communicator precisely because of his ability to sell his ideas through unfriendly media. From Spiro Agnew through George Bush (at times) to Newt Gingrich, conservative politicians who attack the media aggressively are cheered by their own hard-core supporters but lose public support and fail to advance their own ideas.

Lesson #4: Coalitions of interested nongovernmental groups are critical in policy battles. Political leaders should never ignore interested parties. Sometimes in policy battles it is necessary to single out an opposition group as the enemy, as is the case with trial lawyers in tort reform. But it is preferable to build allies, and successful strategies cannot ignore potentially interested groups. The Clinton health care plan failed in no small part because many interested parties, including insurance companies and doctors, were hostile while others, such as hospitals, were not enthusiastic supporters. While television advertising was the most visible of coalition efforts against the Clinton health plan, business, insurance, and medical groups played key early roles in educating their members and the public about problems with the plan.

In some sensitive areas, consensus among outside groups is essential to policy progress. The Religious Freedom Restoration Act, a bill to limit judicial and governmental restrictions on religious practices, was approved easily because backers built a coalition of conservative and liberal groups interested in religious liberty questions. Financial services deregulation is likely in the 105th Congress because backers have worked out compromises among competing industry segments. In many cases, the opposition of only one strongly interested group is sufficient to defeat a policy initiative.

STRATEGIES FOR MOVING AN AGENDA THROUGH CONGRESS

As the foregoing discussion implies, reforming the government process has more to do with the skillful management and use of existing leadership prerogatives than with procedural reforms in Congress or structural reforms in the executive branch. While procedural and structural reforms can be critical, they should not be seen as ends in themselves, and only rarely should they become leaders' top priorities. When procedural reform issues do take top priority, it usually is because an existing government structure or procedure is a substantial barrier to a popular policy objective. Committee reform in the House was urgent at the beginning of the 104th Congress because the committee system had evolved into a special-interest-dominated swamp in which the general interest too often was lost. Committee reform was not merely an efficiency exercise, but an effort to restore more central control and a greater responsiveness to general interests to the congressional policy process. Budget reform today is properly a top priority because the current budget process is biased toward increasing government spending. Reforms should be designed and marketed with policy goals always in mind. If budget process reforms are not explained in terms of lower spending and taxes, they will not have the public support needed to secure their adoption.

In devising procedural reforms, modesty is also necessary: Unintended consequences are sometimes the most significant. Watergate-era campaign finance reforms were intended to reduce the role of money in politics but in fact have had precisely the opposite effect. For this reason, as well as for practical reasons, it is usually better to pursue reforms on an incremental basis rather than attempt a central redesign of an entire procedural system. Conservatives are wise enough to know that they cannot micromanage national activity; they should apply the same modesty to political reform schemes.

STRATEGIES FOR MOVING AN AGENDA THROUGH CONGRESS

- Policymakers must develop ways to centralize decision making.

- Congressional leaders should attempt to control rather than reform committees.

- Government should be made more transparent to make officials more accountable.

- Truth in testimony rules should be established.

- Congressional freedom of information should be considered.

- Casework, ombudsmen, and taxpayer advocates are valuable in establishing a citizen-oriented attitude in Congress.

- Congress should use oversight and other powers to influence the executive branch.

- Creating good public liaison is essential to building alliances.

- More effective hearings and oversight are needed to change the terms of debate.

- It is important to know when and how to use commissions.

- Major reforms of the budget process should be enacted.

- Steps should be taken to reform the campaign finance system.

Particularly in the Senate, rules reforms are difficult because of the requirement for a two-thirds majority to end debate on them. Far more than in the House, Senate procedures are based on custom rather than on strict adherence to written rules in any case. For Senate leaders in particular, rules reforms may be less productive than exploring the innovative use and management of existing powers. Filibusters, for instance, might be limited better by forcing objecting Senators to hold the floor and debate (as opposed to the current practice of laying a matter aside for the two days required to secure a cloture vote to cut off debate) than by attempting to change the relevant rule (Rule XXII) itself. The informal prerequisite of "holds" (delaying floor consideration of a measure due to the objections of one or a few Senators) would be altered best by the Majority Leader's establishing new practices in legislative scheduling. Attempting to limit holds through a Senate rule would only formalize the practice and could lead to making it an even more formidable legislative hurdle.

In thinking about changing the legislative process, the concept of separable design, process, marketing, and management efforts is critical. Party leaders typically are best at moving the legislative process itself and often are indispensable as managers. But conceptual and design duties often are best delegated to legislators based on committee positions or detailed knowledge of an issue; and marketing efforts, which are essential to overall success, often are best conducted by organizations outside of Congress. In other words, party leaders should attend to the process of creating an agenda and rely on others to fill in its details. They must recognize the need for active allies outside the legislature—not merely in campaigning, but also in policy adoption after elections—and recruit and incorporate such allies accordingly.

STRATEGY #1
Policymakers must develop ways to centralize decisionmaking.

Conservatives are used to thinking in terms of Jeffersonian federalism as the best way to maintain popular control of government. But within a given governmental institution, centralization of authority tends to produce more conservative outcomes. Even in a liberal administration, for instance, the White House tends to be more conservative than its Cabinet agencies, and Congress as a whole tends to be more conservative than its committees. Centralization of decisionmaking within a single governmental institution tends toward conservatism because it promotes general over special interests and because it promotes greater accountability, giving citizens more control over the government. If a politician is able to excuse an action because a bureaucrat or committee was responsible, citizens are denied the ability to control their government.

Conservative House and Senate leaders already have begun to apply this principle by centralizing agenda-setting and by giving party organizations more control over committee chairmen. House Republicans gave the Speaker effective authority to choose committee chairmen to ensure that committees would be more responsive to a party agenda. Beginning with the 105th Congress, Senate Republicans actually will vote on a party agenda composed of items which receive a three-quarters majority within their Conference. Senate Republicans also are introducing a new process for nominating and ratifying committee chairmen that is designed to impose more overall party control. House leaders might consider a formal process, similar to that adopted by the Senate, to adopt a broadly supported agenda and build support for it. While such a process is bound to produce some controversy, attempting to forge party unity and defining party obligations at the beginning of a Congress through such a process is far better than attempting to impose party discipline later on.

Prior to the last Congress, many reformist Republicans had viewed many of their own party's members of the Appropriations Committee as part of the problem. In the 104th Congress, Appropriations may have been more successful than any other House committee in advancing the Republican agenda because of reforms designed to impose on its members more responsiveness to central direction.

STRATEGY #2
Congressional leaders should attempt to control rather than reform committees.

Centralization can go too far: The 100 days process enervated House committees, losing a valuable potential resource. Because committees were bound in virtually every detail, they became a barrier rather than an aid to the legislative process. Further, the expertise, vetting, and support-building functions which committees are capable of performing were largely lost. The Appropriations Committee became critical to the conservative agenda because of its innate power. It was able to advance that agenda because leaders gained control of it instead of diluting its power through reorganization or reform efforts.

House leaders and party organizations then should focus on setting a broad agenda, rather than on attempting to settle every detail, and decentralize execution in committees. As long as committee members understand that their allegiance is to the whole body rather than to their own committees, their responsibility to handle the details is not likely to be abused. If committees are reliably responsive to an established agenda, they can perform design and marketing functions which otherwise are almost irreplaceable. Committees are able to develop and employ the expertise necessary to address complex issues and strike delicate balances among competing goals. Through the hearing process, committees are able to market proposals by generating publicity, identifying and rallying potential supporters, and addressing opposition concerns.

Thus, the committee reform process should be a means of exerting control over committees rather than simply attacking or bypassing them. The task force system employed in the House in the last Congress was largely ineffective because it attempted to bypass rather than to control and use committees. Task forces can be useful, but they should be set up to assure that the results feed back into the legislative process, normally though committees. In the House, the Speaker might use his power to appoint select committees in instances where the routine committee process might fail due to divided jurisdiction and vested interests.

In addition to budget reform, financial services legislation might be an ideal topic for a select committee in the House. Rather than attempt to strengthen the Banking Committee against potential objections from the Commerce, Agriculture, and other committees, the Speaker could create a combined panel with a joint interest in creating good legislation rather than defending turf. Industry segments would be at least somewhat more inclined to identify acceptable compromises rather than to exploit divisions among committees. In general, the central decision to produce legislation would be strengthened against the centrifugal forces of the normal committee process.

While jurisdictional reorganization and further consolidation of committees in both the House and Senate might enhance central control of their agendas, it is improving legislative efficiency, not attacking committee powers, that should be the foremost goal of reorganization efforts. Overall, efforts to better discipline committees are likely to provide more benefits, with lower political costs, than jurisdictional reorganization.

STRATEGY #3
Government should be made more transparent to make officials more accountable.

The key to maintaining citizen control of government is to make officials accountable to citizens by making government and government processes transparent. If government functions are too complex for citizens to understand readily, then functions should be devolved through federalism or privatization. Blueprints for those functions are included in other chapters of this book.[6] The resulting, smaller federal government would be more amenable to central control and more readily transparent.

Transparency exposes, and therefore limits, narrow interests and helps bring public pressure to bear on policy questions. Transparent systems also help build public support necessary for complete policy success. Within the congressional process, there are several steps leaders can take both to expose and limit special interests and to enlist public support for a broader agenda.

Three specific legislative reforms would help promote transparency in Congress and the executive branch: exposing government-funded lobbying activities, providing better disclosure of information within Congress, and improving constituent casework practices.

STRATEGY #4
Congress should establish truth in testimony rules.

Republicans fought a major battle in the 104th Congress to restrict lobbying by government grantees. Requiring taxpayers to pay for efforts to secure even more taxpayer dollars is simply absurd. Opposition by recipient groups, congressional liberals, and President Clinton limited the success of that effort. In the 105th Congress, conservatives should renew their efforts to end coerced subsidies for narrow political agendas, beginning in Congress itself, with a truth in testimony rule. Between 25 percent and 50 percent (depending on the committee) of nongovernment witnesses testifying before congressional committees are government grant recipients. Often, witnesses fail to disclose their direct interest in the programs on which they are commenting. Congress should require witnesses to disclose the amount and source of any government grants, as proposed in H. Res. 486 by Representative John Doolittle (R-CA) in the 104th Congress. Such disclosures would change the dynamics of

---

6 See Chapter 2, "Restructuring, Closing, Consolidating Federal Agencies and Programs"; Chapter 3, "Transferring Functions to the States"; and Chapter 4, "Transferring Functions to the Private Sector."

congressional hearings away from appeals by special-interest advocates and toward a more serious examination of government programs.

Congress also should continue efforts to expose and restrict lobbying by government agencies, government grantees, and labor organizations which are the recipients of special legal and funding provisions.

STRATEGY #5
Congressional freedom of information should be considered.

Congress could build better public understanding and support through a congressional freedom of information act, ensuring that critical legislative information is available to the public via the Internet. The House Task Force on Committee Review and the Senate Rules Committee have proposed steps to make information more widely available; Congress should expand these reforms into a comprehensive system based on affirmative disclosures rather than require citizens to seek disclosable information (as is the case with executive branch freedom of information procedures).

STRATEGY #6
Casework, ombudsmen, and taxpayer advocates are valuable in establishing a citizen-oriented attitude in Congress.

Casework — investigating individual constituents' problems with the federal government — is a legitimate function of Congress. But an overemphasis on casework by many Members represents an unfair electoral advantage for incumbents, detracts from Congress's legislative functions, and may even provide an excuse for failing to address systemic problems with government by making it easy to fix faults on a piecemeal basis. In addition, casework can provide an excuse for exercising undue influence on behalf of special interests. Two major scandals of the 1980s, the "Keating Five" banking scandal and the HUD scandal, involved congressional constituent service efforts. Congress can take steps to reduce the negative effects of an overemphasis on casework while preserving the right of constituents to individual representation in difficult cases.

The House Task Force on Committee Reform has recommended the establishment of a central office of casework efforts in the Library of

Congress. The Senate should join the House and move ahead with this proposal. This office would be able to handle routine inquiries, such as tracking constituents' lost Social Security checks. In handling a larger volume of requests, this office should be able better to identify patterns of complaints and recommend systemic solutions. Such an office also might provide individual Members of Congress with a mechanism to investigate politically sensitive cases which may raise substantial issues, but without necessarily taking sides.

Congress might extend this principle further by exploring the establishment of ombudsmen and taxpayer advocates in major federal agencies. In addition to providing another mechanism for resolving problems, having an ombudsmen in federal agencies would help instill a more citizen-oriented attitude within agencies. Ombudsmen also would provide a central point of contact for congressional casework requests, likely making agency responses more efficient. Agencies with major adjudication responsibilities also might be required to employ taxpayer advocates with the responsibility for monitoring and presenting evidence against requests for benefits and other government relief.[7]

STRATEGY #7
Congress should use oversight and other powers to influence the executive branch.

More often than not, conservatives in Congress have to work with a non-conservative executive branch and try to influence executive actions critical to conservative policy successes. Until conservatives enjoy veto-proof majorities, passing legislation will be a largely ineffective method for influencing executive actions. In fact, a central purpose of influencing the executive branch is to change presidential calculations about what legislation to sign. In addition, there are many steps Congress can take short of passing laws to influence the executive branch. Thus, as with overall policy efforts, congressional relations with the executive branch should be viewed as a management task.

---

7 Heritage Foundation Bradley Fellow James L. Payne discusses this issue in his forthcoming publication, currently entitled *Rethinking Welfare: Expecting More from the Poor—and From Ourselves.*

Congressional leaders should note the disproportionality in this regard between Congress and the executive branch. The executive branch has a huge network of legislative affairs offices at the White House, in the Cabinet, and into the small agencies. That network exists principally to monitor and influence what Congress does. Congress in turn devotes substantial resources to monitoring and influencing the executive branch through its committees and the General Accounting Office, among other routes. But executive monitoring activity in Congress is essentially uncoordinated, and legislative efforts to influence the executive branch are sporadic.

House and Senate leaders should establish structures to coordinate oversight activity which should be focused on policy rather than scandal issues. It is not that Congress should overlook evidence of malfeasance in the executive branch, but that oversight efforts should have broader purposes. Overemphasizing scandals fails to advance policy objectives and makes it too easy for liberal opponents to dismiss oversight activities as mere politicking.

Congressional efforts to influence the executive branch are best conducted through oversight in part because more generic management and control efforts are usually disappointing. Substantial leeway in administration is guaranteed by the separation of powers doctrine and is essential to executive branch management. Thus, Congress cannot prescribe every possible executive action. Further, attempting to do so often exacerbates bureaucracy, creating overlapping and conflicting mandates which frustrate sound decisionmaking. In many cases, congressional efforts to place generic limitations on the executive branch have made it more difficult for Congress to exercise control over subsequent executive branch activities. For instance:

- **The War Powers Act** has made it more difficult for Congress to address overseas troop deployments, introducing a procedural wrangle into already difficult questions.

- **The Administrative Procedures Act**, passed by a Republican Congress in 1946 to control the actions of New Deal agencies, makes it more difficult for Congress to address individual regulatory issues.

- **Independent counsel procedures** often get in the way of congressional investigations of executive branch wrongdoing.

- **The 1974 Budget Act**, intended to write the executive branch out of overall budget policy, has failed and has been replaced by an ad hoc series of budget summits.

Within the executive branch, these types of generic controls tend to decentralize and bureaucratize power, making the President less accountable to the public and to Congress. Congress should particularly avoid attempting to limit the number of political appointees as a means of attempting to control the executive branch. In the long term, the President's appointees are Congress's allies in maintaining political control of the bureaucracy.

Hearings can be a particularly effective way for Congress to review military deployments and other issues in foreign affairs. The constitutional division of responsibilities and the impossibility of legislating guidelines for unpredictable situations make it especially difficult for Congress to legislate on foreign affairs. Conducting oversight hearings may be the only way for Congress to express its views and to ensure that Administration actions are subject to proper review.

When Congress does find it necessary to impose legislative controls on the executive branch, they should be as simple as possible. Complex procedures only exacerbate long-term problems with the bureaucracy. Congress's objective should be principles clear and simple enough that they do not need too many regulations. This approach also will help avoid convoluted interpretations by the judiciary.

Congressional leaders also should recall that partisan control will change and that executive-legislative relations therefore should be managed with broad governmental and policy goals in mind, not merely for the sake of partisan advantage.

Since direct legislative efforts to influence the executive branch are difficult, and perhaps ultimately self-defeating, congressional leaders should examine indirect methods of doing so. One obvious route is public opinion. While Congress is unlikely to be able to match the drama of a President's calling on the public to write Congress, congressional leaders can work to build and direct public opinion in their behalf through the media, through interest groups, and through the hearing process. The 104th Congress's success in getting President Clinton to sign a welfare bill quite similar to bills he earlier had opposed was achieved in part by the publicity generated by sending the bill to the White House three times, and by congressional leaders' persistence in pursuing the issue.

STRATEGY #8
Creating good public liaison is essential to building alliances.

As discussed in the introductory and lessons sections of this chapter, building coalitions of interested organizations and citizen groups is a critical part of the policy process. Building public opinion in this fashion also can help to box in the President, forcing him to address or acquiesce in legislative priorities. This strategy can be particularly effective with a President sensitive to public opinion and unfettered by consistent ideology.

As with inter-branch relations, congressional leaders should first realize that they are at a relative disadvantage against the executive branch, where there are offices and personnel dedicated largely to public liaison functions. In the last Congress, House leaders insisted that committees have staff employees responsible for this function, and that committees prepare an outreach plan. Senate leaders would do well to emulate this system, and House leaders should continue to expand the staff resources and level of professionalism dedicated to this function.

Good public liaison begins at the agenda-setting stage; it is not enough merely to appeal for support once decisions already have been made. Liaison staff should identify all organizations potentially interested in a determined policy area. Friendly or potentially friendly groups should be consulted as to their policy preferences. Discussions with possibly hostile groups should be opened in an effort to address or forestall opposition.

Group leaders should have regular access to congressional leaders, and leadership or lead committees should coordinate an outreach effort to make congressional speakers available for conventions and media opportunities. Public liaison efforts should be conducted with extended time frames in mind. It takes large membership groups several months to prepare materials, notify members, and ask them to respond on a single simple issue. Efforts are far more effective if educational efforts are carried out over an extended period, giving organization members an opportunity to see and hear from congressional leaders and allowing group members to work and lobby in their own communities.

STRATEGY #9
More effective hearings and oversight are needed to change the terms of debate.

Conservatives learned in the 104th Congress that conducting effective hearings is a more difficult process than they expected. Compelling witnesses are hard to find, and information about how government programs are running can be difficult to uncover. Effective hearings and oversight require adequate time and often require detailed research. Staff or staff teams should be assigned to a topic for at least several months— and ideally for the duration of a Congress. Several weeks at least should be allowed to prepare for a single hearing or series of hearings. Evidence, allegations, charges, and claims should be well researched. Staff should interview all witnesses before a hearing.

At a hearing, the chairman should take pains to defend witnesses against unfair attacks from liberals. On many committees, former chairmen possess detailed knowledge and an aggressive style, and may have access to information from the Administration. During the 104th Congress, some witnesses were personally attacked by liberal committee members, a practice which chairmen rarely allowed in previous Congresses.

When dealing with Administration or hostile witnesses, committee members should avoid asking questions to which they do not already know the answer. Asking a seemingly hard question to which a witness has a disarming answer can cause investigators to lose control of a hearing and to lose their policy point. A proposed House rules change would allow committee chairmen to allocate time in investigative hearings beyond the five minutes normally allowed each member. In the 104th Congress, Administration witnesses sometimes provided rambling answers, eating up the five minutes allotted a single member and allowing questioning to pass to a more sympathetic committee member. Committees and their members should have the opportunity in investigative hearings to pursue a line of questioning to its logical conclusion, as long as minority members then are provided equal time for their questions.

Media coverage is often a key test of a successful hearing. Committee media relations staff should contact specific editors and reporters prior to a hearing instead of relying on a press release to generate coverage. Staff should provide pre-hearing briefing material to interested reporters to make the story easier to follow and more likely to be covered. Timing a hearing to coincide with the release of a newsworthy study can magnify media attention. Committee leaders might schedule such hearings even if they suspect that they will disagree with the study conclusions (for instance, when a study was conducted by the Administration) in order to present the opposing case right away.

Committee staff assigned to a topic should survey investigative agencies such as the General Accounting Office and interested nongovernmental groups to identify any studies in progress and to establish likely completion dates. Committees with jurisdiction over economic policy and other areas in which there are regular government statistical releases should be aware of regular release dates from the Bureau of Labor Statistics, Census Bureau, and other agencies. Records of government research grants may also provide leads to researchers and should include study duration dates. If time allows, staff might charter or encourage studies from respected groups. If a topic is of ongoing interest and an agency can be expected to conduct an objective study, a committee could even mandate such a study in an authorization or appropriation report.

When possible, committees should arrange for the release of a study at a hearing or to have the authors testify on the day the study is released. In many cases, investigators or researchers will be willing to brief committee staff on preliminary findings and may be flattered to be asked to release a study at a hearing or to testify the same day or soon thereafter. Conservative committee staff should not write off executive agencies in this regard. Policy disagreements within an Administration or the simple desire for attention can lead executive officials to cooperative efforts with Congress.

For general investigative efforts, committee staff should not overlook government documents and information available on the Internet and in other government databases. In many respects in the computer age, the investigator's job is not finding information, but identifying useful information. Government grants, reports, and publications are available through various government databases, and Congress generally has access to data and reports not available to the public. Federal agencies are required by law to have information resource management (IRM) plans.

Staffers should review the IRM plans for agencies within their jurisdiction to identify databases which may be of interest to their committee.

The first witnesses make the most news, both because they set the tone for a hearing and because some reporters will have to file stories before hearings have been completed. By tradition, committees often call Administration witnesses first. This practice is appropriate when reviewing a budget request or an Administration legislative initiative. However, in cases in which Congress and the Administration have significant differences, committee chairman may wish to alter the hearing format. In the summer of 1996, for instance, the Senate Finance Committee held a hearing on the National Governors' Association's welfare reform plan. Despite the fact that Congress was sympathetic to the governors' plan, the Finance Committee's first witness was Health and Human Services Secretary Donna Shalala, who testified in opposition to elements of the governors' proposals. While it is appropriate for Congress to hear the views of Administration officials responsible for a particular policy area, it has no obligation to allow hostile Administration officials the first opportunity to comment on proposals developed in Congress or elsewhere outside of the executive branch.

As with other areas of congressional activity, hearings and oversight will be better conducted if they are coordinated and managed by the leadership. The Senate leadership has announced its intention to focus especially on oversight in the coming Congress. Rather than assign all committees to conduct oversight, leaders should identify committees and subcommittees with appropriate expertise and jurisdiction and plan oversight in specific areas. As a general proposition, oversight topics should relate to policy objectives. Oversight of the management of the Superfund program, for instance, would be an obvious first step in an effort to reform the program. Establishing that the program is failing to clean up waste sites provides the rationale for reform and disarms the reflexive liberal claim that conservative reforms are environmentally damaging.

STRATEGY #10
It is important to know when and how to use commissions.

When progress on an important issue in the routine political process bogs down over an extended period, calls for a commission often are heard. A few commissions have worked so well that some politicians and advocates are now eager to refer every thorny problem to a commission. But commissions cannot serve as fail-safe answers to every politically difficult issue. There are some issues, such as overall budget policy, which it would be clearly inappropriate to delegate to any commission, and many other situations in which commissions would not be likely to succeed. Some consideration about what commissions can or cannot do might clarify what kinds of issues could be advanced through commissions and what conditions are necessary for commissions to be successful.

Among recent commissions, the two most widely cited successes are the 1983 Social Security Commission and the Base Closure Commissions which have operated under separate 1988 and 1990 laws. Historically, scholars cite the Hoover Commissions on government reform as landmark successes. In all three cases, a high degree of consensus about what the commission needed to do existed before the commissions were appointed. Underlying the Hoover Commission was a broad agreement that the federal government needed to be more active in more areas. Institutional rivalries between and within the executive and legislative branches had made the specific reorganizational step difficult. The Hoover Commission was able to fill in important details and to overcome institutional inertia.

In 1983, Social Security trust funds were on the verge of going bankrupt. In 1982, Democrats had defeated dozens of Republicans with charges about GOP plans to reduce benefit growth, but Democrats were unwilling or unable to support tax increases to replenish the trust funds. It was obvious that some combination of tax increases and benefit cuts was the only possible route to avoiding bankruptcy for Social Security. For political reasons, politicians in both parties were afraid to advance proposals; the 1983 Social Security Commission therefore provided both a forum for specific discussions and a political shield against partisan attacks. In the base closure case, Congress and the executive branch agreed that changes in defense operations, external threats, and the declining budget made significant reductions in the basing network essential. Yet no elected official was willing to allow a base in his district to be closed without a fight, and congressional practice generally allowed a few interested Members to prevail on constituency-related questions. A commission removed the congressional suspicion that closures might be politically manipulated by the executive branch and provided the cover of a compelling national interest to balance local reservations about closing particular bases.

In the 1980s-era commissions, an impending budget crunch was also a critical element in creating the necessary consensus and generating the political will for action. When consensus or urgency is absent, commissions face more limited prospects. The 1992 Joint Commission on the Organization of Congress (JCOC) was able to generate a reasonable degree of consensus that the congressional committee system was too complex and autonomous, and that minority rights were not well balanced with majority prerogatives to move a legislative program. Despite this consensus, the absence of urgency about solving these problems made it impossible for the commission to forge a real consensus on details and unattractive for legislative leaders to face the institutional opposition to the recommendations.

The Kerrey-Danforth Bipartisan Commission on Entitlements was also formed in response to, and helped further to define, a consensus that growth in entitlement programs needed to be curbed. Yet crisis points for most programs (and for the overall budget) are several years away, so the sense of urgency which appears necessary for politicians to address politically volatile programs was absent, and the commission's recommendations had no legislative effect. The Kerrey-Danforth Commission, however, helped clarify the genuine problems facing entitlement programs and outlined potential solutions which may be of use in the future.

Thus, commissions can serve useful purposes even when immediate legislative action is unlikely. The 1988 Reagan privatization commission was unable to generate legislative progress because congressional liberals were not convinced that privatization was useful or necessary. Now that budget limitations have made it clearer that privatization may be socially as well as economically beneficial, the detailed plans outlined by the Reagan commission have formed the basis for real privatization efforts.

The National Commission on Economic Growth and Tax Reform (the Kemp Commission) was appointed by leaders of one party, making it unlikely that immediate legislative action would result. Realizing this, the commission focused on clarifying the need for tax reform through an extensive hearing process and laying out fundamental principles (rather than legislative details) of tax reform. The commission clearly advanced the cause of tax reform and probably has laid the basis for a specific plan when political circumstances are more favorable.

Commissions can serve a variety of policy purposes in designing, marketing, and advancing issues procedurally. Those proposing and designing commissions should know what results it is reasonable to expect given the degree of consensus that exists on an issue and the sense of urgency or commitment to action within the government. When it is unrealistic to expect immediate legislative action, commissions should be designed with longer-term goals in view. Several design elements should be kept in mind:

- **Copycat commissions do not work.** The Joint Commission on the Organization of Congress was patterned closely after the 1946 La-Follette-Monroney Commission which substantially restructured the congressional committee system. But because political conditions and the needs of Congress were substantially different in 1992, a similarly structured commission failed. The first Hoover Commission was so satisfactory that numerous copycat efforts were attempted (including a second Hoover Commission), none of which were nearly as successful as the first. Efforts today to model commissions on the base closure commission process are equally likely to be disappointing. Commissions must be designed for the conditions of a particular issue and time.

- **All parties must be at the table.** To produce immediate legislative action, all significant parties must be at the table. Unless a single party enjoys an overwhelming majority in Congress, a partisan commission cannot be expected to overcome the institutional and political barriers which probably caused its appointment. Partisan commissions can produce a party consensus or advance the public case for an issue, but those more limited goals should be acknowledged. The same is generally true of commissions appointed by Congress or by the executive branch without the participation of the other branch. A congressional commission on downsizing the executive branch, for instance, is unlikely to produce short-term results over objections from the President and his executive agencies.

- **Legislators are not required.** The presence or absence of legislators is not, in general, a critical factor in a commission's success. The Social Security Commission was composed largely of legislators and succeeded; the JCOC was composed exclusively of legislators and failed. The successful Base Closure Commission and the Hoover Commission included no sitting politicians. While the administrative or legislative nature of a particular commission's task might usefully guide its composition, simply removing an issue from politicians or getting the key (elected political) figures together is not enough, by itself, to resolve a problem.

This history and these lessons produce different conclusions as to the prospects for success for commissions commonly proposed today. It may well be that the policy consensus and political conditions are now ripe for a successful entitlement commission.[8] A similar consensus does not exist in the area of government downsizing, despite the President's declaration of the end of big government. Legislators considering a downsizing commission should recognize that a commission may be able to advance the public case for government downsizing and to identify principles and steps which might be employed in eliminating or consolidating agencies. But chartering a commission to devise a specific executive branch reorganization plan without executive branch participation is likely to be frustrating and pointless. As discussed in more detail below, it is similarly unrealistic to expect a campaign finance commission to bridge partisan divisions with a specific legislative plan, though a properly designed commission might be of use in clarifying issues and identifying options for action.

STRATEGY #11
Major reforms of the budget process should be enacted.

A consensus exists that the current congressional budget process is unsatisfactory. Some consensus exists as to needed solutions: reducing overlapping and repetitive procedures, reducing the time devoted to budget matters, better enforcement of budget targets and policies, and producing earlier and more complete agreement between the President and Congress on budget policy.

---

8 See Chapter 8, "Solving the Problem of Middle-Class Entitlements."

Crises such as confrontations over debt limits and continuing resolutions have provided the impetus for significant, but less than comprehensive, reforms three times in the past decade. The likely approval by Congress of a balanced budget amendment in 1997 may provide the urgency necessary to spark action on a comprehensive budget process overhaul along the lines of this existing consensus. A balanced budget amendment will make it essential that Congress and the President are able to agree on firm spending, taxation, and deficit levels and enforce them throughout the budget process. The likely introduction of this element of urgency should focus the budget process reform efforts.

The Budget Process Reform Act (H.R. 4285) introduced in the 104th Congress by Representative Christopher Cox (R-CA) with 224 cosponsors is well designed and represents a moderate-conservative consensus on a sound budget process. Senate Majority Leader Trent Lott was the lead Senate co-sponsor of the earlier version of the legislation, with 16 Senate co-sponsors. To secure adoption, however, sponsors must win both the support or acquiescence of the President and sufficient bipartisan support in the Senate to overcome a potential filibuster, which requires a two-thirds vote (67 members) because of the reform measure's affect on Senate rules.

In terms of the policy process, the Cox package is excellently designed but needs additional attention in process and marketing to ensure its adoption. Existing majority support might enable House supporters to pass the measure quickly or with only a cursory legislative effort. But the need to build support in the Senate and executive branch argues for a more deliberate process in the House.

Budget process reforms in general, and the Cox legislation in particular, would be an ideal topic for the appointment of a House select committee. The Committees on Budget, Appropriations, Government Reform, and Rules share jurisdiction over the bill, and Ways and Means and other committees would be affected significantly by any budget reform. The Budget Committee would have difficulty addressing systemic reform efforts for much of the winter and spring while attending to the annual budget resolution.

By requesting testimony from executive branch officials on budget reform proposals, a select committee could involve the Administration in budget reform discussions at an early point instead of ignoring it or waiting for a crisis to open discussions. If Administration officials are generally friendly to proposed changes, the select committee could begin defining elements of common ground. If executive officials are hostile, supporters of the reforms could begin early to address the arguments and concerns that they will face as the proposal moves toward adoption. The committee's hearing process could re-examine details of the proposal and build support, both within the government and among the public, for budget process reforms.

While the Speaker could appoint a Select Committee on the Budget Process on his own initiative, it may be preferable to create a committee by resolution of the House. In this fashion, the issue could be brought up for an initial discussion and vote as early as the first day of the new Congress. The House could go on record as favoring budget process reform and singling it out as an important issue while providing for a process to vet and publicize the proposed reforms more fully. Such a resolution also could provide minimal staffing for the select committee with the expectation that staff from the committees which normally would have jurisdiction would also devote time and expertise. A select committee might be authorized for one year initially, in hopes that budget process reforms could be achieved in that period. Reauthorization, if necessary, would give the House as a whole a second opportunity to address the issue, which might be productive if progress was not rapid.

Among its early activities, the select committee might address potential enforcement and other process issues related to the proposed Balanced Budget Amendment (BBA) to the Constitution, which is likely to come up for a House vote in the spring. Since many of the concerns about a BBA are enforcement-related (whether it would give courts power to order tax increases or result in Social Security benefit cuts), discussions oriented toward the practicality of imposing budget discipline through annual reviews and budget caps would address some of the most serious questions about a BBA. The Judiciary Committee, which has jurisdiction over constitutional amendments, does not have the expertise to address budget enforcement issues (nor probably should they be addressed in the amendment itself), making it useful for another committee to explore those questions.

Balanced Budget Amendment discussions would build support for the Budget Process Reform Act as the logical follow-on to the amendment itself. The legislation might, for instance, be revised to include overall budget targets keyed to the Balanced Budget Amendment's phase-in period. The committee might also consider other budget-related issues, including the Byrd Rule (limiting the permissible subject matter in reconciliation legislation, subject to a three-fifths vote) and other Senate procedures which could affect balanced budget enforcement efforts in significant ways. While traditions of deference and comity limit the way in which a House committee might address Senate procedures, no serious effort to reform the budget process can ignore the interplay of differing rules and procedures between the House and Senate.

Senate leaders should consider a similar means of addressing budget process reform. The Senate does not have procedures for select committees equivalent to those in the House, though there are precedents for Senate select committees, including the committee which originally developed the congressional budget process. Given that a majority of the Senate may not yet be committed to a comprehensive budget process reform along the lines of the Cox proposal, Senate leaders may be more comfortable with a task force, which does not imply an absolute commitment to legislation.

As in the House, Senate leaders would begin to build the case for budget process reform if they create a task force through a Senate resolution rather than simply appoint it on an informal basis. A formal resolution would elevate the status of the effort, establish a deadline toward which to work, and provide an early discussion and test of support within the Senate for budget reform. A task force created by Senate resolution can also hold official hearings, providing a more vigorous public effort and more serious discussion with executive branch officials than an informal task force would allow. As in the House, the Senate task force should be chartered to look into an overall budget reform, including issues related to a Balanced Budget Amendment.

The objective of House and Senate leaders should be to elevate the issue of budget process reform, to link it to the adoption of a Balanced Budget Amendment (probably strengthening both causes), to force interested parties within and outside Congress to raise and address seriously any concerns about proposed reforms, to engage the executive branch in the same serious discussion, to enlist the support of nongovernmental organizations, and to build public support and enthusiasm for budget reform. As outlined above, specific procedures in the House and Senate may differ, but any effort much less structured than those recommended is likely to fail. In particular, leaving initial work on the issue to the Budget Committees is almost certain to produce a damaging delay in addressing the issue because of the need to produce an annual budget resolution. Even though Budget Committee chairmen may be enthusiastic backers of proposed reforms, it may be better for other Members to coordinate the process reform effort to ensure the early and concentrated attention necessary to its success. In addition, the Senate Appropriations and other committees may have institutional concerns about proposed reforms which might be addressed more productively by a task force than by the Budget Committee, which is an interested party in any reform effort.

STRATEGY #12
Steps should be taken to reform the campaign finance system.

Consideration of reforms in the campaign finance system should begin with a re-examination of the reasons for the widespread dissatisfaction with the American political system. Americans are concerned about the role of money in politics, but they are concerned with money largely as a symptom of the lack of genuine citizen control of and involvement in democratic politics. Americans feel that their government is insulated from them, controlled by special interests, and unresponsive to average citizens' concerns. Money is an issue because it appears to be a means by which special interests exercise disproportionate influence in the political system. It is not even interest group participation per se, but its disproportionality and a sense of improper advantage, that concerns average citizens.

Most campaign finance proposals, including the McCain-Feingold and Smith-Shays proposals which enjoyed widespread support in the 104th Congress, are not crafted to address these fundamental concerns. These proposals would limit candidates' spending and fundraising in return for free and reduced-rate broadcast advertising and postage. The bills would do little, however, to limit special interests or reduce incumbent advantages. They would only make campaign financing even more complicated and bureaucratic, erect new roadblocks to vigorous citizen participation in politics, and eventually make citizens even more cynical than they are today. This has already been the result of the 1972 and 1974 Federal Election Campaign Act (FECA), which bureaucratized and regulated the exercise of fundamental political freedoms through electoral campaigns. The most popular pending bills propose to address problems created by overregulation with more new regulations.

The first task of conservatives, then, is to broaden the discussion to the topic of political reform and not allow liberals to focus on campaign financing and regulatory schemes. Merely regulating politics is not the way to defeat special-interest influence, because regulation is a game the special interests always win.

Term limits are the nuclear weapon in the battle for citizen control of politics. Even if term limits are looked upon as a regulatory scheme, it is manifest that simple regulations are better than complex ones: A term limit statute or amendment can be written in a paragraph or two; campaign financing schemes take scores of pages of legislation, thousands of pages of regulations, and perpetual administrative and judicial processes to judge individual cases.

Before endorsing a campaign finance commission whose charter would be to draw up additional regulations, conservatives should address concerns about special interests directly and fundamentally. House Speaker Newt Gingrich has committed to making term limits the first substantive vote of the 105th Congress. This is an important step, both symbolically and substantively. Realistically, however, that amendment is likely to fall short of the two-thirds majority necessary for House approval, and House leaders must not simply drop the issue of term limits for the duration of the Congress.

Through committees, task forces, or other means, conservative leaders must continue the discussion of term limits, both to remind citizens of conservatives' commitment to limiting government power, including their own, and to help build public support for term limits. In the campaign finance discussion more narrowly, conservatives must strive to present citizen control rather than government regulation as the antidote to special-interest influence in politics. Special-interest advantages such as government or compulsory dues funding should be attacked vigorously and on a continuing basis, and continually linked to a pro-citizen political reform agenda. One of the elements of this agenda should be a discussion, though committee hearings, of the possibility of term limits for federal judges. The concerns with judicial imperialism[9] might well be addressed with the same tool that has been applied to overweening executives and legislatures. The objective of a second term limits vote in the House toward the end of the 105th Congress would be a useful focus for these activities.

Given controversies that arose during the presidential campaign, a push to appoint a campaign finance reform commission may be overwhelming. Even those narrowly interested in campaign finance reform should review the conditions necessary for the success of commission efforts to assess what might reasonably be expected from such a commission. It is difficult to see any existing broad consensus between political parties, given the Democrats' close ties to the most vigorous special-interest groups — labor unions — and Republicans' understandable desire to eliminate unions' existing campaign-related advantages. If a commission came up with a split-the-difference compromise, its proposal might wind up being shelved or defeated through the efforts of a variety of interested parties.

Expanding rather than narrowing options may be as important to the solving of campaign finance problems as it is to broader political reform questions. But asking how to promote broad-based citizen involvement in politics is very different from chartering experts to come up with a new regulatory scheme for campaign financing.

A commission, properly designed, might be able to clarify some of the issues at stake in the political reform debate, to identify areas of common ground, and perhaps even to enunciate principles on which more detailed debates could continue. But ordering a commission to devise a specific plan when no broad consensus exists is begging for failure which, again, will only increase citizen cynicism. A commission in such circumstances would be forced either to accept a lowest-common-denominator plan (which would disappoint those most interested) or to recommend steps likely to be vigorously opposed by significant interests (inviting defeat of the proposal). Campaign finance reform advocates above all would be

---

9 See Chapter 7, "Reining in the Federal Judiciary."

best served by a commission which would conduct research and promote discussion on principles instead of dividing over details.

In addition to broadening the discussion at the highest level, Congress should narrow discussions over details to steps which may be achievable right away. The public's number-one concern about campaign financing is for adequate and understandable disclosure of political spending. There are numerous steps Congress easily could take to provide more complete and more understandable disclosure of campaign spending. But disclosure improvement proposals have been held hostage in past Congresses by campaign finance reform advocates themselves, who apparently fear that incremental steps might reduce the political pressure for their more ambitious schemes.

For 20 years in this fashion, self-proclaimed good government groups have stopped achievable incremental campaign reform efforts. Conservatives should point out that the perfect should not be made the enemy of the good. Leaders should charge relevant committees with moving a disclosure improvement bill very early in the Congress, and should condemn those holding out for more ambitious schemes for stopping possible progress. Combining, in a single bill or through contemporaneous consideration, a disclosure improvement statute with a broadly chartered commission and posing real action against future commitments might be the most effective responses to those who vainly hope to take politics out of political fundraising laws. Senate leaders should consider coupling a term limits vote with any campaign finance discussion in the Senate.

CONCLUSION

Reviewing the mixed record of the 104th Congress, conservatives have concluded reasonably that they need to learn better how to govern. Governing more effectively does not imply reflexive compromising, though it will entail more prudence about what is achievable in a limited amount of time and in a given set of political circumstances. At the same time, conservatives must strive to change the definition of the possible by improving their own ideas, changing and better managing the governmental process, and continually promoting their proposals. Reforming Congress and the rest of the federal government to achieve conservative ends will require some new laws and congressional rules, but the competent and innovative use of existing and inherent powers is at least as important as new statutes in achieving conservative governance.

In general, management of the committee system and other legislative processes will produce better results than attempting to revamp procedures on a broad basis. One clear exception to this general rule is the congressional budget process, which was designed with the aim of abetting spending increases. Changes in that process are essential to conform to an era of budget restraint and to the likely passage of a balanced budget amendment in particular. Congressional leaders should make budget reform a top priority and should establish mechanisms, such as select committees or task forces, to ensure that budget reform legislation receives early and concentrated attention.

Congressional leaders should consider the overall policy process of defining, marketing, and securing adoption of a policy program, and should devote their efforts to managing that overall effort as well as to directing the legislative process, which is only one element of policy success. Initiating policies from the legislature is certainly different from, and probably more difficult than, doing so from the executive branch. But legislative leaders enjoy a broader set of tools well-adapted to both incremental and long-term policy efforts. Conservative legislative leaders must set their sights accordingly—not lower, but further out.

Chapter 2

RESTRUCTURING, CLOSING, AND CONSOLIDATING FEDERAL AGENCIES AND PROGRAMS

Ronald D. Utt

Any meaningful government reform agenda must include as one of its major components a comprehensive effort to weed out and eliminate those programs and departments that have outlived their usefulness or whose activities are more properly performed at the state or local level. With two centuries of accumulated responsibilities, the federal government must stretch its limited resources across literally thousands of such programs. Forced to divide its attention between the important and the trivial tasks associated with public service, the federal government no longer is able to perform its core functions particularly well. It often must ask the most important agencies and departments to compromise with, and surrender resources to, those that are nonessential and even marginal.

In order to review and discuss the reallocation or disbanding of such federal activities, policymakers need to understand the general framework of the republic known as the United States. America *is* a nation of states. Both the Founding Fathers and the Constitution presumed that there would

The author would like to thank The Honorable Donald H. Rumsfeld, The Honorable Robert W. Kasten, Jr., the Honorable James C. Miller III, and Dr. Richard W. Rahn for their contributions to this chapter. The views and opinions expressed here, however, are entirely the responsibility of the author.

always be a distinct division of responsibility between the federal government and the states, and between the states and the communities within them. For much of American history, this division was scrupulously maintained; the federal government focused exclusively on issues that were national in scope, such as defense, international relations, customs, immigration, and interstate commerce. Over time, however, and largely during this century, the federal government began creating new and larger responsibilities for itself, gradually absorbing responsibilities that previously were the sole province of the states.

Such a shift from state and local responsibility to federal control has occurred in education, housing, health, welfare, urban issues, law enforcement, and transportation. Yet after decades of involvement at the federal level, and despite an infusion of billions of dollars, there has been no appreciable improvement in performance in these areas. Indeed, many of these services experienced a substantial diminution in quality once the federal government became involved. For many, it is difficult to remember, let alone even imagine, the level of urban quality—whether in jobs, crime control, education, or fiscal stability — that characterized American cities before the Department of Housing and Urban Development (HUD) was created. Just restoring that level would signify a major improvement today.

In addition to these endeavors, the federal government attempts to perform services that are unessential at any level of government and best left to voluntary arrangements between individuals or between individuals and commercial enterprises. Still other activities rendered obsolete by the passage of time and changes in the economy continue, fully funded and looking for justification. Many of the programs created during the New Deal fall in the former category, while the multibillion dollar farm support program, with its origins in the 19th century, fits the latter. In many cases, these programs have absorbed billions of dollars in resources that should have been left with the taxpayers to spend according to their families' needs and preferences.

The first major effort to pare back a century of involvement in obsolete or marginal government programs was initiated by the Reagan Administration in its first term. But despite an extensive agenda of worthy targets, laid out initially in the President's Program for Economic Recovery, only a few programs were shut down, and many of those that had experienced significant budget cuts under Reagan had sizable amounts of money restored later in the decade as a Congress unsympathetic to reform and subject to well organized special-interest groups sought to preserve the status quo.

More than a decade later, in 1995, the 104th Congress convened and immediately adopted an even more ambitious agenda than President Reagan's to shut down, reform, and consolidate government agencies and programs. Its proposals included terminating four Cabinet-level departments (Education, Housing and Urban Development, Energy, and Commerce) and dozens of major independent programs (such as the National Endowment for the Arts and the Appalachian Regional Commission).

While Congress succeeded in meeting only a fraction of these goals, just pursuing such an ambitious agenda yielded far more success than had been achieved previously by President Reagan. While all of the Cabinet departments survived largely intact, more than 250 other programs, offices, divisions, and independent agencies were put out of business. And while a number of factors contributed to these successes, a key factor in itself was the sheer number of targets selected, which helped to spread political opposition to the cuts across a wide battlefront and allowed the reformers to breach the line of defense at a number of weak points.

The lessons learned from these partially successful efforts can be refined and reapplied to many of the targets for closure that slipped through the cracks during the 104th Congress. Given the detritus accumulated from a century of federal expansion, the 105th Congress should conduct a comprehensive review and overhaul of the entire federal establishment; the objective should be nothing less than a new federal system that is focused on the efficient provision of essential national services and that delegates to the states responsibilities that are more appropriate to local operation.

A History of Expansion. Over the past two centuries, the federal government has undergone dramatic change, most frequently getting larger in costs, number of employees, number of objectives pursued, and number of agencies, departments, and bureaus created to pursue those objectives. How many separate offices and divisions exist within the 15 Cabinet-level departments is not known, but the number must be in the thousands. In addition, each of 95 independent government agencies, including fairly large ones like the Agency for International Development, oversees hundreds of separate divisions and departments.

Although new departments, agencies, offices, and divisions have been added over time to reflect America's changing needs, few deletions or shutdowns ever occur when those needs or problems have been solved or diminished. An extreme example of this phenomenon has been the continued funding of the National Helium Reserve, established in 1925 to ensure a steady supply of helium for U.S. dirigibles while denying it to German zeppelins. This former national defense priority diminished in importance and use with the advent of fixed-wing aircraft and peace with Germany, yet the agency did not receive any substantive public scrutiny until the 1980s.[1]

A more typical yet much more costly example of this failure to change with the times has been the continued funding of the Department of Agriculture, created on May 15, 1862, by President Abraham Lincoln with a budget of $115,000. At that time, at least five out of ten American workers were employed in agriculture, which was the single largest sector of the economy, accounting for about one-fifth of the gross national product (GNP). Today, agriculture accounts for just over 1 percent of the GNP and utilizes only 2.5 percent of the workforce. Yet with more than 105,000 employees, the Department of Agriculture is the fourth-largest of the 15 Cabinet departments, behind only the Departments of Defense, Veterans Affairs, and Treasury. Many of its costly and intrusive programs were created during the Great Depression to halt the decline in farm incomes. Although the "problem" solved itself five decades ago, the Department and its costly programs live on.

Redundancy, Obsolescence, and Other Problems. Overlapping functions and redundancy are common problems in a federal establishment that is good at creating and expanding programs but seldom capable of deleting and consolidating them. In the field of civil rights enforcement alone, there are several independent commissions, as well as numerous divisions and offices within Cabinet-level departments, all with overlapping civil rights responsibilities. The independent agencies include the Commission on Civil Rights and the Equal Employment Opportunity Commission. Within the executive branch, the Civil Rights Division of the

---

1 Proposed during the Reagan Administration, and again by the House of Representatives, permission to privatize the Helium Reserve was enacted into law in the last days of the 104th Congress.

Justice Department plays a lead role in civil rights enforcement, but Housing and Urban Development still maintains a Division of Fair Housing and Equal Opportunity. The Department of Labor maintains an Office of Equal Employment Opportunity and Affirmative Action, while the Department of Education maintains an Office of Civil Rights which contains 17 separate branches and six levels of management. Even the Foreign Agriculture Service of the U.S. Department of Agriculture includes a "Civil Rights Staff Coordinator" in the office of the Administrator.

A good illustration of how such top-heavy bureaucratic redundancy and overlap hurt both the taxpayer and the targeted beneficiaries is the group of congressional scholarship funds that honor distinguished Americans. According to the President's FY 1996 budget, the Harry S. Truman Scholarship Foundation planned to spend $1.13 million in overhead to provide just $2 million in scholarships, while the James Madison Memorial Fellowship Foundation planned to spend $986,000 in overhead to provide only $1,008,000 in fellowships to students. The Barry Goldwater Scholarship Foundation and the Morris K. Udall Scholarship and Excellence in National Environmental Policy Foundation, although worthy in purpose, are top-heavy as well, with bureaucratic burdens that diminish their ability to achieve their mandated goals.

One way to measure the social cost of this waste is to recognize that a dollar spent on administrative overhead is a dollar denied a student or scholar. Given the small size of each of these programs, it makes no sense to maintain five separate accounting departments, five mailrooms, five travel budgets, five costly executives, five executive assistants, and five versions of all of the other functions necessary to operate a scholarship program. A proposal to consolidate these scholarship funds in a single entity to reduce overhead and thereby increase the funds available to scholars was ignored by Congress and the heads of these five programs; today, each fund continues to operate as inefficiently as it did in the past.

The time is right to close and consolidate agencies. The reasons that unnecessary agencies and programs should be closed or consolidated can be discussed using three general criteria: Either they suffer from redundancy or obsolescence, or their creation was, simply, a big mistake. These categories are not mutually exclusive.

Agencies are redundant if their primary tasks or key elements of these tasks are performed equally as well by other agencies or departments in the government. The direct cost of such redundancy is substantial and can be measured in the billions of dollars devoted to duplicated overhead. But more significant costs should be measured in what was not accomplished, such as money that was unavailable for scholarships in the previous example, or the duties and responsibilities that fell between the cracks because agencies and personnel pursuing similar or related objectives failed to coordinate their efforts. In the case of overlapping agencies that are responsible for oversight of safety concerns, a lack of coordination could be catastrophic.

Obsolete agencies are those that were established to perform functions which once were deemed important but have become unnecessary, whether because the functions are no longer as important as they once were, the problems that led to their creation have since been solved, or the issues have become insignificant as the economy has changed in structure or emphasis. Although obsolete agencies are less common than redundant ones, they are usually more costly in terms of the direct and indirect costs they inflict on society.

The Department of Agriculture (DOA), in its current configuration, is obsolete; its mission still reflects the needs of a society that ceased to exist with the advent of the industrial revolution. Although the DOA performs a variety of tasks, including tasks unrelated to agriculture, its chief function emerged first as a Depression-era palliative—to sustain farmers' incomes by propping up the price of the raw agricultural products they raise and sell. This is accomplished by restricting how much they can grow; determining what, if anything, their competitors can grow; limiting how much, if any, of the product can be imported; and paying a cash subsidy when the actual sale price falls below a targeted amount. While farmers benefit directly from these schemes, it is the consumer who must pay twice for this program— first for artificially inflated prices at the store and, second, in the $7 billion in taxes needed to prop up the program.

Despite the substantial prosperity that now characterizes America's agricultural sector, dozens of costly economic development programs are still operated by the Department of Agriculture. Its Office of Rural Economic and Community Development, for instance, continues to operate a rural electric and telephone program providing subsidized loans to the tax-exempt rural cooperatives that produce and distribute electricity to rural residents.

Earlier this century, the Department of Agriculture created an agriculture research and extension service to provide farmers with information on modern farming techniques and scientific advances. Although the communication of such information is no longer a problem and some of America's best school systems are located in states that are rural or heavily oriented toward agriculture,[2] the DOA still maintains a costly education program employing nearly 10,000 workers at its Office of Research, Education, and Economics. The DOA also operates many programs that replicate services provided elsewhere in the federal establishment. For example, the DOA even operates a rural housing program in competition with similar programs operated by HUD.

The Department of Agriculture illustrates how an agency that was established to fulfill a series of missions considered important a century ago and again during the Depression has continued to find ways to spend taxpayers' money. Its missions have long since been fulfilled, and agriculture now represents a much smaller segment of our economy, but DOA's share of the budget does not reflect these facts.

The obsolescence of the Department of Agriculture is shared by several other departments and agencies as well, especially the Department of Transportation (DOT), whose predecessor organizations played an important role in creating and constructing the interstate highway system four decades ago and in encouraging commercial aviation even before that. Today, it has become an obstacle to improved transportation services by discouraging innovation, monopolizing most of the financial resources available to transportation, and centralizing all decisionmaking on regional or local transportation issues. Other obsolete agencies include the General Services Administration, the Corporation for Public Broadcasting, the Government Printing Office, the Bureau of Indian Affairs, the Departments of Labor and Commerce, the Arms Control and Disarmament Agency, the Interstate Commerce Commission, the Pennsylvania Avenue Development Corporation, the Tennessee Valley Authority, the U.S. Postal Service, and four federal Power Marketing Administrations.

---

2 Based on student performance in math proficiency, the top ten states were Iowa, North Dakota, Minnesota, Maine, New Hampshire, Nebraska, Wisconsin, Idaho, Utah, and Wyoming.

The third main reason for closing down an agency is the acknowledgment that even its creation was a big mistake and that its continued existence has done little or nothing to resolve the problems that suggested its establishment in the first place. Indeed, in some cases, the agency that was created may have exacerbated the very problems it was expected to solve. The U.S. Department of Housing and Urban Development is perhaps the archetypal example of such federal mistakes. Created in 1965 to stem and reverse the steady decline in American cities, it has presided instead over their collapse. Since the creation of HUD, older cities have continued to decline in population, jobs, taxpayers, and businesses. Crime has risen substantially, education standards have declined, budgets are strained, and the levels of commercial and cultural activities are pale shadows of what they once were. Indeed, merely restoring the "troubled" urban environments that existed on the eve of HUD's creation would amount to a major success by today's standards.

Symbolic of how far our cities have fallen after three decades of HUD guidance is the discovery that some U.S. mayors recently attended a conference sponsored by the Agency for International Development to gain helpful hints for governing their communities. Thanks to one such conference and a trip to Africa by several of his staff, Mayor Kurt L. Schmoke of Baltimore was inspired to implement a new immunization program for the city when he discovered that Kenya's rate of childhood immunization (96 percent) exceeds that of Baltimore (62 percent).[3] When our cities become eligible for our own foreign aid programs, it is time to rethink our nation's urban policy, and getting rid of HUD would be a good place to start.

The Department of Energy (DOE) is another big mistake. Created in 1977 as President Jimmy Carter's response to high energy prices, DOE's command-and-control efforts in the energy crisis proved counterproductive and served only to exacerbate the crisis by interfering with the market's attempts to bring forth more fuel supply and to encourage conservation. While the energy crisis and the long lines at the gas pumps have long since passed, the Department of Energy lives on. Other notable mistakes include

---

3 The AID program is called Lessons Without Borders. See Kelly Couturier, "Baltimore, U.S. Cities Find Community-Building Models in Developing Countries," *The Washington Post*, June 10, 1996, p. A20.

the Appalachian Regional Commission, the National Endowments for the Arts and Humanities, the Legal Services Corporation, the Administrative Conference of the United States, the Advisory Commission on Intergovernmental Relations, Amtrak, the Federal Transit Administration, the Agency for International Development, the Department of Education, the Small Business Administration, the Commission on Fine Arts, the Office of Government Ethics, and the Railroad Retirement Board.

LESSONS LEARNED

Most of the federal programs that have been suggested for termination have been around for a long time (and so have the proposals to terminate them). Their longevity has allowed policymakers to accumulate a substantial record of what works and what does not in terminating agencies. Because the record of failed attempts exceeds that of successful ones, there is a much better record of what does not work. In looking back over the past several decades, it appears that what does not work is targeting a single program or using appeals that depend on logical arguments like wasted money, program inefficiencies, and market distortions. However compelling these cases may be, efforts to close the targeted agencies and programs are often doomed to defeat by countervailing political pressures.

Lesson #1: The political imbalance between program beneficiaries and taxpayers in general must be addressed. Despite the marginal benefits or unintended social costs associated with the continuation of low-priority programs or obsolete agencies, experience shows that they will be exceptionally resistant to reform, elimination, or downsizing. In a democracy, this should seem intuitively implausible, because these programs benefit a relatively small number of people compared to the size of the taxpaying public that pays for them. Ironically, it is precisely this imbalance of interest that protects these programs, since the few people serviced receive substantial per capita benefits and the cost per capita for each taxpayer is too modest to notice. It is also true that those who are responsible for the very sustenance of a program or agency will be intensely involved in preventing its possible demise.

A case in point involves Amtrak, the federally funded rail passenger service which has survived 25 years of termination efforts from several Presidents and from Members of Congress. Amtrak receives $750 million per year in federal subsidies, which implies a $47 per passenger per ride

---

LESSONS LEARNED

- The political imbalance between program beneficiaries and taxpayers in general must be addressed.

- Congressional committees involved in agency oversight tend to expand programs and frustrate efforts to close them.

- Terminations will succeed only if somebody has a large financial stake in the outcome.

- Terminations can be achieved if they are part of a comprehensive agenda and are accompanied by strong political support.

- Successful terminations require the relentless effort of key politicians.

---

subsidy. A businessman (a typical consumer, since 75 percent of Amtrak riders have annual incomes in excess of $40,000) who rides the train once a week from Baltimore to New York costs the taxpayers nearly $2,500 a year in subsidies. Weighed against this subsidy is a per-taxpayer cost of less than $7 per year, or about two cents a day.

As a consequence of this cost/benefit imbalance, whenever the issue of funding for Amtrak comes before Congress, passengers vociferously support the continuation of service while the taxpayers who gain little from its demise say little about the outcome. Indeed, so committed are Amtrak's riders to the continued existence of a subsidized railroad that they voluntarily support and fund two Washington-based lobbying organizations—the National Association of Railroad Passengers and the United Rail Passenger Alliance—to help preserve it. Their presence is not lost on congressional committee members.

Unfortunately, this same political imbalance works to encourage the development of new programs as well. An example is the 1996 creation of the National Sheep Industry Improvement Center. Funded by $50 million from the government, this program mainly supports 1,773 ranchers with annual lamb or wool businesses of $50,000 or more, or per-rancher benefits of $27,000 against a taxpayer cost of just 43 cents per year. Given the size of the benefits to the sheep ranchers, it is certain that elected officials who support continuing this program will be rewarded with campaign contributions, honoraria, and opportunities for travel to attractive destinations. The National Sheep Industry Improvement Center can be expected to have a long and fruitful life.

Such examples abound throughout the federal establishment and help explain the tenacity with which beneficiaries defend their programs. They also explain why the taxpaying public is indifferent to reform, given the modest and uncertain nature of the prospective reward. Many federal programs were cut or terminated in the FY 1996 budget, which reduced the projected budget deficit from over $200 billion to an estimated $107 billion. The loss of subsidies by scores of privileged groups was not offset by an associated tax relief package, which may explain why so many of the targeted agencies ultimately survived the scare and why so little follow-up occurred in the making of the FY 1997 budget.

Lesson #2: Congressional committees involved in agency oversight, by their very nature, tend to expand programs as well as frustrate efforts to close them. Added to the political imbalance among constituents of a program—those who benefit are few, while those who pay are many—is the pressure within the congressional committees charged with its oversight. The congressional committee structure vests substantial power in long-serving Members of Congress who, in turn, derive substantial power from their ability to allocate billions of dollars among vested constituencies. Any reform effort that would limit or end such discretionary power (whether through termination, consolidation, or devolution) is likely to be opposed by Members of Congress who currently benefit from such discretion. Continuing with the example of Amtrak, for well-placed Members of Congress, Amtrak represents a politically positive opportunity to bring costly services to their cities and states at an affordable rate.

Lesson #3: Terminations will succeed only if somebody has a large financial stake in the outcome. Individual efforts to terminate a program can succeed when they are supported by entities that have a large financial stake in the outcome. For example, efforts to privatize Conrail were opposed initially by the work force and dependent shippers in the Northeast. However, their financial concerns were offset by the prospective financial gains that might accrue to the investment community and to the private railroads that hoped to acquire the valuable asset.

More often than not, such efforts to achieve a balance of interests are unsuccessful and do not result in the desired reforms because the entrenched interests have accumulated long-standing political credits through years of campaign support. The persistent failure of the food processing industries to end or modify the government sugar and milk programs that keep the prices of these products stable and benefit farmers is a classic example.

Lesson #4: Terminations can be achieved if they are part of a comprehensive agenda and are accompanied by strong political support. Notwithstanding the long record of failure, some policymakers and their supporters have succeeded in dramatically reducing and terminating programs. These successes, however, have been few and far between, confined largely to the budgets for FY 1982 and FY 1996. Even in those years, most of the targeted programs survived, and full funding was often restored within a few years to those that had been cut back.

Those successful budget campaigns had two things in common: 1) they followed immediately upon overwhelming and unambiguous electoral mandates to reduce the size of government, and 2) they were part of a comprehensive overhaul effort during which virtually all government programs were scrutinized. President Reagan's Program for Economic Recovery proposed substantial cuts or terminations in 85 major programs and linked these changes to substantial across-the-board cuts in individual and corporate income taxes. In the end, only a few of these programs were actually terminated, but many more were substantially reduced or reformed in ways that would require less spending in the years to come. Although the electoral mandate was important, as was the linkage to substantial tax relief, a key reason for success was the assault across a wide programmatic front that successfully weakened the ranks of supporters.

For example, cuts in mass transit subsidies might bring opposition from mayors, governors, unions, and transit managers; but by attacking across a broad front and putting at risk dozens of federal programs, the reformers forced mayors and governors to divide their focus in order to hold onto, for example, their Urban Development Action Grants or Economic Development Administration assistance, and unions in general were forced to protect extended unemployment benefits and trade adjustment assistance. This left only the transit unions and a few local bureaucrats to carry the burden of resistance, which proved inadequate. With this strategy repeated more than 85 times, and with the lines of communication to otherwise sympathetic Members of Congress clogged with the lamentable pleas of groups of aggrieved program dependents, resistance collapsed. Reformers made significant progress in eliminating or reducing the scope of existing, entrenched government programs.

Fourteen years later, the 104th Congress used the same combination of an electoral mandate and a comprehensive reform package to reach a similar outcome which, in terms of programmatic spending changes and terminations, was more far-reaching than President Reagan's had been. This most recent exercise yielded more terminations and cost reductions, as well as important entitlement reform in welfare programs and more privatizations, than had occurred during the entire eight years of the Reagan Administration. Once again, with so many programs under assault, pleas by beneficiaries and program managers often fell on deafened ears.

The 104th Congress's assault on hundreds of programs brought to Washington hundreds of special interests intent on preserving their benefits. The halls of Congress were filled with popular entertainers who wished to preserve funding for the National Endowment for the Arts, as well as teachers and students working on behalf of the Department of Education and busloads of public housing tenants demonstrating against public housing cuts. Their pleas were so distracting that a petition signed by several dozen academics who sought to preserve the Administrative Conference of the United States seldom made it past the summer interns in the congressional offices. As a result, the Administrative Conference of the United States was one of nearly 270 separate spending items, offices, divisions, or agencies eliminated in their entirety in 1995.

Lesson #5: Successful terminations require the relentless effort of key politicians. An essential ingredient of any effort to achieve a controversial political goal, such as terminating government programs, is a determined and dedicated leadership that is willing to take on the project, devote considerable time and energy to it, and demonstrate a willingness to engage in daily political combat until the issue is won. While good planning, sound strategy, and a willingness to compromise and accommodate are also essential, they are no substitute for old-fashioned hard work and determination.

One reason such qualities are so vital is that reformers invariably will be opposed by well-organized groups — frequently represented by well-funded and well-staffed trade and professional associations—whose sole purpose is to preserve the status quo and prevent reform. These lobbying groups represent individuals, related groups, institutions, and businesses whose livelihoods often depend exclusively on some government subsidy, privilege, or entitlement and who stand to lose money and privilege should the reformers win. For this reason, reformers must bring to the fight the same level of determination as their opponents. Otherwise, the chance of success will be very small.

Some of the successful legislative struggles of the recent past illustrate the importance of both a good strategic plan and strong leadership from the top. The much-heralded Defense Base Closure and Realignment Commission (Base Closing Commission), which probably will serve as a model for many such commissions in the future, can attribute much of its success to the dogged leadership of Representative Richard Armey (R-TX). Britain's successful privatization program would not have happened without the determined leadership of Prime Minister Margaret Thatcher. And Speaker Newt Gingrich's appointment of Representative Scott Klug (R-WI) to manage the House's privatization initiatives was instrumental in achieving an unprecedented number of privatization successes during the 104th Congress.

STRATEGIES FOR CLOSING FEDERAL PROGRAMS

Although electoral mandates for budget cuts have been few and far between, and the budget cuts are often beyond the control of individual elected officials, Congress can still pursue an effective program to close, downsize, or consolidate programs. Past experience suggests that the likelihood of success is greater if such a program is part of a comprehensive and far-reaching reform program that puts as many bureaucracies as possible at risk while providing some tangible rewards for the taxpayer. Without a comprehensive effort, those who depend upon the targeted programs for jobs, privilege, and subsidies will work aggressively to ensure that the effort fails, and will likely outnumber and outfight those who would reform the program.

STRATEGIES FOR CLOSING FEDERAL PROGRAMS

- Congressional leaders should make a strong case for comprehensive bureaucratic reorganization.

- Congress must conduct a strong marketing effort.

- Congress should identify as many targets as possible.

- Policymakers must neutralize opposition from as many beneficiary groups as possible.

- Congress should use legislative vehicles to advance comprehensive reform.

Experience is the best teacher. Following the 1994 election, which represented a strong mandate for smaller and less costly government, several proposals for fundamentally restructured government quickly emerged. One of these proposals would have closed the Department of Housing and Urban Development. Sensing both the risk involved and the turn in public sentiment, HUD Secretary Henry Cisneros associated himself with the spirit of the reform effort and proposed a bold plan which would have greatly diminished HUD's command-and-control approach, ended the worst excesses of the failed housing programs, and significantly reduced HUD's staffing. But when the smoke cleared, HUD in all of its manifest waste was still standing, and the Senate and House committees of jurisdiction (the Senate Committee on Banking, Housing, and Urban Affairs and the House Committee on Banking and Financial Services) had approved new housing legislation that would have entrenched some of the worst aspects of HUD policies even more deeply while reversing what few fundamental reforms had occurred over the past decade or more.

What happened was a classic case of the exercise of power by an Iron Triangle — a coalition comprised of the industries and institutions that benefit from the status quo, the congressional committees of jurisdiction, and the work force of a bloated federal bureaucracy. While the freshmen were well organized and had good leadership, they were no match for an industry that risked losing billions of dollars in annual subsidies,. or for the members of congressional committees who allocated those dollars and wanted their influence and prestige maintained.

Trusting in a vague public dissatisfaction with HUD programs, the freshmen who wanted to end HUD and overhaul the federal housing assistance programs went to battle with few allies beyond a couple of supportive think tank experts. Against them were arrayed the more than 3,000 local Public Housing Authorities, real estate developers and builders, tax-exempt financiers, captive nonprofit housing assistance organizations, real estate-related trade associations, and scores of university academicians whose chances for lucrative research grants or consulting agreements might end with the end of federal involvement in housing. Both committees of jurisdiction and the freshman reformers were overwhelmed by the massive and well-organized lobbying effort engineered by the managers of the nation's public housing authorities and supported by other components of the real estate industry. While Secretary Cisneros also was a target of the lobbying effort, relations between Congress and the President had deteriorated to the point where cooperation between Secretary Cisneros and the freshmen was impossible. Many mayors, fearful of losing their share of $4 billion per year in community development block grants, also weighed in to oppose the HUD reforms.

Once energized, these lobbies succeeded not only in putting an end to the reform effort, but also in rolling back past reforms and reshaping America's housing laws in ways that would enhance public housing's role in excess of anything experienced in the past. Missing from the effort to reform HUD were effective House and Senate leaders willing to step in between the factions to ensure that a compromise solution would adhere to the spirit of the new Congress's overall objectives and the 1994 mandate from the electorate.

The lobbying by the special interests involved in this ordeal was highly effective. Ironically, however, the resultant legislative proposals pandered so far to the self-interest of public housing authorities that the House-Senate conference on the bills collapsed in discord, and neither bill was enacted into law. Because of this, the 105th Congress now has an opportunity to start afresh, learning from the mistakes of its predecessor and implementing the fundamental changes needed to overhaul HUD and its abysmal housing programs. In summary, a more promising approach for policymakers to take in trying to restructure an agency such as HUD would include elements that have been learned from the experiences of the freshman Republicans in the 104th Congress:

- **Incite public sentiment for reform.** Take the issue to the public and expose, in overwhelming detail, the pervasive waste within HUD and the horrific conditions that characterize many public housing projects. On-site press conferences would be very effective, and both culpable Washington officials and those who manage the local projects could be questioned to good effect during congressional oversight hearings. HUD's own inspector general reports, which offer a bonanza of frightening examples, would be essential. Efforts to identify sympathetic outside experts and advocates who can speak to the press and testify before Congress should be made from the outset. And linking reform of federal housing assistance to the newly reformed welfare system as completing the work begun by the 104th Congress would capitalize on previous success.

- **Leave no HUD stone unturned.** All of HUD's policies and programs should be scrutinized carefully in order to defuse the inevitable special-interest opposition. This includes the FHA mortgage insurance program and community development block grants. The first has considerable support from the home-building, real estate, and housing finance industries, but these special interests could be mollified by spinning off FHA into an independent government corporation which ultimately could be privatized. Community development block grants, an old-fashioned pork-barrel project beloved by mayors, could be eliminated in favor of more aggressive enterprise zone efforts or a comprehensive urban redevelopment strategy that relies on economic growth, not federal handouts.

- **Mobilize key beneficiaries.** Those who will benefit most from reform must be identified and mobilized; this includes HUD's chief victims, the residents of the deplorable public housing projects. Often poor, of limited education, and easily manipulated by the public housing managers, they are natural prey for those who wish to maintain the current system. They must be apprised of how their lives will improve with well-crafted reform; they also should be invited and encouraged to testify on behalf of reform. Surveys and extensive anecdotes indicate that assisted tenants prefer vouchers over public housing.

- **Involve the congressional leadership.** Congressional leaders must be convinced of the need for each type of reform and must be active and visible participants in the whole process. The past disinterest and neutrality demonstrated by the leadership in Congress encouraged the committees of jurisdiction to pay too much attention to the vocal opponents of reform.

- **Start where the 104th Congress left off.** Comprehensive reform legislation developed and introduced during the 104th Congress by Representatives Sue Myrick (R-NC) and Sam Brownback (R-KS) and by Senator Lauch Faircloth (R-NC) represents an excellent starting point for the 105th Congress in 1997.

Implementing the Elements of Comprehensive Reform

The previous discussion of failed attempts to reform HUD clarifies why a comprehensive plan for reforming each government agency is necessary. A number of specific steps can be taken by reformers to maximize their efforts, to bring as many supporters as possible over to their side, and to diminish the strength and effectiveness of the opposition. These steps include the following strategies.

STRATEGY #1
The congressional leadership should make a strong case for comprehensive bureaucratic reorganization.

Whenever they make the case for a comprehensive overhaul of the federal bureaucracy, policymakers must focus consistently on the positive benefits of closing programs: program improvements, better benefits, tax relief, and more choices. The potential for substantial budgetary savings that can be applied to tax reduction or program consolidation and improvement should be emphasized, but not to the exclusion of programmatic concerns. Reformers also must emphasize the across-the-board nature of the effort and the distant origins of many of the targeted agencies and departments, and then link their proposed changes to the tangible improvements that inevitably will result from a re-engineered government that is better able to deal with the new challenges of the 21st century.

Stressing such broad positive themes also would help to unify the various efforts in the minds of the public and the media. For instance, the theme of modernizing or re-engineering government to position it for the challenges of the next century could build on President Clinton's highly visible "reinventing government" efforts.

While the National Performance Review was comprised largely of gimmicks, managerial mumbo-jumbo, an absence of principle, and inflated accomplishments, the effort nonetheless created the very clear public impression that government was broken and that the President should fix it. Congress could build on this theme and substitute an alternative set of proposals for the thousands of bureaucratic NPR stratagems that are being portrayed as meaningful reform. Another theme might be creating new consolidated Cabinet departments that can deal with new challenges more effectively.

STRATEGY #2
Congress must conduct a strong marketing effort.

Congress must make the case for reform in language and terms that the electorate will find most appealing. Efforts to express the goals of reform in terms of deficit reduction or spending moderation are doomed to failure if opponents counter with tales of individual woe and human misery. Efforts simply to terminate programs that one group deems useless or obsolete can seem unduly negative if they are not presented as part of a broad positive theme. Although the public would be hard-pressed to describe the benefits of the Departments of Housing and Urban Development, Energy, Commerce, and Education, in the last session of Congress a program that proposed shutting them down was seen as extreme, mean, and vindictive.

To counter the inherent negativity associated with efforts to make reductions in money, employees, or departments, any proposed reforms should be expressed in terms that emphasize people-oriented benefits. For example, HUD should be closed down not to save money, but because it operates some of the most dangerous and squalid housing in the U.S. It should be replaced by, say, a welfare reform initiative that empowers its beneficiaries by giving them choice, self-reliance, and independence. The Department of Transportation should be closed down because today's transportation problems for the most part affect local and regional areas, and often are too serious to be resolved by distant bureaucrats in Washington.

To do this effectively requires a coherent plan that defends and explains the reforms in terms of how they will improve the lives of Americans. Closing DOT and turning its functions back to the states, for example, should be justified as an effort to improve transportation services by getting rid of costly, counterproductive mandates and by allowing local and regional discretion as to how the money will be used. Making this case requires a clear demonstration of how those who benefit from the status quo will try to thwart this objective. Such advance planning and detailed justification will be required across the board, and the Cabinet departments that remain will become the repository of responsibilities that fall under the appropriate and necessary functions of a national government.

STRATEGY #3
Congress should identify as many targets as possible.

Chances of success will be greatly improved if a large number of programs and departments are considered, with targets for reform stretched across a wide range of government functions. Reformers must resist the temptation to be too careful or thorough, or to limit the focus of the reform effort to just a few manageable targets. Experience suggests that dividing the opposition while undertaking overly ambitious efforts yields proportionally more successes than do efforts that target just a few problem areas.

Nonetheless, a reasonably detailed plan for the outcome of the reforms and a rationale for the effort are essential in overcoming the predictable charges of negativity and the perceptions that someone's vital benefits and services will be denied. For example, the federal land management functions which are scattered through several agencies could be consolidated into one as redundant and duplicative positions and departments are shut down. This applies as well to many of the safety functions performed by various divisions within the Departments of Health and Human Services, Labor, and Transportation.

In cases where programs are terminated outright with no consolidation at the national level, educational efforts must be made to show how the states will do a better job of providing the service than Washington has done. This was done for the successful welfare and Medicaid reforms. In other cases, when it is the private sector that will take over or expand the existing coverage, the benefit to the taxpayers and the program's recipients should be highlighted. For example, most Americans are unaware that most weather forecasts come from private weather services, not the National Weather Service in the Department of Commerce. Without a preemptive educational program, Americans might believe that terminating the National Weather Service would mean an end to free daily weather forecasts.

STRATEGY #4
Policymakers must neutralize opposition from as many beneficiary groups as possible.

While those who depend on government programs will always be skeptical of reforms that translate into fewer resources and staff, there also will always be some segment of the beneficiary class that is amenable to program improvements. Their interests should be addressed directly. Winning such groups to the side of reform will serve to diminish the sheer size of the opposition and offer alternative views to potentially neutral but influential parties in the process, such as elected officials and journalists.

Perhaps the most important beneficiaries that must be addressed are the congressional committees with formal jurisdiction over programs targeted for termination. Their ability to allocate billions of dollars directly to various classes of beneficiaries gives them significant influence and political power. During the 104th Congress, much of the impetus and many of the detailed plans for reform came from the freshman class and junior members, while much of the most effective opposition came from committee chairmen within their own party. Efforts to shut down HUD, Commerce, Energy, and Education — specific goals of the freshman Republicans—were unsuccessful; none of their proposals was adopted, or even seriously considered, by the responsible committees or actively supported by the leadership.

At present, congressional transportation committees annually distribute $40 billion to projects that often are in the districts of committee members or that will go to their influential constituencies. This, in turn, leads to larger campaign contributions. All of this power and influence will be reduced to some extent when most of these programs are devolved to the states. But there is no substitute for strong congressional leadership at the top to induce reluctant committee members to cooperate, or to mobilize a majority of the Members of Congress to support reform.

STRATEGY #5
Congress should use legislative vehicles to advance comprehensive reforms.

The 105th Congress will benefit by building upon the considerable legislative successes of the last Congress. While the 104th Congress did not terminate or restructure as many targeted agencies as it initially proposed, its members and ad hoc task forces developed legislative vehicles that could be used to overhaul much of the federal structure. These legislative vehicles should be reviewed, modified if necessary, and reintroduced in the 105th Congress as part of the comprehensive reform effort.

Applying the Strategies:
A Proposal to Restructure the Federal Government

Although the 104th Congress made many changes and reforms in government, these successes were merely a fraction of its good intentions. Those programs, departments, offices, divisions, and agencies that managed to survive these efforts provide the 105th Congress with an excellent starting point. But first, Congress should clarify for the public its vision of what a restructured government would be like, and how it can better address the needs of the country as America enters the next century. A key component of this vision should be a renewed commitment to determining the proper role of government and to focusing on responsibilities that are truly national in scope. Then Congress should embark on an end-of-the-century housecleaning and dispense with hundreds of obsolete and redundant programs and agencies that do nothing more than reflect the needs of a bygone era.[4]

Such a vision should seek to limit the number of Cabinet departments to five — the Departments of Defense, State, Health and Human Services, Justice, and Treasury. Other departments would be downgraded to, or consolidated within, bureaus; this includes agricultural concerns, natural resources, the collection and dissemination of national data and statistics, safety concerns, and other independent agencies. This would be

---

4 This proposal follows closely the recommendation included in *Rolling Back Government: A Budget Plan to Rebuild America*, ed. Scott A. Hodge (Washington, D.C.: The Heritage Foundation, 1995).

accomplished through consolidation, major restructuring, the devolution of some responsibilities to states, and the termination of entities that are obsolete or obvious failures.

To accomplish and defend this new vision, Congress should perform a serious review of the existing federal structure. In addition to providing Congress with the rationale for making specific reforms, this review can suggest the disposition and rearrangement of the main functions that belong to the federal government. The following agencies lend themselves to such a review.

- **The Department of Agriculture (DOA).** Most Department of Agriculture spending aimed directly at farmers constitutes a highly restrictive central planning system. This system should be eliminated. It should be noted that very little of the farm price support program goes to small family farmers: Some 60 percent of farm payments goes to 15 percent of the farmers with gross farm sales in excess of $100,000 annually. Programs dedicated to agriculture represent only about 34 percent of the Department's budget. The remainder is allocated to forestry, rural development, and food distribution (mostly food stamps).

  Under a comprehensive reform proposal, the Department's complex apparatus of commodity support programs and production controls would be terminated, and farmers would be encouraged to take full advantage of the burgeoning world market for food. The 1996 Freedom to Farm Act was a good start for reforming a government function, but much more needs to be done in the next congressional session. The Forest Service would be merged with the three other land management agencies, and the lands not sold would be transferred to the new Bureau of Natural Resources. The food stamp program would be folded into the welfare block grants going to the states. The Rural Housing and Community Development Service and the Rural Utilities Service would be closed.

- **The Department of Commerce (DOC).** Created in 1903, the Department of Commerce has a budget of roughly $3.6 billion per year and a work force of nearly 35,000, but it lacks a clear focus and obvious goals. Even its own inspector general admitted that it has evolved into a "loose collection of more than 100 programs delivering services to about 1,000 customer bases."[5] According to the U.S. General Accounting Office (GAO), Commerce "faces the most complex web of divided authorities" from sharing its "missions with at least 71 federal departments, agencies and offices."[6]

Given the duplication and redundancy associated with much of Commerce's activity, a comprehensive reform proposal would require that the Department be dismantled. Obsolete and outmoded programs would be terminated, while duplicative programs would be consolidated within other departments. The Census Bureau would be made into a separate agency with other government-wide data collection agencies as part of a new U.S. Bureau of National Statistics. The Patent and Trademark Office would be transferred to the Department of the Treasury.

- **The Department of Education (DOE).** The Cabinet-level Department of Education was established in 1979 with functions previously housed within the Department of Health and Human Services. Proponents of a separate department argued that it would provide greater efficiency and accountability, provide formal federal recognition of the paramount role played by education in our society, and be more responsive to the needs of school districts, students, parents, and teachers. Since its creation, the Department has more than doubled its budget from around $15 billion to over $31 billion. More than 240 categorical programs exist within the Department today, which is 100 more than in 1980. Despite widespread public concern and the continual increase in funding, the Department of Education has done little to deal with the decline in student performance. But its activities have encouraged an unhealthy reduction in parental and local community control of education. Unfortunately, at a time when more than 80 percent of parents support school choice vouchers and more and more communities are seriously considering giving them a try, Secretary of Education Richard W. Riley stands shoulder-to-shoulder with the teachers' unions and remains adamantly opposed to vouchers.

A comprehensive government restructuring would close down the Department of Education entirely. Most of the Department's funds currently pay for technical assistance, clearinghouse information,

---

5 *Ibid.,* p. 26.

6 *Ibid.*

programs that teachers neither need nor have time to implement, and bureaucratic overhead, as illustrated by the 17 branches of the Department of Education's Office of Civil Rights in downtown Washington, D.C. Only a fraction of its $31 billion budget actually makes it into the classroom. Under a comprehensive reform plan, the money that now funds Education Department programs would be transferred to the states as a block grant with few strings attached. Data gathering and dissemination functions would be transferred to the new Bureau of National Statistics, while the student loan program would be transferred to the existing, and long since privatized, Student Loan Marketing Agency (Sallie Mae).

- **The Department of Energy (DOE).** The Department of Energy was created as a Cabinet-level department in 1977 by President Jimmy Carter to better address the war-related energy problems that emerged during the early 1970s. Shortly after DOE's creation, the Organization of Petroleum Exporting Countries (OPEC) embargo on oil collapsed and world energy prices returned to their former level, where they have largely remained. Despite the absence of any viable problem to solve since then, DOE has grown in both budget and function, and spends 155 percent more today than when it was formed during the energy crisis.

  Any comprehensive restructuring plan should close the Department of Energy and transfer its defense-related work to the Department of Defense, where it more properly belongs, and its primary research work to universities or the National Science Foundation. Commercially oriented research work would be offered to the private sector, along with transition assistance to help in the formation of industry-supported laboratories modeled along the lines of the privately run and sponsored Gas Research Institute or the Electric Power Research Institute, which is funded entirely by the voluntary contributions of electric utilities. Other commercial energy functions, such as the power marketing administrations, would be privatized.

- **The Department of Health and Human Services (HHS).** HHS would remain a Cabinet-level agency, but its costly collection of entitlement programs would be fundamentally overhauled in ways that would give states more choice in operating the programs and that would allow beneficiaries more choices and meaningful incentives, which would lower costs. The health programs (including Medicare, Medicaid, and the Public Health Service), welfare (including Aid to Families with Dependent Children), and the Social Security system collectively cost the government $700 billion—nearly three times what the government spends on national defense. Moreover, these programs represent the fastest-growing portion of the budget, and future projections indicate that unless fundamental reforms are adopted now, Medicare will soon go broke and Social Security may follow soon after.

Any comprehensive reform plan should build on the success achieved in reforming the welfare system during the last session of Congress, applying similar comprehensive reforms to Medicare and Medicaid. With respect to Medicare, vouchers or "medichecks" would be provided to beneficiaries to allow them either to remain within the existing system or to join Preferred Provider Organizations (PPOs) and other point-of-service plans. Additional reforms would be adopted for various co-payments and premiums. Medicaid would be restructured into a block grant and returned to the states, to be provided to eligible beneficiaries under the new welfare reform requirements. Social Security also would be overhauled in a way that provided greater choices to participants and private-sector partnerships in its operations.

- **The Department of Housing and Urban Development (HUD).** HUD should be closed down, and all low-income housing assistance should be consolidated into a single welfare block grant to be used at the discretion of the states in a manner consistent with the objectives and guidelines of the new welfare reform law. The states would be encouraged to use the housing portion of the grant for vouchers and certificates as a way to release the poor from HUD's deplorable public housing projects. The pork-barrel Community Development Block Grant program would end, saving $4 billion per year, and the Federal Housing Administration's mortgage insurance program would be privatized.

- **The Department of Labor (DOL).** Created in 1883 as a bureau and elevated to the status of independent agency in 1913, the Department of Labor has grown to become one of the largest regulatory agencies in the federal government: It is currently responsible for administering and enforcing over 180 federal statutes applied to 10 million employers with over 100 million workers. Other major responsibilities include administering the Unemployment Insurance Compensation program in partnership with the states, as well as Job Training and Employment Services operations which include 160 separate and overlapping programs within the federal establishment.

A comprehensive restructuring would close DOL, and those activities worth maintaining would be transferred to the states, which already operate key components of the program. Specifically, the existing patchwork of federal job training programs, as well as vocational education efforts, would be consolidated, simplified, and then transferred as a block grant to the states. The marginal federal involvement with the Unemployment Insurance program also would be ended, and the program would be operated entirely by the states. Other programs such as the one for black lung disease would be transferred to HHS, data collection efforts would be transferred to the new Bureau of Statistics, and regulatory efforts under Davis-Bacon and Section 13(c) of the Urban Mass Transit Act of 1964 would end when the regulations are repealed.

- **Department of Transportation (DOT).** The Department of Transportation was created in 1966 to consolidate the many federal programs addressing America's transportation needs. Its key components are the National Highway Administration, which funds federal highway construction and repair with money collected by the federal fuel tax, and the Federal Aviation Administration, which funds airport construction and redevelopment, operates the air traffic control system, and oversees the safety of air travel. Other major DOT functions include the Federal Transit Administration, the U.S. Coast Guard, and the Maritime Commission.

Federal involvement in transportation fulfilled its chief objectives years ago with completion of the interstate highway system and the establishment of a commercial aviation industry. A comprehensive reform plan should close the DOT by devolving responsibility for all surface transportation programs (highways, bridges, transit, and rail) to the states with the fuel tax to fund them. Airport construction and development also would become a state responsibility, and the air traffic control system would be privatized or reorganized as an independent government corporation. All that would remain under federal jurisdiction would be the transportation safety responsibilities and the Coast Guard, which would be transferred either to the Department of Defense or to the Department of Justice in recognition of its important law enforcement functions.

- **Department of Veterans Affairs (VA).** The Department of Veterans Affairs would be organized as the Bureau of Veterans Affairs within the Department of Defense. Tasked with responsibility for the specific needs of our veterans, the current system is notorious for the low quality of services provided, particularly in health care. As the second-largest Cabinet department, with 225,000 employees, VA all too often has misdirected its efforts toward maintaining and protecting the lucrative jobs of its enormous work force and resisting executive branch management reform proposals that would allow the VA to do more with less.

  A comprehensive reform plan would reorganize the VA within the Department of Defense, modernize it, and re-target it to help low-income veterans with disabling service-connected injuries. All new construction would be halted, and existing facilities would be reviewed systematically to determine their suitability for use. All remaining benefit programs, such as housing loans and education assistance, would be reviewed and improved to prevent inefficiency and abuse.

- **Environmental Protection Agency (EPA).** The Environmental Protection Agency would be required to cease several of its costly and ineffective practices. Wastewater treatment grants and future contributions to the revolving loan fund would be terminated. Federal involvement in local water treatment activities encourages communities to build infrastructure beyond their needs and discourages them from developing innovative and less expensive solutions. EPA would reorganize its abatement, compliance, and control functions to act as an enforcement entity over independent certified auditors.

- **United States Postal Service (USPS).** The Postal Service would be fully privatized, and other delivery services would be allowed to compete with it in the collection and delivery of first-class mail. Public dissatisfaction with the cost and quality of basic postal services is long-standing and stems chiefly from the legal monopoly of the USPS. The private sector has demonstrated that it can outperform the Postal Service in the delivery of packages and overnight shipments, and extending competition and private-sector efficiency to regular postal services would benefit American consumers and businesses. Just how far the USPS has fallen in esteem and interest is indicated in Vice President Albert Gore's recent annual reinvention of government report, which recounts successful negotiations and cost-saving agreements between the government and Federal Express for overnight service but makes no mention of the USPS as a "competitive" service.

- **Small Business Administration (SBA).** The Small Business Administration would be closed, and all existing SBA loans to private businesses would be securitized and sold to the secondary loan market. Created in 1954, the SBA has never been an important factor contributing to the growth of entrepreneurship or the number of new businesses. Only two-tenths of 1 percent of all small businesses in the United States receive SBA loans.

- **Agency for International Development (AID).** The Agency for International Development's foreign aid program would be closed, and America's foreign aid would be linked more closely to U.S. security interests and to concrete actions by recipient countries to establish market economies. Despite 30 years of effort, most recipient countries in the developing world remain mired in poverty. Foreign aid has not worked, and formerly poor countries that have made the transition to prosperity have done so largely through changes in their domestic policies, not with funds provided by foreign donors. Indeed, it is often the availability of such financial support that encourages poor countries to avoid taking the sometimes unpopular but necessary steps needed to spur sustainable development.

- **Other Independent Agencies.** In addition to the current 15 Cabinet departments, about 95 independent government agencies are organized as commissions, corporations, boards, agencies, councils, and foundations. Almost all are focused on narrowly defined issues or missions, and many share the same obsolescence as the larger departments at the Cabinet level. Examples include the National Endowment for the Arts, the Appalachian Regional Commission, the Legal Services Corporation, and the Corporation for Public Broadcasting.

The 104th Congress succeeded in shutting down a number of the less well-known agencies — including the Pennsylvania Avenue Development Commission, the Administrative Conference of the

United States, and the Advisory Commission on Intergovernmental Relations—while devolving several others, such as the Delaware River Basin Commission and the Susquehanna River Basin Commission, both of which were devolved to the states that share these rivers. These additional independent agencies should be revisited and reviewed by the new Congress for targeted reorganization, reform, consolidation, or closure. The five scholarship funds honoring Barry Goldwater, Morris K. Udall, Harry S. Truman, Christopher Columbus, and James Madison should be consolidated as well to reduce their substantial collective overhead and free more money for scholarships.

Also amenable to consolidation into either the Department of Defense or the Department of State are the duties performed by the East-West Center, Arms Control and Disarmament Agency, Defense Nuclear Facilities Board, Japan United States Friendship Commission, North-South Center, United States Institute of Peace, and Nuclear Waste Technical Review Board. Aspects of the State Justice Institute and the Commission on Civil Rights could be consolidated into the Department of Justice. Among the many other independent agencies that should be closed down because they are either redundant or unsuitable for a national government are the Advisory Council on Historic Preservation, Appalachian Regional Commission, Commission for the Preservation of America's Heritage Abroad, Commission of Fine Arts, Corporation for Public Broadcasting, FDIC Affordable Housing and Bank Enterprise, Legal Services Corporation, Marine Mammal Commission, National Capital Arts and Cultural Affairs, National Capital Planning Commission, National Foundation for the Arts and Humanities, Neighborhood Reinvestment Corporation, and Office of Government Ethics.

CONCLUSION

Throughout government, examples such as those presented here abound. Studying them helps to show how Congress can enact a genuinely comprehensive reform program that conforms to the electoral mandate to make government smaller and more effective. Each element of a comprehensive reform plan should be structured so that the positive purpose in changing a program is highlighted.

Every case targeted for restructuring or termination will present clear examples of how and why the federal government has failed to provide the quality and quantity of service and function originally intended. These failings should be identified clearly and colorfully, and solutions should relate directly to genuine improvements in the status quo, even when the beneficiaries are the taxpayers. While many of these initiatives could be pursued piecemeal, as part of a multi-year strategy policymakers should take advantage of the momentum that a one-time, across-the-board effort creates, diminishing the influence of the special interests in the process. Government can be restructured to operate as the Founding Fathers envisioned. With a tangible, well-planned strategy, Members of Congress who are serious about reform can make it happen.

Chapter 3

TRANSFERRING FUNCTIONS TO THE STATES

Douglas Seay and Robert E. Moffit

The American conservative movement emphasizes personal freedom and responsibility and demands that government give back to Americans control over their lives. At the center of that demand is a firm belief that government must always be directly and immediately accountable to the governed. As the Founding Fathers so eloquently explained in writing after writing, and on the floors of Independence Hall and Congress, the closer government is to the people and the more directly the people can influence its decisions, the less likely it will become abusive or tyrannical. The laws it passes are more likely to be effective and satisfying to the citizens and ones they will gladly follow. President Thomas Jefferson phrased it best when he argued that local government, of all government, is the most naturally democratic, precisely because it is closest to the everyday lives of the people.

This is the basis of federalism. The political framework guaranteeing this exercise of personal liberty and responsibility and the proper checks and balances between state and federal governments already exists. The Constitution, established by the Philadelphia Convention of 1787, delineated the "few and defined" powers of the federal government. The Bill

The authors would like to thank William Beach, Edwin Meese III, Thomas C. Atwood, Ronald Utt, Pat Wilson, David M. Mason, Emily Stimpson, and Adam Meyerson for their suggestions and contributions to this chapter. The opinions and views expressed, however, are solely the responsibility of the authors.

of Rights, adopted on March 4, 1789, enumerated the God-given rights of the people and the powers residing in the states. Conservatives across the United States, however, wonder whether the federal government has not indeed crossed the line, and are scrutinizing the relationship between the government in Washington, D.C., and their own local and state governments to make sure the checks and balances still apply.

As Americans head into the 21st century, the accumulation of federal program failures, especially since the 1960s, has been cause enough for a reinvigoration of America's older tradition of self-government. But the arguments for returning more power to the people at the state and local levels are not solely because of problems with federal programs. Recent and highly effective local government solutions to major problems — exemplified by the stunning achievements of New York City in reducing crime in the past few years—have led many to agree that local governments can deal with local problems in more effective ways than can a bureaucracy miles and miles away. A restoration of federalism as it is embodied in the Constitution, and the pursuit of bringing programs closer to home through devolution, have become eminently plausible over the past four years. To carry out such an agenda, however, Members of Congress need not only to refresh their own understanding of the federalist character of the American Republic,[1] but also to exercise the political will to usher in a new era of self-government.

Devolution. One of the principal successes of the 1994 Contract With America was to alter the terms of the national debate in Washington on the issues of federalism and devolution. Members of Congress voiced a new willingness to allow state and local governments a greater freedom to deal with a number of intransigent economic and social problems that federal programs either had not solved or actually had made worse. Several proposals were put forward advocating the transfer of select limited functions from the federal to state and local governments, a process now commonly known as "devolution." The underlying assumption is that by

---

1 A study of the classics of American government is recommended, especially *The Federalist Papers* by James Madison, John Jay, and Alexander Hamilton. See also Orestes A. Brownson, *The American Republic* (New Haven: College and University Press, 1972), and Felix Morely, *Freedom and Federalism* (Chicago: Henry Regnery Co., 1959).

giving the states greater responsibilities and freedom in these areas, a number of innovative approaches will be tried. Officials in Washington may still establish the general goals and principles for the use of federal funds, but the states will experiment with approaches to meet those goals. The best of these state efforts will be copied and adapted by other states, and their unsuccessful elements will more easily discarded, in sharp contrast to the federal programs that have lumbered on for decades.

Federalism. Federalism also has achieved greater currency as a term heard throughout the corridors of Congress, but generally it is defined so vaguely that it has little specific meaning. Although devolution and federalism often are used interchangeably, they are, in fact, distinct subjects. Whereas devolution concerns the transfer of selected functions from Washington to state and local governments — in essence a reshuffling of government functions from one level to another—federalism concerns the constitutional structure of federal-state relationships and the ability to check and balance each other's movements. The principal goal of devolution is more effective and efficient government programs, while that of federalism is ensuring that government is constrained within enforceable limits.

This difference between federalism and devolution is best seen in the new welfare system, the first major federal program ever to be devolved to the states. In addition to several other reforms built into it, the Welfare Reform Act of 1996 expanded the limits within which the states could experiment with approaches to welfare reform while remaining subject to certain basic conservative goals and principles established by Congress. In part, this new approach breaks away from federal micromanagement of programs and uses the states as testing grounds for new innovative programs that are more effective than those currently in place. The expectation is that the best of these will spread to other states once their success has been demonstrated.

A Conditional Trend. Following in the footsteps of welfare reform are a range of proposals for devolving other programs under consideration in Congress, including transportation and unemployment insurance. Conservatives and others have hailed, and opponents decried, the major accomplishment this trend represents, but it must be stated that this new agenda of devolution is not a true and complete transfer of power from Washington to the states. Although it does represent a welcome loosening of federal micromanagement in several areas of policymaking, the allotted freedoms given to states are carefully circumscribed and heavily conditioned. At best, the current proposals for devolution represent a unilateral transfer of functions from Washington to the states, and not a transfer of power or fiscal responsibility. This trend is better looked on as a conditional grant that is reversible at any time, regardless of the wishes of the states.

Moreover, although it is true that many state officials would prefer that federal mandates and restrictions be virtually eliminated in order to free them to engage in even greater experimentation, others less nobly seek to use the federalist argument to frustrate the fundamental reforms that Congress intended through the welfare legislation. Many of the reforms championed by conservatives, including some contained in the federal legislation, are certain to be resisted by state bureaucracies for reasons of ideology or plain old-fashioned self-interest. For example, much of the welfare establishment in some states would like to reduce or eliminate the new work requirements for recipients, either because they are opposed to such requirements in principle or because their own jobs would be much more difficult and their performance more empirically measurable.

Making Devolution Real. It could be debated endlessly whether or not Washington should be in the business of requiring certain reforms of the states, however needed they might be. But the federal government will continue to be the principal source of funds for these programs. Yet real devolution is not simply collecting money in Washington and handing it over to the states to spend as they wish. Nor is that true federalism. As long as Congress raises funds through taxation, it has a responsibility to see that the money is spent wisely and for productive purposes. In fact, for Washington to provide federal money to state and local governments with no strings attached would be the worst of all worlds for taxpayers because it would further decrease accountability by government. In that situation, the federal government would collect the taxes but, once the money was transferred to the states, could honestly say it had little control over how the funds were spent or misspent by the states.

A far better approach for many federal programs would be for Washington to step out of the picture entirely. In devolving a program, supporters of devolution in Congress and the Administration should reduce the federal government's own tax take by a level equivalent to its current funding for that program. The states then should be informed that they are free to choose between two options: impose their own taxes to fund the program or return the money to their citizens. In either case, federal responsibility and interference for each program would end, and so would the federal government's responsibility for funding.

Only then, when state and local officials are subjected to the discipline of having to justify their programs and expenses directly to their taxpayers, would real pressure for reform come to bear. And only then would taxpaying citizens actually be able to exercise control over what their government does with their money. Ironically, many of the state officials who are eager advocates of getting "free" federal money with "no strings attached" have been and will continue to be very much opposed to real devolution, which will require ending federal funding and returning not only operational control, but also fiscal responsibility for programs to state officials.

The Fight on Two Fronts. It might seem contradictory to advocate that the Congress reduce Washington's power over the states while mandating reforms in the programs devolved to the states. But this duality is merely a reluctant acknowledgment of the severe constitutional distortions of the past several decades, within which conservative reformers in Congress must operate. Over this period the federal government eliminated virtually all restraints on its powers while reducing those of the states to mere vestiges of what they once were.

Restoring a balance between the federal government and the states, including the reimposition of binding limits on Washington, must be a central long-term goal for conservatives and policymakers. This goal cannot be accomplished, however, through self-restraint; any succeeding Congress or Administration easily could elect to resume the former excesses and erase any gain in restoring constitutional order. Self-restraint is most likely to be practiced only by conservatives; a renewed activism by liberals can be expected when they regain their hold on the purse strings. A continuing aggrandizement by the federal government, the unchallenged triumph of liberal policy prescriptions, and the still-birth of conservative reforms would be the most likely results of this strategy.

The seeming conflict of conservative goals disappears when divided into short-term and long-term objectives. Reform of policy cannot wait, and conservatives should use their existing power to advance the conservative policy goals, including an expanded use of devolution. But they must couple this with a long-term federalist agenda of restoring a constitutional structure to the federal government that permanently reduces Washington's control and financing of functions that properly belong to the states. As long as Washington's official funding and control of decision making remains intact —i.e., as long as constitutional reforms that impose binding limits on these have not been put in place—conservatives have little option but to accept the realities of the situation and seek to change them. As long as Washington retains the power to make government policy and the responsibility to pay for government functions, those wielding that power will exercise their own agendas. Thus, devolution should be regarded only as a first stage in this process of re-establishing federalism, allowing much-needed reforms to take root, but it must not be an end in itself. A complementary agenda for developing true federalism is needed to make the changes permanent.

LESSONS LEARNED

The most important lesson learned thus far by anyone who works in or works with or simply observes the federal government is that Washington's power is easy to expand but incredibly difficult to contract. Hard-won victories in reducing Washington's power are easily overturned by succeeding Administrations and Congresses, even by those who have publicly pledged to the same goals.

For example, the regulatory relief achieved during the Reagan years was quickly undone by the Bush and Clinton Administrations, for in those eight years the issuance of new regulations reached record levels, as the chapter on regulatory reform demonstrates. Even when the President himself has committed to reducing the federal government's power, the coalitions against true reform are sufficiently powerful to render impotent all but the most determined efforts. There is little incentive in Washington to limit the federal government other than that which the elected officials will bring to the task. Only a President who is personally committed to this objective and who focuses his Administration on the problem, especially through his appointments, can be expected to succeed. And only a Congress with a leadership committed to the same goal can hope to enact a legislative agenda toward that end. Surprisingly little assistance will be forthcoming from the states, which have assumed an "AWOL" posture, perhaps due to the fact that for so long they were sidelined from the national decision making process even in areas directly affecting them.

LESSONS LEARNED

- Governors and other state politicians may not always stand up for federalism if they receive "free" federal cash.

- It is not wise to trust the policy advice of professional bureaucrats who represent the individual states in Washington.

- Do not bypass state governments when devolving programs to local governments.

- Carefully crafted block grants, which can limit the powers of the federal government, can also lead to revenue sharing and new categorical programs.

- Regulatory reform and judicial appointments can slow or stop the growth of federal mandates, and can promote federalism.

- Even conservatives, once in Congress, have been guilty of "federalizing" power and authority when the federal government has no jurisdiction.

But there are good grounds for optimism. The emergence of devolution is only the latest incarnation of a long and popular political tradition that celebrates the advantages of limited decentralized government. The most common arguments in favor of transferring authority from Washington back to the states are the strongest, and include the benefits of experimenting with solutions in 50 "laboratories," the ability of the public to better monitor and control both government policies and the use of their tax dollars, and the resulting efficiencies produced by the combination of these two forces at work.

The trend over the past 60 years of centralizing decision making in Washington has resulted in a wide variety of problems. Besides the enormous expense and disappointing, even dismal, failures of the federal efforts in areas such as welfare and crime, centralization of programs in Washington has produced inflexible and ill-crafted programs imposed on unwilling communities. The monopoly these programs have enjoyed for so long—primarily by forbidding state and local governments from modifying or competing with them — has prevented more effective and less catastrophic approaches from being attempted and eliminated the ability for anyone to measure the federal failures or successes, because there are no independent programs with which they can be compared. Thus, even well-meaning federal officials have insufficient empirical information to intelligently modify politically driven agendas that dominate discussion on Capitol Hill.

Governors Have Had Success. With his innovative approach to welfare reform, Governor Tommy Thompson of Wisconsin demonstrated that, given a chance to do so, states have a better chance of accomplishing the stated objectives than the one-size-fits-all approach invariably favored by Washington. Successes are more easily copied, and mistakes avoided, by other jurisdictions and states, and programs actually can be compared in terms of cost and effectiveness. And, at the state and local levels, individuals and communities have a much better chance of having real input into the programs that run their lives, especially by the re-establishment of the connection between the taxes they pay and the services they get.

This evisceration of the capacity of the American public to govern themselves in local matters is the most powerful argument behind a revival of federalism. Over three decades, Americans have had to accept forcibly imposed social reconstruction against which they have voted repeatedly, from forced busing for racial balance in schools to the dismantling of the criminal justice system and the ensuing explosion of violent crime and the dramatic decline in the quality of life in urban areas and other communities. This was all done in their local communities even as they were forced to foot the bill through record taxes and a $6 trillion national debt.

By building on these politically powerful sentiments, conservatives have a potent opportunity to re-craft the restoration of the balance of power between the states and the federal government. But policymakers must learn from experiences in the past and remember some important, hard-earned lessons.

Lesson #1: It is not wise to trust the governors to stand up for federalism if they are offered "free" federal cash. In 1988, with the compliance of the Reagan Administration, Congress passed what purported to be a major overhaul of the federal welfare system. The legislation's congressional sponsors solemnly promised to put welfare recipients to work and to change the welfare system for the better. The 1988 welfare reform bill was the latest chapter in the historic failure of federal welfare reform. Taking advice from the governors, Congress forged a bipartisan reform that resulted in a $100 billion increase in welfare spending in five years. Welfare caseloads climbed; and less than 7 percent of welfare recipients, it turned out, had been required to work.

In 1996, the governors, working through the National Governors' Association (NGA), proposed a "welfare reform" measure that virtually eliminated real work requirements for welfare recipients and virtually abandoned any serious attempt to reduce illegitimacy. Only because policy groups throughout Washington successfully had redefined the terms of the national welfare reform debate since 1988 was it possible to thwart the specific measures that would have undermined serious congressional reform in 1996. Moreover, the dogged determination of those in the House and Senate who had mastered the crucial details of welfare policy made it virtually impossible for governors, let alone the Clinton Administration whose plan mirrored the governors' proposals in key respects, to impose their proposals effortlessly on the welfare reformers in Congress.

In dealing with governors, it is essential for policymakers in Washington to focus on their specific state welfare problems and try to assist them in ways that do not compromise conservative principles. The governors as a group often will seek the lowest political common denominator: a quick and easy access to "free" federal money. Those in Congress who support reform should remember this; many governors are willing to accept expanded federal control if it accompanies increased federal funding.

Lesson #2: It is not wise to trust the policy advice from professional bureaucrats who represent the individual states in Washington. Conservatives, like legislators in general, should be cautious in seeking the advice of lobbyists who represent narrow business interests that often are hostile to a real free market. They also should be wary of the policy prescriptions of self-interested state bureaucrats working inside the Washington Beltway.

For example, during Congress's consideration of Medicaid reform in 1996, the NGA formally proposed that federal assistance be converted to block grants and that the entitlement status of the huge Medicaid program be ended. At first glance, the plan looked good, but a close reading of the fine print revealed that it preserved many of Medicaid's worst features while giving state officials an opportunity to make a potentially disastrous run on the federal treasury.[2] And, as described above, the NGA's proposed 650-page welfare reform plan abandoned the goals of reducing illegitimacy and adopting genuine work requirements.[3] Only the determination of conservatives in Congress and reform-minded policymakers ensured enactment of a true welfare reform bill more in line with the provisions of the Contract With America than with the versions of welfare reform pushed by the Clinton Administration or the NGA.

On state interests, conservatives must find ways to deal directly with the governors, bypassing the bureaucracy as much as possible. On institutional matters affecting federal-state relationships, they should rely on the solid advice of conservative state legislators and such organizations as the American Legislative Exchange Council.

Lesson #3: Do not bypass state governments when devolving programs to local governments. During the 1930s, there was a dramatic increase in the authority of the federal government to develop solutions for the conditions of the Great Depression; the federal government's involvement in local problems did not recede with the end of that national emergency. Rather, the federalization of decision making gathered even more momentum in the 1960s. Under President Lyndon Johnson, the Great Society agenda successfully promoted an enormous expansion of federal programs. To get around the troublesome necessity of persuading state officials to cooperate with Washington and absconding with their formerly autonomous areas of responsibility, the Johnson Administration relentlessly handed out federal money with ever more detailed conditions attached, under the Orwellian title of "Creative Federalism." More than 200 new categories of federal grants were created from 1964 to 1968, which was more than all those created in the first two centuries of the United States; total funding for grants doubled in a mere four years. Moreover, Congress responded by creating new Cabinet-level organizations, such as the Departments of Housing and Urban

---

2 See John C. Liu, "Key Changes Needed in the Governors' Medicaid Proposal," Heritage Foundation *F.Y.I.* No. 89, March 12, 1996.

3 See Robert Rector, "Welfare Reform Fraud Once Again: Examining the NGA Welfare Plan," Heritage Foundation *Backgrounder* No. 1076, March 18, 1996.

Development and Transportation, and existing agencies and departments were encouraged to step up their regulatory activities.

Through regulatory devices of the 1960s, state and local governments became little more than agents of the federal government, reduced to implementing the political agenda of Washington. The federal government now dealt directly with cities and counties and rural communities, and it issued regulations in areas once regarded as the inviolable preserve of states and local municipalities. "Creative Federalism" was creative in finding ways to get around the constitutional separation of powers, but it had nothing to do with federalism.

One consequence of funneling of funds directly from Washington to Main Street has been the troublesome, chronic problem of waste, fraud, and abuse of taxpayers' money. In the federal Food Stamp program, which was structurally untouched by the 1996 congressional welfare reform, local stores redeem the government stamps. In South Carolina, a retailer redeemed $300,000 in food stamps even though his "stores" were 12 ice cream trucks. Likewise, in Alameda County, California, a pizza parlor averaged $3,500 per month in food stamp sales although it did not sell foods for home preparation. Of the $26.3 billion spent on the Food Stamp program in 1996, an estimated 10 percent will be lost to such instances of fraud and abuse.

Lesson #4: Carefully crafted block grants, which can limit the powers of the federal government, also can lead to revenue sharing and new categorical programs. In contrast to his predecessors, President Ronald Reagan campaigned on a specific message of restoring limits on Washington's authority, and he persisted with this agenda after assuming office. Setting the tone in his first inaugural address, he declared: "the Federal Government did not create the States, the States created the Federal Government." His agenda of federalism was part of a larger program halting the expansion of the federal government and included such measures as reducing growth in federal spending, promoting tax cuts, and imposing a moratorium on federal hiring.

In the first Reagan budget, the 1981 Omnibus Budget Reconciliation Act, a large number of federal programs were consolidated into nine block grants in which state and local governments were given far greater freedom to fashion programs. The Administration was not successful in returning responsibility and funding for welfare and food stamps to the states, even though the federal government assumed the responsibility for the enormously expensive unfunded Medicare mandate. Unlike President Richard Nixon, President Reagan viewed the inherited federal grant system as a problem to be eliminated, not reformed. Block grants were specifically viewed as a means for reducing the control of the Washington bureaucracy, a kind of halfway house for the eventual federal disengagement of certain programs altogether.

Although block grants can be an instrument for returning political decision making to the states and localities, policymakers should be cautious. Through block grants, the federal government can become a "back door" tax collector for the states; unfortunately, many state officials acquiesce simply because it usually means a greater availability of federal funds. In addition, once a new block grant program is created, unless its terms and duration are made clear, it stands a good chance of becoming just another expensive and permanent federal program.

Lesson #5: Regulatory reform and judicial appointments can slow or stop the growth of federal mandates, and can promote federalism. Regardless of whether they stem from the federal bureaucracy or from Congress, the many mandates imposed on state and local governments have had the effect of producing enormous waste and thwarting the local innovations that normally would accompany devolution. Priorities and procedures are decided at the national level and imposed without regard for differences among regions and localities or even the wishes of the taxpayers who must foot the bill, for these programs have first call on local resources. Absurdities abound: To comply with the Clean Water Act of 1977, the state of Arizona must monitor and regulate the Salt River to meet swimming and fishing standards, even though the river is dry all but two weeks a year. And the city of Anchorage, Alaska, whose water supply was too clean for it to comply with a requirement from the Environmental Protection Agency (EPA) that organic matter be reduced by 30 percent, was forced to arrange for two local fisheries to dump their waste into the river upstream so that the city could remove it.[4]

---

4 Thomas Atwood and Chris West, "Home Rule: How States are Fighting Unfunded Federal Mandates," Heritage Foundation *State Backgrounder* No. 1011/S, December 1994, p. 2.

The sheer volume and cost of unfunded mandates is enormous. The National Conference of State Legislatures (NCSL) has identified at least 192 unfunded mandates on the states, ranging from the Americans with Disabilities Act to regulations governing underground storage tanks. The U.S. Conference of Mayors and Price Waterhouse estimate the cost of these requirements on 314 cities in 1994–1998 at $54 billion. According to the EPA, state and local governments will spend $137 billion to comply with the Clean Water Act alone.[5]

In scrambling to meet and pay for requirements imposed by Washington, state and local governments often are forced to ignore local priorities. Taxpayers already laboring under record-high taxes understandably resist even further increases. The Unfunded Mandates Act of 1995 was the first step in reducing the torrent of unfunded mandates from Congress, but fiscal pressures on these jurisdictions continue to mount as the costs of existing mandates climb and as the federal bureaucracy adds to the regulatory burden.

One of the best ways to help the states is simply to slow or stop altogether the growth of the federal government's regulatory intrusions. This is easier said than done, however, and will require more than general expressions of intent. A very important component of Reagan's federalism agenda was regulatory relief in which centralized management and review of proposed regulations played a key role. By executive order, President Reagan required all new federal regulations to be evaluated by a special White House council that not only ensured the new regulations were actually necessary, but also greatly reduced their volume.

Unlike those of his predecessors, Reagan's appointments to the Supreme Court and the federal judiciary took on a markedly pro-federalist character. Insufficient opportunity for further appointments prevented the emergence of a Supreme Court dedicated to reaffirming the Constitution, but the Supreme Court did take many steps in that direction, resulting finally in 1995 with the *Lopez* decision in which, for the first time in 60 years, it struck down a federal law based on the

---

5 Douglas Seay and Wesley Smith, "Federalism," in Stuart M. Butler and Kim R. Holmes, eds., *Issues '96: The Candidate's Briefing Book* (Washington, D.C.: The Heritage Foundation, 1996), p. 417.

Commerce Clause, and resurrected the 10th Amendment from the constitutional limbo into which decades of liberal judicial activism had consigned it.

Lesson #6: Even conservatives, once in Congress, have been guilty of "federalizing" power and authority when the federal government has no jurisdiction. Although all conservatives profess to work toward re-establishing a limited government that is close to the people, once they take office in Washington, they frequently stray from that goal. To a certain degree, this is a reflection of the extent to which the constitutional system has been distorted, leaning ever more in the direction of centralizing decision making in Washington.

Even the 104th Congress, with its clear commitment to advancing the goals of devolution and federalism, proved to be less than immune to the temptations of federal power. For example, the Church Arson Prevention Act of 1996 made church arson a federal crime, despite the fact that this crime was already illegal in all 50 states and that no conspiracy or other interstate aspect was ever demonstrated that might justify federal involvement. Nevertheless, the measure passed unanimously in both houses of Congress in a near-frantic effort by Members who did not want to be seen as uncaring.

Another glaring example is crime legislation. The Clinton Crime Bill of 1994 federalized a long list of offenses that always had been within the exclusive purview of state and local governments. No session of Congress passes without a proposal for the federalization of even more aspects of the state and local criminal justice system.

A third example exists with health care. The regulation of health insurance has been traditionally a state function. Nonetheless, the most significant feature of the Kassebaum-Kennedy bill, enacted by the conservative 104th Congress and signed into law by President Bill Clinton in August 1996, was the imposition of an unprecedented level of federal regulation on the health insurance market. The new health care reform law also sets up a powerful data collection apparatus at the federal level, including the collection and storage of personal medical information, and it adds six new federal crimes under the pretext of combating fraud and abuse in the health care system.

STRATEGIES FOR TRANSFERRING FUNCTIONS TO THE STATES

The first nine-and-a-half decades of the 20th century were a time of almost unbroken expansion of the powers of the federal government. Now there is literally no subject on which it will not legislate. Looking back at this period ten years from now, it may be those powers reached flood stage and finally began to recede in the latter part of the 1990s; and 1997 could be the year in which the ebb tide began. Americans know that centralization of authority in Washington has created many problems, but powerful political, economic, and ideological interest groups committed to the status quo are strenuously opposed to any curtailing of their power and benefits. If reformers in the 105th Congress and in the Administration are to carry out the mandate of the people—expressed so loudly in the Reagan elections and in 1994—and permanently limit the federal government's power, they must commit themselves to a specific agenda to that end, one that goes beyond mere legislative tinkering and aims at nothing less than a restoration of the Constitution's integrity.

Although each of the three branches of the federal government has expanded its power and jurisdiction, the burden of constitutional reform and of returning government programs to the states and local communities, where people can more clearly get involved, falls mainly on the shoulders of Congress. Only Congress has the constitutional authority, or even the likely inclination, to impose the necessary limitations on the three branches of the federal government. Only Congress, of course, can reform its own abuses. In addition, Congress has enormous freedom to reshape the executive branch by deleting or adding functions that fit the federalism format. Congress can also reform federal agencies through the budget process and help to level the playing field with the states. And Article III of the Constitution plainly gives the Congress tremendous (but often unexercised) authority over the federal judiciary. In short, there can be no abuses by the executive branch, the federal courts, or Congress itself that Congress does not choose to allow.

The states are the only potential counterweight with the requisite capabilities for checking and balancing the federal government as a whole. But there is still much that can be done by Congress and the Administration to improve the situation in the short term and to make the long-term task of imposing limits on the federal government more feasible.

STRATEGIES FOR TRANSFERRING FUNCTIONS TO THE STATES

- The President should put the prestige of his office behind a rebirth of federalism.

- The President should call for and preside over a Devolution Summit.

- Congress should work with allies among the governors and state legislatures to pursue an aggressive strategy of devolution.

- The appropriate legislative vehicles should be developed for devolving specific agencies and functions.

- The states should be encouraged to share information and experience in taking over programs once reserved to the federal government.

- Think tanks and foundations should provide technical advice to the states to help them implement innovative reforms.

- Use hearings to showcase stories of state, local, and private-sector success in combating serious social problems, and combine these with an evaluation of federal programs in these areas.

- The federal waiver process should be streamlined and federal agencies forced to cooperate with state officials.

- A second legislative offensive should be launched immediately against unfunded federal mandates.

- Sponsors of bills should be required to cite the specific constitutional authority for their legislative initiatives.

- The federal bureaucracy should be reined in.

- Hearings should be held on the practice of federalizing crimes under state and local jurisdiction.

- The private sector should be used to enhance the cause of devolution.

- Congress should assert its authority to rein in the federal courts.

- An effort should be made to explain to the American people why the United States needs to enact a balanced budget amendment.

- States should be given the authority to call for discrete constitutional changes.

STRATEGY #1

The President should put the prestige of his office behind a rebirth of federalism.

The President, more so than any other public official, can revive Americans' appreciation of their political heritage of federalism. An Administration dedicated to restraining Washington and promoting federalism has many resources at its disposal, even in the face of an unfriendly Congress. There is, of course, the famous "bully pulpit" by which the President can help set the national agenda and marshal the necessary public support for restoring limits on Washington and helping to revive the authority of the states. And, regardless of whether or not his party controls Congress, a President possesses an enormous influence on shaping the legislative agenda, especially by means of the annual budgets he submits and signs or vetoes.

As head of the Administration, the President directly affects the regulatory function of the federal agencies. President Reagan demonstrated how requiring centralized review and approval of proposed regulations could reduce the number of regulations radically while preventing a bureaucracy from enacting whatever it wanted. Presidents Bush and Clinton both gave free rein to the issuance of regulations, with the result that record levels were recorded in both Administrations. A new Administration should re-impose the former limits with the explicit goal of reducing both the overall number and the extent of new regulations, and review all existing ones with a mandate to eliminate or reduce the maximum number possible.

One action easily taken by the President in support of federalism would be to issue an executive order to all executive agencies that instructs them to deal with state governments as co-equals of the federal government. All new regulations should be required to cite the specific constitutional authority of the executive branch and Congress to engage in the relevant area of policy. The Administration can maintain a bias toward disallowing proposed regulations if such authority cannot be conclusively demonstrated.

A second executive order could instruct agencies to grant state requests for waivers immediately unless the relevant agency could present compelling reasons to deny or modify it. The burden of proof should rest with the agency, however, and not the states, and an automatic approval should be mandated after a set and short time limit.

STRATEGY #2
The President should call for and preside over a Devolution Summit.

To further meet the popular call to reform government and to bring it closer to the people, the President should call a Devolution Summit of governors and state legislative leaders in early 1997 to discuss the direction, form, and content of future devolution initiatives. Input from the states has been largely absent from the debate in Congress, and from the decision making process. Devolution to date largely has been a series of unilateral measures initiated by Congress, and thus has reflected the federal government's view of devolving power and authority almost exclusively. There has been some reallocation of functions, but what has occurred has been as a conditional grant by Washington, under terms entirely of Washington's design, which can be retracted or altered at will. This is not evidence of a restoration of the sovereignty of the states and a constitutional balance between the federal government and the states but merely that the federal government has changed its preferred method of operations which it has felt free to impose on the states.

Conservatives realize that the decentralizing aim of devolution cannot be achieved through unilateral actions of the federal government. The President can play an invaluable role by providing the focus and impetus for the indispensable cooperation of the states by holding a Devolution Summit, and making it one that is not merely a public relations event where passive state officials are briefed on Washington's latest changes of rules and on their newest duties. Here the President must not act in his role as head of the executive branch of the federal government but as President of the country, committed to a restoration of a constitutional balance.

The Devolution Summit agenda must be both comprehensive and forward-looking, with an opportunity for the states to weigh in on all issues and design their own preferred agenda. It should allow them to address their functional relationship with Washington. The President should not seek to determine the specific content of this summit, but rather should use his presiding role to ensure that something substantive does in fact emerge and that it represents the interests of the states.

STRATEGY #3

Regardless of the President's views on restoring federalism, conservatives in Congress, working with allies among the governors and state legislatures, should pursue an aggressive strategy of devolution.

Much of what the federal government now does is clearly beyond its constitutional authority, to say nothing of its competence level. Therefore, conservatives in Congress attempting to revive the fundamental charter of the American Republic must not shy away from the task of tackling head-on the federal government's unconstitutional overreach. In the legislative process, simply cutting down add-ons is not an acceptable solution; letting block grants with loose strings attached pass through is an open invitation to additional abuse, because both Washington and the state governments escape any direct accounting for how the money is used. It would be far better if the taxes were left in the states to begin with, with the acknowledgment that Washington might not always agree with the voters or the legislatures.

The most direct method of reducing the federal government's involvement in areas in which the states should hold authority is for Congress to close down or privatize outmoded, unnecessary federal agencies and departments, eliminate wasteful or inappropriate programs, and transfer remaining functions to other federal agencies or to the states, as appropriate. There are many reasons for such a retrenchment, including achieving greater efficiency by eliminating waste and duplication, freeing states and the private sector from unnecessary federal restrictions and mandates, and bringing government itself closer to the people.

Governors who are willing to take on new tasks and state legislators who wish to exercise more control in areas where the federal government has usurped their authority are natural allies. Conservatives in Congress should seek them out, getting feedback on possible devolution initiatives and working with them directly to develop the strategies of implementation. They should also seek the help of conservative associations which accumulate data on the state level and can help define the parameters of reform, like the American Legislative Exchange Council and the State Policy Network, an association of state-based think tanks.

If the states are to be useful in tackling Washington's overextended powers, a way must be found to focus their attention and energies collectively on this subject. If the President does not call for a Devolution Summit of state leaders, then conservatives in Congress should do so. As long as conservatives hold fast to the rule that the federal tax take and the responsibility for funding will be returned to the states along with whichever programs are devolved, assembling the states to encourage collective action on their part is one of the most promising ways to build support for restructuring the federal government. Having state leaders advance their own downsizing agenda for Washington is more likely to secure their active participation than simply asking them to sign on to one originating from Congress. And state leaders, acting with broad support from their state's voters, can bring enormous political influence to bear on Washington if they can be persuaded to act collectively. High on any summit's agenda must be the compiling of a list of and timetable for federal agencies and programs to be eliminated or restructured, as well as a clear plan for transferring the remaining functions to the states.

STRATEGY #4
Congress should develop the appropriate legislative vehicles for devolving specific agencies and functions.

In addition to devolving welfare, there are several steps Congress can take to devolve major portions of other federal agencies and functions, particularly in areas such as transportation, housing, job training, and unemployment insurance. Supporters of devolution in Congress already have developed the appropriate legislative vehicles. For example, Representative John Kasich (R-OH) and Senator Connie Mack (R-FL) introduced in the 104th Congress the Transportation Empowerment Act (H.R. 3850; S.1907). Although this act retains a core of functions for the federal government—most prominently the Interstate Highway system — it devolves most of the federal government's current control over transportation policy, and it turns over to the states almost all of the tax on gasoline now collected by the federal government along with responsibility for roads, mass transit, and other transportation-related activities.

Although opposition exists in states that currently are net recipients of federal funds, much of their resistance is based on the erroneous assumption that the Mack-Kasich proposal will cut the amount of money available to them. Conservatives in Congress, meeting with the governors of these states and key legislative leaders, should explain that it is estimated that the federal government wastes 25 percent to 30 percent of the available funding on a large federal bureaucracy that frequently performs the work that the states can do easily. It is also important to note that the government drives up the costs of highway projects through the imposition of unnecessary mandates. Economist Gabriel Roth estimates these mandates may add up to 20 percent of total spending on transportation.[6] Governors and state legislators should know that most of the federal money now wasted would become available to the states through devolution.

Finally, Congress should remind governors and state legislators that Washington's politically driven allocations of money not only divert available funds to often-unnecessary uses, but prevent state officials from addressing the real needs close to home. For example, for Fiscal Year 1996, 84 percent of the transportation funding allocated to Pennsylvania was earmarked by Congress for major highway construction, of which 70 percent was mandated for highway construction in central Pennsylvania (coincidentally including much of the district of Representative Bud Shuster (R-PA), chairman of the House Committee on Transportation and Infrastructure). The relationship of this allocation to the state's actual needs is unlikely to be close, and the way the money was used certainly would have been different if the state had been able to determine for itself the best use of its own citizens' tax dollars. Pennsylvania officials concede that the burden of decisions that are made for political reasons in Washington "severely limits the ability of the Department [of Transportation] and the State Transportation Commission to allocate funds to other projects that may be of higher priority." They had little choice but to accept these special-interest projects rather than risk losing the "associated federal funding."[7]

The best way of ending this abuse and waste is to devolve the programs fully, including the federal tax take and responsibility for

---

6 "Paying for Roads," *The Journal of Commerce,* July 25, 1996.

7 Pennsylvania General Assembly, Legislative Budget and Finance Committee, "Performance Audit, Department of Transportation Pursuant to Act 1981–35," June 1996, p. 187.

funding, so that the states and local jurisdictions can make their own decisions regarding local needs. If full devolution is not immediately attainable, conservatives in Congress should work with state officials and legislators to identify and eliminate provisions in federal programs that are not in accord with state and local priorities. The state officials responsible for administering these programs, and the state legislators who must vote to raise the taxes to pay for them, are the best sources of information regarding which provisions of federal programs are wasteful, unwanted, and unneeded. But these officials are often reluctant to go public because of well-founded fears of fiscal retribution. Conservatives in Congress, working with such like-minded organizations as American Legislative Exchange Council and the State Policy Network, should develop their own information networks in each state and actively seek to publicize as much as possible of the absurdities dictated by Washington in order to produce a restraining effect on Congress's use of politically motivated set-asides.

STRATEGY #5
The states should be encouraged to share information and experiences in taking over programs once reserved to the federal government.

When major programs (such as welfare) are devolved to the states, the states are often ill-equipped actually to run the programs or are simply too inexperienced. For devolution to work well, states may need help; in particular, they would benefit from sharing the experiences of more innovative states. In addition to legislating devolution, Congress can and should play a very important role in helping the states carry out their new responsibilities. Congress could assist the states in developing the new policies and procedures at the state and local levels that devolution will demand and for which the states are currently unprepared.

Existing state organizations such as the National Governors' Association, the National Conference of State Legislatures, and the American Legislative Exchange Council also can help. But the need may be too great for these organizations to satisfy by themselves, especially as this role would have to compete with their traditional functions. Instead, what is needed is an organization whose entire focus is on providing the states with the necessary information and expertise. There are many models for such an organization, but the most suitable would be the establishment of a nongovernmental, nonprofit foundation funded and directed exclusively by the states. This foundation would act as a nonpartisan, nonpolitical consultant to the states for the specific purpose of providing information and expertise on those programs that Congress has chosen to devolve.

Regardless of which form this organization might take, it should be a state-sponsored and state-controlled effort; Congress should not attempt directly to establish or control any such organization, as its involvement would inevitably diminish the utility to the states. What is needed is for the states to establish their own organization, one in which the information flows pass directly between themselves, bypassing Washington altogether.

STRATEGY #6
Congress should require federal agencies to share data with the states.

For policymakers who support devolution, encouraging states to develop their own resources and information flows among themselves—not through Washington—and encouraging them to act collectively vis-à-vis the federal government, should be high priorities in general. In addition, resurrecting the ability of the states to challenge, block, and even lead Washington is crucial to the reimposition of effective limits on the federal government.

More substantively, Congress should insert language in the appropriate bills to instruct federal agencies to assist the states with all available means, including free access to the relevant federal data banks. Given that officials in many federal agencies may see their future organizational survival and the success of state efforts to be in direct conflict, they may have little willingness to cooperate with the states, an attitude which an unfriendly Administration might encourage through sheer inaction. To eliminate this potential obstruction, Congress should use its legitimate authority over the agencies to mandate cooperation with clear performance criteria. And if the states established their own organization, Congress could order the delivery to it of all relevant federal data banks, free of charge, thereby largely ending the states' dependence on the federal bureaucracy's goodwill and responsiveness to requests for information.

STRATEGY #7
Conservative think tanks and foundations should provide technical advice to the states to help them implement innovative reforms.

When advocates of devolution are successful in achieving legislation to move functions to the states, that does not of itself mean that these functions will be devolved in ways that stimulate innovation and achieve the policy objectives of the devolution legislation. The danger is that a governor or legislature will tend to turn to the bureaucracies and interest groups now operating the federally run programs for advice on how to design and operate the devolved program. This is an urgent danger in the case of welfare, in which the states are implementing the reforms enacted by Congress in 1996. In many cases those advising governors on how to "end welfare as we know it" will be the same people who bitterly opposed the reform, such as most state welfare officials. These individuals will seek to weaken or undermine the purpose of the reform. Conservative think tanks at the state level, together with national research groups, must provide governors and legislatures with alternative technical advice so that states are not dependent on the welfare establishment.

Two developments in recent years hold great promise for devolution and for conservatives. The first is the growth of free market-oriented, state-based think tanks, the most prominent of which are grouped together in the State Policy Network. More than 35 states now have them, ranging from fledgling organizations to well-established institutions such as Michigan's Mackinac Center for Public Policy. Second, national organizations such as The Heritage Foundation have developed extensive computer modeling capabilities applicable to the national economy and that of the individual states. Working together, these two types of groups have created an unprecedented capability to design programs and forecast their effects, giving their policy recommendations a level of specificity once available only to the national government's well-staffed agencies, such as the General Accounting Office (GAO) or the Congressional Budget Office (CBO). For such capabilities to be utilized, however, accurate and detailed data are needed, information that often only the federal government possesses or has the capability to collect. By mandating that the data from federal agencies be made freely available to these and other organizations, the power of the bureaucracy to block or frustrate reforms through denial of information can be eliminated.

Finally, conservative institutions must be actively creating a policy infrastructure similar to that of the Left. For many years, liberal organizations at the national and state levels have worked together to achieve the liberal agenda, and this effort has been backed by moderate and liberal grant-making foundations. For example, the Robert Wood Johnson Foundation and other grant-makers have funded technical experts to help write legislation at the state level to advance health care reforms based on managed competition. Major think tanks, such as the Urban Institute, currently are working very closely with the states on health policy design issues. Yet the conservative think tanks and grant-makers are not competing in a serious way for this type of involvement in program development or this level of access to program implementation. They must begin to do so in welfare, health care, and other areas to achieve the full realization of any reforms at the state and local levels.

STRATEGY #8
Congress should showcase state, local, and private-sector success stories in combating serious social problems combined with an evaluation of federal programs in these same areas in its hearings.

Congress can use congressional hearings to highlight state and local success stories, including the success stories of private and nonprofit organizations that are dealing with some of America's most difficult social problems in housing, job training, crime prevention, and teen pregnancy. The hearings should be used to elucidate how local officials or community activists have dealt with these various problems; what specific obstacles they encountered, including restrictive federal rules and regulations; how they overcame these obstacles; and what lessons could be imparted to others who are engaged in similar efforts.

One of the most effective means of promoting federalism is to make public the cases of abuse. Every state, every district has its list of judicial and regulatory horror stories, from federal judges ordering the release of tens of thousands of violent criminals from prison on spurious grounds to the enormous costs that Washington casually passes on to state and local governments as a consequence of its endless regulations. Every committee and subcommittee has the opportunity through hearings to bring these often-unbelievable activities to the light of public scrutiny. They can force officials from the executive branch to reveal unflattering data and elements of decision making that otherwise would remain hidden. Each state must fight its battles individually, and virtually none can command sufficient attention to make the problem a national one. But through well-publicized hearings, Congress can demonstrate the widespread pattern of federal abuse. Armed with information and appropriate public outrage, the crafting of corrective legislation and attempting to marshal support for it would become markedly easier.

Meanwhile, Congress also should establish a joint committee to undertake a serious evaluation of federal programs, especially the numerous social programs that liberals in Congress and elsewhere deem indispensable.[8] The project could outline the comparison of the actual results of rigorous, scientific evaluations of those programs with the promises — or initial mandate and mission — in the original authorizing legislation. This evaluation could include an evaluation of the modifications and missions of the programs; the monies spent over the past 40 years on these programs; and the populations served and the numbers of persons affected by them. Much of the rigorous evaluation work could be conducted by the GAO and the Congressional Research Service. In the meantime, congressional committees with jurisdiction over federal programs should schedule hearings, giving the directors of these programs an opportunity to testify on their effectiveness and measuring their results against national trend data. A body of evidence will make it easier for Congress to determine which programs are working and which are not, and which might be more profitably turned over to state and local authorities.

---

8 Conservatives in Congress should realize that their liberal colleagues are not going to be caught unprepared for the fight over devolution. The Urban Institute will be conducting a $20 million multi-year study of the impact of devolution, focusing upon its effect on state budgets, services, and beneficiaries of government services. The Annie E. Casey Foundation has committed $10 million to the project.

STRATEGY #9
**Congress should streamline the federal waiver process and force federal
agencies to cooperate with state officials.**

The thicket of regulations that govern all aspects of federal programs
can stop any attempt by the states or local governments to innovate or
even improve current practices. One of the most innovative governors,
Governor Tommy Thompson of Wisconsin, has described the mind-
numbing process by which even minor waivers must be approved, with
the federal bureaucracy calling all the shots. In addition to having to
compile a vast amount of studies, paperwork, projections, and descriptions for each individual request,

> [A]ny difference of opinion [between state and
> federal officials] in any one of those parts of the
> waiver request can tie up the process for months
> in back-and-forth negotiations, or ultimately doom
> your request if you can't convince them to see it
> your way.... [W]e spend weeks debating back and
> forth, submitting and resubmitting the proposal. It
> makes you want to tear your hair out, but you
> can't get mad, because they might say no .... [I]f
> Washington does grant a waiver, it usually
> amounts to far less of a reform than what was
> originally requested.[9]

By contrast, the Reagan Administration had a far more welcoming
attitude toward state requests for waivers; they were rightly viewed as
the first steps in encouraging the states to innovate and ultimately to take
back policy areas monopolized by Washington. Waiver requests for
welfare reforms, for instance, were hashed out in a one-day or two-day
meeting of the top federal and state officials. After an agreement was
reached, lower-level federal officials were ordered to "make it happen."
Success in these efforts triggered innovation in other states and helped to
build support for reform at the national level. The same process should be
used in other areas, such as environmental policy.

---

9 Tommy G. Thompson, *Power to the People* (New York: HarperCollins, 1996),
   pp. 36-37.

In areas or agencies that have been devolved only partially or which remain tightly controlled by Washington, Congress can legislate a greater responsiveness on the part of federal agencies to requests from the states for waivers by imposing a short time limit — such as two weeks to a month—for the agency to respond, with automatic approval granted for a request that did not receive a definitive response in that period. The burden for justifying any decision should be shifted entirely from the states to the agencies that should be required to establish a clear-cut case, based on empirical evidence and not mere policy differences, for rejecting all state requests.

Such legislation would encourage innovation at the state level in those areas that have not been fully devolved. Currently, even the most promising plans face a seemingly endless series of bureaucratic obstructions that can choke off reform efforts before they even get started. The model welfare reform plan in Wisconsin introduced by Governor Thompson — an effort whose success eventually provided much of the inspiration for the federal Welfare Reform Act of 1996 — required the individual approval of 172 waivers.[10] The effort needed to obtain those waivers was an unnecessary and truly burdensome addition to the already considerable investment of time, money, and political capital required to design and put together a new state program on welfare reform.

Experience has demonstrated that only the most committed of state leaders are willing to embark upon such an unnecessarily difficult process. Through the simple expedient of reducing the federal bureaucracy's ability to veto state initiatives without demonstrable cause, and thereby reducing the need for states to act as supplicants before those same agencies, Congress can advance the goals of localized program development, program efficiency, and better service to the taxpaying public.

---

10 *Ibid.,* p. 37.

STRATEGY #10
The 105th Congress should launch a second legislative offensive immediately against unfunded federal mandates.

The Unfunded Mandates Reform Act of 1995 was intended to be a barrier to the further imposition of financial burdens on state and local governments, and in turn on the private sector. Although celebrated by its backers as a major victory, its long-term utility remains questionable. To begin with, it left existing mandates untouched and applies only to future mandates. More important, it imposes little or no restriction on Congress's ability to impose additional unfunded mandates. The principal obstruction raised is allowing Members to invoke a point of order which would force the relevant chamber to officially recognize that the proposed measure is indeed an unfunded mandate. A simple majority vote would be needed to proceed. Assuming that the measure had enough support to pass in the first place, this is a restriction that is easily transgressed. Finally, it is unclear whether the reduction in new unfunded mandates is a result of the legislation or is more a consequence of the 1994 election of a Republican Congress that pledged a reduction in unfunded mandates. If it was the latter, then a new Congress with a different outlook could change the situation overnight, with little recourse left to the states.

As budget pressures on the federal government climb in the coming years, the temptation to continue to legislate while passing the costs on to state and local governments will become increasingly irresistible, regardless of whatever pledges may have been made. Programs devolved to the states accompanied by block grants could see that funding gradually dry up, leaving the states with yet another burdensome level of mandates but without the promised funding. A comprehensive solution to this problem may require a constitutional amendment, but there are more incremental steps a new Congress could take to improve the situation. The Unfunded Mandates Reform Act could be amended to apply to existing programs as they come up for regular reauthorization, forcing Congress to reimpose or alleviate the burdens on a case-by-case basis. The majority needed to proceed with an unfunded mandate after a point of order is called could be increased to a qualified majority, such as a three-fifths, in each house.

There are even simpler methods of advancing this goal, such as enforcing provisions already enacted. For example, the Unfunded Mandates Reform Act, Section 23, states that the committee report of any bill must contain an "explicit statement on the extent to which the bill or joint resolution is intended to preempt any State, local, or tribal law, and, if so, an explanation of the effect of such preemption." This requirement appears to have been honored only in the breach or in the most cursory fashion.

STRATEGY #11
Congress should start requiring bill sponsors to cite the specific constitutional authority for their legislative initiatives.

There have been a number of proposals to require that a proposed bill cite Congress's specific constitutional authority to legislate in that area, with the hope that some of the more egregious abuses can be curbed by subjecting them to public scrutiny and potential ridicule. Senator Ted Stevens (R-AK) introduced the 10th Amendment Enforcement Act in 1996, which was quickly supported by then-Majority Leader Robert Dole. Companion legislation was introduced in the House by Representative John Shadegg (R-AZ). Senator Stevens's bill would have changed the Senate rules to allow any Senator to raise a point of order regarding the cited constitutional authority and force a vote on that specific issue, with a requirement that 60 affirmative votes would be needed in order for the bill to proceed. The procedural barrier erected could not stop a Congress that was intent on a course of action, but the requirement that it declare its intent to do so publicly might give many Members pause for thought.

The proposed Act also would have removed the ability of executive branch agencies to preempt state and local law automatically with their own rules or regulations. It required that any such rules or regulations be narrowly tailored to achieve the specific goals of the statute, that the scope of preemption be explicitly described, that state officials be notified and allowed to comment on the proposals, and that each agency periodically review its published rules with a mandate to continually revise them to minimize their impact on state and local government powers. The Act also instructed the federal courts to interpret any ambiguities in favor of "preserving the authority of the States and the People." Senator Stevens's proposed bill died with the 104th Congress, but its reintroduction in the 105th Congress should be a high priority.

STRATEGY #12
Congress and the Administration should start reining in the federal bureaucracy.

Far too often, Members of Congress identify a problem, call a press conference, hold hearings, and try to enact legislation to "solve" the problem, but bypass the states' rights or responsibilities in the process. In the enforcement of the broad federal statute, the all-important details of framing the rules and regulations to "solve" the problem are "delegated" to federal agencies and departments. Congress too often delegates this rulemaking authority to the agencies without attaching clear standards for implementation, and thus the agencies are invariably left a wide degree of discretion in implementing the law. This pattern not only undermines the rule of law, but also encourages judicial "reconstruction" of the law,[11] which undermines the authority of Congress itself.

Not only should Congress stop this abdication of legislative responsibility and make sure that any delegation of power to a federal department or agency is accompanied by clear statutory language specifying what the agency can and cannot do, but it should clearly instruct federal officials to defer to state and local officials in the drafting of federal rules that will have an impact on the responsibilities of the state and local governments.

Representative J. D. Hayworth (R-AZ) introduced the Congressional Responsibility Act in the 104th Congress and sought to reverse Congress's delegation of its lawmaking function to the executive branch. It required that rules and regulations issued by the executive branch be approved by Congress before they take effect. These rules and regulations have the force of law; certainly, state and local governments are required by the courts to abide by them. The Act not only would have restored to Congress its constitutional function of making all the laws, but would have given the states and local governments a means of having their interests and those of their citizens taken into account. The requirement of congressional approval would have a welcome chilling effect on the

---

11 For the classic description of this continuing problem, see Theodore J. Lowi, *The End Of Liberalism: Ideology, Policy and the Crisis of Public Authority* (New York: W.W. Norton and Co., 1969), pp. 297-303.

federal bureaucracy's current freedom to legislate for the country, as well as on Congress's ability to escape responsibility for abuses imposed by the executive branch.

STRATEGY #13
Congress should hold hearings on the practice of federalizing crimes under state and local jurisdiction.

Since 95 percent of all violent crimes come under state and local legal jurisdiction, it is incomprehensible that there are now over 3,000 federal crimes on the statute books. According to a January 1996 article by Edwin Meese and Rhett DeHart for *Policy Review,* there are few crimes that fall outside the jurisdiction of federal authorities, from carjacking and drug dealing to disrupting rodeos. The Clinton Administration's 1994 federal crime bill added two dozen more federal crimes to the duplication of offenses already illegal under state and local law. The 1996 Kassebaum-Kennedy health insurance reform bill added a half dozen more.

Congress should end this counterproductive practice by building public support for the elimination of ineffective and duplicative laws and programs. This can be done through a process of congressional hearings to review all federal anti-crime programs to determine their effectiveness in combating crime. Moreover, conservatives in Congress should initiate a thorough review of all federal statutes, determining which ones duplicate or impinge upon local law enforcement authorities and then repealing them.

STRATEGY #14
Congress should use the power of the private sector to enhance the cause of devolution.

Privatization can play a key role in a devolution strategy. Among the quiet successes of the 104th Congress is that it enacted more privatization of federal functions in one year than occurred during the eight years of the Reagan Administration, the last Presidency in which privatization got serious official backing. Congress can continue to build on these initial successes and promote more widespread privatization, not only in the management and administration of the federal government, but also in social policy through the sale of public housing to tenants and vouchers to make private-sector alternatives available to those who currently get services from government monopolies. Perhaps the most promising step in this direction is the comprehensive urban policy embodied in Saving Our Children: The American Community Renewal Act of 1996, sponsored by Representatives J. C. Watts (R-OK) and James Talent (R-MO).[12]

Under the Watts-Talent bill, the private sector would engage in creating jobs and businesses in areas characterized by poverty and distress through so-called enterprise zones. Low-income parents would be entitled to education scholarships for their children, financed out of existing federal funds, to be used at a public, private, or religious school of their choice. Tax credits, refunding up to 75 percent of a taxpayer's contribution to any private charity engaged in direct services to the poor (up to a cap), would encourage a greater reliance on the use of effective charitable organizations to assist the poor. And under the Watts-Talent bill, tax credits would also be available to private employers who hire persons who are welfare recipients or high-risk youth, the very persons who have the greatest difficulty in securing real, permanent jobs in the private sector.

STRATEGY #15
Congress should assert its constitutional authority to rein in the federal courts.

No area of the federal government has exceeded its constitutional boundaries more egregiously than the federal judiciary. Its sins are both those of commission and those of omission: It not only has seen fit to exercise virtually unlimited authority on its own, but has proactively removed all constitutional obstacles that might keep the executive and legislative branches of the federal government from doing so as well. Its arrogance has brought it to the point where there is no federal, state, or local law or ordinance which it cannot set aside at will; no state constitution or popular referendum it need respect; no tradition, institution, or individual beyond its reach.

---

12 For a discussion of the Watts-Talent legislation, see Robert Rector and Christine Olson, "Saving Our Children: The American Community Renewal Act of 1996," Heritage Foundation *Issue Bulletin*, No. 228, July 29, 1996.

The judicial branch has restructured all facets of the criminal justice system in minute detail, and in the process has crippled it; it has stripped communities of their ability to exercise control over their environment and allow their citizens to exercise self-government; and, in its hubris, it has even ordered the imposition of taxes on otherwise free people who had rejected them in a referendum. It sees fit to rewrite the federal Constitution, adding new "rights" that exist only in the imaginations of liberal ideologues or deriving doctrine from the subjectively perceived "penumbras" of the Framers' carefully crafted constitutional text.

For example, in an October 12, 1985, speech to Georgetown University Law School students, Supreme Court Justice William Brennan stated that the death penalty is "under all circumstances cruel and unusual punishment and prohibited by the Eighth Amendment," despite the fact that capital punishment is explicitly recognized by the Constitution, that Congress and state legislatures have specifically provided for it, and that the public overwhelmingly supports it, according to all polls on the subject.[13] Federal judges also have ruled that prisoners have a right to on-site law libraries in order to pursue their appeals, including law clerks to help them with their research and preparation, all at public expense. Delaware Attorney General Charles Oberly II has stated that this has resulted in state prisoners having better access to law materials than he does.[14] A direct result has been an explosion of frivolous lawsuits by prisoners against state prison administrations, which rose from a mere 218 in 1966 to 53,713 in 1993.[15] There is no area of American society that has escaped this idiosyncratic and heavy-handed intrusion, and every Supreme Court term is a time in which the Constitution reemerges in a new and unexpected form.

The attitude of the federal judiciary toward state and local governments has been nothing short of contemptuous. Federal courts routinely invalidate state laws, overturn popular referenda, suspend sections of state constitutions, take over state and local government functions for decades at a time, and impose extensive and idiosyncratic

---

13 William J. Quirk and R. Randall Bridwell, *Judicial Dictatorship* (New Brunswick, N.J.: Transaction Publishers, 1995), p. 6.

14 Wesley Smith, "Jailhouse Blues," *National Review*, June 13, 1994, p. 40.

15 *Ibid.*

changes at enormous cost to the local taxpayers. These federal judicial abuses and their practical impact on local communities can be staggering. For example, Judge Norma Shapiro in Philadelphia has ordered the release of tens of thousands of violent felons from prison on spurious grounds of "overcrowding." In one year alone, police re-arrested thousands of these released prisoners on other charges, including 79 murders, 959 robberies, 2,215 drug deals, 701 burglaries, 2,748 thefts, 90 rapes, 14 kidnapping charges, 1,113 assaults, 264 gun-law violations, and 127 drunk-driving incidents.

In another example, Judge Russell Clark in Kansas City took over the local school system and ordered so many costly changes that several schools are now empty because the county cannot afford to operate them. When a tax rate increase to fund these imposed changes was defeated in a local referendum, Judge Clark astonishingly ordered the collection of the taxes anyway, treating the electorate's decision as mere contempt of court. He later remarked that perhaps he had "created too expensive a school system," a revealing commentary on who really wields power at the local level.

The excesses of the federal judiciary have been allowed by those whose constitutional responsibilities include supervision of the courts. Thus, the failing is not that of the federal judiciary alone, but of the legislative and executive branches as well. There are many things Congress can do to correct this problem. The President, for his part, should appoint only those individuals to the federal bench who have demonstrated a commitment to preserving the integrity of the written Constitution. The Senate should refuse to confirm any appointee who cannot demonstrate a convincing record in this regard.

The Senate of the 104th Congress had many opportunities to require such standards of the Clinton Administration's judicial nominees but routinely approved those nominations without dissent, including overwhelming approval of those nominees with the worst constitutional record. One such example was federal Judge Lee Sarokin of New Jersey. In 1990, Judge Sarokin ruled in favor of a homeless man in Morristown who had brought suit against the town with the help of the American Civil Liberties Union because he had been asked to leave the public library in which he had spent his days stalking, staring down, and speaking loudly and belligerently to library staff and patrons. Judge Sarokin's ruling stated that

> if we wish to shield our eyes and noses from the homeless, we should revoke their condition, not their library cards .... [T]he cause of the revulsion may be of our own making....[The library] cannot condition access on behavior, appearance, or hygiene [because it is] an unreasonable wealth classification.

The total cost to the city reached $480,000; Judge Sarokin was appointed by President Clinton to the U.S. Court of Appeals and was confirmed by the Senate.[16]

Senators and commentators alike point to the Senate's tradition of deferring to the President's right to nominate, but this courtesy is difficult to justify when the result is so thoroughly damaging to the country as a whole. One might reasonably ask what is the point of requiring the Senate's "advice and consent" if it is routinely granted even to those whose qualifications are suspect? Senators can clearly do better than relying on the rating system of the American Bar Association, which is extraordinarily biased against conservatives, and can broaden consideration of the fitness of judicial nominee—for example, in terms of their sensitivity to public safety — to include constitutional experts that have been impaneled by law enforcement organizations. Ultimately, however, it is the Senate's duty to determine the fitness of nominees to the federal judiciary.

Most important, conservatives in Congress should work to dispel the notion that Congress is powerless to act against an abusive judiciary. An unbiased reading of Article III of the Constitution clearly indicates that congressional authority over the federal judiciary is enormous. Not only does the text unambiguously declare that fact; it also was the expressed opinion of the individuals who were the principal authors of Article III and of the first Judiciary Act, the law establishing the federal courts. One

---

16 Wesley R. Smith, "Don't Stand So Close to Me," *Policy Review*, No. 70 (Fall 1994), p. 48.

such author, Oliver Ellsworth of Connecticut, later served as a chief justice and continued to expound this view on the Supreme Court.

Congress and the Administration should recall that James Madison, the Father of the Constitution, and both Presidents Thomas Jefferson and Abraham Lincoln were stouthearted opponents of the modern doctrine of judicial supremacy.[17] Nevertheless, in recent decades the erroneous idea that the courts are somehow above the Constitution as the final arbiter of the meaning of the Constitution has gained considerable currency. But this is an opinion without foundation. Under Article III, Sections 1 and 2 of the Constitution, Congress has explicit authority over the appellate jurisdiction of the courts; indeed, even the creation of the lower federal courts is left to the discretion of Congress. Congress also has some power over the jurisdiction of the U.S. Supreme Court. Congress in particular has a sworn duty to oversee the federal judiciary and act to prevent its abuses, abuses which cannot occur without congressional complicity.

STRATEGY #16
Congress must make an effort to explain to the American people why the United States needs to enact a balanced budget amendment.

Passage of a balanced budget amendment should be at the forefront of the agenda of the new Congress. Had it been in place two decades ago, the U.S. population would have been spared the burden of a $6 trillion debt that continues to grow. Conservatives in Congress, in every forum and at every opportunity, should explain that the mounting debt means higher interest payments, which crowd out spending on other national priorities, and that unrestrained deficits are likely to result in a lower standard of living for all Americans, not just for our children and grandchildren. Moreover, at every opportunity, the American people should be told that the absence of a limit on spending also has allowed

---

17 There is a rich literature in the field of political science on the subject. See, in particular, Louis B. Boudin, *Government By Judiciary* (New York: William Godwin Inc., 1932); Walter Murphy, *Congress and The Court: A Case Study In The American Political Process* (Chicago: University of Chicago Press, 1962); Patrick B. McGuigan and Randall Rader, *A Blueprint For Judicial Reform* (Washington, D.C.: The Free Congress Education and Research Foundation, 1981).

Congresses and Administrations to escape making necessary, although temporarily unpopular, decisions on reforming federal entitlements. The result has been mounting fiscal pressures to make the options less, not more, politically palatable, and substantively more draconian.

Conservatives in Congress can build political support for a balanced budget amendment by highlighting the successful experiences of the states. Despite the fact that 30 percent or more of state budgets are controlled by the federal government through mandates and other impositions, virtually every state is required by its own constitution to balance its budget every year. This fiscal rectitude extends to tax cutting, an area in which states have demonstrated that balanced budgets and tax reductions not only are not incompatible, but also are very much a net positive for the man in the street. Consider the October 1996 report from Congress's Joint Economic Committee called *Tax Cuts and Balanced Budgets: A Tour of Lansing and Trenton*. Michigan and New Jersey both cut taxes and increased economic growth, measured not only against their past performance, but also against that of their neighbors. The report also shows that along with these economic benefits, deficits did not increase.

Several versions of balanced budget amendments for the federal government have been proposed. The 104th Congress voted on one introduced by Senator Paul Simon (D-IL); the House passed it by the necessary two-thirds majority, but it failed in the Senate by one vote. Although successful passage of this proposal would have been a major step forward, for the next attempt Congress should consider adding provisions to close off anticipated avenues of escape. One of the most important additions would be a requirement that both houses muster a supermajority in order to raise taxes. This finally would end Washington's ability to continue to increase spending effortlessly while removing its ability to use the requirement of a balanced budget to justify new taxes.

STRATEGY #17
Congress should give states the authority to call for discrete constitutional changes.

One of the core constitutional mechanisms is the system of checks and balances between the federal government and the states. As part of that mechanism, the Framers included a provision to allow the states to bypass an obstructionist Congress and amend the Constitution themselves, but only through a Constitutional Convention.

For many people, the prospect of a Constitutional Convention conjures up images of a wholesale rewriting of the document, and this fear has made the calling of such a convention all but impossible, allowing Congress to maintain an unwarranted monopoly on proposing amendments. Progressively stripped of their functions and their ability to protect their citizens from federal overreaching, the states have been unable to use the one instrument remaining to them to correct this situation because of the insurmountable obstacles surrounding a convention. To overcome this obstruction, Senator John Ashcroft (R-MO) has introduced a constitutional amendment (S.J. Res. 58) that would eliminate the need for a Constitutional Convention by allowing two-thirds of the state legislatures to propose an amendment. Congress would have an opportunity to vote down the amendment, or to submit its own version alongside that of the states, with ratification by three-quarters of the state legislatures needed for adoption.

Considering the high hurdles any proposed amendment would need to overcome, and the broad national agreement required for passage, no one could argue that the result would be hastily arrived at or would lack consensus. In fact, this cumbersome route is likely to be used only when Congress refused to act on a proposal that had overwhelming public support, such as a balanced budget amendment. The most probable outcome of this process would be to spur Congress to action in an attempt to preempt the states whenever their sponsorship of a proposal neared the two-thirds level. By giving the states the ability to force Congress to act on broadly supported measures, Senator Ashcroft's amendment would restore to the states some of the power to act as the check and balance on Washington that the Founders intended them to be.

A more direct method of restoring the ability of the states to serve as a check and balance on the federal government would be a constitutional amendment that would allow the states to veto or force the reconsideration of federal laws and regulations. Whether the number of states required was set at a simple majority of two-thirds or some other number, the effect would be to give them the means of shielding themselves and their citizens from onerous or absurd federal laws and regulations, especially in the form of unfunded mandates. Some versions of this proposal would give Congress the ability to override a veto by the states with a two-thirds majority in both houses, the same amount necessary for overriding a presidential veto. Again, the lengthy and cumbersome process needed to produce action by the states would limit its application to those laws and regulations that were truly burdensome and unpopular.

CONCLUSION

Fearing the twin evils of anarchy and tyranny, the Framers of the U.S. Constitution created a system they believed would be self-enforcing. Trusting neither the written word of the Constitution nor the character of politicians, they brought into being a new system of checks and balances in which the political actors would be pitted against one another. This deliberate opposition was intended to make certain that the energies and ambitions of the competing organs of government were directed against one another, thus allowing civil society maximum protection against arbitrary political power. The threefold division of the federal government into legislative, executive, and judicial branches has proved its durability and effectiveness after two centuries of tumultuous change. The most important division of power—that between the national government and the states— has, however, all but disappeared.

The only lasting solution is to reimpose limits on official Washington— limits that cannot be overridden by those who wield power for the moment. Ultimately, only the states have the institutional resources, the interests, and the political potential necessary to impose and police the limits on the federal government. Restoring their capacity to perform this vital function will require a long-term commitment on the part of those in Congress and the Administration who proudly call themselves conservatives. This commitment includes constitutional as well as legislative changes. Conservatives in Congress can put temporary restraints on the powers of the federal government, including the federal judiciary. They can evaluate, reform, and devolve federal programs to the states. They can reduce or end programs that do not work, waste taxpayers' money, or have a baneful impact on the quality and character of American life. They can thus prepare the ground for a revival of the states as a countervailing political power. The Contract With America was an excellent start; but it was only the beginning for work that will stretch well into the 21st century.

Over the next term, Congress and the Administration will be responding to the daily crises of governing a powerful nation with daunting national and international responsibilities. They will be motivated to accommodate short-term political interest, as all elected officials must, but they should be governed by a vision of genuine self-government for the American people in those matters that directly affect them at the state and local levels. Certainly, they should judge every proposal on its merits. But they should also judge every legislative measure in terms of its contribution to the overall goal of restoring binding limits on the power of official Washington and the balance of power between the federal government and the states.

Those in Congress who uphold the principles of self-government can help the states resume their responsibility to check and balance the federal government. But here, especially, they must follow their own rule: They cannot do for the states what the states will not do for themselves.

Chapter 4

TRANSFERRING FUNCTIONS TO THE PRIVATE SECTOR

Ronald D. Utt

P rivatization — the process by which certain public services and functions are transferred from the government to private-sector providers — is a powerful tool that governments both here and abroad have used to improve service and control costs. Shifting routine government services like waste removal and landscaping, or even sophisticated ones like jet fighter maintenance and space shuttle operations, to the private sector allows businesses that must succeed in a competitive marketplace to offer the same or better service at lower cost. The savings that have been realized through privatization, in fact, average in excess of 25 percent based upon internal government reports, General Accounting Office studies, and a Department of Defense review presented to Congress in March 1996.

The Privatization Record
Privatization has amassed a favorable record that spans decades, nations, and all levels of government. Although the privatization of services and commercial enterprises within the federal government started slowly in the 1980s and has picked up steam only recently, it achieved far more success in

The author would like to thank the Honorable Carol T. Crawford, Representative Scott L. Klug, William G. Reinhardt, Robert W. Poole, and John M. Palatiello for their suggestions and contributions to this chapter. The views and opinions here, however, are entirely the responsibility of the author.

the 104th session of Congress than in any other comparable period, including eight years under President Ronald Reagan. In 1996, Congress, in cooperation with the President, proposed four major privatizations: the Naval Petroleum Reserve at Elk Hills, the Alaska Power Administration, the national helium program, and the U.S. Enrichment Corporation. These were signed into law in 1996 at a combined sale price that could exceed $3 billion to $4 billion.

Notwithstanding this recent success, the continuing political opposition to privatization has limited Congress and the Administration to success in just a few of the thousands of opportunities that abound throughout the U.S. government. One reason for this is the intense opposition created among groups that benefit from the status quo and view any change as putting them at risk. Opponents of privatization typically are the existing workforce, unions that represent various government workers, current federal management, businesses that supply the programs or utilize their services, local communities in which the programs operate, and the elected officials who represent those communities.

Most people, often with no direct stake in particular government programs and sometimes misinformed by supporters of those programs, seem disinterested at best; at worst, they perceive privatization as a risky and costly experiment. The consequence of this misperception is a vacillation between supporting and opposing privatization efforts that can lead to the legislative defeat of any specific project.

Although Americans pride themselves on the dynamism of the U.S. competitive marketplace and the democratic capitalism that has made this nation the envy of the world for its commercial successes, the United States lags behind much of the rest of the world in privatizing government programs and assets. It has not experienced the socialist excesses that led other industrialized countries to nationalize their telecommunications, energy, and transportation sectors, to name just a few; consequently, the United States has proportionately less to privatize.

Nevertheless, the federal government has accumulated many large and inefficient commercial enterprises as well as a staggering amount of land— approximately 700 million acres—that could be managed more productively and preserved if shifted to private ownership. Moreover, anywhere from 50 percent to 70 percent of federal civilian workers routinely perform administrative and service functions that could be contracted out competitively to private-sector providers at considerable savings.

The Basic Techniques of Privatization

The term "privatization" defines the process or act of transferring government assets to the private sector. How the transfer is accomplished is defined by the various techniques used to privatize those services, and the technique that is chosen is often determined by the nature of the government asset or activity as well as the environment in which it operates.

Divestiture. The technique most commonly associated with privatization is divestiture, whereby a tangible asset or an operating enterprise such as a steel mill or telephone company is sold to a group of private investors. This group may include the company's existing workforce and its management, which could acquire some or all of an enterprise through an employee stock ownership plan (ESOP). Europe, Latin America, and newly independent states nationalized many key components of their economies during the middle decades of this century, when such activity was in fashion. For these countries, divestiture has been the predominant privatization technique. It also is the technique associated with British Prime Minister Margaret Thatcher during the 1980s, and with such advanced developing countries as Mexico, Argentina, Chile, and Czechoslovakia in the 1990s. In these and other countries, aggressive programs of privatization have turned inefficient, money-losing state enterprises into competitive, profit-making, taxpaying businesses that provide quality goods and services to consumers. At the same time, the divestitures have provided billions of dollars in revenues to their governments, with the proceeds used to pay off the public debt, reduce government borrowing, decrease taxes, or fund other, more pressing programs.

The United States opted for regulation instead of nationalization as its prime mechanism for redirecting business activity toward a variety of social objectives. Fewer divestiture opportunities exist in the United States in the form of traditional commercial enterprises, although those that do exist represent potential sales revenues to the government of more than $20 billion. These include such ongoing concerns as the Naval Petroleum Reserve, the Bonneville Power Administration, the U.S. Postal Service, Amtrak, the Tennessee Valley Authority, the U.S. Government Printing

Office, the U.S. Enrichment Corporation, and the Corporation for Public Broadcasting.

Other valuable assets include the government's vast land holdings, especially in the western United States. Some of these holdings have been put to commercial use by eligible private businesses in such for-profit endeavors as logging, grazing, skiing, mining, and tourism. A study from 1988 estimated that the commodity-producing lands—about 38 percent of all federally owned land, excluding the national parks and wildlife refuges— might be worth as much as $136 billion.[1] The broadcast spectrum, which is "owned" by the federal government but heretofore has been given away to for-profit broadcasters, is estimated to be worth between $70 billion and $100 billion.[2] Another collection of federal assets with significant market value includes $161 billion in government loans to a variety of individuals and businesses that are held in the portfolios of several government agencies and the U.S. Treasury.[3] The government periodically has sold portions of this loan portfolio to private investors, earning funds for deficit reduction while also reducing the costs incurred by the agencies that must service the loans.

Public-Private Partnerships. Partnerships for infrastructure investment represent an increasingly common form of privatization by state and local governments. In such cases, private investors and businesses, in cooperation with the government, build or operate major infrastructure projects such as wastewater treatment plants, airports, highways, and prisons. In the past, these typically were constructed with government funds and operated by a government workforce, but recent pressures on government to hold down taxes and spending while maintaining or increasing services has encouraged many communities to seek creative solutions in partnership with the private sector.

---

1 Terry Andersen and Don Leal, "Sale of Federal Lands," in *Federal Privatization: Toward Resolving the Deficit Crisis*, Reason Foundation, June 1988, pp. 34–55.

2 David Colton, "Spectrum Privatization: Removing the Barriers to Telecommunications Competition," Reason Foundation *Policy Study* No. 208, Reason Foundation, July 1996.

3 *Analytical Perspectives, Budget of the United States Government, Fiscal Year 1997* (Washington, D.C.: U.S. Government Printing Office, 1996), p. 120.

In a typical case, the government will contract with a private company to finance, build, and operate a public function such as a wastewater treatment facility according to government specifications. In turn, the private company earns its revenues by charging either the community or the residents for the services rendered, usually at prices agreed upon between the government and the company prior to construction. In recent years, the private sector has opened two highways in Virginia and California that will be financed by the tolls paid by those who use the roads. By using the private sector to fund and operate activities that once were considered public works, government can use its own scarce resources to fulfill other duties, such as education and public safety, more effectively.

Vouchers. Another technique of privatization, one that applies primarily to social welfare programs, is the use of vouchers to purchase goods or services provided by the private sector. Government finances the vouchers, but the private sector provides the goods and services. Food stamps, Medicare, Medicaid, VA and FHA loans, and student loans and grants represent voucher or voucher-like federal programs that provide financial benefits to eligible households.

Voucher-based programs rely on the private sector rather than government institutions to deliver goods and services to assisted beneficiaries. Housing vouchers, for example, allow those who need housing to rent better accommodations from private landlords, offering recipients a less costly and more attractive alternative to the much-maligned public housing projects that still infect U.S. cities and communities. By using vouchers, the government is able to harness the expertise and competitive pressures of the private market to provide goods and services it is ill-equipped to produce on its own.

Contracting Out. The last major technique of privatization, and one that is most applicable to the federal government, is contracting out—a process by which basic services, both for and by the government, are provided by private companies operating under contract to the government. Study after study demonstrates that, by utilizing the expertise and management skills available in the private sector as well as the cost benefits of open competition, competitive contracting saves the government an average of 25 percent over what it would cost government to perform the same service. Current federal contracting procedures, described by Office of Management and Budget (OMB) Circular A–76, usually allow existing government agencies to compete for the contract as well; about half of the awarded contracts remain in house as a result of improvements in an agency's efficiency.

The Department of Defense (DOD) has used competitive contracting very aggressively. In March 1996, the DOD reported to Congress that competitive contracting had resulted in an annual savings of $1.5 billion and that more than 600,000 civilian and uniformed positions could be subject to competitive contracting in the near future. Unfortunately, the DOD's aggressive use of contracting out is the exception among federal departments and agencies. Many agencies, such as the National Park Service, seem assiduously to avoid any opportunity to save money and improve services through competitive contracting.

LESSONS LEARNED

Although there have been impressive privatization successes in recent years, they represent a small fraction of the opportunities that exist within the government. The federal establishment appears to remain skeptical— even hostile—regarding the process of privatization.

The attitude of skepticism that pervades Congress and the executive branch is characteristic of both Republican and Democratic Administrations. It is in sharp contrast to the attitude that permeated government in the early years of the United States, when reliance on the private sector and private initiative was the norm. This reliance on the private sector to find ways to solve the country's problems was responsible for achievements that seem unimaginable in today's era of growing dependence upon government solutions and spending.

The Early Years. It is interesting to note that the voyages leading to the discovery of the United States—including those of Columbus, Cabot, and Hudson — and settlements in places like Jamestown and Plymouth were largely commercial in nature, financed and managed by private investors. During both the War of Independence and the War of 1812, the U.S. government relied heavily on private vessels and crews to conduct its naval warfare. Commander John Paul Jones challenged the *Serapis* from the deck of the *Bonhomme Richard*, a joint-venture with a French nobleman, while the U.S. Marines (just 16 of them) stormed the shores of Tripoli accompanied by a large mercenary army that was privately funded and led by William Eaton of Connecticut.

LESSONS LEARNED

- Successful privatization requires dedicated leadership.
- Successful privatization requires that proponents of reform defuse the opposition.
- Policymakers can be successful if they are patient and persistent.
- Privatization requires effective use of legislative vehicles.

Even the Pony Express, which provided "express" mail service from Joplin, Missouri, to San Francisco, California, was a private company. It became successful because it was able to deliver transcontinental mail in less than a week while the U.S. Postal Service needed months to make the trip sailing around Cape Horn. When the Pony Express's feat was surpassed in less than two years, it was not by the U.S. Post Office, but by the invention of a private "high-tech" competitor, the telegraph.

Private money issued by private banks was an important source of financial liquidity on the cash-starved frontier. Most of our great universities, hospitals, and medical schools were and still are private in origin and current operation.

The Reagan-Bush Years. Efforts in the United States to revive this spirit of enterprise through greater use of privatization techniques had mixed results during the postwar era, when most Members of Congress simply defended the status quo. With the exception of the Eisenhower Administration's largely ignored 1955 edict requiring agencies to pursue opportunities to contract out, and the privatization of the Federal National Mortgage Association during the Johnson Administration in 1967—which may well have been the first major privatization effort ever—privatization remained a neglected tool of federal management until the Reagan Administration made it a key component of its efforts to reform government and cut the deficit. Although it was not part of Reagan's initial Program for Economic Recovery unveiled in 1981, privatization became a major Reagan Administration initiative during the mid-1980s in response to the stunning privatization successes achieved by Margaret Thatcher in Great Britain.

By the mid-1980s, the Reagan Administration had developed an ambitious agenda and had recorded two major privatization successes: the sales of both the National Consumer Cooperative Bank and Conrail. It also achieved the dramatic downsizing of the General Services Administration (GSA) from nearly 35,000 employees in 1980 to 21,000 in 1988 through competitive contracting of services to more efficient private-sector providers, saving, according to a 1994 report by the General Accounting Office (GAO), as much as 50 percent in areas like janitorial services. By the middle of the decade, however, it was apparent that the attainment of any further privatization had become bogged down in agency foot-dragging and congressional opposition. In the case of the GSA, former Representative Robert Edgar (D-PA) was instrumental in getting legislation enacted to forbid the GSA from contracting out for guards, elevator operators, messengers, and custodians.

In an effort to overcome such obstacles, President Reagan issued Executive Order 12615, which required departments and agencies to establish and fulfill ambitious privatization agendas and created the Office of Privatization within the Office of Management and Budget to oversee the program. Reagan's executive order also appointed an independent Commission on Privatization to study and recommend opportunities for privatization within the federal government. Although few, if any, of the recommendations that came out of this effort were enacted at the time, several of the programs first proposed, developed, and advocated by the Reagan Administration (the Alaska Power Marketing Administration, the U.S. Enrichment Corporation, the National Helium Reserve, and the Naval Petroleum Reserve at Elk Hills, California) eventually were approved for privatization by the 104th Congress and the Clinton White House. When ultimately consummated, these privatization efforts could yield at least $3 billion in revenues to the federal government.

The Bush Administration supported many Reagan initiatives, but as lesser priorities. In 1992, President Bush issued Executive Order 12803 in an effort to encourage and facilitate the privatization of federally funded infrastructure projects such as wastewater treatment plants and airports, but agency foot-dragging and White House diffidence led to minimal effect.

Successes by Clinton and the 104th Congress. The 104th Congress represented a watershed in American privatization efforts. Many new Members were elected based on insurgent campaigns promising to cut spending and balance the budget, and the electorate sent a loud and clear message to President Bill Clinton and the new Congress that it wanted less talk and more action. The President responded by including in his Fiscal Year 1996 budget a substantial number of proposed privatizations, virtually all drawn from recommendations made in 1988 by President Reagan's Commission on Privatization. This has been the boldest privatization agenda put forth by any American President to date.

In addition to the four programs mentioned above, Clinton included in his 1996 budget proposals to privatize four of the five Power Marketing Authorities.[4] He suggested possible privatization of the Federal Aviation Administration's troubled Air Traffic Control (ATC) system, which the Administration recommended be turned into an independent government corporation. The President's privatization list also included several functions of the GSA and the National Weather Service.

In January 1993, the President issued Executive Order 12893 in an effort to encourage the privatization of federally financed but locally controlled infrastructure. This executive order required the increased use of economic analysis and promoted public-private partnerships to help ensure that infrastructure investments are as effective as possible. President Clinton did not rescind President Reagan's executive order on competitive contracting of government functions, but he did commission a revision of OMB Circular A–76 in an effort to make contracting guidelines simpler and less burdensome to implement. The Clinton Administration also provided Congress with a list of legislative obstacles to privatization efforts that had been enacted by Congress in the past.

The combination of a new commitment to privatization among Members of Congress and the endorsement and support of the President for many privatization projects has dramatically altered the political environment and contributed to unprecedented success. Until 1996, privatization had been a partisan affair, pitting one branch of the government against another; during the 1980s, it was endorsed by a Republican President but opposed by a Democratic Congress; in the late 1970s and early 1990s, neither branch of government was particularly enthusiastic about it. Maintaining the bipartisan cooperation that existed

---

4 Alaska, Southeastern, Western, and Southwestern; Bonneville was excluded.

between the two branches of government throughout the 104th Congress will be helpful, if not essential, in accomplishing further privatization over the next four years. Such cooperation also will be helpful in working with state and local governments that will be directly affected by remaining federal privatization opportunities.

Decisive Steps by State and Local Governments. In this regard, it is fortuitous that local and state privatization efforts also have accelerated. Although performance varies significantly from one jurisdiction to another, selective progress has occurred at both the state and local levels. Certain governors implemented aggressive privatization programs in the 1990s to hold down costs and improve service. Massachusetts, under Governor William Weld, implemented one of the most aggressive state privatization programs, privatizing the functions of more than 20 government services— until the state legislature enacted anti-privatization laws and shut down the program. New York, New Jersey, Virginia, Georgia, and California have ambitious plans for privatizing services and assets, but meaningful measures of progress will have to await their full implementation.

Just as only a few states are leading the way on privatizing services, several mayors are taking the lead in seizing the opportunities that privatization and competitive contracting offer them to cut costs and improve services. Chief among the cities that have implemented these ambitious privatization programs are Indianapolis, Indiana; Charlotte, North Carolina; and Milwaukee, Wisconsin. Many more cities also are contemplating programs, including Washington, D.C., under the direction and encouragement of its congressionally created Control Board.

Recent progress at the national level has allowed the federal government to "hold its own" compared with these enterprising states and cities. The federal government, however, may begin falling behind if the many ambitious local plans under consideration ultimately are implemented. Moreover, although many in Congress and the federal bureaucracy work to maintain the government's monopoly on federally financed infrastructure, many states are forming partnerships with private-sector businesses to speed the development of highways, bridges, prisons, and wastewater treatment plants, and to increase other services while placing smaller demands upon taxpayers.

Extensive Privatization Abroad. Whether performance is measured by the number of privatizations or by the dollar volume of sales or transfers, the United States continues to lag behind the accomplishments of a number of other countries. In infrastructure alone, the United States ranks a distant seventh in its share of $144 billion in private infrastructure investments made over the past decade. In terms of major divestitures (sales of assets), the performance of the United States over the past decade would amount to less than a good year's work for some of the countries leading in privatization programs, such as Britain, Argentina, New Zealand, and Mexico.

In part, this limited performance reflects a paucity of good U.S. targets compared to the opportunities that confront a typical government abroad. Because the United States successfully resisted the trend toward nationalization that gripped most nations during the middle third of this century, the U.S. government possesses only a few bona fide commercial-type enterprises that could be sold, and many of the ones it does possess — such as passenger rail, national defense laboratories, the postal service, and hydroelectric dams — have tended to remain in government hands throughout the world.

But this, too, is changing. Japan, Mexico, and Great Britain are implementing or developing privatization solutions for their government passenger rail systems, while both Sweden and the Netherlands have privatized postal functions. Nevertheless, considering the relative absence of traditional privatization targets, the United States ranks ahead of continental Europe, most of Latin America, and much of Asia, where the targets are more plentiful and the fiscal problems more severe.

Key Tactics in Overcoming Resistance. Those involved with privatization here and abroad realize just how difficult it is to transfer government programs to the private sector, despite the level of success privatization has enjoyed thus far. It has been so difficult and time-consuming because of political obstacles that confront government officials who propose privatizing a government activity or enterprise. The chief obstacles to their efforts most often are the existing federal workforce, including both labor and management; businesses that support the government's programs; local communities in which the programs function; and elected officials who have become financially or politically dependent upon a government activity as it currently exists. All of these groups see privatization, or any fundamental change in the status quo, as a threat to the benefits they already receive.

Resistance to privatization is frequent, virulent, and invariably successful. In the United States, Members of Congress are willing to protect wasteful and inefficient programs because these programs directly benefit some of their constituents. The United States Code, which lists all of the laws enacted by Congress, is replete with congressionally mandated prohibitions against privatization—some of them explicitly reconfirmed within the past year by legislators acting on behalf of constituents' narrow financial interests.

Several key tactics, however, have been used successfully to overcome these obstacles, and they provide Congress and the Administration with several important lessons.

Lesson #1: Successful privatization requires dedicated leadership. Whether at the local, state, or national level, all successful privatization programs have at their helm an elected official who considers privatization a priority, is willing to do battle with its traditional opponents, and is determined to persevere in the face of numerous obstacles and delays. President Reagan and Prime Minister Thatcher both were successful leaders for these reasons. Both delegated responsibility to subordinates who were held directly accountable for developing and implementing effective privatization programs. Reagan created the first Office of Privatization, whose recommendations later became the privatization successes of the 104th Congress.

One of the chief reasons the 104th Congress was successful in places its predecessors so frequently had failed was that House Speaker Newt Gingrich understood the importance of leadership to privatization efforts and appointed Representative Scott Klug (R-WI) to lead these efforts in the House of Representatives. By granting leadership status to this issue, Gingrich signified that privatization would not be relegated to secondary importance in the many congressional committees of jurisdiction. By the closing bell of the 1996 session, the 104th Congress had accomplished more privatizations in two years than the Reagan Administration had accomplished in eight.

Lesson #2: Successful privatization also requires that proponents of reform defuse the opposition. Even with dedicated leadership, privatization efforts will fail if the leader ignores the concerns of its opponents, however frivolous or selfish they may seem. As the record of the past two decades demonstrates, programs that succeed are ones that are open to compromise and accommodate the concerns of existing and potential opponents, especially those who want to maintain the status quo.

Typical of such accommodation is the common practice of providing workers and managers with shares in the new enterprise, on concessionary terms, either at a discounted price or at no cost. Generous severance packages and no-layoff policies also have been used to allay concerns and diminish opposition among managers and workers whose programs are targeted for privatization.

In Great Britain, where privatization has been practiced successfully for more than a decade, workers and customers have been turned into avid proponents who counter the influence of opponents such as labor union officials. In the sale of the government-owned telephone company, for example, workers were allowed to become shareholders in the new company (on concessionary terms), and the public was mobilized by the potential for vastly improved phone service. Moreover, millions of Britons were induced to buy stock in British Telecom (and later in other companies slated for privatization) by the offer of deeply discounted stocks. In the privatization of the British airports, private for-profit airlines that were part of the current system were the most important potential opponents. The government entered into an advance agreement with them on the determination of present and future landing fees, thereby appeasing their concerns and making them allies in the effort.

These lessons are not lost on American privatization proponents; the ten-year effort to privatize the U.S. Enrichment Corporation is a study in how to win through accommodation. Originally proposed in 1987 by officials in the Reagan Administration's Office of Management and Budget, the idea met swift and overwhelming resistance, primarily from officials at the Department of Energy and contractors who ran the enrichment plants. Employees of the contractors and mayors of the communities where the plants were located opposed the effort. In response to their concerns, Congress enacted P.L. 100-202, forbidding the federal government from even studying the privatization of federal enrichment facilities. Despite this opposition, however, the efforts to privatize the U.S. Enrichment Corporation prevailed. In 1992, Congress finally passed legislation allowing the privatization process to begin; and in 1996, it granted final approval for privatization of the government's enrichment activities.

The accommodations and compromises that were necessary to achieve this privatization were spelled out explicitly in both the 1992 and 1996 bills. In addition to subjecting privatization to the oversight of 12 congressional committees and 17 government agencies, the legislation included such requirements as the following:

- **Privatization** could not result in the corporation's becoming owned, controlled, or dominated by a foreign corporation or foreign government;

- **Owners** must abide by the unexpired collective bargaining agreements at the enrichment plants;

- **Employment** must be offered to non-management employees of the predecessor contractor in the event a new contractor or other new employer takes over management of the plants;

- **Post-retirement health care benefits** for any employee who retires after 1993 will be funded by the corporation; and

- **No preferential treatment** in buying new shares in the privatized corporation will be granted to current managers and employees.

An extensive effort in the United States to accommodate both potential opponents and proponents first appeared in the successful effort to privatize Conrail. The Reagan Administration sought initially to sell Conrail to another railroad, Norfolk-Southern, but that generated strong opposition from other railroads. Then Congress proposed selling Conrail through a stock offering, generating wide public interest and support for the sale. Similar compromises were included in 1996 congressional approval for the privatization of other federal enterprises, including the revival of an otherwise unenforceable 19th century California state statute that requires a portion of the proceeds from the sale of the Naval Petroleum Reserves at Elk Hills to be given to the state's teacher retirement fund.

Although these examples offer Congress useful ideas for the form privatization can take, not all privatization opportunities within the federal government lend themselves to accommodating opponents inexpensively or building supportive coalitions. Competitive contracting, for example, usually involves government services that the public does not experience firsthand, such as data processing, vehicle maintenance, accounting, and building security. It involves competing with an existing, well-paid, and comfortable workforce that, for the first time in its existence, runs the risk of losing its job. Likewise, the privatization of the helium or petroleum reserves yields only the vague and unmeasurable benefit of minimal deficit reduction while depriving extant workers and contractors of a steady stream of government wages, revenues, and profits, and university scientists of a subsidized source of helium for their experiments. These types of issues need to be defused through careful planning and promotional efforts.

Lesson #3: Policymakers can be successful if they are patient and persistent. If the recent past is any guide, privatizing a government function may take eight to ten years to accomplish, from the introduction of a reasonably well-developed proposal to the actual divestiture of the asset or enterprise. Although the Thatcher government in Britain was able to implement and fulfill its far-reaching privatization program more swiftly, the prime minister also had the advantage of operating within a system that vested both legislative and executive authority within a single governing entity. The U.S. government, with its checks and balances, separation of powers, and congressional committee system, encourages lengthy deliberation and allows numerous opportunities for the opponents of privatization to delay and obstruct any legislative efforts that would alter the status quo dramatically.

Nevertheless, and as the experience of the 104th Congress demonstrates, fighting for privatization efforts year after year ultimately can lead to success. In 1996, Congress and the President agreed on four major privatization initiatives, all of which had been proposed in the mid-1980s by Reagan officials and proposed again year after year by succeeding administrations with some new modifications to make them more attractive. By 1996, each had garnered enough support to be enacted into law.

Although some portion of this success is attributable to relentless pursuit of the objective and a willingness to make combat-induced modifications, another portion is attributable to proponents being at the right place at the right time, prepared to take advantage of such fortuitous circumstances. A new Congress more amenable to privatization was certainly fortuitous. Lessons hammered home year after year ultimately sink in; success requires patience and perseverance, because no one can accurately predict when the lesson will take hold.

Lesson #4: Privatization requires effective use of legislative vehicles. For years, the legislative process, particularly the appropriations process that funds the programs and agencies, has been used by opponents to prevent privatization. By learning from these defeats, proponents have discovered that the same legislative vehicles and techniques can be used in support of privatization. Some notable successes occurred in this Congress through the creative use of the appropriations process.

One advantage of the legislative process—especially the appropriations process — is that it can provide cover for controversial proposals by combining them with legislative vehicles that simultaneously provide billions of dollars for thousands of other programs. Because typical U.S. privatization proposals tend to attract more committed opponents than supportive friends, such proposals might never pass if offered by themselves. If, however, the proposal is rolled in with a much larger number of more important issues — such as annual funding of the Department of Energy and its 19,000-employee payroll—the concerns of a few Members of Congress or a few dozen employees might not be sufficient to defeat the legislation because so much more is at stake. During 1996, for example, several of the major privatization proposals that were enacted were included in vehicles such as the comprehensive continuing resolution or the defense authorization bill, the latter of which included a bold proposal for contracting out many DOD activities linked to national security programs.

Another legislative mechanism by which Congress can encourage privatization is placing firm limits on an agency's budget. In such circumstances, privatization becomes a solution to those financial limits, particularly if an agency is required to maintain its existing level of service — an objective that can be met only through management and cost efficiencies that are achieved most easily through contracting out.

Another powerful tool would be making legislative changes that eliminate many of the long-standing prohibitions or institutional roadblocks to privatization. Typical of such obstacles are the attitudes and habits of the politicians and bureaucrats who allocate funds and operate the federal highway program. These officials, always hostile to private-sector solutions, traditionally have mandated that federal transportation assistance be limited only to government-owned and government-operated transportation systems, even though there is no legal prohibition on such participation.

One way to overcome such resistance may be simply to eliminate it by devolving the program directly to the states with no limits or mandates on who can participate in it. With 50 states operating 50 separate programs, some inevitably will create opportunities for partnerships with the private sector; and if these privatizations are successful, they will hasten the spread of privatization to other states.

STRATEGIES FOR TRANSFERRING FUNCTIONS TO THE PRIVATE SECTOR

Based on lessons learned from both successes and failures in the United States and abroad, a framework for a strategy emerges that, although certainly not guaranteeing success, will help tilt the odds more in favor of reformers by helping them avoid common pitfalls. The key elements of such a framework are presented and discussed briefly below, followed by prospective case studies in which both strategy and techniques are applied to two existing federal departments.

STRATEGY #1
Congress should establish leadership for privatization in both houses.

In the House of Representatives, finding good leadership involves taking a step like reappointing Representative Scott Klug to the post he held in the 104th Congress as de facto head and coordinator of privatization initiatives. Considering the success this arrangement achieved in the House, a similar position should be established in the Senate with the blessing and support of the Majority Leader.

STRATEGIES FOR TRANSFERRING FUNCTIONS TO THE PRIVATE SECTOR

- Congress should establish leadership for privatization in both the House and the Senate.

- Congress and the Administration should create a new agenda for privatizing specific programs and services.

- Congress and the Administration should develop a marketing strategy for the new agenda.

- Congress and the Administration should develop a privatization plan that provides significant financial benefits for everyone.

STRATEGY #2
Congress and the Administration should create a new agenda for privatizing specific programs and services.

As a result of the unprecedented number of privatization successes that occurred during the last Congress, new targets need to be developed and added to the list of active and prospective opportunities. These new targets could include the two prospective case studies included later in this chapter—the federal transportation program and the National Park Service—or the GSA, which was on President Clinton's privatization list at one time. Other targets could be added to the extent that time and resources are available.

STRATEGY #3
Congress and the Administration should develop a marketing strategy for the new agenda.

Proponents of privatization must develop a compelling case for the changes they recommend. For instance, in privatizing functions within the National Park Service and federal transportation programs, a strong and defensible case can be made for vastly improving services at no additional cost to the public. When discussing the National Park Service, it is essential that proponents make it clear that their chief concern is to improve it, not eliminate it. Such a case could be strengthened by exposing the failings of the service's existing politicized management and how these failings adversely affect America's natural and historic landmarks. Support groups should be developed and organized to help make the case for change. In the case of transportation reform, governors who favor privatization could offer a very effective counter to the industry groups that will attempt to undermine reform and privatization efforts.

STRATEGY #4
Congress and the Administration should develop a privatization plan that provides significant financial benefits for all citizens.

Proponents of privatization must make a more compelling case for what to do with the billions of dollars in federal revenues that would arise from such a sale. In the Czech Republic's mass privatization program, each citizen received a voucher to buy shares in firms. In the United States, candidates for privatization could be placed into a national portfolio of federal assets. If only those federal assets that are now subject to commercial exploitation comprise the portfolio, preliminary estimates indicate a value in excess of $300 billion. Shares in this portfolio given to each taxpayer would have an estimated value of $3,000, which would make a compelling case for shifting these assets to the private sector in order to spread the benefits beyond the current circle of privileged interests.

Applying These Strategies to Two Agencies
A useful way to illustrate how this political approach and these specific privatization techniques can be applied to solve performance and cost problems in government is through prospective case studies of government departments. Two departments were chosen because of the differences in their operations and purposes, which will allow for a fuller discussion of the techniques that government can utilize. The National Park Service, which has a programmatic orientation toward providing services to the public, may illustrate best the versatility of competitive contracting. The U.S. Department of Transportation's capital-intensive nature and commercially oriented activities provide an opportunity to study the creative use of divestiture and public-private partnerships.

Competitive Contracting: Improving Services at the National Park Service. The National Park Service (NPS) was established in 1916 as part of the Department of the Interior with a very specific charge: "to conserve the scenery and the natural and historic objects and the wild life of the nation's parks…leaving them unimpaired for future generations." The NPS oversees 369 sites, ranging from vast and rugged wilderness to historic city structures in 49 states; collectively, these include more than 80 million acres. More than 270 million tourists visit these sites each year—a figure that exceeds the population of the United States by 10 million.

Historically very resistant to management reforms and competitive contracting for basic services, the NPS has responded to congressional and executive efforts to force budgetary restraint by taking its case to the press and the public. For example, in response to modest reductions of less than 5 percent in its FY 1996 budget, NPS Director Roger G. Kennedy went on the offensive with an ominous message to Americans about to embark on their family vacations. In a television interview with ABC News on May 5, 1996, Kennedy warned: "The hours will be shorter, they will find museums closed, they will find some visitors centers that aren't open, they will find trails marked 'closed.'"

Congress had an opportunity at that moment to teach Director Kennedy how competitive contracting could help him utilize the $1.3 billion budget Congress provides him each year more effectively. The NPS's record of fiscal management has not been without criticism, and many feel it indicates that the administration at the NPS mismanages its vast resources and its stewardship of America's most majestic wonders. According to one recent estimate, the NPS maintenance backlog totals $4 billion. On August 21, 1996, NPS Deputy Director Denis Galvin told reporters from *The Washington Post*, "I would describe the general state of most parks as fair to poor and not getting any better."[5]

Part of the problem is an inadequate financial control and management system — a system that has been criticized by the Department of the Interior's Inspector General. As a result, the NPS is incapable of making any meaningful efficiencies in its operations because it lacks accurate information on actual costs. With management largely ignorant of its own financial situation and the cost of various operations, the NPS is not capable

---

5   See Tom Kenworthy and Gary Younge, "Falling Into a Hole at Grand Canyon," *The Washington Post*, August 21, 1996, p. A23.

of choosing more efficient and cost-effective practices: It has no objective standard by which to measure its own performance. As a result, the NPS has mismanaged and allocated its limited resources in ways that lead to excessive costs for routine functions and leave little for maintaining existing services or reducing its repair and maintenance backlog.

One of the NPS's most glaring problems is a failure to adopt modern management practices common to other government agencies for the performance of routine custodial-type functions. Although a love for the environment and for America's heritage encourages many Americans to join the Park Service, staff workers often are asked to perform menial, custodial, and low-skilled tasks that other government agencies contract out. The NPS might better contract out these tasks as well and devote its staff talent and scarce financial resources to more important and valued services.

In the early 1980s, the General Services Administration began to use competitive contracting to provide custodial and routine maintenance services to the many government departments it served. On average, these agencies realized savings of between 40 percent and 50 percent over what it cost them to do custodial work with their own staff. For the more than 2,000 competitive contracts it has awarded since 1978, the Department of Defense estimates its savings averaged 31 percent over what it would have cost to perform those functions "in-house." Comparable savings have been realized in contracting out many other routine services such as maintenance, repair, and landscaping—types of activities that are common to all of the NPS's nearly 400 U.S. sites.

Time after time, the NPS has refused to take advantage of the substantial cost savings that are available through contracting, insisting on using its own staff and equipment to do most of the work required at its many sites. As a consequence of its inefficiency, inflexibility, and tradition-bound management style, modest financial setbacks overwhelm the system and force it to implement service reductions and defer vital maintenance.

Given the importance of national parks to Americans, Congress has the opportunity and the responsibility to require the NPS to fulfill its duties within the adequate budget resources provided. Specifically, Congress can require the NPS to contract out as much as possible and to do much more with less, as other federal departments like Defense have done. In this way, the NPS would be following in the footsteps of a management style already in use at the U.S. National Forest Service, Parks Canada (the Canadian national park system), and the provincial parks of British Columbia, which provide the public with many services similar to those provided by the NPS but with greater reliance on the private sector.

Beginning in the 1980s, the U.S. National Forest Service, a part of the U.S. Department of Agriculture, encouraged its regional managers to utilize contracting out as a way to provide more services during a period of limited budgets. Tasked with the responsibility of balancing the needs of recreation, conservation, and commercial exploitation within a single forest system, Forest Service managers discovered that by contracting out many routine services, they had more time, more staff, and more money to devote to more important and more professional duties.

More recently, Parks Canada instituted a privatization program, based on contracting out specific functions, as part of a comprehensive overhaul to reduce its annual budget from $260 million to $189 million and its staff by 25 percent, or 1,000 employees. Responsible for 36 national parks and 131 historic sites, Parks Canada had no choice but to privatize government functions as the Canadian government attempts to come to grips with national budget problems even more serious than those in the United States. Although opposition to this initiative has come from the employees, the program establishes a transition period of up to three years during which they have the right of first refusal on all contracts for park operations. During this transition period, Parks Canada will negotiate with existing employee groups to take over designated operations at parks and historic sites.

Moreover, even though employees of Canada's park system and some environmental groups have opposed this plan, some park users support it and note the opportunity it represents to upgrade the government's overall focus. According to Harvey Locke, past president of the Canadian Parks and Wilderness Society, "the government is on the right track if divestment of maintenance operations lets it concentrate more on conservation."[6]

An even bolder privatization plan was implemented in the 1980s in the provincial parks of Canada's westernmost province, British Columbia.

---

6 David Crary, "Privatization Plans Anger Canadian Parks Employees," *The Washington Post*, August 9, 1996, p. A24.

Whereas Parks Canada proposes to contract individual functions at the parks, British Columbia contracted out the entire management and operation of each of its parks, assigning just a few government management employees to oversee the private contractors. Savings under the program averaged 20 percent, which has been reinvested in the program to enhance conservation efforts at the parks.

These recent contracting successes suggest that such techniques can be applied to the U.S. National Park Service for the same purpose: to provide the same or better services for less money and thereby release additional resources to fulfill duties now being neglected. Potential areas of opportunity for competitive contracting include all routine campground management and maintenance; all routine groundskeeping and maintenance; all custodial-type functions; and all facilities repair and maintenance, park and site security, and vehicle management and maintenance, as well as participation in the Department of the Interior's Office of Aviation Services, which owns and operates 105 airplanes, including several passenger craft. Other contracting opportunities include data processing, the new parks reservation system, printing, mapmaking, fee collection, and the development and operation of the service's accounting and financial control system.

However great the opportunities may be for contracting within the NPS, getting the NPS or any other bureau within the Department of the Interior to act on them has been difficult if not impossible. Previous Congresses have aided and abetted this reluctance by enacting legislation forbidding the department from contracting out many of its functions, at times including the NPS.[7]

To overcome this resistance, Congress should set forth clear objectives that the NPS would be expected to fulfill within a well-defined time period. The annual appropriations bill for the Department of the Interior could serve as the vehicle for this initiative by requiring, for example, that the NPS provide access to the maximum number of trails, campgrounds, historic sites, museums, visitors centers, and other facilities that the public is

---

7 The Bureau of Land Management and the Fish and Wildlife Service are forbidden from contracting out certain functions, as per P.L. 16 USC 668(a), 43 USC 1707 (204)(a), and 43 USC 1701(e).

accustomed to finding available for the maximum possible number of dates, days, and hours of operation. The only exceptions to this would be those sites that must remain closed because of regularly scheduled maintenance or rehabilitation, periodic reconstruction, or modernization. In sum, the NPS would be forbidden to close any facility for budgetary purposes. At the same time, it would be required to begin to accomplish a defined portion of the deferred maintenance.

Given the NPS's long-standing resistance to competitive contracting, Congress could specify in detail the types of management efficiencies that it expects the NPS to utilize in meeting the total service objective described above. Congress could require, for example, that various NPS activities and functions be subject to competitive contracting within a defined time frame, such as six months from date of passage; alternatively, it could allow them to be phased in over time, with half accomplished the current year and half the next.

There already is substantial legislative precedent for such explicit direction, and some of it has been applied to several of the NPS's sister bureaus. For example, the 1996 Department of the Interior appropriations bill stated that "The Committee expects the [U.S. Geological] Survey to continue to increase its contracting of map and digital data production, with a goal of no less than 50 percent contracting by the end of fiscal year 1997 and no less than 60 percent contracting by the end of fiscal year 1999." Even stronger language was applied to the U.S. Navy; the House Defense Appropriations Subcommittee "directs the Navy to obtain any future photogrammetric services from the private sector. Photogrammetric services currently available in Navy shipyards shall be used only to train Navy personnel on the proper use of this technology tool so that proper specifications can be written and the quality of work and proposals from the private sector can be evaluated." This sampling of proscriptive legislative provisions enacted in 1996 shows how Congress can require agencies to save money and improve service through competitive contracting. The implications for comparable language relating to NPS-type functions should be obvious. Indeed, something very similar could be applied to the 57 employees at the NPS currently engaged in mapmaking.[8]

---

8 Some legislators may be uncomfortable with the implications for "micro-management" that these provisions entail. But these suggestions are positive,

Although the above samples seem explicit, past experience indicates that many agencies simply ignore these requirements in the belief that there will be no congressional follow-up. When there is, many government agencies have been adept at raising extenuating circumstances to explain the "delay." To prevent this resistance, additional or backup language can be added to limit both funds and personnel. For example, because contracting has been found to save between 25 percent and 30 percent on average compared to what the government was paying to perform the service itself, government departments scheduled for competitive contracting could have their budgets reduced by this amount in advance by the appropriations bill. The number of workers that each office can employ also could be limited.

If it is assumed that private contractors will win at least half of the competitive contracting proposals, the appropriations bill could require 50 percent cuts in employment levels in anticipation of the contracts. A generous severance package could be included to facilitate the change. Such management mandates are common within appropriations bills, although in the past Congress used specific employment targets to increase the number of government employees or to protect certain workers by establishing minimum levels that had to be maintained regardless of whether the program or the workers were needed.

Although the National Park Service was chosen to illustrate the application of certain privatization techniques and political strategies that could ensure success, these same techniques can be applied to any government agency in which personnel services of varying degrees of sophistication are the primary product provided by government. This would include the Department of Commerce, the other bureaus within the Department of the Interior, and the General Services Administration. A potential model for such comprehensive contracting is the recent initiative at the National Aeronautics and Space Administration to contract out most space shuttle operations with a six-year, $7 billion contract to United Space, a joint venture between Lockheed Martin and Rockwell Aerospace.

---

forthright, and still leave day-to-day decisions within the department. Compare this to language that Representative John Dingell (D-MI) included in an FCC bill barring the chairman of the FCC, Reed Hundt, from traveling more than 50 miles from the nation's capital on official business for the next two years.

Devolution and Privatization: Improving America's Transportation System. For government agencies whose services to the public are primarily those derived from capital assets in the form of public infrastructure and physical plants of varying degrees of complexity, different privatization techniques apply. The basic principles described in this case study of the Department of Transportation (DOT) also apply to the Environmental Protection Agency and the Departments of Energy and Defense.

Efforts to encourage the DOT to make greater use of the private sector in meeting America's transportation needs have not been successful. With the exception of the creation and vigorous operation of the Office of Private Sector Initiatives during the Reagan Administration, the DOT's leadership has survived every effort by Congress and successive Administrations to get it to place greater reliance on the private sector.

Despite executive orders from both President Bush (Executive Order 12803) and President Clinton (Executive Order 12893) encouraging the department to rely more on public-private partnerships for the provision of basic infrastructure services such as highways and airports, and despite legislation permitting privatization pilot projects, very little has been done. The DOT continues to reject opportunities that would allow for greater private-sector involvement, even those that do not infringe on its core business such as privatizing rest stops on interstate highways.

As the DOT's ability to perform its core functions declines, this reluctance may fade. Deteriorating roads and bridges, worsening highway congestion, frequent cutbacks in passenger rail service, fare inflation in urban transit systems, and the perception that air safety standards are declining have led to growing dissatisfaction in the public, state and local governments, affected industries, and reform elements in both the executive and legislative branches. With transportation service deteriorating across the board, more and more Americans question whether Washington's centralized transportation system can deliver full value for the $40 billion budget entrusted to it. The DOT will find it increasingly difficult to preserve the status quo in the face of popular reform efforts, including various forms of privatization.

The effort to devolve and privatize DOT functions began in earnest in 1996 when Congress introduced an unprecedented number of significant pieces of legislation to impose fundamental reform on virtually all aspects of the department's operations. Such dramatic reform proposals in the past typically came from the "backbenchers" in Congress; in the 104th Congress, most were introduced by leading members of both houses. That such significant reforms were proposed in so many DOT areas by so many leading members of the House and Senate suggests that congressional concern over the DOT's failings runs deep and wide. Among the proposals that could have a key bearing on future transportation privatization are:

- **The Transportation Empowerment Act (H.R. 3840 and S. 1907).** This bill, introduced in the 104th Congress by Senator Connie Mack (R-FL), chairman of the Joint Economic Committee, and Representative John Kasich (R-OH), chairman of the House Budget Committee, would have turned over the responsibilities of the federal highway program, including most of the existing taxing authority, to the states during a two-year transition period. Future federal involvement would have been limited to a two-cent-per-gallon tax to maintain the interstate highway system. This "give back," or full devolution, program would end all federal allocation formulas, all federal mandates, and all federal prohibitions, including those on privatization.

- **The Amtrak and Local Rail Revitalization Act of 1995 (S. 1319).** Introduced by Senator Larry Pressler (R-SD), chairman of the Senate Commerce, Science and Transportation Committee, this legislation, in addition to its important labor and regulatory reforms, would have represented a major first step in moving some financial and decision-making responsibility for Amtrak from the federal government to the states by allowing states to utilize some of their federal highway and transit grants for passenger rail service. The bill also would have allowed states to form regional compacts to direct and fund inter-city rail transportation. Although the reforms were not enacted, Amtrak's federal subsidy has been reduced significantly over the past two years, forcing it to cut service on low-priority, money-losing lines. With federal financial support diminishing, rail passenger advocates and Amtrak officials will have no choice but to work in partnership with the private sector to maintain the system.

- **The Federal Aviation Administration Revitalization Act of 1995 (S. 1239).** Introduced by Senator John McCain (R-AZ), chairman of the Aviation Subcommittee of the Senate Commerce, Science and Transportation Committee, this legislation proposed both to restructure the Federal Aviation Administration (FAA) and air traffic control (ATC) within the DOT and to change the FAA's primary source of funding. Whereas current ATC funding is derived from a passenger ticket tax and general revenues, the new ATC would have been funded entirely from a user fee paid by aircraft owners using the system. H.R. 2276, an alternative reform proposal introduced in the House by Representative Bud Shuster (R-PA), chairman of the House Transportation and Infrastructure Committee, would have moved air traffic control responsibilities from the Department of Transportation to a newly created independent government agency while maintaining current funding sources. These compare to President Clinton's 1996 proposal to create an independent government corporation for the FAA's ATC responsibilities. All of these proposals, although very different in scope, share a similar purpose and have impressive sponsorship.

- **The Federal Aviation Authorization Act of 1996 (H.R. 3539).** Section 310 of this bill, offered by Representative John J. Duncan (R-TN), chairman of the Aviation Subcommittee of the House Transportation and Infrastructure Committee, and passed by Congress on the last day of its 104th session, establishes a pilot project to allow the sale or lease of up to six airports to private investors at the discretion of the Secretary of Transportation and in conformance with a series of conditions. The legislation also would permit the exemption from a number of existing federal laws that work against private ownership or management of airports. Prior to the enactment of this law, Mayor Stephen Goldsmith of Indianapolis already had used what limited authority he held under existing law to contract out the management and operations of the Indianapolis airport. Under Goldsmith's proposal, the private contractor collects no fee unless the city realizes at least a $6 million savings per year. Pressure on Congress to act quickly and creatively was added by the near depletion of the aviation trust fund due to the expiration of the airline ticket tax during most of 1996.

Although only the airport privatization pilot project was signed into law, these legislative initiatives do reflect a positive trend toward devolution, decentralization, and privatization well in excess of anything that occurred in the past. At the same time, competing legislation that would reconfirm or enhance the status quo struggles for acceptance. Despite vast industry and labor support, Representative Shuster's efforts to move the highway and aviation trust funds off budget appears to have died in the Senate, a proposal by Senator William Roth (R-DE) to recreate Amtrak as an entitlement is dead, and a proposal by Senator Robert Byrd (D-WV) to divert another 4.5 cents of the fuel tax into the highway trust fund also is unlikely to go anywhere.

Taken together, the reform bills described above represent the potential for a major shake-up and breakup of Washington's moribund monopoly and centralized control of U.S. transportation policy and operations. Even though only a few of these bills address privatization directly, they all do so indirectly by creating opportunities for states and localities to choose from a larger number of options, some of which certainly would include elements of privatization.

The advantage of this situation lies in the emergence of both public and congressional dissatisfaction with all facets of the system, and the possibility that this dissatisfaction can be used to overwhelm the otherwise intense opposition from the narrow special interests that benefit financially from the current system, however dysfunctional it may be. These special interests typically combine their efforts to protect parts of the system unrelated to their day-to-day industry concerns in the belief that, if one privilege falls, all others may follow. Such involvement by lobbyists in issues only indirectly related to their specific concerns also works to curry favor among key legislators, who, in turn, may well be encouraged to support legislative and other actions of more direct interest to these same lobbyists.

But when the whole system is at risk, unity in opposition to reform crumbles as each industry and bureaucracy struggles to protect its own privilege, leaving other groups isolated and alone to conduct their own battles. With opposition to reform now spread thinly across a wide front, reformers have a much greater chance of success than if they attempted to tackle the issues piecemeal. The chapter on program termination covers this political process in more detail.

Implementing such a process could begin with the prospective enactment of the Mack-Kasich highway devolution bill, which would strip from the DOT (and Congress) nearly two-thirds of the government's transportation budget. With the money and decision-making authority shifted to the states, subsequent spending on surface transportation would conform more closely to local needs; the states would have more usable highway dollars available to them, in addition to an increased ability to leverage these dollars with private-public partnerships.

Devolving the highway trust fund and the fuel tax that finances it also would undermine the centrally managed federal transit program, which benefits from a small portion of the federal fuel tax. With most transit programs entirely local in nature but burdened with costly federal mandates and misdirection, and supported largely by transportation unions, pressure also would build to turn this program back to the states.

Without these programs, the Department of Transportation would oversee only the federal aviation programs — air safety, air traffic control, and airport construction. Operated by the DOT's Federal Aviation Administration, each of these programs has been the subject of recent comprehensive reform proposals from both Congress and the executive branch. The FAA's air traffic control component could be reorganized as a user fee-financed, independent agency or government corporation (for future privatization), and the airport construction and renovation program could be devolved to the states, cities, or regional authorities. Airport funding would be at the discretion of the local authorities and could be financed through some variation of a facilities user charge, the now-reauthorized passenger ticket tax, and aircraft landing fees, as well as from profits and other revenues that would arise if these airports were privatized.

The task of disassembling a major Cabinet department and redistributing its functions and duties may seem daunting and without precedent. With so many prominent Members of Congress recommending dramatic changes in key DOT sub-functions, however, all that is missing for a successful effort is the high-level political leadership needed to mobilize and bring these disparate forces together, and to make the case to the public that a decentralized program would bring more money and more transportation benefits to citizens without an increase in taxes.

CONCLUSION

Despite strong opposition from special interests opposed to privatization of government services and agencies, the evidence of privatization's cost-worthiness continues to build.

To privatize the Department of Transportation, an organized combination of legislation introduced in the 104th Congress could form the basis of an "omnibus" transportation reform package, with some modifications. The combination of a strong endorsement by the leadership in Congress and cooperative interest on the part of the President could set in motion the successful overhaul of transportation policy with major privatization components. In the case of the National Park Service or any other service-providing department, the best vehicle for encouraging or requiring competitive contracting is the annual appropriations bill, which traditionally serves as the mechanism for most management-oriented policy changes.

These two case studies illustrate the applicability of various privatization techniques to federal programs with diverse structures and purposes. In each case, the opportunity to provide improved services at lower cost represents the most compelling and most attractive attribute of this controversial program. To date, many privatization initiatives have focused on obscure government operations whose improved service would not have much effect on the typical American. By focusing on more visible and more troubled government entities, Congress has the opportunity to build on its successes and take the case for privatization directly to the public.

Chapter 5

EMPOWERING FAMILIES AND COMMUNITIES

Adam Meyerson

P resident Clinton has said that "the era of big government is over." The challenge today is to begin a new era of self-government through which Americans can rebuild society. The foundation for this renewal must rest on strong families, active religious faith, rejuvenated civic associations, accountable local governments, a vigorous market economy, and private charities to help those who fall between the cracks.

Sixty years of liberalism have left America's social fabric in tatters. There is an epidemic of child abuse, nearly half a million children languish in foster care, and crime is rendering vast sections of America's cities uninhabitable. More black men are in jail or prison than in college. Most public schools in poor neighborhoods are not teaching the basics, much less adequately preparing students to compete in the 21st century job market. America's streets, schools, and airwaves are filled with coarseness, violence, and disrespect for women and children. And the strongest and most reliable safety net any child can have—a family with a mom and dad who love each other and stay together—is collapsing.

This situation is repugnant to all Americans, whether they are liberal or conservative. President Clinton expressed this dismay beautifully in a 1993 speech at the Tennessee church where Martin Luther King, Jr., gave his final

The author would like to thank Doug Bandow, Patrick Fagan, Jessica Gavora, Ron Haskins, David Kuo, Joe Loconte, Jennifer E. Marshall, D. W. Miller, Robert Rector, Michael Schwartz, Matthew Spalding, John Walters, and Robert Woodson for their suggestions and contributions to this chapter. The views and opinions expressed, however, are solely the responsibility of the author.

sermon. The President imagined what Dr. King would say were he alive today: "He would say, 'I did not live and die to see the American family destroyed. I fought for freedom,' he would say, 'but not for the freedom of people to kill each other with reckless abandon; not for the freedom of children to have children and the fathers of the children to walk away from them and abandon them as if they don't amount to anything. This is not what I lived and died for.'"

The standard liberal response in recent decades — putting more money into more government programs—has failed. As Senator Robert Dole said in his acceptance speech at the Republican convention in August 1996, "The state is now more involved than it has ever been in the raising of children, and children are now more neglected, abused, and mistreated than they have been in our time." The collapse of the family and the explosion of crime have coincided with the spending of $5.4 trillion on means-tested poverty programs over the last 30 years. Many school districts with the highest spending—Washington, D.C., for example, with $9,000 per student — achieve the worst scholastic results. And the vast infusion of federal money into urban renewal has been accompanied by population declines of 25 percent or more in cities like Detroit, Philadelphia, Baltimore, Cleveland, and St. Louis.

The standard conservative response to poverty — stimulating economic growth through market capitalism — also has failed to remedy America's social crises. Economic growth, entrepreneurship, deregulation, cuts in capital gains taxes, and the lowering of marginal tax rates that hit the poor hardest are all essential to the conservative alternative to the liberal welfare state. But the experience of the last 15 years has demonstrated that economic prosperity alone is not sufficient to save the family. The percentage of out-of-wedlock births rose during the Reagan boom. The 13-year-old and 14-year-old "superpredators" now terrorizing America's towns were born during the Reagan years.

The cultural challenge for public policymakers is to help repair the fabric of American life: to put the family back together, to reduce sharply the crime and drug abuse that devastate so many lives and neighborhoods, to improve education, to protect families from the appalling violence and pornography and coarseness in the popular culture. To do this, they must find new ways to instill a stronger sense of personal responsibility and to empower Americans to take control of their own lives. This means giving parents greater control over the upbringing and education of their children. It means strengthening civic institutions without developing the dependency and loss of mission that come with a government subsidy. It means encouraging respect for religion without endangering America's tradition of church-state separation; building on the welfare reform of 1996 to discourage able-bodied adults from developing a long-term dependency on government assistance; and empowering citizens to assume again the primary responsibility for helping the needy through religious, charitable, and civic institutions.

These are issues on which conservatives in Congress can still set the agenda. President Clinton won re-election in part because, on many issues, he ran as a cultural conservative. Most of his conservative speeches and actions—from saying Dan Quayle was right about the two-parent family to signing legislation overturning barriers to transracial adoption and issuing guidelines on how to teach about religion in public schools—have been "me-too" endorsements of rhetoric and initiatives long championed by conservatives. The most prominent example, of course, was the President's signing of the GOP's 1996 welfare reform legislation which abolished Aid to Families with Dependent Children (AFDC) as a federal entitlement, devolved some responsibility for welfare to the states, and sent a clear signal that society expects able-bodied welfare recipients to work. The voters rewarded the President for embracing such conservative initiatives; if he continues to value his political popularity in a second term, he will be receptive to others.

LESSONS LEARNED

Over the past 15 years, as the cultural crises in American society have steadily worsened, conservative ideas of self-government have gained greater prominence. There is growing recognition of the importance of family, religion, and civic institutions, and the idea that centralized, bureaucratic government has exacerbated the nation's social crises has gained wide currency among policymakers and the public. But conservatives sometimes have struggled to find the best way to garner public support for their principles and translate them into public policy. Fortunately, the political successes and setbacks of the 1980s and 1990s have yielded valuable lessons for shaping the conservative agenda of self-government.

LESSONS LEARNED

- The most effective way to talk about "family values" is to stress the importance of making sure that each American child grows up with both a mother and a father.

- Conservatives have not found a comfortable vocabulary for arguing that religion should take a more central place in American life.

- The most effective strategy for promoting school vouchers is to encourage, monitor, and publicize the growing number of local voucher experiments.

- The best way to combat Hollywood's moral rot is not through censorship but through the bully pulpit strategies of embarrassment and boycott.

- Federal leadership can make a crucial difference in addressing great cultural ills.

- The best way to develop a strategy for empowering low-income people is to learn from those who have demonstrated success.

- Conservatives have been seriously damaged by unfriendly relationships with leading charitable institutions.

Lesson #1: The most effective way for conservatives to talk about "family values" is to stress the importance of making sure that each American child grows up with both a mother and a father. This lesson is clear and fundamental. No longer is there any doubt that illegitimacy and divorce are harmful to children. Social scientific evidence shows unequivocally that among whites as well as blacks, the collapse of the family is the most important cause of crime, poverty, academic failure, and personal unhappiness in America today. The evidence is so overwhelming that liberals who four years ago mocked Vice President Dan Quayle's "Murphy Brown" speech now acknowledge, in the words of President Clinton, that "there were a lot of good things in [the Murphy Brown] speech. This country would be better off if more babies were born into two-parent families. Too many kids are growing up without family support." Liberals will not necessarily sign on to conservative proposals for putting the family back together, but they nod their heads in agreement when conservatives describe the harm caused by the collapse of the family.

How were conservatives able to win broad recognition of the benefits of two-parent families? One reason is that racial politics has changed. In liberal circles, it used to be considered racist to talk about the dangers of illegitimacy. Daniel Patrick Moynihan was ostracized from the liberal establishment in 1965 when he warned that America's black communities would be hurt by an out-of-wedlock birth rate then surpassing 25 percent. Now that black illegitimacy has reached 70 percent, more and more African-American political, cultural, and religious leaders are recognizing that the collapse of the family is devastating their communities. And with illegitimacy among whites exceeding 25 percent and rising rapidly, liberals feel more comfortable with plain talk about a problem that affects whites too. Conservatives also have discovered ways to talk about the family with no invidious racial distinctions, such as pointing out that there is little difference between white and black criminality when the studies take into account family structure. Both blacks and whites who grew up with two parents have low crime rates; both blacks and whites who grew up in broken homes have high crime rates.

Conservatives have used the collapse of the family to undermine the legitimacy of the federal welfare state. Proponents justify government anti-poverty programs primarily in the name of children. But that argument falters in the face of clear evidence that the enormous expansion of federal, state, and local anti-poverty programs over the last 30 years has coincided with skyrocketing rates of illegitimacy and divorce that have devastating effects on children. Conservatives furthermore have exposed the disastrous incentives of welfare programs themselves. They have shown how federal welfare programs discourage both marriage and work and have the unintended effect of subsidizing and promoting unwed motherhood. By reducing the penalties for divorce or nonmarriage, the easy availability of welfare also discourages mothers and fathers from reconciling their differences and staying together.

Conservatives are in the driver's seat on this issue. Liberalism in the last 30 years has sought to diminish individual responsibility for raising children and to augment collective ("state") responsibility. This impulse is summed up best in First Lady Hillary Clinton's slogan "It takes a village to raise a child," with its implication that America is a national village in which everyone is responsible for everyone else's children. Conservatives countered effectively with the answer that it takes a family—mothers and fathers—to raise children. At the Democratic convention, the First Lady was forced to backtrack and to say that "parents first and foremost are responsible for their children," though she also went on to make the breathtaking assertion that "it takes a President" to raise a child. It is time to make her backtrack again. The experience of the last few years suggests that conservatives will win the argument if they continue to emphasize that it takes a married mother and father, not a government, to raise a child.

Yet conservatives have shown they can occasionally mishandle this issue by becoming too preachy or sanctimonious, or by impugning the "family values" of their opponents. Such approaches usually backfire. On a subject as close to Americans' hearts as marriage and the family, it is important for political leaders not to be self-righteous. Many audiences resent a tone of moral superiority. Moreover, since all political leaders are human—which is to say, since all have at least some character flaws—the self-righteous politician is likely to be branded a hypocrite when his own shortcomings are exposed.

A number of leading conservative politicians have obtained divorces while their children were still minors. This should not disqualify them from the debates over parental responsibility; on the contrary, they may be able to add sensitivity and wisdom learned from the sadness of their own experience. It does mean, however, that they and their political allies need to approach debates on parental responsibility in a spirit of personal humility. Cultural conservatives run a great risk when they frame a debate over who has the best and strongest personal commitment to family life. It is more effective to argue over who has the best ideas for putting the family back together and for repairing the fabric of American life.

Lesson #2: While conservatives have broken down barriers to religion in the public square by emphasizing such principles as religious freedom and religious expression, they have not found a comfortable vocabulary for arguing that religion should take a more central place in American life. One of the great cultural achievements of conservatives in the last 15 years has been to convince political leaders across the ideological spectrum that it is wrong for government to discriminate against religious believers and institutions. By emphasizing principles that draw the assent of liberals, such as religious freedom, freedom of expression, and nondiscrimination, conservatives have been able to build powerful left-right coalitions to break down barriers to religion in the public square, including public schools.

The Equal Access Act, which requires public secondary schools to treat student-initiated and student-led religious meetings the same as other student gatherings, became law in 1984 after passing both houses of Congress by overwhelming margins. It passed with the support of such diverse groups as the American Civil Liberties Union, the American Jewish Congress, the National Evangelical Association, and the Christian Legal Society. The law embodies two principles attractive to liberals: nondiscrimination and freedom of expression for students. The Religious Freedom Restoration Act of 1993, also approved by overwhelming bipartisan majorities in Congress, says that government may interfere with religious practices only if it can show that the regulation or action in question furthers a "compelling governmental interest" and is the least restrictive way to further that interest.

In 1996, the Clinton Administration issued guidelines suggesting that public school curricula make more room for teaching *about* religion. The guidelines also suggested that it is constitutionally appropriate for public school students to write or give oral presentations about religious subjects.

The "charitable choice" provision of the 1996 welfare reform legislation, which was added by Senator John Ashcroft (R-MO), was approved by 67 Senators on a point of order without much debate on the Senate floor. The provision is a landmark in public policy because it insists that government respect the religious freedom of groups with which it does business. Religious organizations may receive state contracts for social services without having to remove their religious symbols, change their internal governance structure, or change their hiring practices. Moreover, if states give contracts for such services to private organizations, they are required to treat religious and secular organizations equally.

Three safeguards in the charitable choice provision helped win the support of those who otherwise might have objected to the legislation on church-state grounds. First, the law prohibits federal expenditures for religious worship, instruction, or proselytizing unless aid is given in the form of a voucher which enables a beneficiary to choose a social service provider from a range of religious and non-religious alternatives. Faith-based organizations receiving non-voucherized state welfare contracts can conduct religious activities only with monies received from private sources. Second, faith-based providers receiving state contracts may not discriminate against beneficiaries on the basis of religion, lack of religious belief, or a refusal to participate in a religious practice. Third, any beneficiaries who object to receiving services from a faith-based organization have a right to demand that the state provide them with services from an alternative (non-religious) provider. The charitable choice provision in the welfare legislation is a model for public housing, drug and alcohol rehabilitation, and other areas of public policy where religious groups have been reluctant to take government contracts for fear of losing their religious mission.

Conservatives have been less successful, however, in convincing the electorate that religion should play a much more central role in American life. Few people worry about private renewal or revival of faith within religious communities, but many Americans are worried that public expression of faith by energized, religiously committed groups and movements will lead to religiously inspired bigotry, discrimination against religious minorities, and an accentuation of religious conflict. In many parts of the country, conservatives will be on the defensive in talking about religion until they can overcome these fears.

Lesson #3: The most effective strategy for promoting school vouchers is to encourage, monitor, and publicize the growing number of local voucher experiments. Conservatives correctly have united around school vouchers, or "opportunity scholarships," as one of their central reform ideas. Vouchers clearly would benefit students and parents and would improve the quality of education in much of the country, especially in many inner cities. Vouchers make schools accountable to parents, not to bureaucrats. And because parents, not government officials, would choose which schools their children will attend, vouchers avoid the church-state complications that can accompany government support for religious institutions.

Vouchers also are good long-term politics. Vouchers unite most of the conservative movement while helping create potential new constituencies, particularly in low-income black and Hispanic communities. Libertarians like the emphasis on choice and competition. Many religious conservatives like the opportunity to assist parents who want to send their children to religious schools. The most important source of conservative opposition comes from those who fear that vouchers will lead to much greater state regulation of private and religious schools. One way to reduce this fear would be to overturn the "Grove City" legislation of 1988, which applies federal civil rights regulations to colleges and universities whose students receive federally subsidized loans — a close analogy to the sort of regulation that could accompany school vouchers.

Vouchers so far have failed to win approval in legislatures and at the ballot box every time they have been proposed as a federal or statewide initiative. It is highly unlikely that a major federal initiative for vouchers — e.g., converting Chapter I education funds for disadvantaged students into vouchers — could pass Congress in the short term. Momentum is gathering in the states, however, for targeted and limited voucher programs, such as those in Milwaukee and Cleveland, that enable low-income parents in big cities to send their children to private secular or religious schools. Unfortunately, the Milwaukee program is still tied up in the Wisconsin courts. More recently, Mayor Rudolph Giuliani has proposed sending the bottom 5 percent of New York City public school students to Catholic and other religious schools.

Targeted vouchers provide opportunity to low-income students who, by universal agreement, are badly served by public schools. In both Milwaukee and Cleveland, thousands of parents have sought to take advantage of this opportunity to give their children a better education at safer schools. Hundreds have participated in public rallies supporting this opportunity, and they have been joined by growing numbers of black pastors, school principals, and even some elected officials. When the teachers unions, the civil rights establishment, and the majority of local elected officials continue to oppose such vouchers, they reveal their intent to remain profiteers of a corrupt, failing system that stands in the way of opportunity for children of the poor and denies the parents of those children the right to decide what is best for them.

None of the conventional arguments of the teachers unions can apply to targeted vouchers for the poor: The public schools will not suffer "cream-skimming" (the loss of students from middle-class families); nor will vouchers promote "white flight" from the schools, because most of the participating families are black and Hispanic. And the unions' argument that public education will suffer if taxpayer funds are spent on private education falls on deaf ears in cities such as Cleveland and Milwaukee where it is hard to imagine how public schools could be much worse. Litigation initiated by the Institute for Justice and other conservative public-interest law firms has reinforced the impression that union leaders are more concerned with their own financial interests than with the education of poor children, because the attitudes of union officials are often exposed in discovery proceedings and courtroom arguments.

Targeted programs also can overcome the less vocal resistance to vouchers that comes from many suburban parents who are happy with the public schools in their communities and have made great sacrifices in order to live in better school districts. Such parents are fearful of any diversion of funds to private schools from their children's own public schools. Many are also fearful that vouchers or inter-district public-school choice will bring in children from more violent neighborhoods and increase the exposure of their own children to crime, drugs, and sexual promiscuity. Targeted programs minimize the tax exposure, and programs focusing on private schools rather than inter-district choice can assuage the fears of suburban parents.

Lesson #4: The best way to combat the moral rot pervading Hollywood productions, song lyrics, and the art world is not through censorship but through the bully pulpit strategies of embarrassment and boycott. America is a free country. An artist is free to take and show photographs of sadomasochism among adult homosexuals. A gallery or museum is free to display a crucifix suspended in urine. A record company is free to distribute songs like those of Tupac Shakur or Snoop Doggy Dogg that promote the killing of "niggas" and denigrate women as "hos" and "bitches." Adults are free to look at graphic nudity on a movie or home video screen. And professors are free to teach the principles of Nazism, Communism, nihilism, or radical feminism.

At the same time, there is broad public agreement, sustained by the federal courts, that free expression has some limits. Production and possession of child pornography is illegal. Communities may set obscenity standards and limit the public display of sexual materials. A number of additional restrictions seem to win broad public consensus, such as a prohibition on graphic representation of necrophilia in film and song lyrics. There also could be much tighter restrictions on the sale and distribution of salacious materials to children without the consent of their parents. Nevertheless, freedom of expression remains one of America's most cherished values, and conservatives have learned that it is politically prudent to target narrowly any efforts to use government to censor offensive expression.

One of the central freedoms in America, however, is the freedom to fight back against filth, coarseness, and blasphemy. Conservative political leaders have found two successful ways to wage a culture war consistent with the principles of a free society.

First, conservatives have made a principled case that taxpayer dollars should not fund blasphemous or offensive art, and have shown that restrictions on such funding do not hamper artistic freedom. As Senator Jesse Helms (R-NC) put it so well in the debate over funding for the National Endowment for the Arts, "There is a fundamental difference between government censorship, the preemption of publication or production, and government's refusal to pay for such publication and production." This distinction is consistent with a free society, not a threat to it. "I do not propose that Congress 'censor' artists," said Helms. "I do propose that Congress put an end to the use of federal funds to support outrageous 'art' that is clearly designed to poison our culture. Those who insist on producing garbage should be required to do it on their own time and with their own money. The taxpayers should not be required to pay for it." Conservatives also have come up with a good rule of thumb for these decisions: If it would be inappropriate for a work of art to be shown in the Capitol, or to be read or described in a public congressional debate over C-SPAN, it should not be funded by taxpayers.

Second, conservatives have discovered how to use public shame to put moral and economic pressure on corporations that profit from the pollution of our culture. An excellent model is the campaign William Bennett has led against "trash TV" talk shows and hyperviolent, misogynistic, racist, pornographic, and sexually perverse song lyrics. Partly as a result of Bennett's campaign, Time Warner sold its 50 percent interest in Interscope Records, a leading label for "gangsta" rap, and sales of rap music fell from 10 percent of the total music market in 1991 to 6.7 percent in 1995. Meanwhile, Procter & Gamble withdrew all its advertising from four television talk shows, and a number of trash talk shows have folded in the last year.

Two important features of Bennett's leadership are valuable for conservatives who want to follow his example. Bennett has deliberately taken the issue out of partisan politics, building a bipartisan, multiracial coalition that includes Senators Joseph Lieberman (D-CT) and Sam Nunn (D-GA) and C. Delores Tucker, chairwoman of the National Political Congress of Black Women. Bennett reasons that social pressure will be strongest if it is broadly based and his moral arguments will carry the greatest weight if they do not appear to be designed for political advantage.

Bennett's strategy also aims at maximum embarrassment for his targets. He does not rail against Hollywood or the music industry in general. He does his homework, citing specific song lyrics that are so offensive that executives of the companies that produce them refuse to recite them in public. Although Time Warner has sold Interscope, which also distributes the albums of a number of groups responsible for pornographic music, Bennett has not yet succeeded in his campaign to drive hyperviolent and pornographic "gangsta rap" and "death metal" music to the fringes of the recording industry. However, his embarrassment-and-boycott strategy is a potent model for conservative political leaders. And he offers a useful benchmark for corporate responsibility: A company should not distribute a song lyric or movie scene unless its president would be prepared to describe its content in a public meeting.

Lesson #5: Federal leadership can make a crucial difference in addressing great cultural ills. Political leadership is powerful, as the Reagan-Bush success in driving down drug use shows. Between 1979 and 1992, monthly use of an illegal drug fell by half, from 24 percent to 12 percent of the population age 12 and over. Monthly cocaine use between 1985 and 1992 fell by 78 percent, from 2.7 percent to just 0.6 percent of the population age 12 and over. This was a spectacular achievement, and it should embolden national political leaders to address other seemingly intractable cultural ills. Naysayers said the war on drugs would be a total failure. They were wrong. The fall in drug use during the Reagan-Bush years was caused by a variety of factors, including a belated recognition of the health and safety dangers of marijuana, a shift in popular attitudes after the cocaine-related deaths of leading athletes and actors, the well-organized awareness efforts of private groups such as the Partnership for a Drug-Free America, and tougher enforcement of anti-drug laws in many local jurisdictions.

The political leadership of both Reagan and Bush was crucial in reducing the scourge of drugs. Four aspects of their leadership tactics proved to be essential:

- High-level executive attention from the President ensured that the drug war was a top priority for government agencies. Under President Reagan, a Cabinet-level national drug policy board chaired by the Attorney General met monthly to coordinate federal efforts. The President frequently attended these meetings, reinforcing their importance within his Administration. President Bush appointed to the high-visibility post of National Drug Policy Director William Bennett, who eloquently took the anti-drug message to communities around the country.

- First Lady Nancy Reagan was mocked, at first, by cultural elitists for her "Just Say No" campaign. But those three words had enormous power. She was saying clearly that drugs were wrong; by so doing, she inspired and reinforced the efforts of parents, schools, churches, and civic institutions that were promoting a similar message.

- There was a clear distinction between state and local authority and federal authority. The "feds" focused on interstate and international drug trafficking, leaving responsibility for local enforcement to police and sheriffs. Clear delineation of responsibility is essential to any task.

- Finally, while the Reagan and Bush Administrations went along with congressional Democrats in providing generous funding for treatment, they kept their emphasis on law enforcement and interdiction. If the government really wants to be serious about curbing drugs, they maintained, it is important to curb supply as well as demand.

The wisdom of the Reagan-Bush approach is obvious in retrospect. When the Clinton Administration in its first three years abandoned all four parts of the Reagan-Bush strategy, drug use among teenagers skyrocketed. The Reagan-Bush drug war achievements suggest that federal action can address similar cultural ills in the next four years. Drugs, of course, continue to be an excellent target, and perhaps President Clinton will want to take a page from the book of his predecessors. Alternatively, he might want to address another great ill, such as the collapse of the family; he probably can give only one great moral crusade the kind of priority that President Reagan gave to the drug war.

Lesson #6: The best way to develop a strategy for empowering low-income people is to learn from success: to listen to teachers, service providers, and grassroots leaders in low-income communities who have succeeded in promoting personal responsibility. One of the most destructive features of the welfare state has been the culture of failure it has promoted among the poor. Most scholarly and journalistic work on poverty in recent decades has focused on the degrading lives of poor people who have failed to advance economically. Almost no attention has been paid to the success stories of poor people who have created strong community institutions or risen from poverty and dependency. Liberalism seems almost to have celebrated the culture of failure as a vindication of liberal ideas about the inherent unfairness of capitalism and American society. Liberals have promoted the notion that low-income people, especially blacks and Hispanics, are helpless victims: victims of racism and discrimination, victims of poverty, victims of their own uncontrollable sex drives and other appetites, victims of economic forces beyond their control. This worldview is perverse: Even if the odds are stacked against them, it is a self-defeating prophecy to discourage the poor from striving to build a better life. Liberalism's victim mentality has ignored the capacity of poor people to learn from the success of others and to make intelligent decisions about lifting themselves out of poverty. The culture of failure also has encouraged the poor to be wards of the state, permanently dependent on the helping professions: Victims have to be helped; they cannot help themselves.

By contrast, a growing number of conservatives have emphasized the culture of success among low-income people and some of the service providers who work with them. These conservatives celebrate achievement, not failure. They publicize the work of grassroots organizations that have succeeded in bringing families back together, teaching responsible fatherhood and motherhood, sharply reducing crime, improving private and public schools in low-income neighborhoods, and promoting entrepreneurship and economic opportunity among the poor. These conservatives ask grassroots self-help promoters what government can do differently so they can be even more effective in offering opportunity for the poor. In many cases, the response has been to get government out of the way. In some cases, it requires using government to provide temporary help for those who do not want permanent dependency.

This ask-listen-empower strategy has been effective in helping faith-based drug and alcohol rehabilitation centers to accumulate outstanding track records in turning lives around. For instance, Bob Cote of Denver's Step 13 program testified before the Senate Labor and Human Resources Committee that drug addicts and alcoholics were cashing Supplemental Security Income (SSI) disability payments at liquor stores and bars, undermining street-based "rehab" programs such as Step 13. As a result of this testimony, Congress cut off SSI payments linked to alcohol and drug addiction. Teen Challenge in San Antonio explained how Texas's state credentialing requirements for counselors prevented the organization's being licensed as a drug treatment center despite its outstanding record in rehabilitation. This prompted Governor George Bush to set up a 16-member task force on how to free faith-based charities from unreasonable state regulation. And the Watts-Talent Community Renewal Act includes provisions designed to make it easier for successful faith-based substance abuse rehabilitation centers to win state certification.

The Republican leadership of the Wisconsin State Assembly set up a task force of 28 grassroots problem solvers to put together a report on "strategies to promote the self-sufficiency of low-income residents of Wisconsin." The task force was coordinated by the National Center for Neighborhood Enterprise, assisted by a small-business incubator called Community Enterprises of Greater Milwaukee. It is a model for what might be done at the national level. One of the task force's principal recommendations was that recipients of public assistance be able to choose their service providers. It also recommended vouchers for such services as job training, elder care, substance abuse treatment, child care, technical assistance to businesses and nonprofits, adult day care, and services for the homeless.

During the 1980s, Representatives Jack Kemp (R-NY), Richard Armey (R-TX), and Steve Bartlett (R-TX) visited public housing projects to hear tenants, many of them single mothers, explain the benefits of resident management initiatives. In sharp contrast to what is known about most of the nation's public housing, they learned how projects with resident management were safer and better maintained, and how they promoted entrepreneurship, education, and upward mobility among tenants and their children. Kemp then introduced legislation to help facilitate tenant management. Kemp and Armey advanced their legislative agenda by building an alliance with Democratic delegate and Black Caucus member Walter Fauntroy (D-DC). But even more important, they realized that their greatest political asset was the support of public housing tenants themselves. Kemp and Fauntroy held a press conference at the Kenilworth-Parkside housing complex in Washington, D.C., one of the shining stars of tenant management; the enthusiastic support of residents there led to a "60 Minutes" story and other favorable media coverage. Tenant management organizer Kimi Gray brought hundreds of low-income women to lobby Congress on behalf of the Kemp-Fauntroy amendment, which, despite the vigorous opposition of the public-housing authorities and the powerful American Federation of State, County, and Municipal Employees (AFSCME), passed the House unanimously in 1987. Today, the more than 100 resident management initiatives across the country are mostly thriving islands in a sea of decay and desperation.

Lesson #7: Conservatives have been seriously damaged by unfriendly relationships with leading charitable institutions. Conservatives face a troubling dilemma in the politics of devolution. They want to return responsibility for helping the poor from Washington to where it historically belongs—state and local governments and private charity— but many of the country's leading charities insist that the federal government should keep the leading role. For example, during the debate over welfare reform, organizations such as Catholic Charities, the Salvation Army, the Young Women's Christian Association, and the Lutheran Social Ministry strongly opposed the welfare reform of 1996. Their arguments did not prevail, but the continuing opposition of such charities poses two special problems for conservatives. First, with their enormous prestige and credibility in the human-services arena, the opposition of major charities to the conservative agenda is politically harmful. Second, the conservative alternative to the liberal welfare state depends on a reinvigorated charitable sector that currently seems unwilling to accept that challenge.

Private charities should be natural allies for conservatives, but recent experience reveals three causes of serious strain. Many leading charities receive as much as two-thirds of their income from federal, state, and local government funding. Not only do they resist efforts to reduce federal spending on programs from which they immediately benefit, but many think of themselves as part of a political coalition for a larger federal government and therefore will defend programs that benefit their partners in this coalition. For example, leading charities and philanthropies will resist voucher programs that are opposed by teachers unions and other public-sector unions.

The professional staffs of many leading charities and philanthropic foundations have been strongly influenced by left-liberal ideas like the bean-counting obsession with "diversity"; a reluctance to severely punish criminals; a belief that poverty is unrelated to personal behavior and results primarily from discrimination and an absence of economic opportunity; and an unwillingness to label such behaviors as unwed motherhood, sexual promiscuity, and drug abuse as morally wrong. Indeed, left-liberal ideas probably are entrenched more strongly in the charitable and foundation world than in any other part of American society, with the possible exception of universities.

New social service organizations are emerging which are based on more conservative values of personal responsibility. A prototypical example is Habitat for Humanity, which helps low-income people build their own homes and fosters such conservative principles as private ownership, self-help, and sweat equity. Even here, though, there is a danger that these organizations will become part of the coalition for a larger federal government and will grow lukewarm to the conservative reform agenda. The Clinton Administration is moving aggressively to fund such organizations. Habitat for Humanity, for example, not only uses AmeriCorps' paid "volunteers," but has just been awarded a $25 million grant from the Department of Housing and Urban Development.

STRATEGIES FOR EMPOWERING
FAMILIES AND COMMUNITIES

The next few years offer conservative policymakers and other leaders a wide array of opportunities to build on conservative successes on the cultural battlefield.

STRATEGY #1
Conservatives should engage the public in a great debate over the next few years on whether and how public policy should support and reinforce marriage.

As noted earlier, conservatives have won the intellectual and political debate over the importance of the two-parent family for children. The next challenge is to explore how public policy can make it more likely that the overwhelming majority of children grow up with a married mother and father. In certain important areas of public policy — e.g., Social Security payments, pensions, and the tax treatment of health insurance — the law already favors marriage. In others, such as tax and welfare policy, public policy actively discourages marriage. Perhaps no policies hurt marriage as much as the no-fault divorce laws currently in place in 49 states; but family law has been, and ought to remain, the bailiwick of state rather than federal government. There are many areas in which federal political leaders can make an important difference in promoting marriage:

Taxes. In the great tax-reform debate to come, a central question will be whether tax policy should be made to favor marriage instead of undercutting marriage as it does today. There are three dominant reform ideas in conservative discussion of taxation. One is the principle of neutrality — that government should not use the tax system as an instrument of social engineering. A second is the principle of simplicity and fairness—that all income should be taxed only once and at the same rate. A third is the principle that tax policy should encourage investment and growth—for example, through a consumption tax or low marginal rates on income. All of these principles would remove some of the current penalties against marriage, but none embodies a preference for marriage. As conservatives lay the philosophical and political groundwork for major tax reform over the next few years, they must

---

STRATEGIES FOR
EMPOWERING FAMILIES AND COMMUNITIES

- The public must be engaged in a great debate over the next few years on whether and how public policy should support and reinforce marriage.

- Greater parental responsibility needs to be encouraged by giving fathers and mothers more control over the upbringing and education of their children.

- Greater public appreciation needs to be generated regarding the role of religion and religious believers in healthy societies, while affirming a commitment to the separation of church and state.

- A public policy strategy should be developed for encouraging citizens to involve themselves in their communities and empowering them to take primary responsibility for the needy.

- The connection in public perception between compassion and government spending needs to be severed.

- Conservatives should identify and learn from community heroes in every congressional district.

- Conservatives should engage leading charitable organizations in friendly debate.

- America should mount a national campaign to triple or quadruple the number of adoptions.

---

decide whether such a preference should be combined with the other reform principles.

One of the most significant but seldom talked-about features of the Armey-Shelby flat tax proposal is that it ends marriage penalties for dual-income couples while also making it easier for married mothers not to work. Under any flat tax or consumption tax, dual incomes would no longer push married couples into a higher tax bracket. But perhaps most significant, the large personal exemption ($10,700 per parent and $5,000 per child) would reduce the tax burden on lower-income families and make it much easier for mothers with children to stay at home. This almost certainly would make marriage much more attractive for lower-income women.

There is enormous potential for a broad-based coalition among economic and social conservatives on behalf of the Armey flat tax or similar tax-reform proposals. Before such a coalition can be built, however, Members of Congress and outside conservative groups must decide whether it is important to favor marriage in the tax system. There is a steep price for generous personal exemptions: The tax rates are higher than they otherwise would be. The next year or two will be the perfect time for conservative political leaders to begin this debate.

Welfare. Welfare has had devastating effects on marriage in recent decades. As Robert Rector of The Heritage Foundation has documented, AFDC and other means-tested poverty programs essentially have offered a single mother with two children the following contract: Receive the equivalent of between $8,500 and $15,000 per year (depending on place of residence) but agree not to work and not to marry someone who works. Rector calls this offer the "incentive system from hell." In effect, the federal government offered rewards for illegitimacy and intentional single motherhood—and got what it paid for.

The welfare reform of 1996 does not promote marriage directly or end the subsidization of illegitimacy. However, its work requirements reduce slightly the incentives for out-of-wedlock births. Though the number of recipients who will be required to work is still quite low—a state typically needs to get only 18 percent of its caseload working by 1999 — many women with children will have to work as a condition of getting assistance. Marriage to a working husband suddenly will look much more attractive. (The incentive to marry will be even stronger in states such as Wisconsin that have more stringent work requirements.) The welfare reform also creates a new $50 million-a-year education program to promote sexual abstinence and provides bonus funding to states that reduce illegitimacy without increasing abortion rates. Should any states achieve this goal, conservatives will want to give them enormous national publicity and attention.

Political leaders may wish to debate how to go further in reforming welfare not only by removing the remaining incentives for illegitimacy and divorce in poverty programs, but also by actually using public assistance to promote marriage. Should married couples receive preference in public housing and rent vouchers? Should the Earned Income Tax Credit be more generous for married couples, or perhaps be provided only to married couples? Should men who marry welfare mothers be allowed to fulfill the mothers' work requirements under the new welfare legislation? Should welfare authorities give some sort of dowry to men who take women off welfare by marrying them? There are downsides to such approaches. They might encourage greater dependency on welfare among married people, for example, and might be unfair to mothers who truly have been deserted or are otherwise unmarried through no fault of their own. But it would be helpful to start debating what public assistance can do to favor marriage. As responsibility for poverty programs shifts to state capitals, this debate should take place primarily at the state level; but in the transitional period, there is still a strong role for federal action.

Report on the Family. Every year, the President delivers a few significant reports to Congress, the most notable being the Economic Report of the President. It is time to add an Annual Report to Congress on the State of the American Family. This would be a comprehensive report to Congress on the state of marriage, divorce, abortion, cohabitation, stepfamilies, parental time devoted to children, and the relationship between family structure and such indicators as educational attainment, religious practice, and income. Such a comprehensive report could be compiled from the large national surveys that the federal government already undertakes. The extra cost would be small and could easily be diverted from within other parts of the overall research budget that Congress allocates to the social sciences every year.

Sex Education. Congress should hold hearings to explore why sex education programs in high schools and junior high schools have failed to reduce teenage out-of-wedlock pregnancies. Hearings also should be held on private programs, such as Elayne Bennett's Best Friends and Kathleen Sullivan's Project Reality, that have outstanding track records in reducing teen pregnancy by encouraging abstinence. Similar hearings also could be held by the bipartisan National Campaign to Prevent Teen Pregnancy, established recently in response to a challenge from President Clinton with the goal of reducing the teen pregnancy rate by one-third by 2005. One of the most significant features of the campaign is its acknowledgment that "part of a strategy for reducing teenage pregnancy should be a more overt discussion of religion, culture, and public values."

Homosexuality. A renewed focus on how public policy can make it more likely that children will grow up with both a mother and father gives conservatives a vocabulary for talking about homosexuals, a vocabulary that recognizes their rights as citizens of a free country without according them special status or approval. Public policy gives special privileges and protections to marriage because it is the most important institution for the raising of children. Homosexuals are free to form their own lasting unions and to make their own personal commitments to each other, but it trivializes marriage to give such unions the special protections of the law or the subsidies that are intended to help mothers and fathers raise children into upstanding citizens.

STRATEGY #2
Policymakers should encourage greater parental responsibility by giving fathers and mothers more control over the upbringing and education of their children.

In November, Colorado voters defeated an initiative amending the state constitution to guarantee that "the right of parents to direct the upbringing and education of their children shall not be infringed" by government action in, for example, sex education, school counseling, and medical examinations without parental consent. In Congress, the Parental Rights and Responsibilities Act sponsored by Senator Charles Grassley (R-IA) and Representative Steve Largent (R-OK) gives parents the right to direct or provide for the education of the child; make a health or mental health decision for the child, with exceptions involving imminent harm or life-threatening conditions; discipline the child, including reasonable corporal punishment; and direct or provide for the religious and moral formation of the child. Whether or not this initiative catches on in other states, it clearly reflects the profound anxieties of many parents that they are losing their power to shape their children's upbringing.

Liberals have their own approach to giving parents more control. They use government to regulate corporations in order to give parents more flexibility in making family decisions. The most prominent example is the Family and Medical Leave Act of 1993, which requires employers to give workers a three-month leave of absence without pay (but with medical benefits) to care for a new child or a sick relative. Conservatives opposed this legislation on the grounds that it was costly, intrusive, inflexible, and for the most part unnecessary since most employers already gave such leaves of absence. But by framing the case for the law in terms of the parental rights that conservatives usually support, President Clinton and other liberals put conservatives on the defensive. Perhaps the best way to respond is to emphasize that, though providing family and medical leave is usually the right thing for companies to do, mandating this as a benefit can be costly to both companies and employees, and the federal government should not decide for employees whether they would like to receive compensation in the form of leave or higher wages. Federal benefits for families should take the form of extra tax relief or expansion of the Earned Income Tax Credit for poor families, leaving employment contracts to voluntary negotiations between employers and employees.

In the war over popular culture, conservatives should empower and encourage parents to make informed choices for their children. The Motion Picture Association of America already enforces a rating system for movies, and the recording industry began placing warning stickers on albums that contain explicit materials after a campaign in the mid-1980s by Tipper Gore and others. The objective of the V-chip legislation signed by President Clinton was to stimulate technology and rating systems that would enable parents to keep offensive programs out of their homes. Parents would be given even more power if they were required to give explicit consent before their children could gain access to explicit materials. For example, MTV could be scrambled on TV sets unless parents deliberately unscrambled it, and record stores could be prohibited from selling recordings with offensive lyrics to minors without parental approval.

This informed-choice approach offers conservative political leaders a model for challenging moral relativism and ideological extremism in college and university education without threatening the important principle of academic freedom. Parents are rightly concerned about both the ever-increasing tuition bills they are paying and the debts their children will accumulate. Congress has a legitimate interest in this subject because of its own role in subsidizing student loans. Congress would not threaten academic freedom by holding hearings on why college costs are rising so quickly and whether parents are getting their money's worth for the tuition—as much as $100,000 for four years—they pay for each child's undergraduate education. These hearings also could offer an opportunity to examine the ideological and moral nature of courses that students are taking so that parents could become better informed consumers of higher education.

Perhaps no other reform can do more than educational choice to empower parents in the upbringing of their children. Although school funding is primarily a state and local responsibility, federal legislation can be used as a catalyst to encourage state and local voucher initiatives. The Watts-Talent Community Renewal Act, which incorporates the principle of targeted school vouchers in its strategy for empowerment zones, is an excellent vehicle for jump-starting voucher movements at the grassroots level. Parents and students who have benefited from vouchers can be brought to testify on Capitol Hill; or perhaps better yet, congressional hearings can be held in schools where large numbers of low-income students could benefit from vouchers.

The teachers and principals in religious and secular private schools should figure prominently in these media and publicity strategies. Not only are they eloquent spokesmen for vouchers, but it is important to make these accomplished and dedicated teachers and principals heroes in the education profession. But it is just as important to win friends for school vouchers among public school teachers. All good teachers know how important it is for parents to be involved more actively in their children's education; it is important that public school teachers learn from their private school counterparts how parental choice has helped them as teachers.

The unions will fight school vouchers bitterly. Their opposition will be ferocious, well financed, and well organized. But teachers and principals need not and should not be enemies of reform. No education reform worth achieving can win widespread acceptance without strong support from many teachers and principals. The next challenge for the voucher movement is to win such strong support.

STRATEGY #3
Congressional leaders should encourage greater public appreciation of the role of religion and religious believers in healthy societies while affirming a commitment to the separation of church and state.

A revival of religious faith and observance is central to the conservative ₁vision of American citizenship and self-government. This notion — that faith commitment helps create and sustain the moral communities that make self-government possible — is a theme sounded in nearly every important proclamation on religion in American life, from George Washington's Farewell Address to Dr. Martin Luther King's evocation of the prophet Isaiah in his "I Have a Dream" speech. While it is beyond the power of Presidents, legislators, and judges to lead a religious revival, national political leaders can help encourage greater respect for religion and religious believers.

First, they can point out that religion offers answers to many of the great social crises of our times. Government, for example, cannot build and sustain healthy marriages or teach children to be hard-working, responsible, and virtuous. The family will be restored not primarily by public policy, but by private character-building institutions that touch the souls of men and women and inspire them to be more responsible husbands, wives, and parents. This is, above all, the task of religion.

"Lock 'em up" policies in criminal justice are likewise necessary but insufficient to address the catastrophe of crime. The root cause of crime is spiritual, a hardening of the heart that makes a man or woman indifferent to the rights of others. This is the founding credo of Charles Colson's Prison Fellowship, the most successful and extensive outreach to prisoners in America today. Colson's Christian-based organization has helped thousands of former criminals lead productive lives outside prison walls. It offers hard proof that the most effective institutions in criminal justice will be those that create moral communities and transform individual attitudes and behaviors. In inner cities, no institution does this more than the black church.

Religion is similarly the great wellspring of charity and voluntarism. Nearly half of all charitable gifts are given to churches and other religious organizations. Weekly churchgoers give 3 percent of their income to charity; those who attend church less than once a month give less than 1 percent. Religious revival dwarfs tax incentives as a means to encourage more involvement with charity.

It is similarly important for conservative political leaders to humanize the Christian Right so it is better understood by all Americans. Though the Christian Right frequently is vilified by liberals and the national media, it is one of the most constructive forces in American culture. In the tradition of Mormons, Jews, and others whose religions are characterized by a strong charitable culture, conservative Evangelicals and Catholics run schools for low-income children. They operate maternity homes that give unwed mothers the love and support they need to choose life over abortion. They go into our cities' meanest streets and rescue gang members, drug dealers, and prostitutes from lives of violence, addiction, and desperation. Name a social ill afflicting our cities — poverty, unemployment, illiteracy, illegitimacy — and you will find a religiously affiliated program attacking the problem with prayer and sweat and a small army of volunteers. Conservative political leaders can draw public attention to these programs by regularly visiting and attending services at churches, synagogues, mosques, and other religious institutions that are leading the moral revival in their communities.

Conservative political leaders also can stress the central role of religion in American history: the importance of the Great Awakening in the American Revolution, the religious character of the anti-slavery and civil rights movements, the historic contribution of churches and synagogues to the creation of so many colleges, hospitals, and charities in the 19th century. Conservative political leaders can argue that it is consistent with this tradition for religious leaders to speak out on great moral issues of the day such as abortion and homosexuality, and that it is outrageous— indeed un-American—for anyone to try to stop them from doing so.

National political leaders can pray publicly and seek divine guidance on momentous occasions. In his first official speech as President after the death of Franklin Roosevelt, Harry Truman drew from the Bible as he addressed a joint session of Congress: "At this moment I have in my heart a prayer. As I have assumed my duties, I humbly pray Almighty God, in the words of King Solomon, 'Give therefore thy servant an understanding heart to judge thy people, that I may discern between good and bad: for who is able to judge this thy so great a people.'" So long as it is done in an ecumenical spirit, such public prayer is completely consistent with religious freedom and American tradition.

Religious conservatives are correct when they criticize court rulings that threaten and belittle religious expression in our common culture. The Supreme Court and the lower federal courts often have used the Establishment Clause of the First Amendment as a club to browbeat religious freedom, especially in our public schools. Justice Antonin Scalia has aptly criticized the High Court's *Lemon*[1] test — a standard to determine when government action violates the separation of church and state — as a "ghoul in a late-night horror movie" continually "frightening little children and school attorneys."

The Religious Equality Amendment is a laudable effort to clarify the religious liberty rights of all citizens, especially those in public schools. The Christian Coalition has said it seeks an amendment that "allows voluntary, student and citizen-initiated free speech in non-compulsory settings." This is an important statement, for it is vital for religious conservatives to proclaim their commitment to religious freedom and the separation of church and state. It is important to insist that the powers of government not be enlisted to proselytize any faith. And it is important to be sensitive to the concerns of religious minorities, especially those with children in public schools. Just as many conservative Christians want to protect their children from sex education classes that contradict their moral teachings, so members of religious minorities may want to protect their children from prayers—which are nothing less than acts of worship —that contradict what they are taught at home.

STRATEGY #4
Members of Congress should develop a public-policy strategy for encouraging citizens to involve themselves in their communities and empower them to take primary responsibility for the needy through their support of and participation in charitable, religious, and civic organizations.

When Representative John Kasich (R-OH), chairman of the House Budget Committee, travels to his district and around the country, he likes to ask his audiences how many think they could do a better job than federal bureaucrats in picking which charities can serve their communities most effectively. Usually, 299 out of 300 hands go up. This is a powerful current in public opinion. One of the central challenges for

---

1 The *Lemon* test, as defined by Chief Justice Warren Burger in *Lemon v. Kurtzman* (1971), holds that "First, the statute must have a secular legislative purpose; second, its principal or primary effect must be one that neither advances nor inhibits religion; finally the statute must not foster 'an excessive government entanglement with religion.' "

conservatives is to find ways to give Americans the tools to make the decisions they are ready and eager to make.

One approach would be through tax credits for charitable giving that go beyond the current deduction for those who itemize gifts to charity. However, tax credit approaches run contrary to the objectives of flat-tax proponents and other conservative tax reformers who are trying to simplify the tax system. It also is probably best not to limit tax credits to organizations that are defined specifically as "poverty-fighting"; some of the most effective poverty-fighting groups may be churches, Boy Scout troops, libraries, and other organizations that would fail to qualify under such a definition. But the great advantage of the tax credit approach is that it is a highly effective vehicle for driving home Representative Kasich's question. Indeed, one of the best ways to make the case for federal spending cuts is to tie those cuts, dollar for dollar, to tax credits for families. This encourages families to take more responsibility for the needs in their community and to find out which charities are the most effective and the most consistent with their values.

Policymakers in Washington need to find ways to help civic institutions in their districts without direct government subsidy. One of the most effective ways to do this is to identify and overturn federal regulations that are interfering with their work. For example, the Clinton Labor Department has made life much more difficult for one of the most important community institutions in suburban and rural America: volunteer fire departments and rescue squads. Prodded by the International Association of Firefighters (an AFL-CIO affiliate), the Clinton Labor Department has barred professional firefighters who work elsewhere in their county of residence from volunteering to protect homes and lives in their own communities. This restriction not only robs firemen of the freedom to volunteer their services in their own free time, but also denies volunteer firehouses some of the best expertise available to them. The firefighters union so far has blocked legislation sponsored by Representative Herbert Bateman (R-VA) that would overturn this restriction, but if America's 1.2 million volunteer firemen and rescue workers (about 80 percent of the total) mobilize, conservatives can win this battle against union bullying.

Representative Rob Portman (R-OH) has come up with an innovative way to promote citizen initiatives in his Cincinnati district. Portman's constituents were upset about rising drug use among teens, and Portman wanted to address their concerns without adding to the $13 billion that the federal government already was spending annually on drug control programs. He helped establish the Coalition for a Drug-Free Greater Cincinnati, bringing community activists already involved in anti-drug work together with business leaders, religious leaders, the media, parents, young people, and law enforcement officials. As a result of his work, every leading media outlet in the area is running anti-drug public service announcements and advertisements; some of the radio spots were recorded by a popular local rock band. Health care providers are offering financial discounts to businesses that adopt certified drug-free workplace programs. And parents in every school district are receiving practical training on steps to keep their children drug free. Portman's anti-drug work is a new model of constituent service that avoids pork-barrel spending and is custom-made for the revitalization of community institutions.

STRATEGY #5
Conservatives in Congress should seek to sever the connection in public perception between compassion and government spending.

Nothing in the public discourse is more harmful to the conservative agenda than the widespread notion that the measure of America's compassion on any given issue is the amount of federal (and state and local) spending directed to it. In the next few years, there are at least three major ways that conservatives can discredit this false and destructive equation.

The first way is to dramatize the absence of any correlation between government spending and desirable outcomes in education, health, and lifting children out of poverty. Wall charts of the sort that William Bennett used to display at press conferences are an excellent model. As Secretary of Education, Bennett would put up charts comparing the ranking of state performance in student achievement with similar state rankings for per-student educational expenditures. There was absolutely no correlation between the two. Similar comparisons for government medical expenditures would be very revealing if policymakers highlighted states such as Utah, which has some of the lowest spending on medical care but also has the best health outcomes.

Second, conservatives must expose the great failure of the War on Poverty. During the coming year, the Left can be expected to mount a major assault on the welfare reforms of 1996. Hundreds of horror stories of neglect, abuse, and even starvation will be widely publicized and blamed on the end of the AFDC entitlement and the transfer of responsibility for welfare to the states. Conservatives should prepare for this by emphasizing the success stories of states such as Wisconsin that have provided opportunity to families formerly on welfare, and by reminding Americans over and over just how cruel and tragic life for America's poor was under AFDC. It will be important to show how much child abuse occurred in the welfare rolls in recent years, how many juvenile offenders came out of the AFDC population, and how many children raised on welfare went on to become welfare mothers themselves.

Third, it is important to conduct research on and publicize faith-based, business-based, and other private organizations that achieve better results at lower costs than government social programs. Existing research shows clearly that religious schools teach inner-city children more effectively at less than half the cost of public schools. Congress can hold hearings to investigate why. Congress can ask the General Accounting Office to study whether, as is often asserted, faith-based drug and alcohol rehabilitation centers have a much greater success rate at lower cost than most secular and medical therapies. Similarly, legislators can commission analyses of programs such as Prison Fellowship that seek to rehabilitate prisoners through religious conversion, asking how recidivism rates of prisoners in such programs compare with rates for control groups.

Conservatives ought to build their own cadre of social science advisers and develop their own data procurement and analysis strategy. Congress funds hundreds of millions of dollars worth of social research each year, yet most of the analytic work done with this money supports a non-traditional view of family and community. For instance, research by Richard B. Freeman demonstrates the power of regular religious worship in moving inner-city children out of poverty; but the welfare research community, massively funded by the federal government, has totally ignored this finding despite two major national debates on welfare since Freeman's findings were released in 1985.

Conservatives ought to use their influence to insist that research and analysis of their questions and concerns are conducted. The social science community, though not naturally so inclined, is quite capable of analyzing the data to answer questions of high interest to conservatives. Two of the most powerful variables for developing the capacities of children are marriage and regular religious worship. Social scientists can investigate this claim from many angles, and the national debate will be advanced if Congress insists that some of the research money address these issues.

The National Results Council, a privately funded organization, plans to develop comparative performance measures for vocational rehabilitation, teen pregnancy prevention, job training, and other human services programs. Many similar evaluation systems will be needed. Congress also can encourage research at colleges and universities through federally funded social science programs. Over the next two decades, Congress should call upon academia to stimulate thousands of dissertations on private-sector programs that work. Committees should encourage testimony from teachers and principals at outstanding private and religious schools that receive vouchers; teachers at public schools who defy their unions and go the extra mile for their students; police officials who dramatically cut crime; tough-love juvenile justice programs that turn children around by setting high moral standards; private legal aid programs that help poor people better than the Legal Services Corporation; private colleges that offer better job training than government programs; and restaurants that provide better nutrition at a lower cost than government school lunch programs.

STRATEGY #6
Policymakers can identify and learn from community heroes in every congressional district.

Every congressional district, every rural or metropolitan area, has success stories about grassroots heroes who already embody the conservative alternative to the welfare state. Members of Congress can visit them, listen to their stories, discover the principles that led to their success against the odds, and find out the principal obstacles (including government regulation) to their being even more effective. Such visits offer two vitally important benefits for conservatives in Congress.

First, they provide real-life examples that illustrate the conservative vision of self-government in a caring society based on personal and community responsibility. If conservatives are to articulate an alternative to the welfare state, it is essential to provide examples showing conservative ideas and principles at work. And for politicians, nothing is more persuasive than stories from their own districts or metropolitan areas. Conservative Senators or Representatives ought to be able to point to four or five religious and civic organizations in their districts or states that are providing care or opportunity for low-income people without encouraging long-term dependency on government. Political leaders can then explain that many more such organizations are needed if America is to become again the kind of self-governing republic that conservatives envision.

Second, conservative Members of Congress may learn ways they can be helpful to grassroots community organizations, and thus over time build constituent service relationships with low-income communities. The liberal approach to such a question is to channel taxpayer money to such organizations. Conservatives can help them garner publicity for efforts to raise private money, bringing private donors or TV crews along when they visit effective community groups. They can hold private fund-raisers. They can even hold congressional hearings at the sites of effective community organizations.

Members of Congress who have done this in the past have found it best not to begin these visits during election campaigns, but to conduct them throughout the term. Successful grassroots leaders usually do not get much attention from politicians and usually will welcome and respond warmly to visits from Members of Congress and their staffs. They will be even more appreciative if the visit is aimed at learning and helping, and does not appear to be just another political ploy.

Congress itself could hold national awards ceremonies to salute the work done by individual members of civic institutions. President Bush honored over 1,000 "Points of Light," one every day, and in many cases he or a Cabinet member visited the institutions honored. He invited winners to White House luncheons. In such ways, President Bush helped stimulate media attention and generate financial rewards for good works, but his strategy also encouraged winners to learn from each other. At one three-day event sponsored by Walt Disney World, 550 Points of Light winners met in Orlando to exchange ideas and information, hold press conferences, and establish informal networks. In January 1993, President Bush also issued "The President's Report to the Nation" on the Points of Light movement, which is a gold mine of stories about remarkable civic heroes who, as the President described, were "ordinary people who reach beyond themselves to touch the lives of those in need, bringing hope and opportunity, care and friendship."

The Points of Light initiative would have advanced conservatism better had it been carefully integrated into a political strategy for providing a conservative alternative to the welfare state. President Bush used his daily Points of Light to emphasize the importance of community service and buttress his campaign to reform liability laws. But he made clear that he did not want his celebration of successful private programs to be used as an excuse for government no longer to fund activities in the same areas. By contrast, the 105th Congress could use awards ceremonies to credential a new set of experts: grassroots problem solvers with practical experience in the field.

STRATEGY #7
Conservative policymakers should engage leading charitable organizations in friendly debate.

The self-government agenda will not succeed without the eventual cooperation of leading charities. Conservatives must build bridges to them, starting with their board members and volunteers who tend to be less ideologically liberal than their professional staffs. Conservative political leaders can publicly acknowledge the danger of overburdening philanthropy with too many responsibilities. The charitable world is terrified that, in this age of devolution, philanthropy is going to be asked to shoulder many more responsibilities than it can handle. Government is in trouble partly because it tried to do so much that it could do nothing very well. The same fate could befall charities. Conservative political leaders could help lead a great debate about the comparative advantages of philanthropy as opposed to the other great institutions of society — business, the family, and government.

However, conservatives must recognize that the principal weakness of most private charitable organizations in America today is that they are dominated by the same permissive, value-free philosophy that motivates most public-sector welfare bureaucracies. If private-sector philanthropies are to play a positive role in America's future, the ethos of these institutions must be utterly transformed.

Conservatives also must articulate a principled case against the seductive lure of government money for social service organizations. Initially, this money can prompt a burst of new energy through larger staffs and more volunteers. But over time, it becomes addictive. Charities become less responsive to their beneficiaries and more responsive to bureaucrats and the staff of key congressional subcommittees. They pay less attention to their mission and more attention to strengthening the political coalitions that ensure the preservation of their contracts. And with contracts come regulations that sap their spirit. Congressional hearings could reinforce this argument by asking the officials of charities that do not accept government money to explain their reluctance to do so. It also would be helpful to ask charities that do accept government money to reveal the percentage of their budget that comes from private donations and the percentage that comes from the federal taxpayer.

Not all charities that take government contracts abandon their missions, but many do. If a charity must take government money, it is best to keep it to a minimum. It is even better to funnel public funding to charities through individual vouchers rather than through direct contracts. Vouchers empower the people helped by the organization's services; more important, an agency that does not serve its clients well will soon be out of business.

It is also essential to abolish AmeriCorps, one of President Clinton's favorite programs. Modeled on the military, AmeriCorps has many culturally conservative attributes. It is dedicated to service, volunteerism, and duty to country. It sends its members to many fine organizations such as Habitat for Humanity that promote personal responsibility. But for all its emphasis on personal responsibility, AmeriCorps is a deeply irresponsible program. It is a federal organization parachuting into local communities to solve local problems—for example, by helping a charter school in Oakland, a church-based community service program in Dallas, and a police cadet program in New York City. Many of these are worthy causes, but AmeriCorps usurps local responsibility. Local governments and private funders have the greatest stake in the success of such programs. They also are best able to hold them accountable for how money is spent. But these local institutions are less likely to seek or finance promising solutions if they think AmeriCorps will do it for them.

It will not be easy to abolish AmeriCorps. President Clinton will fight strenuously to protect it, and he will be aided in the wars of public opinion by highly credible organizations (such as Habitat for Humanity) that believe they have benefited from AmeriCorps. Conservatives in Congress will have to invoke the testimony of organizations that have refused the help of AmeriCorps members, as well as dissenters in organizations that have accepted it. They should hold investigative hearings on the enforcement of regulations governing AmeriCorps, because it is likely that over time these regulations will seriously undermine the flexibility and volunteer spirit of the receiving organizations. And conservatives should reiterate that citizens in their communities are better equipped than federal bureaucracies to decide which charitable organizations are the most effective.

STRATEGY #8
Congress and the Administration should mount a national campaign to triple or quadruple the number of adoptions.

Three terrible tragedies in America — the tragedy of abortion, the tragedy of children growing up in single-mother families, and the tragedy of inadequate foster care—could be alleviated by an enormous increase in the number of adoptions. Only about 50,000 American children are adopted each year by non-relatives (when relatives are included, the number is closer to 100,000). There are nearly 500,000 children in foster care. Increasing the number of adoptions each year to 300,000 or 400,000 would offer much more hope for children who need good homes.

President Clinton and the First Lady, to their credit, have talked frequently about the importance of adoption. Over the objections of the National Association of Black Social Workers, the President signed GOP legislation overturning barriers to transracial adoption. Increasing the number of adoptions is an ideal issue for the bully pulpits occupied by the First Lady and the President.

The President has said he wants to make abortions "safe, legal, and rare." One way to make them rarer is to lead a campaign encouraging adoption and suggesting to expectant mothers that it is better to give a child up for adoption than to have an abortion. This message could be reinforced by support, such as that proposed by Senator Dan Coats (R-IN), for maternity homes that offer unwed mothers food, shelter, medical care, and an opportunity to pursue their education as they carry their baby to term—and, it is hoped, to adoption. If the President really believes it is best for children to have two parents, he should recommend that single mothers, if they cannot marry, give their children to mothers and fathers who can provide the loving parental care the children need.

A campaign to increase adoption also would address one of the greatest tragedies of the welfare state. American taxpayers spend $12 billion a year on a foster care system that is unspeakably cruel to children. Perhaps a third of children in foster care are well-served by the system: They have food, shelter, and a friendly foster family to take care of them while their parents work themselves out of temporary difficulties. But hundreds of thousands of children are trapped in a foster care system that denies them what they need most: permanent homes, a last name, a mother and a father. There are 90,000 children in foster care who have been there for longer than three years. Countless others are returned to their birth parents only to be abused again and returned to foster care. Every year, 15,000 foster children "graduate" from the system at age 18, and 40 percent of them go on welfare. Close to 50,000 children are legally free to be adopted but continue to languish in foster care. This is primarily an issue for the states, but it is important to look carefully at whether federal regulations are preventing parents who might want to adopt these children from doing so.

The politics of adoption is tremendously complicated. There are bitter disputes between those who support and those who oppose open adoption. Among conservatives, there are bitter disputes between those who think the foster care system is too aggressive in taking children from their birth parents and those who think it is too permissive in dealing with parental child abuse. There are bitter disputes about how much income parents should make to be able to adopt. And there certainly will be bitter disputes about whether homosexual couples should be permitted to adopt. Perhaps this is why few political leaders have dared to step into this thicket. But the best safety net any child can have is a loving father and mother. President Clinton says he wants to preserve the safety net. The best way to do that is by giving more children mothers and fathers. Adoption helps to do that.

CONCLUSION

Many, perhaps most, conservatives are deeply uncomfortable with the vocabulary of self-government or citizenship. If conservatives are to lead America from the era of big government to the era of self-government, perhaps the biggest challenge is to win the united support of the conservative movement. Building coalitions is important, as the strategies outlined above illustrate.

The vocabulary of citizenship is an essential complement to tax reduction and simplification and other reform objectives of economic conservatives. Taxes cannot be cut, and the deficit cannot be reduced, unless certain responsibilities now handled by the federal government are returned to families, businesses, and community institutions across America. To build the political case for this reform effort requires careful attention to the rebuilding of families and civil society itself to make sure that these institutions are strong enough — and are perceived by voters as strong enough—to act on their rightful responsibilities.

The vocabulary of cultural conservatism and self-government also is one of the most effective ways to talk about racial issues. Any strategy for eliminating mandated affirmative action has to be combined with a strategy for solving the problems that disproportionately affect black America. The evidence is mounting that religious and community institutions in black America are leading the way in solving such problems as family breakdown, crime, and educational collapse.

Yet the self-government movement has hurt its own image, in the view of many conservatives, by putting too much emphasis on increasing charity and volunteer efforts. Many conservatives are more interested in market capitalism and entrepreneurship, national defense, or tough law enforcement; they are afraid the citizenship movement relies on everyone's joining a Rotary Club or volunteering at soup kitchens to solve society's problems. Self-government begins within the family, putting emphasis on taking care of one's own children, one's own spouse, and one's own aging parents. It involves worship at a church or synagogue or mosque to reinforce moral beliefs. It affirms the need for serving in the military. It means accountability for local government. It means helping our neighbors and communities when they are in need and not taking advantage of others' generosity. Good citizens can responsibly own a business, create their own wealth, and produce goods and services that their customers value. In the end, the debate can be about who serves his community more, the volunteer at the soup kitchen or the fast food franchise owner who offers job opportunities producing low-cost food and generating tax revenue.

Self-government is conservatism's positive vision for America. The era of big government is indeed over. It is time to let the era of self-government begin.

Chapter 6

DOWNSIZING AND IMPROVING THE FEDERAL CIVIL SERVICE

Donald J. Devine and Robert E. Moffit

In their efforts to downsize the federal government and improve its management, reformers in Congress face the toughest interest group in Washington: the permanent government.[1] The permanent government is a diverse network; it includes the career civil service, its bipartisan allies in Congress and their staff, and a côterie of federal unions, as well as managerial and professional associations. It includes conservative and moderate Members of Congress with large civil service constituencies, liberal Democrats ideologically zealous in expanding federal programs, federal union leaders opposed to changes in federal pay and benefits or private-sector performance management, and federal managers' organizations that, regardless of their differences with unions, invariably unite in defense of common interests. Its influence extends into academia and certain public policy institutions which are dependable advocates for bureaucratic interests.

The authors would like to thank Patrick Korten, George Nesterczuck, and Patrick Pizzella for their contributions to this chapter. The views and opinions expressed here, however, are entirely the responsibility of the authors.

1 The authors use this term to include long-term congressional staff as well as the career civil service that comprises the bureaucracy. The term was used by Morris Fiorina in *Congress: The Keystone of The Washington Establishment* (New Haven: Yale University Press, 1977).

Nonetheless, if the President and Members of Congress exercise the political will and determination to make serious changes, they can. Both Presidents Jimmy Carter and Ronald Reagan showed it could be done. Over the next several years, the downsizing of the federal workforce will continue, but it should be managed properly and based upon clear policy objectives and sound management principles. This will take a coherent approach to government management that stresses both political leadership and accountability.

Policymakers within the Administration and Congress must show a willingness to call public attention to the weaknesses of the current system and the need to base personnel management decisions on performance. Their efforts need to focus on the elimination of duplicated positions and functions throughout the federal bureaucracy, and they must be ready to make significant changes in federal pay and benefits. Finally, they must find ways to build public support for transferring functions to states, communities, and the private sector, and for a smaller and leaner federal workforce for the functions that remain, while building federal employee support for a solid package of portable private sector-style benefits for their personnel.

Obstacles to Change. For all of its commitment to change, the 104th Congress was unable to enact any major civil service reform. The major House initiatives of 1995 that were begun were stopped in the Senate. In 1996, both President Clinton and congressional Republicans wanted to delay federal retiree cost of living adjustments. They failed to do so. The President and congressional Republicans also wanted to make major changes in civil service benefits. They were frustrated in their attempts to do so. Those in the 105th Congress who seek such changes and the Administration will continue to face major obstacles to their efforts to reform the federal civil service.

First, all too many people who come to Washington with the goal to reform government fail to understand or appreciate the immense power of the federal employee network, its political sophistication, and the intensity of its resistance to serious change. Second, far too many would-be reformers do not have a clear conception of federal management approaches and what model of government administration they should adopt in trying to make government work. For all of the recent rhetoric about "reinventing government" and making government work better to serve the American people, the federal establishment and its powerful allies on Capitol Hill—both Republicans and Democrats—are well-prepared to resist any serious reform such as connecting pay or retention to job performance. The federal establishment, as the Clinton Administration has proven conclusively, finds the rhetoric of reform tolerable, even as the workforce shrinks, as long as there are no real consequences for managers or employees based on job performance and as long as federal benefits remain generous and untouched.

Misunderstanding the Power of the Network. Washington's notorious Iron Triangle—the alliance of the federal bureaucracy, congressional staff, and Beltway interest groups—is perhaps strongest in resisting civil service reform. When it comes to federal pay and retirement issues, Congressmen and staff are self-interested judges in their own cause; and the public employee associations are generally staffed with big-government liberals from Capitol Hill who often take their generous federal benefits with them into the private sector. Federal unions are committed to strengthening their political clout, as evidenced in the weakening of Hatch Act restrictions on partisan political activities among federal workers; but, historically, their ability to do so depends on Democratic control of Congress. Although business groups often vaguely identify with improved government management, they are most concerned with buying access to Capitol Hill and often will hire well-connected, senior liberal congressional staffers to represent them in Washington. Although conservative advocacy organizations often use rhetoric about the need to get "government off our backs," mastering the boring details of civil service laws and regulations so critical to the actual functioning of the bureaucratic system they dislike is far less attractive than pursuing the hotter social and economic issues.

Challenging the bureaucratic culture means challenging powerful congressional interests, regardless of party or ideological inclinations. In terms of federal personnel management, it makes no difference whether or not the overall Congress is friendly to the Administration. The levers of legislative power on federal personnel issues are too often in the hands of Members of Congress who owe more to the political support of the permanent government than the philosophical attractiveness of serious civil service reform. Conservatives in Congress must also be prepared to accept the fact that their colleagues, happily preoccupied with the "big stuff," are ready to dismiss the dry-as-dust, often mind-numbing federal personnel management issues as backwater issues not worth the energy, effort, or inevitable political pain. This is, of course, the greatest single psychological advantage enjoyed by the permanent government.

Individuals coming to change the way Washington works will be educated quickly to the influence, power, and resourcefulness of this sophisticated network. Overwhelmingly, the federal civil service is composed of many fine, capable, and competent individuals, but they nonetheless compose an establishment. They are also financially well off: the average annual salary for a full-time federal employee in Washington, D.C., is $50,694.

This Washington establishment is generally united in its opposition to changes in federal pay and benefits policy that would bring the federal civil service more in line with competitive market rates and private-sector management practices.[2] It also understandably favors the perpetuation of its own bureaucratic power.[3] Jealously guarding paychecks, pocketbooks, and power, the permanent government has too much at stake to offer anything less than stout resistance.

That is why conservatives in Congress, bent on disrupting long-established ways of doing things, must be prepared—as President Jimmy Carter did in his campaign for passage of his historic Civil Service Reform Act of 1978—to expend serious political capital, sweat the details of personnel policy, and demonstrate political resourcefulness. With a clear agenda for reform, and the willingness to pursue it as both Presidents Carter

---

2 At the ground level of agency management, private-sector managers would find the paralysis that can strike the civil service system as absurd. For example, Dr. James Felsen, a physician with the Public Health Service, did "virtually nothing" for three years after an internal dispute with his superiors, and still collected an annual salary of $117,000 per year, including an annual $15,000 bonus for no work during these three years. HHS officials decided that there was "insufficient evidence" for firing Felsen. See Stephen Barr, "HHS Reassigns Physician It Can't Fire," *The Washington Post*, September 30, 1996, p. A21.

3 In 1988, the National Commission on Public Service, for example, including such prominent Washington insiders as Robert S. McNamara and Donna Shalala, argued that the President should reduce the number of political appointees because putting them into positions of authority over "talented" young career civil servants discourages them and blocks them from career advancement. More recently, a task force of the Twentieth Century Fund, a New York-based public policy organization, has also called for sharply cutting back on political appointees.

and Reagan proved, Congress and the executive branch can accomplish major changes in the way government is run.

Misunderstanding Competing Theories of Government Management. The permanent government resists serious change because, in the end, they are fighting for their pay, their generous benefits, and their jobs. But it is a profound mistake to view the recurring struggle between agents of change and Washington's permanent government as merely a struggle over pay or power. Like most political struggles, this conflict also exists on a higher level. The apologists of the permanent government, regardless of their partisan affiliation, are animated by a well-established theory of government administration, the public administration or scientific management model. Historically, it is identified most closely with Presidents Woodrow Wilson and Herbert Hoover. This model emphasizes the Progressive ideal of following a value-free, scientific program that can be technically derived by neutral career public officials adhering to objective management and policy principles. It relies upon career officials to lead the political appointees, including the President, by teaching them the scientific solution residing within the wisdom of the expert civil service and then engineering the solution into a program of action. Theory determines practice. In spite of America's democratic political tradition, many senior career officials in government and their allies in academia really believe in this ideal.

Indeed, this public administration model of government administration is now the norm. It has dominated discussion of government reform since the rise of the modern administrative state—especially since President Franklin D. Roosevelt's New Deal in the 1930s. Professor Wilson of Princeton University brought the new administrative theory, learned from his studies in Germany and Great Britain, to the academy in the United States, where it provided the vision with which the new welfare state could be managed. Wilson believed the separation of powers was "manifestly a radical defect in our federal system that it parcels out power and confuses responsibility." His solution was to centralize power in the national government and, particularly, in the hands of the presidency. The presidency was to be staffed by the nation's top experts, who would determine the proper "scientific" answer for the nation's problems. With the exception of a hiatus under President Dwight D. Eisenhower, the administrative model remained unchallenged until the presidencies of Jimmy Carter and, especially, Ronald Reagan.

Policymakers in Congress, as well as the Administration, should be guided in their efforts by an alternative model of government administration: the cabinet government or political administration model. Advocated in recent years by Presidents Eisenhower, Carter, and Reagan, this model was the norm for presidential government throughout most of American history. It emphasizes political responsibility—providing presidential leadership to committed top political officials and then holding them and their subordinates personally accountable for achievement of the President's election-endorsed and value-defined program. These Cabinet and sub-Cabinet officials then suffuse this program throughout the labyrinth of a bureaucracy often resistant to change.

President Clinton has followed neither approach. Evidently lacking any clear conception of government administration, the Clinton Administration seems to be lurching from a "high-spoils" approach (a crude version of the political management model epitomized by firing of long-time employees in the White House travel office and the use of a political trickster to head the office of personnel security) to turning the Administration over to federal labor unions in the President's October 1993 executive order (a bizarre distortion of "public administration" giving de facto daily management and policymaking authority of federal agencies to labor-management councils). Although Clinton's reduction in the federal workforce has been substantial, two-thirds of that number is attributable to downsizing of the Department of Defense, reflecting the end of the Cold War rather than his "reinventing government" initiative, as Robert J. Samuelson noted in an article on "Bumper Sticker Politics" in *The Washington Post* on September 25, 1996. Worse, the vaunted Clinton management reforms have done little to downsize the bite on the taxpayer. Total federal spending is $189 billion more in 1996 than in 1992, a 14 percent increase. More important, since 1993 the number of civilian Full Time Equivalent positions (FTEs) has declined by 11 percent, but the total cost of the civilian workforce has increased by 4.5 percent, from $111 billion to $115 billion.[4]

---

4 Scott Hodge, "Reinvention Has Not Ended the 'Era of Big Government,'" Heritage Foundation *Backgrounder* No. 1095, October 15, 1996, p. 6.

LESSONS LEARNED

Congress and the Administration can draw on an ample supply of historical experience for why reform is not only necessary, but very possible. Since the Hoover Commission of 1947 and World War II, numerous blue ribbon panels have been assembled to find ways to streamline or downsize the federal government, but their impact has been disappointing. Joseph A. Califano, Secretary of the Department of Health, Education and Welfare (HEW) under President Carter, remarked in *Governing America: An Insider's Report from the White House and the Cabinet:*[5]

> The key commissions of the 1960's and the 1970's that had studied government organization —groups chaired by Ben Heineman, Sr., for Lyndon Johnson and Roy Ash and John Connally for Richard Nixon—had recommended essentially the same structure: consolidation, fewer departments and no Department of Education.

By building on initiatives embodied in these commissions, the Civil Service Reform Act of 1978, and on the experience of the Reagan Administration in attempting to implement it, supporters of reform can learn from the successes and failures, mistakes and missed opportunities of the Reagan, Bush, and Clinton presidencies. For Congress this will mean making legislative decisions to advance the cause of a smaller and limited government and not merely reshuffling, reorganizing, or "reinventing" government agencies and programs. For executive branch officials it means making proposals for legal changes early. If contemplating administrative changes, if existing law allows, they should "just do it." Delay is a deadly enemy of change. Proponents of reform in Congress should recognize that real change is worth it, and they must be prepared to fight a series of continuing battles with the representatives of the permanent government.

---

5 Joseph A. Califano Jr., *Governing America: An Insider's Report from the White House and the Cabinet* (New York: Simon and Shuster, 1981), p. 278.

LESSONS LEARNED

- To reform the federal bureaucracy, Congress must insist on clear accountability and the crucial distinction between career and non-career employees and functions.

- Political appointments should be made in a timely fashion.

- Political appointees must be in charge of policy.

- There must be a clear rationale for reducing the size of the federal workforce and making management changes.

- Key management decisions should not be delegated to the career bureaucracy.

- The Civil Service Reform Act of 1978 can be used to improve management and accountability.

- Good management and contracting out services can save the taxpayers billions of dollars.

- Federal workforce reduction should be planned and implemented in a systematic fashion.

- In reforming the Civil Service Retirement System and other federal employee benefits programs, Congress must be prepared to use the congressional budget process as the way to get serious changes enacted into law.

Lesson #1: For successful reform of the civil service bureaucracy, it is important to insist on clear accountability and the crucial distinction between career and non-career employees and functions. The failure to understand or appreciate the distinct functions of career and political appointees is a recurrent source of pain and embarrassment for executive branch officials. For a recent example of this, advocates of reform need look back no further than the continuing controversy over the Clinton Administration's so-called Travelgate affair—the circumstances surrounding the abrupt firing of seven long-established employees in the White House travel office. The FBI was misused to investigate, and the Department of Justice to indict, the employees. We still do not know all of the facts surrounding this scandal. We do know that a friend of the

President and First Lady wished to provide air services to the White House media, and the President's cousin was poised to run the whole operation from the Executive Office of the President.

Commenting on an early internal Administration report on Travelgate, veteran political columnist David Broder wrote in an article in *The Washington Post:*[6]

> The report can be commended for candor. But what it revealed was a saga so shoddy, so saturated with petty manipulations, snooping and spying, rampant cronyism and tacky deceits that it made you cringe. It also confirmed an abuse of the FBI's role—in summoning agents into a situation without even so much as a by-your-leave to the attorney general, and then pressuring them for action—that it made you wonder if anyone on that young staff had learned the hard-earned lesson of Watergate.

Mr. Broder's observation preceded the court decision that exonerated travel office chief Billy R. Dale from any wrongdoing. It is still not known exactly what motivated the series of actions called "Travelgate." The false charges against Dale look as if they were contrived to cover the fact that he was fired for political reasons, possibly under orders from Hillary Rodham Clinton. Yet there was no reason for this apparent suborning of justice. No one has a right to hold a job in the White House; since the travel office is within the White House, its occupants are not formally subject to civil service hiring or protection procedures. But from the very beginning, the Clinton White House team did not openly claim the right to appoint its own people to this office. Contrast this with the actions of the Reagan Administration, which early in the President's first term made it clear that it would use its right to do so even in far more sensitive inspector general positions charged with investigating waste, fraud, and abuse in federal agencies. Instead, the Clinton team actually encouraged the remarkable view that the only legitimate reason for decisive action regarding personnel in a White House office is corruption.

---

6 David Broder, "Talk Is Not Enough," *The Washington Post*, July 14, 1993.

Thus, the long-time occupants of the White House travel office were not removed according to the assumed—and legitimate—right of a new Administration to bring in its own people. That apparently sounded too Reaganesque, so the claim was circulated that widespread corruption existed in the financial affairs of the travel office. Although the motives for the action are not known, it is clear that personnel not involved in financial matters were dismissed with the rest. It is also known that politically important friends of the President and his wife had asked for such changes previously, and that several employees subsequently were returned to duty. And, of course, it is clear that an innocent, long-serving federal manager was falsely accused of engaging in criminal acts. Even so, the underlying problem was that there was no personnel theory at all—unless it was simple spoils—guiding any of these personnel decisions.

Another garish example was the appointment of Craig Livingstone as head of personnel security at the White House. This position, too, can be filled properly by a political appointee, yet it does not appear that any previous administration had filled such a sensitive position with so partisan a person. Livingstone, after all, was a low-level political operative who dressed in costumes to ridicule opponents and who has been accused of "dirty tricks" in a Democratic nomination contest. Was it prudent to appoint such a person to a job that included reading sensitive FBI personnel files? As it turned out, Livingstone had secured at least 900 FBI files of past Republican White House appointees, a fact that, once discovered, raised great outcries of invaded privacy and possible political abuse, and that caused major political damage to the President. In House hearings on June 26, 1996, Livingstone was forced to resign. Here was a position best filled by a career functionary who could handle this sensitive information in a professional manner, but apparently no one at the White House considered this basic tenet of personnel policy.

During the Reagan Administration, one of the principles of Reagan management that agency heads found to be the most difficult to follow was his insistence on a clear dividing line between political and career functions, so that each was respected. This policy was neither brazenly political nor mindlessly bureaucratic, but a balance of both political and bureaucratic missions. At least during his first term, Reagan's Administration team was comfortable justifying the role of political appointees as leaders and protecting the Chief Executive's appointment authority against congressional attempts to usurp or subvert that right. As a result, the Administration was also comfortable in limiting job shifts to the career service by political appointees.

Nonetheless, Reagan's Office of Personnel Management (OPM) periodically came under great pressure from various quarters to politicize the career service by allowing political appointees to convert to career civil service status. This happens in every Administration, Democrat or Republican. But the OPM generally was successful in limiting this in the first term, arguing that it was proper to create more political positions and respect the professional autonomy of the career service. The prevailing view in the OPM at this time was that once a political appointee received career protection, he or she became more often a careerist in outlook, with new institutional loyalties to the permanent government and less interest in presidential objectives. This Reagan management philosophy promoted the Administration's policy agenda while reinforcing sound administrative principles.

This has not been the policy of the Clinton Administration. So-called careering-in abuses at the Consumer Product Safety Commission (CPSC) and the Pension Benefit Guarantee Corporation (PBGC) led Civil Service Subcommittee Chairman John Mica to request in July 1996 that the General Accounting Office (GAO) probe 50 agencies. Instances include a former law school classmate of Hillary Rodham Clinton who transferred from a career position to a political one at the PBGC but who remained as a career official. And at CPSC, the sister of President Clinton's former campaign manager apparently tailored a career job for a politically connected former assistant to a Democratic Congresswoman.

In addition to fostering these abuses, the Clinton Administration agreed to federal union demands to weaken the Hatch Act prohibition on political activity by career employees, creating a major breach in the division between career and non-career status by politicizing careerists. Career civil servants are permitted to become more politically involved in partisan political campaigns. As they do, they will become subject to increased political pressure from unions and politically active supervisors. The likelihood increases, too, that political careerists will be tempted to use government power more often to threaten clients. (Some, such as the regulators of business, could be very threatening indeed.) Finally, political appointees will be attracted to "careering-in" for their own protection without losing their ability to act politically. This is why career associations, like the National Academy of Public Administration, have opposed such changes.

Lesson #2: Political appointments should be made in a timely fashion. While the White House was expending enormous energy and political capital on filling minor positions in the small travel office, peering into hundreds of FBI files, and politicizing career positions and laws, the Clinton Administration was, incredibly, leaving the management of the most important government agencies in the hands of permanent career officers. For example, *New Yorker* columnist Sidney Blumenthal reported in June 1993 that "Bruce Lindsey, Clinton's close friend and constant companion, has been sentenced to the personnel office, where piles of resumes literally towered to the ceiling and sometimes fell over. Lindsey would slowly send appointments up to Clinton who would roll many of them back down." The result of this situation became evident in long vacancies in key policymaking political jobs.

Because vacancies in appointments give more power to career officials, this approach might be adequate in the parliamentary systems of Europe. There the career-dominated models of government permit very few political positions below the cabinet ministers. Likewise, one could square it within the framework of the American political tradition if Clinton were consciously following Wilson or Hoover and trying to restructure the U.S. government along those lines. But in not following a consistent model at all, an Administration is set adrift, stumbling on policy, maladroit on the selection of key individuals, frequently crossing the line between political and career officialdom, and confusing on the basic function of hiring and dismissing career personnel.[7]

---

7 The consequences for policy without political appointee oversight were painfully evident at the Department of Justice during the series of Clinton White House delays in filling the Attorney General's position. In response to inquiries on the Department's 1993 budgetary and legislative agenda, the Department "issued a sparse one page statement that listed three initiatives, all of which had already been proposed. There was little indication of any change in priorities. Meanwhile, other agencies held news briefings to discuss their spending plans." Joe Davidson, "With Its Highest Positions Yet Unfilled, Justice Department Remains in Disarray," *The Wall Street Journal*, February 24, 1993.

The first step for a new Administration is to adopt one of the two standard administration models and focus resources toward implementing that standard in managing its operations. For conservatives, the choice is easy: The Administration should follow President Reagan's example.

Lesson #3: Political appointees must be in charge of policy. Political appointees are an integral part of an effective Administration. Even the temporary absence of political appointees who can speak authoritatively for the Administration can be a source of frustration for Members of Congress who are trying to hammer out the details of legislation without clear communications on sensitive matters of public policy.

Examples are numerous. During the spring of 1982, Reagan's team at the OPM had been locked in tough and tedious negotiations with Democratic House and Republican Senate staff on legislation to establish permanent "alternative work schedules," or flexible working hours, for federal employees. Although both the Reagan Administration and the federal employee unions favored extension of "flextime" to the entire workforce, the Administration insisted on management's rights to direct the program. During negotiations, the legal authority for the temporary flextime program was likely to expire, and House and Senate leaders sought a temporary extension to continue the program while OPM and congressional staff hammered out a final compromise bill. Senior career staff at the Office of Management and Budget (OMB), insulated from Hill negotiations and therefore utterly ignorant of the political dynamics, flatly opposed such a simple extension and declared that a "hang tough" posture would force congressional capitulation at the conference table.

Having soundly beaten House Democrats in a previous floor vote, the Reagan team at the OPM knew very well that this threat was politically silly. When notified of the OMB's instructions, House Republicans, including some of President Reagan's strongest allies, were enraged and told Reagan's team at the OPM that there would be no Republican leadership support on the floor for such an inflexible position, which guaranteed a political embarrassment for the White House. Only at the very last minute, as the temporary extension provision was literally heading for a full debate on the floor of the House, was the OPM's political leadership able to override OMB career staff and reverse an official position, just hours before the floor vote. This gave both the

Reagan Administration and Congress the breathing space they needed to complete negotiations on a permanent authorization for the flextime program. The final compromise bill embodied the management rights provisions upon which the Reagan Administration insisted.

Only the American Federation of Government Employees (AFGE) opposed the flextime bill on final passage because its leadership found the management rights provisions so repugnant. For the Reagan Administration, it was a good outcome. But it could have been consummated more easily and without an unnecessary loss of congressional goodwill if the process had been left entirely in the hands of the political leadership responsible for settling the issue.

Congress always should give consideration to the views of senior career officials on technical matters of administration and take advantage of their impressive institutional memory, except on matters of Administration policy, in which the most politically sensitive questions are sure to arise. For example, following the terrorist bombing of the World Trade Center in New York City in 1993, Representative Romano Mazzolli (D-KY), a member of the House Judiciary Committee, was frustrated in trying to refashion federal policy on the admission of aliens into the United States because the Clinton Administration kept sending over career staff who represented the Immigration and Naturalization Service (INS) but who could not speak authoritatively for the Administration. Seeking commitments from senior career officials who cannot or will not speak on behalf of the policy agenda of the Administration is a waste of valuable time.

Lesson #4: A clear rationale must be set forth for reducing the size of the federal workforce and making management changes. Reforming bureaucracy has been a major stated goal of every recent Administration. Yet only two, those of Eisenhower and Reagan (in the case of the non-defense sector), actually achieved any significant reductions in its numbers *and* successfully imposed their managerial leadership upon the bureaucracy. These Administrations were successful because they used such broad-scale management tools as eliminating personnel along with entire functions of government, setting reduction targets and monitoring them, and focusing upon political responsibility. They did not try to use scientifically engineered efficiencies at the margins of agencies. President Clinton decided to use a micro-planning approach highlighting "engineering" as the means for his National Performance Review—his so-called reinvention of government, which in terms of managerial results was not as productive.

The Political Responsibility Model. The rationale used by the Reagan Administration in creating management efficiencies and reducing the size of the workforce was a clear understanding of cabinet government and the political responsibility model of administration. The President set the policy, while the politically appointed Cabinet members and their subordinate officers were to implement it, all in accord with the President's mandate expressed in the election. Under this model, the government is managed at the top by the President and his political officials, who, in turn, work through career senior executives to direct the staff of the career civil service. The focus is on people and managing personnel.

To understand how this management model works, it is important first to understand how the federal government is organized. There are several key groups within the federal bureaucracy that should be differentiated whenever analysts, politicians, and the media discuss reducing the civil service workforce. When reporting federal civilian employment figures, the media routinely include the independent Postal Service—which is not directly managed by the President—in their government employment totals. Journalists also do not distinguish between defense civilian employment (which President Reagan, for example, wanted to expand to win the Cold War) and domestic non-defense civilian personnel (which Reagan planned to cut). Rarely are political and career officials separately identified. Such clarity, however, is essential because the civilian personnel system is immensely complex. As pictured in Chart 6.1, it has many discrete elements.

The Reagan Administration began its tenure by focusing upon the appointment of the top presidential and non-career appointees because Reagan understood how critical these were for its success. The Administration focused on training and support for its senior political appointees in its first, second, and fourth levels to give them the management tools they would need to perform successfully. In a major series of reports on the bureaucracy at the time, *Washington Post* reporter Paul Taylor noted, "The Reagan Administration has moved more aggressively, more systematically, and more successfully than any in

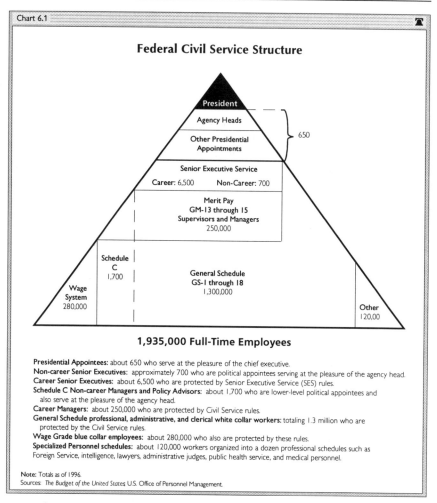

Chart 6.1

Federal Civil Service Structure

President

Agency Heads

Other Presidential Appointments

650

Senior Executive Service
Career: 6,500   Non-Career: 700

Merit Pay
GM-13 through 15
Supervisors and Managers
250,000

Schedule C
1,700

General Schedule
GS-1 through 18
1,300,000

Wage System
280,000

Other
120,00

1,935,000 Full-Time Employees

Presidential Appointees: about 650 who serve at the pleasure of the chief executive.
Non-career Senior Executives: approximately 700 who are political appointees serving at the pleasure of the agency head.
Career Senior Executives: about 6,500 who are protected by Senior Executive Service (SES) rules.
Schedule C Non-career Managers and Policy Advisors: about 1,700 who are lower-level political appointees and also serve at the pleasure of the agency head.
Career Managers: about 250,000 who are protected by Civil Service rules.
General Schedule professional, administrative, and clerical white collar workers: totaling 1.3 million who are protected by the Civil Service rules.
Wage Grade blue collar employees: about 280,000 who also are protected by these rules.
Specialized Personnel schedules: about 120,000 workers organized into a dozen professional schedules such as Foreign Service, intelligence, lawyers, administrative judges, public health service, and medical personnel.

Note: Totals as of 1996.
Sources: *The Budget of the United States* U.S. Office of Personnel Management.

modern times to assert its policy control over the top levels of the bureaucracy."

The Clinton Administration provides a dramatic contrast in personnel management. President Clinton frittered away critical months by focusing on the ethnic and gender diversity of his appointments, delaying them, and contributing directly to the lack of strong agency management during his first two years. There was nearly universal criticism for

Clinton's management of the executive branch during those two years. Unfortunately, he had not consistently followed a model for personnel management.

In reducing the size of the career government, the two administrations took different paths as well. The Reagan Administration set the goal of reducing domestic government employment by 75,000 FTEs, and it set targets for each operating agency to meet. Throughout the period it monitored the progress of agencies through a new, monthly personnel accounting process. At the end of Reagan's first term, Reagan's Administration had achieved its goal because the President rallied support from his own top political management, his Cabinet officers, and his sub-Cabinet management team.

By the time the Clinton Administration took office, the monthly accounting system no longer existed, and personnel reductions were driven by the budget. In the first two years of Clinton's term, 97 percent of the reductions came from defense as a direct result of the downsizing policies set under his predecessor, George Bush. In the past two years (1995–1996) most reductions in non-defense personnel were forced by the decisions of the Republican-led Congress on federal spending. Indeed, pressure exerted by the 104th Congress reduced the number of federal employees at 29 of 39 major government agencies.

To summarize, the Reagan reductions in the bureaucracy were planned by pre-set personnel goals, whereas Clinton reductions largely were achieved by the pressure of external forces. President Reagan, in his first term, obtained almost precisely the domestic reductions he targeted. President Clinton's "reinventing government" through the National Performance Review (NPR), of course, had little effect upon the personnel reductions that were made. In fact, of the 1,203 original NPR action items specified to make the government work better and cost less, the GAO found that, by January 1996, only 294, or 24 percent, had been completed. Although President Clinton had done his best to protect his favorite domestic welfare agencies, he basically was propelled by events and circumstances beyond his control to make reductions.

For proponents of reform, again the lesson is to learn from the Reagan years: Plan, encourage, and monitor the progress in personnel reductions through a chain of political leaders placed throughout the government.

Lesson #5: Key management decisions must not be delegated to the career bureaucracy. Government management does not have the private-sector luxury of using bottom-line profit-and-loss statements to measure success. Government budget figures tell only what was spent last year, not whether the program or its staff were successful (e.g., made a "profit"). In government, the only real replacement for a private-sector, financial statement form of management is personnel management. In government, this inevitably becomes political personnel management. An effective career force is essential, but it cannot be led without strong political managers. Indeed, political appointees in the top positions can make or break any Administration.

Managing and leading people is what efficient government is all about, even more so in the sprawling national bureaucracy. Although President Carter was successful in passing the Civil Service Reform Act of 1978, which implemented this principle, he tended to rely too much on the Executive Office of the President and viewed management too much like managing a small state from the governor's mansion, or an engineering problem to be solved by tools retained from an earlier occupation. Although the White House Office must play a central role in planning, it would be more effective if it delegated the effort to a leaner Executive Office staff and if "line-function" Cabinet and major agency heads were included more in the top management team. Placing trusted political appointees who are dedicated to the President, rather than to their own personal or narrow agency agendas, throughout the bureaus of government is the secret to controlling both the management and policy processes.

This in turn means that the Office of Presidential Personnel (OPP) must make appointment decisions upon loyalty first and expertise second, and that the whole governmental apparatus must be managed from this perspective. Picking appointees who are "best for the job" merely in terms of expert qualifications can be disastrous for an Administration genuinely committed to change, because the best qualified are already in the career positions and are part of the status quo, the permanent government. Yet cabinet government is not simply a spoils system, either, so expertise cannot be ignored. If the Reagan Administration failed on a few early appointments based upon the loyalty criteria, the Clinton team tended to fail on expertise.

The Office of Personnel Management is the central federal agency managing the federal workforce, and it must play a critical part in developing a team, managing the Senior Executive Service, and overseeing Schedule C positioning. Because political appointees are so critical to an Administration's success, they need special attention: They need presidential access, though limited depending upon rank and importance; they must receive special training in political responsibility for the tasks and agencies they are to manage; and they must be exempted from actions otherwise affecting the personnel process, such as hiring freezes. In return, they will be better able to manage the morass that lies below them.

Presidents Carter and Reagan fought to give political executives the tools they needed to manage the bureaucracy. For a few short years it worked. More was accomplished with less, and measures of productivity increased, as personnel were cut. Yet decisions of both Presidents Bush and Clinton removed essential management tools from the very political executives that were the focus of the Carter reforms and, in Clinton's case, actually sought to transfer management authority to a new entity called labor-management councils.

Clinton's decision to use collective-like councils (even if they are not union-dominated) will weaken the direct political-to-career management link that is essential to the cabinet model of government. It will strengthen, however, the permanent government. Incredibly, conservatives in the 104th Congress, perhaps motivated more by political hostility to the President than by a commitment to increase the power of career staff, proposed cutting the already tiny number of executive branch political appointees—which would weaken not only the President's control over the execution of his policy agenda, but also his overall management of the government. Advocates of reform in the 105th Congress and the Administration should realize that reducing the number of political appointees to weaken political control has been a long-sought goal not only of unions, but of the career manager-dominated American Society of Public Administration (ASPA) as well.

It is political appointees, in the end, who must be held accountable. It is expecting too much of subordinate career executives and union leaders to make difficult and always politically sensitive decisions about such issues as pay, hiring, firing, and performance ratings independent of political executives who represent the President as the Clinton Administration has proposed. Only political appointees, because their rewards come directly from the President and not from the system, have any incentive to resist the dominant cultural pressures and make tough decisions. Without such political leadership, when the President gives an order, there is no reason to assume anything would happen down the line in the bureaucracy. For this reason, all of the responsibility must rest with the political agency head.

Turning control of these management decisions over to unions makes even less sense. Unions exist entirely to get more for their members in an environment in which the public demands less. To the extent President Clinton's plan shifts power to the labor-dominated councils, "reinventing government" will prove to be simply a political gift to the federal unions. In a perverse way, however, the Clinton Administration recommendation acknowledges that responsibility should lie with the agency head. Its proposal gives decision-making power to the labor-management councils, but it also recommends that recourse for abuses committed upon employees should be taken against the political agency head. There is no ignoring the fact that democratic government, at some level, must place responsibility in the hands of political appointees who represent the elected executive.

President Carter's management reforms recognized this and moved the responsibility down the management chain to successively lower-level political executives, then to career executives and managers, and finally down to the level where the work was performed. All were bound together by a performance appraisal and performance reward system which rewarded those who successfully enacted the policies set by the President within the laws of Congress. Although employee work groups and organizations can be useful in some situations, and employee input and needs must be considered by management, effective government management requires strong agency leadership communicated through successive subordinate officials. To the degree a mission is simplified, the easier leadership becomes. The reforms implemented by the Reagan Administration were based upon a management theory appropriate to the organizational reality of government. Leadership, simplicity of mission and work, and political responsibility were the essence of this reality.

Labor-management councils, in fact, are rare enough in a private sector that uses the bottom line to limit their abuse. The Clinton proposal is untested; and the federal workforce is too important to be used as guinea pigs in this kind of management experiment in a government that has no profit-and-loss bottom line. The Administration should return to the principles of the Carter-Reagan reforms and make them work, using intelligent and dedicated leadership and sound management principles.

Lesson #6: The Civil Service Reform Act should be used to improve management and accountability. The Civil Service Reform Act of 1978 (CSRA) applied sound principles of performance management to the daily workings of the federal government. Central to this law is Title 5, U.S. Code 2301(b), which requires that "recruitment, selection, and promotion" are to be determined "solely" on the basis of "relative ability, knowledge and skills"; that "appropriate incentives" are to be provided to encourage "excellence in performance"; and that "employees should be retained on the basis of their performance."

Backed by the Carter statute, the Reagan Administration created a comprehensive and standardized employee performance appraisal system, tightened employee discipline systems, implemented a merit pay system for managers and executives, and increased flexibility in assignments of the Senior Executive Service. The Reagan Administration wanted to expand these reforms from the executive ranks to establish a direct link between pay and all monetary awards and performance, and to eliminate the automatic nature of within-grade pay increases, for all General Schedule employees. Reagan attempted to increase the role of performance as the basis of employee retention in reduction-in-force efforts in federal agencies too, to extend the performance principle throughout the entire work force.

President Carter had prepared the way. He was elected on a platform promising to reform the bureaucracy, and he did. President Carter did not tell anyone that he had fulfilled his promise to reform the bureaucracy, however, and what this success meant. He did not highlight his accomplishments, even to his own managers, and thus he received only the negative news generated in the media by the unions and others who opposed his efforts. So the CSRA yielded few tangible results under Carter; to a great degree, time simply ran out on his term. But from day one, Reagan and his team used the tools of the CSRA, and they kept the issue of reducing the size of the government while increasing its efficiency firmly in the daily news, generating countervailing support from a public that praised their efforts.

President Clinton's National Performance Review supports performance in principle, yet it devolves control over government systems to the agencies and unions, and therefore to the very entities which historically have resisted directly linking performance and accountability. More important, the Administration responsible for issuing the NPR is itself going in a different direction. This is discernible in three areas: the Federal Employee Performance Appraisal System, reduction-in-force procedures, and merit pay.

The Federal Employee Performance Appraisal System. Performance appraisal means nothing if it is not, in the words of David Osborne, celebrated author of *Reinventing Government*, tied directly to "real consequences" for success or failure. Before the enactment of the CSRA, performance appraisal in the federal system used a three-tiered rating system in which 99 percent of federal employees received a "satisfactory" rating at the middle range of performance. The Carter Administration, realizing this was meaningless, created a five-step performance appraisal system, which rated job performance as "outstanding," "exceeds fully successful," "successful," "below successful" (needing improvement), and "unsuccessful." The Reagan Administration enforced this new system, spreading the ratings over at least four of these categories so that performance levels could be distinguished more clearly and rewards distributed accordingly, even if relatively few were actually rated unsuccessful and fired for poor performance.

Instead of strengthening this performance appraisal system, the Clinton Administration's OPM aggressively encouraged agencies to adopt a two-level, pass-fail system. This is even more primitive than the federal employee appraisal system that was scrapped by President Carter, and it effectively would end any serious appraisal of job performance in the federal workforce. If work is not even appraised, it is not possible to reward those who perform it best (which could not be considered a victory for anyone except, possibly, the permanent government).

Reduction-in-Force Procedures. Reduction-in-force (RIF) procedures are the rules for laying off federal employees. Historically, one of the biggest federal management problems has been the policy of laying off federal workers with little consideration given to how well they perform.

Four factors govern the decision to lay off federal workers: tenure, veterans preference, seniority, and performance. The main goal of the Reagan Administration, amid strong opposition from federal employee unions and their allies in Congress, was to upgrade the role of performance relative to seniority, enforcing the legal principle that employees should be retained on the basis of performance. After months of negotiation with interested parties, regulations were issued, only to be blocked by an appropriations rider added in the Democratic House blocking reform in the following years. Indeed, an unfortunate byproduct of the Clinton OPM guidance supporting a pass-fail system was to further lessen the role of performance relative to seniority in RIF procedures. The result is that it is now even easier for top performers to be laid off during agency consolidations or reductions in force. This result is hardly consistent with improving efficiency or providing positive consequences for good performance in the federal workforce.

In September 1996, the Civil Service Subcommittee of the House of Representatives again proposed bills to increase modestly the weight given to performance and to expand veterans preference, but given the predictable unity of federal managers and federal unions on the issue of performance ratings, and the Clinton Administration's unwillingness to give support to this measure, it is no surprise that these bills died in the Senate. A number of key Senators who remained anonymous were opposed to giving more weight to performance and to increased veterans preferences, and another victory by the permanent government was secured.

Merit pay. According to a 1994 survey of major U.S. companies, 90 percent used a system of merit pay for performance.[8] This is not the case in the federal government. While the Clinton Administration lobbied furiously to get its huge tax and budget package through the 103rd Congress, Representative Eleanor Holmes Norton (D-DC) sponsored a provision in the legislation that would eliminate all bonuses and cash

---

8 Robert J. Samuelson, *The Good Life and Its Discontents: The American Dream in The Age of Entitlement, 1945-1995* (New York: Random House, 1995), p. 120.

awards for good performance among federal employees. "As soon as I heard that [incentive bonuses] were gone," said a bewildered and shocked Vice President Gore, "I said 'that's ridiculous. That's not going to happen.'" Although it did not happen in that budget bill, the entire pay-for-performance system created by Carter in the CSRA in 1978 and implemented by Reagan in 1981 for the managerial corps has been effectively eliminated nonetheless.

After implementing merit pay for executives and managers, beginning in the summer of 1982, the Reagan team at the OPM entered 18 months of negotiations with House and Senate staff on extending merit pay to the entire workforce. Long and detailed talks between the OPM and Democrats and Republicans in Congress ensued, and a final agreement was reached in 1983 that supposedly assured passage of legislation creating a new Performance Management and Recognition System (PMRS) for all GS-13 through GS-15 employees. Meanwhile, the OPM issued regulations to expand the role of performance throughout the entire workforce. But congressional allies of the permanent government, led by Representative Steny Hoyer (D-MD), stoutly resisted this extension of pay-for-performance and, with strong union support, blocked OPM administrative pay reforms through the congressional appropriations process.

But it got worse. The original merit pay system for federal managers (GM 13–15 grade levels) expired on September 30, 1993. The Bush Administration did nothing. And, to date, nothing has been done by the Clinton Administration to reinstitute the federal merit pay program for managers or to extend one to the remainder of the workforce. This must be considered a resounding victory for the permanent government.

President Clinton's NPR proposes decentralizing decisions like performance management, merit pay, pay classification, merit hiring, and management leadership rights and giving authority for those decisions to the agency bureaucracies that are at the heart of the problem. The President, instead, should stoutly champion his right to manage the executive branch, to make performance appraisal meaningful, to protect better performers during reductions in force, and to reward better performers with higher pay. Instead, President Clinton is eliminating the central role of individual performance in making personnel decisions. The President also should direct the OPM to make performance once again the center of its personnel reward system, teaching entrepreneurial attitudes and executing the other management reform policies initiated by Presidents Reagan and Carter.

Lesson #7: Good management and contracting out can save the taxpayers billions of dollars.[9] Even with some modest declines in personnel over the years, the federal bureaucracy with its duplicated functions and programs is still a bloated target for management and budgetary reform. Personnel costs (wages and benefits for 1995) equal 18 percent of total domestic spending, and other administrative overhead adds roughly 4 percent more. With expenditures for management so large, even minor efficiency gains will translate into big savings.

If management theory is correct that performance-based management yields more efficient and better work with fewer staff, that pay based upon performance results in greater productivity, and that central oversight of agency operations with decentralized decision making by line managers uses resources more efficiently, then even a 1 percent efficiency gain on payroll cost would total more than $1 billion a year in savings. Federal retirement alone accounts for a little more than 4 percent of all domestic spending. While tougher options are possible, simply limiting the federal retiree cost of living (COLA) increases to the dollar amount available to persons enrolled in the Social Security system, as The Heritage Foundation has suggested, would make it possible to save $729 million in the first year and $5.2 billion over five years.

Contracting out federal functions to the private sector will have an even greater effect. Virtually no one outside of the federal government, including the representatives of the Clinton Administration, thinks the comparability measurements between federal and private-sector pay scales are accurate. The permanent government supports existing comparability measurements because they suggest, against all common sense, that federal workers are grossly underpaid.

During the Reagan Administration, the OPM conducted an independent study in the 1980s and found that federal pay was in fact about 11 percent above that for comparable jobs in the private sector. If one uses that estimate today, contracting out the work conducted by only

---

9 See Chapter 4, "Transferring Functions to the Private Sector."

half of the existing federal employment could reduce expenditures by $5.6 billion per year. Reagan's OPM also estimated pension benefit costs, in its most conservative estimate, as 4.3 percent of payroll higher than the private sector. Using that estimate, if contractors were paid the private pension rate, the government could save an additional $2.2 billion per year.

In adopting the policy of contracting out as a management strategy, proponents of reform in Congress will have to address practical questions regarding separation costs. This would argue for a more gradual implementation of outsourcing and that contracting savings would be slightly offset by higher pay for the higher-skilled contract managers who would remain in the government. Nonetheless, the OPM studies conducted in the 1980s give some idea of the sizable permanent savings to the taxpayers available from personnel reductions. As the number of personnel is cut, other overhead reductions are produced. For example, reduction of space used in overpriced federal buildings and facilities alone would result in billions of dollars more in savings to the taxpayer.

If one goes beyond personnel into the programs and functions performed, even greater savings are possible. After carefully taking out the effects of interest payments and savings and loan bailout costs, Heritage Foundation scholars Scott Hodge and Robert Rector have shown that the domestic spending Reagan targeted declined from 14.8 percent of gross domestic product to 12.2 percent under his initiatives. Cato Institute scholar Stephen Moore documents that the growth rate of real government spending under Reagan was one-third that of the next closest Administration since World War II. The Republican-controlled 104th Congress went even further. When the 1996 budget process came to a close, it had made real cuts in discretionary spending. All told it eliminated 270 federal programs, agencies, offices, and projects, and helped to reduce the deficit to the lowest levels since 1982. Still more would have been accomplished had President Clinton not vetoed the earlier congressional budgets.

The 1996 Republican platform proposed to eliminate the Departments of Commerce, Housing and Urban Development, Education, and Energy. It promised the elimination, defunding, or privatization of agencies that have become obsolete or redundant, or are of limited value, such as the National Endowment for the Arts and Humanities, the

Corporation for Public Broadcasting, and the Legal Services Corporation. 1996 Republican presidential candidate Robert Dole said these major governmental changes only require political will, but a sound personnel and administrative plan already in place would help assure Congress and the public that the $110 billion in savings Mr. Dole targeted actually could be realized.

Lesson #8: Federal workforce reduction should be planned and implemented in a systematic fashion. Cutting federal jobs is difficult. It is also probably inevitable. Even the Clinton budget shows that as many as 100,000 positions should be cut in the next four years. The unions and managerial associations will protest vigorously. The career managers will resist having fewer subordinates to spread the work and build their empires. And political appointees will try desperately to avoid the hard decisions that attract unwarranted press attention. The good news is that it can be done in a rational and systematic fashion—President Reagan showed how.

Then-Governor Reagan promised during the 1980 presidential election to reduce the size of the bureaucracy. Once in office he clarified his goal to decrease non-defense FTE personnel by 75,000. Table 6.1 shows that between 1981 and the end of the Reagan's first term in 1984, non-defense federal FTE employment went down by 78,650, thereby exceeding his goal. The decrease in number of employees, the "head count," actually was 105,484. Significantly, about 90 percent of the decrease had been achieved by the end of the first year. Early, bold, and determined action (in the form of a total freeze on hiring followed later by a more flexible, managed freeze and rigorous monitoring) allowed the target to be achieved.

By the end of Reagan's second term, non-defense employment totals had nearly edged back to the levels under Jimmy Carter. The problem was that the energy generated in the first term largely had dissipated and clear plans and goals were not set, so the natural forces of bureaucratic growth reasserted themselves. The reductions achieved in the core Great Society agencies generally held firm, but personnel grew in agencies that had received less presidential attention.

Although the two Reagan terms are instructive in their different ways, so is the presidency of his successor in the White House. President Bush said he, too, would cut the bureaucracy, but he never made clear

Table 6.1

Federal Personnel Staffing from 1981-1996

Agency	Employment, Carter End 1981	Employment, Reagan 1st 1984	Employment, Bush Beginning 1990	Employment, Bush End 1993	Employment, Clinton 1996	Change, Reagan 1st 1981-84	Change, Reagan-Bush 1981-93	Change, Clinton 1993-96	Total Change, 1981-96
Non-Defense	1,163,646	1,084,996	1,169,370	1,187,929	1,134,900	-78,650	24,283	-53,028	-28,746
Civilian Military	937,700	1,011,532	1,021,163	931,800	800,000	73,832	-5,900	-131,800	-137,700
Total Civilian	2,101,346	2,096,528	2,190,533	2,119,729	1,934,900	-4,818	18,383	-184,828	-166,446
Agriculture	121,000	108,986	110,755	111,021	105,500	-12,014	-9,979	-5,221	-15,500
AID	5,616	5,115	4,526	4,454	3,400	-501	-1,162	-1,054	-2,216
Commerce	36,347	32,305	34,858	36,682	35,200	-4,402	335	-1,482	-1,147
Corps of Engineers	32,330	28,681	28,259	27,444	27,600	-3,649	-4,886	156	-4,730
Education	6,634	5,025	4,596	5,032	4,800	-1,609	-1,602	232	-1,834
Energy	18,675	16,708	16,815	19,960	19,700	-1,967	1,285	260	1,025
EPA	12,861	11,412	15,155	17,917	18,100	-1,149	5,056	183	5,239
Gen. Services Admin.	32,758	25,572	19,447	19,858	16,200	-7,186	-12,900	-3,658	-16,558
HHS/SSA	154,000	136,969	117,817	125,704	123,600	-17,031	-28,296	-2,104	-30,400
Labor	21,647	18,577	18,050	18,265	16,700	-3,070	-3,383	-1,565	-4,947
NASA	22,727	22,080	23,829	24,947	21,800	-647	2,220	-3,147	-927
Nuclear Reg. Comm.	3,448	3,441	3,188	3,377	3,200	-7	-71	-177	-248
HUD	15,703	12,437	13,264	13,837	11,900	-3,266	-1,866	-1,937	-3,803
Interior	81,747	73,245	71,233	74,000	70,500	-8,229	-7,747	-3,500	-11,247
Justice	54,422	58,244	79,082	97,968	106,300	3,822	43,546	8,332	51,878
Office of Pers. Man.	7,133	5,710	5,702	6,158	4,000	-1,423	-975	-2,158	-3,033
Panama Canal	9,138	8,137	8,293	8,603	9,000	-1,001	-535	397	-138
Small Business Admin.	4,704	4,238	5,316	4,637	4,300	-466	-67	-337	-404
State	22,887	24,139	25,633	26,012	23,700	1,252	2,925	-2,312	813
Transportation	68,055	61,130	64,863	70,212	63,900	-6,925	2,157	-6,312	-4,155
Treasury	124,264	123,155	155,931	161,964	153,300	-1,109	36,700	-8,664	29,034
Tenn. Valley Authority	44,752	31,952	23,716	23,000	16,400	-12,800	-21,752	-6,600	-28,352
USIA	7,636	8,167	8,598	8,679	7,300	531	1,043	-1,379	-336
Veterans	209,575	218,545	214,040	221,518	223,700	8,970	11,943	2,182	14,125
Other	45,587	41,414	43,506	57,382	50,300	-4,173	11,795	-7,082	-4,587

Note: Figures are for Fiscal Years. All figures reflect full time equivalent (FTE) employment. Clinton 1996 figures are based on Office of Personnel Management estimates.

Sources: The Budget of the United States; U.S. Office of Personnel Management.

beforehand what programs were to be targeted, even in the general terms of the second Reagan Administration. Nor did he detail plans specifying how or to what degree this should be accomplished after he entered office. Consequently, the domestic bureaucracy under President Bush actually increased 24,283 (more if budget sleights of hand are corrected) during his term. Conversely, through congressional pressure and to a great degree against Bush's desires, uniformed military personnel declined and civilian military employment decreased by 5,900.

Clearly, the largest personnel reductions have been made under President Clinton, but most of the cuts had already been set in motion before his term. The Federal Restructuring Act of 1994 sets a target of 272,900 FTE reductions by the year 2000. By the end of Fiscal Year 1996, 75 percent of the projected reductions will have been taken out of the Department of Defense. Non-defense employment will have been reduced by only 4 percent. If President Clinton had been given his way on national health care reform, the bureaucracy would have ballooned under his watch. After all, the Clinton plan would have added at least 59 new specialized agencies, bureaus, offices, panels, and related staff.

Personnel Reduction Patterns. Table 6.1, in outlining the personnel reductions, shows the different patterns that evolved during the conservative Reagan, the more moderate Bush, and the congressionally pressured Clinton Administrations. There are actually five patterns:

> **Pattern #1:** Both Reagan and Bush were tough on foreign aid (the Agency for International Development), government engineering projects (the Corps of Engineers and the Tennessee Valley Authority), Education, the General Services Administration, Health and Human Services, and the Small Business Administration.

> **Pattern #2:** Although Reagan was significantly tougher on a second set of agencies (Agriculture, Housing and Urban Development, Interior, Labor, Office of Personnel Management, and the Panama Canal Commission), the Bush Administration held up reasonably well, too.

> **Pattern #3:** Both Administrations weakened in the face of the Departments of Justice, Veterans Affairs, and State, and the United States Information Agency, presumably because of

historic Republican support of law and order and veterans issues, and upholding the flag abroad.

Pattern #4: Presidents Reagan and Bush differed the most over the regulatory agencies. Bush seemingly just could not say no—whether at the Environmental Protection Agency, in major Cabinet departments (for example, when it came to Treasury tax agents, who were perversely added to the budget as "savings" to increase revenues, or to Commerce and Energy overseers), or in independent ("other") regulatory bodies.

Pattern #5: The Clinton Administration presented a very different pattern. Defense accounted for 71 percent of the 184,829 FTE personnel reductions in the civilian workforce from the last Bush year of 1993 to 1996, most of these targeted before Clinton entered office. When the 9,100 FTE representing bank examiners and liquidators no longer required for the completed savings and loan cleanup are included, 76 percent of Clinton's reductions are accounted for. Otherwise, the reductions looked much like the two Republican administrations in Patterns 1, 2, and 3, except that agencies hit hard by both Reagan and Bush, such as the Department of Education and the Department of Health and Human Services, or by Reagan alone, such as the EPA, were somewhat protected from further large reductions. The fact that Republican favorites like the Departments of Justice and Veterans Affairs showed the only significant growth and that Great Society programs were not increased shows the Republican Congress had more to do with the domestic pattern than the President.

Even with 53,029 Clinton non-defense cuts, domestic bureaucracy was still 49,904 higher than the 1984 low point under President Reagan. Much had grown back under President Bush and a Democratic Congress. By the end of 1996, non-defense employment was only 28,746 below the point at which Reagan began. Although the Republican 104th Congress clearly tried to restore the Reagan pattern, the reverses of the Bush years could only begin to be corrected. It would take adoption of Congress's vetoed 1995 balanced budget plan to return to the employment levels of 1984. President Clinton went further than President Bush in reducing the domestic bureaucracy, but he clearly was forced in that direction by a

Republican Congress dedicated to cutting domestic federal spending. Nevertheless, Clinton did minimize the personnel cuts for some of his protected favorites. It is only President Reagan who met the bureaucracy reduction targets he actually planned. He did it by setting his goals early, monitoring progress, and achieving the targets before the affected interests coalesced. That must be the model for any future Administration wishing to reduce the size of bureaucracy or "end the era of big government" as both political parties now profess to desire.

Lesson #9: In reforming the Civil Service Retirement System and other federal employee benefits programs, Congress must be prepared to use the congressional budget process as the way to get serious changes enacted into law. *Washington Post* cartoonist Herblock calls federal retirement the government's sacred cow of entitlement programs. Members of Congress, congressional employees, federal employees and annuitants, and many of Washington's power elite who gained access to the retirement system earlier in life fight to the death to preserve their very generous benefits. This means that a meat-ax occasionally will be better than a scalpel. Because liberals in Congress, as well as conservatives and moderates with large federal employee constituencies, always will present obstacles to serious changes in the committees having jurisdiction over federal personnel programs, advocates of reform must be prepared to make fundamental changes rather than simple business-as-usual decisions chipping away at the margins.

The political opposition, especially on Capitol Hill, to any such changes always will be ferocious. In 1994, Representative Tim Penny (D-MN) criticized federal pensions and their total cost, including the unfunded liability that reached $1.1 trillion at the end of Fiscal Year 1992. In response, the Federal Government Service Task Force, a caucus of 56 Members of Congress, commissioned the Congressional Research Service (CRS) to refute the Congressman's charges. Covered under the very same federal pension system, the CRS proved happy to do so, noting that it is unseemly to be concerned about the unfunded liability of the federal pension system because the federal government is not going to disappear and thus payments on the liabilities are not going to be due all at once. Translation: This is not a problem, because the taxpayers will simply foot the extra bills.

Of course, federal pensions are far more generous than typical private-sector pension plans. Compared with their private-sector counterparts, federal employees retire earlier and enjoy automatic COLAs and a richer pension annuity. A federal employee with a pre-retirement income of $25,000 under the older of the two federal retirement plans would receive at least $200,000 more over a 20-year period than a person with the same pre-retirement salary in the private sector. The Reagan Administration tried both an incremental reform strategy and the strategy of creating a whole new retirement system to emulate private-sector plans more fairly. On the whole, the blunt meat-ax approach was more successful.

During the Reagan years, many specific provisions of the pension program were reformed, generating considerable savings. Federal pensions are fully indexed for inflation, a practice that is extremely rare in the private sector. In the 1970s, the cost of these adjustments was compounded by paying the index twice per year. A provision called "look back" allowed a retiring employee to receive the previous year's COLA in addition to his immediate pension, and a 1 percent "kicker" on top of that. The twice-a-year, look-back, and kicker were all removed in 1981 as part of the Reagan budget package. The Reagan Administration also reduced an excessive 32 percent rate of disability retirement by 58 percent without significant complaints, and saved $1.2 billion in the process. An additional $2 billion was saved through a large number of small changes in the formula used to compute the benefit. Every change resulted in very strong reactions from the retirees, the career workforce, Members of Congress, and congressional staff, their powerful allies. Significant, although limited, savings were made, but the political costs were steep.

The major change in the federal civil service retirement system was a byproduct of the 1984 fundamental revision of the Social Security laws. When federal employees were required to pay Social Security taxes, a whole new federal retirement system became mandatory. This permitted a real reform. The cost under the old Civil Service Retirement System (CSRS) of 51.3 percent of payroll (including disbursements for unfunded liability) was reduced to 28.5 percent of payroll (including Social Security contributions and the employer match to the Thrift Savings Plan) under the new Federal Employees Retirement System (FERS). More of the costs were shifted to employees, but the system was made more portable, allowing participating employees to keep more of their funds if they did not stay in government until retirement. This was a major advantage to the 40 percent of employees who received few or no benefits under the old system because they left before retiring. By 1995, 46.8 percent of employees were under the new system, and the government's costs as employer were cut by more than half (21.5 percent of FERS payroll vs. 44.3 percent of CSRS payroll). Over the long run, the change to the new system will save scores of billions of dollars.

STRATEGIES FOR DOWNSIZING AND IMPROVING THE FEDERAL CIVIL SERVICE

In downsizing government and improving the federal civil service, proponents of reform should not inadvertently make matters worse. As the Clinton Administration was forced to meet its promised personnel reductions, it decided to meet as many as possible through early retirement. When it announced its plan to buy out personnel reductions with early retirement, normal retirements went down from 42,000 to 28,000 in one year. Why retire now if the government will pay a bonus to retire next year? Over the fiscal years 1993 to 1995, 110,000 buyouts—at an average cost of $24,500 each—were made at a total cost of $2.8 billion. Fifty percent were already eligible to retire, and another 22 percent were eligible for early retirement without paying a bonus. This is such poor personnel policy, and so very costly to the Treasury and the pension system, that it can be seen only as a political payment to the labor unions so they would not publicly object to the reductions, which—in a first for unions facing personnel cuts—they did not.

STRATEGY #1
If Congress sets up another commission for cutting federal agencies, make sure there is the political will to staff it correctly and to follow through with its recommendations.

Understandably, advocates of reform in Congress will be tempted to establish yet another bipartisan commission on the reorganization of the federal government. The argument for such a commission is that a comprehensive approach, with a take-it-or-leave-it ("base closure") feature, is superior to a piecemeal approach to eliminating or reducing

---

STRATEGIES FOR DOWNSIZING
AND IMPROVING THE FEDERAL CIVIL SERVICE

- If another commission for cutting federal agencies is set up, the political will must exist to staff it correctly and follow through with its recommendations.

- The duplication of federal programs and functions must be ended.

- Public support must be built for a new and modernized federal personnel system.

- Support must be built among federal workers and the public for market-based reform and portability of federal retirement benefits.

- The core-spoke-rim model should be promoted as the ideal for federal employment.

- Public support must be built for restoring merit principles to federal hiring procedures.

- Public support must be built for market-based reform of the federal pay system, with oversight by the Office of Personnel Management.

- The Administration should take managerial control of the government back from the federal bureaucracy.

---

the size of Cabinet departments, agencies, or bureaus. Reformers should beware that, with only notable exceptions, in Washington the major function of a commission is to avoid making decisions and to delay action on tough problems. That is one of the reasons they are so popular. Moreover, as Secretary Joseph Califano has noted, the most serious recommendations of these commissions are largely ignored.

Government reform, like tax reform, is a perennial feature of the political scene. It is also a perennial failure of American politics. For such a reorganization commission to succeed, it would have to be staffed with persons who have expertise in government management and the civil service system and yet have no personal or political interest in the preservation of the pay scales, perks, or positions of the permanent government. The President would need to appoint his own key policy people to such a commission, set rigorous deadlines, adopt its recommendations to reduce the size and scope of government as his own policies, and invest the requisite political capital early in his first term to get the job done. Otherwise the new commission is likely to go the way of its predecessors.

STRATEGY #2
Congress must end the duplication of federal programs and functions.

Taxpayers are understandably bewildered by the size and cost of the federal government. The Government Performance and Results Act of 1993, for example, requires all federal agencies to define their mission, establish goals and objectives, and measure and report their performance. This is akin to asking affected career employees to draft a "mission statement with a future." Congress, not the bureaucracy, should be setting agency goals and drafting agency mission statements. Instead of waiting for federal agencies to justify their existence—although a worthwhile exercise—proponents of reform in Congress should order the GAO to identify every office of the federal government with a program budget, beginning with the departments and federal agencies and continuing downward through the sub-Cabinet agencies and into every division and unit of the federal government. The quality of congressional oversight would be improved mightily if Congress got a printout describing every unit of government that has a finance officer, plus a description, in plain English, of the mission or the goals of every unit in every division within every department or agency. If reformers are serious about making rational personnel reductions, they do not need a commission. They should determine what functions the federal government ought to perform, what should be turned over to the states or local jurisdictions, what should be privatized, and what should be terminated altogether. In the meantime, they can start eliminating the duplication of functions and clarifying the roles and responsibilities of federal agencies and departments.

STRATEGY #3
Congress and the Administration should work to build public support for a new and modernized federal personnel system.

Civil service reform is not a sexy issue. Therefore, generating broad public support for "good government" initiatives is likely to be difficult, considering the general public's short attention span, which is supported by mass media that like to report on conflict or scandal rather than the substance of policy. Nonetheless, it can be done. President Reagan seized the public relations offensive by firing federal air traffic controllers union members who, he emphasized, had broken their oaths and gone on strike in disregard of the interests of the general public. President Reagan defined the issue, and the public clearly supported him. President Clinton, likewise, staged events in which huge volumes of rules and regulations were wheeled out onto the south lawn of the White House to demonstrate the need to "reinvent government."

Policymakers in Congress and the Administration should follow President Clinton's example and call attention to absurdities in existing federal personnel and management rules and practices that defy common sense. At the same time, advocates of reform should pursue a "high road" campaign for government reform that focuses on the need to spend taxpayer dollars wisely and improve the efficiency and effectiveness of government service.

STRATEGY #4
Conservatives in Congress should build support among federal workers and the public for market-based reform and portability of federal retirement benefits.

It is paradoxical that the components of the federal benefit system that work best and are most popular among federal workers are driven largely by market forces of consumer choice and competition rather than bureaucratic micromanagement. In the Federal Employees Health Benefits Program, for example, federal workers and their families can choose from almost 400 private plans nationwide, offering a wide variety of benefits at competitive premiums. In 1997, according to the OPM, average total premiums will rise by only 2.4 percent.

Although incremental reform of the CSRS need not be abandoned, pursuing a more fundamental reform of the federal retirement system is likely to prove more fruitful. For the future, the more promising alternative is to create a third, fully portable and individually directed system based upon 401(k) private plans, much like those found in the private sector, where the employee is fully vested and can move assets right from the beginning. A fully portable plan removes the major impediment to employee mobility and would facilitate future workforce restructuring. Such a plan, fully paid for by the government with no employee contribution, would be more valuable in attracting new people into government employment and less costly to the taxpayer. Contributions could be invested in indexed common stock funds to generate higher rates of return than Treasury bonds. In 1995, for example, the common stock fund in the Thrift Savings Plan of the FERS program yielded federal employees a dramatic 37.41 percent gain.[10] Reformers should dramatize the tangible benefits of a portable new system, including returns on private-sector investments, for both employees and the taxpayers.

STRATEGY #5
Policymakers in Washington should promote a core-spoke-rim model as the ideal for federal employment.

Congress and the Administration should promote the value of a new "core, spoke, and rim" organizational model of government. A core federal government workforce would consist of expert, highly compensated individuals serving as executives and managers and implementing the federal programs by managing the contractors who would perform the great majority of the work on the "rim" of government. This approach would build upon current experience.

Contractors are already a predominant part of the work provided by national government. Perhaps as many as 8 million contractor employees dwarf the 2 million federal civilian employees. Millions of state government employees also implement numerous federal rules. No one knows with absolute certainty the total number of employees involved in performing federal work. The problem is that the federal government is still organized as if it were functioning in the 1930s, when federal civilian employees performed all the work and federal managers tried to direct it all.

---

10 The "F" fund, another private mutual fund option for federal employees, saw an 18.31 percent gain. The "G" fund, investments in government securities, had a modest 7.03 percent performance. See *The Federal Employees News Digest*, Vol. 45, No. 23 (January 22, 1996), p. 1.

In between the core federal civil service and the rim of the expanded contractor work force, temporary employees would make up the "spokes" in such a model. Temporary employees could be used to take up increases in workload demand whenever more core work is generated than the basic workforce could fulfill.

Such a model puts a premium on flexibility, just as it does in the private sector, and gives federal agencies and programs an opportunity to staff up and staff down as the needs arise. This is where the Clinton "reinventing government" reforms go most astray. Rather than increase flexibility, they further bureaucratize the existing system with their partnership councils, an additional level of labor-management involvement. They propose to decentralize functions further down the management chain, making them less accountable. They propose to enhance protections for formerly temporary employees. They also propose to divide central management authorities, duplicating work in each agency.

For the new core workforce, the OPM should be ordered to transmit to Congress a compensation system built on performance that rewards program savings and timely mission accomplishment as directed by the President. The new federal classification system should be broad-banded to allow agency flexibility in paying employees, but under tight OPM supervision to counteract the inevitable tendency of agencies (shown in the demonstration studies already conducted) to inflate compensation schedules. Although input from employees and even unions is helpful, final decision making on mission accomplishment made by top agency management must be a central requirement within the overall framework of the President's priorities.

STRATEGY #6
Congress should work to build public support for restoring merit principles to federal hiring procedures.

Because a higher quality of permanent employee is required by the core-and-rim staffing system, it is important that employee selection based upon knowledge, skills, and abilities is restored. Congress should initiate hearings on the status of merit selection in the current system and what is being done to improve it. The OPM should immediately seek to end the sweetheart consent decree, entered into during the last days of the Carter Administration, that abolished its Professional and Administrative Career Examination (PACE), which was used to select superior college graduates for government employment. The decree—which was to last only five years—already has allowed the federal courts to control hiring for 15 years.

There is a sound reason to centralize hiring. General ability tests such as PACE are better in selecting qualified individuals than are any of the separate tests for particular occupations, and they are more cost-effective as well. The reason courts have ruled otherwise is that some minorities, on average, achieve lower scores on these generalized exams (the so-called disparate impact) than non-minorities. Certainly, an argument could be made for some temporary remedial affirmative action, but to be denied an entry examination for 15 years deserves some notice and redress. The courts have agreed to review the decree if the Uniform Guidelines on Selection Procedures are reformed. Advocates of reform in Congress should accept this challenge and return federal hiring to merit selection based on the knowledge, skills, and abilities of the applicants.

Just as the law requires hiring to be based upon skills, it also calls for retention and reward based upon good performance. The unions oppose performance-based retention and favor seniority. On September 25, 1996, the House of Representatives voted on H.R. 3841, the Omnibus Civil Service Reform Act of 1996. Although it received 228 votes, it failed to reach the two-thirds support needed for passage under suspension of the House rules. The bill failed because of union opposition to a section specifically increasing the weight given to employee performance or when conducting reductions in force. A statement of opposition was circulated on the floor of the House that spells it out succinctly: "The American Federation of Government Employees, the National Treasury Employees Union, and the National Federation of Federal Employees all oppose the bill because of the section giving greater weight to subjective performance ratings and less weight to seniority in deciding which Federal workers are laid-off when an agency shrinks."

The Federal Managers Association also opposed the bill, and the Senior Executives Association failed to endorse it. The Clinton reforms promoting pass-fail performance effectively achieve the union goals. Indeed, the apparent purpose of much of the Clinton personnel reforms is to shift totally to labor-management control and away from political oversight. The likelihood that such a system will lead to higher standards of performance and more action against poor performers is *nil*. Unions just do not thrive being tough on employee performance or discipline. True labor reform would amount to eliminating the expensive and duplicative labor grievance apparatus and reestablishing a true merit system. Indeed, an expert core workforce will depend on and therefore demand strong merit-based hiring, open to all and stressing the skills of the applicants.

The Clinton reforms propose placing greater reliance on labor-management committees, and would duplicate the examining function, classification function, and performance management support in every agency of the government, at much greater total cost. Oversight would be left to the unions and lower levels of management. The OPM has been shown to be a more cost-effective and objective alternative, with selections costing $10 to $15 less per applicant than agency systems. The more efficient, responsible, and cost-effective alternative for the federal workforce is a core-spoke-rim model structure based on the principles of the Civil Service Reform Act of 1978.

STRATEGY #7
Congress and the Administration should build public support for market-based reform of the federal pay system, with oversight by the OPM.

Ordinary taxpayers' wages are determined by the market, which relies on the normal interaction of supply and demand. Although the official government pay comparability studies claim that federal employees are underpaid by over 30 percent relative to other workers in the private sector, all other indications are that the national government actually overpays employees relative to the private sector or state government. In the first place, federal "quit rates" are much lower than in the private sector. Where private-sector rates range between 10 percent and 25 percent (depending upon the industry), federal turnover never has exceeded 7 percent. After employees vest in the retirement system, virtually no one leaves, as reflected by annual quit rates of below 3 percent.

Second, whenever federal vacancies are announced widely, the lines of those seeking federal government work are staggering. Not too long ago, an announcement for a few dozen blue-collar jobs generated a queue of 3,000 applicants. Even jobs announced with limited publicity generate ten applicants for every vacant position. Although the OPM's independent study conducted in the 1980s found that the federal government paid 11 percent more than the private sector, attempts to reform the pay system and to change the comparability study have failed. Political pressure from employees and unions and Members of Congress who defend their interests has so far prevailed.

The obvious solution is to move closer to a market model for federal pay. A smaller core workforce is the start of a reformed pay system. With more work contracted out to the private sector, the market will set at least those wages directly. With fewer remaining positions, a rational pay system will be easier to implement and administer. A rationalized pension plan would further limit compensation distortions. But the need for a neutral agency to oversee pay decisions becomes even greater. The central Office of Personnel Management has the knowledge of various agency operations which is needed to assess true requirements in the federal workplace. For many years, through its Special Pay Rates program, the OPM has determined when existing pay was inadequate to meet the agency requirements, and it used its authority sparingly to set pay rates when that was warranted.

The OPM should establish an initial pay rate for each occupation and region of the country and adjust it up or down based upon quit rates and applicant-to-position ratios necessary to attract the right people. Agencies should set job qualification requirements, subject to the OPM review, to assure a quality workforce. Knowledge, skills, and ability (KSA) tests should be used to hire the best candidates from the applicant pool. Although the process should be well advertised and open to all, selection must be based upon the KSAs of the applicants.

For the system to operate, Congress must not micromanage the process. If they do, it simply will not work. The OPM must be allowed the flexibility to set real pay rates, based upon the market realities of supply and demand. If Congress cannot resist getting involved, the only other solution is to fully privatize every federal function possible or devolve them to the states and live with the current irrational system for the rest.

STRATEGY #8
The Administration should take the managerial control of government back from the bureaucracy.

President Clinton has promised to "reinvent" government to make it efficient and responsive. His sweeping plans to reform management and increase efficiency, however, conflict with his promise to government unions to involve them in every level of decision making. President Clinton, for obvious political reasons, has made labor's support of reform a high priority, and it is unnatural to expect unions to support real management reforms that do not involve union bargaining. Nor will they favor personnel reductions that cut into their membership base. Still, in a *Washington Post* article entitled "Reorganization Report Goes to Clinton Today" by Stephen Barr on September 7, 1993, Vice President Al Gore insisted that employee involvement "has made all the difference" between the Clinton Administration's efforts and all previous efforts at reform. President Clinton reportedly has bragged even to the AFL-CIO leadership that his federal sector reforms were "unprecedented."[11]

In fact, NPR recommendations, taken as a whole, are a significant shift away from the personnel management philosophy of President Carter's Civil Service Reform Act and its implementation under President Reagan. President Carter stoutly resisted union involvement in management decisions, despite threats by labor allies in Congress to derail his reform legislation. And both the Carter and Reagan Administrations consistently and vigorously defended management rights before the Federal Labor Relations Authority (FLRA).

Besides resisting union encroachment in management decisions, Presidents Carter and Reagan gave great support to building incentives that reward individual civil servants for good work. To be sure, they did support allowing bureaus to retain the money saved from management improvements—so-called innovation funds—as a reward for unit efficiencies, but not to the exclusion of individual rewards for productivity gains. Under President Clinton, however, authority for both programs is to be decentralized to the agencies themselves, where they

---

11 Stephen Barr, "Organizing for Empowerment," *The Washington Post*, October 13, 1993, p. A19.

can be expected to wither because the agencies historically have opposed them.

The NPR recommendation to devolve personnel hiring further to the agencies is even stranger because most hiring was decentralized already under the Carter and Reagan reforms. Simplification of how work is classified in the government has been a goal of all recent Administrations. But to give the agencies unsupervised power over such classification —which ultimately determines pay—is not only novel, but an invitation to abuse, especially when combined with a policy of more union involvement.

Decentralizing management and personnel policy works in the private sector because there is a financial bottom line against which to measure the success or failure of the decentralization efforts. But that is not the case in government. Moreover, decentralizing an Administration from the center to the agencies takes management and political leadership from top political executives, especially the President, and transfers it to the career bureau managers and, in the case of the Clinton Administration, to the unions as well. That makes it extremely difficult for an Administration to assure that agencies either carry out broad policy or operate efficiently. These Clinton proposals effectively will shift decision making to the permanent government deep within the bureaucracy.

If President Clinton were siding consciously and consistently with the public administration management philosophy embodied by Woodrow Wilson and Herbert Hoover, it at least would be a rational and understandable approach. Instead, he is seemingly bereft of an understandable governing rationale or philosophy of government management. By deferring to the unions, presumably for raw political purposes, he has departed from all coherent models for public administration. If the purpose is to turn management over to partnership councils—and his executive order of October 1, 1993, suggests it is—President Clinton at least should explain and defend this radical course of action to Congress.

The inevitable result of such a course would be to make government itself unaccountable. Unions are, at best, responsible to their members. At worst, they represent the permanent government acting on its own interests rather than the desires of the electorate. Placing decision making in the hands of the career bureaucracy puts the interests of the permanent government first. Democratic government is supposed to put the interests of the people first, as those interests are expressed through the electoral process. The people direct the government and its bureaucracy through the Congress and the President. The President, especially, is expected to press his program through the lowest levels of the executive branch to enact his popular mandate. His subordinates are tasked with enacting the President's program—not bargaining with labor unions or independent career officials over what should be done.

The first act of the President should be to revoke the executive order establishing labor partnership councils. If that is not feasible, Congress should use an appropriation rider to deny use of funds for further implementation. Then the President and Congress should return to the tested cabinet government principles established with such hard work on a bipartisan basis by Presidents Carter and Reagan—and make them work. They have been proven to be effective when they receive the proper commitment from the Chief Executive and his political subordinates. The people deserve to have a responsive government which only a hierarchical cabinet government can deliver.

CONCLUSION

Politicians running for office often promise constituents that they are going to change the way Washington works. Delivering on that promise when the subject is federal personnel management turns out to be a much tougher task. Yet if Congress or the Administration pursue only modest reforms in federal management or simply back away from the task altogether, it should not be assumed that nothing will happen. In the absence of planned and determined action, powerful congressional and bureaucratic interests will step in to define the civil service agenda for them.

Advocates of reform in Congress are capable of changing the way Washington works. They must do so by heeding the solid lessons of both the Carter and Reagan Administrations, basing their reforms on the twin foundations of political responsibility and performance management, emphasizing managerial accountability and making sure that job performance has consequences. At the same time, they must maintain the bright line between career and non-career positions and functions, support the proper roles of each, and avoid blurring the distinctions or confusing these roles, which will be a guaranteed invitation to scandal or embarrassment to the President. Because further federal workforce reductions are almost inevitable, they should be managed carefully by the Administration and its Office of Personnel Management, with strong congressional oversight. Finally, as has been done with other entitlement programs, reformers should not hesitate to use both legislation and the congressional budget process to get significant changes in the federal benefits program. It has been done before; it can be done again.

In creating a smaller and leaner federal government for the 21st century, Congress is tasked with building broad public support for comprehensive reform, redefining the roles and functions of the federal government, ending duplication of functions and programs, and introducing more efficiency into its organization, staffing, pay and benefits structure. Advocates of reform can argue such a case, not only to the general public, but also to new federal employees, a class of civil servants who will staff the core workforce of the federal government, serving in well-compensated jobs with portable benefits not unlike those available in the best private corporations. Moreover, such a 21st century workforce will appreciate the premium put on performance and accountability, and applaud the restoration of merit principles in hiring and retention. With a more efficient and effective federal government, America's taxpayers will be well served.

Chapter 7

REINING IN THE
FEDERAL JUDICIARY

Edwin Meese III and Rhett DeHart

America's Founding Fathers created a democratic republic in which
elected representatives were to decide the important issues of the
day. The role of the judiciary, while vitally important to the
Framers, was to interpret and clarify the law—not to make law itself. The
Framers recognized the necessity of judicial restraint and the dangers of
judicial activism. James Madison wrote in *The Federalist* No. 48 that to
combine the judicial power with that of executive and legislative authority
was "the very definition of tyranny," while Thomas Jefferson believed that
allowing only the unelected judiciary to interpret the Constitution would
result in judicial supremacy. "It is a very dangerous doctrine to consider the
judges as the ultimate arbiters of all constitutional questions," wrote
Jefferson. "It is one which would place us under the despotism of an
oligarchy."[1]

Unfortunately, the federal judiciary has strayed far beyond its proper
functions, in many ways validating Jefferson's warnings about judicial
power. In no other democracy in the world do unelected judges decide as
many vital political issues as they do in the United States. If the federal
government is to be returned to its proper role, the federal judiciary must
first be returned to its appropriate role.

---

1 "Letter to William Jarvis in 1820," *The Writings of Thomas Jefferson*, ed. Paul Leicester
Ford, 10 vols. (New York: G. P. Putnam's Sons, 1892-1899).

The Proper Role for the Federal Judiciary: Interpretation

Under the modern doctrine of judicial review, the federal judiciary can invalidate any state or federal law or policy it considers inconsistent with the Constitution. This doctrine gives the federal judiciary awesome power. When unelected federal judges exceed their constitutional role of interpretation and impute their personal views and prejudices into the Constitution, the judiciary becomes simultaneously the most undemocratic and the most powerful branch of government.

It is important to remember how difficult it is to reverse or amend federal court decisions. When a Supreme Court decision is based on the Constitution, the decision usually cannot be reversed or altered except by a constitutional amendment. Such constitutional decisions are virtually immune from presidential vetoes or congressional legislation. Abraham Lincoln warned of this in his *First Inaugural Address* when he wrote:

> [T]he candid citizen must confess that if the policy
> of the government, upon vital questions, affecting
> the whole people, is to be irrevocably fixed by
> decisions of the Supreme Court... the people will
> have ceased to be their own rulers, having, to that
> extent, practically resigned their government into
> the hands of that eminent tribunal.

Unfortunately, because the past four decades have been marked by instances of rampant judicial activism, many of the most important political issues in the United States have been usurped by the federal judiciary. When the most important social and moral issues are removed from the democratic process and decided by unelected judges, citizenship suffers because people lose the political experience and moral education that come from resolving difficult issues and reaching a social consensus. In the swearing-in ceremonies for Chief Justice William H. Rehnquist and Associate Justice Antonin Scalia, President Ronald Reagan explained how judicial activism is incompatible with popular government:

> The Founding Fathers were clear on this issue. For
> them, the question involved in judicial restraint
> was not—as it is not—will we have liberal courts
> or conservative courts? They knew that the courts,
> like the Constitution itself, must not be liberal or

conservative. *The question was and is, will we have government by the people?* [Emphasis added.]

When federal judges exceed their proper interpretative role, the result is not only constitutional infidelity, but, as the following section shows, very often poor public policy.

Judicial Excesses

There are numerous cases that illustrate the consequences of judicial activism and the negative effect it has had on our society. Activist court decisions have had an adverse impact on nearly every aspect of public policy. Among the most egregious examples are:

- **Imposing** racial preferences and quotas;

- **Creating** a "right" to public welfare assistance;

- **Weakening** criminal procedures;

- **Lowering** hiring standards;

- **Interfering** in state legislative reapportionment;

- **"Discovering"** a right to an abortion;

- **Overturning** state referenda.

Imposing racial preferences and quotas. In *United Steelworkers of America v. Weber*, 443 U.S. 193 (1979), the Supreme Court held for the first time that the Civil Rights Act of 1964 permits private employers to establish racial preferences and quotas in employment, despite the clear language of the statute that states: "It shall be an unlawful employment practice for any employer... to discriminate against any individual because of his race, color, religion, sex, or national origin...." Critics contend that had the *Weber* decision turned out differently, racial preferences in the private sector would not exist in the United States today. The *Weber* decision is a classic example of how unelected government employees and federal judges have distorted our civil rights laws from a color-blind ideal to a complex and unfair system of racial and ethnic preferences and quotas that perpetuate bias and discrimination.

Creating a "right" to public welfare assistance. In addressing social welfare, the Supreme Court, in *Goldberg v. Kelly*, 397 U.S. 254 (1970), created the idea that welfare entitlements are a form of "property" under the Fourteenth Amendment, and therefore welfare recipients are entitled to an extensive and costly hearing process before benefits can be terminated on the grounds that the individual is not eligible. The Supreme Court turned a charitable benefit into a "right" that enables a welfare recipient fraudulently to receive benefits during the lengthy legal proceedings without even having to reimburse the government when the lack of eligibility is confirmed. The result has been thousands of welfare workers tied up in hearings and less money available for the truly needy. For example, by 1974, a staff of 3,000 was needed to conduct the *Goldberg* hearings in New York City alone.

Weakening criminal procedures. In a revolutionary change in criminal procedure that began with the case of *Mapp v. Ohio*, 367 U.S. 643 (1961), the Supreme Court imposed a new national requirement on state courts by requiring the exclusion from criminal cases of any evidence found to be the result of an "unreasonable" search or seizure. In so holding, the Supreme Court overruled a previous case, *Wolf v. Colorado*, 338 U.S. 25 (1949), which had allowed each state to devise its own methods to deter unreasonable searches and seizures. In doing so, the Supreme Court acted like a legislature rather than a judicial body. As a dissenting justice stated, the *Mapp* decision invalidly infringed upon the states' sovereign judicial systems and forced on them one federal procedural remedy that was ill-suited to serve states with "their own peculiar problems in criminal law enforcement."[2]

A major criticism against the *Mapp* decision is that nothing in the Fourth Amendment or any other provision of the Constitution mentions the exclusion of evidence; nor does the legislative history of the Constitution indicate that the Framers intended to require such exclusion. Experts have argued that there are many other remedies that will deter police misconduct without acquitting criminals, such as civil lawsuits against reckless government officials and internal police sanctions such as fines and demotions.

Since *Mapp v. Ohio*, the exclusionary rule has had a devastating impact on law enforcement in the United States. One recent study estimated that

---

2   367 U.S. 681 (1961).

150,000 criminal cases, including 30,000 cases of violence, are dropped or dismissed every year because the exclusionary rule excluded valid, probative evidence needed for prosecution.

Five years later, in *Miranda v. Arizona,* 384 U.S. 436 (1966), the Supreme Court determined new rules for the admissibility of confessions in all criminal trials in the United States and again radically changed the criminal procedure of every state and the federal government. Specifically, the Supreme Court ruled that the admissibility of statements obtained during police questioning was now to be limited by the Fifth Amendment's prohibition against compelled self-incrimination, which previously had been held to apply only to testimonial evidence in court proceedings. This led to the requirement that suspects must be warned of the right to remain silent, that anything they say can be used against them in a court of law, and so forth. This was a dramatic change from the numerous prior decisions that already excluded involuntary statements or confessions in which the "totality of the circumstances," rather than arbitrary requirements, were used to determine whether a defendant had "free choice to admit, to deny, or to refuse to answer."

The dissenting justices argued that the *Miranda* rules would discourage confessions and severely impede criminal investigations, and that the decision was a "deliberate calculus to prevent interrogations, to reduce the incidence of confessions and pleas of guilty and to increase the number of trials."[3] One dissenting justice predicted that "in some unknown number of cases the Court's rule will return a killer, a rapist or other criminal to the streets and to the environment which produced him, to repeat his crime whenever it pleases him."[4] This proved to be prophetic. It is estimated that each year *Miranda* results in over 100,000 criminal cases, including 28,000 violent cases, that cannot be prosecuted successfully because of these court-created rules.

Lowering hiring standards. In *Griggs v. Duke Power Co.,* 401 U.S. 424 (1971), the lawsuit challenged a company's requirement of a high school diploma and a general aptitude test as a condition of employment. Specifically, the suit argued that because the diploma and test requirements

---

3 384 U.S. 541 (1966).

4 *Id.* at 542.

disqualified a disproportionate number of minorities, those requirements were unlawful under the Civil Rights Act of 1964 unless shown to be related to the particular job in question.

The Supreme Court ruled that, under the Civil Rights Act of 1964, employment requirements that disproportionately exclude minorities must be shown to be related to job performance, despite the employer's argument that the diploma and testing requirements were implemented to improve the overall quality of the work force. Moreover, the Supreme Court held that "Congress has placed on the employer the burden of showing that any given requirement must have a manifest relationship to the employment in question."[5]

Critics of the *Griggs* decision note that nowhere in the Civil Rights Act of 1964 does it state that an employer must show that a neutral employment requirement has a "demonstrable relationship"[6] to the job in question. Also, critics note that under §703(h) of the act, an employer is explicitly authorized to use aptitude tests of the sort the employer used in *Griggs*. The *Griggs* case has lowered the quality of the U.S. workforce by making it difficult for employers to require high school diplomas and impose other neutral job requirements. It also forced employers to adopt racial quotas in order to avoid the expense of defending hiring practices that happen to produce disparate outcomes for different ethnic groups.

Interfering in state legislative reapportionment. In the case of *Reynolds v. Sims*, 377 U.S. 533 (1964), the Supreme Court directly interfered with the ability of states to apportion their legislatures and, in effect, arbitrarily amended nearly every state constitution. The controversy in *Reynolds* involved the Alabama legislature, neither chamber of which was apportioned according to population. Instead, due to the failure to adjust for population changes, a minority of rural voters elected a majority of state representatives and senators. When this was challenged as a violation of the Equal Protection Clause of the U.S. Constitution, the Supreme Court made

---

5 401 U.S. 432 (1971).

6 "The court cited not a line in a committee report, not a colloquy on the floor of either house of Congress" to support its holding. See Michael Gold, *Griggs' Folly: An Essay on the Theory, Problems, and Origin of the Reverse Impact Definition of Employment Discrimination and a Recommendation for Reform*, 7 Indus. Rel. L.J. 429, 480-481 (1985).

the surprising ruling that both chambers of state legislatures must be apportioned strictly on a population basis. In what became known as the "One Man, One Vote" decision, the Supreme Court opined that even legislative apportionment plans that allow one chamber to be based on geographical or political boundaries constitute impermissible vote dilution.

The justices who opposed this ruling contended that state legislative apportionment was a fundamental state issue in which the federal government should not intrude. Further, the dissent stated that both the text and the history of the Fourteenth Amendment prove that the Equal Protection Clause does not limit the power of the states to apportion their legislatures. "It is difficult to imagine a more intolerable and inappropriate interference by the judiciary with the independent legislatures of the states,"[7] the dissent lamented. "These decisions cut deeply into the fabric of our federalism."[8]

Ironically, the *Reynolds* decision prevents states from modeling their legislatures after the U.S. Congress. This abrogation of state authority is so extreme that it might have upset the whole constitutional agreement if the possibility of such a decision could have been foreseen in 1787.

"Discovering" a right to an abortion. In *Roe v. Wade,* 410 U.S. 113 (1973), the Supreme Court considered the constitutionality of a Texas statute that prohibited abortion except to save the life of the mother. After a long discussion of the ancient attitudes and practices of abortion dating to the ancient Greeks, the Supreme Court examined the statute in question. Although it acknowledged that the Constitution does not mention a right of privacy explicitly, the Supreme Court held that a right of privacy nevertheless exists under the Constitution for rights "implicit in the concept of ordered liberty."[9] The Court ruled that "the right of personal privacy includes the abortion decision," and it invalidated the Texas statute under the Due Process Clause of the Fourteenth Amendment.[10] The Supreme Court then went on, in a blatantly legislative fashion, to proclaim a precise framework limiting the states' ability to regulate abortion procedures.

---

7 377 U.S. 615 (1964).

8 *Id.* at 624.

9 410 U.S. 152 (1973).

10 *Id.* at 153-154.

The dissent in *Roe* pointed out how the Court, in order to justify its ruling, somehow had to "find" within the scope of the Fourteenth Amendment a right that was unknown to the drafters of the Amendment. The dissent noted that, when the Fourteenth Amendment was adopted in 1868, there were at least 36 state or territorial laws limiting abortion, and that there was no question concerning the validity of those laws at the time. "The only conclusion possible from this history is that the drafters did not intend to have the Fourteenth Amendment withdraw from the States the power to legislate with respect to this matter."

Also, the dissent criticized the Supreme Court for exceeding its judicial authority and assuming a legislative function. "The decision here to break pregnancy into three distinct terms and to outline the permissible restrictions the State may impose in each one, for example, partakes more of judicial legislation than it does of a determination of the intent of the drafters of the Fourteenth Amendment."

One of the most pernicious aspects of the *Roe* decision is that it removed one of the most profound social and moral issues from the democratic process without any constitutional authority. For the first 197 years of America's existence, the abortion issue was decided by state legislatures, with substantially less violence and conflict than has attended the issue since the *Roe* decision. No matter what one's view may be about abortion, it is clear that the Founders did not establish the United States as a democratic republic to have unelected judges decide the most important issues of the day.

Overturning state referenda. In *Romer v. Evans,* No. 94–1039, May 20, 1996, the Supreme Court even negated a direct vote of the people. This case involved an amendment to the Colorado constitution enacted in 1992 by a statewide referendum. This "Amendment 2" prohibited the state or any political subdivisions therein from adopting any policy that grants homosexuals "any minority status, quota preference, protected status, or claim of discrimination."

The Supreme Court ruled that the amendment was unconstitutional, claiming that Amendment 2 did not bear a "rational relationship" to a legitimate government purpose, and thus violated the Equal Protection Clause of the Fourteenth Amendment.

The state of Colorado contended that this amendment protected freedom of association, particularly for landlords and employers who have religious objections to homosexuality, and that it only prohibited preferential treatment for homosexuals and placed them in the same position as all other persons who are nonminorities. But the Supreme Court rejected these arguments and imposed its own idea of what motivated the citizens of Colorado, claiming that "laws of the kind now before us raise the inevitable inference that the disadvantage imposed is born of animosity toward the class of persons affected."[11]

In a scalding dissent, one justice stated that Amendment 2 "prohibits special treatment of homosexuals, and nothing more."[12] Furthermore, the dissent argued that the only denial of equal treatment caused by Amendment 2 is that homosexuals may not obtain "preferential treatment without amending the state constitution."[13]

Noting that under *Bowers v. Hardwick*, 478 U.S. 186 (1986), states are permitted to outlaw homosexual sodomy, the dissent reasoned that if it is constitutionally permissible for a state to criminalize homosexual conduct, it is surely constitutionally permissible for a state to deny special favor and protection to homosexuals. The Supreme Court's decision, the dissent charged, "is an act not of judicial judgment, but of political will."[14]

Critics argue that the *Romer* decision is the pinnacle of judicial arrogance because six appointed justices struck down a law approved by 54 percent of a state's voters in a direct election, the most democratic of all procedures. In one of the most egregious usurpations of power in constitutional history, the Supreme Court not only desecrated the principle of self-government, but set itself up as the moral arbiter of the nation's values.

Although this representative sample of Supreme Court decisions demonstrates the widespread impact of judicial activism, other federal courts have usurped executive and legislative functions within their jurisdictions. In nearly every state, federal, district, and appellate courts are

---

11 No. 94-1039, at 14.

12 *Id.* at 13.

13 Dissent at 3.

14 *Id.* at 4.

substituting their judgment for that of local officials and are trying to manage everything from prisons and mental hospitals to grammar schools and athletic leagues. Often they are aided and abetted by extremist lawyers, funded at taxpayers' expense, who bring the cases that serve as the vehicles for judicial activism.

As criminologist John DiIulio described in a recent article, a single federal judge in Philadelphia imposed a population cap on the city's jails and used her small army of court aides to micromanage the jail system. The results were predictable: "In one 18-month period alone, the cap resulted in 9,723 re-arrests of individuals who had been freed because of the decree. While free, they committed 79 murders, 90 rapes, 701 burglaries, 959 robberies, 1,113 assaults, 2,715 drug-dealing crimes, and 2,748 thefts."[15] It is not surprising, therefore, that many observers believe that such activist judges have indeed brought about the despotic oligarchy against which Thomas Jefferson warned.

LESSONS LEARNED

As the federal judiciary has exceeded its proper constitutional role, there have been attempts in the past to introduce proper restraints on the activities of federal judges. Some of these attempts have been successful, although others have not. Along the way, those who seek judicial reform have learned some important lessons.

Lesson #1: Presidential appointments to the federal courts are critical in promoting or restraining judicial activism. A President's understanding of the constitutional role of the judiciary, and his selection of judges who share that view, are the most important factors in determining whether the federal courts follow the judicial restraint inherent in constitutional government or the democratic process is subverted by judicial activism. These factors also affect the quality of justice dispensed by the federal judicial system. As Clint Bolick of the Institute for Justice[16] has written, "the Reagan and Bush Administrations resolved to restore the judiciary to

---

15 John S. DiIulio, "Questions for Crime-Buster Clinton," *The Weekly Standard,* September 2, 1996.

16 "Clinton's Judges: A Preliminary Analysis," *Issue Analysis,* Goldwater Foundation, April 1996, p. 2.

LESSONS LEARNED

- Presidential appointments to the federal courts are critical in promoting or restraining judicial activism.

- The Senate confirmation process is ineffective in blocking activist judges.

- The American Bar Association has forfeited its position as an objective source for the evaluation of federal judicial nominees.

- Congress contributes to judicial activism by giving the federal courts more power.

- Current means of amending the Constitution seldom are effective in correcting judicial activism.

- Congress has the power to limit the jurisdiction of, and more closely regulate, the federal courts.

---

its assigned Constitutional role and to halt what they perceived as unfettered judicial activism." This was in contrast to the prior decades, in which "the power of the federal judiciary increased dramatically... the courts recognized new rights and responsibilities that were not clearly anchored in law," the public was subjected to numerous "judicial inventions," and many judicial results "were procured by liberal activist groups seeking social outcomes they could not achieve through [democratic] legislative processes." The willingness of Presidents Reagan and Bush to invest "substantial political capital in securing confirmation of judges committed to judicial restraint... remains one of the most important and enduring legacies" of their administrations.

By contrast, say Bolick and other observers of the courts, the judges appointed by President Clinton—which make up nearly one-quarter of the whole federal judiciary—have made the courts "more liberal, moving them perceptibly toward the kind of judicial activism that characterized the federal courts before the election of Ronald Reagan." Clinton's appointments to the Supreme Court have solidified its liberal wing, and the lower federal courts have become more sympathetic to criminals and criminal defendants, more disposed toward expensive remedies in civil actions, and "more hospitable generally to novel legal theories and to a more sweeping exercise of judicial power."

Lesson #2: The Senate confirmation process is ineffective in blocking activist judges. Recent experience shows that the Senate confirmation process is conducted in a manner that favors liberal activist judges and is hostile toward nominees who understand and are committed to judicial restraint. To illustrate the disparity in treatment, one need only compare the confirmation battles of Chief Justice William Rehnquist, Judge Robert Bork, and Justice Clarence Thomas to the perfunctory confirmations of Democratic nominees Ruth Bader Ginsburg and Stephen Breyer.

During Bork's confirmation process, for example, he was labeled repeatedly an extremist, despite an unblemished record as an attorney, public official, law professor, and appellate judge. By contrast, Justice Ruth Bader Ginsburg had a lengthy record of liberal causes, including an active role in the Women's Rights Project of the American Civil Liberties Union (ACLU), an organization committed to promoting judicial activism. In sum, Ginsburg had a record far more "extreme," albeit in a different direction, than Bork. Yet Ginsburg was confirmed 96–3 by the Senate with little or no serious discussion of her philosophy or her involvement with the ACLU, while Bork's nomination was rejected after his judicial philosophy was exhaustively examined, and ultimately distorted.

The same disparity in confirming justices exists with respect to nominees for the lower federal courts. Although numerous prospective Reagan and Bush appointees were forced to undergo grueling examinations—with some being rejected or forced to withdraw—a very different situation has occurred regarding the Clinton nominees. As Thomas L. Jipping of the Free Congress Foundation has written:[17]

> Mr. Clinton appointed 202 judges in his first term, 25 percent more than President Reagan in his first term and 13 more than President Bush. The Senate did not defeat a single Clinton nominee, either in the Judiciary Committee or on the Senate floor,

---

17 Thomas L. Jipping, "Stacking the federal bench," *The Washington Times*, October 8, 1996.

and took a roll call vote on just four nominees, approving the other 198 by unanimous consent without a minute of floor debate.

Lesson #3: The American Bar Association has forfeited its position as an objective source for the evaluation of federal judicial nominees. For four decades, the American Bar Association (ABA) has played a semi-official, but very important, role in the selection of federal judges. Its Standing Committee on the Federal Judiciary has been given the authority to obtain extensive information about potential nominees from other lawyers, judges, and other sources. The ABA then provides evaluations of judicial nominees to the President and the Senate Judiciary Committee. In years past, this has been a valued means of analyzing the professional qualifications of potential judges.

But, as revealed in a careful study by the nonpartisan Capital Research Center,[18] the ABA has fallen from a "proud professional organization to a political pressure group." From its shameful role in the Bork nomination, in which four members of the Standing Committee rated him "not qualified," to "its support for a raft of left wing policy prescriptions, the ABA has lost all claim to be an unbiased voice of the legal profession. It has become just another Washington lobby...." For example, the following is a representative sample of the official positions of the ABA on issues before the 104th Congress: The ABA supports federal funding for abortion services for the poor; supports racial and ethnic preferences; supports the ban on assault weapons; opposes efforts to outlaw flag burning; opposes restrictions on the exclusionary rule and habeas corpus appeals; and opposes welfare reform legislation that would restrict payments to mothers having additional children. These political issues, which are unrelated to the legal profession, have so politicized the ABA that it no longer can claim to be a neutral organization that is able to evaluate judicial candidates objectively.

The appearance of ideological bias has been compounded by evidence concerning the ABA's judicial evaluations themselves. Recently, the Senate Judiciary Committee reviewed the ABA's handling of nominations

---

18 "By One Vote Lawyers' Group Picks Controversial President-Elect," *Organization Trends*, Capital Research Center, Washington, D.C., October 1996, p. 1.

by Republican and Democrat Presidents in which the candidates had similar professional and academic qualifications. The Senate Committee found that those nominated by Democrat Presidents were consistently rated higher than Republican nominees who had similar or better credentials. As the Capital Research Center study concludes, "these facts have led many to regard the ABA's evaluation process as fundamentally biased."[19] For a discussion of the proper ABA role in the confirmation process, see the Strategy section that follows.

Lesson #4: Congress contributes to judicial activism by giving the federal courts more power. When Congress enacts legislation that creates new causes of action and new federal crimes, it necessarily expands the jurisdiction and the power of the federal judiciary. Not only is this federalization often poor public policy, but it also contradicts constitutional principles. As he wrote in *The Federalist* No. 45, Madison envisioned a far narrower role for the federal government than exists today:

> The powers delegated by the proposed Constitution to the federal government are few and defined. Those which are to remain in the State governments are numerous and indefinite. The former will be exercised principally on external objects, as war, peace, negotiation, and foreign commerce....

One of the largest recent expansions of federal law is the federal criminal code. Although the Constitution gave Congress jurisdiction over only three crimes, there are more that 3,000 federal crimes on the books today, and this number grows with each congressional session. Hardly any crime, no matter how local in nature, is beyond the jurisdiction of federal criminal authorities. Federal crimes now range from serious but purely local crimes like carjacking and drug dealing to trivial crimes like disrupting a rodeo. Although many of these crimes pose a real threat to public safety, they already are outlawed by the states and need not be duplicated in the federal law. Since these offenses are tried and appealed in federal court, the federalization of crime increases the power of the

---

19 *Ibid.,* p. 4.

federal judiciary and further invades the province of state and local governments.

The federalization of the law also has included environmental and regulatory legislation. Such federal statutes as the Clean Water Act, the Americans with Disabilities Act, and the Resource Conservation and Recovery Act regulate activities that occur entirely within the states and bear little connection to the federal government. These statutes greatly increase litigation in the federal courts and provide federal judges with a policymaking power through statutory interpretation and implementation. This threat to the balance between federal and state jurisdictions also endangers individual liberty and constitutional rights, particularly when criminal penalties are attached to what traditionally have been civil and administrative matters. For a discussion of how the federalization of the law can be reduced, see the following Strategy section.

Lesson #5: Current means of amending the Constitution seldom are effective in correcting judicial activism. As mentioned earlier, only a constitutional amendment can overrule the constitutional rulings of the federal judiciary; a mere statute will not suffice. Obviously, the amendment procedure set forth in Article V of the Constitution is difficult and lengthy—a desirable limitation to avoid hasty changes to conform to the passions of the moment. But history has shown that even the most egregious court decisions—particularly those that affect the balance of power between the national government and the states—seldom have been amenable to correction by constitutional amendment. One reason for this is that Congress, which is a source for initiating such an amendment, is loath to give up federal power. The other method of amending the Constitution—by constitutional convention—has never been tried because of uncertainty over how such a convention would be organized and what its powers would be. The fear that such a convention body might exceed its grant of authority and do violence to traditional concepts of constitutionalism in effect has negated its usefulness. For a discussion of a new method of amending the Constitution that avoids the unpredictability of a convention and gives the states a greater opportunity to rein in the federal judiciary, see the following Strategy section.

Lesson #6: Congress has the power to limit the jurisdiction of, and more closely regulate, the federal courts. Congress has a great deal of power over the jurisdiction of the lower federal courts. Article III, § 1 of the Constitution provides that "[t]he judicial power of the United States, shall be vested in one supreme Court, *and in such inferior Courts as the Congress may from time to time ordain and establish*" [emphasis added]. It is well-established that, because Congress has total discretion over whether to create the lower federal courts, it also has great discretion over the jurisdiction of those courts it chooses to create. In fact, in the past, Congress has withdrawn previously granted jurisdiction from the lower federal courts because of dissatisfaction with their performance, and in the belief that state courts were the better forum for certain types of cases. The Supreme Court repeatedly has upheld Congress's power to do so.

For example, Congress restricted the jurisdiction of the lower federal courts in the Norris-La Guardia Act of 1932 and the Emergency Price Control Act of 1942. In *Lockerty v. Phillips,* 319 U.S. 182 (1943), the Supreme Court upheld the Emergency Price Control Act, which withdrew from the lower federal courts jurisdiction to restrain the enforcement of price orders. In upholding the withdrawal of jurisdiction, the Court stated that:

> [T]he Congressional power to ordain and establish inferior federal courts includes the power "of investing them with jurisdiction either limited, concurrent, or exclusive, *and of withholding jurisdiction from them in the exact degrees and character which to Congress may seem proper for the public good."* [Emphasis added.]

Likewise, in *Lauf v. E. G. Shinner & Co.,* 303 U.S. 323 (1938), the Supreme Court upheld the Norris–La Guardia Act, which imposed restrictions on the jurisdiction of federal courts to issue labor injunctions. The Supreme Court ruled that "[t]here can be no question of the power of Congress thus to define and limit the jurisdiction of the inferior courts of the United States." Modern Supreme Court decisions, such as *Palmore v. United States,* 411 U.S. 389 (1973), also have upheld Congress's power to restrict the lower federal courts' jurisdiction.

In the 104th Congress, Congress successfully used its power over the jurisdiction of the lower federal courts. For example, the Prison Litigation Reform Act of 1995 reduced the discretion of the federal courts to micromanage state prisons and to force the early release of prisoners. The act also makes it more difficult for prisoners to file frivolous lawsuits, of which an incredible 63,550 were filed in federal court in 1995 alone. In addition, Congress passed the Effective Death Penalty Act of 1995. This act limited the power of the federal courts to entertain endless habeas corpus appeals filed by prisoners on death row, and thus significantly expedited the death penalty process. For a discussion of additional areas in which Congress should consider restraining the jurisdiction of the federal courts, see the Strategy section below.

The U.S. Supreme Court. Congress also has some authority to limit the jurisdiction of the Supreme Court and to regulate its activities. Article III of the Constitution states that the Supreme Court "shall have appellate jurisdiction, both as to law and fact, *with such Exceptions, and under such Regulations as the Congress shall make*" [emphasis added]. Although it should be recognized that there is a debate over the scope of Congress's power to regulate and restrict the Supreme Court's jurisdiction and its ability to decide particular types of cases, there is a constitutional basis for this authority. An impressive array of legal scholars concede that Congress has broad power to curtail the jurisdiction of the Supreme Court.[20]

In the only case that directly addressed this issue, the Supreme Court upheld Congress's power to restrict the Court's appellate jurisdiction. In *Ex Parte McCardle*, 74 U.S. 506 (1869), the Supreme Court unanimously upheld Congress's power to limit its jurisdiction, stating:

> We are not at liberty to inquire into the motives of the legislature. We can only examine into its power under the Constitution; *and the power to*

---

20 See, for example, Gunther, *Congressional Power to Curtail Federal Court Jurisdiction: An Opinionated Guide to the Ongoing Debate*, 36 Stan. L. Rev. 895 (1984); Berger, *Congressional Contraction of Federal Jurisdiction*, 1980 Wis. L. Rev. 801; Wechsler, *The Courts and the Constitution*, 65 Colum. L. Rev. 1001 (1965); and Van Alstyne, *Constitutional Restraints upon the Judiciary: Hearings Before the Subcommittee on the Constitution of the Senate Committee on the Judiciary*, 97th Cong., 1st Sess. (1981).

> make exceptions to the appellate jurisdiction of this
> court is given by express words. What, then, is the
> effect of the repealing act upon the case before us?
> We cannot doubt as to this. Without jurisdiction,
> the court cannot proceed at all in any case.
> [Emphasis added.]

Although some respected constitutional scholars argue that Congress cannot restrict the Supreme Court's jurisdiction to the extent that it intrudes upon the Court's "core functions," there is no question that there is more authority under the Constitution for Congress to act than it has exercised recently.

STRATEGIES FOR REINING IN THE FEDERAL JUDICIARY

There are a number of strategies that can be used to confine the judiciary to its proper constitutional role. These include:

STRATEGY #1
The Senate should use its confirmation authority to block the appointment of activist federal judges.

When a President is one who is likely to appoint judges who exceed their constitutional authority and usurp the role of other branches, the Senate can restrain the judiciary properly by carefully exercising its responsibilities under the "Advise and Consent" clause of Article II, § 2, of the Constitution. Normally, the Senate Judiciary Committee conducts a hearing on the President's nominees. Those nominees that are approved by the committee or submitted without recommendation go to the full Senate for a confirmation vote.

Unfortunately, in recent years, the confirmation process has been relatively perfunctory. There has been a reluctance on the part of the Senate to question a nominee closely to ascertain the candidate's understanding of the proper role of the judiciary. The Senate committee hearing provides an excellent opportunity to discern a judicial candidate's understanding of a constitutionally limited judiciary. It also provides a public opportunity for judicial-watch organizations to testify on behalf of or against a particular nominee. The Constitution established Senate

---

STRATEGIES FOR
REINING IN THE FEDERAL JUDICIARY

- The Senate should use its confirmation authority to block the appointment of activist federal judges.

- The American Bar Association should be removed from its special role in the judicial selection process.

- Congress should utilize its power to limit the jurisdiction of, and to regulate, the federal courts.

- The states should join together to persuade Congress to initiate a constitutional amendment that allows the states to amend the Constitution without the approval of Congress.

- Congress should avoid the federalization of crime and the expansion of litigation in federal court.

---

confirmation to ensure that unqualified nominees were not given life-long judgeships. Senators, in carrying out this important responsibility, should ascertain a prospective judge's commitment to a philosophy of judicial restraint and constitutional fidelity. In doing so, they should review carefully all the opinions, legal articles, and other materials authored by the candidate; the report of the background investigation conducted by the Federal Bureau of Investigation; and information obtained from judges and other attorneys who have had opportunities to view a candidate's work.

In questioning and evaluating a judicial nominee, it is important for Senators to ensure that the potential judge has an intellectual understanding of the constitutional principles involved and a moral commitment to follow them. The extent to which one has been tested in the crucible of philosophical conflict may indicate his or her dedication to constitutional values. It is important to be sure that prospective judges have the ability to resist the blandishments of the liberal establishment and to value the approval of those who uphold the original precepts of the Constitution through a jurisprudence of limited judicial power.

When the nomination of a prospective judge comes to the floor of the Senate, each nominee should be voted on individually. This not only gives the entire Senate information about each candidate, but also impresses upon the prospective judge and the public the importance and responsibility of each new member of the judiciary. In addition, voting on each nominee individually is a means of holding each Senator responsible, through his or her vote, for each judge appointed to the federal bench.

STRATEGY #2
The American Bar Association should be removed from its special role in the judicial selection process.

Because the American Bar Association has shown itself to be a politicized special-interest group, it should be removed from any official role in evaluating judicial nominees and should be treated the same as any other partisan political group, such as the American Civil Liberties Union or the National Rifle Association. It would be able to testify before the Senate Judiciary Committee concerning the potential judge, but it would not have any special status or authority.

In place of the ABA, as a means of ascertaining the information available from judges and lawyers who have a detailed knowledge of the work and background of a judicial candidate, special fact-finding committees could be appointed by the Senate in each of the 94 federal judicial districts. The lawyers involved in these small committees would be selected for their objectivity, ideological neutrality, and understanding of the constitutional role of the judiciary. They then could obtain the detailed information necessary for the Senate to evaluate a candidate, and could provide that information directly to the Judiciary Committee without subjective comments or evaluation.

STRATEGY #3
Congress should utilize its power to limit the jurisdiction of and regulate the federal courts.

Article III of the Constitution gives Congress the power to regulate the appellate jurisdiction of the Supreme Court through such exceptions and under such regulations as Congress shall make. It also provides that Congress may ordain and establish federal courts inferior to the Supreme Court. This means that Congress can restrict the jurisdiction of the federal courts in appropriate circumstances. The following issues are ripe for such action:

- **Same-Sex Marriage.** One issue over which Congress might consider restricting the jurisdiction of the lower federal courts is same-sex marriage. No area of the law has been more a province of the states than domestic relations. Nevertheless, the possibility exists that some federal judges will "discover" a constitutional right to homosexual marriage, and thus remove the issue from the democratic process. For example, the Hawaii Supreme Court recently indicated that it would recognize homosexual marriage, which could impose its ruling on the rest of the nation under the Full Faith and Credit Clause of Article IV, § 1. This possibility motivated Congress to pass the Defense of Marriage Act, which enabled the states to refuse to recognize a same-sex marriage enacted in another state. The Defense of Marriage Act does not, however, prevent the federal judiciary from usurping this issue. Congress should consider going one step further and remove the jurisdiction of the lower federal courts over same-sex marriages to ensure that this cultural issue is decided by the legislative process in each state.

- **Private School Choice.** Another issue Congress might consider restricting the jurisdiction of the lower federal courts to determine is private school choice. Some radical groups like the American Civil Liberties Union argue that if the government gives a tuition voucher to a family that then chooses to use the voucher at a religious school, this would violate the First Amendment's Establishment Clause. Under current Supreme Court precedents, however, school vouchers are almost certainly constitutional. Nevertheless, certain individual federal judges have indicated they would invalidate private school choice plans under the Establishment Clause. Moreover, if the personnel of the Supreme Court change and additional activist justices are appointed, one of the most promising educational initiatives in recent years could be crushed by judicial fiat. Thus, in order to ensure that private school choice is not usurped by the federal judiciary, Congress should consider restricting the jurisdiction of the federal courts over this issue.

- **Judicial Taxation.** Another possibility is for Congress to prohibit the lower federal courts from ordering a particular remedy that is inappropriate for judicial imposition. Under this strategy, rather than deprive the federal courts of all jurisdiction over a particular issue, Congress can impose restrictions on federal court jurisdiction to issue certain remedies. As mentioned earlier, this strategy was used successfully in *Lauf v. E. G. Shinner & Co.*, 303 U.S. 323 (1938). In *Lauf*, the Supreme Court upheld provisions of the Norris-La Guardia Act that prohibited the federal courts from issuing labor injunctions, even though the act did not completely deny the courts jurisdiction over labor disputes.

A particular remedy that Congress should deny to federal judges is the ability to levy judicial taxation. "Judicial taxation" refers to federal court orders that require a state or local government to make significant expenditures to pay for court-ordered injunctions. For example, one federal judge ordered the state of Missouri to pay for approximately $2.6 billion in capital improvements and other costs to "desegregate" the school districts in St. Louis and Kansas City. In requiring Kansas City to maintain the most lavish schools in the nation, the federal judge actually issued an order increasing property taxes to pay for his court-ordered remedies.

To allow appointed, life-tenured federal judges to order tax increases is literally taxation without representation. Under the Constitution, only Congress can lay and collect taxes. Our Founding Fathers would be appalled at the thought of federal judges raising taxes. In *The Federalist* No. 48, Madison explained that in our democratic system, "the legislative branch alone has access to the pockets of the people." Consequently, Congress should consider restricting the jurisdiction of federal courts to order the federal government or any state or local government from raising taxes in any circumstance.

- **Use of Special Masters.** Federal courts should be prohibited from utilizing "special masters" to micromanage prisons and jails, mental hospitals, and school districts. In the past, courts have appointed these special masters to oversee illegitimate judicial excursions into the province of the legislative and executive branches. Moreover, the use of special masters has been a form of taxation, in that state and local governments are required to pay their salaries and expenses — which often have been extravagant. In some cases, special masters have had large numbers of staff members to help them in carrying out the court order. Without these special masters, federal judges would have to restrain themselves because they would not have the time or resources to manage prisons or other institutions.

STRATEGY #4
The states should join together to persuade Congress to initiate a constitutional amendment that allows the states to amend the Constitution without the approval of Congress.

One reason judicial activism is so dangerous and undemocratic is the difficulty of reversing or amending federal court decisions. When a decision of the Supreme Court or a lower federal court is based on the Constitution, the decision cannot be reversed or altered except by constitutional amendment. Such constitutional decisions are immune from presidential vetoes or congressional legislation.

The Constitution's amendment procedure led Lord Bryce to conclude in his 1888 study, *The American Commonwealth,* that "[t]he Constitution which it is the most difficult to change is that of the United States." This difficulty in changing our Constitution has encouraged judicial activism and allowed the federal courts to "twist and shape" the Constitution, as Jefferson predicted, as an "artist shapes a ball of wax." The reason that the difficult amendment procedure encourages judicial activism is simple: Life-tenured judges are less likely to show restraint when the possibility that their rulings will be rejected is slight. Woodrow Wilson touched upon this fact in his 1908 book, *Congressional Government:*

> The process of formal amendment was made so difficult by the provisions of the Constitution itself that it has seldom been feasible to use it; *and the difficulty of formal amendment has understandably made the courts more liberal, not to say lax, in their interpretation than they would otherwise have been.* [Emphasis added.]

Consequently, one strategy to rein in the federal judiciary is to amend the Constitution's amendment procedure in Article V to allow the states to amend the Constitution without Congress's approval and without a constitutional convention. Under this proposal, two-thirds of the states, by resolutions of their legislatures agreeing to an identical amendment to the Constitution, would transmit that amendment to Congress for submission to all the states for ratification. If the legislatures of three-fourths of the states then ratified the amendment, it would become part of the Constitution. Congress's role in this process would be purely ministerial.

This process would give the states co-equal power with Congress to inaugurate the amendment process and would provide a further check on the power of both the federal courts and Congress. Furthermore, this proposal would avoid the uncertainty of a convention and still be a very deliberative process.

STRATEGY #5
Congress should avoid the federalization of crime and the expansion of litigation in federal court.

Whenever Congress enacts a new federal criminal statute or a statute creating a cause of action in federal court, it enlarges the power and authority of the federal courts and provides more opportunities for judicial activism. At the same time, the federalization of crimes that traditionally have been within the province of state and local governments upsets the balance between the national government and the states. By exercising restraint in its own legislative power, Congress also can limit the power of the federal judiciary. Additional steps that Congress can take in restoring federalism include the following:

- **Recodify the U.S. Code.** One approach to reducing the federalization of the law would be to rewrite the entire federal criminal code. Critics note that, in the present code, important offenses like treason are commingled with insignificant offenses like the unauthorized interstate transport of water hyacinths. The Federal Courts Study Committee found that the current federal criminal code is "hard to find, hard to understand, redundant, and conflicting."[21] Ideally, Congress

---

21 Sara S. Beale, in *Working Papers and Subcommittee Reports*, Report to the Subcommittee on Workload regarding Federal Criminal Caseload of the Federal Courts Study Committee, 1990, at 106. Cited in Thomas A. Mengler, "Federal Criminal Jurisdiction: A Report to the Long Range Planning Committee of the Judicial Conference of the United States," December 21, 1992, p. 40.

would recodify only those offenses that legitimately belong under federal jurisdiction. Due to the highly political nature of crime, some commentators suggest the creation of an independent commission, modeled after the Base Closure Commission, to recodify the federal criminal code.

- **Include a federalism assessment in legislation.** This idea was proposed by President Reagan's 1986 Working Group on Federalism. It would require that federal legislation contain an assessment discussing the factors necessitating a national solution, any efforts the states have taken to address the problem, the legislation's effect on state experimentation, and a citation of Congress's constitutional authority to enact the proposed legislation.

- **Create a Federalism Subcommittee in both Judiciary Committees.** Also proposed by President Reagan's Working Group on Federalism, this idea would establish a federalism subcommittee which would attempt to ensure compliance with federalism principles in all proposed legislation.

CONCLUSION

The Framers of the Constitution intended that the federal judiciary play a vital role in America's representative democracy. None of the above material should be interpreted as an assault on the very existence of the judiciary. It is important to remember, however, that in no other democracy in the world do unelected judges decide as many vital political issues as they do in the United States. When viewed objectively, judicial reform is actually a nonpartisan issue. The "conservative" activist Supreme Court of the 1920–1930s, which struck down as unconstitutional minimum wage and other mild labor reforms, was as repugnant to constitutional democracy as the "liberal" activist Warren Court.

In recent decades, the legislative and executive branches have been very meek in responding to activist federal judges. As a result, perhaps no issue is more in need of attention and effort than judicial reform. The strategies listed above illustrate some ways in which the judiciary can be restrained in a proper and constitutional manner. It is to be hoped that these and other strategies will be used successfully to rein in the federal judiciary.

Chapter 8

SOLVING THE PROBLEM OF MIDDLE-CLASS ENTITLEMENTS

Stuart M. Butler and John S. Barry

If Congress is ever going to restore the federal government to its proper size and scope, it must devise an effective strategy to control the growth of middle-class entitlements. Not only are these entitlements the driving force behind the growth of government, but they embody one of the most inappropriate and inefficient of the many roles government has assumed for itself—government as manager of personal finance.

Middle-class entitlements include such tax-financed expenditure programs as Social Security, Medicare, and subsidized student loans. Unlike other programs, these programs do not need legislation to grow — they need legislation to stop growing. Without firm action and a shrewd political strategy to achieve that action, the autopilot nature of entitlements will cause government to grow even if tough steps are taken to curb other federal programs.

Even worse, middle-class entitlements have created a powerful constituency for larger government within the very segment of the population that traditionally has been most hostile to any expansion of government power. Some programs, particularly Medicare and student

The authors would like to thank Grace-Marie Arnett, Enid Borden, Michael Carrozza, Robert Moffit, Stan Sokul, and Mark Tapscott for their suggestions and contributions to this chapter. The views and opinions expressed in this chapter, however, are solely the responsibility of the authors.

loans, have such a large middle-class constituency that conservatives risk eroding their political base by raising even the possibility of curbing entitlements. These programs foster a disturbing notion among the middle class that government has an inherent responsibility to ensure that they are insulated from the vicissitudes of life and get their perceived "fair share" of the economic pie. Liberals, because they understand this only too well, see proposals for entitlements, including required "private-sector" entitlements in the form of employer mandates (an element of the Clinton health plan), as a political wedge they can use to lock the middle class into supporting larger government.

Fortunately—even though we have learned it the hard way—we have learned a great deal over the last 15 years about the politics of entitlements and how these programs can be restrained or even ended. Thanks to these hard lessons, conservatives can be much more optimistic about devising a strategy to control the explosive growth of entitlements.

How Entitlements Have Grown

The Social Security Act of 1935, part of Franklin Roosevelt's New Deal, sowed the seeds of many of today's federal entitlement programs. Before the Act was passed, all federal funds had been approved and spent on an annual basis; Social Security, however, launched something new: federal spending without annual accountability.

After passage of the Social Security Act, entitlement spending increased, accounting for 27 percent of total spending by 1965, the year Medicare was created. Over the past 30 years, entitlement spending has nearly doubled, reaching 49 percent of total federal spending in 1995. Today, Social Security is the largest entitlement program, consuming a full 42 percent of all federal mandatory program spending. The others include Medicare (20 percent); Medicaid (11 percent); the various welfare and unemployment programs (14 percent); and agriculture subsidies, education, training, and veterans benefits (13 percent).

All estimates indicate that entitlement spending will continue to rise for the foreseeable future. The Bipartisan Commission on Entitlement and Tax Reform concluded in 1995 that by 2030, under current law, entitlement spending will consume all federal tax revenues collected. This means that unless taxes are raised, the government will have to borrow money to pay for every discretionary program, including national defense, interstate highway construction, and foreign diplomacy.

There are two overriding reasons for the rapid growth of entitlement spending. First, the number of people eligible for payments has increased steadily as new programs have been created and old ones expanded. The Social Security Act of 1935 alone has been amended more than 20 times. The institution of Medicare in 1965 increased the payroll tax and expanded old-age payments to include medical costs. The number of federal student loan guarantees (and, more recently, direct student loans) has increased steadily over the past two decades. And unemployment insurance and welfare programs have increased in scope ever since President Lyndon Johnson initiated his War on Poverty in 1964.

Second, demographic trends have caused levels of spending to grow. The unique characteristic of entitlements is that one need only meet certain criteria to qualify for benefits. Therefore, it is difficult to set an upper (or lower) limit on the amount of money spent on an entitlement program in any single year. Spending levels are determined partially outside of statute. As large groups of Americans move through demographic phases that qualify them for entitlements, spending naturally increases. For example, as

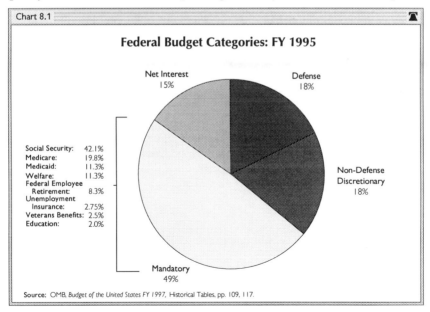

Chart 8.1

Federal Budget Categories: FY 1995

Net Interest
15%

Defense
18%

Social Security: 42.1%
Medicare: 19.8%
Medicaid: 11.3%
Welfare: 11.3%
Federal Employee
Retirement: 8.3%
Unemployment
Insurance: 2.75%
Veterans Benefits: 2.5%
Education: 2.0%

Non-Defense
Discretionary
18%

Mandatory
49%

Source: OMB, *Budget of the United States FY 1997*, Historical Tables, pp. 109, 117.

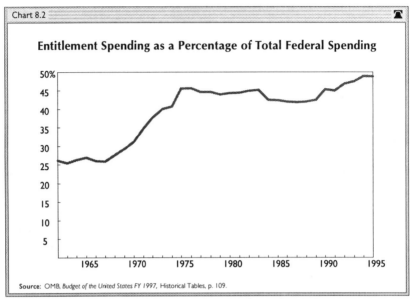

Chart 8.2

Entitlement Spending as a Percentage of Total Federal Spending

Source: OMB, *Budget of the United States FY 1997*, Historical Tables, p. 109.

the Baby Boom generation retires, the number of people receiving Social Security benefits will increase rapidly; so, therefore, will federal spending. In the case of some defined benefit programs, such as Medicare, the cost of supplying the benefit has grown rapidly, pushing up overall program costs (see Charts 8.1 and 8.2).

How Middle-Class Entitlements Expand Government

The growth of middle-class entitlements represents the gradual seduction of what once was the most anti-government segment of the American population. This process has taken many decades. It has been successful not only because the political architects of these programs have designed them so skillfully, but also because attitudes toward risk and security among ordinary Americans have changed.

The Success of Liberal Tactics. The Depression shocked Americans into accepting a far larger role for government in the form of new entitlements to such things as housing and farm support and, of course, comprehensive Social Security. But as Carolyn Weaver of the American Enterprise Institute has pointed out, there was wide opposition to a compulsory social insurance pension program. Roosevelt carefully maneuvered Congress into accepting a pay-as-you go program virtually guaranteed to grow as more and more Americans came to believe they were merely getting back what they had paid into it.

Describing the program as a trust fund (nothing more than an accounting trick) accomplished two things, both of them essential to securing broad middle-class support for a program actually in structural deficit: 1) It reinforced the idea that people were just getting back money they had paid into the program, and 2) it encouraged the entirely erroneous assumption that the trust fund would be balanced over time. It also helped plant the seeds of middle-class indignation against any who might try to reduce the benefits already "paid for" by elderly Americans. Roosevelt believed that the payroll tax/trust fund arrangement meant "no damn politician can ever scrap my Social Security system." It is no coincidence that the same payroll tax/trust fund mechanism forms the heart of the Medicare hospital program, the social insurance component of the political compromise legislation of 1965 (the other component being subsidized insurance). Yet, as both Medicare and Social Security have matured in a financial sense, the chronically unbalanced condition of the trust funds has become a political liability and may be creating the political conditions necessary for major reform.

In recent years, the precarious condition of the social insurance trust funds has led liberals to avoid proposing large new social insurance programs as a way to expand government and lure the middle class. There is deep skepticism among Americans about the wisdom of letting the government run a large insurance program. This has led, among other things, to liberal entitlement programs that subsidize—but also regulate— private financing instead of replacing it with a hands-on government program. One example is the student loan program (although the Clinton Administration did try to nationalize the program's banking feature). Such efforts, it is claimed, merely help out the "financially strapped" middle class, (the middle class always thinks of itself as "financially strapped" and worthy of financial assistance), and thus should not threaten middle-class values.

Another way to enact *de facto* new entitlement programs has been to finance government-controlled activity by hiding the cost within the private sector. This is the essence of the drive to create new entitlements "paid for" by mandated employer spending. This has the advantage of widening government influence through programs that, unlike payroll or income taxes, involve no direct cost to recipients; workers typically do not realize that mandated employer spending means a reduction in their own compensation. Crucial to this strategy is the campaign to establish in the minds of Americans the notion that corporations are community institutions with moral and financial obligations to their workers and other "stakeholders." Once businesses are viewed as community institutions rather than as private organizations, it is easier for middle-class people to feel comfortable about demanding unpaid services from them.

The Clinton health plan epitomized this strategy. Clinton strategists talked constantly of the "obligations" of employers and how their plan was a "private-sector" solution to gaps in the health care system. And when the plan was defeated, the primary reason was not that Americans had failed to respond to that particular message, but rather that they had become persuaded that their choices and access to medical care would be reduced and bureaucratized.

Notwithstanding the defeat of the Clinton plan, modern liberals well understand how to exploit entitlement programs to unite middle-class interests with their own objective of larger and more pervasive government. If one proposal fails, another more refined one will be tried: A revamped Clinton health plan focusing on children, for example, is already in the making. The rich political prize of strong middle-class support for government is central to this liberal strategy. As summarized by Democratic tactician Stan Greenberg in a 1991 American Prospect article, "Democrats are for 'everybody,' not just the 'have-nots.' That means defending and enlarging social insurance initiatives that reach the lower and middle classes rather than constructing safety nets that protect only the poor."

The Middle-Class Attitude Toward Entitlements. The general attitude of middle-class Americans toward entitlements makes it much easier for liberals to defend or expand such programs, and much harder for conservatives to dismantle them. As journalist/economist Robert Samuelson explains in his book The Good Life and Its Discontents, middle-class expectations have changed in recent decades. Samuelson argues persuasively that Americans have come to expect not merely the opportunity to seek happiness and security, but the guarantee of financial stability and improvement as well as fulfillment in their lives. Americans increasingly have come to the conclusion that they are entitled to the good life and that it is only appropriate for government, and even private institutions such as businesses, to create programs that guarantee an entitlement.

This widespread middle-class belief in an entitlement society makes tackling entitlements a politically treacherous matter. But unless these programs are curbed, and unless the middle class is freed from psychological dependence on them, it will be impossible to constrain the growth of government and restore the federal government to its proper role. Fortunately, the period from Reagan to Clinton provides many important lessons that can help conservatives construct a successful strategy.

LESSONS LEARNED

Given the seemingly inexorable growth of entitlements during the last 20 years, it might seem that the only lesson to be learned is that the pessimists are correct: Entitlements are the "third rail" of politics and best left untouched. According to this view, the best that can be achieved is small, technical adjustments that do not threaten these programs but still might achieve sizable savings over time. Some feel that even these savings are not worth the risk. Experience, however, suggests a number of lessons—some sobering and some salutary — that should make conservatives more optimistic about the prospects for needed reform.

Lesson #1: It is crucial to prepare and educate the public thoroughly before a plan to reform an entitlement program is released. It is not possible to push through major entitlement curbs without anyone's noticing. Nor is it possible to craft a logical and reasonable reform behind closed doors and then simply unveil it and expect Americans to embrace it. They will not. They will savage the plan and denounce its architects. Even if politicians of both parties privately concede the need for reform and agree that a given proposal is reasonable, it would be naïve to assume that one's political adversaries will refrain from joining in the general bloodletting.

For example, it was widely recognized by experts in the early 1980s that the retirement portion of Social Security (OASI) was likely to run out of money within a few years despite a huge payroll tax increase enacted under President Carter. In its 1981 annual report, for example, the Social Security Board of Trustees concluded that the program could run out of money by 1983 or even late 1982. The Reagan Administration responded by quickly developing a bold plan to deal decisively with this crisis.

LESSONS LEARNED

- The public must be educated about the need for reform of an entitlement program before any plan to reform it is released.

- Those who would be affected by a change in entitlements must be made to feel that the reforms will bring them greater security.

- Provider constituencies that would gain from entitlement reform must be brought into the process.

- Commissions have their uses, but they also have their limitations.

- The focus of efforts should be on structural reform of the programs themselves, not on achieving short-term budget savings.

During the 1980 campaign, Reagan had pledged not to cut benefits for current beneficiaries, and his advisers were confident they had developed a way to save the system that was in line with that pledge. The proposal developed by the White House would simply have delayed a cost-of-living (COLA) increase by three months while reducing benefits for those retiring early — though full benefits still would have become available for these Americans at age 65. It seemed a reasonable proposal that beneficiaries and workers alike could support.

But when the package was announced on the eve of its scheduled transmittal to Capitol Hill for what many aides assumed would be quick passage, the uproar was so fierce that it became clear there was no point in formally handing it over to anyone. Groups representing the elderly characterized it as destroying the golden years of senior citizens. The Democrats, delighted at the prospect of halting the Reagan bandwagon, employed similar denunciations. House Speaker Thomas P. O'Neill, for example, declared that "cutting benefits for those who retire at age 62 is a sneak attack on Social Security." In large part because neither the need for action nor the available options had been explained in advance to confused and anxious seniors, these denunciations struck home. The firestorm was so fierce that Republicans quickly ran up the white flag: Senator Robert Dole introduced a resolution that was a slap in the face to the White House. The resolution declared, among other things, that "Congress shall not precipitously and unfairly penalize early retirees." It carried 96–0, and this humiliation — born of a failure to prepare the ground with the elderly—contributed to Republican losses in 1982.

The main reason good intentions and financial logic are no protection against public condemnation is that the vast majority of middle-class Americans have only a rudimentary understanding of entitlement programs. Many cannot even distinguish among these programs, and few have any real idea about their financial condition. For example, polling in January 1995, as the new Congress was taking office, indicated that almost two-thirds of Americans interpreted a campaign pledge not to cut Social Security benefits as a pledge also not to cut Medicare. Similarly, despite the huge imbalance between the amounts typically paid into Medicare and Social Security and the benefits actually received under these programs, a poll presented at a July 1995 American Association of Retired Persons (AARP) conference by Public Opinion Strategies pollster Bill McInturff showed that 67 percent of seniors saw Medicare as merely providing benefits for which they already had paid, while 74 percent felt this was true of Social Security.

Given such a high degree of public misunderstanding, it was reasonable to assume that the 1995 Republican proposals to transform Medicare would have suffered an even more hysterical reception than Reagan's 1981 Social Security reforms. Although the indication by House Republicans that they would achieve significant budget savings by reforming Medicare triggered strong opposition, it was remarkable how tempered that opposition actually was. There was no panicky Republican flight and no unanimous Senate resolution. Although the legislation eventually was vetoed by President Clinton, the wonder is that it ever made it to his desk with any chance of being signed into law.

While there are many lessons to be learned from this, one of the most important is that the House leadership recognized at the outset that it would be necessary to convince Americans there was a real crisis in Medicare that threatened not just the elderly, but future generations expecting to receive Medicare benefits. The House leadership's strategy was to convince Americans, including a solid portion of the elderly, that the crisis was real and needed decisive action — and to do it *before* a detailed proposal was unveiled and pushed through Congress. This was something learned from the Clinton health bill debacle, in which an intense but superficial education campaign was followed by the thud of a numbingly detailed legislative package that nobody other than a few policy wonks could understand and even White House officials found impossible to explain. The result: The campaign lost momentum as the plan was picked apart and public support withered away.

The failure of the Clinton health plan helped shape a very different strategy for the Republican Medicare proposal: Treat the 1995 Medicare Trustees Report predicting bankruptcy in a few years (as previous reports had done to little fanfare) as a bombshell in order to shock Americans into realizing the problem and accepting immediate reform. The report's release in the spring of 1995 was followed by a barrage of hearings, press briefings, and studies from organizations supporting reform. Throughout the resultant public discussion of the seriousness of the crisis and the general outlines of proposals for reform, however, the House leadership (and later the Senate leadership) carefully avoided releasing a legislative plan and repeating Clinton's mistake. By not presenting a target to divert attention from the education campaign, they retained the ability to craft a final plan after first assessing public response to various options.

The education campaign was surprisingly successful. According to surveys conducted by a major polling firm, American Viewpoint, those who had heard recent reports of Medicare's financial problems rose from just 14 percent of Americans in April 1995 to 34 percent (57 percent among those over 65) by June; the proportion of Americans believing it would go bankrupt jumped from 37 percent in April to 63 percent (and over two-thirds of Americans aged 18 to 54) in June; and 70 percent of the 63 percent who in June expected bankruptcy in seven years were persuaded that "Republicans in Congress" were trying to do what is best for all Americans.

This advantage eroded later in the year as the Medicare plan became entangled in the tax debate, and this came back to haunt Republicans as public debate degenerated in the 1996 election cycle. But the experience of 1995 suggests strongly that is possible—and necessary—to mount an effective educational campaign on entitlement reform. The 1995 Medicare campaign is all the more remarkable because it took place as just one element of a political battle to achieve sweeping changes in many policy areas. At the time, Republicans complained to their leaders that so many political battles were taking place simultaneously that they found it hard to maintain their focus. Nevertheless, the Medicare educational campaign was remarkably successful.

Even Social Security, a program about which there has been little real discussion of reform in Congress in recent years, carries considerable potential for successful public education. Many Americans already are very skeptical that the program will be there when they retire. According to 1996 polling by Public Opinion Strategies for the Cato Institute, 70 percent of Baby Boomers and Generation Xers hold that view. There is close to 80 percent support among these groups for a private "opt out" alternative to Social Security — and even 47 percent support among seniors, with just 14 percent actually opposed. It would seem that a carefully crafted education campaign building on these attitudes would make it possible to construct a powerful constituency for radical reform.

Lesson #2: Using any savings from entitlement reform to pay for changes that benefit unrelated constituencies most likely will backfire. Those who feel affected by the change must be made to feel that the reforms will bring them greater security. Americans generally do not like cutting or reducing the growth of programs, even if that is what is needed to save them. A common tactic in building support for any such "painful" change is to combine it with a "pleasurable" change that either mollifies the same constituency or creates a new constituency for the overall reform. Thus, part of the tactic of Reagan's 1981 economic package was to build public support for a spending slowdown by using part of the "proceeds" to finance an across-the-board tax reduction, thereby building a self-interest constituency for the spending curbs. Similarly, the 1995 congressional plan to balance the budget did not merely contain spending reductions; it also contained a tax break aimed primarily at a key constituency—families with children.

Despite the general soundness of this combination strategy, experience shows that its implementation can easily come unglued when middle-class entitlements are part of the equation. Generally, tax cuts or deficit reduction should appeal most strongly to the middle class, and thus help win middle-class support for reductions in entitlements. As mentioned earlier, however, Americans brought up in the entitlement age are strongly wedded to the idea that entitlements represent security and that receiving them is a matter of economic justice. Therefore, reforming—and even cutting—benefits to maintain the goal of security can be acceptable; but if a proposal appears to threaten the long-term security associated with an entitlement — even if it provides the instant gratification of a tax cut — or appears to give "my money" to someone else, there will be political trouble. Polling shows that even younger working Americans not directly affected by a change in a retirement entitlement generally perceive that they will have to pay the bill in the event their elderly parents face financial hardship. For this reason, the perception of "taking benefits" from seniors to reward younger Americans may not necessarily win the support of the younger group.

This is one reason Reagan's Social Security reform collapsed so quickly. Not only did it seem confusing and threatening to workers nearing retirement, but it also seemed to be robbing Peter to pay Paul, this time with tax relief. The 1995 Medicare proposal got entangled in the same damaging accusation, undermining the success of the earlier educational campaign. For one thing, it appeared that Medicare was to be "cut" simply to balance the rest of the budget. Because most Americans do not understand that the system actually siphons off money from the rest of the budget, critics were able to argue successfully that the elderly's money should not be diverted to achieve some goal that is not only arbitrary and unclear, but also of doubtful value to most Americans. Even more damaging, the Budget Act made it necessary to include the tax cut provisions in the same legislation as the Medicare changes. This allowed critics to make the fatal charge that "health care for seniors is being cut to pay for tax cuts for the rich."

The lesson to be learned from these episodes is that rather than link sensitive entitlement changes with what Americans generally would see as unrelated benefits, such as a tax cut, deficit reduction, or an unrelated new program, it would be much wiser to link the change to related reforms that increase the general sense of personal economic security. Thus, Medicare entitlement reforms might be proposed in the general context of health care security. Clinton understood this connection. In his health plan, Medicare changes that in many ways were just as threatening as recent Republican proposals were wrapped up in the general quest for health care security. The Clinton plan failed for reasons other than its very significant Medicare entitlement changes. Similarly, the Republican Medicare plan gained traction with Americans because of an emphasis on "strengthening" the Medicare system and improving choices.

The key to passing other entitlement reforms might be to link them to related proposals which help achieve the objective of the entitlement. Linking Social Security benefit reductions to steps to improve the general financial security of the elderly, such as allowing diversions of payroll taxes into IRAs, would have a good chance of success, especially in light of the declining public confidence in Social Security. So might linking proposals to curb student loans with proposals to enable families with children to increase their savings for education and other purposes.

To see how linkage can work, consider Congress's successful reform of agriculture programs in the 1995–1996 session. This is the most radical reform of farm programs in 60 years. It will phase out the largest farm subsidy programs (income entitlements) payable to farmers. Yet it passed with remarkable ease; most journalists still have to be reminded that it even occurred when they review the actions of the 104th Congress. How could this happen, especially after even modest subsidy reductions in the past had been blocked amid denunciations that cutbacks would destroy the family farm and rural life as we know it? The key was a decision to link the entitlement phase-out with the sweeping away of government control on the amount and range of crops that farmers could grow. Farmers were offered the right to control their own livelihood and freely exploit the huge opportunities in world markets—made more attractive by international trade agreements—in exchange for giving up a highly bureaucratic and restrictive government subsidy system.

Lesson #3: Provider constituencies that would gain from entitlement reform must be identified and brought into the process. Reforming an entitlement by changing the way financial security is achieved or medical services are provided also changes the present flow of huge amounts of money. This increases the likelihood that a constituency for the reform can be created among the commercial or service professions that would gain from it. One reason privatizing Social Security wins such wide public support among Americans today, for example, is that they are familiar with potential alternatives such as IRAs and 401(k) plans.

This is no accident. In the early 1980s, privatization strategists reasoned that it would be difficult to persuade Americans to take a chance on privatizing Social Security. Working people might be growing more skeptical about the system, but they would be unlikely to support private alternatives merely in theory. Strategists therefore sought to build a universal, working private alternative running parallel to Social Security *before* pushing strongly for privatization. This explains why there was such an effort to make IRAs generally available. With IRAs in place today, Americans already are familiar with large retirement accounts which they own and control, and the idea of allowing them to transfer Social Security payroll taxes into these accounts involves familiar devices that imply benefits with little risk. The availability of IRAs has generated much wider support for "medisave" accounts (medical IRAs) as at least a partial alternative to traditional Medicare.

A crucial political force in the growth of IRAs, and probably in any major future campaign to privatize Social Security, was the involvement of financial institutions that would handle the money. In the 1980s, banks, mutual funds, and similar institutions lobbied actively for IRAs and promoted them once the legislation was enacted. Similarly, Congress was able to pass sweeping Medicare reform (which later was vetoed) in part because reformers paid careful attention to the need to create a plan that could energize certain provider constituencies while mollifying others. In designing the voucher-type alternative to traditional Medicare, Congress specified that such vouchers could be used to enroll in plans organized by physicians. This plan, along with other reforms that benefit doctors, helped galvanize American Medical Association support, particularly since reform offered the prospect of a viable fee-for-service Medicare alternative to the seemingly remorseless growth of managed care.

Even more intriguing were the surprisingly muted position of the AARP and the active support of some other elderly organizations. Elderly groups usually are the destroyers of Medicare reforms. AARP grumbled loudly about the constraints placed on Medicare spending, but it also was quite open to the idea that private plans be offered to seniors. The reason: AARP was well aware that with this reform, large organizations held in high regard by the elderly, such as AARP, would have the inside track in organizing and marketing such plans. AARP's business antennae are well tuned; it already operates the second-largest mail order drug business in America, and it makes considerable money selling supplemental insurance.

Lesson #4: Commissions (and similar bodies) have their uses, but they also have their limitations. The suggestion is often made that the best way to deal with the treacherous political waters of entitlement reform would be to appoint a commission of experts to propose a solution, with Congress promising to act on the commission's recommendations. Since members of a commission would not be concerned about re-election, the argument goes, they would be able to discuss controversial matters and recommend tough reforms. Politicians could distance themselves from the commission's deliberations, saying that a panel of dispassionate experts was tackling the issue. When the panel submitted its report, lawmakers would have the political cover needed to vote for a package of changes.

In support of this approach, proponents point to such commissions as the 1982–1983 Social Security Commission and the Base Closure Commission, established in 1988. Each was generally considered a success. The Social Security Commission defused the funding crisis of the early 1980s, while the Base Closure Commission — whose recommendations Congress considered in a single up-or-down vote — ended decades of congressional paralysis over closing obsolete military installations.

Overlooked in this recommendation, however, are other commissions that ended in failure. The high-profile Grace Commission, for instance, in 1984 issued a no-nonsense report pointing to billions of dollars of wasteful federal spending that could be eliminated. Yet the report led to virtually no action and merely collected dust, as did the 1988 report of the Commission on Privatization. Proponents of a commission on Medicare also conveniently forget the fact that a Bipartisan Commission on Entitlements and Tax Reform (Kerrey-Danforth) issued its report just last year only to see its proposals completely ignored.

Why do some commissions succeed while others turn into forgotten failures? And why, even though there seem to be certain key ingredients for success, are these ingredients not easily found today when one is considering what to do about Medicare or other major entitlements?

For a commission to be successful, it must have the full, enthusiastic, and bipartisan support of all political leaders in the White House as well as in Congress. Without this support, a commission report simply becomes associated with one faction or another and fails to provide political cover for controversial actions. The commissions dealing with base closings and Social Security had this "buy-in" from the political leadership, but President Clinton and the Democratic leadership paid no attention to the report of the Bipartisan Commission on Entitlements, and its proposals were ignored. Thus, unless there is a strong, visible commitment by Washington's leadership, in advance, to act on the recommendations of, say, a Medicare commission, setting up such a panel will not lead to decisive political action; it will merely use up valuable time.

The snag is that other ingredients have to exist in the policy mix before leadership support is likely. A review of previous efforts suggests that commissions can be a success in some combination of only two situations: when the task at hand is only to find a short-term fix rather than a structural solution, or when there actually is full agreement in Congress and the White House as to what action is needed and the commission simply provides political cover. The Social Security Commission, for example, patched together a temporary fix for the retirement program and gave political cover but did not try to address long-term structural questions of equity and efficiency; in fact, the commission-driven changes made by Congress made the system an even worse deal for future Americans. In the case of the Base Closure Commission, there was universal acceptance in Congress and the Pentagon that dozens of expensive bases needed to be closed. The problem was that Members of Congress and Presidents flinched from entering the political minefield of deciding which bases should go. The requirement for up-or-down acceptance of the whole report very neatly got everyone off the hook.

Commissions can be quite helpful in certain instances by highlighting a serious problem or presenting a range of options and recommendations. This is a limited purpose, however; and while it can help further the debate, it is rarely effective in moving forward a reform if there is not widespread buy-in by the political leadership. Thus, the 1988 Commission on Privatization laid out many useful proposals but did virtually nothing to build momentum for privatization at the time because of strong congressional opposition. On the other hand, once the Clinton Administration and the 1995 Republican Congress embraced privatization, the commission's proposals turned out to be practically a blueprint for successful legislation.

In the case of entitlements, commissions also may have this limited role. The 1995 report of the Medicare Trustees (not technically a commission but having that role) undoubtedly helped the public education campaign because proponents of reform were able to publicize the bipartisan report's conclusion that Medicare is bankrupt. Similarly, while the Bipartisan Commission on Entitlements failed to provide momentum for reform, its findings may help crystallize options at some point in the future.

The problem is that resorting to a commission now probably would not advance the campaign for Medicare reform, and most probably would set back the campaign. The problem has already been identified, and the options well-developed. Setting up, say, a year-long commission to analyze the problem or present a list of options would simply leave us at exactly the same place one year later. At this stage in the debate, expecting a commission to spearhead a successful specific reform is naïve. The plain fact is that, at the moment, there is no consensus on what structural reforms are needed—only that major reforms must be made: Is it time to means-test the program? Should Medicare be transformed into a defined-contribution system? Should the entire program become a full, Canadian-style government program? There are deep ideological and practical disputes of this kind which proponents would be unwilling to devolve to a commission, and which probably would need the decisive victory of one particular viewpoint before a Medicare commission could be used to give practical reality to a new political consensus. Without such a leadership agreement going into the creation of a Medicare commission, the enterprise is likely to be ignored or to fall apart, and the Medicare crisis to deepen through inaction.

Social Security, on the other hand, might be more amenable to a commission-driven long-term solution. There is surprisingly widespread public support for reforms that would permit working Americans to devote at least a portion of their payroll taxes to a private savings plan. This quiet consensus may permit Congress to build on the current Social Security Advisory Council's general support for a private option and to create a commission to recommend future concrete reforms.

Lesson #5: The focus of any effort should be on structural reform to the programs themselves, not on achieving short-term budget savings. The political blood that has to be shed to achieve significant budget savings in the short term can prove fatal to more substantive long-term reform of the sort embodied, for example, in the 1981 Social Security reform package and the attempt to effect short-term savings in the 1995 Medicare reform proposal. Focusing on politically acceptable ways of relieving short-term financial pressures can lead to bad long-term policy. The 1983 Social Security rescue package chose the comparatively easy route of raising payroll taxes and forcing previously exempt workers into the system, among other things, and this had the effect of increasing the long-range liability of the system and reducing the effective rate of return.

The lesson of recent years is to forego short-term budget savings and focus entirely on structural reforms and delayed-impact changes that do not pose a significant threat to current beneficiaries and that also convey the theme of strengthening personal economic security, promising large savings and improvements over time.

Certain small changes now, some of which might not take effect until many years in the future, can have a large effect on entitlement spending levels. For example, one popular recommendation is to change how the Consumer Price Index (CPI) is calculated. The CPI is the government's measure of inflation—the increased cost of living—and is used to adjust benefit payments through annual cost-of-living adjustments (COLAs). There is a growing consensus that the CPI overstates the actual rate of inflation, and therefore that annual COLAs are larger than necessary. Adjusting the CPI downward so that it better reflects the actual rate of inflation would mean a small change for individual beneficiaries but a huge savings for the federal government because of the large number of people receiving those payments. A downward adjustment of only one-half of one percentage point, for example, would produce savings of some $38 billion over the next six years in Social Security alone. These savings, by the power of compounding, would continue to increase in the future.

Another popular short-term reform is to increase the retirement age for Social Security recipients. When Social Security was created in 1935, the average life expectancy was 61.4 years. With the retirement age set at 65 years, many workers never reached an age where they were eligible for benefits. Today, the average life expectancy is over 75 years and increasing. Thus, the average retiree can look forward to more than ten years of entitlement benefits. Increasing the age at which retirees are eligible for entitlement benefits would take into account this increased life expectancy. It also would mean huge savings.

STRATEGIES FOR SOLVING THE PROBLEM OF MIDDLE-CLASS ENTITLEMENTS

Before using these lessons to design a strategy for reforming particular middle-class entitlements, it is important to bear in mind four broad background points that will shape the general environment for reform. These are:

- The **demographic "window of opportunity"** now available for reform.

- The importance of **the idea of personal control of wealth** as an antidote to the demand for entitlements.

- The need to deal with entitlements as **stand-alone bills dealing with financial security**.

- The **importance of blocking liberal efforts** to "privatize" entitlements through mandates on companies.

A Demographic "Window of Opportunity." The next few years will offer an unparalleled opportunity to tackle entitlements, particularly those associated with retirement. The first Baby Boom generation is hitting age 50. This powerful constituency is no longer composed of people who see themselves as indestructible youngsters for whom retirement is a distant prospect commanding little attention and no planning; it is a constituency of graying married couples with children. These Americans are now contemplating their own mortality, and financial security in retirement is very important to them, as is the financial future of their children.

These 76 million Americans, born between 1946 and 1964, constitute a huge and active voting bulge in the political system. Compared with today's elderly, who also are concerned about financial security, the Baby Boom generation of voters differs in two crucial ways: First, the Baby Boomers have enough time before retirement to take advantage of an alternative to a traditional entitlement (for instance, by putting aside a large amount of money in an IRA as an alternative to Social Security); and second, they are far more familiar than many of today's elderly with innovative alternatives to traditional programs. Most, for instance, already have IRAs, and many are used to having a choice of medical plans, including managed care, at their place of work. These alternatives are not as threatening or unknown to them as they are to many of the elderly.

Moreover, the *post*-Baby Boomers generally referred to as Generation X are quickly becoming the largest potential voting block in the nation. This is a generation that firmly believes Social Security and Medicare will not be there when they retire: In an oft-quoted poll, more members of this young generation expressed belief in UFOs than in the solvency of federal retirement programs.

Thus, an effort to reform the major federal entitlement programs should be thought of as affecting not just one powerful voting group—the elderly —but these younger generations as well. Shifting demographics and the concerns of younger voting blocs may well present an unparalleled opportunity to build a constituency for the reform of retirement entitlements among the non-elderly. But this opportunity must not be misunderstood. Simply pitting the young against the elderly, for example, overlooks the fear among middle-aged Americans that curbing retirement programs for today's elderly might just shift costs to their adult children. Rather, it is a question of fashioning a proposal that builds support among the middle-aged.

The political window of opportunity is likely to be a temporary one (see Chart 8.3). If reform proposals are not enacted over the next few years, the Baby Boomers will be very close to retirement with less financial room for maneuver and more perceived reasons to resist proposals that might affect current retirees.

Offering Security Through Control of Wealth. Boiled down to its essence, the central issue of all middle-class entitlements turns on one word: "security." Social Security implies you will be able to retire with the knowledge that you can afford all the necessities of life and the luxuries you expect after working hard for many years. Medicare means that if you get very sick in retirement or become disabled during your working life, you will not be wiped out financially. Subsidized student loans mean that your son or daughter will be able to go to college.

In each case, a government program claims both to provide security and to be a family's cash manager and investor. The key to entitlement reform, then, is to convince Americans that government is not the best institution to carry out these functions and that private alternatives provide more security

Chart 8.3

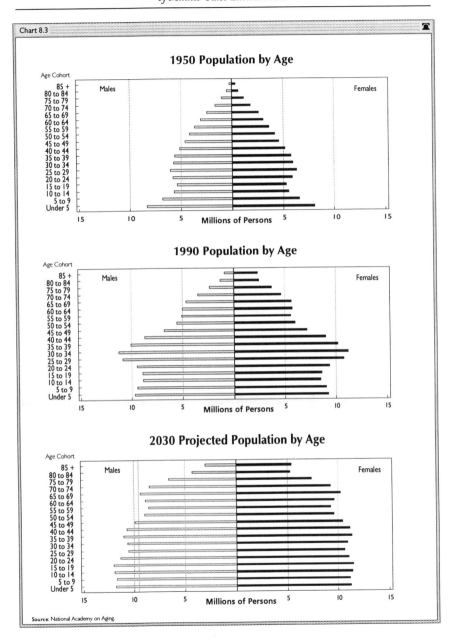

1950 Population by Age

Age Cohort

Males   Females

Millions of Persons

1990 Population by Age

Age Cohort

Males   Females

Millions of Persons

2030 Projected Population by Age

Age Cohort

Males   Females

Millions of Persons

Source: National Academy on Aging.

and a better return on their investment. In other words, if reforms are portrayed as providing more security through better alternatives, they stand a good chance of succeeding. If, on the other hand, they are portrayed simply as cutting entitlements in order to achieve some other objective like balancing the budget, they will be perceived as threatening security and unfairly reducing a return on investment to benefit someone else, in which case they almost certainly will fail.

Besides being made to see the potential for greater financial returns with private alternatives, the public must understand the crucial concept that security can be attained better under personal control through ownership of wealth than by social insurance owned and controlled by government. Americans instinctively believe this idea, and reform proposals must be designed so that they enable it to take hold. For this reason, the plan to allow retirees to control the cash value of their Medicare benefits, and to decide how to spend them, has great political potential. It also is why basing Social Security reform on a plan that allows people to opt out of the program in favor of private savings is so attractive. And it is why proposals to give Americans greater incentives to save for their children's education need to be linked to curbs on student loans: A savings option would mean that a child's education could be paid for without either parents or children having to incur a huge burden of debt.

The Need for Stand-Alone Bills Dealing with Financial Security. From Ronald Reagan's first attempt to deal with Social Security to Congress's 1995 attempt to reform Medicare, it is clear that folding entitlement reform into a large package of unrelated budget changes is a recipe for public confusion and political disaster. Just as structural welfare reform was accomplished in 1996 only after it was separated from measures dealing with the budget so that its case could be made in isolation, so the general strategy for entitlement reform must be made within a debate focused on financial security and not within the debate over the budget.

Furthermore, to build intergenerational support for reforms, the stated goal must be financial security, not "curbing entitlements." Medicare reform, for instance, must be proposed within the context of "strengthening retirement health care," in conjunction with other related measures dealing only with retiree health care. Similarly, Social Security reform must be proposed within the context of "greater retirement income security," along with such steps as repealing the estate tax and encouraging working people to save for their retirement.

The Importance of Efforts to Block "Privatized" Entitlements Through Mandates. While the expansion of government-funded entitlements over recent decades has been alarming, a more insidious development has been the recent pattern of requiring employers to act as social service agencies. For instance, pressure has grown for requiring employers to provide free or subsidized health care, family leave, and child care. These demands are hard to fight, and there is strong public support for such mandates. But there are good reasons to oppose them even while recognizing that steps may be needed to help address the underlying concern.

For one thing, mandates constitute a political free lunch for lawmakers, allowing them to create new entitlements by hiding the cost from families. Proponents of these mandates suggest that employer-sponsored services somehow are paid for by business, as distinct from direct taxes and payroll levies used to finance government-sponsored entitlements. Unfortunately, many conservatives in the 104th Congress went along with new mandates in such areas as health care to mollify constituents. The reality, of course, is that the way business actually pays for such services is by deducting the cost from worker compensation. These mandates may be a free lunch for politicians, but they are no free lunch for employees.

Even worse than the accounting fraud implicit in these mandates is that they extend even further the general notion of entitlement, especially the idea that large institutions, both government and business, somehow must guarantee security and improvement, absolving middle-class individuals and families from responsibility.

For these reasons, further attempts to add new middle-class entitlement mandates must be fiercely resisted. The Clinton health plan, the most dramatic example in recent years, failed. But recent new regulations on employer-sponsored health insurance, enacted by the Republican Congress, show just how attractive these mandates are to politicians—and hence what a danger they pose to good policymaking.

These general themes, and the lessons of previous attempts to reform programs, suggest specific techniques for enacting needed reforms in the three major types of entitlements.

Strategies for Social Security Reform:
Assuring Retirement Income Security

Building support for Social Security reform means following a clear design: Reform must give working Americans the right to place some of their Social Security payroll taxes into a private account, trimming future Social Security benefits accordingly. In addition, it must maintain a basic safety-net pension plan for all recipients and guarantee existing retirees inflation-proof benefits.

Polling shows that even though Americans are not familiar with the financial details, they already are very skeptical about the likelihood that Social Security will provide them with the income security they need in retirement. To build public support for reform, this general insecurity about Social Security needs to be focused through an education campaign that gives Americans a clear idea of current shortcomings and attractive alternatives. Absent from this campaign should be the idea that many retirees receive far more from Social Security than they paid in. Most of the elderly do not believe that, and making the case only heightens their anxiety, anger, and resistance to change. Most young Americans also assume that cutting excessive retirement benefits just means that they will have to help their parents as well as worry about their own retirement.

An ideal education campaign would be an "inside-outside" activity, with reformers in Congress and the Administration working in tandem with outside organizations on a consistent and comprehensive campaign. Such a campaign should be designed specifically to:

- **Explain** the nature of Social Security.

- **Require** that comparative rates of return are published.

- **Focus** on groups for whom Social Security is a particularly bad deal.

- **Protect** current beneficiaries.

- **Promote** an "opt-out" choice as part of a general goal of greater retirement security based on individual financial control.

- **Build** a coalition against permitting the government to invest private retirement savings.

- **Achieve** spending control gradually through cumulative changes, not short-term savings.

STRATEGIES FOR
REFORMING SOCIAL SECURITY

- The nature of Social Security must be clearly explained to the American people.

- The Social Security Administration should be required to publish the rates of return on contributions to the Social Security program.

- Congressional committees should focus on the specific groups for whom Social Security is a particularly bad deal.

- Congress should protect current beneficiaries.

- Congress should promote an "opt-out" choice as part of the general goal of greater retirement financial security based on individual control.

- A coalition against permitting the government to invest private retirement savings should be organized.

- Congress should seek gradual spending control through cumulative changes in the program, not through short-term savings.

STRATEGY #1
An effective campaign to reform Social Security must clearly explain the nature of the Social Security program.

Some 40 percent of Americans assume that under the present Social Security system, they have a real account with their own money in it, like savings in a bank, and that this is kept for them, with interest, until they retire. To build support for change, reformers in Congress need to make clear to Americans how the Social Security system actually works: that it is a program in which the government spends every penny paid into the system, and in which benefits have little to do with contributions made. This education campaign must include hearings, high-profile studies, and similar steps to raise public awareness.

STRATEGY #2

The Administration or Congress should require that the Social Security Administration provide each American with information on the rate of return on their Social Security contribution, so it can be compared with other retirement investments.

Americans with stocks, mutual funds, or bank savings are used to glancing through money magazines or newspapers to compare rates of return, and to switching their money accordingly. But although workers can get information on their Social Security contributions and probable yearly payments if they request it, and starting in 2000 all workers will receive estimates of their benefits, this information is not in a rate-of-return format, so it is not easily compared with a mutual fund or private annuity.

The Administration could instruct the Social Security Administration to provide rate-of-return information to all workers so that comparisons could be made. This calculation should include contributions made by the employer. This information could be made available to newspapers and financial magazines, leaving no doubt about the value of the investments in charts comparing Social Security with private retirement savings. Most Americans would suffer "sticker shock" when they saw the low or even negative returns on their payroll contributions and the dismal performance of Social Security compared with private alternatives.

Whether or not the Administration issued such an instruction, Congress could require it, in the interests of full disclosure. Moreover, even if Congress flinched from this, there is nothing to stop individual Members from requesting the General Accounting Office to analyze the rates of return for "typical" individuals and to compare them with typical private alternatives. Private accounting and economics organizations could issue similar information to journalists, just as they do for tax proposals.

STRATEGY #3

Congressional committees should focus on specific groups for whom Social Security is a particularly bad deal.

Some groups fare badly under the current system. For example, the typical African-American male born today has a life expectancy of less than 66 years. This means that, on average, he can expect to receive

Social Security benefits for just a few months after a lifetime of paying into the system if he retires at 65 (in fact, almost half of all African-American males born today will collect no Social Security benefits at all). And if he, or any other American, dies before retirement, his decades of forced saving though Social Security do not constitute an estate (like an IRA) to pass on to his children. In general, minority Americans do very badly under this form of annuity system, which has the effect of transferring their savings to other retirees. An IRA-type system, on the other hand, would mean a bigger nest egg to spend during retirement or to pass on to the individual's spouse or children.

Congressional committees and outside organizations could highlight these shortcomings through hearings, town hall meetings, and similar public events. The "war story" approach of highlighting typically tragic cases can be very effective in creating the political environment for change, as its use to build early momentum for the Clinton health plan clearly shows.

STRATEGY #4
Any reform must protect current beneficiaries.

Because current beneficiaries have little or no ability to reorganize their finances to adjust to changes in the system, any reform of Social Security must be combined with an ironclad commitment to pay specified benefits to current retirees, and perhaps to those close to retirement. This would accomplish two things: It would calm the fears among elderly Americans that Social Security might be taken away from them, and it would deflate that charge whenever it is made by opponents of entitlement reform. It is also a necessary step in making sure that today's workers do not feel that a structural reform could leave them having to provide greater financial support to their parents.

A guarantee might take the form of a "Social Security Bond," with a status similar to that of a Treasury bill, that a retiree could put in a safe deposit box. This would indicate a specific inflation-adjusted stream of annual benefits for the beneficiary and his or her survivor, guaranteed by the full faith and credit of the U.S. Treasury. While calculation of these benefits, particularly the inflation adjustment, still would be subject to intense debate (many experts contend, for instance, that the Consumer Price Index needs to be adjusted downward, and this would affect benefits), the political bottom line is to make sure that current beneficiaries are sufficiently protected and satisfied with that protection.

STRATEGY #5
An "opt-out" choice should be promoted as part of a general goal of greater retirement financial security based on individual control.

Various proposals put forward over the years would privatize Social Security based on an opt-out approach. Countries from Chile to Great Britain have instituted partly privatized systems with great and (in Britain's case) bipartisan support. Under this arrangement, workers would be given the right to divert some portion of their current Social Security payroll taxes into a retirement savings plan such as an IRA. Under most proposals that have been aired, the worker would still be required to pay something into the traditional system to finance a basic minimum pension and to help pay the benefits of current retirees. Most proposals would require the worker to place opt-out money in a relatively secure retirement account instead of using it, for example, to buy real estate.

To build general support for this approach, it should be portrayed as part of a general initiative to improve retirement financial security, not simply as a plan to "reform Social Security" or to dismantle Social Security (the charge critics surely will level). To win support, Social Security reforms should be part of a comprehensive set of proposals to help Americans accumulate wealth and other forms of financial protection for their own retirement, to help them build a nest egg for their children, and to reduce the potential for seniors to become a burden on their children. For example, the choice to opt out of Social Security might be combined with greater opportunities to open and build tax-deferred retirement accounts: opportunities that could be created by increasing the amounts that can be contributed to IRAs, making spousal IRAs more available, giving greater tax incentives for long-term care insurance, and repealing the estate tax. In each of these proposals, the theme should be to make future retirees more independent by enabling them to accumulate, keep, and control their own wealth. Combining all these elements around a central theme changes the focus from reforming or improving Social Security as it is to improving financial security.

Since the current Social Security System produces such dismal returns compared with private programs, it may be possible to build strong backing among Americans who might relish the rewards but not the potential risk of a private option. One method might be to require private plans to purchase an insurance policy for enrollees that would guarantee at least the return that the individual would have obtained by remaining entirely within Social Security.

STRATEGY #6
A coalition against permitting the government to invest private retirement savings should be organized.

The notion of individual control as the ultimate source of security is a powerful weapon against liberal attempts to hijack the opt-out idea and turn it into a new program that would allow government to exercise greater control over the economy and personal savings. The liberal "reform" strategy involves requiring workers to place their opt-out funds into an account that would be controlled and invested by government, either directly or through some quasi-independent board. The Clinton Administration even argued that existing trust fund money should be invested in private stocks. The danger, of course, is that this money would become a huge pool for government-directed investment in the economy — an industrial policy planner's dream. Government officials then could use other people's savings to invest in all sorts of trendy enterprises rather than seek the best return, as competing managers must do. In addition, the government investing agency inevitably would insist that the companies it invests in comply with its affirmative action, "social responsibility," and other similar objectives.

This alarming possibility makes it all the more important that, from the outset, the legislative design of a general reform gives private financial management institutions such as mutual funds, banks, and life insurance companies the right to manage the pool of new money and be held directly accountable to individual workers and retirees. Just as these institutions had an interest in providing powerful backing for the expansion of IRAs, this direct financial interest would help secure their backing for individual rather than government control of the funds. In addition, ordinary Americans need to be reminded that a government bureaucrat is hardly likely to invest their money wisely.

STRATEGY #7
Spending control should be achieved gradually through cumulative changes, not short-term savings.

Just as the public financing of entitlements tends to become a burden mounting slowly over time, so should a wise political strategy for dealing with it involve incremental structural changes and modifications that amount to huge benefits over many years. Trying to reform entitlements to gain quick budget savings invariably engenders enormous opposition from people who perceive reforms as cuts, and often leads to bad policy. Ronald Reagan's 1981 decision to delay a planned benefit increase, for instance, triggered an avalanche of righteous indignation, as did Congress's attempt last year to institute changes perceived as an immediate cut in Medicare.

The potential long-range financial impact of structural reform means that it even makes sense to "spend" money now, if necessary, to achieve greater financial benefits in the long run. One of the concerns about opt-out approaches under the current pay-as-you-go Social Security system, for instance, is that allowing workers to divert some of their payroll taxes would make it more difficult to maintain the level of current benefits. But the potential reduction of long-term liabilities associated with opting out with a corresponding reduction in benefits is so large that it would be worth whatever creative accounting is necessary (such as "off-budget" borrowing or selling federal assets) to cover the short-term shortfall.

Strategies for Medicare Reform: Achieving Health Care Security

Reform of the Medicare program should be designed around the following efforts: making Medicare a defined benefit program; giving retirees the cash value of their Medicare benefits and the right to decide what private health plan they wish to be in; and allowing retirees to remain in the current system if they wish.

Until 1995, it was generally assumed that the only way to achieve any control of Medicare spending was to impose even tighter price controls on doctors and hospitals and turn a blind eye to the damaging effect such controls have on the quality and availability of health care for seniors. Today, there is much more interest in market-based reforms. The reason: Although the 1995 Medicare reform package ultimately fell to a Clinton

---

STRATEGIES FOR
REFORMING MEDICARE

- Americans need to be convinced that Medicare as it now exists provides inferior medicine and poor financial security.

- Americans need to be convinced that Medicare must be restructured, and the focus should be on structural reform, not short-term savings.

- The public must be shown that a reformed Medicare system would be comparable to the FEHBP.

- Current beneficiaries must be protected.

- Congress should make enhancing "health care security" the focus of reform.

- Provider constituencies must be attracted to the cause.

- Bipartisan support must be built first, then reinforced with a commission.

---

veto, it demonstrated that an education campaign can change public attitudes regarding reform.

Congress's education campaign in 1995 was far from well-crafted. It was just one of many efforts by an increasingly tired and confused Congress to sell controversial proposals to an increasingly confused public. Despite its limitations, however, it achieved a remarkable degree of success.

Taking into account the lessons and missed opportunities of the 1995 political battle, an education campaign to prepare public opinion for Medicare reform would need to include the following elements:

- **Convince** Americans that Medicare provides inferior medicine and poor financial security.

- **Convince** Americans that Medicare cannot be sustained for long.

- **Compare** a reformed Medicare system to the Federal Employees Health Benefit Program (FEHBP).

- **Protect** current beneficiaries.

- **Focus** on "health care security."

- **Attract** provider constituencies to support reform.

- **Build** bipartisan support first, then reinforce it with a commission.

STRATEGY #1
For any reform to work, Americans must be convinced that Medicare provides inferior medicine and poor financial security.

Even if Medicare were financially efficient and operating with a surplus, it would provide second-rate medical care. Americans value the seeming financial security provided by Medicare; they need to understand that it provides very inadequate financial protection and that its out-of-date structure leads to bad medical care. Congress should hold hearings and well-publicized town hall meetings, for instance, and showcase senior citizens who are unable to obtain the medical care they need because of the shortcomings of the rigid benefits system, such as the lack of an out-patient prescription drug benefit. Also showcased should be senior citizens who have incurred huge costs because of a lack of catastrophic protection under Medicare. These cases should be contrasted with examples of senior citizens under private plans, including the plans covering Members of Congress and federal workers that provide far better benefits and financial protection.

STRATEGY #2
Americans need to be convinced that Medicare cannot be sustained for long and must be restructured. And reformers should focus on obtaining that structural reform, not in seeking unachievable short-term savings.

In 1995, the Medicare Trustees report was used effectively to convince many Americans that Medicare is in deep financial trouble and cannot continue for more than a few years without drastic cutbacks, unacceptable tax increases, or structural reforms to make it operate more efficiently. Over just a few weeks, the idea of a financial crisis in Medicare became accepted by an overwhelming majority of Americans.

While the immediate aim in 1995 was to convince seniors to accept changes, it would be better in the future to focus on current workers. The message should be that traditional Medicare will not be there for them and that they should support reforms giving them financial help to join (or stay in) a health plan they think is right for them. Focusing too much on the immediate crisis tends to trigger denial and allows opponents of reform to declare that "we won't let the system collapse" and "we won't let them take away your Medicare." Focusing on the long-term problem and on current workers allows proponents of reform to talk about forestalling a crisis through prudent and medically beneficial changes.

However, learning the lessons of 1995 and 1996 means not allowing opponents of reform once again to accuse reformers of "cutting" too deeply. The best way to do this would be to accept virtually any Medicare savings proposed by President Clinton — rather than face another unwinnable battle over "cuts" — and focus on long-term structural reform. If the savings proposed by Clinton proved insufficient, it would be he who had let Medicare go broke.

STRATEGY #3
A reformed Medicare system should be compared to the FEHBP.

The 1995 Medicare reform plan was a version of the plan covering Congress itself, the Federal Employees Health Benefits Program. While they differ in technical ways, the new plan followed the FEHBP by giving seniors the cash support to purchase a private health plan of their choice from among competing plans offering different benefits at different prices. While the comparison was made from time to time in 1995, there was no sustained campaign to show seniors that, as an option, they could have the same health plan current and retired Members of Congress have. Ironically, Clinton won public support for his health plan by claiming it was the same as Congress's plan even though it bore little factual resemblance to it.

This comparison to the FEHBP should be a key part of the public education campaign. Americans assume, with good cause, that Congress will make sure its own members have the best health program available. The FEHBP also provides an existing working model, and as such reduces the "leap in the dark" anxiety that leads to public resistance to a proposed change; the untested and artificial alliance system in the Clinton plan, for instance, raised considerable public concern. Finally, raising public knowledge about the FEHBP would deal with the host of criticisms and questions about a choice in health care: How can people really make choices? Would the system be stable? Would people like it? How easy is it to compare plans?

STRATEGY #4
A new Medicare plan must protect current beneficiaries.

Just as has been argued for Social Security, Medicare reform can succeed only if current beneficiaries who resist change are allowed to remain under the current system. The 1995 plan allowed the elderly to remain within a completely unreformed system if they wished. The calculation was that the private alternatives generated by the voucher-style option would be so much more efficient, and so much more attractive, that fewer and fewer seniors would decide to remain in the traditional system; hence, Speaker Gingrich's remark that the bureaucracy running the traditional Medicare system would "wither on the vine" because the demand for that option would decline sharply over time.

Keeping the traditional system as an option will need to be a central feature of future reform proposals. Very likely, as proponents of a defined benefit or voucher system argue, in the first few years a large majority of elderly Americans would choose to take the cash value of their benefits to enroll in a private plan of their choice. Most "young" seniors have experience with plans that offer many choices, good benefits, catastrophic protection, and innovative ways of providing care at a more reasonable cost. They often criticize the current Medicare system as out-of-date and would be very open to a private option. Moreover, even if the private option achieved a modest decline in the growth of future costs, the impact on Medicare's future outlays would be considerable. Thus, a reform plan could prove to be quite generous to the very elderly who are most likely to remain in the traditional system.

STRATEGY #5
Enhancing "health care security" should be the focus of reform.

As noted earlier, President Clinton won strong early public support for his health plan by understanding that the core issue for most Americans was not "cost control" or "managed care" but financial security. He argued successfully for some time that all the elements of the plan were merely technical devices to achieve that one overarching goal. Only when major parts of the plan were seen to conflict with that goal did support begin to collapse.

Based on the experience of the Clinton plan and the 1995 reform plan, Medicare reform is far more likely to succeed if it is put forward within the context of a general plan to assure health care security in retirement. Linking Medicare reforms to other reforms that would help achieve the goal of security would build a wider constituency for changes in Medicare.

For example, Congress should propose building on the Kassebaum-Kennedy health reforms by making it even easier for working Americans to choose a health plan they like no matter where they work, without tax penalty, and with the right to remain enrolled without undue premium increases, even if their health condition deteriorates. With that as the next stage in health reform for the working population, converting Medicare into a voucher program simply becomes a method of allowing Americans to keep the coverage they like in retirement instead of facing the insecurity of having to change to a different system with different doctors and benefits. Similarly, pressing to expand the medisave provisions in that legislation — for example, by making these accounts more widely available—would make a medisave option merely a logical extension of the present reforms, and provide the security of a health system that does not abruptly change for the worse upon retirement.

STRATEGY #6
Provider constituencies that could benefit from the reforms should be targeted.

The 1995 Medicare plan took the first important steps toward building constituency support in the health care industry in favor of Medicare reform. It did this in several ways. One was by crafting provisions in the legislation that appealed directly to physicians, including the explicit opportunity, through a relaxation of anti-trust restrictions, for physician-led plans to compete for Medicare patients. Another was the wide freedom of private plans to offer additional benefits and different methods of delivering care as a way to compete for Medicare enrollees. This meant that pharmaceutical companies, medical specialties not well covered under that current Medicare program, and more innovative managed care plans had a vested interest in the reform and generally supported it even though it included limits on the growth of Medicare spending. Similarly, the potential opposition of some elderly organizations was defused because the plan gave these organizations an opportunity to profit by marketing their own plans to the elderly.

A new reform plan should garner even stronger support from these and other powerful constituencies such as organized labor. Union-sponsored plans are among the most popular in the FEHBP, and are big money-raisers for such unions as the Mailhandlers. Proposals to include union-sponsored plans as an explicit option in the 1995 Medicare plan were dropped, largely because of opposition from conservatives. This was a tactical mistake that should not be repeated in the next reform plan. Strong self-interested union support not only would mean crucial backing, but also would help build support among older blue-collar workers, many of whom would see a union-sponsored Medicare plan as a more secure way to receiving their health care.

A strong effort should be made to explain to religious organizations the potential for church-sponsored plans, both as revenue generators and as a way to construct plans that would be more sensitive to the needs of congregants. The greatest political benefit of such an effort could be support within the African-American community, where apprehensions about the current medical system tend to be greatest.

STRATEGY #7
Bipartisan support should be built first, and then reinforced with a commission.

Despite the rhetoric surrounding Medicare in the 1996 elections, there is considerable potential for a bipartisan plan to achieve structural reform of Medicare. The untold story of the 1995–1996 debate on the issue is that while there was a heated debate about the amount of savings that should be sought in Medicare to stabilize the program's finances, there also were the makings of a consensus on the deeper structural reforms needed. The plan pushed through by Republicans presented rather mainstream ideas. The consensus of Republicans and many Democrats was to move away from a defined benefit program to a defined contribution system, and make it possible for retirees to turn their Medicare benefits into a cash contribution to use in choosing an acceptable private health plan. These ideas were vigorously opposed by many top Clinton officials and by liberals in Congress, but the makings of a bipartisan congressional coalition were there.

As early as possible in 1997, reformers should move quickly to solidify this potential consensus. For instance, reformers on Capitol Hill should bring together think tanks as diverse as the Brookings Institution, American Enterprise Institute, Heritage Foundation, and Progressive Policy Institute, each of which has pushed defined-contribution proposals, to emphasize the strong similarities in their approaches. In addition, the Republican leadership should meet with conservative Democrats to develop an agreeable framework for legislation. With re-election safely behind him, and with the knowledge that a Medicare bankruptcy would sully his second term, there is a reasonable possibility that President Clinton would join in designing that consensus plan.

Once a broad consensus plan could be hammered out, then and only then would it be appropriate to assemble a commission to develop the details of a legislative proposal. With the backing of the leadership in Congress and the White House, a commission could provide the political cover for enactment. Calling a commission into being before bipartisan consensus has taken firm shape, however, would virtually guarantee the political demise of structural reform.

Strategies for Reforming Student Loan Programs: Affording Higher Education

Any general reform of student loan programs should do at least three things: replace the current system of government-run debt financing of higher education with private savings-financing; make it more attractive for American families to save money for their children's education than to rely on the federal government and incur years of costly debt; and reduce students' and universities' reliance on federal assistance in general.

Intuitively, most Americans are aware of the shortcomings of the current options available for financing higher education. While median household income has increased by 82 percent over the past 15 years, the cost of public higher education has increased a staggering 234 percent. Private tuition costs have increased even more rapidly. At the same time, a college education is becoming more and more necessary for economic prosperity. The General Accounting Office reports that in 1980, the average college graduate earned about 43 percent more than the average high school graduate. Today, the difference in earnings between these same two

---

STRATEGIES FOR
REFORMING THE STUDENT LOAN PROGRAM

- Students and parents need to be made aware of the great costs and inefficiencies inherent in the federal loan programs.

- Reform efforts should be targeted on middle-class families and students.

- American families need to know why private savings, not loan indebtedness, is the best way to pay for higher education.

- Greater incentives should be developed to encourage private savings to finance higher education.

- Private savings institutions such as commercial banks and mutual funds need to be educated about the benefits of increased savings for higher education.

workers is more than 70 percent.[1] Thus, as families find it increasingly difficult to pay for college without incurring tremendous debt, the cost of not going to college makes these sacrifices difficult to avoid.

To be effective, an education campaign to build support for reform of the student loan entitlement should:

- **Help** students and parents understand the great costs and inefficiencies inherent in federal loan programs.

- **Target** middle-class families and students.

- **Explain** to American families exactly why private saving, not loan indebtedness, is the best way to pay for their children's higher education.

- **Provide** greater incentives for private savings to finance higher education.

- **Inform** private savings institutions, such as commercial banks and mutual funds, of the benefits they derive from greater customer saving for higher education.

---

1 U.S. General Accounting Office, *Higher Education: Tuition Increasing Faster Than Household Income and Public Colleges' Costs*, GAO/HEHS-96-154, August 1996.

STRATEGY #1
Effective reform of the student loan program can come about only if students and parents are aware of the great costs and inefficiencies inherent in federal loan programs.

One lesson learned from the 1995–1996 federal budget debate was that the public must be informed about the inadequacy of current programs if these programs are to be eliminated or reformed. Otherwise, opponents can portray reform as the "gutting" of a program or as an attempt to harm its stated beneficiaries. Consider just two examples.

Conservatives in Congress failed to eliminate any of the four Cabinet-level departments slated for termination. Part of the reason for this failure was that the public never understood how wasteful—and in some respects harmful — these departments are. Reformers never communicated to the American public that the Department of Housing and Urban Development (HUD) is an integral part of the nation's failed welfare system which, despite spending more than $5 trillion since 1965, has left the urban poor worse off today than ever before. HUD policies have forced poverty-level Americans to live in decrepit and inhumane conditions while lining the pockets of many often-corrupt property developers and landlords. If the American public had been made aware of these realities, it might have been possible to eliminate HUD, and opponents might not have been able to get away with portraying reformers as cold-hearted thugs interested only in throwing poor people into the streets.

With respect to means-tested federal welfare programs, on the other hand, reformers achieved notable success. The reason: The American public came to realize that the current system was broken. This was no accident. Conservatives have spent years educating people about the rising levels of illegitimacy, family breakdown, crime, and dependency associated with the federal welfare system. Once the American people understood that these problems were a direct result of the current system, reform was inevitable. In other words, a basic understanding of a program's failure is necessary if significant reform is to get off the ground.

The same is true with regard to federal student aid. Unless reformers are able to communicate to the voters that these programs are inefficient, poorly managed, and expensive for both taxpayers and students, any attempt to reform student aid will be painted simply as a radical cut in government support for higher education, and the debate will be over before it even begins.

STRATEGY #2
Reform efforts must target middle-class families and students.

Success in this debate depends to a significant degree on reaching America's politically powerful middle class. The current system of federal student loans and grants is a bad deal for middle-class families. These families typically work hard; but after taxes and other costs of daily life, they still cannot save enough to cover their children's college costs, so they turn to direct federal loans or federally guaranteed loans. The result: Parents and their children are forced deeply into debt.

STRATEGY #3
American families need to understand why private saving, not loan indebtedness, is the best way to pay for their children's higher education.

To cover tuition and fees at an average public university for four years, a student today would have to take out loans of roughly $14,000. Adding interest charges and taking into account federal subsidies, this amounts to a total debt of $19,802, or $165 a month for ten years. This means this student would enter the workforce saddled with a debt equal to the cost of a new automobile. At the same time, however, if the parents picked up the tab, they would wind up with less money for their own retirement.

Consider the alternative. If the parents of this student who attended an average public university had saved just $31 a month from the time the student was born, the accumulated savings would have covered the entire cost of tuition and fees. Instead of paying nearly $6,000 in interest, the family would have earned more than $7,000 in interest. Graduating students could enter the workforce debt free, and parents would be able to save more for their retirement or for whatever else they view as important.

Public hearings are one way to highlight both the value of higher education and the advantages of savings over debt in financing that education. Congress should hold public hearings — preferably field hearings and town hall meetings to reach as many people as possible—

about the value of a college degree and the advantages to families of saving for their children's education instead of incurring piles of debt through government loans. Oversight hearings also should be held on the inefficiencies of the current system and the problems a direct loan program will create. These oversight hearings would bring accountability to the federal loan agencies while educating American families on the benefits of savings vis-à-vis the current system of debt.

Also, as will be discussed below, the banks and stock funds that would manage education savings should be encouraged to educate their customers on the advantages of tax-deferred savings for college. America's commercial banks have established elaborate retail operations that reach nearly every family in the country. Therefore, they are in a uniquely advantageous position to educate the families with whom they interact on a daily basis.

STRATEGY #4
Greater incentives should be developed to encourage private saving to finance higher education costs.

Federal taxes alone now consume nearly 25 percent of the average family's income. This is the primary reason American families find it so difficult to save for their children's higher education.

Even a minor tax reform, such as the $500-per-child tax credit proposed as part of the congressional Balanced Budget Act of 1995, can have a tremendous impact in this area. If a young family with a newborn child were to invest the $500 credit in an "education savings account" each year for 18 years, the cumulative savings (assuming a 5 percent real rate of return) would cover more than four years of tuition at the average public university adjusted for inflation. Instead of borrowing money for their children's education, parents could save the money and avoid greater debt.

In addition, the use of tax-deferred IRAs for education should be considered within the context of the current tax structure. Such a plan, perhaps called an "edusave" account, would allow parents to withdraw savings from their IRA for their children's education without incurring a tax penalty or having to pay the money back into the account. Instead of borrowing from the federal government, parents would be using their own savings and would have the incentive to save for education within the framework of IRA accounts. Such an "edusave" system also would allow parents to plan their lifetime spending and savings better. Knowing that they could withdraw funds for their children's education, parents might save more than they would need for retirement alone. Such a system would encourage dependence on the family rather than dependence on the federal government.

Ultimately, adopting some form of a flat rate income tax is the best answer. The current system of tax deductions, loopholes, credits, varying rates, and pages and pages of forms would be replaced with one simple low rate. A flat tax would reduce the tax burden on most of America's families; thus, they would have more after-tax income that could be set aside for their children's higher education. Moreover, under most flat income tax proposals, the double taxation of savings inherent in the current system would be eliminated. This would end the current bias toward consumption and end the existing penalty against savings.

Other options to promote savings also should be considered. One idea is for universities or private banks to issue bonds that are redeemable in years of education rather than dollars. Nine states currently offer such programs for public colleges, and many more are poised to do so. Although each is different in its details, the general idea is that parents can purchase a semester or year of education now for 15 to 20 years in the future when their child is ready for college. These programs essentially lock in the cost of higher education at today's tuition rates. Some states have expanded their programs to include public and private schools. Massachusetts' "U. Plan," for example, currently includes some 75 in-state schools.

These state plans are attractive because of tax benefits given at the state level and, as of last year, by the federal government. State plans do not tax the interest that builds up on bonds purchased by parents, and with the recently enacted deferment of federal taxes on these bonds, these plans offer a better deal than private market alternatives. If Congress were to give similar tax relief for a private market for bonds issued by private colleges, there could be a surge in private savings for college. With this change, the Ivy League or any other consortium of schools could establish similar education bond savings systems that would encourage families to save for school rather than incur mountainous debt.

STRATEGY #5
Private savings institutions such as commercial banks and mutual funds should be educated about the benefits of increased savings for higher education.

The current system of federal aid, replete with a guarantee against default and an interest rate floor, provides many banks with a guaranteed source of income. Profits also are guaranteed for the relatively few companies in the secondary student loan market. Like any other self-interested constituency, these firms are valuable allies in the fight against increasing the scope of direct student loans. The organizational power of these financial institutions and the front-line contacts they have with students should be employed to build support against direct federal loans and for private-sector alternatives.

Money management companies such as mutual funds and investment banks are a potentially valuable ally in reforming higher education financing away from debt and toward savings. Because they currently enjoy a huge increase in business from tax-advantaged individual retirement accounts as established in the 1980s, these companies certainly would benefit from any expansion of these savings vehicles. For the same reason, they should be enrolled to fight for policy measures that would increase opportunities for Americans to save for higher education instead of piling up debt. Private money management companies already are very active in supporting Social Security privatization efforts and should view private higher education savings programs as inroads to the next generation of savings customers.

Moving away from the current system of loans and toward savings may be opposed initially by banks that currently benefit from government guarantees. However, this resistance can be countered by reminding banks that they also would benefit from increased savings through increased deposits. These additional funds could be used to underwrite investments that are more profitable than simple student loans. In addition, instead of being locked into one source of income, banks could dedicate these increased deposits to the most profitable investments.

Modernization of the financial sector also would help to defuse any initial resistance from banks benefiting from the current system of loan guarantees. Financial sector modernization would allow banks to offer an unlimited range of financial products, including mutual funds, and these additional products and services in turn would give banks even more profitable options to pursue when investing increased education savings.

CONCLUSION

Because of the growing impact of middle-class entitlements on the size and scope of the federal government, and because the entitlement mentality has encouraged the middle class to turn to government, conservatives must find ways to break the cycle of entitlement dependency. History shows that this will be no easy task. Conservatives have shed much political blood over entitlements with little to show for it. Nevertheless, if the hard lessons are understood, and if careful but aggressive steps are taken to reframe the public debate, Congress can achieve reforms that clearly are in the interests of all middle-class Americans.

Chapter 9

RETHINKING REGULATION

Angela M. Antonelli and Adam Thierer

Federal regulation today is vast in scope and staggering in its impact, both on individuals and on the U.S. economy. Before the 104th Congress convened, few of the reform efforts undertaken during the 1980s and 1990s had done much to stem the growth of regulation. By 1995, the scope, size, and cost of the federal regulatory system had reached an all-time high. Today, some 55 federal regulatory agencies and more than 130,000 staff employees develop, implement, and enforce a myriad of regulations, with more than 2,000 new federal rules issued every year. Regulations now are estimated to cost $677 billion a year—almost $7,000 per household, or about 19 percent of a family's after-tax budget.

The experience of the last 20 years yields some hard and clear lessons for conservatives. Put simply, conservatives who understand the problem have yet to make an effective case for reform. Success in the future will come when the American public understands that the objective of reform is not to dismantle public health, safety, and environmental protections, but to bring common sense to the process by which federal regulators make decisions about whether and how to regulate. Everyone—conservative and liberal, Republican and Democrat—wants a clean, healthy environment and safe food and consumer products. The key to reform is to communicate effectively that scarce economic resources are not being allocated efficiently

The authors would like to thank Wendy Lee Gramm, James MacRae, Jeff Holmstead, Susan Eckerly, Edward L. Hudgins, John S. Barry, John Shanahan, Ronald D. Utt, Mark Wilson, and William Laffer for their suggestions and contributions to this chapter. The views and opinions expressed, however, are solely the responsibility of the authors.

to achieve these goals. Effective regulatory reform means smarter regulation.

During the 1980s, the Reagan Administration's reform efforts proved more difficult to implement than originally expected, in large part because of an overall failure to explain the need for change to the American people. Other than modest steps toward economic deregulation of the energy, communications, and transportation industries and a new administrative review process that enjoyed some success in holding back new rules that were either unnecessary or too high in cost when measured against their expected benefits, the Reagan Administration could do little to reverse the trend toward more regulation—particularly "social" regulation designed to protect environmental quality, workplace safety, and health and product safety—that had begun in the 1970s.

While the Reagan Administration achieved modest success in slowing the growth of government regulation, the Bush and Clinton Administrations not only failed to continue this trend, but essentially reversed it. President Bush actively supported the enactment of a number of statutes—the Clean Air Act of 1990, the Oil Pollution Act of 1990, the Americans with Disabilities Act, and many others—that drove regulatory costs, often with little corresponding benefit to the public, to all-time highs. He also failed to discipline appointees who pursued aggressive regulatory policies that conflicted with his own administration's priorities. Only after the economy slipped into a recession did President Bush act to make sure that federal agencies were establishing only rules that were clearly necessary and sensible; it proved to be a case of too little too late.

Although Bill Clinton effectively used the explosion of regulation against President Bush during the 1992 campaign with a pledge to "stop handing down mandates and regulating you to death," his record on regulation as President has been achieved more by accident than by determination. What stopped President Clinton from achieving a far worse record than President Bush's was the congressional election of 1994. For example, the President's 1993 health care reform plan would have brought one-seventh of the national economy under government control and would have been the largest single expansion of regulatory authority since the New Deal. During 1995 and 1996, the new congressional regulatory agenda sought to return common sense to regulatory decisionmaking by enacting a number of new statutes which move toward a more flexible and efficient system that will cost Americans less and achieve the same or higher levels of public health, safety, and environmental protection.

When a Republican majority took control of the House of Representatives for the first time in 40 years, its policy blueprint—the Contract With America—included reforms intended to address the problem of increasingly expensive, ineffective regulation. Unlike the Reagan, Bush, and Clinton Administrations, the 104th Congress had a regulatory agenda designed not just to slow or stop harmful federal regulation, but to *reduce* the role of the federal government. The 104th Congress also made it a priority to take on for the first time the rapid expansion of major health, safety, and environmental programs which have increased steadily since the 1970s. The costs of these social regulations, particularly environmental regulation, had almost tripled over the last 20 years, rising from about $80 billion in 1977 to more than $220 billion in 1995.

Although the 104th Congress, because of its commitment to improving the regulatory decisionmaking process, did help to ensure that the Clinton Administration would not continue the rapid rate of increase in regulations that cause more harm than good, it was unable to achieve many of its most ambitious goals. Unfortunately, the 104th Congress had failed to study the lessons of the Reagan Administration, which also had great regulatory reform ambitions, and the heroic but largely futile efforts of the Council on Competitiveness to force agency regulators during the latter half of the Bush Administration to apply sound principles like cost-benefit analysis and the consideration of market-based alternatives to their regulatory decisions. Conservatives made some of the same mistakes again in their transition to leadership simply by taking on too much too fast, assuming the need for reform was obvious to the American people and failing to build coalitions and grassroots support in their home districts for their ambitious agenda. At the same time, the Clinton Administration used Congress's missteps to its own political advantage and soon painted conservatives in Congress as extremists intent not on improving the system, but on dismantling it entirely. In spite of this, however, the 104th Congress still managed to achieve a number of important goals of the boldest regulatory agenda in 20 years.

While public opinion surveys seem to suggest that many Americans today believe government regulation costs too much and usually does more harm than good, many of the efforts of the 104th Congress to reform social regulation for the first time in 20 years met considerable resistance. Conservatives mistakenly believed that building broad-based support for reform was simply a matter of illustrating how federal regulators frustrate and humiliate ordinary citizens. But this falls far short of what needs to be done to reverse 20 years of social regulatory excess. Because most Americans want environmental, health, and safety protections to be preserved, they need to be assured that reform does not mean dismantling this foundation. Unless conservatives can convince Americans of this, it will be impossible to achieve fundamental reform.

Why Regulation Matters

Government regulations affect all Americans: from the food they eat and the medications they take to how they use their private property and run their businesses. Although the direct costs of regulation typically are imposed on businesses and state and local governments, ultimately they are passed on to American consumers in the form of higher prices, reduced wages, reduced returns on investments, or reduced quality and availability of products and services. In addition, regulation can increase the cost of employing workers and thus act as a tax on job creation and employment.

How the federal government regulates is important because it has a significant impact on the economy. Professor Thomas Hopkins of the Rochester Institute of Technology has estimated the direct annual cost of complying with federal regulations to be $677 billion in 1996 (see Chart 9.1), and this estimate is likely to be low because it does not take into consideration either the direct costs that are not measured or the indirect effects of regulation on labor and productivity. A recent study by Richard Vedder for the Center for the Study of American Business shows that in addition to the costs of complying with regulations, the long-term costs of reduced productivity are high (see Chart 9.2). Federal regulations cause $1.3 trillion in economic activity—roughly equivalent to the entire economic output of the U.S. Mid-Atlantic region (New York, Pennsylvania, New Jersey, Maryland, Delaware, and the District of Columbia)—to be lost each year. Vedder explains that when a business must devote resources to implementing regulatory mandates, those resources are used less efficiently because the firm is forced to operate in a more costly and less productive manner. This significant "drag" on productivity denies workers a higher standard of living. Other studies have drawn similar conclusions. A 1995 study by the Employment Policy Foundation found that 19 percent of the

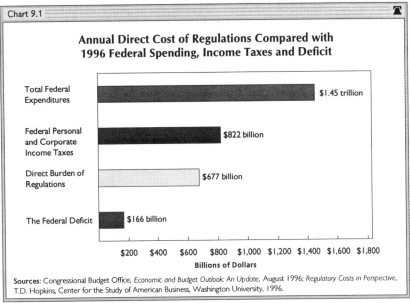

Chart 9.1

Annual Direct Cost of Regulations Compared with 1996 Federal Spending, Income Taxes and Deficit

Total Federal Expenditures — $1.45 trillion

Federal Personal and Corporate Income Taxes — $822 billion

Direct Burden of Regulations — $677 billion

The Federal Deficit — $166 billion

Billions of Dollars: $200 $400 $600 $800 $1,000 $1,200 $1,400 $1,600 $1,800

Sources: Congressional Budget Office, *Economic and Budget Outlook: An Update*, August 1996; *Regulatory Costs in Perspective*, T.D. Hopkins, Center for the Study of American Business, Washington University, 1996.

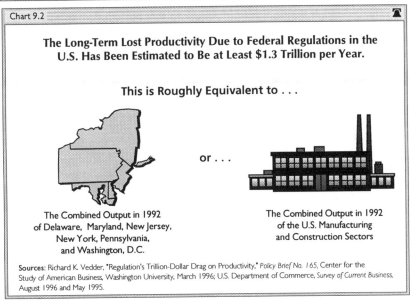

Chart 9.2

The Long-Term Lost Productivity Due to Federal Regulations in the U.S. Has Been Estimated to Be at Least $1.3 Trillion per Year.

This is Roughly Equivalent to . . .

or . . .

The Combined Output in 1992 of Delaware, Maryland, New Jersey, New York, Pennsylvania, and Washington, D.C.

The Combined Output in 1992 of the U.S. Manufacturing and Construction Sectors

Sources: Richard K. Vedder, "Regulation's Trillion-Dollar Drag on Productivity," *Policy Brief No. 165*, Center for the Study of American Business, Washington University, March 1996; U.S. Department of Commerce, *Survey of Current Business*, August 1996 and May 1995.

productivity slowdown during the 1970s is directly attributable to regulations published by the Occupational Safety and Health Administration (OSHA) and that nearly half of the slowdown in long-term productivity can be explained by rising government regulatory activity.

Many regulations today are either unnecessary or poorly designed, as well as needlessly inefficient and expensive. Federal regulatory agencies have not developed a system for making rational, well-informed decisions on how to allocate limited resources efficiently to maximize health, safety, and environmental protection. The objective of reform is to help government to shift its resources from ineffective regulations to more efficient ones, and business to devote its resources to becoming more innovative and productive.

Although the amount of money the federal government spends each year to administer its regulatory programs—almost $17 billion in 1996—is significant, it is trivial when compared with the costs imposed on businesses, private citizens, and state and local governments. For example, a ban on a particular product, such as chlorofluorocarbons (CFCs), may cost very little to enforce and may even entail very little in the way of direct compliance costs, such as paperwork requirements or litigation, for the private sector. Yet the full economic cost might be very heavy in terms of higher prices and reduced choices for consumers. For example, some elderly, who often live on limited incomes, might no longer be able to afford to buy air conditioners because the changes mandated by the CFC ban have made them prohibitively expensive.

Increasingly, regulations impose enormous costs on businesses in such areas as paperwork, permits, equipment, worker training, attorneys fees, and recordkeeping (see Charts 9.3 and 9.4). They also increase the costs of goods and services, reduce innovation and economic growth, and fail to do what they are supposed to do. Mandated requirements, such as family and medical leave, while instinctively appealing, actually affect an employer's decisions about whether and when to hire an additional worker, which worker to hire, how much to pay the worker, and how long to keep that worker.

Regulation is becoming the most politically convenient way to carry out public policy because it typically does not require substantial direct taxation or government spending. This is particularly appealing in an era of budgetary restraint. When government regulates, large numbers of people

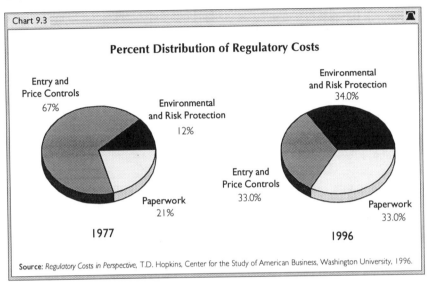

Chart 9.3

Percent Distribution of Regulatory Costs

Entry and
Price Controls
67%

Environmental
and Risk Protection
12%

Paperwork
21%

1977

Environmental
and Risk Protection
34.0%

Entry and
Price Controls
33.0%

Paperwork
33.0%

1996

Source: *Regulatory Costs in Perspective*, T.D. Hopkins, Center for the Study of American Business, Washington University, 1996.

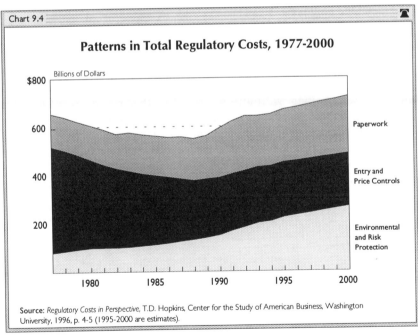

Chart 9.4

Patterns in Total Regulatory Costs, 1977-2000

Billions of Dollars

$800

600

400

200

Paperwork

Entry and
Price Controls

Environmental
and Risk
Protection

1980   1985   1990   1995   2000

Source: *Regulatory Costs in Perspective*, T.D. Hopkins, Center for the Study of American Business, Washington University, 1996, p. 4-5 (1995-2000 are estimates).

are forced to spend money to do something that a few federal employees have decided is good for society. There is nothing to stop these unelected officials from regulating as if it cost nothing, even when the costs of a particular rule far exceed its benefits, because the costs of regulation are largely hidden. Regulation acts as a hidden tax because the direct and indirect costs of implementation are passed on to the private sector—consumers, employees, employers, and stockholders—making those costs harder to measure and track. If conservatives are to succeed in fundamentally changing the role of the federal government in regulation, they must help the American people understand the economic consequences of regulation. This means making these hidden costs less hidden in a way that is easily understood and that shows their impact on people's daily lives and standard of living. If Congress fails to control the use of regulation as a substitute for spending, the benefits of efforts to control expenditures and balance the federal budget will be significantly diminished.

With respect to social regulation, a look at the indirect costs tells us that supporters of the current regulatory system who claim increased regulation always saves lives are simply wrong. Even well-intentioned regulations can cost lives. A 1994 Harvard University study examined 500 life-saving interventions and concluded that more than 60,000 lives are lost every year due to the current command-and-control regulatory system,[1] which squanders billions of dollars on eliminating risks that are negligible or nonexistent while failing to protect the public from others that are much more serious. Among the more serious risks that could be reduced are crime; disease (through the use of vaccinations); harm from hurricanes and earthquakes; or the presence of nonpoint sources of water pollution (runoffs from agriculture, mining, forestry, and construction) rather than point sources which, although easier to regulate and monitor, are not the primary sources of water pollution.

The American public needs to know how a decision to allocate resources in a particular way keeps those resources from being used in ways that could save more lives or produce other, more desirable outcomes. A world of

---

1 Tammy O. Tengs, "Optimizing Societal Investments in the Prevention of Premature Death," doctoral dissertation, School of Public Health, Harvard University, June 1994, p. 2.

competing needs and limited resources requires intensely studied decisions about how best to allocate resources to achieve the greatest benefits to society. Cost-benefit analysis is a tool for doing this.

Conservatives must not walk away from the public debate over the importance of cost-benefit analysis. Although conservatives in the 104th Congress called for the use of cost-benefit analysis in developing regulations, critics asserted successfully that the costs and benefits of regulations are difficult to quantify, and that it is difficult to place a dollar value on human life that may be saved by a regulation. They made it appear that cost-benefit analysis was the single criterion on which all decisions would rest and that, given its imprecision, this would result in the elimination of many important protections.

Cost-benefit analysis is intended to be one of several decisionmaking tools. Contrary to what critics suggest, the goal of such analysis does not mean stating a final conclusion in dollar terms; it simply means enumerating the gains and losses of a decision in the most understandable terms possible. Remarkably, this commonsense procedure, used by people every day in making decisions in their personal lives, has been deemed too radical for the federal government to use regularly in making decisions about how to protect public health, safety, and the environment.

The American public actually has little or no information on the benefits and costs of regulation. One way to make the case for change is to use effective examples of the huge costs of regulations and the trivial benefits they provide and then—which is even more important—to contrast them with actions not taken that would provide greater benefits, such as saving more lives. The American people need to feel they have as much right to engage in dialogue over regulatory priorities as they have to debate federal budget priorities.

Conservatives need to invest the resources to challenge agency analyses of the impact of regulation on the economy. All too often, the only analysis that is done is prepared by federal regulators who have little incentive to make rational regulatory decisions, and there is little independent outside analysis to verify how well this work is done. Conservatives would benefit greatly from investing in third-party, independent research organizations with the technical tools needed to comment and peer review the quality of analysis done by federal regulators.

The Presidential Track Record:
Controlling the Regulatory Burden

The Nixon Years: A Tidal Wave of Regulation. The great explosion in federal regulation began when President Richard Nixon signed legislation creating a host of new regulatory agencies, including the Environmental Protection Agency (EPA), Occupational Safety and Health Administration (OSHA), Consumer Product Safety Commission (CPSC), and National Highway Traffic Safety Administration (NHTSA). Nixon also signed a number of major pieces of regulatory legislation, including the 1970 Clean Air Act and the 1973 Endangered Species Act, and imposed specific controls on areas ranging from noise pollution to pension programs, in addition to general wage and price controls. The brief presidency of Gerald Ford continued and expanded the red tape of the Nixon years, although Ford did remove most of Nixon's wage and price controls.

The Carter Term: Regulatory Ebb and Flow. President Jimmy Carter's record on regulation was mixed. From the early 1920s to the 1970s, the federal government had major and growing responsibility in regulating industries like transportation, communications, finance, and energy, either by controlling prices and services or by establishing financial standards of safety and soundness. By the late 1970s, momentum built for removing the heavy hand of government to allow industries to rely on market forces. In the late 1970s, Congress passed four major pieces of legislation that deregulated airlines and air cargo and liberalized the regulation of trucking and railroads. Further, Carter removed restrictions on the rate of interest that banks and other depository institutions could pay their depositors and took the first important steps toward the eventual decontrol of oil prices. Finally, Congress passed and the President signed into the law the Paperwork Reduction Act of 1980 that gave the White House Office of Management and Budget the responsibility for reviewing and eliminating unnecessary and costly federal paperwork requirements imposed on the public. Despite a number of positive steps, however, President Carter also tightened environmental regulations, created the Department of Energy, and tried to impose race and sex quotas on businesses.

The Reagan Resistance: Stemming the Tide. One of the major goals of Ronald Reagan's bid for the presidency was to reverse the social regulatory expansion initiated in the early 1970s under President Nixon. However, President Reagan proposed relatively little legislation to change things. His main legislative strategy was to try to block, through the use or threat of presidential veto, legislation that would have increased red tape and slowed the rate of economic growth. More important, Reagan took steps to reduce the volume of administrative rules issued by government officials. Among his most important actions were:

- **Issuing** Executive Order 12291, requiring all executive branch agencies to estimate the benefits and costs of new regulations they wished to issue and to select regulatory alternatives that maximized net benefits to the extent permitted by law;

- **Designating** the Office of Information and Regulatory Affairs (OIRA) within the White House Office of Management and Budget (OMB) as the central office for evaluating the cost-benefit analyses of regulations developed by the agencies;

- **Establishing** a Task Force on Regulatory Relief, headed by then Vice President George Bush, to oversee federal regulators and to identify and address the most burdensome federal regulations;

- **Appointing** to most Cabinet departments and independent agencies individuals who recognized the need to return common sense to regulation; and

- **Significantly reducing** the staffing of most regulatory agencies.

The Reagan Administration's inability to implement more fundamental change in the federal government's role in regulation was due largely to the success of its opponents. These critics of reform claimed the moral high ground very early and put the Administration on the defensive in trying to explain why its reforms would not hurt women and children while benefiting corporate America.

The Bush Resurgence: Rising Regulatory Waters. Although President George Bush claimed to want to return common sense to regulatory decisionmaking, his presidency was characterized by a serious resurgence of regulation with enormous costs and little benefit. During his four years, the annual number of pages in the *Federal Register* rose by more than 9,000, or about 16 percent; the staffing level of federal regulatory agencies increased sharply, with 21,254 new bureaucrats added for an all-time high of 125,666 regulatory employees; and the amount of money the federal government spent each year administering its regulatory programs soared (see Table

9.1). Measured in constant 1987 dollars, federal regulatory spending grew by
only $782 million over the entire course of Reagan's two terms in office,
from $8.8 billion in Carter's last year to $9.6 billion in Reagan's last year.
Bush increased federal regulatory spending more than twice as much as
Reagan and in only half the time; in constant dollars, regulatory spending
under Bush grew by $1.7 billion, from $9.6 billion to $11.5 billion.

Table 9.1				

Measures of Federal Regulatory Activity: 1975-1996

	Total Number of Pages in Fed. Register	Total Federal Regulatory Employees	Total Federal Regulatory Spending (Millions of Dollars)	Total Number of Pages in the Code of Federal Regulations
1975	60,221	102,243	$7,079	71,224
1976	57,072	107,834	6,954	72,740
1977	65,603	108,788	7,650	84,729
1978	61,261	115,032	8,004	94,151
1979	77,498	119,800	8,491	98,032
1980	87,012	121,791	8,785	102,195
1981	63,554	117,209	8,313	107,109
1982	58,494	106,415	7,895	104,938
1983	57,704	101,303	7,654	105,654
1984	50,998	101,847	8,232	111,830
1985	53,480	102,192	8,418	105,935
1986	47,418	101,933	8,237	109,509
1987	49,654	101,804	8,993	114,337
1988	53,376	104,412	9,562	117,480
1989	53,841	107,017	9,737	122,090
1990	53,620	114,640	10,218	126,893
1991	67,716	118,519	10,530	125,331
1992	62,928	125,666	11,454	128,344
1993	69,688	129,577	11,885	132,228
1994	68,108	128,566	11,808	134,196
1995	68,419	130,929	12,004	138,186
1996	68,000*	131,919	12,400	Unavailable

Note: *Estimated. Employees are Full-Time Equivalent employees. Spending figures are in 1987 dollars.
Source: *Federal Register, Budget of the United States, Code of Federal Regulations;* various years.

Some of the blame for this growth in regulation lies with the individuals
President Bush appointed. With only a handful of exceptions, these
appointees were far more prone to issue regulations and support regulatory
legislation than their Reagan predecessors. For example, although EPA

Administrator William Reilly maintained that he tried not to impose undue regulatory burdens on businesses and households, he and his agency were at the forefront of the regulatory buildup. A case in point: Just days after George Bush had been sworn in as President, the EPA and the Army Corps of Engineers significantly expanded the scope of federal wetlands regulations. Land that had standing water for as little as seven days per year could be subject to federal control as a "wetland," as could land that was dry at the surface but moist within 18 inches of the surface. In some cases, this meant prohibiting farmers from planting crops on their own land and stopping home gardeners from planting flowers. In one case, a man was jailed for clearing away old tires and putting fill dirt on his own land as a base for a garage. Similarly, civil rights and antitrust officials at the Department of Justice and antitrust officials at the Federal Trade Commission expanded the scope of their enforcement activities well beyond that of their predecessors under Reagan.

The principal driving force behind the growth in regulation during the Bush Administration often was legislation encouraged by political appointees in direct conflict with the President's own priorities. Several laws in particular resulted in a surge of new regulation:

- **The 1990 Clean Air Act Amendments.** Environmental regulation accounts for the largest share of the recent regulatory explosion. Bush promised during the 1988 campaign to support a new clean air bill, and he was instrumental in securing its passage. Estimates of the cost of the legislation varied, but all have been huge. Murray Weidenbaum, former chairman of the Council of Economic Advisers under Reagan and now Director of the Center for the Study of American Business at Washington University in Saint Louis, estimated that the law would "cost an added $25 billion to $35 billion a year, over and above the more than $100 billion [already] spent annually on all pollution controls." Economist Paul Portney of Resources for the Future, a Washington, D.C., think tank specializing in environmental issues, estimated that the new law would cost between $29 billion and $36 billion a year while providing only about $14 billion a year in benefits.

- **The 1990 Americans with Disabilities Act (ADA).** Although described as a "civil rights" bill by its supporters, including President Bush, the ADA does much more than simply prohibit discrimination against the disabled. It also requires owners of private businesses, apartment buildings, restaurants, and stores to make—at their own expense—various physical modifications in their premises, such as widening doorways and installing wheelchair ramps, in order to accommodate the disabilities of current and potential employees, tenants, and customers, regardless of the cost and even if better and cheaper alternatives are available. Hotels and auto rental companies must absorb the extra expense of including wheelchair lifts on all their new pickup vans, and public transit systems must install wheelchair lifts on all new buses. It has been estimated that the cost of the ADA, though difficult to calculate, is similar to that of the 1990 Clean Air Act.

- **The 1991 Civil Rights Act.** Ostensibly an attempt merely to restore civil rights law to where it stood before a series of Supreme Court decisions in 1988, this legislation radically changed federal employment discrimination law. It made it easier for employees to sue employers, harder for employers to defend themselves successfully when they are innocent of any actual discrimination, and more expensive for employers when they lose. The new law allows the proportion of workers of various races in an employer's workforce to be used as *prima facie* evidence of discrimination; in addition, instead of requiring the plaintiffs to prove the employer guilty, it requires the employer to prove that he is innocent, thereby shifting the burden of proof from plaintiff to defendant.

  The additional costs of litigation and fines act like a tax on employment. With each new job an employer creates, his recordkeeping burdens and chances of being sued increase. Even if an employer tries to avoid litigation by using quotas when hiring minorities and women, he can never eliminate the risk of being sued over the racial composition of his work force. Moreover, an employer who uses quotas risks being sued for deliberate discrimination by those whom the quotas exclude. And even if the employer is lucky enough not to be sued, his work force will be less productive because he was forced to hire by race and sex instead of by merit. Thus, no matter which way an employer turns, the cost of creating jobs and employing people will have risen.

- **Other Regulatory Burdens.** Other legislative initiatives signed by Bush include the 1989 increase in the federal minimum wage, the Oil Pollution Act of 1990, the Nutrition Labeling and Education Act of

1990, the Pollution Prevention Act of 1990, and increased authority for the Securities and Exchange Commission (SEC). When all of Bush's regulatory initiatives are added together and combined with increases in staffing and budgets at various federal regulatory agencies and the more vigorous and far-reaching enforcement policies adopted by so many of Bush's key appointees, it becomes clear that Bush was responsible for an enormous increase in federal regulation. Indeed, according to a *National Journal* article entitled "The Regulatory President," American business under George Bush experienced "the most imposing over-all extension of regulatory authority since Nixon."

There were a few bright spots in the effort to stem the tide of costly and ineffective regulation during Bush's term; but once again, it was a case of too little too late. Shortly after he was inaugurated, for example, Bush created the Council on Competitiveness, headed by Vice President Dan Quayle. The Council's task was to review major new regulations with a view to injecting common sense into regulatory decisions whenever possible, and to act as a referee when different executive branch agencies disagreed.

The Council's staff was quite small, however, and reviewed only a handful of the annual flood of regulations that the executive branch issued. The Council was able to intervene in drafting only a few dozen regulations, whereas the total number of regulations issued by agencies within the executive branch was on the order of 2,000 to 3,000 per year. Moreover, even when the Council did review an issue, it had to deal with agency personnel, many of whom resented having their authority to manage the economy questioned or curtailed, and a Democratically controlled Congress that played politics with the Council's activities. Lack of cooperation—and sometimes outright resistance—by the agencies made the Council's task even more difficult and limited its effectiveness.

Another source of dashed expectations was OMB's Office of Information and Regulatory Affairs, the agency responsible for ensuring that new regulations would not cost more than the benefits they provided. Despite the urging of his most loyal advisers, including Vice President Quayle, White House Counsel C. Boyden Gray, and Council of Economic Advisers Chairman Michael Boskin, President Bush failed to give OIRA the support it needed to assure that regulations maximized their benefits to society. Instead, Bush listened to OMB Director Richard Darman—the same adviser who persuaded the President to break his solemn "no new taxes" promise to the American people—and did not push a recalcitrant Congress to appoint a permanent head of OIRA. Because Bush had not given it the support it needed, OIRA was preoccupied with defending itself against congressional attacks instead of with taking the offensive to ensure that regulations were sensible.

Recognizing the burden that regulation places on the economy, President Bush in January 1992 announced a 90-day moratorium on most new regulations. As part of the moratorium, regulatory agencies were instructed to evaluate their existing regulations and to develop initiatives that would streamline regulation and create jobs and economic growth. A few agencies announced constructive reforms during this period; the Food and Drug Administration, for example, proposed new procedures to expedite its approval of new drugs, and the Securities and Exchange Commission took steps to make it easier for smaller businesses to raise capital by selling stock. But as the magnitude of the regulatory crisis became apparent, the original 90-day moratorium was extended by an additional 120 days, to the end of August.

There is only so much that a moratorium focused mainly on new regulations can accomplish. While less new red tape is a relief for business, the regulations put into place during the Bush Administration continue to burden the economy. Unfortunately, since most of these new regulations were mandated by legislation which the President signed, they cannot be repealed without the cooperation of Congress.

The Clinton Presidency: Riding a Congressional Wave of Reform. The Clinton Administration's record on regulation is arguably better than that of the Bush Administration; but it could well have been just as bad—or even worse—without a Republican-controlled Congress committed to putting into place principles to test whether federal regulations were necessary, sensible, and more beneficial than harmful. Thus, it comes as no surprise that the Clinton Administration's record on regulation seems to suggest a slower rate of activity.

Overall, the record of the Clinton Administration is much more like the Bush Administration's record than the Reagan Administration's. The Clinton Administration has done no better than the Bush Administration in holding federal agencies accountable for adhering to sound regulatory principles. For example, on September 30, 1993, President Clinton issued

Executive Order 12866 ("Regulatory Planning and Review"), replacing a Reagan Administration executive order requiring executive branch agencies to submit proposed regulations with a cost in excess of $100 million to OMB for review and approval. In the new executive order, the Clinton Administration reaffirmed its commitment to using the best scientific and economic data; using analysis to inform decisionmaking; considering flexible, cost-effective performance standards; and allowing early public participation in an open and accountable regulatory process. However, the Clinton Administration actually has reviewed only about 800 rules—about one-third the number reviewed during the Reagan and Bush Administrations—to see whether they meet the principles outlined in E.O. 12866.

In addition, there is little evidence that the order has had any significant impact or that the White House is encouraging agencies to comply. An April 1995 study by the Institute for Regulatory Policy examined all EPA proposed and final rules published in the *Federal Register* during the second six months after the Clinton executive order took effect. Based on an analysis of 222 substantive rulemakings, the study found only six for which the demonstrated benefits justified the costs involved. In addition, only 14 examined regulatory alternatives, and only eight of these specified that the most cost-effective rule had been adopted. Federal agencies currently are doing fewer analyses of rules because the Clinton Administration is not enforcing its own regulatory review executive order, and the Administration's delegation of oversight of most rules to agencies has failed miserably. In fact, a September 1996 report by the U.S. General Accounting Office (GAO) indicates that the Administration does not require any type of cost-benefit analysis for the majority of rules it reviews.

Soon after the 104th Congress took office, the Clinton Administration initiated a number of steps that made it look as though it was serious about its promise to produce smarter regulations. For example, on February 21, 1995, the White House directed federal agencies to conduct a review of their existing regulations to determine which should be eliminated and which should be streamlined, updated, overhauled, or otherwise improved. However, by the end of 1996, the Administration had made no real progress. For example:

- At the end of 1992, the Code of Federal Regulations, the annual accumulation of all federal regulations in effect, filled 199 volumes and

128,344 pages. By the end of 1995, the CFR had grown to 205 volumes and 138,186 pages—almost 10,000 pages of new executive branch rules in just three years (see Table 9.1).

- A number of costly new rules with potentially little benefit are being developed. On May 3, 1996, the Administration published its 1,700-page semiannual agenda of federal regulations, which presents very brief descriptions of all planned regulatory actions. It contains 4,500 new rules in development that will cost at least $11 billion.

- While EPA claims to be streamlining various permitting, review, and reporting requirements for a number of programs, the Clinton Administration simultaneously is pushing forward with burdensome regulatory initiatives, such as expanding the universe of sources that must report as part of the Toxic Release Inventory. Critics argue that last year's expansion will mean as much as $331 million in compliance costs with little or no benefit.

- The Administration, while asserting that it is committed to sound science, is pursuing federal guidelines on cancer assessment to make it easier to regulate or ban substances despite the lack of sound scientific evidence that they pose any risk. Virtually all scientists who conduct statistical analyses to determine cancer risks (or any other analyses, for that matter) use confidence levels to determine the likelihood that their results are accurate. But the EPA proposed new rules in April 1996 that would eliminate the current requirement that EPA use confidence levels in doing risk assessments. Under this new rule, EPA would be able to conclude that something is dangerous on the basis of evidence that would fail under any rigorous scientific study.

- In a September 1996 report, the GAO concluded that more than 50 percent of agency actions to eliminate rules from the Code of Federal Regulations were taken because the regulations were obsolete. For example, the Veterans Administration said it was eliminating a regulation providing lump-sum payments to veterans involved in an incident in Texas in 1906. The GAO further concluded that "it did not appear that the CFR pages being eliminated would reduce substantively the regulatory burden."

The Clinton Administration has done little to change how federal agencies regulate the public. In fact, it has worked tirelessly to block the enactment of comprehensive reform legislation that would have codified the principles found in the President's executive order. This legislation would have done more than anything else to make sure that agencies made the smarter regulatory decisions that the Administration has claimed it wanted. The Administration continues to take the position that fundamental reform can and should be achieved through administrative change, not through statute. The Clinton Administration's lack of commitment to making any real improvements, however, only reinforces the need for Congress to establish a statutory roadmap for federal regulators to follow in making decisions that includes commonsense, well-defined analytic standards that all rules must meet.

The 104th Congress: The Boldest Agenda in 20 Years. Not unlike the Reagan Administration, the 104th Congress was under assault from opponents of reform who scared the American public into believing that reform would have disastrous consequences. The Clinton Administration went from being an "agent of change" in 1993 to the protector of the status quo in 1995. While abdicating any legislative agenda of its own, the Clinton Administration was very successful in frightening the American public and blocking much of the 104th Congress's social reform agenda. Nevertheless, the 104th Congress's record of accomplishment was still the boldest in the past 20 years. While the accomplishments of the preceding 20 years focused on freeing industries to rely on market forces ("economic deregulation"), the 104th Congress for the first time tackled basic programs and the costly and ineffective expansion of major health, safety, and environmental regulations to carry out these programs.

The 104th Congress stands alone in the scope and scale of its reform efforts. In a two-year period, it introduced legislation to reform many of the largest environmental statutes, such as the Safe Drinking Water Act, Superfund, the Endangered Species Act, and others like the Food, Drug and Cosmetic Act and the Occupational Safety and Health Act. It tackled many other areas of economic regulation as well, such as agricultural subsidies, telecommunications, and tort reform. The goal of this Congress was to impose discipline on the federal regulatory process and fundamentally change how the federal government and the American people think about regulation, particularly public health, safety, and environmental regulation.

Unfortunately, the 104th Congress failed to bring about the desired changes in environmental, public health, and safety regulations. Once again, opponents of reform were able to capture the moral high ground with surprising ease. In many cases, supporters of federal regulatory agencies effectively depicted those who supported change in brutally inhuman terms, suggesting a willingness to sacrifice helpless women and children to evil business interests.

Alarmists did a good job, in this first round, of convincing the American public that regulatory reform was just another term for the rollback of important public health, safety, and environmental protections. As a result, Congress still has not seen many of its most ambitious efforts signed into law. Many in Congress believe they lost the battle to reduce the burden of regulation and cut away the approximately $700 billion in red tape that strangles American businesses and consumers. However, conservatives should take to heart the many hard lessons learned during the legislative battles of the 104th Congress.

LESSONS LEARNED

In retrospect, conservatives have learned a number of important lessons in trying to carry out a regulatory reform agenda.

Lesson #1: Change must be approached slowly and incrementally. Conservatives tried to improve 20 years of social legislation in less than two years. This agenda was far too ambitious, particularly in light of the complexity of some of the scientific issues involved. Achieving fundamental change will take years, just as it has taken years to get where we are today.

Lesson #2: For successful reforms to pass, it is imperative that a positive vision is conveyed and that advocates of reform stick to it even when the momentum shifts. Unfortunately, when the opponents of reform began to be effective in portraying conservative reformers as extremists intent on destroying important protections, conservatives backed away too quickly and conceded defeat. When the momentum shifts, conservatives must hold their ground, maintain a positive vision, and stay on message. They can do this by taking every opportunity with the media and local constituencies, for example, to affirm their commitment to a clean environment, safe consumer products, and healthy workplaces.

For example, concern for the environment should not be conceded as the sole province of professed "environmentalists." Conservatives also are

---

LESSONS LEARNED

- Change must be approached slowly and incrementally.

- For successful reforms to pass, it is imperative that a positive vision is conveyed and that advocates of reform stick to it even when the momentum shifts.

- Americans need to see that there are alternatives to government intervention and to understand exactly how these alternatives would benefit them.

- The need for change is not always obvious to the public. Americans need to understand how current government solutions fail them.

- Conservatives need to recognize messages that simply do not work.

- Special interests that represent themselves as "public" interests can hurt rather than help reform.

- Advocates of reform must never underestimate the emotionalism, commitment, and confidence of those who support the current system.

- Conservatives need to work with natural allies, not the opposition.

- People are policy.

---

concerned about the environment, and they must remind the public that the real debate is about how best to protect the environment: through government intervention or market-based incentives. The same is true about how the federal government regulates particular industries, such as the telecommunications, transportation, or utility sectors of the economy. What distinguishes conservatives is a belief that it is possible to do a better job of protecting the environment and to do it in a way that strengthens, not weakens, the economy. It is possible to have both a cleaner environment and a healthy economy, but the current system is failing.

Lesson #3: Americans need to see that there are alternatives to government intervention and to understand exactly how these alternatives would benefit them. For people to be willing to accept change, they must see that there are successful alternatives to the current system. It is not enough for conservatives to point out how the current system fails the American people. They also must invest in the analysis that shows how reform, such as reliance on market-based alternatives, will benefit them. They must show that health and economic well-being will be enhanced through reform. This can be done with case studies or more sophisticated economic analyses that show how higher productivity, higher wages, and more jobs can be created while existing levels of services or protections are preserved and improved.

Lesson #4: The need for change is not always obvious to the public. Americans need to understand how current government solutions fail them. Advocates of reform need to show the public, in very concrete and simple ways, how Americans are let down by the current system. People need to know how much of their earnings is affected by regulations imposed on their employers. They need to see how their employers and state and local communities are disadvantaged by federal mandates and how this affects, for example, the quality of their education and public safety. They need to understand that more lives can be saved if federal regulators can prioritize and address the risks they face more effectively. Conservatives have become better at using anecdotes and making things easily understandable to most Americans, but they still have a long way to go.

The 104th Congress should have used oversight hearings much more frequently and aggressively to show how the federal regulatory system hurts the American people. Conservatives must press regulators to explain the motivations behind their proposed regulatory actions, who pays and who benefits, and to what extent the Administration is consistent in carrying out its own regulatory principles. Once the regulation is in place, if it truly is more costly and provides significantly less benefit than the agency predicted, Congress has a record to show just how poor a job of decisionmaking regulators are doing.

Lesson #5: Conservatives need to recognize messages that simply do not work. Historically, conservatives have tended to convey the idea that there is a trade-off to be made between environmental or other types of protections and the demands of economic growth. This has been interpreted as shorthand for rolling back decades of protections. Balancing costs against a child's life is a losing proposition. However, conservatives *should* show the public that a decision to invest resources to save 20 lives might mean that these resources will not be available for some other action that actually would save 200 lives. The public needs to understand the differences between the benefits a rule produces and the benefits foregone by taking that action. If conservatives can show that their policies enhance economic growth while doing a better job of protecting the environment and public health, reform will be possible. Again, smarter regulation equals more protection and a stronger economy. A recent Danish study concluded that countries with the highest levels of regulation suffered from the slowest economic growth.[2] Moreover, reduced economic activity due to regulation actually increases risks because living standards are reduced and mortality rates are raised.

The American people do not believe that every regulation is a bad regulation; thus, conservatives will meet considerable resistance to change if they convey the perception that the objective of reform is no regulation at all. Certain terms, however, give this impression. Among the worst, for example, are "deregulation" and "regulatory relief." Even the term "reform" has acquired a negative connotation with the public. Conservatives need to convey the message that most appropriately reflects their objectives: the need for smarter regulation. This can be accomplished through the use of sound analytic principles in the regulatory decisionmaking process. Smarter decisions about whether and how to regulate will enable the American public to enjoy higher levels of protection at less cost.

Lesson #6: Special interests that represent themselves as "public" interests can hurt rather than help reform. As economist Robert McCormick of Clemson University has noted, "when the flag of public interest is raised to support regulation, there is always a private interest lurking in the background."[3] There is hardly a regulatory program that

---

2 "Two rules good, four rules bad," *The Economist*, October 12, 1996, p. 85.

3 Robert E. McCormick, "A Review of the Economics of Regulation: The Political

does not benefit some industry or subset, most often at the expense of consumers or rivals. Understanding that most groups have some kind of agenda of their own will ensure that conservatives do not make the mistake of naively charging forward with reforms that come from just one group or perspective and that benefit one particular industry, thereby opening themselves, however unwittingly, to charges of favoritism or backroom dealings.

Lesson #7: Advocates of reform must never underestimate the emotionalism, commitment, and confidence of those who support the current system. Supporters of the current system can be expected to play politics with people's lives. For example, supporters of the status quo have not hesitated to argue that women would be denied life-saving mammograms and that the nation's food supply would not be safe from deadly *e. coli* bacteria. Both are untrue. Even worse, these scare tactics prevent improvements in regulatory decisionmaking that actually would allow Americans to devote more resources to activities that they know save lives. Reformers should ask—and keep asking—how many people have died because of the failures of the current regulatory system. To some degree, conservatives need to approach their reforms with the same level of emotionalism, commitment, and confidence to keep the moral high ground.

Lesson #8: Conservatives need to work with natural allies, not the opposition. The Clinton Administration's success in slowing the conservative agenda in Congress was based on its willingness to work with its Democratic allies on Capitol Hill rather than with the Republican majority. Conservatives in previous Administrations have forgotten that negotiating with the opposition on the Hill while ignoring allies sabotages not only their allies, but their own policies, and thus allows the opposition to dictate terms and determine the outcome. The Clinton Administration has enjoyed this success because many Republican successes on regulatory issues have come through compromise with Democrats. The Clinton Administration, for example, received more of

Process," in *Regulation and the Reagan Era*, ed. Roger E. Meiners and Bruce Yandle (Oakland, Cal.: The Independent Institute, 1989), pp. 27-28.

the credit than congressional Republicans for the 1996 Food Quality Protection Act and reform of the Safe Drinking Water Act.

One of the most important reasons the Administration was so effective is that it really had no agenda of its own and largely reacted to the agenda set by Congress. In doing so, it developed and maintained a cohesive message and unified voice. It proved much more difficult to get hundreds of Members of Congress to agree on and communicate a cohesive message on any one of the dozens of legislative initiatives undertaken. Thus, over time, instead of taking the initiative, conservatives in Congress allowed themselves to be maneuvered into a defensive position on regulatory issues. The Clinton Administration soon assumed the offensive position, successfully arguing that many of its initiatives were far superior to anything that Congress was suggesting. This often was the story that appeared in the press, further adding to the resistance to change and leading Congress to give up many of its attempts at reform, fearing bad publicity and outright defeat. With such an ambitious policy agenda, Congress was not able to benefit as it could have from individuals and groups who might have tackled the opposition and deflected some of the public attention on controversial issues.

Lesson #9: People are policy. Because elected leaders cannot closely monitor every issue 24 hours a day, it is vital that they be able to trust their staffs to represent their views during the policymaking process. If conservative policymakers want to ensure their policies are implemented in a principled fashion, they must ensure their staff members are as conservative as they are. This is particularly important when considering who will fill staffing positions on committees that deal specifically with regulatory policy. Too often, conservatives in Congress have been willing to hire staff simply because they had some previous experience on a particular committee or on Capitol Hill in general. But people are policy, and a more liberal staff only undermines the conservative agenda.

STRATEGIES
FOR REFORMING REGULATION

If Members of Congress hope to craft successful reform initiatives in the future, they not only must learn how to communicate the costs and adverse consequences of over-regulation more effectively, but also must develop a sophisticated set of principles and feasible strategies to deal with the many

---

STRATEGIES FOR REGULATORY REFORM

- Congress should write smarter legislation.

- Congress should pursue aggressive oversight and implementation of its new regulatory review authority.

- The budget and appropriations process should be used to effect change in the regulatory structure.

- Congress should scrutinize agency enforcement activity.

- Congress should establish procedural reforms.

- Congress should allow for judicial review.

- Congress should identify regulatory policy objectives and priorities.

- Conservatives should invest in the analysis needed to show how government solutions fail the American people.

- Conservatives can make a more effective case for private alternatives to government regulation.

- Conservatives must improve their message, develop a positive vision, and stick with it no matter what happens.

- Conservatives should build effective coalitions that support reform.

---

different regulations and bureaucracies that comprise the regulatory state. How advocates of change should formulate these strategies will depend on which types of regulations they hope to improve or eliminate. More specifically, different strategies will be needed to deal with different goals for social and economic regulations.

Economic Regulation: The Goal of "Complete Withdrawal." Supporters of regulatory reform should pursue a strategy of "complete withdrawal" in the field of economic regulation because there is little to no remaining justification for federal involvement in such sectors of the American economy as electricity, natural gas, communications, transportation, aviation, agriculture, and banking. These sectors should be completely freed from outdated, counterproductive barriers to entry, licensing and tariffing laws, price controls, and other economic regulations that make markets less competitive, discourage efficiency, and lessen overall consumer welfare. Specific areas of economic regulatory reform that conservatives should consider pursuing under this strategy include:

- **Electricity and energy** regulations;

- **Banking** statutes and other financial regulations;

- **Telecommunications** rules; and

- **Transportation** regulations.

Because these issues are technical and less provocative in nature, they are not likely to evoke either a strong response or a sense of urgency in the general electorate or in the media. Lives typically are not at stake. Members of Congress need to work cooperatively with other interested parties to craft legislation and recognize that parties likely to be hurt by a more competitive industry will use the "consumers will be adversely affected" argument to lead the public to believe that reform will harm the average person. This inevitably leads to the addition of counterproductive, needless, and costly measures that supposedly protect consumers but really protect only those industry players who succeeded in getting the changes made.

Social Regulation: The Goal of "Commonsense Regulation." A different approach should be followed with social regulation. Those who support reform of social regulations should pursue a strategy of "common sense" over the next few years. Social regulations include statutes or rules that are intended to protect citizen or worker health and safety, accomplish environmental and other goals, or promote civil rights objectives. Targeted reforms will be necessary to contain the social regulations that have become egregiously counterproductive and potentially life-threatening. Examples would include:

- **Comprehensive reform** of food, drug, and medical device laws;

- **Reform** of Superfund;

- **Reform** of antiquated workplace laws and labor regulations;

- **Reform** of the Endangered Species Act; and

- **Protection** of property rights.

A much more convincing case must be made for changes in the way public health, safety, and environmental regulatory decisions are made. These social regulatory reforms will require a more broad-based educational effort aimed at winning popular appeal and changing the terms of the debate in the media. Grassroots coalitions must be formed, and great care must be taken when considering how to educate the public about reform initiatives.

Strategies for Change. Congress can craft numerous strategies and policies to implement both the goal of complete withdrawal in the area of economic regulation and the goal of commonsense regulation in the area of social regulation.

STRATEGY #1
Congress should begin writing smarter legislation.

Successful reform requires Congress to recognize that it often has been a large part of the problem. Beginning with the Nixon presidency, Congress has countenanced a significant expansion of the discretionary power of administrative agencies. Although a number of theories purport to explain why this shift occurred, it is sufficient here to point out that the end result was a Congress that increasingly designed legislative language to evade responsibility for making policy decisions. The rise of "goals" statutes in the 1970s put tremendous pressure on agencies to turn out rules by the dozens and by the hundreds. As Cornell political scientist Theodore Lowi points out, a "goals" statute ordains an outcome like a "cleaner environment"[4] and delegates to the agency all of the power to make all the rules to achieve this goal. Because Congress delegates responsibility for a whole abstractly defined, open-ended system, the agency is given no priority or guidelines, so everything becomes compelling: The agency keeps shooting arrows in the air, hoping that one will hit its target.

With little to balance or check this growth in administrative discretion and power, there was a massive increase in social regulatory activity in the 1970s that has continued until the present day. Congress needs to reverse this trend. Abuse of agency discretion is at the heart of the problem that Congress must solve. Regulators gain power by regulating

---

4 Theodore J. Lowi, *The End of the Republican Era* (Norman, Okla.: University of Oklahoma Press, 1996), p. 75.

as much as possible, and there is little today to stop them from regulating as if it cost nothing.

Conservatives especially can work to remedy this problem by blocking any regulatory legislation that is crafted with open-ended mandates for change. When Congress can be certain that a particular problem exists (and is properly a subject of federal action), it must develop a legislative solution to it, state what the goal of the statute should be, and require federal regulators to apply commonsense principles in developing the regulations to implement the law. Conservatives also must apply these principles in all efforts to reform existing statutes, from banking laws to Superfund.

Statutory changes are critical to success in fundamentally reforming the current system because administrative changes have failed. The continued growth of regulation from Reagan to Clinton clearly demonstrates this. The current system also needs to be reformed to force federal regulators to allocate scarce economic resources to achieve the most good. The concept of smarter regulation is an important one. The following principles are key elements of this concept and should be incorporated, to the extent practicable, into all legislative and regulatory policies.

- **Cost-Benefit Analysis.** Federal agencies should be required to evaluate the costs and benefits of all new regulations. Critics will argue that costs and benefits can be difficult to identify or hard to quantify, and this is true to some extent. Nevertheless, it is very useful to begin to get agencies to think more systematically about the economic impact of new regulations by requiring an accounting and weighing of the costs and benefits of their decisions to the extent possible. Agencies also should be required to provide Congress with information about the costs and benefits of the laws it passes.

- **Risk Assessment and Risk Management.** The purpose of risk assessment needs to be changed from a safety assessment (from asking questions like "what is a safe level?") to a real risk assessment ("what is the risk?"). Risk assessment methods need to be improved (for example, by using sound scientific methods), and agencies need to establish a clear distinction between assessing risks and deciding how to manage them. Federal agencies should work closely with the scientific community to improve risk assessment guidelines. Today, agencies too often allow policy decisions about how to manage risk to influence the determination of risk. Only when a risk is identified should a policy decision be made about how to handle it.

- **Risk-Based Priorities and Public Education.** Government has a responsibility to inform the public of risks and to minimize the distortion and exaggeration of those risks. By using risk comparisons, federal agencies can help people to understand the familiar risks they face every day (such as being struck by lightning) and how these familiar risks compare with unfamiliar risks (such as exposure to a particular chemical in the community).

- **Market Incentives and Performance Standards.** Whenever regulation is necessary, it should be accomplished to the extent possible by setting a goal and allowing the market to decide how it will achieve that goal. For example, instead of requiring businesses to use specific technology to reduce pollution, a regulation should mandate the amount of pollution reduction and allow businesses to decide how they will achieve that reduction. Each business then has the freedom and the incentive to adopt the least costly means of achieving the goal for itself, minimizing the total cost burden that compliance imposes on the economy. In contrast, command-and-control regulations provide no incentive for the regulated entity to exceed a regulatory goal.

- **State and Local Government Flexibility.** If states and localities truly are to be the laboratories of experimentation that the Founders envisioned, the federal government must be willing to share power with them and, in many cases, allow them complete and unfettered latitude to act as they wish. More important, Congress should continue and expand the effort, initiated with passage of the Unfunded Mandates Reform Act, to ensure that Washington is not passing along the costs of federal regulations to unsuspecting state and local government officials, as well as to the private sector.

- **A Minimal Paperwork Burden.** In 1995, about one-third of the costs of regulation—about $200 billion—was due to paperwork. Most Americans fill out some kind of federal paperwork, such as tax forms or forms to obtain government benefits. Businesses also must maintain a bewildering array of records to demonstrate compliance with environmental, workplace, and other rules. Almost 90 percent of all federal paperwork is required by federal regulation. Even a modest reduction in the total paperwork burden imposed on the public—almost 6 billion hours or the equivalent of 2.8 million full-time employees—can save Americans hours of time and hundreds of millions, if not billions, of dollars in lost productivity.

In addition to incorporating these principles into every piece of legislation, conservatives in Congress also should work to enact general reform legislation that requires federal agencies to follow these principles whenever they develop regulations. Incremental statutory reforms can contribute to significant changes in whether and how the federal government regulates. Passage of one comprehensive reform bill that captures all of these principles is extremely difficult to accomplish because it is hard to reach agreement among all interested parties. Those who object to the cost-benefit standard might have no problem with the risk assessment methods outlined in the legislation, yet disputes over cost-benefit still might hold up positive risk assessment changes. Each principle, separated from the others, would accomplish important changes in the regulatory decisionmaking process by improving the information available to support more significant change in the future.

Thus, Congress should consider taking on only one or two of the principles in a single bill. As a start, for example, advocates might consider moving only legislation that would require federal agencies to improve the way they conduct risk assessments. If Congress codifies a set of principles for smarter regulation, it also should require that federal regulators go back and review all existing regulations to make sure they also meet those principles.

STRATEGY #2
Congress should pursue aggressive oversight and implementation of its new regulatory review authority.

Congress needs to pursue an aggressive oversight strategy—including oversight hearings and studies by the U.S. General Accounting Office—to hold the executive branch accountable for implementing its own stated regulatory principles and initiatives. In addition, field hearings that allow business owners and other Americans adversely affected by particular regulations to talk about their own experiences can give the policy debate a much more realistic, human dimension. The 104th Congress failed to do this well. In addition to a few field hearings, for example, there was one hearing at the end of the 104th Congress on the Clinton Administration's compliance with its own executive order.

Conservatives outside of Congress also did not do a particularly good job of communicating widely the information gathered from the hearings that were held, and more needs to be done during the 105th Congress. An aggressive oversight strategy will help build a record which reformers can use to justify the need for change. In addition, confirmation hearings should be used to alert Congress whenever individuals who clearly have a career record of supporting government intervention at any cost, and whose actions show them to be at odds with the Administration's own regulatory principles, are appointed to key regulatory staff positions.

Beginning in 1997, implementation of the new Congressional Review Act of 1996 will have a significant impact on all future regulatory reform efforts. Congress expects to receive from federal agencies as many as 10,000 documents for review each year. It will be very difficult for conservatives to argue for fundamental change if they review 10,000 rules every year and can find fault with few or none of them. Thus, Congress stands to lose credibility from ineffective implementation or outright neglect of the Act. On the other hand, if federal agencies believe that Congress has the political will to tackle economically significant or otherwise important new regulatory initiatives, they will be much more inclined to take the necessary care in the development of regulations, following sound cost-benefit and risk assessment principles, to make sure they hold up under scrutiny.

Effective implementation of congressional review of rules will mean a serious commitment on the part of conservatives in Congress, the business community, and the academic and public policy research community to putting in place the mechanisms for identifying, prioritizing, and challenging agency rulemaking. This includes a number of steps, including:

- **Establishing** a joint congressional committee on regulation that is the central place through which all rules are sent and initially reviewed. The committee would work with other relevant House and Senate committees of jurisdiction to determine the appropriate course of action on rulemaking. The rulemaking record, for example, could be examined in periodic hearings that involve both agency officials and the regulated community. Alternatively, a joint task force could be tasked with making recommendations to the committees of jurisdiction, with the committees retaining authority for any action. Absent a joint committee, there needs to be one committee in the House and one in the Senate, with each given sole jurisdiction for implementing the Act.

- **Demanding** that federal agencies submit to the GAO consistent and concise information on the extent to which rulemaking complies with statutory requirements and an assessment of the adequacy of the cost-benefit analysis, risk assessment, and other types of analyses required. The GAO does not need additional resources to do this job and should be able to reallocate positions and fill any open slots with economists and others to conduct these initial reviews on behalf of the congressional committees.

- **Establishing** vehicles for identifying rules for review. Conservative research organizations, the business community, and the academic community can help Congress identify rules for review and provide timely analysis to show why particular regulations are harmful or a drag on the economy. These organizations can play a critical role in undertaking research on the economic impact of regulations and in offering more direct challenges to agency economic impact analyses.

- **Building and highlighting** the regulatory record. Congressional review of rules offers a tremendous opportunity to pass on information that cannot be filtered by federal agencies. Information on harmful rules must be sent back to local congressional districts and the media to help build the consensus for reform.

Finally, Congress should revisit and strengthen the Unfunded Mandates Reform Act of 1995 to extend the point of order to private-sector mandates. In addition, the point of order should be subject to override only by supermajority vote and not by a simple majority as is now the case.

STRATEGY #3
Congress should use the budget and appropriations process to effect change in the regulatory structure.

In addition to specific statutory reforms, the legislative branch can pursue deregulatory strategies by using the appropriations process to reach its goals. That is, if conservatives believe it is politically impossible to eliminate unilaterally the unnecessary regulations that burden the economy and consumers, an alternative might be to downsize the particular agencies that carry out those regulations.

For example, with deregulation of the telecommunications industry and the pending liberalization of electricity markets, both the Federal Communications Commission and the Federal Energy Regulatory Commission can and should be downsized if not eliminated. Just as airline deregulation during the 1970s included a successful effort to eliminate the Civil Aeronautics Board because it was doing more harm than good, deregulation of other economic fields cannot be considered complete until the agencies overseeing them are radically downsized or eliminated. At a minimum, conservatives should outline a strategy for phasing out such agencies gradually over five to ten years.

On the social front, it is unlikely—and in some cases undesirable—that certain health and safety regulatory agencies will be eliminated. This does not mean, however, that these agencies cannot be forced to live under a strict budget and streamline their operations to ensure they are carrying out only essential duties. Unfortunately, a common mistake is to push for budget cuts without making the case for them. One need only turn to the wealth of government reports generated by the agencies' own inspectors general or the General Accounting Office to find examples of millions of dollars in fraud, waste, and abuse that highlight areas ripe for elimination because they just do not work. In addition, agency budget justifications should include details about what regulations will be issued and enforced during the fiscal year, both to show how well the agency is prioritizing its resources and to facilitate a more effective debate on whether those priorities are reasonable.

Conservatives should not shy away from a strategy of using the fiscal budget process to improve the quality of regulations. However, one of the lessons learned by conservatives in the 104th Congress was that using narrowly targeted appropriations riders was a political liability. Many of the riders were put in place to benefit very specific interests. This seriously damaged the ability of conservatives to refute the claim that reform represented little more than a rollback of important protections on behalf of big business. Nevertheless, riders can be beneficial if they are reasonable. In particular, "report riders" that require agencies to report on their compliance with the Administration's regulatory executive order or particular statutes can help identify real problems and facilitate congressional oversight hearings.

Conservatives also must resist efforts by opponents of reform to link appropriations to specific regulatory reform action items which Congress may task agencies with performing. A clever tactic of opponents is to require specific and separate appropriations for such actions, knowing that conservatives might feel obligated to vote against "new" spending. Similarly, if conservatives cannot control the appropriations process, it would be too easy for regulatory reform initiatives simply to be defunded. Too often, federal agencies receive generous appropriations that allow them to continue to look for new problems to solve at great cost but with little benefit. Conversely, they have more than ample resources to carry out legislative requirements to reexamine and reduce, as appropriate, the number and burden of their regulations. Ostensibly cutting an agency's appropriations while really cutting reform efforts is not acceptable.

Using the budget process can be effective when it focuses federal regulatory agencies on their most important priorities and mission. It also should make more information on the level and costs of regulations available to the public. When federal agencies submit their budget justifications, they must explain why additional funding is needed. Curtailing or cutting off their spending will force federal regulatory agencies to be more efficient. In simplest terms, an agency with less funding is an agency than can do less harm.

STRATEGY #4
Congress should scrutinize agency enforcement activity.

Although federal authorities obviously will need to enforce regulations that remain on the books, there are right and wrong ways for them to do so. Unfortunately, federal regulators have been known to engage in overzealous and potentially unconstitutional enforcement and seizure actions. Such abuses of regulatory power occur throughout government. Regardless of what enforcement action an agency feels is necessary, regulators should be required to:

- **Give fair notice** and warning to regulated parties when enforcing federal statutes.

- **Work cooperatively** with regulated entities by providing technical assistance and information on how to comply with federal regulations. Those responsible for enforcing federal rules should not be given incentives, such as bonuses, based on the frequency and amounts of penalties levied against violators.

- **Be unarmed** when on duty. Federal, state, and local law enforcement authorities can provide whatever protection federal regulators feel is necessary to carry out their responsibilities. There is little need for EPA or Food and Drug Administration authorities to carry guns when they visit businesses.

Rather than work cooperatively with businesses and individuals, the Clinton Administration has proposed legislation that would freeze assets for noncompliance with federal environmental standards. The "shoot first, ask questions later" strategy of enforcement is government run amok. Treating businesses and individuals like drug dealers when they violate an environmental standard (or any other standard that they might not even know exists) is wrong. In addition, federal bureaucrats too often have gone overboard and failed to recognize that the loss of jobs and other damage done to businesses and employees far exceeds any harm caused by the violation.

STRATEGY #5
Congress should establish procedural reforms.

Advocates of reform should consider a simple set of procedural tools to guide all regulatory decisionmaking. This will ensure that when regulations are deemed necessary, scarce economic resources can be allocated more efficiently to achieve the most good for society. The following principles and policies will help achieve this goal:

- **A Regulatory Budget.** The President and Congress should establish a federal regulatory budget that places a ceiling on the total estimated cost that can be imposed on the economy each year by all federal regulations. Just as the annual federal budget allows policymakers and the public to debate and decide what programs to support and which ones to scale back and eliminate, information on regulatory costs and benefits would clarify which regulations do the most good for the money spent, thereby helping responsible officials set regulatory priorities that, in addition to being more effective, minimize the burden on the economy. If the budget total was reached by existing regulations, an agency wishing to add a regulation with further costs would have to repeal or modify an existing regulation which imposed the same or greater cost.

A regulatory budget would place a politically accountable limit on the total burden that could be imposed on the economy by federal regulation. It also would give agencies a strong incentive to review existing regulations to discover which ones could safely be eliminated or modified to reduce costs. In other words, government would be forced both to prioritize its regulations and to maximize the overall benefits to society.

- **A Regulatory Reduction Commission.** Congress could take advantage of the success of the Defense Base Closure and Realignment Commission model to form a Regulatory Reduction Commission to assist deregulatory efforts. The Base Closure Commission avoided political manipulation by independently compiling a list of obsolete or unneeded military bases to be closed. This list was then voted on as a package by the full Congress, making it impossible for individual bases to be excluded simply to appease a single legislator and ensuring that political considerations did not override rational policy judgments concerning the overall need to downsize military base expenses.

A Regulatory Reduction Commission established along the lines of this model could help Congress and the executive branch weed out the many needless, repetitious, and counterproductive regulations that remain on the books at the federal level. The Commission simply would recommend to Congress that a list of such regulations be voted on as a package, thereby increasing the chances that all would be eliminated.

STRATEGY #6
Congress should allow for judicial review.

Although it is the least attractive forum in which to bring common sense to regulation, the courts provide an important avenue for checking the reasonableness of agency actions and preventing those that are clearly unconstitutional. Today, the courts often consider whether agencies have exceeded their statutory authority. Typically, courts will defer to a federal agency on regulatory matters as long as the agency has made a "reasonable" interpretation of the law. Once a court decides that an agency is acting within its authority, it may turn to questions about whether the agency has followed its required public notice and comment process or statutory deadlines, or has abused its discretion by acting "arbitrarily and capriciously." Regardless of what the court considers, however, it typically has little impact on making sure that federal agencies make sensible decisions.

Thus, judicial review also should apply to any statutory standard, such as cost-benefit analysis, established to improve the quality of regulatory decisionmaking that an agency must follow. If Congress wants to ensure that federal regulators faithfully implement the scope and intent of the laws it passes, allowing judicial review of decisionmaking principles—for example, judicial evaluation of the impact of rules on small business—would help ensure that federal regulators make sensible decisions by subjecting them to an additional layer of accountability.

Finally, it goes without saying that the presidential power to appoint federal judges is itself an important area of reform strategy. The President must ensure that judges appointed to the federal courts share an understanding of the constitutional limitations of regulatory agencies and their policymaking powers, a strong belief in property rights and states' rights, and a general deference to Congress in matters of regulation. If the President appoints judges with such credentials, they will help both Congress and the Administration make smarter regulatory decisions.

STRATEGY #7
Congress should identify regulatory policy objectives and priorities.

Conservatives in Congress, as well as the Administration, should adopt principles similar to those embodied in Reagan Executive Order 12291, such as cost-benefit analysis, sound science, and risk assessments, to guide them in their legislative agenda. In 1997, the legislative agenda must be modest and incremental, and must take on those issues about which there has been considerable debate and on which bipartisan progress already has been made.

Superfund and repeal of Glass-Steagall—the law which separates commercial and investment banking—are examples of issues on which significant progress has been made and agreement often has been close. At the same time, statutes that are up for reauthorization, such as the Endangered Species Act, need to be handled more effectively than they have been in the past. On a number of other important legislative reforms, such as FDA and OSHA reform, property rights, and utility deregulation, building the case for reform will require considerable additional investments of time and resources; it may not be until 1998 or beyond that fundamental changes can be achieved.

STRATEGY #8
Conservatives should invest in the analysis needed to show how government solutions fail the American people.

Conservatives can analyze regulations and the regulatory process in a number of ways. For example, they can:

- **Examine** the costs and benefits of regulation. Federal agencies are the only ones that examine the economic impact of rules, and their analyses typically go unchallenged by the academic and policy research community. More of an effort needs to be made to create a private, independent organization that does what OMB's Office of Information and Regulatory Affairs would do it if were supported: review agency economic impact analyses and critique and challenge them as appropriate. In addition to helping improve the quality of the analysis performed by agencies, this would give conservatives the information they need to make the case for reform more effectively.

- **Reveal** the ways in which politicians and bureaucrats are captured by special interests and act out of self-interest. This is one way to help show how the government currently fails Americans. Is a regulation really going to protect mine safety, or will it just eliminate non-union small mines? Does the Endangered Species Act really protect species, or does it simply help support organizations like the Sierra Club?

- **Show** how reform would benefit the American people. Conservatives need to communicate down to local communities their alternative vision of reform and what this vision would mean to these communities in terms of lower priced goods, higher productivity and wages, and so on.

STRATEGY #9
Conservatives can make a more effective case for private alternatives to government regulation.

This has long been the weakest link in making the case for reform. In the future, conservatives must show, with real examples, how market-based alternatives are superior to government intervention. Examples from home and abroad are equally suitable for this purpose. The forces of the marketplace are powerful tools in the effort to change individual and institutional behavior. They can achieve superior environmental objectives at less cost and with less opposition than the traditional command-and-control approach. For example, the use of property rights and marketable permits is more effective in controlling water pollution than government-mandated specific technologies and proportional reductions in discharges. The reason: People have incentives to find cheaper, better ways to reduce pollution.

STRATEGY #10
Conservatives must improve their message, develop a positive vision, and stick with it no matter what happens.

A positive vision for reform is critical. Although conservatives have begun to master the use of horror stories almost as effectively as the liberals, these stories alone are not enough. Public dismay at such stories does not signify broad-based support for deregulation. Americans understandably fear that if the regulatory "safety net" were dismantled, the country would return to the days of billowing smokestacks and burning rivers.

In some ways, this almost requires conservatives to take time out to develop their own new dictionary for communicating about regulation. Negative terms such as "deregulation" and "relief" should be avoided because they are too easily misinterpreted and presented as extreme. They should be replaced with a more positive vision that reflects actual policy objectives. The objective of change is to make federal regulators produce only rules that are necessary, efficient, effective, and "smart." For example, after 20 years of environmental regulation which in many cases led to significant improvements, it is necessary to reexamine the current system to make sure that—given the changes in technology and improvements already made—America continues to invest in environmental protection in the most efficient manner possible. Americans want a clean, safe environment, but they also want jobs and a high standard of living; the goal is to make sure that we do the best we can to maximize both.

Being right has little or no value if no one is aware of that fact. Those in Congress who favor reform need to maintain more frequent and deeper contacts with the media. Today, information is disseminated, and ideas gain respectability, through the media. All advocates of regulatory reform, but especially conservatives, need to be out meeting the press, giving them newsworthy information about the important things they are trying to accomplish for *all* Americans.

STRATEGY #11
Conservatives should build effective coalitions that support reform.

Members of Congress need to work with the business community, as well as with conservative national and state-based policy research and grassroots organizations, to help set the regulatory agenda. Once they have done that, they must then work with these groups to carry out this agenda. Every initiative must be handled differently. Not all groups will support all initiatives. Even within the environmental movement, there will be strong differences from issue to issue. It is critical to take the time to determine which groups are likely to be supportive, which ones oppose reform, and which ones might be persuaded by good information and education. For each organizational category, there should be plans on how to make allies more effective, how to respond to opponents' attacks, and how to get the support of those that still have not taken a position.

Unfortunately, the 104th Congress did not heed these simple plans. The House of Representatives moved quickly to pass a comprehensive regulatory reform bill, unfunded mandates legislation, the Paperwork Reduction Act, and other initiatives within the first 100 days. Moving quickly worked well in this case because the opposition did not have enough time to react effectively. Unfortunately, Republicans in the Senate were more willing to work with liberals than with their own natural allies in developing regulatory legislative proposals. The consequence of this was that natural conservative allies were shut out of the debate and the momentum behind the coalitions of business and policy research groups withered. In the end, the more conservative members of the House of Representatives felt abandoned as they tried to keep their agenda on track despite impasses in the Senate.

The Conservative Role. If conservative Members of Congress are unwilling to take active roles in promoting policy initiatives for fear of being left stranded when the going gets tough, the entire conservative movement will suffer. Unfortunately, by early 1996, conservatives in the House of Representatives had given up on most of their social regulatory agenda because the Senate's inclination to ignore them took the steam out of their efforts. Groups began to splinter and resort to self-interested lobbying, moving away from the larger goals of regulatory reform. This gave the Clinton Administration, unions, and other groups ammunition with which to exploit the public perception that regulatory reform really meant just giving breaks to special interests.

In the end, advocates of reform attempted to salvage some of the elements of the program that were largely procedural in nature and that could not be connected directly with any particular adverse regulatory action, as well as those that generated little if any opposition from any group. In addition, organizations representing small business were successful in their attempts to get the 104th Congress to require that federal agencies pay special attention to the impact of regulations on them. Unfortunately, this approach played into the hands of opponents of reform who tend to believe that big business can afford to pay for expensive yet ineffective regulation but that small businesses cannot afford the cost and therefore should be treated differently. This belief loses sight of the overall goal of bringing to an end the promulgation of regulations that impose huge costs and produce little benefit to society. In the long run, it also probably takes some of the steam out of more comprehensive reform efforts.

As conservatives undertake a new regulatory agenda in 1997 and beyond, they must understand that each issue needs to be reformulated in several ways to make it acceptable to a variety of interests. Each issue is worthy of its own special coalition of business interests, national and state-based policy research organizations, and grassroots organizations. Once a coalition is formed, one nongovernmental organization should serve as a clearinghouse for communication and coordination among the members of that coalition. And once the initiative is launched, the coalition must maintain a positive vision, support conservative legislators and policymakers with the analysis they need, and stay on message even when the going gets tough.

CONCLUSION

Rethinking regulation and producing more sensible regulations will take time. Experience gained during the Bush and Clinton Administrations and the 104th Congress clearly shows that conservatives need to rethink how they have presented regulatory issues to the American people. The reality is that social regulation today is the fastest growing element of the overall cost of regulation. The challenge for conservatives is to help people understand that while significant benefits have been achieved, after 20 years the federal government's approach has become outdated and ineffective.

Not all regulations are good regulations. Some have seriously adverse effects on the national economy, our health, and our well-being. The challenge is to show in concrete ways how the federal regulatory system fails the American people and to present alternatives that will be of greater benefit to Americans. If conservatives balance economic growth with lives, they will lose. As long as they mistakenly assume that frustration over red tape equals an invitation to undertake reform without explaining how current protections will be maintained, they will lose. Conservatives need to start with a positive vision that shows how their alternatives will stimulate economic growth and offer consumers better products at lower prices while promoting higher levels of public health, safety, and environmental protections.

As the 105th Congress looks to 1997 and beyond, its conservative members should begin by giving serious thought to a new dictionary of regulatory language. At the same time, they need to take small steps to build the types of information that will support their reform efforts. For example, the concept of a regulatory budget which requires agencies to keep track of the costs of regulations can engage the public more actively in a dialogue similar to the debate over the federal budget. Congress can start with reforms in areas where the public generally recognizes problems inherent in the system. The challenge, however, will be to make sure that the American people clearly understand how alternatives to the current failed system will improve their lives and their standard of living.

Chapter 10

WINNING THE BATTLE FOR A FAIRER TAX SYSTEM

Daniel J. Mitchell

America's tax system is convoluted, anti-growth, and morally bankrupt. Decades of tinkering and social engineering have made the tax code a national embarrassment. Record amounts of taxpayers' income are confiscated by government each year, leaving Americans with little faith that the system is being applied evenly. Behaviors that should be rewarded—such as work, savings, and entrepreneurship—create added tax penalties. And to add insult to injury, tax laws have become so incomprehensible that even the so-called experts have no idea how to fill out the hundreds of forms correctly.

Fortunately, however, the very fact that the tax system is so unpopular and deeply flawed presents policymakers with an historic opportunity for sweeping reform. Moreover, since the tax code's problems have been analyzed so extensively, there is no mystery about what needs to be done: Washington policymakers can no longer claim ignorance. It is widely recognized, for instance, that high tax rates, bias against savings and investment, and complexity are slowing the economy and causing incomes to stagnate. Likewise, it is no secret that the combination of multiple tax

The author would like to thank Cesar Conda, David Burton, Steve Entin, and Bruce Bartlett for their suggestions and contributions to this chapter. The views and opinions expressed, however, are solely the responsibility of the author.

rates and special loopholes means that citizens are not treated equally under the law.

Not only are the tax code's problems well-documented, but so are the solutions and the evidence to support them. If tax rates are too high (and they are), lower them. If double taxation of savings hurts the economy (and it does), tax income only once. If the estate tax destroys family businesses and takes capital out of the economy (and it does), repeal it. If capital gains taxes undermine America's international competitiveness (and they do), eliminate them.

While a number of specific steps are possible, by far the best course of action would be for Congress to enact fundamental, comprehensive reform of the tax code. A flat tax that taxed all income just once and at one low rate would yield immense benefits to American citizens and to the Internal Revenue Service. Not only would the economy's growth rate accelerate, but the sordid special-interest deals that characterize so much of the tax code would be eliminated.

These solutions to the myriad problems of the tax code are well-known and strongly supported by more than just conservatives. The more difficult question is how to move sound policy proposals through the cumbersome political process. As in any human endeavor, there is no simple cookie-cutter formula that will guarantee success. Enacting pro-growth tax reforms will not be easy. Many politicians relish the power and control that comes with a heavy tax burden. Likewise, fundamental reform will be resisted by anyone in Washington who benefits from manipulating the tax code to create special preferences, exemptions, deductions, shelters, and loopholes.

But there is much to be learned from history. The contentious tax battles fought over the years have shown policymakers which strategies are most successful and which ones present pitfalls and dangers. The major tax changes — whether positive or negative — implemented over the last 15 years provide valuable lessons for improving the nation's economy and restoring the public trust in government.

LESSONS LEARNED

The last 20 years have taught policymakers some hard lessons about what kinds of proposals they should offer when seeking to lower or increase tax rates. These lessons — from who benefits from each proposal to whether package deals and commissions should be used—should be reviewed before Congress begins considering any new tax legislation in 1997. Looking back over the last two decades reveals that success occurred when conservatives were on the offensive and that failure resulted when pro-tax forces had the initiative. The key to victory in building support for—and enacting—the Reagan tax cuts, needless to say, is to regain the offensive.

On the Offensive:
Building Support for, and Enacting, the Reagan Tax Cuts

President Reagan's primary focus was to restore the economy and reduce the size of government. It is worth noting that the tax cut legislation was entitled the Economic Recovery Tax Act to drive home that message. Tax cuts were a logical prescription for achieving both of Reagan's goals, as was the effort to slow the growth of spending. Policymakers saw considerably less success in this latter area than they originally hoped. Reducing the deficit, which is viewed as a desirable result of an Administration's overall fiscal policy, was not the driving force.

Lesson #1: Changes in the tax code will not work unless the focus of reform is on improving America's economic growth and reducing the size of government, and unless everyone benefits from the reforms. In the 1970s, then-Representative Jack Kemp (R-NY) and Senator William Roth (R-DE) began to promote their view that tax rates could be reduced by one-third. They argued that the top tax rate at the time—70 percent— was a disincentive for work, savings, and investment. They also publicized the fact that many taxpayers were being pushed into ever-higher tax brackets because of inflation even though their real purchasing power was stagnant or falling.

As economic conditions began to deteriorate in the late 1970s, Kemp's and Roth's efforts received increasing publicity, and the Republican Party began to unify around the idea of pro-growth tax rate reductions. Perhaps most important, presidential candidate Ronald Reagan adopted "tax cuts" as a central plank in his campaign. Reagan went on to win a landslide

---

LESSONS LEARNED
Building Support for Tax Cuts

- Changes in the tax code will not work unless the focus of reform is on improving America's economic growth and reducing the size of government, and unless everyone benefits from the reforms.

- Advocates of tax reform must take advantage of circumstances.

- History matters. Do not let the enemies of smaller government misrepresent the 1980s.

---

victory, which was followed in August of 1981 by the enactment of a 25 percent across-the-board tax cut phased in over several years.

A handful of suggestions emerge from the debate during this period. First, it is important to make sure everyone benefits. As Chart 10.1 illustrates, improvements in the economy and economic hard times affect all Americans. Second, reform efforts should focus on economic growth and the size of government. Opponents of Reagan's tax cuts argued that they represented a major windfall for the rich. This rhetoric, however, did not hurt the reform process. Even though the public recognized that wealthy taxpayers would benefit from lower tax rates, lower and middle-income taxpayers did not object, since their payments to the IRS declined as well.

Finally, one person can make a difference: Every Senator and Representative can help create the climate for reform. There is little doubt that Kemp's relentless advocacy of lower taxes and economic growth made the difference. While he was sometimes caricatured as "Johnny-One-Note," his determination, stamina, and hard work were necessary in order to capture the imagination of the American people and overcome the inertia of many Senators and Representatives who were afraid to challenge the status quo.

Lesson #2: Advocates of tax reform must take advantage of circumstances. Supporters of across-the-board tax rate reductions, such as Kemp, Roth, and Reagan, made several wise decisions. They articulated the pro-growth message, they made sure that the vast majority of taxpayers saw a tangible benefit, and they included reform of

Chart 10.1

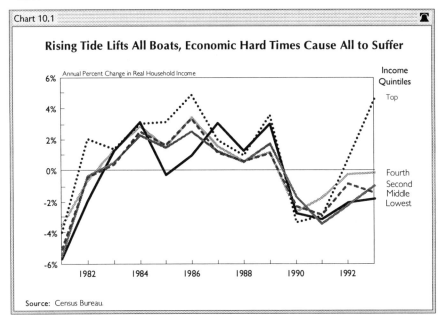

Rising Tide Lifts All Boats, Economic Hard Times Cause All to Suffer

Annual Percent Change in Real Household Income

Income Quintiles

Top

Fourth
Second
Middle
Lowest

Source: Census Bureau.

the business side of the tax code to ensure support from that community. Perhaps just as important, however, they tailored their proposal to the existing economic climate. The late 1970s was a dismal time in our nation's history. The economy was wracked by double-digit inflation, growth was sputtering, incomes were falling, government regulation had created huge disruptions in energy markets, and there was a sense that the nation was somehow doomed to an era of perpetual stagflation.

Advocates of lower tax rates explicitly addressed this issue, arguing that there was nothing wrong with America. Instead, the blame belonged to government—specifically, a tax system that punished people who added to the nation's wealth. By showing voters that tax cuts were a way to overcome the gloom-and-doom outlook of many in Washington, tax cutters were able to garner the maximum level of support.

Fortunately, the economy is not nearly as weak today as it was when Jimmy Carter left office. Nonetheless, its performance since Reagan left office has been mediocre. Moreover, it is likely that there will be an economic downturn sometime in the next four years. Should that occur, supporters of tax reform need to replicate the success of the late 1970s by pointing out that any such weakness in the economy can be cured by adopting the right tax policy.

Lesson #3: History matters. Do not let the enemies of smaller government misrepresent the 1980s. Reagan's early victory on tax cuts was significant. Not only did he reduce tax rates by 25 percent, but his 1981 legislation imposed indexing to keep taxpayers from being pushed into higher tax brackets as a result of inflation, even though this did not go into effect until 1985. Reagan, however, was victimized by poor timing. Although no serious economist links the two events, the 1981–1982 recession, caused primarily by the high inflation of preceding years, kicked in just about the time Congress was enacting the tax cut legislation. The resulting higher unemployment rates, falling incomes, and greater demands on government programs combined to increase the budget deficit, especially in 1981.

Opponents were quick to blame these tax cuts for the rising level of government borrowing. Ironically, not only did the recession begin before tax cuts went into effect, but the tiny reduction in tax rates that went into effect in the last three months of 1981 was overwhelmed by previously legislated payroll tax increases and bracket creep. As a result, the economy actually received a significant tax hike in 1981; yet opponents still blamed the recession and higher deficits on tax cuts.

Indeed, it was not until sometime in the latter half of 1982 that the economy received a net tax cut, which meant that the era of rising deficits occurred almost entirely during a time when taxes were rising rather than falling. Nevertheless, the opposing side was quick to act by taking advantage of the fact that the public did not understand the difference between the time a tax cut became law and the time it actually went into effect. Hence, it became the "conventional wisdom" that tax cuts caused the deficit.

The Holding Pattern: 1982–1988

Congressional advocates of tax reform should beware of package deals that combine a tax hike with budget "cuts." With depressing regularity, politicians decide that the deficit is a crisis. The solution, they claim, is a combination of higher taxes and spending cuts. The higher taxes are approved, but not the promised spending cuts. As a result, the Reagan Administration spent too much time after 1981 fending off proposal after

---

LESSONS LEARNED
The Holding Pattern: 1982–1988

- Policymakers should not be swayed by opponents of tax cuts and their assurances of spending cuts in the future.

- Static revenue estimates lead to bad policy.

- Using summits and commissions to resolve budget crises is not always effective. Invariably, the reports coming out of these summits and commissions increase pressure on Congress to raise taxes.

- Experience gained from the debate on the 1986 Tax Reform Act demonstrates that support of public opinion leaders is crucial.

- Tax reform must lead to one rate.

- Bold steps will work, generating more enthusiasm than halfway measures.

- Trying to maintain revenue "neutrality" can cause good policies to be offset by bad ones.

- Itemized deductions are not a minefield if handled properly.

---

proposal to increase taxes. On occasion—most notably in 1982, 1984, and 1987—the White House even got roped into holding budget summits for the alleged purpose of reaching agreement on reducing the budget deficit. Invariably, however, the result was higher taxes, higher spending, and higher deficits.

Guidelines for tax reform that emerge from these episodes include:

Lesson #1: Policymakers should not let themselves be swayed by opponents of tax cuts and their assurances of spending cuts in the future. These "cuts" never materialize. In the years following the 1981 legislation, the Reagan Administration was lured into accepting several congressionally approved tax increases for the alleged purpose of reducing the deficit. In retrospect, many of these revenue bills were quite small compared to the record-breaking tax increases of the Bush and Clinton years, but they still proved harmful to the economy and resulted in higher deficits since Congress was freed from any need to control government spending.

Lesson #2: Static revenue estimates lead to bad policy. Deficits actually increased following the tax increases imposed during the Reagan Administration. Higher spending, however, was only part of the reason. Another systemic problem was the use of models that assumed higher taxes would have no impact on economic behavior. As a result, revenue projections routinely overestimated the amount of taxes that would be collected.

Lesson #3: Using summits and commissions to resolve budget crises is not always effective. Invariably, the reports coming out of these summits and commissions increase pressure on Congress to raise taxes. Even though the Social Security system had been bailed out in 1977, it became apparent in the early 1980s that the Social Security system was heading toward financial crisis. The weak economy and high tax rates of the 1970s hindered job creation, and this limited the amount of payroll tax revenues flowing into the Social Security fund. The number of beneficiaries continued to grow, of course, creating the politically charged question of how to pay for benefits in the future.

The National Commission on Social Security Reform, which was created to address this issue, recommended a significant tax increase and an expansion of the number of people forced to participate in the system. That tax hike, especially when combined with the 20 million new jobs created by the Reagan boom, alleviated the short-term fiscal imbalance in Social Security. Absolutely nothing was done, however, to address the system's long-term problems.

The Social Security system's own Trustees now admit that the system will begin to suffer a budget shortfall in less than 15 years. Defenders of the status quo argue that this looming deficit is not a problem because the Trust Fund has enough reserves to keep the system solvent for another 15 years. There is only one problem with this statement: The Trust Fund is no better than a hoax because it is filled with nothing but IOUs.

With a growing consensus that something must be done to address Social Security's fundamental problems, the experience of tax reformers in the early 1980s offers several important perspectives that policymakers can use to avoid making the same mistake a second time:

- **An atmosphere of crisis, unless properly managed, can result in horrendous policy decisions.** The 1983 Social Security bailout legislation resulted in a huge tax increase that did nothing to address long-term structural problems with the government's retirement scheme. Many lawmakers, even while recognizing that they were simply papering over the problem with higher taxes, felt they had to act to avert the imminent bankruptcy of the Social Security system. Had the President or some other significant political force used this perception to win concessions from defenders of the status quo, desirable reforms might have been possible.

- **Commissions are useful only if their members understand the nature of the problem and are capable of developing solutions.** The Social Security Commission of the early 1980s was a failure because membership was heavily skewed in favor of those who favored the status quo. It was no surprise that the Commission wound up supporting a huge increase in payroll taxes as a way to postpone genuine reforms until a later date.

Lesson #4: Experience gained from the debate on the 1986 Tax Reform Act demonstrates that support of public opinion leaders is crucial. The 1986 tax reform debate yielded a number of very important lessons for lawmakers and policymakers who favor a flat, simple tax system. In 1984, when President Reagan proposed that the American tax system be overhauled, he directed the Treasury Department to produce a report on how best to fix the tax code. After the election, the Treasury Department produced two separate reports. The central theme of each report was that current high tax rates were inhibiting economic growth and distorting behavior, even after the rate reductions phased in during the previous years.

Reagan's tax reform proposal did not endorse a flat tax, however. Though the idea had gained popularity during the early 1980s, a flat tax was seen as too dramatic to be politically feasible. Instead, the proposed reforms called for lower tax rates, fewer tax brackets, and some limits on deductions.

Congress began working on tax reform in 1985 and by the following year had produced a bill that contained only two rates: a 15 percent bracket for most Americans and a top rate of 28 percent. In addition, the corporate tax rate was reduced, though the actual tax burden on business income was increased because of provisions such as depreciation and the alternative minimum tax (both of which force businesses to overstate their taxable income) and increased double taxation (a higher capital gains tax rate and limits on individual retirement accounts). While there was considerable complaining about the bill, primarily because of its bias against savings and investment and the lack of simplification, it was adopted by comfortable margins in both houses of Congress and was signed into law by the President.

Interestingly, while the American people supported tax reform in general, there was never a strong outpouring of support for any of the tax reform proposals that were up for debate. Instead, the legislation was propelled in part by a consensus view that the economy would perform better if tax rates were lower and there was less distortion caused by preferences and penalties in the tax code. With the flat tax a major agenda item in today's political climate, the 1986 Tax Reform Act offers key suggestions for policymakers to consider.

While the phrase "conventional wisdom" may be shopworn, one side nonetheless will enjoy a distinct political advantage if it is able to dominate the press coverage, policy proposals, and academic debate on an issue. The 1986 tax reform push was helped by such a confluence of opinion. The trade issue is a comparable example: Notwithstanding all the political pressure to impose protectionist legislation in recent years, lawmakers have moved in the opposite direction, promoting increased openness and expanded trade. Proponents of the flat tax need to mimic this success by making available to key groups and individuals the wealth of existing information on the benefits of tax reform. Given the political wrangling that occurred over the flat tax in late 1995 and early 1996, this may seem a tall order, but the politically inspired attacks on the flat tax should be seen as the exception rather than the rule.

Lesson #5: Tax reform must lead to one rate. The 1986 Tax Reform Act was supposed to be a compact between politicians and taxpayers: Individuals would agree to give up certain deductions and allow an increase in the amount of income subject to double taxation, and politicians would cut tax rates. As history as shown, however, it did not take long for the politicians to renege on their part of the bargain. In both 1990 and 1993, legislators increased tax rates. This, of course, is hardly surprising; but it was disappointing that many taxpayers acquiesced in the increases because someone else was paying the tab. Had tax reform advocates in 1986 succeeded in creating a flat tax, however, it is unlikely that subsequent administrations would have had such an easy time playing divide and conquer and raising tax rates.

A great example of the political advantages of a single-rate tax comes from Massachusetts. Although considered a very liberal state, Massachusetts actually has a flat tax. Many state politicians, needless to say, would like to change this system since it restricts their ability to raise more revenue, but repeal requires a vote of the people. Pro-spending lobbies therefore have put this issue on the ballot several times, most recently in 1994 with a proposal that would have eliminated the flat tax by raising taxes on the "rich" and lowering them for everyone else. Fortunately, the voters saw through this appeal to class and rejected the referendum by a stunning margin of 69 percent to 31 percent. This response was perfectly logical: The voters realized that, under a one-rate tax system, it was hard for politicians to raise rates since all taxpayers would be adversely affected. Despite a promise that most of them would get a tax cut, voters realized that eliminating the flat tax would allow politicians to use divide-and-conquer tactics, and that ultimately all taxpayers would have more of their income seized.

Lesson #6: Bold steps will work, generating more enthusiasm than halfway measures. The American people supported the notion of tax reform in 1985–1986, yet there was never any groundswell of grassroots support for the specific legislative proposals being debated (nor, for that matter, was there any significant public opposition). This tepid response almost certainly was related to the fact that the 1986 legislation did not appear to be represent any dramatic change. The very things that cause taxpayers to be excited about the flat tax—one rate, radical simplification of the tax code, an end to special-interest politics and social engineering— were absent in 1986. While it is true that some of these features today will arouse opposition that was not apparent ten years ago, the trade-off is worthwhile.

This is not to say that enacting a flat tax will be easy. Even though some polls show that as many as two-thirds of voters support a flat tax, there is little question that a negative campaign can drive down those numbers. Attacks by Republicans against the flat tax proposal during the presidential primary process in 1996 caused the plan's support to drop to a level even with that of the opposition.

Other tax reform plans, however, fare even worse. There is overwhelming opposition to reforms such as a value-added tax that taxes consumption directly. Such a proposal would have many of the same economic benefits as the flat tax, but the little grassroots support it enjoys is based on the unsustainable claim that no tax collection agency would be required. Moreover, tax reform plans that attempt explicitly to maintain the principle of income redistribution fare even worse. The so-called USA (unlimited savings allowance) tax has some desirable features, but its continued reliance on a discriminatory rate structure and needless levels of complexity make it impossible to sell.

Lesson #7: Trying to maintain revenue "neutrality" can cause good policies to be offset by bad ones. The 1986 Tax Reform Act is best-known for reducing the top tax rate to 28 percent. But because of a requirement that the legislation not affect total federal tax collections, lawmakers were forced to raise taxes elsewhere. Much of the revenue loss associated with lower personal income tax rates was offset by higher tax rates on savings and investment. Higher capital gains taxes, more double taxation of savings, and depreciation provisions that force businesses to overstate their income all were included in the bill, and offset the gains made by the lower tax rates.

The 1986 legislation could have been improved dramatically if lawmakers had decided that the primary goal of reform was simply to create a sound tax system that did the least possible damage to the economy. This approach, of course, would be criticized by some as increasing the deficit (though the attacks would come from those who care about the deficit only when tax reductions are being discussed but conveniently forget about the issue when new programs are being debated).

The best response to this attack would be to include spending savings in the overall plan and avoid increases in government borrowing. Should that approach fail, however, the benefits of genuine tax reform would still be large enough to justify a short-term increase in the deficit.

Lesson #8: Itemized deductions are not a minefield if handled properly. The best approach to overall tax reform is to eliminate loopholes that allow some taxpayers to shelter their income from tax. This would make the tax system more neutral and permit a lower rate. Politicians often fear this approach, but to the limited extent it was used to finance lower rates in 1986, it worked.

- **Eliminating consumer interest on borrowing.** Specifically, the deductibility of consumer interest on things like auto loans and credit cards was eliminated in the 1986 Tax Reform Act. This was accompanied by substantial complaints and ferocious lobbying from certain interest groups. In the final analysis, however, the change went through, and there is no evidence that there was even the slightest adverse effect on any segment of the economy. Moreover, there were no negative political consequences for lawmakers who supported removing the deduction.

- **Itemized deductions such as state and local taxes.** Doing things opposed by special interests often carries no political cost. This is especially important when considering the frustrating issue of itemized deductions. There was an effort in 1986 to eliminate the state and local tax deduction, a feature which worked to the benefit of a small number of high-tax states. Oddly, it proved very difficult to create a coalition from the vast majority of states which were net losers from the existing deduction. In states with no income tax, for example, retaining the deduction would have provided no benefit to taxpayers, but the higher marginal rate resulting from retention would have hurt taxpayers. It turned out that the politicians in these states cared more about the political cover they received from the deduction, even though taxpayers would have paid lower taxes if the deduction had been ended. Lawmakers almost certainly could have eliminated the state and local tax deduction without any adverse consequence, but they made a mistake in focusing on rallying the support of politicians with an interest in maintaining a stake in bigger government regardless of whether their constituents suffered.

- **Home mortgage interest and charitable contributions.** The biggest challenge for supporters of a pure flat tax will be overcoming objections from those wishing to keep the home mortgage interest or charitable contributions deductions. While no serious effort was made in 1986 to challenge these deductions, the debate in the last two years suggests that these will be two of the most sensitive issues. In some sense, this is good news. The fact that the debate has focused so heavily on itemized deductions indicates that the most important goals—having only one rate and taxing income only one time—may be relatively easy to achieve. Even if there are concessions on these deductions, therefore, proponents of fundamental tax reform will have solved 95 percent of the tax code's problems by winning the really important battles.

But this does not mean that supporters of tax reform should not fight for the "pure" version of the flat tax. While one or two itemized deductions may seem innocuous, the existence of any deduction becomes the best argument for the creation or restoration of others. This kind of political wrangling puts pressure on politicians to raise the rate for the purpose of so-called revenue neutrality. Perhaps even more important, the creation or restoration of any deduction undermines support from those who are drawn to tax reform because they see a flat tax as a way to abolish all preferences and social engineering.

- **Set the rate low enough to give everyone a tax cut, and allow taxpayers to choose to continue to use the current system if they do not yet trust the new one.** There are two ways of trying to overcome the political obstacles created by these sensitive deductions. First and foremost, supporters of tax reform need to set the rate low enough to guarantee that virtually every taxpayer receives a tax cut. Polling data show that taxpayers who are concerned about deductions become much less worried if they can be assured that their total tax bill will go down. One problem, however, is that voters have learned to doubt the promises of politicians — particularly when it comes to the tax issue. One way to address this legitimate distrust would be to allow taxpayers to stick with the current system.

The Bush/Clinton High-Tax Years

The Tax Hikes of the 1990s. The tax hikes of 1990 and 1993 underscored once again that raising tax rates harms the economy and does little to raise revenue. After the 1990 tax increase, the economy entered a recession; and while it would be foolish to claim that the tax increase was the sole reason, it is quite reasonable to believe that the lengthy budget negotiations dampened economic activity and helped cause the recession, and that the imposition of the tax hike was partly responsible for the length of the recession and the economy's subsequent anemic recovery.

LESSONS LEARNED
The Bush/Clinton High-Tax Years

- To reduce or eliminate the capital gains tax, voters must understand how a capital gains tax inhibits growth and directly affects ordinary families and businesses.

- Personnel are policy. Politicians should have staff members committed to sound economic policy.

- A unified conservative position can sharpen the debate.

The 1993 tax increase also failed. Tax revenues in the high-tax 1990s have been growing more slowly than they did during the tax-cutting 1980s. It is true that the deficit has come down, but this is due to the Administration's reductions in defense outlays combined with a relatively good performance on controlling the growth of domestic spending (helped, of course, by the election of a more conservative Congress in 1994). Tax revenues actually are no larger, as a percentage of the economy, than they were in 1989 before the record tax hikes of 1990 and 1993.

Like those of the 1990 budget deal, the lessons of 1993 are very straightforward. After running as a fiscal moderate and promising middle-class tax cuts, President Clinton reversed field and proposed to Congress a record tax increase. Even with Congress dominated by the President's own party, however, the legislation was passed with hardly a vote to spare in either the House or the Senate, and President Clinton was forced to drop his call for a major energy tax (the BTU tax) that would have affected all taxpayers adversely.

The record tax increase, not surprisingly, had an adverse impact on the economy. Combined with the ill effects of the 1990 tax hike, the Clinton tax increase has contributed to the economy's worst seven-year performance since the end of World War II. Even more disturbing is the impact of this slow growth on families. According to Census Bureau data, the average household has lost nearly $1,500 of income (adjusted for inflation) since Ronald Reagan left office.

The lessons from this period are clear:

Lesson #1: To reduce or eliminate the capital gains tax, voters must understand how a capital gains tax inhibits growth and directly affects ordinary families and businesses. In 1989, the Bush Administration proposed reducing the capital gains tax rate. The proposal was modest, calling for a 45 percent exclusion that would have lowered the rate from 28 percent to 15 percent. Moreover, there were several restrictions on taxpayers seeking to take advantage of this lower rate. The Administration's proposal was further weakened in Congress: The exclusion was lowered to 30 percent, which meant the rate would drop to only 19.6 percent. The House of Representatives enacted this proposal by a wide margin, but the Senate proved to be more difficult. Despite concessions, Senate liberals led by Majority Leader George Mitchell mounted a filibuster. While supporters were able to corral a majority of votes, they never came close to the 60 votes needed to invoke cloture.

The Bush Administration's failure to obtain capital gains tax relief was not surprising, given the rules of the Senate. What was disappointing, however, was the inability of proponents to rally public support for the measure or to punish those who resisted. If public arguments were any gauge, the Bush Administration's proposed capital gains tax cut was driven primarily by a desire to increase government revenues. As a result, the law was written to encourage investors to sell long-term assets (on which they would pay the lower tax rate), but only secondary attention was given to how the law could be structured to promote growth (by stimulating new savings and investment).

Revenue maximizing undermines growth maximizing. One casualty of the focus on revenue maximization was that it became very difficult to argue credibly that Bush's capital gains tax proposal would have a substantial growth effect. Politicians thus were able to make the distribution of tax benefits a key issue.

A capital gains proposal that was focused on growth, by contrast, would have been more attractive and would have generated a larger level of support from savers, investors, and entrepreneurs. The other side would have continued its opposition, but a growth-maximizing capital gains proposal would have stimulated countervailing pressure, especially if supporters used specific examples to show how real-world businesses and investors would respond in ways that led to more jobs and higher incomes.

To illustrate how the growth argument could have been used, consider the issue of international competition. Many of America's major trading partners, such as Germany, South Korea, Taiwan, Holland, Hong Kong, and Singapore, do not tax capital gains. Others, including Japan, tax them only at a very low rate. In a global economy, there is no question that tax burdens, particularly on savings and investment, have an impact on a country's competitive position. The fact that America has one of the highest capital gains taxes in the world could have been used—and still should be used—to promote sound improvements in current tax policies.

Lesson #2: Personnel are policy. Politicians should have staff members committed to sound economic policy. From the beginning, the key challenge to the Bush Administration was how to comply with the Gramm-Rudman Deficit Reduction Act without raising taxes. Unfortunately, the President's appointees, such as Budget Director Richard Darman and Treasury Secretary Nicholas Brady, did not seem to take this challenge seriously. As a result, the Administration's 1989 budget was a disheartening combination of budget gimmicks and minor tax increases that, while estimated to meet the deficit law's target, in reality put off all hard decisions until the following year.

When the 1990 budget debate began, the conventional wisdom held that there was no way to close the gap between the projected deficit and what the Gramm-Rudman law required. The best course of action would have been to postpone the deficit reduction targets while avoiding any tax hike. Unfortunately, liberals in Congress completely dominated the budget debate, drawing the Bush Administration into a budget summit during which the White House made every concession imaginable and then some. The result: the largest tax increase in history up to that time and emasculation of the Gramm-Rudman Deficit Reduction Act through elimination of fixed deficit targets. Freed from any constraint, Congress increased domestic spending by record amounts. To the extent that black clouds have silver linings, however, the 1990 budget fiasco did teach several important lessons:

- **The wrong personnel can undermine the success of good intentions.** There is little doubt that the Bush Administration set the stage for disaster when the President appointed to key positions individuals such as Richard Darman and Nicholas Brady who had neither the inclination nor the ability to fight for the no-new-taxes/deficit reduction position that Bush effectively articulated during the campaign. If no other lesson is learned, policymakers should recognize the importance of filling key positions with those who have the fortitude needed to resist the temptations of special-interest politics.

- **Violating a promise to voters is political poison.** The 1990 budget deal is a prime example of how not to conduct negotiations. The liberals entered the year hoping to force Bush off his no-new-taxes vow and to escape the fiscal discipline imposed by Gramm-Rudman. They got everything they wanted and more—higher tax rates, record increases in domestic spending, and the gutting of the Gramm-Rudman deficit reduction plan.

Lesson #3: A unified conservative position can sharpen the debate. One of the major lessons of the 1993 tax hike is that there were no defections from the field of Republican opponents. Every single Republican opposed Clinton's record tax increase, which crystallized in voters' minds that there was a genuine difference between the two parties. This was especially important after the failures of the Bush Administration and helped lead to a landslide congressional victory for Republicans in 1994.

Preparing for Tomorrow's Battles: Regaining the Offensive

The 1995–1996 Flat Tax Debate. Although there was never any serious prospect that it would come up for a vote, the flat tax has been one of the dominant tax issues in recent years. In basic terms, the flat tax applies to all income but taxes it only once, at one low rate. In addition to its economic growth features (one low rate, elimination of the bias against savings and investment, and dramatic simplification), the flat tax attracts considerable support because it would radically simplify the Internal Revenue System and severely restrict special-interest manipulation of the tax code.

While the flat tax concept has existed for decades, it did not penetrate the public consciousness until the early 1980s, when two Hoover Institution scholars published a book explaining how the idea worked. The boomlet of rhetorical support was overtaken by the Tax Reform Act of 1986, however, and the flat tax as an issue faded into the background until 1994 when Representative Richard Armey (R-TX) re-introduced the proposal. The idea received a further boost when the Republicans took control of Congress and Armey suddenly became the Majority Leader, second only to Speaker of the House Newt Gingrich in rank.

LESSONS LEARNED
Preparing for Tomorrow's Battles

- Debate should be focused on the problems and unpopularity of the current system, and highlight key principles of reforms that address those problems.
- Peripheral issues will bog down reform.

The flat tax vaulted even further into the public eye when magazine publisher Steve Forbes proposed it as the centerpiece of his 1996 campaign for the Republican nomination for President. Using his own financial resources to bring the flat tax to a wide audience, Forbes attracted considerable support and won two of the presidential primaries, but political opponents within the Republican party stopped his momentum by raising doubts about his flat tax plan. Ironically, arguments that probably would not have had much credibility coming from Democrats were raised by Forbes's opponents, many of whom had endorsed most or all of the principles of the flat tax just months before. Their new opposition eroded support for the flat tax across the country.

Senator Robert Dole's eventual capture of the Republican nomination, and his call for a 15 percent across-the-board tax cut, once again pushed the flat tax onto a back burner. Dole felt compelled to make a vague commitment to fundamental tax reform at some future point should he win the White House. Now that Bill Clinton has been re-elected, the flat tax may well re-emerge as the consensus position of congressional Republicans.

The non-legislative flat tax battle of the last two years provides at least two useful lessons:

Lesson #1: The debate should be on the problems and unpopularity of the current system, and should highlight the key principles of reforms that will address those problems. The present tax code is extremely unpopular. Taxpayers resent the complexity, fear the audits, and rightfully suspect that special interests get special privileges. Needless to say, most taxpayers also think they are paying too much. Supporters of tax reform need to tap into these concerns and explain that this anger is justified. They need to specify the ways in which the current system is broken. It is particularly important to stress that this is not necessarily the fault of individual IRS agents (although, as in any organization, the IRS will have its share of bad employees); rather, the fault lies primarily with the deficiencies of the tax code as it now exists.

The flat tax has several very popular features which should be the focus of supporters' arguments. Fortunately, these features also tend to be the fundamental building blocks of a sound tax system. Most notably, policymakers should stress that a fair, pro-growth tax system must have only one rate, must tax income only one time, and must use a form that fits on a postcard for easy filing. Reform that satisfies these principles will be successful. Indeed, these principles will allow supporters of the flat tax and sales tax to unite their energies, since both proposals comply with the key points: one rate, one application, one form.

Lesson #2: Peripheral issues will bog down reform. One of the ironic aspects of the tax reform debate is the degree to which trivial topics dominate the headlines. The flat tax, for instance, was attacked by housing lobbyists who feared the loss of the home mortgage interest deduction. The arguments these lobbyists used proved false, and the flat tax emerged reasonably unscathed, but the discord was a distraction and used up time and resources that could have been used to promote key principles.

Supporters of tax reform should devise readily understood illustrations to explain why these other arguments should be discounted. To those who seek to maintain the home mortgage interest deduction, for example, lawmakers could point out that it if they were to reserve the current system for those who wish to deduct home mortgage interest and tax the interest income of the mortgage holder, those homeowners would not be subject to the lower interest rates for which other borrowers were able to qualify. The key point is that issues like itemized deductions are minor compared to the goal of achieving one rate applied just one time.

STRATEGIES FOR ENACTING A FAIRER TAX SYSTEM

It is imperative that policymakers, both in the next Administration and in Congress, apply these lessons in ways that will help bring about fundamental reform of America's cumbersome, unpopular, and corrupt tax

STRATEGIES FOR
ENACTING A FAIRER TAX SYSTEM

- It is important to act fast if you have the votes.

- Advocates of tax reform must understand their goals.

- Policymakers should target key constituencies.

- To convince voters they share these goals as well, it is important to understand your constituents, and not to confuse special interests with the voters at large.

- Tax reform should include a tax cut for all income classes.

- Growth and tax cuts will trump the Left's fairness argument.

- Comprehensive tax reform may be easier than fixing problems one by one.

- The goal of implementing just one tax rate must not be compromised.

- The congressional leadership should take steps to modernize the revenue-estimating process.

- Personnel are policy; therefore, staff members should be chosen wisely.

- Conservatives should use the CBO, the JCT, the GAO, and various tax-writing and appropriations committees to highlight deficiencies in the current system.

- Congress should consider enacting legislation to repeal the current tax code by a specified date in the future.

- Policymakers should allow a safety hatch during the period of reform.

system. This means that supporters of tax reform must clearly understand what they are trying to do and develop strategies for winning popular support while figuring out ways to overcome the obstacles that are sure to be set up by special interests inside the Beltway.

A few simple steps—structural and political—must be taken if tax reform is to become a reality. While some of these proposals may seem obvious, however, it is not entirely clear that policymakers fully understand their importance. Failure to adopt these simple strategies would be a tactical mistake, and would open up opportunities for opponents to attack and destroy even the most sincere and popular tax reform.

STRATEGY #1
If you have the votes, act fast.

It is vital to strike while the iron is hot. The prospects for dramatic change are always greatest in the first year following an election. Reagan's tax cuts probably would not have attracted the necessary Democratic votes, for instance, had he waited until 1982. Simply stated, battles delayed often are battles lost.

For 1997, achieving an across-the-board tax cut will require decisive action. Delay and equivocation will be taken as a sign that newly elected officials are not committed to a pro-growth, smaller-government agenda. Moreover, such weakness will undermine prospects for fundamental reform after the 1998 mid-term elections. In the event there are not enough votes in Congress or the President is hostile, supporters of pro-growth tax policies should focus on the long term.

STRATEGY #2
Advocates of tax reform must understand their goals.

A prerequisite of successful governance by any legislator is a deep understanding of one's goals. Conservatives have a mixed record of success in Washington because of a mistaken belief that balancing the budget is the number one goal of fiscal policy. This is short-sighted. While avoiding debt is an important moral and political issue, it is a relatively minor economic concern. The number one goal should be smaller government and sustainable economic growth through a system of taxation that rewards work and investment, and that focuses on clear and simple messages to the taxpayers of America.

A proper understanding of the issues can lead to important conclusions about the focus of government policy in general, especially with regard to balancing the budget. Policymakers would do well to remember that:

- **The deficit is not what matters; the real problem is government.** Budget deficits are not desirable, but they are only a symptom of too much government. More specifically, there is no reason to believe that the economy would benefit if deficit-financed government spending was replaced by tax-financed spending. Either way, government takes resources from the productive sector of the economy. Proponents of big government understand this very well, which is why they focus on the symptom rather than the disease. They know they can exploit concern over the deficit to win support for higher taxes, which they then can use to fuel even more new spending. Even in the best of circumstances, higher taxes are a poor substitute for spending discipline.

- **Spending should be reduced even if the budget is balanced.** The myopic fixation on budget deficits has had one positive impact: Many lawmakers resist new programs or attempt to reduce existing programs in hopes of reducing government borrowing overall. To the extent that the right thing is being done for the wrong reason, however, there is an automatic limit to the progress that can be made. For instance, would the need for less spending disappear if some huge new source of revenue was uncovered by the Treasury and the budget somehow was balanced tomorrow? Would we suddenly no longer have such counterproductive, wasteful, and duplicative programs? The answer, of course, is that government indeed should be reduced, but that years of "deficit" rhetoric may have convinced the public that the job will be done once the budget has been balanced.

  Once again, the other side already has learned the appropriate lesson. The recent drop in the budget deficit has taken much of the wind out of the sails of those who have been using the level of government borrowing as the primary argument for spending reductions. As a result, President Clinton spent much of the 1996 campaign season endorsing one new government program after another. But while these new proposals were designed to be rather small in terms of overall budget impact, that was not the point: The environment for fiscal discipline had eroded even more.

- **The tax system should be fixed regardless of short-term revenue impact.** Misplaced deficit concern also is used by proponents of big government to block long-overdue tax changes. Viewing the deficit as the most important issue gives the pro-tax lobby tremendous power. As long as they refuse to reduce the growth of government spending, they can block tax cuts. But blocking tax cuts also keeps the

economy from growing at a faster rate, and this slower growth can
then be used as an argument for even more government.

Perhaps the best way to look at this issue is to ask a question.
Although tax revenues increased by 99.44 percent during the 1980s, it
is likely that there was a modest revenue decline (compared to what
tax collections would have been) in the first few years after the tax
cuts went into effect. The question, therefore, is: "Should Ronald
Reagan have abandoned his tax cuts until Congress demonstrated a
willingness to enact immediate offsetting spending savings?" The
answer, clearly, is "No." Failure to enact the Reagan tax cuts would
have condemned the economy to continued "stagflation" — the
combination of inflation and low growth that characterized the
1970s. Fortunately, President Reagan understood what was required;
because of his determination to persevere, the nation enjoyed its
longest-ever period of economic expansion.

- **A lower budget deficit will not generate noticeably lower interest
  rates.** Opponents of tax relief, Republican as well as Democrat, argue
  that a balanced budget should be the most important goal because
  the economy will benefit from dramatic reductions in interest rates.
  But while economic theory suggests that higher deficits should bid up
  interest rates, statisticians and other economists have yet to find a significant relationship between the two. Over the last 30 years, for instance, interest rates have been more likely to climb when the deficit
  falls, and vice versa. This does not mean the theory is necessarily
  wrong, but it does help illustrate that, in world capital markets of tril-
  lions of dollars, even shifts of tens of billions of dollars in the U.S.
  budget deficit are not likely to have any noticeable effect.

  On this issue more than any other, the accumulated data are
  overwhelming. As Chart 10.2 illustrates, the presumed relationship
  between budget deficits and interest rates is nonexistent. Rather than
  move in the same direction, as politicians of both parties often
  presume, the two are more likely to move in opposite directions.

- **Lower interest rates are not the key to growth.** Pro-tax politicians
  also argue that lower interest rates will boost the economy by stimulating new investment. Once again, however, there is little evidence
  to support this claim. America has gone through periods of very high
  real interest rates and very low real interest rates, and the economy

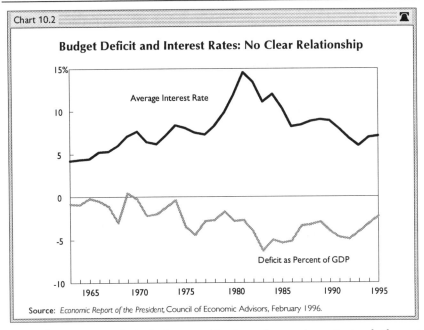

Chart 10.2

Budget Deficit and Interest Rates: No Clear Relationship

Source: *Economic Report of the President,* Council of Economic Advisors, February 1996.

does not march in lockstep with these fluctuations. Instead, the evidence suggests that a more important variable is the after-tax rate of return. In other words, whether interest rates are high or low, investors will put up money for a project if they expect to make a profit. If, however, the tax burden erodes the expected return on investment, they will forego the opportunity.

Good examples of this occurred in the 1930s and 1980s. In the 1930s, America had very low interest rates, but there was almost no investment. Investors obviously looked at the bad economic climate, and at the higher tax rates imposed by Presidents Hoover and Roosevelt, and wisely chose to hang onto their money. The economy, of course, suffered. Conversely, in the 1980s, interest rates were at relatively high levels; nevertheless, the investment climate was good, tax rates were falling, and investors responded accordingly.

- **Any tax reform more than likely will be a futile exercise if it does not result in a single-rate system.** As the 1986 Tax Reform Act demonstrated, a tax code with multiple tax rates is not stable. While the number of tax rates was reduced to two and the top rate fell to 28 percent—which, while still too high, was at least a dramatic improvement over the 70 percent rate that existed when Reagan took office— it did not take long for politicians to go back on the commitment they had made to voters. The Bush tax increase in 1990 boosted the top rate to 31 percent, and Clinton's record tax hike in 1993 pushed it still higher to nearly 40 percent.

The question, of course, is how to prevent a recurrence of this mistake. One answer is to make sure that the tax system winds up with just one rate. Not only is this sound economic policy, allowing dramatic simplification of the tax code, but it also has an important political impact. When there is only one low rate, taxpayers understand that they are all in the same boat. Efforts to raise taxes become much more difficult. If the politicians try to raise the rate, all taxpayers suffer and thus are united in their obvious incentive to resist. But even if politicians attempt to create a second rate to be paid by the "rich," it will be much harder to enact than it would be with a tax system that already is riddled with several rates.

Taxpayers, rich and poor alike, recognize that the creation of a second rate gives politicians carte blanche to tax all taxpayers at a higher rate. A good test of this theory at the state level is to review the situation in Massachusetts. Massachusetts has a statewide flat tax that is an obstacle to the spending lobbies because the only way it can be eliminated is by referendum. Several times, most recently in 1994, voters were asked to replace this tax with a "progressive" tax that proponents claimed would make the "rich" pay more and reduce taxes for everyone else. By a vote of 69 percent to 31 percent, Massachusetts voters rejected the referendum.

STRATEGY #3
Policymakers should target key constituencies.

Editorial writers are a key group since they presumably have the time and inclination to look at the larger picture. Given the overwhelming evidence that a flat tax will boost growth, the opportunity exists to reach all but the most ideologically rigid of this group. One good indication that this may be happening is that both the *Washington Post* and *New York Times* have editorialized in favor of the flat tax.

Another major target is the business community, which can be reached through individual companies or trade associations. Most businesses recognize that a flat tax would be good for business, but they also fear change. In particular, business leaders worry that a flat tax could result in higher tax burdens on capital or that the process could be derailed and captured by those who want to use the exercise as a way to raise taxes. Leaders of the tax reform movement can ease these fears by clearly demonstrating that they would kill the bill themselves rather than allow this to happen.

STRATEGY #4
To convince voters they share these goals as well, understand your constituents. Don't confuse the special interests with the voters at large.

Because of the strong adverse reactions to be expected from pro-spending groups, efforts to enact pro-economic growth tax and budget policies will require better political skills. This is particularly true when the media appear to be ideologically hostile. Fiscally responsible lawmakers need to take their message directly to the people. To help sell the message of lower taxes and less government, policymakers should employ the following themes to demonstrate to voters why change is needed.

- **The economy is the worst in 50 years.** Defenders of the status quo have done a good job of undermining the rationale for change by convincing voters that the economy is doing fine. This is due in part to the Clinton Administration's technique of comparing its record to that of the Bush Administration. By almost all measures, Clinton has outperformed Bush, but this is misleading since both Administrations followed very similar policies of raising taxes and creating bigger government. When the Reagan years are compared with the Bush/Clinton years, however, the Reagan era of lower tax rates and less government control wins handily. Even more revealing is the fact that the years since Reagan left office represent the worst seven-year period in our economy since the end of World War II.

  Shedding a dogmatic attachment to party labels is important in any tax debate. One of the most compelling historical arguments for lower tax rates is provided by the experience of the Kennedy Administration. One of the original supply-siders, John F. Kennedy presided over steep reductions in the tax burden on capital and introduced across-the-board tax rate reductions that went into effect after his death. Because Kennedy was a Democrat, however, some Republicans are loath to talk about the success of his policies. Not admitting the successes implemented by policymakers on the other side of the political fence is the political equivalent of cutting off one's nose to spite one's face.

Finally, policymakers need to understand that growth does matter and find ways to convince voters that they stand to derive real benefits from an expanding economy. Increasing the economy's growth rate by just one-half of 1 percent, for instance, means $5,000 of additional wealth for an average family of four after just ten years. Federal Reserve Governor Lawrence Lindsey points out that increasing growth by this amount will mean $300,000 of higher lifetime income for the average household.

- **Real income has been falling.** One consequence of stagnant growth is that real incomes, adjusted for inflation, are declining. While there has been a modest upswing in the last two years, the average family still has lost nearly $1,500 in income since Reagan left office. The combination of falling incomes and higher taxes during the post-Reagan years has not exactly been a recipe for higher standards of living.

Annual income figures are worth considering particularly because they clearly contradict the liberals' persistent claim that the rich got richer and the poor got poorer during the 1980s. The Reagan years were the only period in the last 20 years when the poor were better off. In addition to helping convince liberals of the moral necessity of tax cuts, these figures, properly used, can serve as persuasive evidence for journalists seeking an honest story.

- **The tax system bears much of the blame.** Taxes are not the only economic policy that can hinder growth, but they certainly rank near the top. There is every reason to fear that the tax increases imposed on the American people in 1990 and 1993 are the main reason the economy's growth rates have been so dismal. Indeed, one of the most effective strategies for those who want to cut taxes is to cite history. America has enjoyed three major periods of tax rate reduction: during the 1920s, the 1960s, and the 1980s. In every case, the economy boomed, tax revenues rose, and people prospered. Conversely, every period of higher tax rates — the 1930s, the 1970s because of bracket creep, and the 1990s—has been one of sub-par economic performance and stagnant incomes.

- **The tax system is unfair to everyone but politicians and special interests.** Proponents of big government should be forced to defend what they have wrought, but this means more than just revealing how government wastes Americans' tax dollars; the unfair, economically destructive way government raises those tax dollars also must be exposed. Reformers must continually remind voters of two things: how much time-consuming paperwork is generated by the IRS and how frequently the tax code is changed as politicians try to manipulate the economy.

  Members of the tax-writing committees receive more campaign contributions, including PAC dollars, than the average Member of Congress. This does not necessarily mean they are bad politicians; sometimes contributions come from those who simply are trying to protect themselves from tax increases. In too many cases, however, campaign dollars are given in the hope of getting a special loophole added to the tax code. One of the biggest benefits of tax reform is that it would end this sordid game. Both those who are paying to avoid even higher taxes and those who are trying to buy special treatment could put their money to more productive uses.

- **Tax reform can defang the IRS.** Not only can lawmakers in Congress legitimately criticize the IRS for case after case of excessive force and mistaken application, but they also can show the public a reasonable solution. Under a flat tax, the 480 forms now in use would be replaced by two postcard-size forms. Today's complex array of preferences, deductions, credits, loopholes, exemptions, and shelters would be replaced by a simple one-rate tax system.

  More specifically, lawmakers can explain in simple English how radically different America would be under a flat tax. They can emphasize to the public that the only questions the IRS should be able to ask the average taxpayer are the amount of income he or she makes and the size of the family he or she supports. No longer would taxpayers be forced to fill out and then justify potentially hundreds of unclear, confusing, and ever-changing questions. And because double taxation would end, no longer could the IRS force Americans to reveal the amount and composition of their assets. Once money is made and the flat tax proportion of it has been paid, no one in the government should be permitted to intrude into the personal lives of Americans.

Supporters of tax reform should always carry the two postcard-size forms that are the only forms required under the flat tax. Voters are naturally suspicious whenever someone in Washington promises huge benefits without putting the promise in writing. The postcards are a wonderful reinforcement because they prove that taxes really can be filed simply and quickly. They can help policymakers and reformers generate considerable grassroots support, especially if the message is linked to how a flat tax ends the power of special interests to manipulate the tax code.

STRATEGY #5
Tax reform should include a tax cut for all income classes.

Policymakers sometimes face a choice between tax cuts that will maximize growth and tax cuts that will generate the most political support. Some of the tax cuts that would have the biggest impact on growth, for instance, such as repealing the estate tax, cutting the top income tax rate, and reducing the capital gains rate, do not benefit all voters. While legislators should never shy from arguing for these changes, it is wise to include tax provisions in any pro-growth package that benefit the largest possible number of voters, and certainly all taxpayers. That is the beauty of the flat tax; it is also why candidate Dole promised Americans a 15 percent across-the-board tax cut.

STRATEGY #6
Growth and tax cuts will trump the Left's fairness argument.

No matter what tax cut is proposed, the Left will argue that it is unfair because upper-income taxpayers will benefit. This claim will not be terribly effective if other taxpayers also are enjoying a reduction in their tax burden, but lawmakers should not neglect the importance of the growth argument. The public wants to believe in a brighter future, and there is considerable acceptance of the notion that federal taxes and spending are a drag on the economy.

STRATEGY #7
Comprehensive tax reform may be easier than fixing problems one by one.

The problems of the tax code are so numerous that fixing each of them individually could take years. This is one of the best arguments for a flat tax. High tax rates, double taxation of interest income, depreciation, alternative minimum tax, foreign tax rules, capital gains taxes, double taxation of dividends, the estate tax, pension laws, deductions, phaseouts, and complexity—just a few of the major flaws in the current system— would all disappear in omnibus flat tax legislation. This fact alone should generate a strong base of support for quick approval of flat tax reform.

It is very important to focus the tax debate on taxing income only once. Every economic theory — even Marxism — agrees that capital formation is the key to economic growth. It is therefore self-defeating to continue to take more and more money out of the pockets of taxpayers when they invest or save and create more capital to spend. Rather than focus on taxing entities (e.g., corporations, individuals, and estates), and thereby continuing to tax the same people's income at various stages through economic growth, policymakers must focus on income at its source. To popularize this notion, supporters of tax reform can state simply that the IRS (and the U.S. government) should come to taxpayers with its hands held out only once.

STRATEGY #8
The goal of implementing just one tax rate must not be compromised.

This point cannot be repeated too often. One tax rate is not just good for the economy and not just an important element in simplifying the system; it also is the key moral argument for tax reform. The American people believe in fairness, and fairness means equal treatment under the law, which they believe to be a constitutional right. The only tax system which satisfies that goal is one which taxes Americans at a single rate. Moreover, a tax reform plan that leaves in place more than one rate is an invitation to future politicians to raise rates and create new rates.

STRATEGY #9
The congressional leadership should take steps to modernize the revenue-estimating process.

Under the leadership of House Ways and Means Committee Chairman William Archer (R-TX), efforts already are underway to examine how the revenue-estimating procedure could be improved. It is very important that the existing, deeply flawed process of static scoring—based on the assumption that taxes have no effect on the economy's performance—be replaced as soon as possible. This is particularly true if lawmakers have a chance to consider tax legislation like the flat tax that would have a strong, positive impact on growth. Perhaps best of all, this type of reform can be effected without legislation. It simply requires leadership and boldness on the part of the chairman and support from other members of the committee.

STRATEGY #10
Personnel are policy. Choose staff members wisely.

Another key to passing sound tax policy is putting the most qualified people in important staff positions. Adversaries on the left routinely use inaccurate analyses produced by the Congressional Budget Office (CBO) and the Joint Committee on Taxation (JCT) to buttress their arguments for or against tax relief. The alternative, however, should not be to create inaccurate analyses which favor conservative proposals; instead, policymakers in Congress and the Administration must concentrate on installing personnel who will generate the most accurate possible figures.

Unfortunately, very few changes have been made at the CBO and JCT, and many important committee staff positions are filled by those who do not understand or share a free-market perspective. It is up to the key Members of Congress to force these changes, and it is within their power to do so. The CBO's director, for instance, controls the CBO staff, and that director is hired by the two chairmen of the budget committees. It should be obvious that the director needs to be someone who not only understands these issues, but also is willing to replace any staff members who hold outmoded, ideologically driven ideas. Likewise, it is the chairman of one of the tax-writing committees (rotating every two years between the House and Senate) who holds complete power over who works for the JCT. This power should be used to hire staff who have the best understanding and ability to do the job.

STRATEGY #11
Conservatives should use the CBO, the JCT, the GAO, and the various tax-writing and appropriations committees to highlight deficiencies in the current system.

Conservatives should use existing government agencies and committees to publish regular, clearly written reports highlighting the need for market-based reforms. This again requires hiring qualified staff who know how to ask the right questions and frame the information as fairly and accurately as possible. Well-grounded papers or hearings could significantly affect the debate on many issues by providing Congress, the Administration, and the public with a better understanding of the parameters of the problems being discussed.

Accurate information is critical to building a consensus among both Democrats and Republicans that the tax system must be reformed, and that the minimum requirements of that reform include a single tax rate, one-time taxing of income, and a simplified system that lets taxpayers file their taxes using a postcard-size form.

STRATEGY #12
Congress should enact a law to repeal the current tax code by a specified future date.

Repealing the current tax code by a specified future date may require jumping some procedural hurdles, but it could be a popular way to begin the necessary debate on tax reform. This approach has the advantage of putting the onus on opponents to justify the current system. Another political benefit is that this approach circumvents contentious questions about which new tax system should be selected and what those plans entail. Thus, this strategy could unite flat tax and sales tax proponents and give nervous Members of Congress a way to vote for tax reform even if they are not yet ready to explain to their constituents why things like itemized deductions should not stand in the way.

STRATEGY #13
Policymakers should allow a safety hatch during the period of reform.

At some point, lawmakers will have to address, specifically and individually, the difficult issues associated with any tax reform. More specifically, since the inherent equality of the flat tax can preempt any effort to invoke the politics of envy, it is safe to predict that opponents will try to scare middle-class voters into believing they somehow will lose. One easy way to deflect that attack would be to allow taxpayers to remain in the current system for a ten-year period if they so chose. Because it is doubtful that very many would do so, opponents of a flat tax would lose momentum, and the chances that the flat tax could be killed by special-interest lobbying would be greatly diminished.

CONCLUSION

Misguided fiscal policy is hindering economic growth and undermining America's ability to compete worldwide. Lawmakers who want to improve the nation's performance should focus on reducing the size of government and reforming the tax system to minimize the penalties on working, saving, and investing. The combination of these policies also will reduce the budget deficit, although this should not be the primary goal.

Making the right tax and spending decisions will not be easy. Too many interest groups benefit from the existing loophole-ridden tax system, and many politicians therefore will resist changing it. Because the nation and its hardworking taxpayers have so much to gain, however, it is critically important that policymakers immediately adopt tactics and strategies that will increase their chances of successfully reforming America's inefficient and abusive tax system.

PART II: FOREIGN POLICY ISSUES

Chapter 11

DEFINING THE U.S. ROLE IN PROMOTING GLOBAL FREEDOM

Kim R. Holmes

Liberty is the quintessential American idea. The belief in individual freedom, unlimited opportunity, and limited government has shaped the history of this country like no other. It lies at the heart of the American dream—a dream shared by millions of people around the world. From the collapse of communism in the former Soviet Union to the triumph of democracy in places like Argentina, South Africa, and Taiwan, the desire to be free has been universal. By nurturing and championing this dream of liberty for others, the United States is grounding its foreign policy in a universal idea that is good both for America and for the world.

Translating this ideal into principles of foreign policy requires that the U.S. support the spread of free trade, free markets, and free governments abroad. There are utilitarian reasons for embracing such policies: Free trade, free markets, and Western-style democracy are good for American interests. They promote international economic growth and stability, create markets for American goods and services, and keep nations open to the free flow of ideas. They help to create the global conditions for economic growth inside the United States, growth which generates more jobs and a higher standard of living for Americans. Free trade and free governments abroad are also good for American security. Democracies with market economies are far more likely to be friends of America than are dictatorships with closed economies.

There also are moral reasons for supporting freedom around the world. Whenever possible, Americans want their government to side with nations and peoples that are resisting tyranny and oppression. Americans believe in liberty not only for themselves, but for all peoples of the world. Americans want to see their character as a nation reflected in their foreign and national security policies. They want to help make the world a better place while confirming the validity of their own values of liberty and democracy at home.

Americans are idealists, but they are not utopians. Being a champion of liberty around the world should never be seen as the totality or centerpiece of American foreign policy. America will always have more to do in the world than promote democracy and free trade. Protecting American security at times may even require measures that do not directly advance these principles: buttressing non-democratic moderate Arab regimes in the Middle East, for example, or imposing stringent trade sanctions on rogue countries like Cuba when national security interests require them.

However, now that the Cold War is over, these instances will be less frequent than before. Freedom and democracy by no means have triumphed in the world, but they have a much better chance of growing now that their opposites — tyranny and dictatorship — lack the legitimacy and material support of a superpower like the Soviet Union. In this environment, the U.S. has more freedom to employ non-military means — trade, private and public diplomacy, and even, in some instances, foreign aid in the form of security and humanitarian assistance — to accomplish what once was mainly achievable only through military means: the preservation and spread of free institutions around the world.

POLITICAL FREEDOM: DEMOCRACY AND THE RULE OF LAW

It has become a truism to assert that Western-style democratic governments are not likely to be enemies of the United States. It is argued that their political pluralism and their focus on commercial activities tend to make them a force for international stability. This is largely true. The key question for U.S. policymakers, however, is not whether this assertion is true, but what it means for U.S. foreign policy. It is true to the point of banality to insist that America should support the emergence of democracy around the world, but how should this be done? This broader question breaks down into three specific ones: 1) How should Americans understand "democracy;" 2) what are the proper means of policy to promote that end; and 3) will there be instances when the U.S. may choose not to support some democratic process because it will lead unintentionally to instability or undermine some other U.S. security interest?

The Meaning of Democracy. Democracy can be defined broadly to include a whole host of institutions and ideas; in practice, however, it is often reduced to the process of elections. This definition is too simplistic and can be misleading. By Russian standards, Russia's recent presidential elections certainly were free and fair, but that does not mean that Russia has all (or even most) of the prerequisites for Western-style democracy. It lacks, for example, a well-developed respect for the rule of law, traditions of political parties and a loyal opposition, and institutional checks and balances that limit corruption and abuses of power. Russia is far more democratic than the Soviet Union, but it is not a democracy like America, Britain, or Germany.

What difference does this viewpoint make for U.S. foreign policy? A great deal. Seen from this perspective, support for the man guaranteeing the election process in Russia, Boris Yeltsin, is not necessarily the same as support for democracy. While President Yeltsin has allowed elections to take place, he has done little to institutionalize the rule of law and a constitutional system that could guarantee democracy after he is gone. Moreover, by launching the war in Chechnya, Yeltsin made a mockery of the democratic principles for which he supposedly stands.

By pretending that democracy in Russia depends solely on the physical and political survival of Yeltsin, U.S. policymakers have done little to encourage the growth of free and legal institutions which are the backbone of Western-style democracy. In fact, the warm embrace of Yeltsin has done nothing to stop either the decline of the real democratic movement around Yegor Gaidar and Grigory Yavlinski (it may inadvertently have accelerated it) or the rising power of the military-industrial complex around Prime Minister Viktor Chernomyrdin. As a result, the process of institutionalizing democracy in Russia has stalled. Because democracy lacks roots in Russia, the process of holding democratic elections could be reversed by some anti-democratic communist or nationalist politician, or even by a populist leader like former General Alexander Lebed, whose attachment to democratic principles is unknown.

It may be true that President Yeltsin is preferable to a communist or a radical nationalist. But that does not mean that institutions of democracy exist in Russia, or that the U.S. has no choice but to support Boris Yeltsin no matter what he does. The mistake is twofold: defining democracy solely in terms of how Yeltsin was elected president, rather than more broadly in terms of how the society and economy are progressing, and then making U.S. policy dependent on the political fortunes of one man.

Another example of advancing a flawed concept of democracy in U.S. foreign policy can be seen in the Clinton Administration's actions in Haiti. To justify its military operation to "restore democracy" in Haiti, the White House claimed that Jean-Bertrand Aristide was the elected ruler of Haiti. Regardless of how Aristide was elected, as president he ruled undemocratically; he even threatened violence against his own people. Moreover, Aristide's successor, President Rene Preval, has presided over the continuation of political murders, the intimidation of the political opposition, and widespread corruption and poverty despite billions of dollars of aid and the presence of U.S. troops guarding the regime. The country was not a democracy under Aristide, and it is not a democracy today under Preval.

In both Russia and Haiti, a higher principle was sacrificed to advance a fraudulent notion of democracy. That higher principle was liberty: the freedom of citizens not only to participate in free and fair elections, but also to enjoy the fruits of their liberty by having a government that, no matter how it was chosen, respects their rights as free men and women. If this principle had been followed, Yeltsin's war in Chechnya would have tempered U.S. support for the Russian president, as would Yeltsin's failure to institutionalize the rule of law and other building blocks of real democracy. If support for liberty, instead of a flawed notion of democracy, had been the rule in Haiti, the U.S. would never have wielded military force to reinstate Aristide — a man who had threatened the liberties of his own people while president.

U.S. support for Yeltsin or Aristide could have been justified if such a policy served some higher security interest. But it did not. In fact, the Clinton Administration's policies on Russia and Haiti have come at the expense of U.S. credibility and security interests. In its obsession with Yeltsin's political fortunes, the U.S. dragged its feet on enlargement of the North Atlantic Treaty Organization (NATO); made unwise concessions to the Russians on the Conventional Forces in Europe (CFE) treaty; and looked the other way as Russia helped Iran build nuclear reactors, supplied China with advanced fighter aircraft, and undermined U.S. policy in Iraq and elsewhere in the Middle East. In its efforts to tie Haitian democracy to the political fortunes of Aristide, the Clinton Administration not only threatened the use of force for purposes for which it was ill-suited (and for which there was no vital U.S. interest), but also tied American prestige and credibility to a regime that is corrupt and increasingly undemocratic—all in the name of "restoring democracy."

Washington will have many reasons to back or oppose any given regime in the world. Sometimes the U.S. will have to overlook domestic practices of foreign countries that are not to its liking. The U.S. does not require Saudi Arabia or Kuwait to be democracies, for example, because America has overriding security interests in having these countries as allies.

However, it makes little sense to sacrifice American security interests in the name of a flawed and narrow notion of democracy, as is now being done in Russia and Haiti. Letting a muddled and idealized conception of a foreign government's domestic arrangements determine the totality of U.S. foreign policy toward that government stands strategy on its head. It not only undermines American security, but makes a mockery of American values. This is a double loss for the United States. In these two cases, Clinton's policy of "enlarging" the world's democracies advances neither the cause of freedom nor the security interests of the United States.

International Stability and the Rule of Law. By far the most important contribution America can make to the cause of liberty around the world is to continue its global role not only as a leader of the Western military alliances like NATO, but as a general force for international stability and the rule of law in international organizations and bilateral diplomacy. America's military commitments to NATO and other allies represent a concrete pledge to safeguard, with military means if necessary, the freedom of these countries. The role of these alliances in ensuring international stability is a tangible contribution by America to creating an environment in which freedom and democracy can grow.[1]

---

1 See Chapter 12, "Defining the U.S. Role in Promoting Global Security," and Chapter 20, "Reforming and Working With the United Nations."

The U.S. has a very important stake in international order and stability. For example, blatant aggression by one country against its neighbor cannot be countenanced by the United States. America may not be able, either directly or indirectly, to stop the aggression with armed force, but its moral authority in the world requires that the aggression at least be condemned diplomatically (and in some cases punished with sanctions). Of course, where America's security is endangered directly, as it was during the Persian Gulf War, direct military action is warranted. While the decision to intervene militarily depends mainly on whether American security interests are endangered, it must be remembered that the U.S. always has a general interest in maintaining international stability. Just because America does not fight does not mean that America does not care.

The U.S. also has a stake in the rule of law, which is an indispensable condition not only for freedom and democracy, but for international stability. As the German poet Johann Wolfgang von Goethe once said, "only law can give us freedom." This is true for domestic as well as international politics. The rule of law as established by international treaties and agreements, whether they are concerned with trade or with arms control, is indispensable to the spread of freedom around the world.

Respect for the rule of law, in the form of the Sino-British Joint Declaration, will be the only thing that protects the liberties of Hong Kong against potential Chinese transgression after July 1997, when the Crown Colony reverts to Chinese rule. Respect for the rule of law, by living up to international trade treaties, is the best way to advance the economic freedom of millions of people who benefit from the trade liberalization provisions of the North American Free Trade Agreement (NAFTA) and other free trade treaties. And respect for the rule of law is absolutely necessary to ensure that Russia complies with the terms of the START II treaty, thereby reducing the nuclear threat to America.

By standing up for these and other international agreements, the U.S. can lay down markers for countries like China and Russia which have spotty histories in living up to international agreements. By insisting that these and other countries conform to international standards and norms of behavior— not only with respect to international agreements, but also in their treatment of neighbors and their own people—the U.S. can encourage the political systems of these countries to adapt to the international norms and expectations of law-abiding democracies.

The best way to achieve this goal is to adopt a carrot-and-stick approach that promises benefits if norms and standards are observed and a denial of benefits if they are not. If China, Russia, or any other country wishes to benefit from trade or any other form of interaction with the U.S., it must keep its word on international agreements regarding trade, arms control, and other issues. For example, the Chinese could be told that the U.S. will not agree to Beijing's entry into the World Trade Organization so long as China is not upholding its obligations in other areas, such as the Missile Technology Control Regime (MTCR) which China has agreed to enforce. By the same token, Russia should be informed that a failure to ratify the START II treaty, or to comply with it, will produce an in-kind U.S. response proportionate to the Russian violation or action. Both Moscow and Beijing want cooperation from the U.S. in certain areas. The U.S. should use their interest in cooperation as leverage in demanding that international obligations are met.

The purpose of this type of linkage is not only to get countries to live up to their international agreements, but also to bolster the credibility and legitimacy of the entire system of international law and treaties. These types of diplomatic trade-offs are intended to raise the price for breaking international promises and obligations by offering rewards for compliance and a denial of benefits or punishment if such promises are not kept.

However, negotiations to ensure compliance with international agreements should never undermine the system of international law itself. Put simply, a country should be punished or denied some future benefit if it breaks international law, but it should never be rewarded unilaterally for simply keeping its word to comply with an international agreement. Benefits should be seen as the result of cooperating with the international community, not as special exemptions or concessions which some rogue state has managed to extract from the U.S. or the international community in return for keeping its word.[2]

---

2 All countries should live up to their international treaty obligations, but international treaties and agreements are not unalterable. All treaties contain provisions that allow participants to seek a redress of grievances or even to withdraw from the treaty. For example, the 1972 Anti-Ballistic Missile Treaty banning the deployment of strategic defenses contains a provision allowing withdrawal after six months notice. Therefore, the U.S. could legally withdraw from the ABM Treaty with six months notice without in any way undermining the

Unfortunately, this rule was broken by the Clinton Administration's Framework Agreement with North Korea. The U.S. pledged to provide financial and other support for the construction of light-water nuclear reactors in North Korea in return for Pyongyang's commitment to freeze its nuclear weapons program. This concession amounted to a bribe to persuade North Korea to keep its word — enshrined in the 1985 Nuclear Non-Proliferation Treaty (NPT)—not to build nuclear weapons. Not only did this negotiating strategy open up a direct U.S.-North Korean channel of communication, which Pyongyang had been seeking for years in order to isolate South Korea, but it also implied that particularly troublesome countries like North Korea actually could be rewarded — as opposed to punished—for breaking treaty obligations. No one is sure whether North Korea's nuclear weapons program really has been frozen (North Korea recently threatened to abrogate the entire agreement), but Pyongyang certainly has learned that it can use an international treaty—the NPT—to extort concessions from the United States and the international community. This lesson will not be lost on other rogue states like Iraq or Iran: Breaking international law pays, and treaties and agreements can be used as a weapon to weaken the regime of international sanctions arrayed against rogue states.

Unfortunately, Fidel Castro needs no instruction from the North Koreans on how to extract concessions from the international community while flagrantly violating international law. He has been challenging international law and norms for years, most recently by shooting down two American civilian aircraft over international waters, and yet some of America's allies accuse the United States of undermining international law with respect to Cuba. The object of their ire is the stepped-up U.S. embargo against Castro's regime.

The U.S. embargo against Cuba is perfectly legal, even by the standards of the World Trade Organization. Article XXI of the 1994 General

---

integrity of the international legal system. By the same token, WTO agreements — the GATT 1994 and GATS, in Article XXI and Article XIV, respectively — allow countries to impose trade sanctions for national security reasons. What matters here is not that countries may want to withdraw from or alter treaties or agreements, but that they seek a change in the treaty's status through the legal means that were established by the treaty itself. In this way, the party seeking change is complying with the original terms of the agreement, and thus is respecting international law.

Agreement on Tariffs and Trade (GATT) states that "Nothing in this Agreement shall be construed to prevent any contracting party from taking any action which it considers necessary for the protection of its essential security interests."[3] Both as a threat to U.S. civilian aviation, as witnessed by the recent downing of two American civilian aircraft, and as a continuing source of instability and illegal drug trafficking, Cuba remains a major national security concern for the United States.

Moreover, it is wrong to suggest that the Helms-Burton Act, which toughens the sanctions against Cuba, applies American law extraterritorially to foreign countries. This law allows Americans to sue foreign companies in U.S. courts only for using or benefiting from confiscated U.S. property in Cuba. In this sense, it upholds the international legal protection of property rights—a right which, while not yet explicitly protected by the World Trade Organization, may be covered in the future if and when the WTO undertakes negotiations on foreign investment. While the Helms-Burton bill does impose restrictions on the activities of offending foreign companies inside the U.S., it imposes no across-the-board trade sanctions against the host country of these companies. Nor does it take any direct action outside the United States—either in foreign courts or against the transportation of foreign commerce — to infringe on the foreign trade of countries which benefit from this stolen property.

There is a principle at stake here, but it is not "extraterritoriality" as Canada and other countries charge. The U.S. government has a right to regulate the activities of foreign entities inside the United States. The U.S. is merely demanding respect not only for its sovereignty (the right to regulate commerce inside the United States), but also for the legal protection of international property rights.

---

3 *General Agreement on Tariffs and Trade*, Article XXI, Section 1(b), 1994, p. 520 (as provided by the WTO).

PUTTING LIBERTY INTO PRACTICE: MATCHING MEANS TO ENDS

The U.S. can and should champion liberty, democracy, and the rule of law abroad. It should seek to enshrine these principles in international agreements and use them as a touchstone in conducting its diplomacy. But it should also recognize that there are limits to what the U.S. can do to change foreign political systems. America can help create the international conditions for the growth of freedom and democracy, but it cannot be the world's policeman. The U.S. does not have the obligation, the will, or the means to guarantee that all democratic groups and nations will succeed in their bids to overthrow tyranny.

These limits exist primarily because America has obligations and interests other than championing liberty abroad. During the Cold War, the Soviet Union was both a military and moral threat. It was the single most important source not only of anti-democratic movements around the world, but of military power which could destroy the United States. Thus, by containing Soviet military power, the U.S. also was holding back the threats to democracy and American security at their source: international communism.

Today the United States faces no such monolithic moral and military threat. Military threats come in all shapes and sizes: from rogue states like North Korea and Iraq to international terrorist groups like Hamas and Hezbollah. The ideological challenge is diverse as well, ranging from radical Islam to anti-Western nationalism in Russia. Since there exists in the world today no single source that threatens worldwide liberty or American security, the U.S. should not try to find a post-Cold War version of the heroic or monolithic Cold War strategy of containment. The times do not demand it. Overseas dragons should be slain only when they threaten America or its allies, not just because they are dragons.

The key question is how to match means and ends: Which tools of statecraft are best suited to promoting freedom, democracy, and the international rule of law? In most cases, traditional tools such as private and public diplomacy, multilateral initiatives, and other means short of war are most appropriate. However, threatening or using force would be most appropriate when, for example, an action by some nation or foreign group threatens not only the general American interest in international law, freedom, or democracy, but a vital U.S. security interest as well. This was the case in Iraq's invasion of Kuwait, which was both a violation of international law and a threat to U.S. security interests in the Persian Gulf.

It was not the case, however, when the Clinton Administration intervened in Haiti in 1994. No conceivable U.S. security interest was endangered by the government of General Raul Cedras. Therefore, the Clinton Administration's military intervention in Haiti was unjustified, doubly so because the purported purpose of the intervention—to establish democracy in Haiti—was not achieved.

How much of a threat these movements pose to U.S. security depends on how aggressive and dangerous they are, and how and where they challenge concrete U.S. security interests. When linked with dictatorships, these movements can become the force behind international aggression and imperialism, which threaten vital U.S. interests. A pan-Arab nationalism fueled the fire of Saddam Hussein's expansionist desires toward Kuwait. By the same token, Islamic fundamentalism is a force for expansionism in Iran, and ultra-nationalism or national communism could serve as the main ingredients of a renascent Russian imperialism.

While it is important to the U.S. that nations generally respect international standards of behavior, it is vital that they do so only in parts of the world where America has vital interests. With this in mind, Washington can decide whether a particular outrage against the international order warrants diplomatic action or the use of military force. Because there are many diplomatic ways to express general disapproval, overwhelming military force—particularly ground troops—should not be used merely to demonstrate U.S. support or endorsement of democracy or international order as abstract principles. Such force normally should be used only when both vital U.S. interests *and* international order or democratic principles are threatened.

However, the U.S. should vigorously support the principles of democracy, freedom, and the rule of law in statements and resolutions in the United Nations and other multilateral organizations. Respect for international law should influence and inform U.S. policy. That is what separates America from, say, Russia or China, whose national interests often are not defined in ways that are consistent with international stability and international law. Nevertheless, a U.S. defense of the international order should be conducted at all times with concrete American interests in mind.

Otherwise, the U.S. will not respond to crises with the appropriate means; it will be miscast as the world's policeman, as the hapless defender of some indefinable and unachievable New World Order.[4]

Americans are realists. They know that the U.S. cannot embark on some open-ended crusade to protect the world's oppressed or to fight for democracy wherever it may be threatened. They know that their moral impulses must be tempered by the recognition that America's resources are finite and that operating in the real world often requires choosing between two evils. As the world has known since Aristotle, choosing the best course of action in the real world is the true test of the moralist; good intentions are not enough. Surely, the same test should apply no less to nations.

Striking a balance between these two demands of morality and self-interest is a major challenge to American statecraft. While certainly not easy, it is not impossible. After all, a balance between the desire to support freedom and the need to defend America's security was achieved during two world wars and during the Cold War as well. And it was achieved by the Bush Administration even after the Cold War ended. Iraq's invasion of Kuwait offended Americans' sense of justice, but it also threatened U.S. strategic and economic interests in the Persian Gulf. As a result, Bush was able to craft a policy that not only enjoyed congressional and public support, but achieved a spectacular military victory as well.

Today this balance has broken down, and American leadership and strength are suffering as a result. Because of its preoccupation with peacekeeping and enlargement, the Clinton Administration has created the impression that America may be willing to fight for democracy in places like Haiti and Bosnia where the risks and level of U.S. interests are low, but not in more difficult places (such as Korea) where the risks and stakes are higher. The Clinton Administration has been indulging itself in easy, low-risk, feel-good policies while neglecting the hard work of protecting America's more important national interests. This is not a matter of good intentions gone awry. It is a matter of neglecting the critically important job of caring for the best interests of the American people.

---

4 See Chapter 14, "Maintaining an Effective Military in a Budget Straitjacket," and Chapter 15, "Planning a Coherent Military Strategy."

America's national strategy must be put back in balance. While the U.S. should declare itself to be the friend of liberty everywhere, it should guarantee only that which it has the will and the means to protect with military power: the liberty of friends and allies vitally important to U.S. interests. For the rest of the world, the U.S. can and should mobilize its resources of private and public diplomacy and foreign aid on behalf of the cause of freedom. This is no small matter. Much can be done short of using force to advance the cause of freedom around the world, and the U.S. should sharpen the diplomatic tools that are best suited to this purpose. As is always the case in devising a national strategy, it is a question of matching means and ends, of finding the proper way to accomplish a desired goal.

To do this, the U.S. needs to pay more attention to protecting and advancing vital national interests: enhancing U.S. national security, ensuring an open international trading system, and maintaining a global balance of power in favor of the U.S. and the West. Achieving these objectives will advance the cause of freedom far more than insincere and insupportable declarations about enlarging the world's democracies.

ECONOMIC FREEDOM: FREE MARKETS AND FREE TRADE

There is more to liberty than political freedom. Liberty must also embrace economic freedom. It is not enough for people to have the right to form a government of their choosing and to have that government, as Thomas Jefferson argued in the Declaration of Independence, protect their rights to life, liberty, and the pursuit of happiness. That government also must protect the right of people to pursue property, as John Locke had argued before Jefferson's time. People must be free to enjoy the fruits of their labor, not only because this freedom produces a prosperous economy for all, but because it is an inalienable right granted by God and protected by government.

Such was the philosophy of America's Founding Fathers. But this philosophy has relevance today for the entire world. It has become obvious even to former communists that free markets are essential to political freedom. Market institutions have been re-introduced into former communist and socialist economies throughout the world over the past ten years. It is no accident that democratic reformers in Russia, Eastern Europe, Latin America, and even Asia also tend to favor democratic capitalism. They

	1997 Index of Economic Freedom Score	Freedom House Rank of Political Freedom
Comparing Economic and Political Freedom: Free Countries		
Hong Kong	Free (1.25)	Not Rated
Singapore	Free (1.3)	Partly Free (5)
Bahrain	Free (1.6)	Not Free (6)
New Zealand	Free (1.75)	Free (1)
Switzerland	Free (1.9)	Free (1)
United States	Free (1.9)	Free (1)
United Kingdom	Free (1.95)	Free (1.5)
Taiwan	Free (1.95)	Partly Free (3)
Bahamas	Mostly Free (2.0)	Free (1.5)
Netherlands	Mostly Free (2.0)	Free (1)
Czech Republic	Mostly Free (2.05)	Free (1.5)
Denmark	Mostly Free (2.05)	Free (1)
Japan	Mostly Free (2.05)	Free (1.5)
Luxembourg	Mostly Free (2.05)	Free (1)
Canada	Mostly Free (2.10)	Free (1)

Table 11.1

Note: Ratings for the *Index of Economic Freedom* range from 1 to 5, with 1 to 1.99 considered "free," 2.00 to 2.99 considered "mostly free," 3.00 to 3.99 considered "mostly not free," and 4.00 to 5.00 considered "repressed." Freedom House's *Freedom Review* rates countries for political and civil freedom with 1 being the most and 7 being the least free.

know, as economist Milton Friedman argued over three decades ago, that "History suggests that capitalism is a necessary [albeit insufficient] condition for political freedom."

There is little doubt that a strong link exists between economic and political freedom. Table 11.1 compares the ratings of the 15 most economically free countries in the world according to *The Index of Economic Freedom*, published by The Heritage Foundation and *The Wall Street Journal*, and the scale of political freedom published by Freedom House.[5] Fourteen countries are rated by both indices. Of these 14 countries, all but three were

5 The *1997 Index of Economic Freedom*, ed. Kim R. Holmes, Bryan T. Johnson, and Melanie Kirkpatrick (Washington, D.C.: The Heritage Foundation and Dow Jones & Co., Inc., 1997).

rated "free" by Freedom House, with two of the remaining three rated "partly free." Only one was rated "not free."

Conversely, countries that oppose political freedom are unlikely to support economic freedom. Table 11.2 compares the ratings of the 15 least economically free countries in the world according to the Heritage Foundation/*Wall Street Journal Index of Economic Freedom* and the Freedom House scale of political freedom. All of these "economies" are rated as "not free" by Freedom House. The similarity within these two charts is no coincidence. Countries that adhere to one form of freedom are more likely to support other types, and vice versa.

Though there are strong links between economic freedom and political freedom, the links between economic freedom and wealth are even stronger. In the 1997 edition of the *Index of Economic Freedom*, Heritage Foundation economists examined the statistical connection between

Table 11.2

Comparing Economic and Political Freedom: Unfree Countries

	1997 Index of Economic Freedom Score	Freedom House Rank of Political Freedom
North Korea	Repressed (5.0)	Not Free (7)
Laos	Repressed (5.0)	Not Free (6.5)
Cuba	Repressed (5.0)	Not Free (7)
Iraq	Repressed (4.9)	Not Free (7)
Vietnam	Repressed (4.7)	Not Free (7)
Somalia	Repressed (4.7)	Not Free (7)
Libya	Repressed (4.7)	Not Free (7)
Iran	Repressed (4.7)	Not Free (6.5)
Azerbaijan	Repressed (4.6)	Not Free (6)
Angola	Repressed (4.35)	Not Free (6)
Myanmar	Repressed (4.3)	Not Free (7)
Zaire	Repressed (4.2)	Not Free (6.5)
Syria	Repressed (4.2)	Not Free (7)
Sudan	Repressed (4.2)	Not Free (7)
Rwanda	Repressed (4.2)	Not Free (6.5)

Note: Ratings for the *Index of Economic Freedom* range from 1 to 5, with 1 to 1.99 considered "free," 2.00 to 2.99 considered "mostly free," 3.00 to 3.99 considered "mostly not free," and 4.00 to 5.00 considered "repressed." Freedom House's *Freedom Review* rates countries for political and civil freedom with 1 being the most and 7 being the least free.

economic freedom and economic growth. Using data collected by Robert
Barro and Jong-Wha Lee on economic growth in 138 countries (all of which
are present in the *Index of Economic Freedom*), the authors examined the
economic benefits that flow from economic freedom. They concluded that
there is strong evidence, both from the emerging field of New Growth
Theory and from their own statistical tests, linking the concepts measured
in the *Index* to higher growth rates and greater prosperity. They also
concluded that introducing the sorts of reforms that would boost a nation's
score on the *Index of Economic Freedom* could well produce massive
improvements in the living standards experienced by people in many of the
world's poorest and least free economies.

This analysis showed that a quarter point (0.25) improvement in a
country's economic freedom score implied a change of 0.3 to 0.54 percent in
its annual growth rate. For example, if a country's gross domestic product
equals $500 billion, a mere quarter point increase in its *Index* score would
result in an additional $22 billion to $41 billion of economic output over a
15-year period.

This relationship is illustrated in Chart 11.1. The bar graph describes the
average annual real per capita growth rate experienced over the 1980–1993
period by nations in each of the Heritage/*Wall Street Journal Index*
categories. For example, nations with "repressed" or "mostly unfree"
economies in the 1997 ranking experienced negative per capita income
growth from 1980–1993. Conversely, "free" and, to a lesser extent, "mostly
free" economies on average experienced positive real income growth over
this period.[6]

The conclusion is inescapable: Economic freedom is not only an
inalienable right which democratic governments should be constitutionally
bound to defend; it also is a practical precondition for economic prosperity.
The surest way to create economic wealth for the most people is for a
government to cut or eliminate taxation and tariffs, privatize state
enterprises, deregulate the economy, and reduce its role in the economy
generally. The key to economic growth is a set of policies to minimize

---

6 Growth figures are from the 1995 *World Bank Report,* and the scores are from the
  1997 *Index of Economic Freedom.*

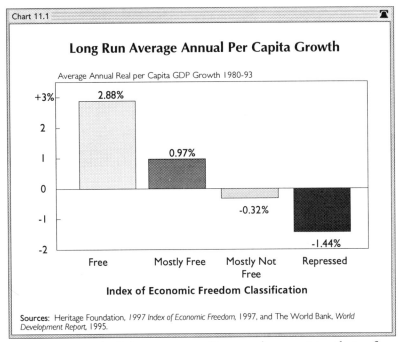

Chart 11.1

Long Run Average Annual Per Capita Growth

Average Annual Real per Capita GDP Growth 1980-93

- Free: 2.88%
- Mostly Free: 0.97%
- Mostly Not Free: -0.32%
- Repressed: -1.44%

Index of Economic Freedom Classification

Sources: Heritage Foundation, *1997 Index of Economic Freedom,* 1997, and The World Bank, *World Development Report,* 1995.

government control of the economy. Conversely, countries that refuse to implement economic liberalization most likely will remain poor.

The Need for Sound International Economic Policy. Over two centuries ago, Adam Smith understood both the moral and practical dimensions of economic freedom. This understanding is as relevant today as it was in the 18th century. People all over the world have rediscovered that to prosper they must first be free. For U.S. policymakers, this understanding is more than an intellectual exercise: It is the beginning of a sound international economic policy. By promoting free markets and free trade abroad, America not only strikes a blow for liberty, but also creates international economic conditions beneficial to the American economy.[7]

---

7 For further discussions of the world economy and the importance of free trade, see Chapter 13, "Defining the U.S. Role in the Global Economy," and Chapter 18, "Building Support for Free Trade and Investment."

Economic freedom is the single greatest factor in encouraging economic growth. The number of possible markets for American goods increases as more countries adopt free trade policies. Additionally, as free trade policies are adopted, countries experience greater economic growth, further increasing the size of potential markets for American goods. Therefore, economic opportunities for Americans increase with the spread of economic freedom.

There has been an explosion of U.S. exports over the past 20 years; the value of U.S. merchandise exports has grown more than 600 percent since 1960. U.S. investment abroad likewise has been mushrooming over the past 20 years; since 1960, income from overseas investments by Americans has grown over 700 percent.[8] Trade with other nations now represents almost 25 percent of total U.S. gross domestic product. This growth has created millions of jobs in America. Using the standard assumptions of the U.S. Department of Commerce, U.S. exports support nearly 14 million American jobs.[9]

Additionally, free trade encourages U.S. businesses to remain competitive and innovative. Competition from foreign products forces U.S. businesses to produce more desirable products less expensively or face decreasing sales. It also allows America to focus its efforts on the products that the U.S. can produce more efficiently than other nations. Instead of trying to supply all of the tennis shoes America needs at great cost in labor and capital, the U.S. imports most of what it needs. Efforts then can be channeled into the high-technology areas in which America is especially skilled. Thus, economic freedom encourages the U.S. to use America's human and physical resources to their greatest benefit.

American consumers also benefit as U.S. standards of living are increased through free trade. Americans are able to purchase higher quality products more cheaply and in greater variety than would be possible if trade were restricted.

---

8 Kim R. Holmes and Thomas G. Moore, eds., *Restoring American Leadership: A U.S. Foreign and Defense Policy Blueprint* (Washington, D.C.: The Heritage Foundation, 1996), p. 111.

9 The U.S. Department of Commerce estimates that every $1 billion of U.S. exports supports 20,000 jobs. In 1996, U.S. exports are expected to be approximately $700 billion.

In addition, America has an interest in a freer international investment climate. Growing international investment is integrating the American economy into the global market. Since 1985, the annual outflow of international direct investment has been growing faster than the exports of both goods and services. More liberal investment laws inside the U.S. and in foreign countries would boost demand for U.S. goods and services overseas, reduce production costs back home, import cost-cutting foreign management techniques and skills, and make U.S. firms more competitive abroad.

Other aspects of international economic freedom that are crucial to America's economic future include such regulatory issues as the protection of intellectual property rights abroad, competition policy, technology, and communications policy. American exports increasingly are based in the service and high-technology industries, which rely heavily on the specialized knowledge protected by intellectual property laws. For this reason, regulatory policies should allow the American private sector the greatest possible freedom from government restraint. Only in an environment of economic freedom can American innovation, which is the envy of the world, reach its full potential.

The U.S. should do all it can to liberalize the world economy. It should not engage in actions that perpetuate the statist economic policies that have caused so much of the world's poverty and misery. In short, the U.S. should not continue its program of economic aid to developing countries. This aid has succeeded only in creating and perpetuating a dependency on foreign assistance in recipient countries.[10]

The strong relationship between economic growth and free-market institutions is particularly weak for those countries receiving significant U.S. foreign aid. Heritage economists analyzed 42 countries receiving foreign aid and found that this assistance is positively associated with declining economies. For every dollar of aid from the U.S., these recipient countries are losing approximately 4 cents in gross domestic product. Heritage economists also found that the rate of economic growth associated with an improved *Index* score is much weaker in countries receiving aid.

---

10 See Chapter 19, "Restructuring and Reforming the Foreign Aid Programs."

Poverty in developing nations will not be solved by income transfers, such as foreign aid, but by encouraging developing nations to initiate economic freedom. Economic freedom will open the economies of these countries to foreign investment, which supplies the capital and jobs that developing nations desperately need, and to trade, which makes available the cheaper goods their people need for improved living standards.

The policy of the U.S. should be clear: America should pursue and expand free trade agreements—both regionally through treaties like NAFTA and globally in the World Trade Organization; further liberalize international investment rules in such venues as the Organization for Economic Cooperation and Development (OECD) and the WTO; ask other countries to accelerate implementation of existing intellectual property rights agreements reached in the Uruguay Round talks of the General Agreement on Tariffs and Trade (GATT); and begin weaning foreign countries from their dependence on foreign economic aid, demanding instead that they rely more on the expanded trade that flows from reduced barriers to international trade and investment.

CONCLUSION

American liberty and prosperity are linked in many ways. A growing U.S. economy both creates more economic opportunities for Americans and strengthens the constitutional order of liberty upon which America's political freedoms depend. America would not be as free as it is today, and its Constitution would not have survived for so long a time, were it not for its phenomenal economic success over the past two centuries. Successive generations of economic growth have made America a largely middle-class country dedicated to both democracy and capitalism. In a very real sense, America remains free because it is prosperous.

A connection between liberty and prosperity exists also in the international arena. Economic freedom, wherever it exists, tends to produce economic growth. Those countries with the lowest taxes and tariffs, fewest regulations, and best protection of private property are also the richest. Economic freedom tends to lay the foundations for the growth of political freedom as well. It is no accident that most of the economically free countries in the world are also the most politically free. Neither is it an accident that the poorest countries in the world are also the most politically repressed.

The drama of liberty unfolding on a global scale has deep historical roots, not all of which are American; but America still plays a critical, important role. In the early part of the 19th century, Thomas Jefferson spoke of America as the "empire of liberty." By this he meant the opportunity to plant the seeds of liberty in what was then a vast unsettled land opened up in the West by the Louisiana Purchase. Today, however, the soil for Jefferson's dream is no longer exclusively American: It is Russian, Chilean, Czech, South African, and Taiwanese. In short, it is a global dream, begun as an experiment in North America over two centuries ago but played out in reality today in every corner of the globe.

Whether this new global experiment succeeds will depend on many things, but a key factor will be whether America remains a global power dedicated to defending its security and military alliances and engaging in free international commerce. Freedom surely would not endure for long in Europe or Asia without America's military presence in those regions. And the global (to say nothing of the U.S.) economy surely would shrink if the U.S. became protectionist or autarkic in its economic policies.

Not only for its own sake, but for the sake of the world, the United States must be committed to a strong national defense, to liberty and the rule of law, and to an open international economy. These are the keys to the kingdom of liberty Jefferson dreamed of so long ago. They are the keys to spreading liberty—in all its forms—around the world.

Chapter 12

DEFINING THE PROPER U.S. ROLE IN GLOBAL SECURITY

John Hillen

Throughout the Cold War, Presidents and public leaders, Democrats and Republicans, had little trouble defining America's role in global security. The United States was the world's democratic superpower—the leader of the free world, willing to go to war around the globe to stop the spread of Communism. Now, five years after the Soviet Union ceased to exist, the chaotic makeup of the post-Cold War world is much more apparent, but America's role in this inchoate international arena has yet to be defined. In the absence of a Cold War threat, U.S. leaders have not clearly articulated their views about the nature of the new world and the leadership role America should play in it. As a result, U.S. strategy—especially during the Clinton Administration—has been inconsistent. It is unclear how U.S. leaders determine where, when, why, and how to use military force, as well as which international conflicts will require American military leadership and which ones will be solved best by the combined efforts of America's allies and other international organizations.

This lack of vision poses a dilemma for policymakers: The U.S. must defend a host of ever-changing global interests, but it must do so with a

The author would like to thank Dr. Richard Haass, Ambassador Charles Lichenstein, Peter Rodman, Bruce Weinrod, Colonel Harry Summers, and Dr. Dov Zakheim for their suggestions and contributions to this chapter. The views and opinions expressed, however, are entirely the responsibility of the author.

diminishing and finite pool of military resources. Because a coherent strategy demands that the U.S. credibly match its political ends to its military means, this dilemma clearly necessitates that U.S. leaders develop and follow a consistent strategy of selective engagement and a new strategy for its military alliances.

The Strategy of Selective Engagement. Selective engagement charts a sensible course between an excessive global military activism that can deplete important American resources on ventures offering little in return and an isolationism that eschews important opportunities to shape events in an increasingly interconnected world.[1] On the one hand, the U.S. does not need to engage in expensive crusades to replace the great ideological and military struggle against the Soviet Union. In unpredictable situations around the world, global activism has produced wasteful and inconclusive military efforts that amount to little more than "tilting at windmills" in places like Somalia, Rwanda, Liberia, Bosnia, and Haiti.

On the other hand, America should not pull up its drawbridge and lose the global influence and power it gained over decades of commitment to global security and democracy. The freedom, security, and prosperity of the United States depend in large measure on two things: the absence of major conflicts in other regions of the world and the ability of the U.S. to maintain unimpeded access to trade and natural resources around the globe. Preserving the freedom and prosperity of the U.S. will require taking an active role in the world—a role commensurate with the singular capabilities of the world's greatest military power.

To mark its course between overworked global policeman and out-of-touch global power, the U.S. must prioritize the national interests it is willing to defend and then allocate its limited resources accordingly. Furthermore, the U.S. must specifically identify its role in security ventures with its allies. An organized alliance led by the U.S. should demarcate a sensible division of labor to take advantage of the differing interests and military capabilities of the alliance members. Only in this way can policy and military leaders ensure that the military forces of the United States are

---

1 See Kim R. Holmes and Thomas G. Moore, eds., *Restoring American Leadership: A U.S. Foreign and Defense Policy Blueprint* (Washington, D.C.: The Heritage Foundation, 1996). This strategy was first developed and presented in this publication.

being used selectively where they are most needed and in ways that are most effective.

Leadership in Global Security. In the aftermath of the Cold War, the role that the United States should assume in global security can be compared to that of the Mayo Clinic in health affairs or the FBI in law enforcement. Each one assumes leadership in a hierarchy of involvement that includes organizations on more local levels. In the realm of global security, the U.S. is faced with a variety of crises around the globe; because of its capabilities and interests, it must play the lead role within a cooperative system of countries and organizations that play important supporting roles. Like the Mayo Clinic in an unhealthy world, rather than make military house calls for every case of insurgent heartburn or colic, the U.S. should support the local "doctors" who fill that function as the need arises. Moreover, the U.S. should be committed principally to intervening where the "illnesses" are truly consequential and when the unique and decisive capabilities of the American military are critical.

This global system explicitly recognizes the interests and capabilities of the members of each alliance, as well as a very important point about the level of U.S. involvement in security challenges that have arisen and will arise in the aftermath of the Cold War: While the U.S. has assumed very large global security responsibilities, it cannot and should not do everything. It should attend to the larger security problems worldwide while its allies and like-minded countries respond to global security needs first in their own regions. The role the U.S. plays in this cooperative system is unique. While many countries can exercise power in local military affairs, only the U.S. can deter and defeat major power aggression in any region of the globe. It is a role that demands the full attention of U.S. policymakers and military strategists on such strategic issues as military preparedness, the prioritizing of security interests, and the effective use of U.S. military alliances.

A NEW STRATEGY FOR U.S. GLOBAL MILITARY LEADERSHIP

Preparing for and implementing this global role for America's armed forces and defending America's national security interests will require that two new policies regarding national security are developed quickly:

- **The U.S. must** develop a policy for the use of American military force which stipulates the criteria used to determine when, where, why, and how American military forces will be engaged; and

- **The U.S. then must** develop a policy to define the depth of the unique role it will play, with its military alliances, as the world's foremost leader in global security affairs.

A Policy Governing When to Use Military Force

While domestic and international political considerations play an enormous role in specific decisions regarding the use of military force, the policy questions affecting decisions about when the U.S. should use its military force fall into the realm of strategy. U.S. military strategy matches the national objectives of the United States (ends) with the manpower and material resources of America's armed forces (means). A military strategy should stipulate exactly what America's goals are and how the U.S. might best use its military force to defend or achieve these goals. The strategy should prioritize objectives, identify potential threats or obstacles to these goals, and earmark the armed forces and military methods by which the objectives will be attained.

The prioritizing of national security objectives is particularly important in the post-Cold War world for two reasons that often work at cross purposes: 1) The U.S., as a superpower, has a complex set of national interests and objectives the world over, and 2) it must defend and promote these interests with a military establishment that has shrunk by some 35 percent in the past six years. This means that, in many instances, the U.S. is trying to do more with less. Keeping America's means equal to its purposes and its purposes equal to its means in these circumstances demands a clear identification of priorities and an honest appraisal of how best to defend them.

Foreign policy has several principal permutations—diplomatic, political, economic, social, and military—but issues concerning the use of military force go to the very core of a great nation's role in the world. The policies surrounding the use of military force show clearly the national interests and objectives of the U.S. and the varying degrees of importance attached to those goals, and the military strategy undertaken becomes the most profound statement of how America views the world and the American role in it. Like no other policy, U.S. military strategy reflects the level of commitment in blood and treasure that the U.S. is willing to make to protect or further its national interests and values.

Objective Criteria for Selective Engagement. Any policy concerning the direct use of military force must be centered on objective criteria addressing not only when to use (and not use) military force, but where, why, and how to use it as well. The criteria chosen, however, cannot be used as a rote checklist, slavishly followed every time the U.S. considers military action. They must be applied carefully, providing a logical methodology for raising and addressing all the more difficult questions that accompany the use of military force. Unfortunately, in the absence of such a logical and disciplined methodology, policymakers have tended to succumb to other influences like short-term political expediency, media-generated urgency, and knee-jerk reaction born of political hubris.

Rather than continue to make military decisions on the basis of such capricious considerations, American policymakers must develop a decisionmaking policy based on the following criteria:

- Military intervention should defend national security interests.

- The use of military force should not jeopardize the military's ability to meet more important security commitments or training for warfighting missions.

- When military force is used, it should be to achieve clearly defined, decisive, attainable, and sustainable goals.

- The use of military force should enjoy congressional and public support.

- The armed forces must be allowed to create the conditions for success.

Criterion #1: Does military intervention defend national security interests? The need to prioritize interests is often exacerbated by the limited pool of military resources available to the United States. Former Secretary of Defense James Schlesinger recently testified before Congress that "the reality of the post-Cold War world is that the U.S. has limited political capital for foreign ventures.... [T]he clear inference is that we should husband that political capital for those matters that are of vital interest to the United States." As far as policymakers are concerned, "political capital" comes in both tangible forms (for example, number of troops, carrier battle groups, or fighter wings) and intangible forms

OBJECTIVE CRITERIA FOR SELECTIVE ENGAGEMENT

American policymakers must develop a decisionmaking policy based on the following criteria:

- Military intervention should defend national security interests.

- The use of military force should not jeopardize the military's ability to meet more important security commitments or training for warfighting missions.

- Military force should be used to achieve clearly defined, decisive, attainable, and sustainable goals.

- The use of military force should enjoy congressional and public support.

- The armed forces must be allowed to create the conditions for success.

(public and congressional support, the willingness to sacrifice). Allocating this political capital would be impossible if all national interests were seen as equally important. Instead, policymakers should discriminate among interests by using the common methodology that determines categories of national interest such as vital, important, and marginal (see Chart 12.1).[2]

Vital National Security Interests. Vital interests that directly affect the national security of the United States or the lives and well-being of Americans abroad must carry immense weight in prioritizing military strategies. Any threat to vital national interests is a threat to the freedom and prosperity of the U.S. itself; America should always be willing to wage war to protect vital national interests and to consider all types of military intervention in order to defend them. Not all national interests are national security interests, and not all national security interests are created equal. As the chart shows, vital national interests are always national security interests. America's vital national interests include:

- **Defending** American territory, borders, and airspace;

---

2 Ibid., Chapter 1. This methodology was developed in *Restoring American Leadership: A U.S. Foreign and Defense Policy Blueprint.*

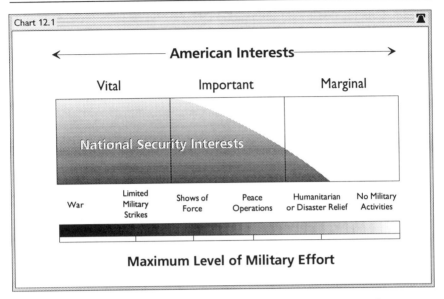

Chart 12.1

American Interests

Vital   Important   Marginal

National Security Interests

| War | Limited Military Strikes | Shows of Force | Peace Operations | Humanitarian or Disaster Relief | No Military Activities |

Maximum Level of Military Effort

- **Preventing** a major power threat to Europe, East Asia, or the Persian Gulf;

- **Preventing** hostile interference by an outside power in the Western Hemisphere;

- **Protecting** the lives and well-being of Americans at home and abroad; and

- **Ensuring** continued access to foreign trade, global resources, and open seas.

Important National Interests. Interests that are less than vital but important enough to warrant major diplomatic, economic, or limited military intervention are known as important national interests. Important interests are not always national security interests (see Chart 12.1), and the level of interest will depend on the gravity of the threat, the national security implications inherent in the interest, and the suitability of a military response to the threat. Some important interests may be threatened by trade wars or humanitarian disasters but are not military challenges. As a rule, the use of military force to defend important national interests should be considered as a last resort. In many cases, diplomatic or economic efforts will be far more effective. Important national interests include:

- **Preserving** general stability in Europe, the Middle East, and East Asia;

- **Promoting** free trade;

- **Encouraging** democracy and economic reform abroad; and

- **Combating** terrorism or illegal drugs.

Marginal Interests. National interests that are rarely interests involving national security can be called marginal interests, and they should not be placed high on the list of priorities requiring a commitment of America's military resources. Threats to marginal interests rarely threaten the United States as a nation, and therefore should be considered marginal from a military perspective. They tend to involve the kinds of problems that do not lend themselves to military solutions, especially if the solutions are imposed by an outside force. Marginal interests include:

- **Political stability and economic development** in parts of the developing world;

- **Humanitarian** concerns; and

- **Environmental** issues.

Economic and political development problems or humanitarian and environmental concerns are solved best by solutions that have been fostered locally and supported by diplomatic or economic support.

Developing a National Interest-Based Strategy. A national interest-based strategy is critical for two reasons: 1) It helps the U.S. decide where limited resources will be applied most effectively, and 2) it helps policymakers form a reasonable calculation about the level of military sacrifice as well as the commitment the nation must sustain for each confrontation. Moral outrage and reactions to transgressions of international law can convince policymakers that "something must be done" immediately. However, only if national interests are clearly threatened and the sacrifices of the American people appear necessary to defend those interests can military action be sustained. As strategist Harry Summers recently observed, "it is the value of the objective that determines the sacrifices made in pursuit of it, in magnitude and duration."[3]

If a policymaker miscalculates the value and threshold of sacrifice that the American people inherently attach to a military effort, a humiliating withdrawal can accompany small setbacks, as happened in Beirut in 1983 and Somalia in 1993. While other moral and legal elements must be factored into the equation, only calculations of national interest can measure accurately what the American people will sacrifice to see military action through to its conclusion. As former National Security Council official Richard Haass writes, "the ability to sustain an intervention over time, and more importantly, despite human and financial costs, is linked directly to the perceived importance of the interests at stake."[4]

Criterion #2: Will the use of military force jeopardize the military's ability to meet more important security commitments or training for future warfighting missions? Balancing the ends and means of a strategy is a complex exercise, and one made more complicated by the uncertain nature of future threats and the necessity for broad and varied contingency planning. The prioritizing of national interests, the identification of national security interests, and an indication of how (and by whom) they are best defended helps to maintain this balance. Given the myriad threats to U.S. interests around the globe and the low degree of predictability about these threats, U.S. forces must be prepared for military operations ranging from full-scale war against another major power to conventional deterrence, punitive airstrikes, humanitarian relief, shows of force, and support for some peace operations. However, U.S. forces also must have an overriding focus that provides purpose and direction, and which is in fact the primary mission of the U.S. armed forces: to fight and win America's wars.

How the Absence of Conflict Affects Military Preparedness. A recurring theme in American history is that, in the absence of conflict or

---

3 Harry Summers, "Achilles Heel of Keeping the Peace," *The Washington Times*, October 17, 1996, p. A20.

4 Richard Haass, *Intervention: The Use of American Military Force in the Post-Cold War World* (Washington, D.C.: Carnegie Endowment, 1994), p. 71.

the immediate threat of conflict, the military loses its focus and *raison d'être*. In times of relative peace, policymakers, unduly influenced by short-term political needs or media-generated urgency, tend to commit the military to every conceivable activity other than training for war. In the first battles of World War II and Korea, Americans paid in blood for this lack of wartime readiness. On the other hand, the many years of vigilant Cold War deterrence kept American forces honed for large-scale combat operations. This was seen most clearly in the extraordinary performance of the U.S. Army VII Corps in Operation Desert Storm. The long-range offensive undertaken by this unit was the centerpiece of the desert victory even though this unit had spent the previous 40 years training for a defensive mission against the armies of the Warsaw Pact in the hills and forests of central Germany. Despite the difference in the theater of operations and the mission, VII Corps adapted quickly because it was trained for warfighting and focused on combat when the unexpected happened in Southwest Asia.

Training for Combat. Warfighting is a complicated business, made especially so in this day and age by the sophistication of the U.S. military's joint warfighting doctrine. This doctrine requires that the operations of all four services be integrated and synchronized for a simultaneous and ultimately devastating assault on an enemy force. The warfighters of the U.S. Army, Navy, Air Force, and Marine Corps are trained to conduct this decisive assault throughout the breadth and depth of enemy defenses, ensuring an overwhelming victory for U.S. forces while minimizing their losses. In order to do this, the services are equipped with the most sophisticated and technologically advanced systems in the world, systems that require years of dedicated and concentrated training. The United States also is famous for conducting the most demanding and realistic battle training in the world, training that requires a sense of urgency and focus in order to be effective.

Unfortunately, in the absence of a clear and present danger that would require warfighting proficiency, policymakers tend to lose their focus on the need for wartime readiness. This is unacceptable. They must allow the military to focus on combat training and keep its powder dry for conflicts centered on threats to vital national interests. For instance, the primary mission of U.S. forces in Europe is to be the linchpin of NATO, a credible military alliance focused on the collective defense of Western Europe. NATO's deterrence capability is rooted inextricably in the warfighting prowess of its core units: the American forces in Europe. That deterrence capability would be eroded if the U.S. presence in Europe was focused on peacekeeping in Southeast Europe.

The same is true of U.S. forces dedicated to protecting national security interests in East Asia, in the Persian Gulf, in the Western Hemisphere, and on the high seas. In the absence of any immediate threat to these areas, policymakers are tempted either to cut these forces or to use them for more peripheral operations. However, history proves that a great power will always need its forces when conflict is least expected. In 1996, the need for a large show of conventional naval power in support of Taiwan was the latest manifestation of the recurring need for a global power with numerous national security interests and the ability to exercise its military power in ways that are persuasive in peace and decisive in war.

To maintain this focus on the most important and consequential security tasks, military missions must be prioritized. Lesser missions must never detract from the capability of a credible military response to the more important security commitments. As Colin Powell stated shortly before he retired:

> [W]e can modify our doctrine, we can modify our strategy, we can modify our structure, our equipment, our training, our leadership techniques, everything else to do these other [lesser] missions, but we never want to do it in such a way that we lose sight of the focus of why you have armed forces — to fight and win the nation's wars.[5]

As a rule, missions such as support for civilian projects, humanitarian relief operations, and peacekeeping should not be conducted by America's warfighting forces. For some support units, a peacekeeping operation provides an opportunity to exercise their wartime tasks, albeit under far more benign conditions. For combat units, however, these sorts

5 General Colin Powell, in remarks to a defense writers' group breakfast, September 23, 1993, quoted in Summers, *New World Strategy* (New York, N.Y.: Touchstone Books, 1995), p. 139.

of operations consume time better spent on firing ranges and maneuver centers, decrease training time, dilute mission focus, and hurt combat proficiency. As Representative Ike Skelton (D-MO) has noted, "peace-keeping commitments may so degrade the armed forces warfighting capability that it will be impossible to carry out the national military strategy."[6] His findings are supported by reports from the U.S. General Accounting Office (GAO) and elsewhere.[7]

America must act like a great power, but it is not the only power. It cannot chase every regional or local crisis to flex its military might. The U.S. must use its military forces wherever American interests are most at stake and where its military role is clear, unique, and decisive. Like its diplomatic and economic strategies, America's military energies must be concentrated on core interests involving relations with other major powers and in key regions of the world. Preventing conflicts between these powers through a credible military presence and respected deterrence strategy is a role that no other nation can play. There are many other nations, however, that can provide competent military forces for the management of local or regional crises, humanitarian operations, or peacekeeping missions. Their capabilities should be used to complement the U.S. role in larger issues of global security.

For these reasons, the U.S. should never shift the main focus of its armed forces to peripheral missions in areas of lesser interest. The U.S. can respond to and support these sorts of operations, but never at the expense of defending more important interests and ensuring 100 percent combat readiness throughout its armed forces. In the furtherance of international peace and security, the U.S. has singular capabilities and singular responsibilities, and its military leaders must not let these capabilities be diluted, lest America lose the warfighting focus that brought it to its state of excellence in the first place.

---

6 Representative Ike Skelton (D-MO), in a speech to the U.S. House of Representatives, October 4, 1993.

7 U.S. General Accounting Office, *Peace Operations: Effect of Training, Equipment, and Other Factors on Unit Capability*, NSIAD-96-14, October 1995, pp. 28-39.

Criterion #3: When military force is used, will it achieve clearly defined, decisive, attainable, and sustainable military goals? The exercise of power, like most other enterprises, demands criteria by which to measure its success or failure in reaching the goal. So it is with military operations. Ultimately, the objectives in military strategy resemble a series of building blocks. Military planners identify tactical military objectives that must be achieved for operational success, operational objectives that will lead to strategic success, and strategic objectives that will deliver the political goal. This coherent relationship between cause and effect enables policymakers to achieve their political goals through the use of military force.

In order for this to happen, however, the use of military force must be oriented around objectives that are clear, unambiguous, and capable of attainment by the forces at hand with minimum casualties. In addition, once attained, the objectives should make a difference in the conflict and contribute directly to an eventual goal. In Vietnam, the costly battlefield victories won by American forces often had little or no ultimate effect on the strategic or political outcome of the war. To ensure that this tragic formula is not repeated in the future, the measurable objectives not only should be decisive, but also should be sustainable and not easily reversed or overturned.

The process of achieving a series of clearly defined, decisive, attainable, and sustainable military objectives is often referred to as an "exit strategy." This term is somewhat redundant, as the word "strategy" (the use of military means to achieve political ends) itself implies an end to or exit from the operation. Good strategy provides an exit because its military and political objectives are linked toward a common purpose and pursued by military forces more than capable of achieving these objectives.

Identifying and working toward clearly defined goals may seem a rather obvious point, but it has been violated with great regularity over the past few years. This was especially evident in Bosnia, where the U.S. substituted time-driven objectives for event-driven objectives — the strategy of just "being there." This strategy violates the profound military dictum of Clausewitz that "No one starts a war—or rather, no one in his senses ought to do so — without first being clear in his mind what he intends to achieve and how he intends to conduct it."[8] Hope is not a method in military operations, and it is a mark of poor planning if the strategy of a military operation is based on "establishing a presence" (as in the 1983 Marine mission in Beirut) and hoping that this presence will affect events in the way U.S. policymakers wish. A U.S. military force can deliver results; it does not hope for them to happen on their own. To deliver results, however, U.S. military forces must have a clear series of military objectives. The achievement of these objectives must be virtually guaranteed and attained through a process where success and failure can be measured unambiguously. Once achieved, the objectives should be sustainable and, most important, should make a decisive difference in the outcome of the conflict.

When policymakers and military planners cannot find clearly defined, decisive, and attainable military objectives, as was the case in Vietnam, they often resort to incremental "may-work" options that are controllable instead of plans that will bring military and political success. This creates an intolerable situation in which the sacrifices made by U.S. military forces and the nation are in vain because policymakers did not lay out clearly why those sacrifices needed to be made, let alone how they were supposed to succeed. This type of military strategy should never again be tolerated in the United States.

Criterion #4: Does the use of military force enjoy congressional and public support? The Framers of the U.S. Constitution clearly intended that both Congress and the President should have a part in decisions about when to use military force. Article I, Section 8 gives Congress the power to raise military forces and the further power to declare war, while Article II, Section 2 gives the President the power to use those forces to wage war. This system was delineated to ensure that neither branch of government abused the country's military powers. Recognizing that a great amount of heated deliberation could mark the congressional debate over whether to declare war, James Madison also convinced the Framers to give the President the power to repel sudden attacks. Madison and the other Framers understood that the Commander in Chief might be

---

8 Carl von Clausewitz, *On War*, ed. and trans. Michael Howard and Peter Paret (Princeton, N.J.: Princeton University Press, 1976), p. 579.

required to act with expediency and even secrecy to ensure that national security is upheld.

Unfortunately, this profoundly important constitutional balance has become somewhat lopsided since World War II. Because modern convention dictates that nations resort to the force of arms without declaring war, the system of checks and balances envisaged by the Framers has broken down. Congress no longer is accustomed to voting on the merits of military action; votes in fact are taken on whether to support American forces after they already have been deployed. Even though none of America's recent military actions have been national emergencies requiring the President to react with secrecy and speed, Congress still has not been included in the decisionmaking process.

This pattern has skewed the nature of the congressional debate, reducing Congress to the status of rubber stamp and check writer for unilateral decisions made by the President concerning when, where, and how to use American military force. Clearly, when the United States engages its honor, prestige, and forces in significant military actions, congressional approval should be a prerequisite. According to most constitutional historians, Congress was designed to act as the embodiment of the political will of the American people. The wisdom of the Framers in this regard remains a relevant matter of policy to this day. In addition, the U.S. should not engage in significant military operations without a clear expression of support from the American public. While the decision to undertake military action cannot be made by polling, the President is responsible for building the case for public support before the decision is made. If the American public does not support a certain military action, the entire operation can collapse after minimum resistance and a few American casualties.

Contrary to the opinions of some contemporary strategists, the American public is not automatically intolerant of casualties incurred through U.S. military action. However, the American public will never tolerate losses in a military action that does not have clear goals and readily apparent benefits that are worth the investment of blood and treasure. As Harry Summers has written, "casualties *per se* are not the limiting factor. It is whether those casualties are disproportionate to the value of the mission."[9] The American public inherently will place a value on a U.S. military effort, and that value will be expressed in the national will to sacrifice and sustain the costs of military action. That value does not exist in the abstract, however; it can be shaped and guided by presidential leadership. This leadership should appear in the form of a clear explanation of the threat to a national security interest, the rationale for why that interest must be protected, and the enunciation of a coherent military and political strategy designed to ensure success at a minimum cost in American lives. If this reasoning is sound, the public will support the mission.

Criterion #5: Are the armed forces allowed to create the conditions for success? Although the case has been made that the U.S. should use military force for objectives that can be achieved decisively and that are politically decisive as well, this does not mean that the U.S. military should be saved for just "the big ones" as some critics charge. The U.S. military does not have to use absolutely massive force to control events in a military action. Limited interventions undertaken with enough force to create the conditions for success, such as the 1986 F-111 raid on Tripoli in Libya, can have a decisive effect.

However, in limited military actions, policymakers often are tempted to restrict military requirements when the purpose is to send a political signal. This happened in 1979 when Iran was threatening Saudi Arabia. It caused national embarrassment when it was revealed that the F-15s which President Carter sent to help defend Saudi Arabia were unarmed. This amounted to an empty political gesture that could have been a military disaster.

If U.S. combat forces are to be used in action, their operations must be completely consistent with the proven operational doctrine of the U.S. military. This doctrine allows U.S. armed forces both the access to resources and the political latitude needed to create and control the conditions for their success, no matter how big or small the tasks and the stakes. It calls for rapid and decisive military action that can be achieved

---

9 Harry Summers, "After the Doubts, Salute and Obey," *The Washington Times*, December 11, 1995, p. A18. See also Eric Larson, *Casualties and Consensus: The Historical Role of Casualties in Domestic Support for U.S. Military Operations* (Santa Monica, Cal.: RAND Corporation, 1996).

at minimum cost through the use of disproportionate force. If the U.S. wants to send a signal through military action, it should signal something significant and unambiguous. Attempting to fine-tune military action to send subtle political signals is reminiscent of some of the absurd rules of engagement used in airstrikes over North Vietnam. Ideally, military action will achieve clear-cut, attainable political goals; and while this ideal does not fit every situation in which the military will be involved, policymakers should strive to replicate it as closely as possible.

The U.S. military prefers rapid and decisive action because that is the kind of action that consistently delivers results. Not only is "overwhelming force" and decisive action consistent with the greatest chance of success, but it also tends to be the least costly way to engage an enemy. American forces should keep the initiative in any military action. The actions of U.S. forces, not the actions of their opponents (or even of U.S. allies), should dictate the pace of events and control the outcome. Even in limited military actions, the use of disproportionate force helps American forces keep the initiative and create the conditions for success. Disproportionate force also helps to minimize the casualties and costs of protracted warfare.

Let there be no mistake: There is nothing ennobling about being engaged in a "fair" fight or an attrition slugfest. There is no advantage in fine-tuning U.S. efforts to attain a marginal advantage or in gearing operations toward playing for a draw. American forces should have every advantage when they are engaged in military action, and they should always seek to win in a rout.

This classic military tenet is both well-founded in military history and particularly well-suited to a military superpower like the United States. When America's military might is employed, action should be swift, decisive, and successful. Many types of military and quasi-military action are inherently resistant to this formula, however. Peacekeeping, for example, relies not on overwhelming force for a "victory," but on the consent and cooperation of local factions. The peacekeepers cannot guarantee the outcome, no matter how efficient their operations. It is for this reason that peacekeeping missions like the U.N. missions in Palestine and the Kashmir carry on for 20, 30, or over 40 years. There is no intrinsic reason why the United States should be involved in these types of protracted operations. In fact, most nations would rather the U.S. not commit ground troops to multinational peacekeeping missions, since many other countries are more "culturally attuned" to the quasi-military work of peacekeeping.

A POLICY ON THE DIVISION OF LABOR FOR U.S. MILITARY ALLIANCES

Throughout American history, the U.S. has implemented its foreign policy objectives and military strategy through its international alliances. In fact, American involvement in these alliances predates the nation itself, beginning with the alliance with France during the American Revolution. Prior to the Cold War, American alliances for the most part were only temporary military partnerships designed for specific crises. Once these crises passed, the political and military arrangements were abrogated or left to atrophy. The Cold War period proved an exception to this pattern, as alliances were characterized by an unprecedented longevity. The principal factors underpinning the durability of Cold War alliances were the global threat of communist expansion, the dominant role of the United States as the political and military leader in its military alliances, and the highly institutionalized and formalized structure of the main Cold War alliances.

With the collapse of the Soviet threat and the end of the Cold War, America's network of Cold War alliances should have been weakened. Remarkably, however, this network managed to survive the aftermath of the Cold War and the subsequent focus on non-traditional (transnational and sub-state) threats for which traditional alliances might not be best suited. In some areas, notably Asia and the Persian Gulf, new threats to the regional balance of power (from China and Iraq) have emerged, while old threats remain poised against the U.S. and its allied interests (in North Korea and Iran). This has sustained the relevance of old alliances, like those the U.S. has maintained with Korea and Japan, and has made critical the more informal alliances that are created as a need arises, such as those with Saudi Arabia, Kuwait, and other Persian Gulf partners. Lesser security challenges like Bosnia have kept highly institutionalized alliances such as NATO occupied in missions quite different from those that had been envisaged during the Cold War; in the minds of some, these lesser challenges also provided new missions for old organizations.

Even though the commitment to contain Communism no longer determines global security objectives, the network of U.S. alliances survives because it is an effective vehicle for protecting vital American interests around the world. Even a greatly reduced American military presence worldwide reflects the preponderance of American leadership in these alliances. Although the mission and the military's presence have been reconfigured, the U.S. armed forces remain as active and involved around the globe as they were during the Cold War. Given the absence of overwhelming threats to U.S. security, it is this active presence that holds American alliances together. Nonetheless, the network of U.S. alliances that formed under the threats of the Cold War is under strain; it must change if it is to continue to serve America's national security interests in different areas of the world.

A converging set of strategic trends is straining America's alliances:

- **The strategic strain** on U.S. armed forces;

- **The diverging military capabilities** of the U.S. and its allies; and

- **The discrepancy** between the interests of the U.S. and those of its allies in regard to many security challenges in the post-Cold War world.

The Strategic Strain on U.S. Armed Forces

The U.S. military, fatigued and overtaxed, has been reduced in size by almost 40 percent since the end of the Cold War even as overseas deployment requirements have grown. Downsizing the military has taken place only on the supply side, not on the demand side. In the past five years, while it has been shrinking, the U.S. military has attempted to maintain a vast network of worldwide, ongoing security commitments, including an array of new operations in such places as Somalia, Haiti, and Bosnia.

This frenetic activity has put an unprecedented strain on the military during peacetime, wearing out men and materiel while denying the U.S. military the opportunity to prepare for the future. The pace of operations in all services currently exceeds the policy recommendations of the respective service chiefs; it also is damaging readiness and morale. On any given day in 1996, the U.S. Army had some 105,000 soldiers permanently stationed overseas and another 40,000 on temporary duty in 60 countries.[10] This

---

10 U.S. Department of Defense, *Defense Almanac*, 1996, p. 18, and G. E. Willis, "On the Road Again," *The Army Times*, July 1, 1996, p. 12.

demand, coupled with a 38 percent reduction in the size of the Army since 1991, means that soldiers are deploying overseas at a rate 300 percent to 400 percent higher than during the Cold War. In a time of relative peace, nearly 15 percent of active duty Army soldiers are deployed on 12-month hardship tours of duty. An April 1996 GAO investigation found some Army units deployed over 210 days per year.[11]

The other services face similar dilemmas. Expressing his concern about the high operational tempo, the U.S. Air Force Chief of Staff set a target of a maximum of 120 days of temporary duty per unit. That target was greatly exceeded by many units, including AWACS units (which averaged 136 days), RC-135 units (168 days), combat air controllers (160 days), EC-130E units (175 days), and some electronic warfare units that spent over 300 days per year on deployments.[12] The high deployment rate of these and other Air Force units is the inevitable result of trying to use a service that has been downsized by some 36 percent to meet military requirements that are increasing.

The Navy also has exceeded its target (and budgeted) operations tempo for the past several years, and predicts that it will do so again in FY 1997.[13] This tempo, coupled with the decline in the number of Navy warships, increasingly is forcing the Navy to "gap" the assignment of aircraft carriers and other warships, a process by which other forces must cover the gap left by the absence of a carrier. This happened most recently in the spring of 1996 when the USS *Nimitz* was rushed from the Persian Gulf to cover the Taiwan-China crisis, which required the U.S. to deploy a squadron of Air Force F-15s to Jordan to continue supervision of the no-fly zone over Iraq. Even more recently, the USS *Enterprise* left the Adriatic in September 1996 to reinforce the U.S. presence in the Persian Gulf during the latest round of confrontations with Saddam Hussein. The sudden absence of the *Enterprise* required the land-based aircraft supporting the U.S. troops in Bosnia to

---

11 U.S. General Accounting Office, "Military Readiness: A Clear Policy Is Needed to Guide Management of Frequently Deployed Units," GAO/NSIAD-96-105, April 1996.

12 GAO report and information provided by the U.S. Air Force Chief of Staff's Operations Group, 1996.

13 Chief of Naval Operations, "Department of the Navy FY 1997 Budget," Washington, D.C., 1996, p. 2-2.

make up for the hundreds of weekly sorties normally flown by the carrier-based aircraft.

Admiral Joseph Lopes, the former American commander in Bosnia, notes that U.S. service members are "busier than hell" trying to keep up with these requirements.[14] Even more worrisome, this pace is not just keeping the Department of Defense (DOD) busy; it is literally wearing out men and materiel, causing former Pentagon planner Robert Gaskin to note that the military is "approaching burnout."[15]

This strain has produced deleterious effects on training, readiness, procurement, retention of service members, and quality of life issues. For instance, the high rate of current operations has strained budgets, equipment, and units to the point where all services have been forced to cancel required wartime training exercises. In only one such example, peacekeeping support duties in 1995 forced three Air Force fighter wings to cancel critical combat training exercises.[16] As a result of these kinds of trade-offs, the GAO found that 28 percent of the services' frequently deployed units are not "combat ready" by DOD standards.[17]

In addition, the money being spent on current operations denies the Department of Defense the funds it needs to invest in recapitalizing the U.S. armed forces. Procurement accounts—money used by DOD to fund new equipment and weapon systems—have dropped nearly 70 percent in the past ten years, precipitating a 1996 rebellion by the Joint Chiefs of Staff, who begged Congress to restore some $20 billion in funding for new weapon systems. In the meantime, current stocks of equipment are heavily used and wearing out. For instance, C-130 aircraft supplying the Bosnia mission are at least 26 years old and flying at twice their normal rate. European-based C-130s had to be supplemented by a squadron from North Carolina

---

14 Tom Philpott, "Is the Navy Now Too Small to Meet the Challenges of an Unstable World?," in *Seapower Almanac* (Washington, D.C.: U.S. Navy League, January 1996), p. 4.

15 Quoted in Art Pine, "U.S. Military Highly Rated, But Strains Begin to Show," *The Los Angeles Times*, March 19, 1996, p. A7. See also Steven Komarow, "Smaller Forces, More Missions Add Up to GI Stress," *USA Today*, October 8, 1996, p. 10.

16 USAF Chief of Staff Operations Group, 1996.

17 GAO, "Military Readiness," *op. cit.*

because, in the words of one aircraft commander, the European-based squadron "ran their aircraft into the ground." New C-130s are not expected until 2005 at the earliest. Admiral William Owens, former Vice Chairman of the Joint Chiefs, warned that the low levels of procurement constituted a "crisis in the defense budget."[18] However, projected DOD budgets do not offer much of a plan other than continuing to live off the capital investments of the Reagan-era military buildup. Because of this, by 2005 all the tanks and most of the U.S. military aircraft will be older than the soldiers or pilots driving and flying them.

Finally, the strain on the U.S. armed forces is having an adverse effect on morale and the quality of military life. The GAO investigation found that "officials in major commands revealed pronounced concerns about personnel problems such as divorces... and lowered retention."[19] The drop in retention rates is especially worrying, given the time and money spent training servicemembers in the increasingly technical and sophisticated business of modern military operations. In 1995, the Navy failed to reach its targets for first, second, and third term reenlistment.[20] This problem was somewhat ameliorated by the shrinking force structure, but it will become acute when the Navy finishes its post-Cold War drawdown. In any event, the services are losing valuable and well-trained personnel because of the extreme pace of operations forced on a shrinking military force.

History suggests that military powers should use the interregnum between conflicts for replenishing military stocks, for training and resting soldiers, and for aggressively experimenting with new doctrines and equipment. The U.S. military, however, is being strained by an already high operating tempo, compounded by a series of peripheral peace operations. Speaker of the House Newt Gingrich (R-GA) has recognized that this effort is "stretching our military [to] the verge of the breaking point."[21] He notes that "at some point somebody needs to stand up and say there is a

---

18 Quoted in John Merline, "Stripping America's Defenses?," *Investor's Business Daily*, July 1, 1996.

19 GAO, "Military Readiness," *op. cit.*

20 Philpott, "Is the Navy Now Too Small to Meet the Challenges of an Unstable World?," p. 6.

21 Speaker Newt Gingrich, from an address at the annual award dinner of the Center for Security Policy, Washington, D.C., September 18, 1996.

minimum size to being the world's only superpower, and we have gotten smaller than that in terms of our regular units, and we have an obligation to insist on a military in which people can serve without being burned out by the sheer constancy of their being used."[22]

Diverging Military Competencies

Since the end of the Cold War, America's allies, especially in Europe, have talked about the need to develop capabilities for military operations independent of—or at least not so dependent on—the United States. In general, this movement toward a larger measure of military self-reliance has been welcomed by the U.S., although the Bush Administration initially sent conflicting signals to Europe about such European-only defense initiatives as the Franco-German Corps and the Western European Union (WEU). Nonetheless, the end of the Cold War marked a time when both the U.S. and its allies recognized the need for those allies to pick up a greater share of the security burden in their own regions. The enthusiasm for this was clearly reflected in 1991 when the European Union (EU) President at the time, Jacques Delors, triumphantly proclaimed that solving the Bosnian crisis would prove to be the "hour of Europe."

Unfortunately, reality is not matching the formal rhetoric, especially when it comes to paying for and developing the military capabilities necessary to undertake an independent security policy. As Professor Eliot Cohen has noted, "two seemingly contradictory trends seem to be at work: a formal effort to develop more independent forces that can operate outside traditional frameworks and operational environments, on the one hand, and on the other increased dependence on the United States in key areas of military power."[23] Moreover, the core competencies of the U.S. military and the militaries of many of our allies are diverging. The U.S. is focused on deterrence and warfighting against aggressive states, while many allies are refocusing their military establishments on peacekeeping and operations other than war.

---

22 *Ibid.*

23 Eliot Cohen, "The U.S. and Alliance Strategies," paper presented to the 38th Annual International Institute for Strategic Studies conference, Dresden, Germany, September 1-4, 1996.

Fiscal Concerns. Fiscal concerns are one of the principal driving forces behind the changing military capabilities of many U.S. allies. While South Korea and Japan have increased their defense spending (markedly so in Japan) since the end of the Cold War, America's European allies have cut defense spending as a percentage of GDP by an average of one-third.[24] Most of these cuts have been precipitated by the need to meet the stringent fiscal requirements of EU monetary integration. As of September 1996, only Luxembourg and Ireland had met the Maastricht Treaty conditions by having a budget deficit less than 3 percent of GDP and a national debt less than 60 percent of GDP.[25] All other EU countries are cutting government spending, both on domestic programs and in defense.

More important, cuts in defense spending have prevented European allies from creating the types of military establishments that could give Europeans more self-reliance and help relieve the strategic strain on the U.S. armed forces. For the most part, European allies (and Canada) are cutting the size of their forces significantly, preparing for regional peacekeeping and other low-intensity conflicts. Many European militaries have moved recently from the conscript system to all-volunteer forces. This move typically halves the size of the force. In addition, there is a shift in the psychological and doctrinal focus of European allies who face no clear and present danger from a major power in the post-Cold War world. The shift from emphasis on territorial defense to a new focus on peacekeeping and operations other than war is prevalent. Canada's new Defense Minister stated recently that "I am a peacekeeper, not a warrior."[26] At an August 1996 ceremony to celebrate the end of conscription in the Netherlands, the Dutch Defense Minister noted that "the draft no longer fitted with the army's role in a world where peacekeeping has taken over from combat."[27]

---

24 Statistics taken from yearly issues of *The Military Balance* (London: International Institute of Strategic Studies).

25 Fred Barbash, "Europe's Quest of Common Currency by 1999 Proving Divisive but Fervent," *The Washington Post*, September 23, 1996, p. A15.

26 Howard Schneider, "Canada's Military Under Attack," *The Washington Post*, October 5, 1996, p. A20.

27 Reuters, "Dutch End Military Draft," *The International Herald Tribune*, September 1, 1996, p. 2.

European allies are no longer investing in military systems that would allow them to project power and conduct sustained warfighting campaigns. With only the smallest of exceptions, they are not investing in strategic airlift and sealift capabilities; strategic logistics systems; space-based command, control, communications, and intelligence (C3I) networks; and modern weapon systems based on revolutionary advances in information technology.[28] The percentage of European defense spending that goes to research and development (R&D) is half the percentage allocated for the same purpose in the U.S. defense budget. The U.S. also spends a much greater percentage on procuring new equipment than almost all its NATO partners.[29] Many European defense analysts have noted that the decision not to invest in these expensive systems has relegated the European allies to an increased reliance on the U.S. for campaigns outside of Europe or any sort of warfighting contingencies.[30] Only a few Europeans, mostly defense industrialists, have criticized this lack of investment in expensive but critical warfighting systems.[31]

Capability Concerns. The divergence between U.S. and allied military capabilities since the end of the Cold War is becoming acute. The U.S. still maintains an enormous quantitative advantage over its allies (in 1996, the entire Canadian Army was only slightly larger than one U.S. division); but it is the qualitative advantage that has exacerbated the trends creating different military competencies between the U.S. and its allies. For example, the U.S. is the only member in its many security alliances that has large

---

28 In addition to statistics gained through publications such as *The Military Balance,* see R. L. Kugler, *U.S.-West European Cooperation in Out-of-Area Military Operations: Problems and Prospects* (Santa Monica, Cal.: RAND Corporation, 1994), and Ronald Asmus, Richard Kugler, and Stephen Larrabee, "What Will NATO Enlargement Cost?," *Survival,* Vol. 38, No. 3 (Autumn 1996), pp. 5-26, esp. pp. 8-11.

29 *The Military Balance, 1995-6,* p. 39.

30 See Philip H. Gordon, "Recasting the Atlantic Alliance," *Survival,* Vol. 38, No. 1 (Spring 1996), pp. 50-51, and Rick Atkinson and Bradley Graham, "As Europe Seeks Wider NATO Role, Its Armies Shrink," *The Washington Post,* July 29, 1996, pp. A1 and A15.

31 See, for instance, the warnings of Robert Bussiere, Vice-Chairman of the Centre d'Etude de Prospective Stategique, about the loss of a European industrial base that can support a wartime footing in *NATO Review,* Vol. 43, No. 5 (September 1995), pp. 31-35.

aircraft carriers, long-range strike aircraft, stealth aircraft, a network of space-based C3I satellites and sensors, advanced aerial surveillance and reconnaissance systems, global lift capabilities, strategic logistics systems, and advanced weaponry based on information technology and the nascent "revolution in military affairs." In Bosnia, 46 of the 48 satellites used by the intervention force for C3I functions belong to the U.S. As Phil Gordon of London's International Institute for Strategic Studies has noted, however, "this dependence isn't unpleasant enough to inspire the Europeans to do what they have to do to get around it."[32]

As a result of this divergence in military competencies, many allies, principally European, are losing the ability to function as useful military partners in warfighting coalition operations such as the Persian Gulf War of 1991. Most of the U.S. allies are likely to be more valuable now as political partners than as military partners. These trends were clearly evident in the Gulf War, where the U.S. completely dominated the military force structure of the 31-country coalition. In terms of numbers, the U.S. provided over 70 percent of the ground troops. The only coalition members with ground forces of comparable quality — Great Britain and France — scrambled to mobilize a division and a brigade, respectively. The U.S. also provided 76 percent of the combat aircraft in the theater and two out of three warships, including all six coalition aircraft carriers that participated in the attack on Iraq.

In some specialized capabilities, the U.S. was even more dominant in the Gulf. Although 11 countries provided combat aircraft, the U.S. completely dominated the command and support functions necessary for launching air strikes: intelligence, targeting information and air tasking orders, command and control aircraft and systems, electronic warfare aircraft, and refueling tankers.[33] For instance, on January 20, 1991, the third day of the air campaign against Iraq, every electronic warfare aircraft in the theater was American. Eleven countries also provided warships, but only American

---

32 Atkinson and Graham, "As Europe Seeks Wider NATO Role, Its Armies Shrink," p. A1, and Brooks Tigner, "Europeans Resist AGS Fast Track," *The Army Times*, October 14, 1996, p. 39.

33 See U.S. Department of Defense, *The Conduct of the Persian Gulf War* (Washington, D.C.: U.S. Government Printing Office, 1992), pp. 109-114 and 218.

warships and a few British frigates had the advanced technologies necessary to operate together in the dangerous waters of the northern Persian Gulf.[34]

This decline in the warfighting capabilities of many of America's allies makes it clear that these countries will be less self-reliant and more dependent on the U.S. in future combat missions. Consequently, the U.S. will have to continue to fund, provide, and train large American military forces that can provide the sort of warfighting capabilities needed to protect America's vital national interests with minimal military help from allies. However, the divergence of military capabilities does not mean that allies cannot help reduce the strain on U.S. forces. In missions such as Somalia, Haiti, and Bosnia for regional peacekeeping, crisis management, and humanitarian relief, U.S. allies with lesser military capabilities still can be major military players. If some European allies choose to have a small military establishment focused on peacekeeping, then render unto the peacekeepers what is theirs.

Matching Capabilities to Roles. Diverging military competencies make it all the more necessary to enforce a new security compact between the U.S. and its allies that matches its members' interests and capabilities to roles and responsibilities. If the U.S. is the only allied power with a strategy that requires large forces capable of global power projection and large-scale, modern combat operations, it should focus 90 percent of its energies and resources on this set of tasks. Conversely, regional allies who have smaller and less combat-oriented military establishments should bear the primary responsibility for local peacekeeping and crisis management. In accordance with the principles listed below, the U.S. can support these efforts with some unique and decisive capabilities, but providing the preponderance of forces in missions like Bosnia runs counter to these principles. Effective management in military alliances takes advantage of diverging military capabilities and uses them to maximum benefit.

Diverging Interests over Security Challenges

The Iraq crisis of September 1996 highlights the final trend that is driving the need for a re-evaluation of America's role in its alliances. This latest round of confrontations with Saddam Hussein reinforced the continuous

---

34 *Ibid.*, pp. 70-81, and Department of the Navy, *The U.S. Navy in Desert Shield and Desert Storm* (Washington, D.C.: U.S. Government Printing Office, 1991).

historical pattern: Alliances and coalitions tend to weaken when there is a shift in the level of the threat their members face. The unity of effort shown by the many members of the Persian Gulf coalition of 1990–1991 was driven by the magnitude of Saddam's aggression against Kuwait and the threat Iraqi forces posed to the entire Arabian peninsula. Only this sort of overwhelming regional threat could have caused the interests of states as different as the U.S. and Syria to converge as they did.

Conversely, the very limited nature of Saddam's aggression against an Iraqi Kurdish faction in August and September of 1996 prompted very different responses from the allies. America's unilateral cruise missile strike was criticized or unsupported by close allies such as France, Turkey, and Saudi Arabia. When the threat is low or the objectives are unclear, alliance members tend to view their interests and courses of action very differently.

Absence of a Unifying Threat. Similarly, the overwhelming threat posed by the Soviet Union and the Warsaw Pact during the Cold War provided a centripetal force that held NATO together. In the absence of that unifying threat, the stakes in local crises such as the crisis in Bosnia are very different for the U.S. and Europe. After all, it is axiomatic that European states should always be more concerned about the situation in the Balkans than the U.S. This is a reflection of national interest which, barring special circumstances, generally decreases with distance (geographic, cultural, or economic). Bosnia is *the* European security problem, and one that affects the vital national interests of the European powers. On the other hand, the U.S., as a global military power, should be more concerned about its security relations with great military powers such as Russia and China. These are security challenges of the first order. The U.S. also should be concerned about security threats of a second order, such as deterring aggressive and well-armed rogue states like Iran, Iraq, and North Korea. These are missions that only the U.S. can perform, in addition to being missions that involve vital U.S. interests. Bosnia, while a compelling issue, is an issue of a third order, on the strategic periphery of U.S. national security interests.

A U.S. commitment to do the heavy lifting for a peacekeeping force in Bosnia incapacitates the combat capability of U.S. forces in Europe. A U.S.-led military effort in the Balkans completely misconstrues the American role in world security, European security, and U.S. military alliances. These alliances and security commitments were created to facilitate the protection of vital American interests in key regions of the world. Alliances like NATO were formed to take advantage of similar or complementary interests among regional partners. In NATO's case, the member nations joined because they had, and still have, a critical stake in ensuring Europe would not be dominated by a hostile power or bloc of powers. Conversely, the U.S. is not involved in European alliances to be the lead police force in solving long-running ethnic disputes in Southeast Europe. NATO was not created for this task and should not let the minutiae of European peacekeeping become its *raison d'être*.[35]

While U.S. alliances and security commitments are structured around the collective defense of key regions against major power threats, most post-Cold War security challenges have been well below the threshold of a major threat. Problems of a third or lesser order, like the ethnic strife in the former Yugoslavia, threaten local and regional security interests more directly than they threaten the global security interests of the United States. These sorts of smaller security threats should be competently addressed by "primary care networks" before they become the responsibility of a U.S.-led alliance of collective defense like NATO. Many Americans question the utility of U.S.-led alliances when the imperative of U.S. leadership forces the U.S. into operations and actions it otherwise might not undertake. This was the case in Bosnia, where preserving the credibility of NATO and the U.S. became the principal reason for the U.S.-led intervention into what Clinton Administration officials themselves called a regrettable mission.[36] In these cases, alliances and U.S. leadership do not function as the means to the ends of U.S. foreign policy, but become ends in themselves.

A Burden That Reduces Military Effectiveness. These three trends do not augur well for the management of international peace and security through a system of enduring alliances. Taken together, they create a nexus in which U.S. alliances become a burden that reduces the effectiveness of U.S. national strategy rather than a network of organizations that multiplies the effectiveness of the U.S. and its alliance partners working together. The

---

35 See John Hillen, "Getting NATO Back to Basics," *Strategic Review*, Vol. XXIV, No. 2 (Spring 1996), pp. 41-50.

36 According to Assistant Secretary of State Richard Holbrooke, "we did not choose this as a test case.... [N]obody wanted it to happen, but that is the hand history has dealt us." Quoted in John Pomfret, "U.S. Builds Arc of Alliances to Contain Serbia's Power," *The Washington Post*, December 19, 1995, p. A28.

convergence of these trends prevents the U.S. from discriminating among security priorities and using its singular military capabilities where they are most needed and most effective. It creates imperatives that force the U.S. to function as a global policeman, expending resources indiscriminately, rather than as a global power capable of applying military force in a coherent and measured manner. A strained U.S. military must clearly prioritize and ask its allies to share the security burden and to take responsibility for local crises that do not threaten the balance of power, critical regions, or key global systems.

The United States enters into alliances because they serve American security interests and are an effective way to protect those interests collectively with like-minded partners. Alliances, both today and in the past, are a "cost-effective" way to protect and promote American interests in many parts of the world. Alliances allow the U.S. to spread limited military resources around the globe and still maintain a position of strength, influence, and leadership in many regions simultaneously. However, the relationship between the U.S. and its allies must be flexible, as it must always adapt to changing political, economic, military, and sociological circumstances.

Regional Devolution. Because of this variance in threats, and the different ways they affect the interests of allies in U.S. alliances, the U.S. should press for a strategy of regional devolution; that is, allies that are closest to the problem, and whose interests are most affected, should be the prime movers in taking steps to mitigate these smaller crises. An "all for one and one for all" approach to every security dilemma, large and small, does not make sense for U.S. alliances (especially when some of America's allies are reluctant to give "all for one" when that "one" is the United States). A more flexible and sensible approach would "deputize" smaller allies by matching their interests and capabilities to different roles and responsibilities.

A new security compact between the U.S. and its allies must be built on this philosophy. Every state in an alliance brings something different to the table, and smart alliance leadership takes advantage of those differences. Differences in the level of national interest should be used to the advantage of alliances, and not as indications of divisiveness or weakness. Those states most affected by a crisis must be able to act and not be emasculated by an overweening dependence on an ally who may have little interest in taking the lead role in addressing the problem. Consequently, the U.S. must promote structures and procedures like NATO's Combined Joint Task Force that allow allies to undertake military roles and responsibilities more in line with their interests and capabilities. This strategy bodes well for local crises because it empowers those regional allies who might have the greatest interest in tackling a regional affair like Bosnia. It also makes sense for the U.S., which must use its finite military power judiciously to deal with many global security issues, not just regional crises that are of much greater concern to allies.

THE PRINCIPLES BEHIND
A NEW SECURITY COMPACT

In the post-Cold War world, the U.S. must press for a new security compact with its allies. This security compact should recognize that America will continue to perform larger global security tasks such as deterring or defeating major powers that threaten the U.S. or regions vital to U.S. interests, or that threaten global systems important to the U.S. such as trade, financial markets, and supplies of energy. In the meantime, allies of the U.S. must attend to the more local dilemmas such as peacekeeping with a lessened reliance on the U.S. Such a new compact will best serve U.S. security interests and address U.S. global security dilemmas by matching the interests and capabilities of America's allies to their roles and responsibilities in regional and global affairs. As Owen Harries has written,

> In deciding when to deploy [military force], Washington should practice the sound federal principle of subsidiarity — that is, allowing problems to be handled at the level closest to the problem. This way, a sense of responsibility can be developed throughout the international system and the United States can reserve its own intentions for the great issues involving its vital interests, acting as a balancer of last resort rather than a busybody and bully.[37]

---

[37] Owen Harries, "Dole's Calculated Pragmatism," *The New York Times Magazine,* September 22, 1996, p. 71.

THE PRINCIPLES BEHIND
A NEW SECURITY ALLIANCE COMPACT

- The U.S. role in military alliances should be focused on collective defense to deter and defeat major power threats to the region.
- The role the U.S. plays in its alliances should remain unique.
- The role the U.S. plays in its alliances should be decisive.

In this way, the U.S. can be a good manager as well as a good leader. A new security compact will allow a smaller, more skillful American military force to continue to protect a wide variety of U.S. interests in a more unpredictable and volatile world.

The U.S. needs to push for a sensible division of labor in its alliances that is based on the premise that while alliance members will share some common goals, not all independent states in an alliance will have the same interests or even similar military capabilities. For example, it makes little sense to pretend that America has the same level of interest in Bosnia as France. It therefore behooves the alliance leader—the United States—to match those interests and capabilities to the different roles and responsibilities that each security dilemma presents. If the U.S. and its allies truly are going to do more with less, then alliance members should undertake national security tasks that are well-suited to their level of national interest and their military capabilities.

Successful managers are successful because they match the talents and ambitions of their employees to certain tasks and responsibilities. A global leader will do the same in military alliances to "stretch" limited resources while maintaining effectiveness. While new alliances are not needed and should not be sought, in order to make its existing military alliances more effective and efficient, the U.S. must put forth a policy that clarifies the principles it will use to govern its superior role in these alliances.

The following three principles should create the framework for a new and more coherent security compact with America's alliance partners:

- **The U.S. role** in military alliances should be focused on collective defense.

- **The U.S. role** in its alliances should remain unique.

- **The U.S. role** should be decisive.

The U.S. Role Should Be Focused on Collective Defense

The post-Cold War world faces a host of security challenges that will require some sort of military response. The majority of these challenges are likely to be local and to require a protracted yet low-level military commitment (such as a variant of peacekeeping) from regional actors with a direct interest in a peaceable outcome. Conversely, more significant military challenges (such as state-to-state aggression) are less likely, but their consequences for the international arena are considerably more serious. American strategists from across the political spectrum agree that the U.S., as the world's only military superpower, must remain focused on deterring and defeating these larger threats in key regions of the world. The U.S. should not squander its power on tangential missions that may be in the media spotlight but are hardly an effective use of finite national security resources.

All U.S. alliances are regional, and all are manifestations of an American commitment to the peace and security of that region. However, this commitment is not without limits. With the exception of North and Central America, the U.S. commitment to regional security in Europe, the Middle East, the Persian Gulf, East Asia, and the Western Hemisphere is one of collective defense, not collective security. Alliances of collective defense, such as NATO, engage states in a collaborative effort to defend against a major threat to the balance of power in the region. As the name implies, the missions of collective defense are defensive in nature, straightforward, and focused. They cause the interests of alliance members to converge in support of common goals. Collective defense seeks to deter through military strength and defeat an aggressor when deterrence fails.

Alliances of collective security, such as the Organization for Security and Cooperation in Europe (OSCE) or the Association of South-East Asian Nations (ASEAN) Regional Forum, on the other hand, seek to provide a forum through which members can organize cooperative responses to many different problems of peace and security, not just major power threats to the region. The missions of collective security are broadly defined and can be proactive in nature. Collective security missions can include many non-military efforts as well as limited or quasi-military interventions. These include humanitarian intervention, support to nation-building, peacekeeping, peace enforcement, or other missions short of full-fledged combat operations. Collective security missions do not offer the same unambiguous goals as collective defense, and often cause the interests of alliance members to diverge, as was seen in the imbroglio among NATO allies cooperating in the U.N. mission to Somalia in 1993. Because of inevitable differences over solutions to the many and varied threats addressed by alliances of collective security, these alliances tend to be much less cohesive and decisive than alliances of collective defense.

The U.S. has a vital national interest in ensuring that Europe, East Asia, the Persian Gulf, and the Western Hemisphere are not threatened by a major power. The U.S. alliances in these areas and elsewhere serve that purpose. Conversely, the U.S. is not in alliances with NATO, Korea, Japan, and others in order to offer American-led military responses to every local or regional security dilemma. The U.S. role of collective defense is clearly tied to enduring American interests that require the singular military capabilities of the U.S. This critical distinction has been lost in recent years, especially in Europe, where local problems such as ethnic tensions and regional squabbles have thrust themselves onto NATO's agenda because of the vacuum left by the fall of the Soviet Union. However, it must be stressed that using NATO for peripheral, ambiguous, and inconclusive security missions, such as that in the Balkans, can serve to erode American public support for a strategic U.S. military role in Europe. "Bring the boys home" will be heard as the rallying cry across the United States if the *raison d'être* for placing the American military in Europe becomes policing local trouble spots on behalf of prosperous European allies.

The U.S. can always support allies who are involved in lesser security challenges in their region. But lesser security challenges that do not threaten the balance of power in the region should be confronted by the allies first. An efficient alliance of collective defense recognizes this imperative and reserves to those members roles and responsibilities that are consistent with their interests. The U.S. should remain focused on the principal mission of maintaining a credible warfighting capability that will deter or defeat a major power threat to the key regions where we have alliances.

The U.S. Role Should Remain Unique

No alliance partner has a series of worldwide military commitments that can come close to matching those of the U.S. In fact, with few exceptions (the U.K. and France, albeit in a more limited fashion), there are no U.S. allies with truly global security responsibilities today. As the world's only superpower with a full range of global security commitments, the U.S. therefore must discriminate over where and when it will use its ever-diminishing set of military means. A key component of this process of selectivity is that the U.S. plays a unique role in its military alliances and does not needlessly duplicate the capabilities of allies whose national security interests are limited to their region alone.

The U.S. increasingly will bring unique and specialized military capabilities to allied combat operations. These capabilities include the ability to project land, sea, and airpower on a global basis; the integration of joint (multi-service) operations under a space-based command, control, communications, and intelligence network; and the ability to field high-technology weapons systems that take advantage of the revolution in information technology and precision guided munitions. If these military capabilities are coupled with the U.S. strategic focus on deterrence and warfighting, one can easily appreciate the evolving difference in military competencies: The U.S. will have a national security strategy concentrated on other major powers and the global balance of power, and the American military establishment will support this strategy through a focus on deterrence and warfighting. Most of America's allies, on the other hand, will have a strategy centered on regional powers and regional problems, with a military establishment leaning toward crisis management and peacekeeping.

A new security compact between the U.S. and its allies must take advantage of that divergence in military competencies. A division of labor in which America's military contribution is predicated on its unique capabilities ensures that the U.S. is using its military resources where they are most needed and most effective. U.S. and allied military capabilities must complement each other and not needlessly duplicate each other's potential. The U.S. and its alliance partners cannot afford the luxury of redundancy in today's world. The military capabilities required by a mission must be identified and then matched to the alliance partner whose capabilities and national interest are best suited to the task. Such a process would recognize the unique assets of each partner and make most effective use of a variety of alliance resources. In other words, alliance management would center on trying to make the whole greater than the sum of its parts.

This means the U.S. should take the lead on missions associated with deterrence and warfighting wherever its military capabilities are truly unique. Conversely, the unique military capabilities of the U.S. should play only a supporting role in local and regional crisis management, humanitarian relief, or peacekeeping-type operations. In those cases, local alliance partners should provide the great bulk of the manpower, with the U.S. using its unique capabilities, such as command and control assets, airpower, intelligence, and logistics, to support the mission.

The U.S. Role Should Be Decisive

This last principle should guide the commitment of U.S. military forces to alliance operations. The American military contribution should be decisive and make the difference between winning and losing or drawing. If allies can protect and defend the security and stability of their regions without U.S. assistance, the American public will balk (and rightly so) at the expense of these worldwide military commitments. This is especially so in alliances in which America's partners are wealthy and prosperous states. It is therefore incumbent on the U.S. that it constantly evaluate the interests, roles, and capabilities of alliance partners while gearing the U.S. military role toward a contribution that will provide the decisive edge.

This calculation will change given the nature of the threat, the requirements of the mission, and the differing capabilities of the alliance partners. In some instances, the U.S. military can be decisive through the limited deployment of small but special capabilities like command and control, logistics, or intelligence assets that dramatically enhance and multiply the effectiveness of a coalition dominated by allies. In others, such as the Persian Gulf War, where the mission requirements are greater, the allied effort might require the U.S. to dominate the force structure, command and control arrangements, and operational planning.

In either case, the U.S. is exercising alliance leadership. Leadership is not just providing the most troops, hardware, and ordnance for every mission. Leadership is getting the most out of an organization by measuring capabilities and requirements, and then tapping into the different resources and talents of the members. As management expert Peter Drucker has noted,

> Effective leaders delegate a good many things;
> they have to or they drown in trivia. But they do
> not delegate the one thing that only they can do
> with excellence, the one thing that will make a
> difference, the one thing that will set standards,
> the one thing they want to be remembered for.
> They do it.[38]

The U.S. leads in its alliances because of the major power security guarantee that only America can deliver and the enormous power it can bring to bear should the need arise. This is the "one thing" that cannot be delegated but that also can be done with excellence, will make a difference, and will be remembered because failure carries with it the gravest consequences for international peace and security. Only America has the resources to perform such tasks.

The U.S. also leads because of the unique and decisive military capabilities it can deploy for almost any manner of operation. The competent strategist will recognize that these are the immutable pillars of U.S. leadership in military alliances. Therefore, the U.S. should not feel trapped into "leading" an ambiguous mission in an area of negligible security interest. If the U.S. attempted to lead everywhere and do everything, it could indeed "drown in trivia" to satisfy a narrow definition of leadership. America leads in its alliances not for leadership's sake itself, but because of the conditions that leadership engenders—conditions that favor both the U.S. and its allies. Leadership should never be defined merely as pleasing as many allies as possible.

Alliance leadership requires that U.S. policymakers, who are committing finite resources to many different alliances and other military contingencies, always calculate the mission requirements before matching them to relative interests and capabilities. Failing to do so could turn American military alliances into a wasting proposition instead of what is known in military lexicon as a force multiplier.[39] An indiscriminate and unbalanced

---

38 Peter Drucker, "Not Enough Generals Were Killed," *Forbes*, April 8, 1996.

39 Benjamin C. Schwarz, "The Arcana of Empire and the Dilemma of American National Security," *Salmagundi*, Winter-Spring 1994, p. 195.

commitment to a worldwide system of alliances can become a burden that needlessly siphons off important American resources instead of effectively multiplying American power and influence.

A Herculean effort to provide the overwhelming preponderance of all resources in every alliance would certainly overextend the U.S., causing it to become a military superpower that is progressively less efficient because it is trying to do too much around the globe. Moreover, as the U.S. struggled to carry on in this role of indiscriminate global superpower, the beneficiaries of this largesse — America's allies — would divert their would-be defense spending to areas such as industry, trade, market penetration, and productivity. Such a "client" relationship, with allies benefiting from the services of the U.S. as security provider, is not acceptable; America's allies must be full security partners. Allies cannot just consume security — they must provide it as well, especially in smaller missions in their regions. It is therefore imperative that the U.S. enforce burden sharing in alliances and reserve for itself military roles that are both decisive and necessary for success.

CONCLUSION

Most Americans would agree that the U.S. must be active in the world, but not so active that the effort wastes American resources and energies in interventions with little or no payoff. Thus, selective engagement is merely a commonsense approach to security policy. Few people would advocate either intervening everywhere or intervening nowhere. In addition, the need for a policy of selective engagement is made all the more conspicuous by the fact that the U.S. faces numerous security challenges that must be addressed with a limited and shrinking pool of military resources.

Nonetheless, common sense by itself will not make it easy to transpose selective engagement into political and military policies that clearly communicate the proper U.S. role in global security. Two policies are needed:

- The U.S. must lay down the criteria that will define when, where, why, and how it might choose to use military force. This sends a very clear message — to allies and adversaries alike — about the nature of U.S. national security interests and how the U.S. plans to protect them.

- After defining its military role through these criteria for the use of force, the U.S. must lay out what is expected of its allies in international security. Specifically, the U.S. must promote a new security compact in its alliances to forestall further confusion about its role in minor post-Cold War security challenges.

Together, these policies lay out America's role in global security. They recognize that there is a hierarchical order to international security that consists of local military powers, regional powers, global military powers, superpowers, and other entities such as alliances, and international organizations like the United Nations. They also recognize that this hierarchy is much more effective if each participant has roles and responsibilities that match its interests and capabilities. These different roles should complement each other. If an organization tries to do too much, it fails. This has been evident over the past few years with the U.N. Similarly, if the U.S. attempts to do too much, as it is doing now, its forces become strained and overstretched while losing focus on their most consequential roles.

The U.S. therefore should concentrate its security policies on major threats such as other great powers or rogue states that can upset the balance of power in key regions. America's allies should take the lead in local crisis management, peacekeeping, and humanitarian relief operations. Such a demarcation with respect to the roles of allies and when, where, why, and how the U.S. will use military force will stand the world in good stead. The U.S. will remain strong and focused on those conflicts that are truly consequential to the family of democratic nations, and allies will take more responsibility for the many minor problems that plague the post-Cold War world. History shows that another major conflict is never far away and is usually unpredictable. The U.S. is the only nation capable of forestalling and combating this eventuality, and it should remain focused on this role in global security affairs.

Chapter 13

DEFINING THE U.S. ROLE IN THE GLOBAL ECONOMY

Bryan T. Johnson

With the end of the Cold War, the United States has witnessed a rise in public indifference to most international issues. After World War II, quite the opposite was true. The United States based much of its economic expansion on the growth of the international marketplace, and many Americans were conscious of how important the health and state of the world economy were to their standard of living at home. Although the United States is better positioned today to add to its own wealth and to improve its standard of living through increased international commerce, there are those who do not recognize its importance. The economic policies U.S. leaders enact in the near future will play a powerful role in overall economic growth, both at home and abroad.

In order to reap the rewards of the growing international economy, the United States must re-establish its leadership in free trade and investment policies. The U.S. economy today is the largest and wealthiest in the world, producing over $7 trillion a year in goods and services. Nevertheless, many of the opportunities available to American businesses are threatened by contradictory U.S. policies toward the global marketplace. If the United States fails to regain its leadership role in the international economy, its economic future will be threatened.

The author would like to thank Brett Schaefer for his suggestions and contributions to this chapter. The views and opinions herein, however, are solely the responsibility of the author.

Why is the global economy so important to the United States? According to the 1996 *Economic Report of the President*, U.S. exports have grown by over 600 percent since 1960, while income from U.S. investments abroad has grown by over 700 percent.[1] The United States remains the world's largest exporter, sending some $735 billion in goods and services overseas each year. These exports directly support one out of every five American jobs. The involvement of the United States in foreign markets plays a large part in its per capita wealth, which (measured in constant 1992 dollars) has increased from around $10,000 in 1960 to over $25,000.

The United States faces very strong economic competition from Asia, Europe, and elsewhere. How the United States meets and challenges this competition will have a direct bearing on the health of its economy and the U.S. standard of living. In order to face this challenge, the United States must develop a more competitive strategy so that it can benefit from the growth in the international economic market. To be more competitive, the United States must try to reduce all barriers to international trade, eliminate unsound international financial policies, reduce regulations on all economies (including its own), protect intellectual property rights, and foster an open international investment climate.

THE IMPORTANCE OF GLOBAL ECONOMIC PROSPERITY

Global economic growth is important to the United States for more than economic reasons. Economic stagnation overseas also breeds instability that can threaten U.S. security. One of the biggest challenges the United States will face in the coming decades is how best to deal with the consequences of economic problems overseas. Unstable and economically stagnant nations suffer from civil unrest, military conflict, famine, pestilence, and mass emigration. These ills affect the access Americans have to foreign markets, create instability in regions vital to U.S. interests, and foster even greater illegal immigration into the United States. For these reasons, international economic growth and trade are vital U.S. interests. Consider the following examples:

---

1 *Economic Report of the President: 1996,* Council of Economic Advisers, Executive Office of the President, The White House, Washington, D.C., 1996.

- **An economic crisis in Mexico could threaten U.S. security.** Mexico can create many problems for the United States, primarily because of the 2,000-mile border the two countries share. Poor economic management in Mexico has caused its economy to slump, leading some 500,000 Mexican citizens to seek to enter the United States illegally each year. Moreover, seriously polluted air and water from Mexico are finding their way into U.S. air and water supplies. Both of these problems could be alleviated if Mexico's economy grew more rapidly, but the Mexican economy actually shrank in 1995.

- **Economic crisis in Russia and the former Soviet bloc is a major obstacle to democracy and reform.** Although many former Soviet bloc countries demonstrated great economic prospects following the collapse of the Soviet Union, little prosperity has developed in Russia and the other former communist countries. This is mostly a result of inadequate economic reform. Russia's economy has shrunk every year since the Soviet Union's collapse, with its gross domestic product (GDP) dropping by 19 percent in 1991, 12 percent in 1992, 11 percent in 1993, 17 percent in 1994, and 9 percent in 1995. This staggering economic loss has given rise to significant political instability, creating an environment that has enabled former communist government officials to regain power in local and federal bureaucracies as well as in the Duma, and a communist candidate, Gennady Zyuganov, to mount a serious challenge to Boris Yeltsin in the June 1996 presidential election.

- **Stagnant economies and declining living standards in many Muslim countries breed a popular discontent that fuels the growth of radical Islamic fundamentalism.** Widespread unemployment in Muslim countries such as Algeria, Egypt, and Iran has created a mass of disillusioned young men who form a reservoir of potential recruits for the radical Islamic groups. These restless poor, called the "dispossessed" by Ayatollah Ruhollah Khomeini, often join militant groups in search of hope and a sense of personal empowerment. This is causing an increase in radical Islamic fundamentalism, which often results in increased international terrorism.

Although it would be impossible for the United States to eliminate poverty everywhere in the world, U.S. international economic policy can contribute considerably to economic growth, which in the long run can alleviate global poverty and reduce international instability. The relevant question for policymakers is how best to deal with the economic causes of instability. The best answer is not the acute therapy of direct military intervention after a problem has gotten out of hand, but the preventive medicine of opening markets to free trade, economic deregulation, and private international investment. These are the best economic treatments for creating the international economic growth needed to boost the U.S. economy, promote international stability, and protect American investments and interests worldwide.

THE IMPORTANCE OF INTERNATIONAL FREE TRADE

Free trade is an important instrument for creating international economic growth. But free trade in the United States is under assault from those who are interested in protecting a minority of noncompetitive industries from foreign competition. This protectionism is potentially very dangerous. A free trade policy is in the best interests of the United States. For example:

- **Free trade creates U.S. jobs.** In 1960, U.S. trade represented only 9 percent of GDP. Today, it represents 23 percent of GDP, according to the 1996 *Economic Report of the President*. Indeed, some 12 million Americans owe their jobs to U.S. exports. The opportunities for overseas sales alone affect a company's investment choices, hiring decisions, and research and development expenditures. Over the past three years, U.S. exports of goods and services have grown by 20 percent, representing one-third of real GDP growth. Moreover, the United States is trading more today with poorer countries. For example, 29 percent of U.S. exports went to developing countries in 1970. Today, 41 percent of U.S. exports go to the less-developed world.

An open and competitive international marketplace promotes the economic prosperity of all countries involved. Open borders allow U.S. firms to increase their production in order to meet the demand of foreign consumers. Open borders enable U.S. firms to hire more workers, pay higher wages, and invest more money in the research and development of new products. Closed borders overseas would have the same impact on U.S. firms as, for example, shutting off the California market would have to a company in New York. Thus, free trade expands markets, which in turn expands sales, which then provides increased capital for U.S. companies.

- **Free trade brings greater prosperity to the United States.** This is achieved by maximizing comparative advantage and economies of scale. No country can possibly produce all the products that its citizens would want to consume. Barriers to trade reduce the ability of companies to sell to other countries the kinds of products they have an expertise in producing. In the past, many Americans were employed in jobs like gluing the soles onto tennis shoes or sewing the labels in sweaters. Today, more Americans are employed in producing supercomputers and semiconductors and in writing computer software. Free trade has allowed the educated and productive workforce in the United States to produce goods and services of greater value than was possible only a decade ago.

- **Free trade increases domestic competition, which in turn spurs innovation.** Supporters of protectionism argue that foreign competition threatens U.S. jobs and the profitability of U.S. firms. This is not the case. In more cases than not, competition forces companies to become more efficient and innovative. For example, it was the competition from Japanese auto companies that forced U.S. auto companies to redesign their products for the domestic market. Indeed, competition is the foundation of the free enterprise system. Without competition, companies are under no pressure to build better and cheaper products. The innovative cycle breaks down, and companies become bloated and inefficient. In the end, consumers pay higher prices, have fewer choices, and are forced to live with an increasing number of shoddy products.

- **Free trade accelerates the flow of technology.** Most of the more expensive products made by industrialized countries today did not even exist two decades ago. Although U.S. manufacturers were responsible for developing a large portion of the technologies used to make these products, this technology more often than not has been developed elsewhere. A country cannot possibly produce all the goods and services consumed by its citizens. Nor can it produce all the technologies necessary for the development of newer and more innovative products. Free trade allows U.S. firms to enter into crucial partnerships with foreign firms. These strategic alliances allow companies to share new manufacturing, marketing, and distributing techniques.

- **Free trade broadens the variety of inputs available to producers.**
  Today, more U.S. companies than ever import the crucial components
  and raw materials needed to manufacture their final products. U.S.
  computer manufacturers, for example, must import certain
  components, mainly low-tech circuit boards, to produce high-tech
  finished goods. The United States could seek to produce all the
  components within its own borders; however, doing this would divert
  labor, capital, and other resources from higher-end production. This
  would be an expensive way to do business. Thus, free trade maximizes a
  U.S. company's ability to produce products like computers while
  leaving the production of the minor components like circuit boards to
  other countries.

The United States benefits from free trade. Jobs are increased; consumers
are satisfied with a greater variety of cheaper goods; industrial costs are
reduced; and the United States is able to remain a leader in new
technologies. Restricting trade for the short-term benefits of a few selected
interests ultimately would harm the United States.

THE IMPORTANCE OF
GLOBAL ECONOMIC FREEDOM

Economic freedom is the ability of people to engage in free enterprise
with minimal government interference or coercion. For a country fully to
enjoy economic freedom, it must have low taxes, free and open borders,
minimal government regulation, the rule of law, and no government
corruption. Armed with such tools, individuals and companies are free to
work and create wealth. Thus, those countries with the highest levels of
economic freedom are the wealthiest, and those countries with the lowest
levels of economic freedom are the poorest.

Such is the conclusion of The Heritage Foundation's *Index of Economic
Freedom.*[2] Displayed graphically, the statistical connection between
economic freedom and wealth is called the Curve of Economic Freedom
(see Chart 13.1). This chart clearly shows that, in general, the more

---

2 Kim R. Holmes, Bryan T. Johnson, and Melanie Kirkpatrick, eds., *1997 Index of
  Economic Freedom* (Washington, D.C.: The Heritage Foundation and Dow Jones &
  Co., Inc, 1997).

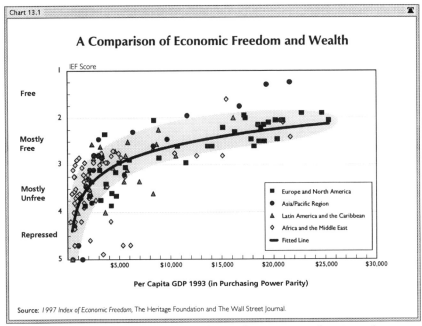

Chart 13.1

A Comparison of Economic Freedom and Wealth

IEF Score

Free

Mostly Free

Mostly Unfree

Repressed

- ■ Europe and North America
- ● Asia/Pacific Region
- ▲ Latin America and the Caribbean
- ◇ Africa and the Middle East
- — Fitted Line

Per Capita GDP 1993 (in Purchasing Power Parity)

Source: *1997 Index of Economic Freedom*, The Heritage Foundation and The Wall Street Journal.

economically free a country is, the richer it is. Likewise, the more economically repressed a country is, the poorer it remains.

This connection also can be seen by examining countries that have used economic freedom as a tool to create wealth and economic growth. Economic prosperity has not been forthcoming in most of the lesser-developed countries primarily because they do not have economic freedom. Rather, most have high taxes, barriers to trade, restrictions on international investment, banking systems in disarray, onerous government regulations, inflationary monetary policies, extensive wage and price controls, and large black markets.

Models of Economic Freedom

The best models of economic growth over the past 35 years are Hong Kong and Singapore, the most successful of the so-called Asian tigers. These countries have experienced phenomenal economic growth rates and have become the envy of the developed world. They achieved their remarkable success largely without foreign aid from the United States or loans from the World Bank. Thirty years ago, they were as poor as other countries that received World Bank loans and foreign aid; however, they walked away from foreign aid and embarked instead on successful programs of economic liberalization. The evidence shows that there is a direct correlation between the economic freedom these countries enjoy and their tremendous economic growth over the past 30 years (see Chart 13.2).

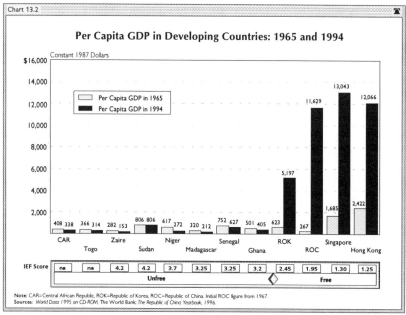

Chart 13.2

Per Capita GDP in Developing Countries: 1965 and 1994

Constant 1987 Dollars

Note: CAR=Central African Republic, ROK=Republic of Korea, ROC=Republic of China. Initial ROC figure from 1967.
Sources: *World Data 1995 on CD-ROM*, The World Bank; *The Republic of China Yearbook*, 1996.

For example, Hong Kong began a massive economic liberalization program after it turned away from large-scale foreign aid in 1965. This liberalization program included reforms in banking and financial services, government regulation of business, and international investment laws. Specifically, Hong Kong abolished almost all import duties and tariffs. Today, it has one of the lowest tariff levels in the world. Hong Kong also slashed income and corporate tax rates, and today remains one of the lowest-taxed countries in the world. After these economic reforms were in place, Hong Kong's economy took off. GDP increased 9.2 percent a year from 1970 to 1980. From 1980 to 1993, it grew an additional 6.5 percent a year. Overall, over the past 35 years, Hong Kong's per capita GDP has mushroomed an astonishing 535 percent, with most of this growth occurring since the beginning of economic liberalization.

Singapore, like Hong Kong, embarked on a course of economic liberalization and achieved the same stunning results. From the late 1960s into the 1970s, Singapore instituted a series of economic reforms aimed at achieving two major goals, the first of which was to promote increased international investment and higher levels of exports. To this end, Singapore opened its market to foreign investors. By 1970, some 80 percent to 90 percent of all manufactured exports were derived from international investment. Singapore also slashed taxes on income and corporate profits. These economic reforms helped increase Singapore's GDP. From 1970 to 1980, GDP grew by 8.3 percent a year. From 1980 to 1993, it jumped an additional 6.9 percent per year. Overall, Singapore's GDP has risen by over 6 percent a year since 1965.

The Asian tigers are not the only countries to develop over the past several decades. In 1973, Chile was the world's second-largest recipient of foreign aid. The World Bank had lent almost $4 billion to Chile since 1965. Under the leadership of Marxist President Salvador Allende, Chile's GDP shrank by 5.6 percent in 1973. In that year, some 75 percent of GDP was created by money-losing state-owned enterprises. In 1973, however, Augusto Pinochet seized power through a military coup. From 1974 until the 1980s, without the crutch of foreign aid, the government of Chile privatized state-owned industries, cut taxes, removed government regulations, freed up the banking system, opened the country to trade, legalized private property, and established a legal and judicial system. As a result, Chile's economy grew 5.1 percent each year from 1980 to 1991. No longer a major recipient of foreign aid or multilateral lending, Chile is rapidly becoming one of the richest countries in Latin America.

Hong Kong, Singapore, and Chile consistently have outperformed all of the developing countries. They have managed to grow economically without foreign aid. When compared with countries that are still dependent on foreign aid, their success underscores the importance of economic freedom as a key factor in economic development. But these selected countries are not the only examples of how economic freedom affects economic growth. Using the *1997 Index of Economic Freedom* rankings as indicators of future economic performance, statistical tests run by The Heritage Foundation further underscore the statistical connections between economic freedom and economic growth. Using one of the largest datasets for inter-country growth comparisons,[3] Heritage analysts found statistically significant relationships at the 99 percent confidence level between the *Index* and country-by-country levels of economic development, and between the *Index* and economic growth rates.[4]

Chart 13.3 shows the type of relationship observed between economic growth and *Index* values. In Chart 13.3, the vertical axis contains real GDP per person in 1991 as a percent of real GDP per person in 1976. The horizontal axis shows the *Index* values for 1997. This graph clearly shows a distinct association between countries with lower *Index* numbers (freer economies) and higher economic growth. In other words, the Heritage analysis of these data strongly suggests that countries with free-market policies grow faster than countries that discourage economic freedom.[5]

Despite the limitations of these and other data used to explore the implications of policy changes on cross-country growth rates, numerous other scholars have found similar and significant relationships between economic growth and public policies. For example, Harvard economist Robert Barro has found a strong positive relationship between growth rates and data that measure the degree to which a country rules itself by law as

---

3 The 138-country dataset modified and expanded by Harvard economists Robert Barro and Jong-Wha Lee. The data are presented in five-year intervals from 1960 and fall generally into seven categories: national income, education, population/fertility, government expenditures, price deflators, political variables, and trade variables. See Robert Barro and Xavier Sali-I-Martin, *Economic Growth* (New York, N.Y.: McGraw-Hill, 1995).

4 William W. Beach and Gareth Davis, "The Index of Economic Freedom and Economic Growth," in *1997 Index of Economic Freedom*.

5 A number of factors outside the sphere of economic policy affect a country's growth rate, including natural disasters, unusual weather, war, pestilence, and the vagaries of economic activity caused by the policies of other countries. Even so, a prudent use of the relationship illustrated in Chart 13.3 is justified; at the very least, it emphasizes a connection between economic performance and public policies that emerged over the 15-year period from 1976 to 1991. In addition, the Heritage analysis compares growth rates ending in 1991 to *Index* numbers based on 1995–1996 data. The *Index*, however, measures institutional dimensions of economic activity that typically change very little over the short run; in fact, a correlation of 96 percent was found between the *Index* for 1995 and the *Index* for 1996. The four-year gap between the two variables probably would not obliterate the relationship that appears to exist between these variables.

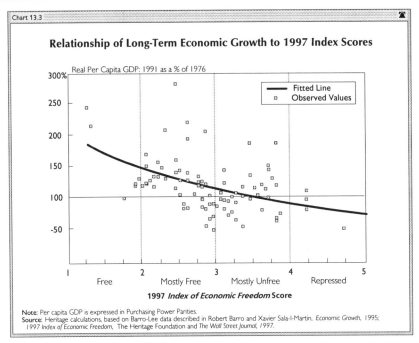

Chart 13.3

Relationship of Long-Term Economic Growth to 1997 Index Scores

Real Per Capita GDP: 1991 as a % of 1976

Fitted Line
Observed Values

1997 *Index of Economic Freedom* Score

1 — Free
2 — Mostly Free
3 — Mostly Unfree
4 — Repressed
5

Note: Per capita GDP is expressed in Purchasing Power Parities.
Source: Heritage calculations, based on Barro-Lee data described in Robert Barro and Xavier Sala-I-Martin, *Economic Growth,* 1995; *1997 Index of Economic Freedom,* The Heritage Foundation and *The Wall Street Journal,* 1997.

opposed to the whims and edicts of political strongmen. He also has found that growth rates in countries in which government consumes less GDP are better than the growth rates in countries in which government consumes more GDP. Barro determined that other policy and institutional or non-economic variables significantly related to growth include the inflation rate, political rights, the fertility rate, years of secondary and higher education, and the initial level of GDP.[6]

The evidence is clear: with economic freedom comes economic growth, and with economic growth comes economic opportunities for the United States. For example, the world's total economic output was $8.5 trillion in 1978. Today, it is over $32 trillion, a 294 percent increase. During that time,

---

6 Robert J. Barro in presentation to Heritage Foundation Roundtable on Economic Growth, June 26, 1996; copies available upon request from The Heritage Foundation. See also Robert J. Barro, "Economic Growth in a Cross-Section of Countries," *Quarterly Journal of Economics,* Vol. 106 (1991), pp. 407–443.

U.S. total exports have grown over 15 times, from $42.7 billion to over $700 billion. Thus, there is a direct connection between growth of the world economy and U.S. exports. Higher exports mean better jobs for Americans, a higher standard of living, and more innovative and competitive U.S. companies. But although economic growth helps expand exports, so also do lower barriers to trade.

Countries with Low Barriers to Trade

Much of the growth in U.S. exports has come not just from economic growth, but also from lower barriers to international trade. Although some pundits continue to debate the merits of protectionism over free trade, it is clear that countries with the lowest barriers to trade also are the wealthiest, and countries with the highest barriers to trade are the poorest. There is a statistical correlation between lower tariff rates and higher levels of economic wealth, just as there is a statistical correlation between higher average tariff rates and lower levels of economic wealth (see Chart 13.4). In other words, countries with lower average tariffs rates generally are richer, and countries with higher average tariff rates generally are poorer.[7] For example:

- **Hong Kong.** There are no tariffs on imported goods in Hong Kong, so goods move freely across the border. This is one of the primary reasons Hong Kong has become a major location for manufacturers. Companies that locate in Hong Kong find it cheaper to import the components they need to manufacture their final products. As these businesses locate in Hong Kong, more people are employed, which results in a higher level of economic growth. In 1993, measured on a purchasing-power basis, Hong Kong had a per capita GDP of $21,560. This makes Hong Kong the fifth-richest country in the world.

- **Singapore.** With an average tariff rate of 0.3 percent, Singapore is quickly becoming one of the fastest-growing and wealthiest countries in the world. Like Hong Kong, Singapore's low tariff rates allow manufacturers to locate in Singapore and conduct business more

---

7 Average tariff rates from Bryan T. Johnson and Thomas P. Sheehy, *1996 Index of Economic Freedom* (Washington, D.C.: The Heritage Foundation, 1996). Per capita gross domestic product figures are from *Human Development Report 1996* (New York, N.Y.: United Nations, 1996) and are expressed in purchasing power parity.

cheaply than in countries with high tariff rates. This has allowed Singapore's exports to grow by over 12 percent a year since 1980, compared with 5 percent growth in the United States.

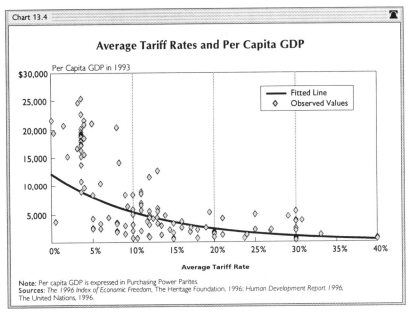

Chart 13.4

Average Tariff Rates and Per Capita GDP

Note: Per capita GDP is expressed in Purchasing Power Parites.
Sources: *The 1996 Index of Economic Freedom*, The Heritage Foundation, 1996; *Human Development Report 1996*, The United Nations, 1996.

The average per capita income level of countries with an average tariff rate of 4 percent or below is over $17,000. But the average per capita income level of countries with average tariff rates above 20 percent is below $2,000.

Tariffs, however, are not the only forms of protectionism a country uses. A country may have a relatively low average tariff rate but still heavily protect its market. Thus, in order to demonstrate fully the connection between free trade and economic prosperity, it is necessary to analyze other forms of trade protection that go beyond tariffs and duties. These other forms of trade protection are called non-tariff barriers. They include such policies as import bans and quotas, strict licensing and labeling requirements, inspection requirements, corrupt customs officials, strict antidumping and antitrust laws, and so on.[8]

These barriers often are hard to quantify. But The Heritage Foundation has been quantifying these non-tariff barriers on a global basis for over three years. The *Index of Economic Freedom,* first published in 1994, includes an in-depth economic analysis of over 100 countries in ten broad economic factors. One of these factors is international trade. The international trade component of the *Index* measures the average tariff rate and non-tariff barriers. Using the *Index,* it is possible to identify the level of overall trade protectionism within a country.[9] As shown in Chart 13.5, the countries with better trade scores also generally are the richest. Likewise, those countries with worse trade scores generally are the poorest. In fact, countries that have mostly free trade to totally free trade policies have an average per capita income level of almost $15,000, whereas countries that have protectionist trade policies have an average per capita income of less than $2,000.

Although it is difficult to determine whether increases in a country's wealth precede free trade policies or free trade policies precede increases in wealth, there still is a correlation between lower barriers to trade and higher levels of wealth. Moreover, the facts indicate that as countries open their borders to trade, they are more likely to become richer.

---

8 There are a few isolated instances in which countries use neither tariffs nor non-tariff barriers to protect their markets; for example, the use of "value-added taxes" to protect markets from the imports of particular goods is growing. A country may have a special tax that applies to imports of particular goods like automobiles; Hong Kong and Singapore both have special taxes on imported automobiles, although the purpose is more to control the number of vehicles on the road in these island nations than to protect the market. It is safe to assume, however, that even with the existence of such special taxes, countries like Hong Kong and Singapore are still unusually open to imports and thus essentially free-trading nations.

9 Based on a comparison of international trade scores in Johnson and Sheehy, *1996 Index of Economic Freedom,* and per capita income levels from *The World Bank World Development Report,* 1995 and 1996 editions, and *World Bank World Atlas,* 1995 and 1996.

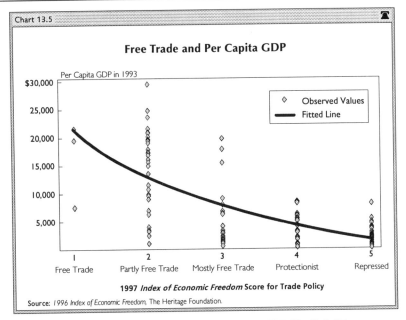

Chart 13.5

Free Trade and Per Capita GDP

Per Capita GDP in 1993

◇ Observed Values
— Fitted Line

1	2	3	4	5
Free Trade	Partly Free Trade	Mostly Free Trade	Protectionist	Repressed

1997 *Index of Economic Freedom* **Score for Trade Policy**

Source: *1996 Index of Economic Freedom,* The Heritage Foundation.

THE PROPER GOVERNMENT ROLE IN PROMOTING TRADE

What is the proper role of the U.S. government in promoting international trade and commerce? One approach generally has the U.S. government involved in subsidizing U.S. exports, as well as acting as a guarantor of investment in targeted less-developed countries. This is the approach utilized by the Overseas Private Investment Corporation (OPIC) and the United States Export-Import (Ex-Im) Bank. OPIC provides subsidized loans for U.S. businesses to invest in foreign countries. The Ex-Im Bank provides aid to U.S. firms to export products to less-developed countries.

Whatever their stated intentions, these programs are aimed more at providing welfare for U.S.-based multinational corporations than at promoting economic development in less-developed countries. The rationale for maintaining U.S. subsidized export and lending programs is that they fill a void. For example, supporters of such programs argue that some countries are ignored by the private sector and that subsidized loans to

U.S. companies help them attract imports and investments. The United States supposedly benefits from increased exports and investment as a result. Thus, supporters argue, in the absence of such government programs, the United States would lose business in less-developed countries.

There is, however, a very good explanation as to why the private sector is not already exporting to or investing in many of the regions in which OPIC and the Ex-Im Bank are engaged: free market conditions do not exist, making purely private economic transactions too risky. Perhaps, for example, the countries do not have impartial judicial systems to ensure the enforcement of contracts; similarly, taxes may be too high or private property may be outlawed.

OPIC and the Ex-Im Bank use U.S. tax dollars to funnel money to regions that have done little to get their own economic houses in order. OPIC, for example, has extended investment guarantees to many countries whose economies are graded as "mostly unfree" or "repressed" on The Heritage Foundation/ *Wall Street Journal 1997 Index of Economic Freedom.* These countries[10] could attract much greater amounts of foreign capital from U.S. direct investment simply by liberalizing their economies. OPIC, by providing an alternative source of foreign capital, discourages economic freedom.

Although many less-developed countries receive subsidies from the U.S. export and investment program, there also are many more developed countries receiving this aid that do not need it. Some countries, like Singapore and the Philippines, have no problem attracting substantial foreign investment and exports from the developed world. These countries already have made progress toward economic reform. OPIC, however, continues to send aid to them. In Singapore, Indonesia, Malaysia, the Philippines, and Thailand, U.S. private investment is substantial (see Table 13.1). Yet, they still continue to receive OPIC aid.

It is clear that these countries have no trouble attracting foreign investment. In fact, Japan is a larger foreign investor in these countries than the United States is. Despite claims by supporters of subsidized exports and

---

10 These countries are: Albania, Cameroon, Cape Verde, Croatia, Djibouti, Egypt, Ethiopia, Haiti, Laos, Malta, Mongolia, Nepal, Rwanda, Somalia, Ukraine, and Yemen.

Table 13.1

OPIC Investments: A Comparison of Economically Free Countries, Their OPIC Aid and U.S. Direct Investment

	Economic Freedom Ranking	OPIC Aid	U.S. Direct Investment
Singapore	Free	$30 million	$12.5 billion
Indonesia	Mostly Free	$210 million	$7 billion
Malaysia	Mostly Free	$146 million	$3.6 billion
Philippines	Mostly Free	$470 million	$2.6 billion
Thailand	Mostly Free	$27 million	$4.6 billion

Sources: "1995 Annual Report," Overseas Private Investment Corporation; *The 1996 Index of Economic Freedom*, The Heritage Foundation, 1996; Bureau of Economic Analysis, Department of Commerce.

investments that U.S. subsidies go only to less-developed countries, the United States devotes some 26 percent of all its investments to the developing world each year. In some cases, this amount exceeds $20 billion annually.

Redefining America's Role in the Global Economy

Rather than use U.S. tax dollars to subsidize selected U.S. companies that otherwise would not invest in risky countries, or that already are investing in countries like Singapore, the United States needs to redefine its role in promoting international economic prosperity. The United States once again must champion the cause of free trade and investment much as it did following World War II. It must become the leader in supporting and promoting free trade and investment worldwide.

It should seek to reduce barriers to trade and foreign investment by using the same agreements that proved so successful following World War II. The leadership role of the United States helped create the General Agreement on Tariffs and Trade (GATT). which began shortly after World War II as a forum to reduce worldwide tariff rates and spur economic growth and prosperity.

Not only did the United States seek aggressively to open Europe to trade and investment after the war, but it also sought to rebuild Japan's economy, primarily through private U.S. investment. The United States used the auspices of the GATT to break down barriers to trade and investment in Europe and Japan. The U.S. leadership role continued in the 1980s, when the Reagan Administration launched a series of bilateral trade agreements with regions like the Caribbean and initiated a free trade area with Israel and Canada. Later, the Bush Administration sought to extend the U.S.–Canada free trade area to Mexico and the rest of Latin America, creating the North American Free Trade Agreement (NAFTA).

But the United States no longer commands a leadership role in these areas. With so much of the future prosperity of the United States riding on how well it meets the challenges of the international marketplace, policymakers once again must establish a U.S. worldwide leadership role in promoting economic prosperity and free trade and opening countries to investment. If the United States succeeds in this effort, it not only will maintain itself as the world's richest economy, it also will become even more prosperous.

The Failure of Foreign Aid

Although economic growth has been slow in many countries for centuries, there seems to be little understanding within the U.S. government bureaucracy of what causes either economic growth or its opposite, economic stagnation and poverty. For decades, the official approach of the United States to alleviating poverty abroad has been the same as its approach to eliminating it at home: enact government policies to redistribute wealth from the rich to the poor. After nearly 50 years, the U.S. international welfare policy has been even less successful than its domestic welfare policies.

Since its inception in 1949, the U.S. economic aid program has been a failure. Most long-term recipients of foreign aid are no better off today than they were before beginning to receive such aid. In fact, many are worse off. Likewise, the World Bank and the International Monetary Fund have shown little success in helping poor countries lift themselves out of poverty. For example, the amount of money lent by the World Bank to the developing world has been substantial, but the results have been far from successful. Indeed, the World Bank's record overall has been one of failure. Despite decades of subsidized loans, most of the world's less-developed countries are no more prosperous today than they were before. Many have even experienced economic declines.

The notion that people are poor mainly because other people are rich is fundamentally flawed. Although giving poor people in foreign countries more money may alleviate some of the effects of poverty temporarily, it cannot work in the long run because it ignores the root causes of poverty. In today's world, in which economic prosperity exists in the global marketplace, poverty is not the natural condition of mankind. It is a condition largely imposed on people by governments. Therefore, the United States should eliminate economic development aid in all its forms.

CONCLUSION

As the world's largest exporter of goods and services, the United States has an interest in global economic growth. Moreover, increasing global prosperity can help alleviate the popular discontent that, in turn, helps fuel regional instability, conflict, and tension. Economic growth and prosperity abroad creates markets for U.S. exports and reduces regional instability or conflicts that can threaten U.S. access to markets, raw materials, and trade routes.

Economic freedom is the foundation of individual prosperity and the economic development of nations. Without it, countries will remain poor, no matter how much money they receive in foreign aid. Thus, in order for countries to grow economically, the overseas economic development policies of the United States must be based on the principles of individual liberty and economic freedom that unleash the entrepreneurial, wealth-creating potential of nations.

International trade and investment are becoming increasingly vital to the U.S. economy. The nation's interests require the elimination or reduction of barriers to trade and investment overseas. The current practice of financing international development by transferring money from richer to poorer nations through international welfare programs does not work. It is time for the United States to pursue a strategy that does work—one that reduces barriers to international trade and investment.

Chapter 14

MAINTAINING AN EFFECTIVE MILITARY IN A BUDGET STRAITJACKET

Thomas Moore

Edmund Burke, the archetypal conservative of the 18th century, warned that eternal vigilance is the price of liberty. During the five decades of the Cold War, it was the vigilance and resolve of Burke's descendants — today's conservatives — that kept the Soviet Union contained until that predatory empire finally collapsed under its own rotten weight.

Since then, the vigilance of conservatives, and especially those of the 104th Congress, has been redirected toward concerns that hit much closer to home. Today, many Americans feel that their own government threatens liberty instead of protecting it because the federal government has slipped its constitutional moorings. Although the Tenth Amendment limits the federal government to specific, enumerated powers, Washington recognizes virtually no limits on its power. It intrudes heavily into every sphere of private and economic life, corrodes everything it touches, and consumes more and more of the citizen's hard-earned wealth through coercive, confiscatory taxation. And as the taxpayer's wealth disappears into the rapacious maw of the federal Leviathan, his liberty goes with it, bit by bit.

The author would like to thank Dr. Dov Zakheim, Dr. Phillip Gold, Senator Malcolm Wallop, and Mr. Kevin McGowan for their suggestions and contributions to this chapter. The views and opinions expressed herein, however, are solely the responsibility of the author.

Little wonder that today's political controversies are on the domestic front, with scant attention to foreign policy and national defense, especially because the fall of the Soviet Union, in the minds of most Americans, has removed any serious threat to the nation's security or survival. The average American is preoccupied with the daily demands of making a living and supporting a family, working harder while keeping less of the fruit of his labor, and while society seems to be disintegrating around him. Even many on the Right, formerly champions of a vigorous foreign policy and a strong national defense, no longer are engaged in the national security debate.

This turning inward at the end of a national conflict is very much in keeping with patterns in U.S. history. It is instructive to see the relevance this tendency has today for the condition of the U.S. military and the nation's overall defense capabilities.

Historic Patterns of Preparedness

After the allied victory in World War I, which was won in large part because of an influx of fresh, strong U.S. troops to break the stalemate on the Western Front, Americans turned inward. They believed they could withdraw behind the unbridgeable barriers of two great oceans and go about their business in a New World untroubled by wars in the Old. But Americans found they could not isolate themselves. As a great maritime and trading power, the United States depended on freedom of the seas and access to raw materials and open markets for its well-being. Inexorably, a peaceful United States began to be touched by a world at war even before the attack on Pearl Harbor in 1941.

Hindsight leads many Americans to believe the Allied victory in World War II was pre-ordained, but it did not seem that way at the time. Americans of the post–World War II generation did not experience the anxiety and terror of the early days of the war when the Axis almost won. The Germans and Japanese racked up a string of victories everywhere against traditionally strong military powers. It looked as if no one could stop them, and it was by only the slimmest of margins that the tide turned, against the Germans at Stalingrad and against the Japanese at Midway. Even at Midway, properly celebrated as a magnificent feat of arms, U.S. Navy airmen lost their lives because their equipment was inferior and their training inadequate—the direct result of neglecting the military during the interwar years. Fortunately, their courage and determination were in no way deficient, and it was these qualities, along with considerable luck, that won the day.

After World War II, the United States demobilized rapidly in 1945; and as a consequence, aggression again reared its head in Korea. U.S. occupation troops in Japan were in a poor state of combat readiness when rushed to stem the tide of the North Korean onslaught in June 1950. Americans and their South Korean allies were defeated time and again. Allied forces were pushed back until the battle finally stabilized around the Pusan Perimeter, and General Douglas MacArthur's brilliant landing at Inchon was able to reverse North Korea's gains.

Today, this historic pattern of a lack of vigilance and concern about foreign policy and defense is being repeated, even in Congress and among those for whom such concerns used to be paramount. The unifying and clarifying threat of the former Soviet Union is gone—even though a variety of other lesser threats continues to grow. But the strong-defense community is not vocal or persuasive enough to overcome the force of this historical pattern. The downward spiral of defense spending cuts continues for the time being, and the choice between Democrats and Republicans is simply one of how steep and how fast the downward spiral will go. In fact, congressional Democrats have pointed out—correctly, one must add—that the Republicans' "front-loaded" defense budget may spend more in the near term, but actually provides less in future years than the planned Clinton budget for the same period. Furthermore, the 105th Congress may be tempted to cut defense even more to pay for promised tax cuts. The result: Today, the United States has too few forces to fight two nearly simultaneous regional conflicts, and too little money to pay for the inadequate forces.

There is, however, more to the historical pattern than neglect and turning inward. The lack of vigilance abroad after winning a war always has encouraged new aggression for which the United States was unprepared. It is safe to predict that today's Age of Chaos will be no exception. Greed, passion, and folly are immutable parts of human character; and somewhere, someday, a new dictator, having observed the lack of U.S. military preparedness, will embark upon some mad venture that threatens America's vital interests or its allies. Sooner or later, there will be another major conflict—or multiple conflicts—that will draw in the United States. In fact, the forces of conflict already are building up steadily around the world—

great power competition, unbridled nationalism, ethnic strife, religious fanaticism, and hunger for newly discovered or diminishing natural resources.

When the inevitable crisis — whether a single event or a succession of converging regional crises — erupts again in the world, the historic pattern shows the American people will rally and do what is needed. Today's apathy and lack of interest in national security will evaporate overnight. But the American people rely on their elected leaders to maintain the tools they will need to do the job. If they find the neglected military instrument rusty and brittle in their hands, they will hold accountable those who let our defenses decline. The blood of their sons, brothers, husbands, and fathers who die unnecessarily will demand it. This is where the strong-defense community can — and must — play a vital role. If experts from this community cannot stop or reverse the historic pattern of postwar neglect, at least they can concentrate their efforts on preserving a military that will remain relatively effective even while wearing a budget straitjacket.

An Effective Military for the 21st Century

National security policymakers constantly must assess the growing dangers in the world in light of human nature and the nature of warfare, and illuminated by the experience of the past. The United States is the watchman on the walls. It has to be vigilant even if others are not, because the United States no longer can afford to be surprised as it was on December 7, 1941, in June 1950, and before the Persian Gulf War in August 1990. The nation ought to have learned its lesson each time; but in this Age of Chaos, no one can accurately predict or anticipate what form the next threat may take. Wise and prudent Americans expect aggression to arise somewhere. Like Napoleon, they believe that "To be defeated is pardonable; to be surprised—never!"

National security policymakers must undertake an overarching goal in this current "interwar" period to negate the damaging effects of postwar neglect of national defense as much as possible. Congress and defense leaders must devote themselves not to achieving the unattainable, but to maintaining a "core" capability—an adequate, viable military force that can survive the initial shock of future conflict, minimize damage to the most vital interests of the United States, and serve as a cadre or base for rapid expansion in the event the conflict is protracted.

No one can say with certainty how much the defense budget and force levels will continue to fall. Today, military forces have been cut by approximately 40 percent from the level of 1990, on the eve of the Persian Gulf War. Clearly, the resources allocated for defense are going to be severely limited in the foreseeable future, and those who support a strong defense policy cannot expect more than marginal gains. Because the nation will not spend more on defense, it will have to spend more wisely. The scarce funds available for defense must go to maintain a flexible, responsive, combat-ready force capable of prevailing in 21st century conflicts.

Americans cannot expect future conflicts to be repeats of the dramatic victory in the Persian Gulf War. The most likely significant difference is that a future aggressor cannot be expected to give away the initiative and allow the United States or its allies six months to build up their forces, as Saddam Hussein did.

To deal with the likely contingencies of future conflict, the U.S. military forces of the future must satisfy the following criteria:

- **U.S. armed forces must be more expeditionary in nature, and able to deploy more quickly to distant trouble spots on shorter warning.** This means they must have adequate sealift and airlift capabilities.

- **U.S. armed forces must be able to force their way into a contested area.** Because there may be no friendly host nation for a U.S. strategic base, the military must be able to enter the theater of operations even if there is little opportunity to build up strength or plan an offensive campaign.

- **U.S. armed forces must be able to operate in terrain** that is unfavorable for mechanized forces, and in weather that restricts air operations.

- **U.S. armed forces must be capable of defeating a more determined enemy** than Iraq proved to be in 1990–1991, including an enemy that enjoys technological superiority (or at least parity) in some areas.

- **U.S. armed forces must be able to maintain a superior operational doctrine,** with close coordination of combined arms; good synchronicity in combat operations; and effective sequencing of close, deep, and rear area attacks. They must be able to combine precision firepower, shock action, a fast tempo, and high mobility to keep the enemy reeling and continually off balance, shattering his moral as well as his physical cohesiveness.

- **U.S armed forces must be able to conduct joint operations** so that the combined effect of air, sea, and ground action is greater than the sum of the parts.

- **U.S. armed forces must maintain high quality in the human component,** because intangible human factors like morale, discipline, courage, training, motivation, stamina, and leadership are decisive in battle. Junior leaders at the tactical level must have a high degree of initiative in fluid combat situations where detailed control from remote headquarters is not possible, and commanders at the rear echelons must be willing to trust the leaders of their forward units. Operational forces must be products of tough, realistic training, such as the kind given at the Army's National Training Center at Fort Irwin, California.

- **U.S. forces must be supported by superior logistics.** There is an old axiom in the military: "Amateurs talk about strategy and tactics; professionals talk about logistics." Although an overstatement, this dramatizes an essential point: modern warfare as practiced by the U.S. military consumes an immense amount of material that must be put in the hands of the operational units on the field.

LESSONS LEARNED

The obstacles to maintaining this kind of highly effective military in a period of national neglect and diminishing resources are many. The lessons learned in confronting these obstacles are interrelated and overlapping, but can be separated and identified as follows:

Lesson #1: Maintaining an effective military is ultimately the responsibility of the President. The main obstacle to maintaining a combat-effective military has been the performance of the President, and concomitantly the policies and priorities of his Administration. As Commander in Chief, Bill Clinton has the primary responsibility to conduct foreign policy and to command the armed forces. If he fails in this office, or if his policies are harmful to the combat effectiveness of the armed forces, it is very difficult for Congress and others to make up the deficiency.

LESSONS LEARNED

- Maintaining an effective military is ultimately the responsibility of the President.

- The tendency to cut the defense budget to pay for growth in domestic spending and entitlements has put military combat readiness at risk.

- The willingness of the American people to spend tax dollars on defense is directly proportional to the level of perceived threat.

- Using the defense budget for non-defense spending, or for so-called defense spending that really is not essential to national security, depletes funds needed to sustain and adequately equip the armed forces.

- Decisions on defense spending should be strategy-driven, not budget-driven.

- The arms control establishment undermines, rather than enhances, the effectiveness of the armed forces.

- The post–Cold War mindset of complacency is a major impediment to the effectiveness of the armed forces.

- A crisis of culture is undermining the effectiveness of the armed forces.

- War remains a dirty, bloody affair that places great demands on servicemen and women.

The old axiom that the fish rots from the head is appropriate to the relationship between the U.S. Commander in Chief and his military forces. Anyone who has worked as a political appointee of a President can attest that the President's character, vision, and priorities affect the actions of the people whom he has appointed. His agenda, stated or even unstated, is a checklist and a shared value system that instructs an appointee on decisions he will make. In this respect, political appointees provide the conduit for a sort of "trickle-down" process. Unfortunately, many of the policies trickling down from President Clinton have seriously undermined the effectiveness of the armed services and the nation's security.

The Commander in Chief may have the primary constitutional responsibility for foreign and defense policy, but Congress has the obligation to intervene when conditions demand, because Congress represents the will of the people and shares in the constitutional responsibility for national security through its oversight and funding roles. The Framers of the Constitution wisely did not place all the responsibility in the President's hands—for just such a time as this. The constitutional system of checks and balances assigns much of the responsibility for national security to Congress. For example, Article I, Section 8 confers on Congress the "Power to...provide for the common Defence and general welfare of the United States...," including the power "To declare war... To Raise and support Armies...To provide and maintain a Navy; To make Rules for the Government and Regulation of the land and naval Forces," and so forth.

Congress can exercise oversight authority for the conduct of foreign and security policy through the "power of the purse," that is, the authorization and appropriation of funds for executive branch agencies. The Senate also has specific national security responsibilities through the confirming of Administration appointments and officers of the armed services and, most significantly, consenting to the ratification of treaties as spelled out in Article II, Section 2 of the Constitution. Unfortunately, many in Congress misunderstand their constitutional role in national security. As a result, Congress cedes too much authority to the Commander in Chief and fails to use the legislative tools at its disposal to check harmful decisions by the President.

Lesson #2: Congress's tendency to cut the defense budget to pay for growth in domestic spending and entitlements has put the combat readiness of the military at risk. Members of Congress whose top priority is national defense must understand the full ramifications of the deficit problem and the looming crisis in the federal government's ability to finance its obligations. The so-called discretionary part of the federal budget, which includes accounts subject to annual authorization and appropriation by Congress such as the defense budget, is shrinking every year in relation to the non-discretionary accounts. In fact, cuts in the defense budget have provided most of the savings in overall federal spending (the so-called peace dividend). Non-discretionary accounts include the entitlements portion of the budget for Medicare, Medicaid, and Social Security, and the "debt service," or interest on the ballooning national debt.

The discretionary part of the budget now represents only 34 percent of total federal outlays. Yet even as entitlements consume the discretionary budget accounts, the financial stability of the entitlement programs is eroding. And thanks to years of profligate deficit spending combined with compound interest, the service on the national debt is increasing geometrically. At current rates of federal spending and growth in the debt, interest payments on the national debt will exceed what the nation pays for its national defense in four or five years.

This looming budgetary "train wreck" puts immense pressure on the discretionary side of the budget at the expense of the defense budget. In short, the future ability of the U.S. government to finance its operations and meet its obligations is being undermined. The bill for decades of fiscal irresponsibility is finally coming due. If this problem is not resolved in the very near future, the United States could experience a level of economic, political, and social turmoil it has not seen since the early 1930s. The political struggle over how much to spend on defense must be understood in this context.

Lesson #3: The willingness of the American people to spend money on defense is directly proportional to the level of perceived threat. During the 50 years of confrontation with the Soviet Union, Americans were willing to sacrifice to keep the United States on an even footing with the Soviets in military capabilities because Moscow threatened vital U.S. interests around the globe, and potentially the very survival of the nation itself. Even though Russia retains a massive nuclear arsenal that could wreak horrible devastation on the United States, the threat of a massive nuclear attack now seems to be a thing of the past. At the same time, the ability and even the intent of some former Soviet republics to challenge the United States and its allies with conventional force have virtually ended. Western victory over communism and the fall of this once-mighty empire were events of great historical magnitude, and Americans can take great satisfaction from the role they and their country played. The fall of the Soviet Union, however, obscures the fact that communism is still alive and well in China, Cuba, North Korea, and even Russia, where the final chapter has not been written and resurgent communists and xenophobic hard-liners are attempting to gain power.

The end of the Cold War has not spelled the "end of history." Instead, the world is seeing a "re-cycling" of history—the violent release of forces previously contained by five decades of superpower confrontation. The post–Cold War era is becoming the Age of Chaos as nations revert to traditional great power competition and regional rivalries. Extreme nationalism, ethnic rivalry, and the rise of a radical, revolutionary version of Islam all pose immediate threats to the United States, its regional interests, and its allies. The ancient enmities between religions, races, and tribes have not gone away, but have been intensified by the information age and the spread of military technology, and have spawned new threats and new challenges to U.S. interests in various corners of the globe. But because these threats are often subtle and insidious, or masked through a strategy of deception, it will be difficult to generate the mass support for heavy defense spending that was possible in the Cold War.

Lesson #4: Using the defense budget for non-defense spending, or for so-called defense spending that really is not essential to national security, depletes funds needed to sustain and adequately equip the armed forces. Compounding the already severe budget problem is the current congressional practice of raiding the defense budget to fund non-defense items or to create jobs back in someone's home state or district. Of course, there is nothing wrong with creating jobs in defense industry per se; the military's hardware has to be built somewhere by human minds and hands. But political considerations often override defense needs in the budget process, and outmoded equipment that the armed services do not need or want often continues to be built simply because the work is done in the state or district of a powerful Member of Congress.

Unfortunately, Republicans are as prone as Democrats to use defense programs as a kind of grand constituent service. Location of a defense program is as important a criterion for garnering congressional support as its usefulness to the armed forces or its role in enhancing combat effectiveness. But in addition to the problem of pork-barrel defense spending, demands to divert scarce defense funds to projects that have even less to do with national defense—for example, breast cancer research or environmental cleanup—have increased steadily. And even though this spending may be for laudable purposes, this practice depletes the funds needed to sustain and equip the armed forces.

Lesson #5: Decisions on defense spending should be strategy-driven, not budget-driven. American defense thinking has not adjusted fully to the end of the Cold War, and U.S. leaders have failed to formulate a strategy appropriate to this new Age of Chaos. The Clinton Administration's Bottom-Up Review (BUR) purports to be a national security strategy, but it is deficient in this fundamental respect. It is based on the capability of the United States to fight and win two simultaneous regional conflicts, but it does not provide force levels adequate to meet such a demand; nor does it provide enough funds to pay even for this inadequate force level.

Political leaders are all too confident that the United States can "get by" safely with ever smaller reduced forces and lowered capabilities, and are incurring the higher risks and smaller margin of error that accompany them. What passes for military strategy today is really a form of accounting or bookkeeping, with defense decisions no more than budget decisions based not on the imperatives of military strategy, but on what political leaders feel the political traffic will bear. This approach does not correct the deficiencies inherent in the BUR. It makes no logical connection between the forces and capabilities required and the funds needed to pay for them. It provides no solution to the chronic underfunding of defense.

A purely budget-driven approach can produce, of course, some marginal gains from "inside" the defense budget (privatizing, cutting bureaucracy and overhead, acquisition reform). Some shortfalls in military capabilities also can be made up by advanced technologies. But the long-term prospects for a budget-driven defense posture are still negative. The unwillingness to engage in rigorous strategic thinking is fundamental to the problem, and it characterizes the denial and flight from responsibility that is typical of today's elites. As long as this approach dominates the strong-defense community, the United States will continue to have a budget-driven strategy rather than a strategy-driven budget.

Lesson #6: The arms control establishment undermines the effectiveness of the armed forces instead of enhancing it. Arms control as it is practiced today does great harm to the nation as a whole by leaving the American people vulnerable to the world's most destructive weapons. But more to the point, its policies have exposed U.S. military personnel and bases abroad to a variety of dangers. The members of the arms control establishment, ensconced in the Pentagon, the State

Department, and the Arms Control and Disarmament Agency (ACDA) and reinforced by liberal think tanks, foundations, the news media, and academia, are a self-perpetuating and self-aggrandizing elite. Like a modern-day pagan priesthood, they ascribe awesome moral properties to inanimate objects that must be propitiated by the mystical process of arms negotiations. Of course, as a practical matter, their shamanistic rituals rarely control any arms except those of the United States; and their promises of universal peace through arms control have not been fulfilled.

The principal example is the 1972 Anti-Ballistic Missile (ABM) Treaty with the then-Soviet Union. It prohibits the United States from deploying an effective defense against strategic or intercontinental ballistic missiles. An unexpected result of the U.S. arms control establishment's dogged observance of the ABM Treaty has been the limiting of defenses against shorter-range or theater ballistic missiles as well. The ABM Treaty was not intended to cover those weapons. A consequence of this expanded version of the treaty is that U.S. forces are more vulnerable to the proliferation of advanced theater ballistic missiles among rogue regimes like Iran, Iraq, Libya, and North Korea. The possibility exists that these regimes also may possess or be developing chemical, nuclear, or biological weapons with which to arm their missiles.

During the Persian Gulf War, the largest single loss of American lives occurred when an Iraqi Scud missile fell on a barracks in Dharan, Saudi Arabia, killing 28 Army Reservists from Pennsylvania. The only defense against Saddam Hussein's Scud missiles was the Patriot PAC2 system. The Patriot, originally designed as an anti-aircraft missile, had been upgraded to give it a limited anti-missile capability. But during the period of the Patriot missile's development and improvement, its anti-missile capability had been deliberately restrained in order not to approach the capabilities that would violate the ABM Treaty. For this reason, the Patriot PAC2 was only minimally capable against Iraq's Scud missile attacks.

In the Dharan incident, the Patriot battery never engaged the Scud missile that struck the Army barracks. The data from U.S. satellites, which detected the Scud launches in Iraq, were not sent directly to the Patriot batteries in Saudi Arabia (and Israel) to warn them of an impending missile attack. Instead, the data were transmitted back to U.S. Space Command in Colorado and then retransmitted to the Patriot batteries in the region. This process ate up precious warning and preparation time. In the tragedy, the missile launch warning and tracking data never reached the Patriot battery in time, and it did not engage the fatal Scud. The logical question is why the launch warning and tracking data were not sent directly to the Patriot batteries in the theater, giving them maximum time in which to engage the incoming missiles. One reason is technical, but another is political—to send the satellite data directly to the Patriot batteries would have raised the specter of an ABM Treaty violation.

Lesson #7: The post–Cold War mindset of complacency is a major impediment to the effectiveness of the armed forces. A complacent mindset exists both among officials charged with responsibility for national security and among the American people at large. One embodiment of this complacency is the fallacy of the "steady state," which assumes that trends and developments are constant, that things will always remain as they are now. In other words, this mindset projects today's conditions upon tomorrow and assumes that because the United States is strong today and there is no major threat facing the nation now, it will always be so. It is the mindset of those who support the status quo.

Another form of complacency arises from the belief that "things take care of themselves." Americans assume that their elected leaders and the military services are doing their job of protecting the nation. Unfortunately, things do not just take care of themselves even in the best of circumstances, and especially not in today's political culture, which has spawned a generation of "leaders" unprecedented for their bad judgment, lack of understanding, and outright neglect of vital national security matters. A proper study of military history shows that complacency almost always precedes military disaster. Today, the mindset of complacency in the United States is stronger than the historical perspective that has forestalled military defeat or disaster in the past.

The issue of complacency and a willing blindness to the country's vulnerability is not an abstraction. It has a practical consequence in that it gets Americans killed. The most recent example is the truck-bombing of a U.S. Air Force barracks at Al Khobar in Dharan, Saudi Arabia, in July 1996. There is absolutely no excuse for this tragedy, especially because Muslim extremists had bombed a Saudi National Guard complex in Riyadh the previous November, killing five Americans. There was ample intelligence warning of another such attack. Yet incredibly, in the aftermath, the Pentagon responded with explanations that used complacency as a justification. "We just didn't take the threat seriously; we didn't anticipate such an attack," characterized Defense Secretary William Perry's testimony before Congress after the Dharan bombing episode, as if failure to anticipate was an excuse. That in itself is the essence of the failure.

In fairness, Secretary Perry was not as much to blame as the uniformed commanders on the scene. If they could not get the cooperation of the Saudi authorities or the U.S. Embassy team to implement the security measures they knew were necessary, then they should have complained incessantly instead of supinely acquiescing. To date, no one has paid for this lapse of leadership. It sends a very disheartening message to the rest of the officer corps: complacency and a "blind eye" no longer are grounds for disciplinary action in the military, even if they result in people dying unnecessarily.

Lesson #8: A crisis of culture is undermining the effectiveness of the armed forces. There is a growing gulf between the nation's ruling elites and the average American. A culture war is being played out in every institution, and the military is by no means immune. The impact of the crisis of culture on U.S. fighting forces has several destructive dimensions, not the least of which is a lack of self-discipline at odds with the demands of combat. Another is that personal feelings have become the only validation of truth and the determinant of what one should do in a given situation. Normally, a military institution with a sound martial ethos can overcome this crisis of culture. The first thing military forces should do is to transform unwarlike civilians into warriors. Some of the best armies in history have been built out of undisciplined human material, which regimental pride, military customs and courtesies, and inspiring leadership turned into effective fighting men.

The ability of the U.S. military to transform civilians into soldiers, however, is being blocked or thwarted by a trend Robert Bork, in *Slouching Towards Gomorrah*, calls "radical individualism" and by a radical social agenda to which liberals are willing to subordinate the nation's security. These radical "deconstructionists" are attracted to the military as a vehicle for their cultural revolution precisely because it is a command hierarchy unique in American society. Policies adopted by those at the pinnacle, such as opening the services to openly practicing homosexuals or putting women in ground combat units, can be imposed down the chain of command by the disciplinary or coercive nature of the institution. And because the American people as a whole have a high esteem for their armed forces, the military's imprimatur can confer a kind of broad cultural legitimacy on the deconstructionist agenda.

Lesson #9: War is still a dirty and bloody affair that places great demands on today's soldier, sailor, airman, and Marine. The demands on today's warrior are at least as great as they were in the past, when battles and campaigns were more protracted and perhaps bloodier, and when the soldier had few of the aids and comforts of modern medicine or battlefield technology. Today's warrior has to be highly intelligent to master and control complex weapons. He has to have initiative, to be a bold and clear thinker as well as tough and brave. In fact, modern warfare is all the more difficult for an intelligent man because he knows the massive lethality of today's weapons and the horrors of chemical-biological warfare.

Although policymakers should support the military-technical revolution, they also must appreciate the dangers in relying too heavily on high technology. Congress must not allow the Pentagon to forget that the battlefield, even the supposed high-tech modern battlefield, is a unique and alien land with logic, rules, and values all its own. Brute strength and sheer guts are still important. In the Falkland Islands War, British paratroopers carried as much as 80 pounds on their backs on the long trek to the battle at Goose Green. In the Persian Gulf War, in addition to a seven- or eight-pound weapon, troops carried combat harnesses and rucksacks with extra ammo, fragmentation grenades, smoke grenades, anti-personnel mine, gas mask, extra clothing and personal items, rations, extra link-belt ammo for the machine gun crew, and spare mortar rounds.

In hot climates, the heaviest of all items is also the most necessary — two or three canteens of water. In addition to these, a radio operator carries a 10-pound radio set and a machine gunner carries a 20-pound M–60 machine gun. A tanker may have to change a thrown track while standing knee deep in mud, wrestling with heavy, unwieldy steel links, or he may have to drag his wounded gunner or loader through the narrow hatch of a burning tank. Anyone who says that modern warfare is an antiseptic, impersonal, push-button affair that no longer demands the traditional martial virtues either is ignorant or is pursuing a deconstructionist political agenda.

STRATEGIES FOR MAINTAINING AN EFFECTIVE MILITARY

To maintain a combat-effective military in a budget straitjacket, Congress and other policymakers must focus on three broad principal objectives: to preserve the integrity and military character of the armed forces, to protect the forces from likely threats, and to provide the forces with the weapons and equipment they need to prevail in all likely conflicts of the future.

Preserving the Integrity of the Forces

In the national security community, the debate on defending the nation is focused almost entirely on the material dimension of the equation—how much to spend on the defense budget, what force levels are needed, and what new equipment and new weapons are needed to replace obsolescing systems. It is self-evident that no nation can prevail in war without adequate means—its troops, weapons, and supplies. Ultimately, however, the most decisive dimension in warfare is not the material, but the moral. The great captains and skilled practitioners of the military arts have always recognized that "in war the moral is to the material as three is to one," as Napoleon Bonaparte said in *Maxims of War*. In 1941, General George C. Marshall called this moral dimension "morale":

> Morale is a state of mind. It is steadfastness and courage and hope. It is confidence and zeal and loyalty. It is *élan*, *esprit de corps*, and determination. It is staying power, the spirit which endures to the end—the will to win. With it all things are possible. Without it everything else, planning, preparation, production, count for naught.[1]

Today's military institution is facing an unprecedented attack from radicals and social revolutionaries, and often has been let down by its own

---

1 General George C. Marshall, in an address at Trinity College, Connecticut, June 15, 1941.

STRATEGIES FOR
MAINTAINING AN EFFECTIVE MILITARY

- An aggressive legislative campaign must be conducted, accompanied by a powerful public information campaign, to preserve the integrity of the armed forces.

- Congress must end the misuse of the armed forces.

- A new congressional commission on national security should be used to implement needed military reforms.

- Congress should squeeze more savings out of the Department of Defense budget, especially in Pentagon overhead and infrastructure, during the budget oversight and appropriation process.

- Congress should commit budget resources to maintaining the technology base and investing in high-technology advances.

- Congress should act to "end arms control as we know it," starting with the 1972 ABM Treaty.

- Advocates of a strong national defense should organize a series of task forces or caucuses, and should include all supporting players and allies.

- Advocates of a strong national defense should cultivate better information sources inside the Pentagon and the armed services.

- Pro-defense coalitions in Congress should cooperate with news and opinion media outlets, never forgetting the value of positive—or at least accurate—media coverage.

- Congress must be more vigilant in exercising oversight and accountability functions.

- Congress must remember that "personnel are policy" and work to place reliable proponents of a strong national defense in key defense policy positions.

- Defense supporters should not fear the veto.

leaders when confronted with an aggressive deconstructionist agenda. Policymakers must act effectively in the moral dimension to preserve the martial character and integrity of the military institution and the moral elements of combat power; they must end misuse of the services in peace operations and efforts to convert the military into a constabulary or social service institution.

History is full of examples of ostensibly well-armed and competent military forces suffering calamitous defeat at the hands of an enemy no better armed or even more poorly prepared in a purely material sense. Congress must not allow the U.S. military to become morally and spiritually hollow. The deconstructionist agenda is having a seriously negative impact on recruiting and retaining qualified personnel in uniform. The best people, those with a sense of honor and purpose and high calling, are being driven out in a subtle and little-noticed process. For example, 45 percent of highly qualified Naval aviators in the mid-range of the officer ranks currently are leaving the service, compared with a normal attrition rate of about 25 percent. This exodus, largely a reaction to the "witch hunt" that followed the Tailhook scandal, must be addressed and reversed.

Combat is the ultimate purpose, the end for which the armed forces exist. All the military's subordinate activities, and all its institutional policies related to personnel, discipline, and promotion, must support the combat mission. This subtle erosion of the warrior ethos must be addressed by policymakers. Congress must institute policies and procedures to reward military leaders who exhibit that spark of initiative that always has characterized the U.S. military.

Ensuring the Safety of the Forces

Congress must ensure that U.S. armed forces have the best protection possible against the threats most likely to result from the proliferation of advanced military technology. Effective battlefield intelligence and warning systems and missile defense systems are needed especially to counter ballistic missiles (possibly armed with nuclear, biological, or chemical warheads) and cruise missiles (both antiship and land-attack). U.S. air crews need protection from advanced or next-generation air defense systems. In addition to better ship-borne defenses against the sea-skimming cruise missiles, the crews of Navy ships need improved protection against naval mines and quiet diesel-electric submarines, especially those operating in noisy, crowded waters like the Persian Gulf.

The kind of protection needed is illustrated by the urgent request in December 1995 from General Gary Luck, commander of U.S. troops in South Korea, to the Pentagon to expedite development and deployment of THAAD, the Theater High Altitude Area Defense system, a follow-on to the Patriot missile defense. The lessons of the 1990–1991 Persian Gulf War were not lost on General Luck; the largest single American loss of life in that conflict came from an Iraqi Scud missile that got through the inadequate protection of the Patriot missile defense system. General Luck understood all too well that a future attack on his forces would be preceded by an all-out launch of North Korea's Scud arsenal, perhaps bearing weapons of mass destruction. Commendably, he wanted THAAD to protect his troops, because Patriot is not fully adequate for the task.

This seems like a perfectly reasonable request, because the Clinton Administration has professed from its first days in office that theater missile defense (TMD) is a top priority. In fact, the Clinton Administration's supposed commitment to theater defense, where the threat is real and present, has been a prime excuse for not pursuing defense of the U.S. homeland against longer-range ballistic missiles. But the Chairman of the Joint Chiefs of Staff, General John Shalikashvili, turned down General Luck's request to expedite THAAD. As a result, development of THAAD, which the Administration says is a top priority, proceeds at a routine, even languid, pace. Meanwhile, the Administration's arms control experts continue their assiduous efforts to limit THAAD's technical capabilities through negotiations with the Russians to expand the 1972 ABM Treaty to limit advanced TMD systems — which the Treaty was never intended to limit in the first place.

U.S. forces abroad also face the threat of terrorism, although for clarity's sake it ought not to be called terrorism. As demonstrated by the tragic truck-bombing at Dharan, Saudi Arabia, in July 1996, it is simply another form of low-intensity or guerrilla warfare against Americans, U.S. allies, and U.S. global interests by rogue states or hostile forces. In this case, it appears to have been the work of radical Muslims, perhaps supported by Iran's revolutionary Islamic regime, who want to drive U.S. forces out of Saudi Arabia and the Persian Gulf region. U.S. forces facing this kind of threat are entitled to better protection, or else they should be re-deployed out of harm's way.

Increasing the Fighting Capability of the Forces

Congress must empower the armed forces with modern, high-technology weapons and equipment to ensure that U.S. military personnel always have the qualitative advantage in combat, even if the size of the force has decreased sharply. This includes strategic lift so the troops can get quickly to where they are needed. Simply buying high-technology hardware, however, without regard to what the forces are being asked to do with it will not suffice. The needed technological empowerment and improvement of the forces must take place in the context of a sound military strategy.

Congress should require the Pentagon to shift defense posture and force planning from a traditional threat- and budget-driven strategy to one based on identifying vital national interests and acquiring the military capabilities needed to defend those interests. Then Congress should ensure that the capabilities inherent in the new technologies are employed with flexibility and adaptability. This will guarantee that U.S. forces are always capable of adjusting to new and unanticipated threats.

Such a strategy will emphasize systems that give the most leverage in combat—space platforms; command, control, and communications systems, including real-time battlefield surveillance, target acquisition, and intelligence; long-range strike platforms that can penetrate enemy air space, survive, and deliver ordnance (for example, additional B–2 bombers); and precision-guided munitions ranging from artillery rounds to cruise missiles. This strategy would connect ends and means, and provide guidance for Congress in allocating funds to procurement accounts in order to replace aging weapons.

To preserve the integrity of, ensure the safety of, and increase the fighting capabilities of the U.S. armed forces, Congress should employ the following initiatives and strategies to achieve these objectives.

STRATEGY #1
Congress must conduct an aggressive legislative campaign, accompanied by a powerful public information campaign, to preserve the integrity of the armed forces.

To roll back the destructive impact of the political correctness in the military that is undermining the unique character and ethos of the military, congressional champions of a strong national defense must sponsor legislative remedies which include the following elements:

- More effective use of the confirmation of Pentagon officials and uniformed officers. Confirmation hearings of senior officials usually are well-covered by the news media, and provide an excellent opportunity to demand the truth, illuminate problems, highlight issues, and extract commitments.

- More directed efforts to eliminate the Defense Advisory Commission on Women in the Service and similar boards and commissions; enforce penalties for lobbying Congress while in uniform and during duty hours unless formally assigned to legislative liaison duty; spotlight how much is being spent on non-readiness functions and social experimentation; and protect uniformed service members who speak truthfully about the harmful conditions caused by that agenda.

STRATEGY #2
Congress should end the misuse of the armed forces.

In particular, Congress needs to use its powers to block the deployment of forces overseas for non-traditional, constabulary, and peacekeeping missions. This effort should include educating the American people that commitments to areas like Somalia, Haiti, Rwanda, and Bosnia that are not of vital interest to national security impose unrealistic and self-defeating restraints on U.S. military readiness. They cause immense stress on the forces and family members, which hurts retention; cost billions of dollars; use up scarce capabilities and resources; dull the warfighting edge of the units deployed; and commit shrinking forces to peripheral missions which take them out of position for response in the event of a real crisis—without providing any national security benefit in return.

A valuable byproduct of this strategy would be the reassertion of the capacity of the United States to act when its interests are threatened. The notion that U.S. power must be legitimized through some international or multilateral entity like the United Nations before action can be taken is contrary to sound national policy. The Clinton policy of "assertive multilateralism" subordinates U.S. national interests to the United Nations and other supranational entities.

Restoring the military to its primary mission of waging war and ending the emphasis on non-traditional, non-combat missions will have two beneficial effects. First, it will reduce both the "wear and tear" on forces and equipment and the immense drain on the defense budget. Second, it will end the subtle alteration of the military from a warfighting institution into a constabulary or global welfare institution and reverse the growing confusion in the minds of the troops about their ultimate purpose, a confusion that saps their fighting edge. If the military is not at war, its mission in peacetime should be training and preparing for war.

The Constitution empowers Congress to cut off all funds for an unnecessary or unwise operation. In cases in which it is not consulted in sufficient advance of a deployment or when the President acts improperly, Congress should use its power of the purse to end funding, or stipulate by statute that the operation must end. A determined Commander in Chief might defy such congressional acts, but defiance carries heavy constitutional freight and political risk. A new war-powers legislative vehicle is not needed for Congress to act.

STRATEGY #3
A new congressional commission on national security should be used to implement needed military reforms.

The FY 1997 Defense Authorization Act, in fact, establishes such a commission, and advocates of a strong national defense in Congress must ensure it is staffed properly and used effectively. This bicameral, bipartisan commission should support Congress in its use of legislative powers to implement reforms instead of just recommending reforms to the executive branch. Its aims should include at least the following:

- **A new look at roles and missions.** In particular, the commission should consider establishing a new armed service—a U.S. Space Force. Space is becoming the decisive theater of modern warfare. Terrestrial forces are critically dependent on space platforms for successful ground, sea, and air operations. None of the existing services has the necessary organization or doctrine to operate effectively in space as a theater of conflict, or to ensure U.S. access to and dominance in space. The time is coming in which a new "space navy" will be needed to perform this vital role.

- **A new national security strategy.** The commission can formulate a new strategy and begin to implement it by legislation. A national strategy should look at options to maintain major overseas commitments (Asia, Europe) that may need to be ended or reduced either because of the actions of host nations or because of pressure of the defense budget. The commission should begin to ask how a large presence overseas can be replaced with less costly and less manpower-intensive missions. One possibility might be to replace large general-purpose combat forces with troops performing more specialized missions—for example, ballistic missile defense and extended air defense. This would still give the United States a politically and militarily significant presence without the burden of maintaining large forces.

Caution is necessary, however, in adopting this approach. Too prominent a pronouncement or too open a discussion about withdrawing U.S. forces and scaling back commitments might tempt a waiting aggressor to ignite the conflict the United States wants to avoid. One notable historical example of this is former Secretary of State Dean Acheson's statement that Korea lay outside the zone the United States was prepared to defend. This proved to be a direct contributing factor in North Korea's invasion of South Korea in June 1950.

In any case, Congress must act to end the mismatch between forces, budgets, and missions inherent in the Bottom-Up Review. The United States does not have adequate forces to fight two nearly simultaneous regional conflicts on the scale of the Persian Gulf War. And the defense budget is not sufficient to pay for its already inadequate forces. This is a prescription for disaster. In five to ten years, the United States might well face multiple, converging crises in which an aggressor in one part of the globe takes advantage of U.S. preoccupation in another (e.g., North Korea and the Persian Gulf). A harbinger is the most recent maneuver by Saddam Hussein into Kurdish areas in Northern Iraq in late August 1996. Once again, the Pentagon had to dispatch troops 6,000 miles from Fort Hood, Texas, while the nearest heavy combat forces were committed to Bosnia, sitting on their hands, while their combat skills and readiness atrophied.

A serious look at U.S. commitments, available forces, and the resources to support them cannot be put off too much longer. The military capabilities of the United States and its allies are diverging. With the exception of Japan, allies are downsizing and reducing capabilities even more drastically than the United States. At the same time, the United States is attempting—in fits and starts—to build a 21st century military force; and allied units in the North Atlantic Treaty Organization may not be interoperable with U.S. forces in another decade. A new compact with the allies is in order, encompassing a new "division of labor" that allows the United States to focus on providing its unique capabilities — for example, logistics, strategic lift, command and control, and air and missile defense—while the allies provide the manpower.

STRATEGY #4
Congress should squeeze more savings out of the Department of Defense budget, especially in Pentagon overhead and infrastructure, during the budget oversight and appropriation process.

One way to do this would be to increase the privatizing and outsourcing of administrative and support functions. Too much money from the Operations and Maintenance accounts goes to maintaining infrastructure, like routine housing maintenance, firefighting capabilities, financial accounting on military bases, as well as depot echelon maintenance, and a host of other administrative and support functions. Considerable savings could be realized by reducing overhead, with the money then applied to genuine needs like modernization of equipment. Some possible targets for congressionally mandated savings inside the defense budget include:

- **Privatizing and outsourcing** the administrative and logistical support of bases, infrastructure, and depot maintenance. Congress has mandated a 60/40 requirement for depot maintenance work. This ratio could be phased down to allow more work to be done by the private sector.

- **Reviewing** the Military Construction (MILCON) budget. Despite a 40 percent reduction in forces, the Pentagon is spending too much on military construction. One option would be a 25 percent to 33 percent across-the-board cut in MILCON, with the savings to be applied to recapitalize modernization accounts.

- **Eliminating** pork-barrel and non-defense items like breast cancer research and environmental cleanup of closed military bases. These may be desirable, even necessary, but should not be charged against the defense budget at the expense of combat readiness.

- **Mandating** continued acquisition reform, including more reliance on off-the-shelf technology and non-developmental items. Less cumbersome and shorter research and development and production cycles are needed. It takes on average 12 to 15 years to bring a new system from drawing board to the field. Much of the high cost of defense equipment results directly from the delays and bureaucratic red tape in the current acquisition process.

STRATEGY #5
Congress should commit budget resources to maintaining the technology base and investing in high-technology advances.

Congress should commit now to robust research and development efforts, and put enough money in future-year budgets for procurement of new systems. The focus must be on key technologies that provide the maximum battlefield leverage or protect the forces and critical battlefield capabilities, such as space platforms for surveillance, targeting, navigation, and communications; improved command and control systems; and precision-guided munitions. The technology emphasis should produce new test-bed units that experiment with emerging technologies in operational settings, learn to maximize their potential, and integrate them into the force. The effort also should include more realistic simulations for training personnel. Now, in a period of relative calm, is the time to allocate substantial new funds to modernization of the forces and to rebuild long-term combat capabilities.

STRATEGY #6
Congress should act to end arms control "as we know it," starting with the 1972 ABM Treaty.

The ABM Treaty is blocking the protection of U.S. forces deployed abroad and U.S. allies from advanced theater ballistic missiles. Other arms control measures, including the Chemical Weapons Convention, the Comprehensive Test Ban Treaty, and the proposed Land Mine Ban, are unverifiable and unenforceable, and would leave U.S. forces vulnerable to increasing threats.

Advocates of a strong national defense should portray arms control "as we know it" as the mentality of welfare-statism writ large and applied to foreign policy. Arms control has the same effect on a national scale as welfare does locally and individually. It kills responsibility and initiative by attempting to make others—in this case the United Nations or multilateral entities or treaty partners—responsible for U.S. security, not Americans themselves. In so doing, it undermines the sovereignty of the nation, just as welfare does to families. It leaves the United States defenseless and U.S. troops in danger in the same way welfare leaves families and individuals demoralized, weakened, and in a state of permanent dependency and near-poverty.

The Senate in particular must reassert its proper constitutional role in consenting to the ratification of treaties, a function that embodies the principle of checks and balances. Senators act as fiduciary agents for the American people to protect them from harmful agreements that might leave them vulnerable or intrude on their freedoms (or both). They have a solemn moral as well as political obligation not to rubber-stamp treaties or merely give them a cursory review. They are duty bound to study, analyze, and subject the claims of the arms control establishment to close scrutiny, and make sure the treaty truly serves the interests of the United States and the American people, not just the narrow interests of the arms control elites. Congress can legislatively nullify treaties that deprive U.S. forces of the protection they need, starting with the 1972 ABM Treaty, the nation's biggest obstacle to developing and deploying the most effective missile defenses.

The Constitution establishes treaties duly ratified as part of the "Supreme Law of the Land." Consequently, many in Congress are intimidated unnecessarily by the prospects of taking on the ABM Treaty. But the Supreme Law of the Land consists of the U.S. Constitution, "laws of the United States which shall be made in pursuance thereof," and then "all Treaties... which shall be made under the Authority of the United States," *in that order*. In other words, treaties are not supreme over statute law, and they are subordinate to the requirements of the Constitution itself. Treaties, like the Constitution and other federal laws, are subject to change or amendment. They are not permanently unalterable like the laws of the Medes and the Persians. It is a settled matter of law that Congress may overturn the ABM Treaty by a simple statute declaring it null and void.

To aid in this effort, advocates of a strong national defense must demonstrate to Congress and to the "deficit hawks" the high costs of compliance with outmoded treaties like the ABM Treaty. A cost-benefit analysis shows that the old Cold War paradigm of arms control is folly, both in terms of security and in terms of economy. In reality, the American way of arms control means that only U.S. arms are controlled, leaving the United States and its forces overseas defenseless and exposed to emerging threats without buying anything in return in the way of security. But it does buy jobs and status for the arms control elite—in ACDA, the State Department, and the Pentagon Office of Compliance, and among the various general counsels' shops in both Departments, from which swarms of lawyers emerge to justify their existence by telling weapons program managers why they cannot take advantage of superior U.S. technology to defend the nation and its troops overseas.

But these parasites cost the taxpayers many millions to house and sustain. Ending arms control, like rolling back the radical social agenda in the military services, has the added benefit of costing nothing but in fact saving millions.

STRATEGY #7
Advocates of a strong national defense in Congress should organize themselves into a series of task forces or caucuses, and should include all supporting players and allies.

Caucuses do not cost much, and they give an official or semi-official standing to the participants, a bully pulpit of sorts, and a structure to bring the news media, private policy groups, and defense industry representatives together with Members of Congress in a synergistic effort to work on the key issues.

STRATEGY #8
Congressional defense champions need to cultivate better information sources inside the Pentagon and the armed services.

These are key allies and can provide essential "combat intelligence" on decisions, policies, and trends that negatively affect the services. Conservatives on Capitol Hill and elsewhere cannot act effectively without good information on what is happening. In fact, sometimes merely exposing a destructive trend or decision is enough to prevent it from happening. Conservatives also need to learn how to practice "security"—how to protect their sources, using the information delivered in such a way that it does not expose the source to political retribution.

STRATEGY #9
Pro-defense coalitions in Congress must cooperate with news and opinion media outlets, never forgetting the value of positive—or at least accurate—media coverage.

It is not enough to decry the prevailing liberal bias in the mainstream media; advocates of a strong national defense must develop their own effective media channels to cover defense issues. News reporting is like artillery support: it softens up the target and keeps the enemy hunkered down in foxholes. Defense advocates must do a better job of cultivating honest reporters willing to cover national security subjects properly. A notable example is the work of a few conservative reporters to expose the Clinton Administration's dishonest and surreptitious attempts to broaden the ABM Treaty to "capture" the most promising new theater defense technologies. By covering this dangerous effort adequately, these reporters gave pro-defense leaders in Congress the information they needed to act effectively. Such reporting helped the cause of ballistic missile defense more than any other single effort by exposing facts that otherwise might not have been revealed.

STRATEGY #10
In using the tools at its disposal, Congress must become more vigilant in exercising its oversight and accountability function.

The Senate must not confirm senior officers who do not uphold what is best for the armed forces and the nation. It is not enough to defer to the President's nominations when the President is actively engaged in undermining the military. In that circumstance, deferring to the President is a failure by Congress to carry its constitutional responsibility to maintain the armed forces. If the Senate proves reluctant to act in this manner, other elements in the strong-defense community must inform, then appeal, then cajole, then criticize, and finally, if necessary, condemn.

STRATEGY #11
Congress must remember that "personnel are policy" and work to place reliable proponents of a strong national defense in key defense policy positions.

Proponents of a strong national defense on Capitol Hill as well as in the private sector need to develop a concerted plan to identify crucial defense policymaking positions in both the executive branch and Congress, especially the professional staff of congressional defense committees, and place conservatives in those positions. These include the House National Security Committee, Senate Armed Services Committee, House Defense Appropriations Subcommittee, Senate Defense Appropriations Subcommittee, and House and Senate Select Committees on Intelligence.

STRATEGY #12
Defense supporters should not fear the veto.

Proponents of a strong national defense on Capitol Hill must learn how to portray a presidential veto in its proper light and turn it to political advantage. President Clinton vetoed the FY 1996 defense authorization bill, which would have provided more funds to maintain U.S. technological superiority, given a pay raise and housing allowance increase for military personnel (including those deployed to Bosnia), and mandated the defense of the U.S. homeland against ballistic missiles. The veto was upheld by a narrow margin, and Congress weakened the missile defense provisions of the bill in order to get it enacted into law. Congress should not allow the short-term legislative agenda to overshadow the more important long-term agenda of restoring the nation's security.

CONCLUSION
Backers of a strong national defense in Congress should remember some basic operational principles that do not constitute a strategy in themselves but do undergird a sound approach to implementing a strategy for rebuilding U.S. defense capabilities. The most important principle is that courage is decisive. The Greek Heraclitus said courage is the ladder on which all other virtues mount. Without it, nothing much can be accomplished. Courage is needed to take on established interests, to weather a storm of criticism or ridicule from the media, and to face down

enraged officials fighting to protect their jobs. Those engaged in policy battles must show moral courage worthy of the valor that American soldiers, sailors, Marines, and airmen show when they are called forth to serve in combat, as they surely will be again.

The second principle necessary to a strong national defense is the presence of inspired, and inspiring, leadership. The nation needs its own Winston Churchill for these "wilderness years," and if it is lucky enough to see one emerging in the embattled halls of Congress, he (or she) needs support and encouragement, not criticism when things do not go exactly the way they would like.

Third, policymakers must stress the importance of clear, honest language. Those who do not support a strong national defense pervert the language because it allows them to distort reality and escape the political retribution that inevitably would follow if they were honest about their goals.

Finally, policymakers should remember that war is a dirty, brutal, ugly, and dehumanizing experience. It exacts a terrible price from all who engage in it. Whether mentally or physically, no one emerges from the crucible of combat unscathed. Conservatives should neither glorify it nor glory in it, but they should understand and help others understand that some things are worse than war. A world ruled by a Hitler or a Stalin or a Saddam Hussein is definitely worse.

The policy objectives proposed herein are simple, but as Clausewitz said in *On War*, what is simple is also very difficult. There will be the inevitable resistance from those who support the status quo. There will also be the usual "fog of war," the confusion and uncertainty that accompany major human endeavors involving large numbers of people. If Members of Congress understand they are engaged in a kind of benign policy battle against the status quo and act accordingly, they will derive a tremendous psychological and intellectual advantage. But policy battles, like combat, require courage. Even though life is not at risk, there are potential losses of reputations and livelihoods for the key players, for example.

Policymakers on Capitol Hill who support defense must learn to think more like military strategists. The misjudgments, missed opportunities, and follies of the Clinton Administration's foreign and defense policies over the past four years have seriously weakened U.S. influence and credibility abroad. Unless Congress and its concerned allies can become more effective, the Clinton failures will lead inevitably to the decline of the United States as a great power, without the means or the will to defend its values and interests.

For the United States, the choice is either to lead or be led. The first choice leads to freedom, security, and greatness; the second, to weakness and submission. For its own well-being, and for that of the entire world, the credibility of the United States as a global power must be restored. Without the credibility that comes from a strong military force, the United States will be reduced to making empty warnings and impotent demarches in times of crisis. Forfeiting national credibility—and moral authority—means possibly having to resort to force when credibility and an image of steadfast resolve could have prevented conflict. But when that moment of crisis comes, the United States may find itself without a military force able to meet the demands of conflict. If the Administration cannot or will not provide this leadership, then Congress, with the active aid of a defense policy community that wants to make America strong again, must hold it publicly and politically accountable. Then, insofar as the Constitution and good public policy allow, they must step into the leadership void to safeguard U.S. national security.

Chapter 15

PLANNING A COHERENT MILITARY STRATEGY

John Hillen

In 1997, the Department of Defense will once again initiate its Quadrennial Defense Review (QDR). In addition, an independent panel mandated by Congress will review American military strategy and defense posture in the post-Cold War world. However, without guidance from the Administration about America's role in global security and a prioritization of its national objectives, it is inevitable that these evaluations of American strategy and force structure will be flawed. The vacuum left by the lack of a coherent explanation of national purpose and strategic direction will be filled with "business as usual" by Department of Defense planners and the military services. The service and joint planners involved in the QDR will continue to use the faulty Bottom-Up Review (BUR) assumptions of the last strategic review. Building a coherent military strategy demands a rigorous policy process that must start at the top, lest other influences at the bottom place the whole process on autopilot and reverse-engineer an American military strategy that does not coherently match means to ends and protect American interests worldwide.

Having a coherent sense of national purpose and strategic direction is critical in crafting effective military policy because such a focus will guide policymakers in determining where, when, why, and how United States military force will be used. In the absence of such policies, both the U.S. and

The author wishes to thank Dr. Dov Zakheim, Dr. Richard Haass, Peter Rodman, and Colonel Harry Summers for their suggestions and contributions to this chapter. The views and opinions expressed, however, are solely the responsibility of the author.

the rest of the world are uncertain about America's security role in the world. Is the U.S. the global policeman or the global firefighter? Will the U.S. military be the vanguard for democracy and human rights, or will it respond only when American interests are directly threatened? Because these questions have remained largely unanswered in the Clinton Administration, brushfires like Bosnia smolder and burn while the international community argues over who should address the problem and how.

More important, ambiguity about America's global role or doubts about the credibility of American military strategy can invite aggression — as happened in Korea in 1950 and Kuwait in 1990. A clear and coherent U.S. military strategy is therefore essential. Such strategic clarity lets the world know what can be expected of U.S. military forces and why. It underpins American credibility in the world and deters potential adversaries. And it encourages U.S. allies or international organizations to address local security challenges in areas that the U.S. does not consider strategically significant.

An examination of America's record in military strategy over the last 50 years shows great successes and great failures. The damage done over the past five years by the lack of a coherent military strategy is obvious. The strategies and approaches taken by various Presidents throughout those years greatly determined these successes and failures. Studying these lessons can help a new Administration, backed by a supportive Congress, create the vital, coherent military strategy the U.S. needs to fulfill its role as leader.

Changing Objectives. Containing the power of the Soviet Union and its client states summarized the U.S. national security strategy for the 40 years leading up to the fall of the Iron Curtain in November 1989. Although the exact goals and methods differed from administration to administration, U.S. military strategy stayed fairly constant. More important, throughout most of the Cold War, devising military strategy was a coherent exercise, with planning conducted from the top down and national goals matched to the means and methods the armed forces would use to advance those goals. National objectives were identified, the roles the U.S. and its allies would play were clearly articulated, and the military means were allocated accordingly. Naturally, this process was not without much partisan acrimony, especially over the amount of military means, which ranged from President Carter's hollow military to President Reagan's rearmament and modernization program. In general, however, the national purpose and strategic direction of the United States were matters of bipartisan consensus.

Conversely, since the end of the Cold War, neither President George Bush nor President Bill Clinton articulated a similarly comprehensive strategic purpose for the United States. Both Administrations failed to answer the questions on which U.S. strategy is grounded: What is the nature of the post-Cold War world? What is the role of the U.S. in that world? and What goals should the U.S. pursue in filling that role? Because they failed to answer those questions, the Bush and Clinton Administrations foundered in their attempts to integrate a complex set of economic, political, diplomatic, humanitarian, and military goals into one comprehensive foreign policy. Furthermore, because those fundamental questions remained unanswered, U.S. military strategy was left to search for its own rationale from the bottom up instead of from the top down. In the absence of clear guidance from the Chief Executive on down about America's national objectives and the U.S. role in global security affairs, American military strategy has been incoherent, hampered by a dangerous gap between ends and means that is likely to worsen over the next five years.

President Bush's call for the defense of a "New World Order" and President Clinton's stated "National Security Strategy of Engagement and Enlargement" turned out to be little more than academic abstractions and rhetorical rallying cries. The New World Order idea seemed to imply that a U.S.-led coalition like that assembled in the Persian Gulf War of 1991 would respond to almost any breach of international peace and security in the post-Cold War world. Engagement and Enlargement also seemed to offer false promises about the extent to which the U.S. would intervene to spread the gospel of democracy and economic freedom. Instead of offering clear policy guidance about America's military role in the world, these broad philosophies let everyone see in them what they would.

Such "strategies" are little help to the military policymaker who must have a definitive sense of national purpose in order to determine the goals that serve that stated purpose. Furthermore, this sense of purpose and the relative importance of its many supporting goals are critical to helping the policymaker allocate national resources and identify methods to be used in pursuit of those goals. A clear enunciation of America's role in global security efforts is needed to help define the roles of its allies and even organizations such as the United Nations or the Organization for Security and Cooperation in Europe. Without this critical first step, all the other processes that go into making strategy — matching ends to means — are disconnected and incoherent.

An Incoherent Strategy. A top-down strategy is one that identifies specific goals, prioritizes them according to their relative importance to national security interests, and then matches the military means to these ends. The current U.S. military strategy, however, is one based on a process known as the Bottom-Up Review. The BUR was initiated by the Clinton Administration in March 1993 as a comprehensive review of the nation's defense strategy and military force structure. However, the BUR attempted to answer questions about what American forces should look like without first answering questions about what they should be used for and how. In the absence of such clear policy guidance about the U.S. role in global security, the BUR assumed that U.S. strategy should focus on the ability to fight two nearly simultaneous regional conflicts. In the meantime, President Clinton had far different ideas about the use of military force and what his Administration was willing to spend on defense.

Thus, while the Department of Defense centered its 1993–1998 planning on being able to re-fight the Korean War and the Gulf War at almost the same time, the Administration was ambiguous about its strategic goals and parsimonious over the defense budgets it was prepared to support. This disconnect laid the groundwork for a damaging gap between ends and means. In his 1994 assessment of the BUR, analyst Andrew Krepinevich wrote that the report's conclusions were "critically handicapped by the Administration's failure thus far to enunciate a clear national security strategy that defines the American military's role in the post-Cold War era."[1] Because of this failure, "the plan offers insurance we probably do not need, at a cost the Clinton defense budget likely cannot afford. Equally disturbing, it may not insure us against the security challenges that we are most likely to face beyond the five-year coverage period."[2]

An incoherent strategy planned from the bottom up has several deleterious consequences. First, because it does not specify goals or

---

1 Andrew Krepinevich, Jr., *The Bottom Up Review: An Assessment* (Washington, D.C.: Defense Budget Project, 1994), p. ii.

2 Andrew Krepinevich, Jr., "Assessing the Bottom-Up Review," *Joint Forces Quarterly*, No. 3 (Winter 1993-1994), p. 23.

priorities, it makes no distinctions about where American military forces should be used and why. As a consequence, the Clinton Administration has used U.S. military forces recklessly, wasting the military on interventions in peripheral conflicts that promise few tangible benefits in return for the sacrifices incurred. Second, this failure to have a disciplined approach to the use of military force has expanded military commitments during a stressful time of downsizing and budget cutting in the armed forces. This dual action has opened up a wide gap between the ends and means of U.S. military strategy, a gap the military is severely strained in trying to close. Third, the long-term effects of this misuse of the military make it difficult for the U.S. to invest in the training and equipment necessary to undertake the more important tasks of international peace and security, both now and in the future. Finally, such an incoherent policy cannot long be supported by the Congress and the American people, especially if they are marginalized in the decisions over American strategy. An imperial President acting without congressional or public support only further undermines American military credibility abroad.

LESSONS LEARNED

When policymakers act without goals and priorities, they have no criteria for deciding when to use military force. Consequently, they have no methodology for addressing the complex set of issues that surround the political and military questions involved in strategic and military policy. In circumstances where the U.S. is not under attack, or required by treaty or law to react militarily to aggression overseas, any number of fleeting political or media pressures can unduly influence ad hoc military decisions.

Instinct, shaped by political and media pressure, is not a reliable guide when deciding where, when, and how a superpower uses military force. President Bush's instincts about the nature of security threats and the ability of the U.S. military to effect change were proven right in the Persian Gulf but wrong in Somalia. President Clinton's instincts about when to use military force have resulted in a series of expensive, strategically insignificant, and easily reversible military interventions in areas of only marginal importance to U.S. security interests. Failed or inconsequential interventions in Somalia, Haiti, and Bosnia have prompted critics to deride this focus on the periphery of the international arena and to characterize the

---

LESSONS LEARNED

- Failure to develop a top-down strategy with clear criteria for military intervention results in squandering American prestige and military resources on expensive operations that offer little in return.

- U.S. forces are not being given the military goals and operational freedom needed to accomplish anything of consequence in military interventions.

- The ends-means gap in U.S. military strategy seriously undermines U.S. credibility, invites aggression from adversaries, causes confusion among allies, and greatly strains the armed forces attempting to make up this gap.

- The failure to plan for critical security challenges means the United States has mortgaged its preparedness for truly consequential threats to focus on near-term peripheral problems.

- The failure to act with the consent of Congress and the American public has made U.S. credibility abroad paper-thin and U.S. troops more vulnerable.

Clinton national security strategy as "an instinct for the capillary"[3] or "foreign policy as social work."[4]

Lesson #1: Squandering American prestige and military resources on expensive operations that offer little in return is the direct result of a failure to develop a top-down strategy with clear criteria for military intervention. A top-down strategy can act as a guide for policymakers in determining when to use military force. As required by law, the President submits a yearly National Security Strategy (NSS), a document that should clearly lay out the Administration's national security objectives. President Clinton's strategy is entitled "A National Security Strategy of Engagement and Enlargement." While the Clinton Administration

---

3 Jonathan Clarke, "Instinct for the Capillary: The Clinton Administration's Foreign Policy 'Successes'," Cato Institute *Foreign Policy Briefing Paper* No. 40, April 5, 1996.

4 Michael Mandelbaum, "Foreign Policy as Social Work," *Foreign Affairs*, Vol. 75, No. 1 (January/February 1996), pp. 16-32.

strategy does address the question of when and how to employ U.S. military forces, it does so without priorities and with criteria and terms that could be interpreted any way at all.

For instance, instead of outlining some tangible and measurable way of ensuring public and congressional support, the National Security Strategy merely states that having a "reasonable likelihood of support from the American people and their elected representatives" will be considered during the decisionmaking process. "Reasonable" must be solely in the eye of the beholder, as fewer than 40 percent of the American people and an even smaller percentage of Members of Congress supported the President's Bosnia intervention initiative.

President Clinton's failure to specify clearly when he would use military force and what he would use it for was highlighted once again on March 6, 1996. Three years into this Administration, National Security Advisor Anthony Lake gave a landmark speech to define President Clinton's new security policy. Despite the fact that the President already had initiated three large and controversial military interventions in 1993–1995 and had no more planned, Lake said that March 1996 "was a good time for this discussion."[5] To further the hypocrisy, however, this ex post facto doctrine for the use of military force was even more vague and ambiguous than the National Security Strategy. In place of constructive policy guidance that would give some indication of how the Administration might make the tough calls, Lake offered up seven broad circumstances that "may call for the use of force or our military forces." Among them: "to counter aggression," "to preserve, promote, and defend democracy," "to maintain U.S. reliability," and "for humanitarian purposes." Such platitudes, however, could never serve to provide guidance for a competent military policy that clearly identifies U.S. interests and objectives while matching those ends to military means and methods. For instance, stating that the U.S. will use force "to counter aggression" is strategically meaningless. It suggests that aggression anywhere, large or small, may require the use of U.S. military force.

5 Anthony Lake, "Defining Missions, Setting Deadlines: Meeting New Security Challenges in the Post-Cold War World," speech at George Washington University, The White House, Office of the Press Secretary, March 6, 1996.

Indiscriminate criteria such as these have provided no constructive guidance for President Clinton in deciding when American military force is most needed and where it is most effective. Ironically, the most successful Administration exercise in this field has been in formulating a fairly competent policy for deciding when to be involved in peace operations. In contrast to President Clinton's early doctrine of "assertive multilateralism," the 1994 Presidential Decision Directive 25 (PDD-25) laid down sensible criteria for the U.S. to consider before launching any multilateral peacekeeping or peace enforcement operation. Following solidly in the tradition of prudence and caution started by Caspar Weinberger, this document listed eight criteria for the U.S. to consider when deciding to support a peace operation, six further restrictions on U.S. participation should American troops be involved, and an additional three criteria for situations in which there was a strong possibility of combat.[6]

Unfortunately, the discerning criteria of PDD-25 often have been ignored (as in Haiti and Bosnia) and have not been reproduced to address a larger spectrum of military operations. The Clinton Administration has shown little desire to comply with the criteria, even when guidelines have been set. The most significant military operations undertaken by the Clinton Administration have been large and expensive multilateral peace operations with little payoff. In Somalia, Haiti, and Bosnia, military interventions have occurred in areas of peripheral importance to U.S. national security, in circumstances where U.S. military power is only marginally effective, and with results that are, as Michael Mandelbaum has argued, at best "provisional, fragile, and reversible."[7]

Lesson #2: U.S. forces are not being given the military goals and operational freedom needed to accomplish anything of consequence in military interventions. The interventions in Somalia, Haiti, and Bosnia lacked military goals that could provide lasting benefits to those countries. In the rare instances where criteria for measuring military success were clearly defined and attainable (such as feeding starving Somalis or manning the zone of separation in Bosnia), the outcome made

---

6 The White House, "The Clinton Administration's Policy on Reforming Multilateral Peace Operations," PDD-25, May 1994, pp. 4–5.

7 Mandelbaum, "Foreign Policy as Social Work," p. 21.

little or no difference to the political goal of the enterprise (such as creating a healed and whole Somalia or Bosnia). In most cases, unambiguous, decisive, and sustainable military objectives could not be defined, so the Administration's strategists substituted timelines, schedules, and deadlines for goals. By substituting time-driven strategy for event-driven strategy, the Administration chose short-term political gratification over competent military policy.

Instead of using American military force for clearly stated purposes with a value relative to the sacrifice entailed, the strategies of Somalia, Haiti, and Bosnia are centered on merely "being there." The withdrawal of American forces is determined by timelines and sharp withdrawal deadlines rather than missions accomplished and objectives achieved. By choosing exit dates over exit strategies, the Administration has chosen a method that guarantees American troops will be present for a stated amount of time, but not necessarily to do anything of consequence. Like virtual reality, this virtual strategy is superficial and delusive. The commitment of American forces must be accompanied by a rigorous assessment of what they mean to accomplish, whether it will make a difference, and whether it will be worth the costs incurred. The attempt to ameliorate this fundamental policy formula with deadlines and artificial timelines amounts to a gross misuse of American military power.

For a superpower, there is nothing to be gained from asking its forces to "be seen" in missions where they are hostage to the whimsy of capricious belligerents, neutrals, or mission partners. Unfortunately, this is the situation the U.S. military was forced to endure in Somalia, Haiti, and Bosnia. In all three missions, the prime determiners of success were not the U.S. military forces, but a combination of Somali warlords, reckless coalition partners, the unreliable command and control systems of the United Nations, suspect Haitian allies, and a nefarious mixture of ethnic chieftains in the Balkans. In each case, despite the tremendous resources available to the U.S. and the unmatched excellence of U.S. forces, the success of the mission was out of American hands.

This is an intolerable situation for a superpower. American forces should not be committed to military or quasi-military operations where they do not have the resources or operational freedom to produce the outcome of their choosing. By no means does this mean the U.S. must operate unilaterally in order to ensure this condition. The U.S. military will operate in multinational coalitions more often than not, but it should never abrogate the responsibility of ensuring that U.S. forces work toward clearly defined goals and with the means and methods to achieve them decisively.

Lesson #3: The ends-means gap in U.S. military strategy seriously undermines U.S. credibility, invites aggression from adversaries, causes confusion among allies, and greatly strains the armed forces attempting to make up this gap. The Clinton Administration's military strategy—the "two-MRC" concept—requires a force capable of fighting and winning two nearly simultaneous major regional conflicts (MRCs). Although the Administration maintains that the U.S. military is capable of carrying out this strategy, the great majority of defense planners, both in and out of uniform, disagree.[8] Compounding this strategic bankruptcy is a July 1994 estimate by the U.S. General Accounting Office that this too-small force is underfunded by some $150 billion over five years.[9] This has produced a double mismatch in America's current military strategy: a force too small to execute the national security strategy and a defense budget too small to fund that inadequate force. By the year 2002, the U.S. will have barely enough active duty forces to fight one regional conflict on the scale of the Persian Gulf War and one contingency operation on the scale of the Panamanian intervention of 1989.

The strain felt in the military as it attempts to make up this gap is examined in Chapter 12, "Defining the U.S. Role in Promoting Global Security." In general, the ends-means gap and the subsequent strain it imposes on the U.S. armed forces have many damaging side effects: Major combat training exercises are canceled; "gaps" appear regularly in the coverage provided by the shrinking Navy to key regions of the globe;

---

8   For instance, see Krepinevich, *The Bottom Up Review: An Assessment*; U.S. General Accounting Office, *Bottom Up Review: Analysis of Key DOD Assumptions*, January 1995; numerous reports from the Center for Strategic and International Studies and The Heritage Foundation; and the testimony of the Joint Chiefs quoted in Rowan Scarborough, "Pentagon Document Lets JCS Talk Frankly," *The Washington Times*, March 15, 1996.

9   See U.S. General Accounting Office, *Future Years Defense Program: Optimistic Estimates Lead to Billions in Overprogramming*, July 29, 1994, and Baker Spring, "Clinton's Defense Budget Falls Far Short Again," Heritage Foundation *Backgrounder Update* No. 242, March 7, 1995.

problems with divorce, quality of life, and re-enlistment are increasing; and money to recapitalize the armed forces for the future is down by some 70 percent since the Reagan years. Defense funding that should go to research, development, and the procurement of future weapon systems and equipment is being siphoned off to pay for current operations. In short, the U.S. military is robbing its future ability to protect vital interests for the near-term "benefits" of involvement in missions such as Somalia, Haiti, and Bosnia. The ends-means gap and the strain on the military steadily degrade the ability of the U.S. armed forces to succeed in more important conflicts, both now and in the future.

Lesson #4: The failure to plan for critical security challenges means the U.S. has mortgaged its preparedness for truly consequential threats by focusing on near-term peripheral problems. As a direct result of the failure to make calculations about national interests and set national priorities, the Clinton Administration has squandered American military power on peripheral ventures and undermined the ability of the U.S. to meet more important security commitments. For instance, the mission to Bosnia requires so many resources from the U.S. forces in Europe that it degrades the combat effectiveness of the North Atlantic Treaty Organization (NATO) as a warfighting alliance for two to three years.[10] In addition, spending billions of dollars in Bosnia and on other peacekeeping operations severely hampers the possibility of shifting funds for current operations to alleviate the crisis in the military procurement accounts. This situation is a direct refutation of the Administration's claimed recognition of the American military's paramount need for a warfighting capability that can deter and defeat armed aggression in areas of vital national interest.

The failure of the Administration to prioritize national security interests is acute, and is manifested in U.S. foreign policy as well as military strategy. The imbalance between core and peripheral interests is

---

10 This includes the time needed to retrain U.S. forces in Europe after they have redeployed from Bosnia. The GAO estimates that even small combat units returning from peacekeeping missions need up to six months of recovery time to train back up to warfighting standards. Larger units (such as divisions) need more. See U.S. General Accounting Office, *Peace Operations: Effect of Training, Equipment and Other Factors on Unit Capability*, GAO/NSIAD-96-14, October 1995, pp. 28-39.

reflected in the fact that the Secretary of State visited Damascus over 25 times between 1993 and mid-1996 while making only one (ultimately humbling) visit to Beijing. This not only displays a poor prioritization of interests, but also reflects a myopic focus on short-term political gain instead of preparedness for the future. History teaches military planners to have a unique perspective: They must focus on the most unexpected and consequential conflicts possible. The insurance provided by the U.S. military must be directed toward meeting those future contingencies through worst-case-scenario planning. The ability to wage a successful fight against major security threats in the future should not be undermined by the feel-good interventions of the present.

Lesson #5: The failure to act with the consent of Congress and the American public means that American credibility abroad is paper-thin and that U.S. troops are more vulnerable as a result. If Congress and the American public do not support a military commitment, the credibility of that commitment is greatly undermined. This was readily apparent in Somalia. When the disaster in Mogadishu exposed the strategic shortcomings of the intervention and the American people questioned whether such costs were commensurate with the value of the mission itself, Congress pulled the plug. Senator Robert Byrd (D-WV) led the successful effort to cut off funds for the mission and forced withdrawal within six months. In 1993, President Clinton had not bothered to consult Congress before convincing the U.N. to undertake a very ambitious mission in Somalia and committing thousands of U.S. troops to support that U.N. mission. The President and American troops therefore had no base of support when their fortunes soured in Somalia.

In contrast, President Bush worked assiduously for months to rally Congress and the American public behind Operations Desert Shield and Desert Storm. Even then, not a single member of the Democratic leadership in either the House or the Senate voted in favor of the Desert Storm resolution. However, by letting Congress decide on the merits of his plan, President Bush ensured that regardless of initial casualties, U.S. forces in the Persian Gulf would be able to prosecute the war with vigor and commitment, knowing the nation was behind them. Conversely, in Bosnia, despite drawn-out peace negotiations in the fall of 1995, President Clinton came to Congress only after American troops were on the ground, thereby forcing Members to forgo judgment on the Bosnian peace plan and giving them only the opportunity to vote in support of

U.S. troops already in Bosnia or on the way. This led to the nonsensical situation in which the House voted overwhelmingly to condemn the mission but support the troops and the Senate voted to stand by the troops but not endorse either the President's decision or the agreement reached in Dayton. U.S. forces must operate with a base of credibility and support, and that requires congressional and public support that is neither lukewarm nor equivocal.

Before the start of Desert Storm, with predictions of up to 20,000 U.S. casualties being cited regularly, over 80 percent of the American public still supported the action. In contrast, public support for the intervention in Bosnia peaked at 40 percent and hovered below that level during most of the debate.[11] If public support is that low, American troops are operating without an important base of national support. In the event the Bosnia mission took a turn for the worse, U.S. troops would be on their own, trying to rescue a mission that the American people do not support. It is fortunate for U.S. troops in Bosnia that no terrorist has figured out that the death of a few dozen GIs undoubtedly would cause public and congressional support for this already unpopular mission to collapse. The U.S. learned an important lesson in Vietnam: Do not commit the armed forces of the United States without the support of the nation. To do so undermines the troops and the mission, and threatens to create another Vietnam-like rift between the American people and their military.

STRATEGIES FOR CREATING A COHERENT MILITARY STRATEGY

Planning a coherent U.S. military strategy involves a top-down planning process, as outlined in Table 15.1. In general, the process involves:

- **Identifying** enduring national goals and principles;

- **Deriving and prioritizing** the national interests of the United States from the goals and principles identified;

---

11 See ABC News/Washington Post Poll in *The New York Times*, December 14, 1995, p. A1, and Wall Street Journal/NBC News Poll in *The Wall Street Journal*, December 8, 1995, p. 1.

STRATEGIES FOR
CREATING A COHERENT MILITARY STRATEGY

- The President should publish an NSC-68 for the post-Cold War world.

- The President should provide detailed and comprehensive guidance in the National Security Strategy.

- The Chairman of the Joint Chiefs of Staff should create a detailed and coherent National Military Strategy in support of the National Security Strategy.

- The Secretary of Defense should allocate military resources through the Defense Planning Guidance, which should be subject to congressional oversight.

- The President must seek congressional approval for the National Military Strategy and the use of force, and Congress must enforce its constitutional prerogatives.

- The President should work to keep the support of the American people.

- The President should publish a National Security Directive on the use of military force.

- The President should promote a new security compact in U.S. alliances.

- **Taking into account** threats to those interests, support from allies for those interests, and U.S. means of influence to develop specific national objectives to support these interests;

- **Deriving** a comprehensive National Security Strategy that identifies and integrates social, economic, political, diplomatic, and military objectives in support of national objectives;

- **Determining** force requirements and the strategies necessary to attain military objectives; and

- **Allocating** military resources to achieve those objectives in accordance with priority interests.

This policy process is manifested in a series of documents and policy statements from the White House, the National Security Council, and the

Department of Defense. In addition, Congress has an oversight role in maintaining the coherence of U.S. military strategy. When this process is complete, not only will the U.S. role in global security be clearly identified; it also will be supported by a coherent military strategy that has matched means to ends throughout the process. Moreover, by stressing the coherence of this military strategy, the U.S. can operate with credibility and determination abroad as allies and adversaries alike know that the U.S. always has the capability to undertake its stated national security objectives.

In its entirety, U.S. military strategy is a series of documents and operational plans published by the Chairman of the Joint Chiefs of Staff, the Secretary of Defense, and the warfighting commanders of the armed forces. However, as seen in Table 15.1, there are several steps that must be taken as a prerequisite to strategic planning. This must be done in consecutive stages, with each stage building on the work of the previous step.

Table 15.1

How to Plan a Coherent U.S. Military Strategy

Action	Documents	Influences
1. Analyze International Security Environment Identify U.S. Role in Global Security Identify & Prioritize American National Interests Identify & Prioritize National Objectives	"NSC-68" for the Post-Cold War World	Enduring American Goals and Principles Changing Global Circumstances and Trends
2. Identify & Prioritize Detailed Objectives - Political - Diplomatic - Social - Economic - Military Integrate Objectives into Comprehensive Strategy	The National Security Strategy	Means of American Influence - Diplomacy - Economic Power - Military Power Foreign Support and Opposition Allies' Interests and Capabilities Adversaries' Interests and Capabilities Other Regional Interests and Circumstances
3. Prioritize Military Objectives Identify Roles, Means, and Methods for Achieving Match Means to Ends	The National Military Strategy	Changing Security Requirements Trends in Military Affairs and Technology Threat Assessments
4. Allocate Defense Resources to Military Objectives Program for Future Requirements and Funding	The Defense Planning Guidance & Other Military Plans & Programming Documents	Force Requirements Defense Funding Other Constraints - Manpower - Materiel - Infrastructure - Industry

STRATEGY #1
The President should publish an NSC-68 for the post-Cold War world.

Presidential leadership is the key ingredient in instituting any comprehensive policy for the U.S. role in global security. While Congress and other executive departments are involved in foreign policy and military planning, the President sets the strategic direction. The President must state authoritatively what he thinks about the state of the world and America's role in that world. The first step in that process is an overarching yet definitive statement of America's national interests, its national objectives in pursuit of those interests, and how it plans to achieve these goals. This should be a comprehensive statement similar to the famous NSC-68 of 1950 which laid the basis for the Cold War strategy of containment. That document looked at enduring American goals and principles in the wake of World War II, as well as threats to those goals from the changing global circumstances of the postwar world, and then laid out both the interests that needed to be protected from Soviet expansionism and the objectives that should be pursued in defense of those interests.

An NSC-68 for the post-Cold War world must emphasize the unique U.S. role in global security. As the world's only superpower, the U.S. must focus its foreign policy definitively on managing relations with other great powers, deterring aggression in key regions around the globe, and protecting those global trading and economic systems that allow the U.S. to exist as a free and prosperous nation. Moreover, the document would prioritize these interests and America's many other interests worldwide. This would ensure that the U.S. has a sensible perspective on the relative importance of its national interests and national objectives. Lesser interests, such as regional stability, human rights, and environmental concerns, must not consume the lion's share of foreign policy resources and energies at the expense of more important or vital national interests. An NSC-68 for the post-Cold War world would order U.S. foreign policy priorities by clearly stating the interests and objectives the U.S. will pursue in 1997 and beyond.

This document will be produced by the National Security Council for the President and should be the result of NSC interagency conferences involving departmental Secretaries and agency heads as well as the deputies' committees. The President will need to provide clear guidance, but the work will be done principally by deputies such as the Undersecretary of Defense for Policy and his counterparts at the NSC, the CIA, and the State Department. The committees should make this document a top priority and ensure that it is finalized and widely publicized within two to three months of the beginning of a new administration.

STRATEGY #2
The President should provide detailed and comprehensive guidance in the National Security Strategy.

An NSC-68 for the post-Cold War world is necessary to lay out the nature of the international arena and America's role in it. However, the interests and objectives in that document should be fairly broad. Subsequently, a more detailed statement of national objectives should be contained in the National Security Strategy of the United States. This document, signed by the President and produced by the National Security Council, is required by the National Security Act of 1947, as amended by Section 603 of the Goldwater-Nichols Department of Defense Reorganization Act of 1986 and codified into law in Title 10, United States Code. In this document, the National Security Council, once again in conjunction with deputies of the relevant executive departments and agencies, will add flesh to the bones of NSC-68 for the post-Cold War world.

The principal function of the National Security Strategy is to take those national objectives previously identified; lay out the specific political, diplomatic, economic, social, and military objectives that must be pursued in order to achieve these national objectives; and specify how they will be integrated and coordinated. For instance, if it is a U.S. objective to help ensure the continued existence of South Korea as a free, secure, and prosperous ally, then there must be political, diplomatic, economic, social, and military goals to support this objective. The State Department and the White House have political and diplomatic goals; the Commerce Department, Export-Import Bank, Agency for International Development, and other agencies have economic goals; the U.S. Information Agency and other agencies have social goals; and the Department of Defense has military goals. The National Security Advisor's task is to integrate these separate objectives into a comprehensive National Security Strategy aimed at achieving the national objectives of the U.S. In addition to this internal coordination, the National Security Strategy must take into account the level of support or opposition from abroad for U.S. national objectives. The positions and capabilities of both allies and adversaries will change the strategy behind specific objectives outlined in the NSS.

For military planners who are preparing to allocate scarce resources, the National Security Strategy must give the military an indication of where their focus should lie. While the NSC-68 for the post-Cold War period would rank the relative importance of national interests and objectives, the NSS must explicitly prioritize national security interests in greater detail. This is necessary because the broad prioritization of national interests does not necessarily reflect the relative need for U.S. military forces or action. For instance, although protecting the Western Hemisphere from outside interference has been a vital U.S. interest since the early 19th century, potential threats to that region are so low that its defense requires few dedicated forces. Conversely, a less important interest may require many more military forces or greater military action as the situation dictates. The National Security Strategy prioritizes objectives with an eye to threats to national interests and potential support from allies with common interests. As former strategic planner Don Snider notes in his critical review of the Clinton Administration's National Security Strategy, unless the NSS offers clear priorities among the national interests, it does not help the Secretary of Defense or the Chairman of the Joint Chiefs of Staff to translate general foreign policy into executable strategy.[12]

STRATEGY #3
The Chairman of the Joint Chiefs of Staff should create a detailed and coherent National Military Strategy (NMS) in support of the NSS.

The actual creation of a military strategy starts at this point. If the NSC-68 for the post-Cold War world and the National Security Strategy have provided a clear and detailed indication of the relative importance of U.S. interests and objectives, then the Secretary of Defense and the

---

12 Don Snider, *The National Security Strategy: Documenting Strategic Vision* (Carlisle, Pa.: U.S. Army War College, 1995), pp. 9–14.

Chairman of the Joint Chiefs of Staff can conduct more specific military planning in support of these objectives. The Chairman, as the principal military advisor to the National Command Authorities (the President and the Secretary of Defense), is responsible for producing the National Military Strategy. The NMS is a broad and unclassified document that in recent years has become a somewhat simple reiteration of military goals first mentioned in the NSS. At best, in its present form it merely expresses the broad objectives of U.S. military forces and the strategy through which they will be attained. The 1995 NMS gives an overview of the international environment followed by macro-objectives, such as "promote stability" and "thwart aggression" through strategic concepts, and capabilities such as "overseas presence," "power projection," and "peacetime engagement."[13]

This approach is flawed. A broad and abstract NMS does nothing to advance a policy on the use of military force. The National Military Strategy should set more exact goals. First, it should identify specific military objectives that support the national objectives outlined in the National Security Strategy. For instance, in support of a national objective in Korea, the National Military Strategy would state that the U.S. will keep at least 30,000 combat troops forward-deployed and combat ready in South Korea in order to deter an invasion or defeat one should it occur. This allows the military to pinpoint clearly defined, decisive, attainable, and sustainable military objectives in support of national strategy. Moreover, by clearly matching U.S. military objectives to national objectives, planners can better see the suitability of U.S. military force in support of national policy goals. Certain national objectives, such as promoting democracy and local stability in the developing world, are not well supported by the use of U.S. military force. It is better to have that debate sooner, when formatting planning documents such as the NSS and NMS, than in the midst of a military operation as happened in Somalia.

Second, the prioritization of national security interests will allow the Chairman to derive a related prioritization of military objectives — something the NMS currently does not address—in much the same way the NSC-68 laid out priorities for the post-Cold War world. Because it

13 John M. Shalikashvili, *The National Military Strategy of the United States of America* (Washington, D.C.: U.S. Government Printing Office, 1995).

lacked strategic guidance from the top, the Bottom-Up Review force made no priorities. As a result, regional warfighting commanders must plan to use the same military units and resources for combat contingencies which the BUR assumes may happen simultaneously. Moreover, the lack of priorities has caused the military to wear out forces on missions of little value while becoming less and less prepared for contingencies of much greater consequence. Since 1993, the U.S. has been rotating infantry, cavalry, and tank battalions through six-month peacekeeping tours as part of the U.N. mission in Macedonia. These units are away from their tanks and fighting vehicles for the entire tour, and their combat skills atrophy considerably. As a result, this mission robs an entire brigade (one-fourth of America's NATO ground force) of the ability to be combat ready. A prioritization of military objectives in the NMS would make it clear that this sort of mission should be among the lowest priorities—much lower than being prepared to deter major power aggression against Europe.

Prioritization should happen early in the planning process to allow the Chairman to discriminate as to where U.S. military forces are most needed. Of course, need creates its own priorities, and history shows that the unexpected is often the norm in military affairs. The Central Command of General Norman Schwarzkopf had a very low priority until the Iraqi invasion of Kuwait in 1990, at which point it became the main effort of U.S. military forces worldwide. Nonetheless, a list of military priorities reflecting national objectives and known threats will give the Chairman of the Joint Chiefs early guidance on how forces can be structured to be most effective (to oversimplify a complex force structure issue, for instance, it is navy-heavy for East Asia, air-heavy for Southwest Asia, and land-heavy for Europe).

The prioritization of military objectives also will benefit more detailed operational planning, such as that contained in the Unified Command Plan and the Joint Strategic Capabilities Plan. Both of these documents give specific planning guidance to the Commanders in Chief (CINCs) of the operational commands, from which they construct contingency plans for military objectives in their areas of responsibility. The Chairman, as their chief spokesman, then can integrate these plans at the national level and provide additional advice to the Secretary of Defense about where and how to allocate resources according to national security priorities. If two or more regional CINCs are fighting over the same military resources, the Chairman must decide the outcome based on national priorities and not CNN's cameras. Finally, the NMS should continue to contain, as definitive statements of policy, the operational necessity for U.S. armed forces to operate in accordance with proven doctrine that emphasizes clear objectives, decisive force, and the means and methods needed to create the conditions for U.S. military (and therefore political) success.

STRATEGY #4
The Secretary of Defense should allocate military resources through the Defense Planning Guidance (DPG), which should be subject to congressional oversight.

The final step in instituting a coherent military strategy takes place at the level of military means (see Table 15.1). This planning is conducted in the Office of the Secretary of Defense (OSD) and runs parallel to the planning taking place between the Joint Staff and the CINCs. The Undersecretary of Defense for Policy produces the Defense Planning Guidance, which is intended to provide more guidance on the resources available for defense and how they should be matched to national security objectives. Thus, while the NMS should be principally responsible for matching military objectives to political objectives, the DPG should be the chief method through which the means are kept in accord with those various ends. Both documents overlap to some extent and are mutually dependent on each other. The OSD needs the Chairman's recommendations for strategic planning, and the Chairman needs a realistic projection of the means likely to be available for the planning period under consideration. The DPG is a critical document because it is the principal link between the joint strategic planning system of the Chairman and the CINCs (which provides operational plans) and the Planning, Programming, Budgeting System (PPBS) of the separate services (which provides guidance for training, programs, and weapon systems).

The competent matching of means to ends helps avoid the gap that exists today between forces and commitments. It also helps reinforce priorities and prevent important and limited U.S. military capabilities from being squandered on missions of little relevance. The DPG currently fails to do this and has allowed the U.S. military to become strained to the breaking point. More dangerously, the current DPG does not recognize the critical need to invest in the future by procuring new weapons for the 21st century and sponsoring an aggressive research, development, and testing program. Because the DPG is a medium-range (five-year) planning document, it begs for clear guidance from the political processes detailed above. In the absence of that guidance, the DPG uses illustrative scenarios as a base for planning that might not reflect the priorities of the President or the military means he is prepared to fund. Thus, instead of becoming the last link in a chain of strategic documents that coherently match means to ends, the DPG has been reverse-engineered to cover up the fiscal and strategic mismatches present in the current Administration's strategy.

A select congressional committee should be formed to provide oversight of this document. This will ensure that the DPG does not provide bureaucratic cover for an ends-means shell game — as it does today.

STRATEGY #5
The President must seek congressional approval for the National Military Strategy and the use of force, and Congress must enforce its constitutional prerogatives.

Military strategy, coherent or not, will not be successful if it is not supported by Congress. The recent pattern of military interventions has left Congress on the sidelines and in an intractable quandary about whether to support ill-defined and poorly planned military missions that already are underway. The President has taken advantage of this situation, knowing full well that Congress will not vote to cancel a new mission if American prestige and honor are engaged and U.S. troops are on the ground. Only in the event of a military disaster does Congress assert itself, pulling the fiscal plug on missions such as U.S. operations in Cambodia during the Vietnam War and U.S. military support for the 1993–1994 U.N. mission in Somalia. This pattern has left only one role for Congress in the policy process surrounding the use of American military force: post-disaster spoiler. It surely is in the nation's best interest that Congress, as the direct embodiment of the people's will, be involved more constructively—and much earlier—in this process.

Conservatives who support a more assertive role for Congress face a dilemma. They have always been against measures, such as the 1973 War

Powers Resolution, which would give Congress more of a voice in decisions about military affairs. Former Senate Majority Leader Howard Baker (R-TN) criticized the Resolution and Congress for "attempting to write in the margins of the Constitution... institutionaliz[ing] a mechanism for casting doubt and uncertainty on the resolve of the United States."[14] On the other hand, the Republican majority in the 104th Congress was understandably frustrated by the political maneuvering of the President that left them helpless to voice effective dissent against the reckless employment of American military forces.

There is no new legislative answer to this dilemma. Producing new legislation akin to the highly controversial, ineffective, and probably unconstitutional War Powers Resolution would merely muddy the waters of the tension and ambiguity that have existed over this issue for over 200 years. The President must have the flexibility and unimpeded authority to act with speed and resolve on behalf of the nation, but Congress must have the opportunity, in the absence of "declaring war," to approve or disapprove significant U.S. military actions. Congress should decide where U.S. troops are used through funding bills, and the President should manage those efforts. This "invitation to struggle"[15] was built into the Constitution as part of the system of checks and balances on the use of American military force, and it should be honored. In operations short of declared war, Congress must make its weight felt through the "power of the purse." If a U.S. military intervention does not meet the criteria of the policy outlined above, Congress should veto the mission by withdrawing the funds.

Unless Congress is willing to cut off funds for a military mission, there is no legal recourse against a President who insists on making poor strategic decisions and then underpins these follies with U.S. credibility and the lives of American troops. However, Congress should reaffirm, in every reiteration of the defense authorization bill, its constitutional mandate to oversee significant military actions and appropriate the resources of the nation to pay for them. The missions to Somalia, Haiti,

---

14 Quoted in Lawrence Di Rita, "Time to Repeal the War Powers Resolution," Heritage Foundation *Executive Memorandum* No. 408, March 31, 1995.

15 Edward S. Corwin, *The President: Office and Powers, 1787–1957* (New York, N.Y.: New York University Press, 1940), p. 200.

and Bosnia were not national emergencies and did not require the President to act with secrecy or undue expediency. There was ample time for a debate over means and methods in these missions, and a reasoned debate in Congress should not be forestalled by the facile argument that "politics stops at the water's edge." Congress should insist — as it proposed in the National Security Revitalization Act of 1995 — that the President consult with Congress before committing American forces to these types of non-emergency operations. If the President ignores these concerns, then Congress has no choice but to vote to reduce or cut off funding for the mission.

STRATEGY #6
The President should work to keep the support of the American people.

Strategy and military policy cannot be run by polls. The American people traditionally have been reluctant to intervene abroad, and presidential leadership is needed to articulate clear goals that produce tangible benefits for the United States. In the absence of a clear and present danger to U.S. national security, such as that presented throughout the Cold War by the Soviet Union, the American people understandably are even more reluctant to support uncertain military adventures. However, according to most polls surveying opinions about foreign affairs, a great majority of Americans want the U.S. to remain actively engaged as a leader in world affairs.[16]

Author Robert Tucker has called this phenomenon "the great issue of American foreign policy today. It is the contradiction between the persisting desire to remain the premier global power and an ever deepening aversion to bear the costs of this position."[17] However, another way to look at this phenomenon is to understand the desire of the American people for a logical and sensible policy of global

---

16 For instance, 65 percent of respondents in a poll taken by the Chicago Council on Foreign Relations ("American Public Opinion and U.S. Foreign Policy 1995," p. 6) and 59 percent of respondents in a poll from the Center for International and Security Studies at the University of Maryland ("An Emerging Consensus: A Study of American Public Attitudes on America's Role in the World," July 1996, p. 5).

17 Robert W. Tucker, "The Future of a Contradiction," *The National Interest*, No. 43 (Spring 1996), p. 20.

engagement, one that preserves American involvement in global activities that are to America's benefit but does not squander U.S. resources on a crusade of global gendarmerie. Americans consistently state that they want the U.S. to remain a global power, but not to become the world's police officer.[18] Walking the line between these understandable desires demands a military policy that discriminates among national interests of different levels of importance and uses American power where it is most needed and most effective.

The American people will support a military policy that provides a level of return commensurate with the national investment. The American people are not intolerant of U.S. casualties per se; they are intolerant of the loss of American lives in a hopeless or protracted military enterprise that does not clearly serve the national interest. This observation is supported by a good deal of empirical evidence. One sociological study of public opinions during the Lebanon intervention of 1982–1983 and the Somalia intervention of 1992–1994 found that public approval of those missions was falling well before the disasters in Beirut and Mogadishu. The study concluded that public approval "is not conditioned by some knee-jerk reaction to casualties. Judging from the responses we have seen to Lebanon and Somalia, it is conditioned rather by the demand that casualties be incurred for some clear and worthy purpose."[19] The innate common sense of the American people, a common sense that can be shaped and informed by presidential leadership, will accept sacrifice for worthwhile military missions. This bodes well for a military policy that ties the use of force to national security interests and the support of Congress and the American people. The bottom line from a policy perspective is that it is folly to undertake significant military actions without the clear support of the American people.

---

18 Along with the surveys previously cited, see Steven Kull, "What the Public Knows That Washington Doesn't," *Foreign Policy,* Winter 1995, p. 104.

19 Professor James Burk, "Public Support for Peacekeeping in Lebanon and Somalia," paper read at the biennial meeting of the Inter-University Seminar on Armed Forces and Society, October 20–22, 1995.

STRATEGY #7

The President should publish a National Security Directive on the use of military force.

A coherent military strategy supported by Congress and the American people will create a sensible policy for the use of American military force. However, policymakers should have the criteria for the use of force in one place instead of having to pick and choose from the hierarchy of plans and documents that make up American military strategy. In this way, policymakers will have a disciplined framework for working through the issues about when, where, why, and how to use military force. This should be a separate national security policy, best expressed as a National Security Directive or Presidential Decision Directive similar to PDD-25 but addressing all manner of military operations. This Directive, created by the National Security Council from inter-agency meetings, must be a firm expression of presidential intent. In contrast, although they had President Reagan's support, the famous Weinberger criteria of 1984 came from the office of the Secretary of Defense as an ad hoc clarification of DOD policy, not as part of a more deliberate and wider set of plans and policy. Because of this, the criteria were challenged by other executive departments (notably the State Department through Secretary Shultz) and never codified or instituted in a more tangible manner. In order to make these new criteria the policy of the entire government, the President must issue a National Security Directive. This will eliminate different interpretations from various branches, agencies, or departments.

STRATEGY #8

The President should promote a new security compact in America's alliances.

America's military alliances come in many different forms. In its strictest sense, an alliance is a commitment for mutual military support against some external actor or actors in some specified set of circumstances.[20] Conversely, collective security organizations like the U.N., the Association of South-East Asian Nations (ASEAN) Regional

---

20 See Stephen Walt, *The Origins of Alliances* (Ithaca, N.Y.: Cornell University Press, 1987).

Forum, and the Organization for Security and Cooperation in Europe (OSCE) are not military alliances. Formal alliances usually are based on treaties (see Table 15.2). These alliances can differ greatly: They can be highly institutionalized multilateral arrangements like NATO; active bilateral defense alliances like those with Korea and Japan; latent bilateral agreements like that with the Philippines; de facto bilateral alliances like the Australia, New Zealand, and United States Security Treaty (ANZUS); or even moribund multilateral alliances like the South-East Asia Treaty Organization (SEATO) or the Rio Treaty.

Table 15.2

Formal U.S. Military Alliances and Treaties

Alliance	Foundation Agreement	Members
NATO	North Atlantic Treaty - 4 April 1949	Belgium, Canada, Denmark, France, Germany, Greece, Iceland, Italy, Luxembourg, Netherlands, Norway, Portugal, Spain, Turkey, U.K., U.S.
Japan	Mutual Cooperation and Security Treaty - 8 September 1951, 19 January 1960	Japan, U.S.
Korea	Republic of Korea Treaty - 1 October 1953	Republic of Korea, U.S.
ANZUS	ANZUS Treaty - 1 September 1951	Australia, New Zealand, U.S.
Rio Treaty Alliance	The Rio Treaty - 2 September 1947	Argentina, Bahamas, Bolivia, Brazil, Chile, Colombia, Costa Rica, Cuba, Dominican Republic, Ecuador, El Salvador, Guatemala, Haiti, Honduras, Mexico, Nicaragua, Panama, Paraguay, Peru, Trinidad & Tobago, U.S., Uruguay, Venezuela
The Philippines	The Philippines-U.S. Mutual Defense Treaty - 30 August 1951 (& 1983)	The Philippines, U.S.
SEATO	SouthEast Asia Treaty - 8 Sept 1954	Australia, France, New Zealand, Philippines, Thailand, U.K., U.S.

Notes: Alliances are defined as formal or informal commitments between two or more states for mutual military support against an external threat. Those alliances listed here are those that are based on formal collective defense treaties between the U.S. and allies. However, as discussed throughout this chapter, the U.S. has other defense commitments and national security interests that are protected through less formal alliances, other mutual defense agreements, or semi-permanent coalitions. This is the case with the Persian Gulf, Taiwan, the Middle East, and elsewhere. In some cases, these less formalized commitments are much more important for defense planners than some dead letter alliances where the treaty remains officially in force (such as SEATO — the South-East Asia Treaty Organization) or some other formal alliance agreements that do not play a significant role in U.S. military planning (such as the Rio Treaty). Because of New Zealand's opposition to nuclear weapons and nuclear powered ships, the U.S. suspended the treaty obligations with New Zealand on 17 September 1986. For practical purposes, the ANZUS treaty is between the U.S. and Australia only. SEATO (the organization) was dissolved in 1975, but the collective defense treaty remains in force.

The U.S. is also involved in more informal military alliances based on other forms of security cooperation. This cooperation can include the supply of military training and equipment, basing rights for U.S. troops or pre-positioned equipment, military training exchanges, or combined military exercises. These informal alliances, in time of need, can act as frameworks for setting up coalitions of those who are willing to undertake specific actions. This sort of arrangement is seen most clearly in the informal alliance between the U.S. and its partners in the Persian Gulf. Finally, there are unspoken but de facto military alliances in which the U.S. national interest is so obvious that there is an implicit commitment to the defense of an ally with which there are very limited or even no formal defense agreements. This is the case with countries such as Israel and Taiwan.

The U.S. needs this flexible array of formal, informal, multilateral, and bilateral alliances in order to protect many different interests against various threats in several key regions around the globe. Nonetheless, in every one of these arrangements, the U.S. must look at how it can best enforce a division of labor in which the U.S. role supports the vital American interests at stake and for which the American military commitment is both unique and decisive. Every alliance must undergo this sort of examination, and the U.S. and its allies must explore structures and procedures that will take advantage of different but complementary interests and capabilities provided by the allies. In this way, the U.S. can make the total effect of the alliance more than the sum of its composite parts.

The North Atlantic Treaty Organization (NATO). Getting European allies to take more responsibility for local security missions in Europe is not merely a matter of political will. Political will can be bolstered by institutional mechanisms and procedures that give European allies the military means for taking on this role. The principal mechanism needed for this task does not need to be invented; it exists now and is waiting to be taken off the drawing board and put into practice. The Combined Joint Task Force (CJTF) is an organizational framework that will allow European allies to borrow NATO resources for European-led missions such as crisis management, humanitarian relief, and peacekeeping. The CJTF, a U.S. initiative proposed in 1993 and finally approved by NATO in June 1996, is the one existing practical measure for moving America's NATO allies toward greater self-reliance in dealing with smaller

European security challenges.

The CJTF allows NATO and Europe a flexible range of military options rather than the one Cold War paradigm of "all for one and one for all." Because Combined Joint Task Forces are force packages that are tailored for specific missions, they can be formed in a number of ways to suit different challenges. A CJTF can be a NATO operation composed of almost any variety of allied units and led either by the U.S. (as in NATO's warfighting structure) or by a European commander. More important, a CJTF can be formed outside of NATO and led by a different European security organization such as the Western European Union or the OSCE. In this case, the CJTF could temporarily "lease" NATO units that would be "separable but not separate" for the duration of the CJTF mission. Finally, a CJTF allows other non-NATO European states to contribute troops, as many have done for the implementation force in Bosnia.

The U.S. Ambassador to NATO, Robert Hunter, called the CJTF "the first significant change in the way the alliance does business since 1966" when the French left the military structure of the alliance.[21] This statement is very true when applied to involvement in small regional military missions such as peacekeeping in Southeastern Europe. In that sort of peacekeeping and other lesser "business," the CJTF gives NATO many options that will allow the allies with the greatest interest in local crises both to take the lead and to have the means to do so. However, the CJTF concept is equally valuable for the protection it gives to the traditional business of NATO and the U.S.: providing a credible combat capability that can deter a major power threat to Europe. Because the CJTF allows flexible options for solving lesser security dilemmas, the U.S. can preserve the role it plays as NATO's warfighting leader, a role that matches its interest in Europe and that cannot be replicated by any other ally.

The CJTF must not atrophy in the committee rooms at NATO headquarters in Belgium. NATO should give the CJTF its debut in the follow-on force that will be present in Bosnia through 1997, 1998, and perhaps longer. In 1997, the Intervention Force in Bosnia (IFOR) should transition from a U.S.-led NATO task force to a European-led NATO

---

21 "NATO Acquires a European Identity," *The Economist*, June 8, 1996, p. 51.

Combined Joint Task Force. The U.S. should still contribute unique and decisive support capabilities to this European-led CJTF, but most of the troops should come from NATO allies. In 1998, any residual Bosnia force should evolve even further, and should be entirely European. Such a force also should be a CJTF, but led by a European organization such as the Western European Union or OSCE and not officially connected with NATO, although it may use some NATO assets and units.

Of all the U.S. alliances, formal and informal, NATO is the one that needs the most reform in pressing for a clear division of labor that matches interests and capabilities to roles and responsibilities. America's NATO allies are prosperous and democratic states. They chose to cut defense spending, chose to cut capabilities, and chose to follow ineffective half-measures in Bosnia for four years. These allies are more than capable of handling European peacekeeping missions with support in key areas from the U.S. Out of all the global security responsibilities facing the U.S. and its many allies, Bosnia is the one that requires the military capabilities of the U.S. the least. Through mechanisms such as the CJTF, the European allies can pick up the slack in missions like Bosnia so the U.S. can attend to the singular responsibilities of a superpower with security interests around the globe.

Japan. During the Cold War, the bilateral U.S. alliance with Japan was the cornerstone of American strategy in East Asia. In the post-Cold War era, this alliance remains critical, especially when China and North Korea pose two of the most salient threats to peace and security in a region of increasing importance to U.S. national security. Moreover, the U.S.-Japan security relationship remains well-balanced, with the U.S. and Japan playing complementary roles that match the interests and military capabilities of each country. The many calls for a fundamental reworking of the U.S.-Japan alliance should not be heeded.

Over the years, many criticisms have been aimed at the structure of the U.S.-Japan defense relationship.[22] Some observers maintain that the U.S. pays too much to maintain some 47,000 troops in Japan when many

---

22 For instance, see Ted Galen Carpenter, "Paternalism and Dependence: The U.S.-Japanese Security Relationship," Cato Institute *Policy Analysis* No. 244, November 1, 1995.

Japanese (especially the Okinawans) are ungrateful and want the troops to leave. Others argue that the Japanese take advantage of America's security blanket to invest would-be defense monies in economic production that eventually is used against the U.S. in unfair trade deals. Still others maintain that in the event of any real major power crisis in East Asia, the Japanese would not support U.S. combat operations unless Japan itself was attacked.

While all these points deserve a hearing and are part of the continuous assessment of the U.S.-Japan alliance, the basic structure of the alliance as it stands serves the U.S. well.[23] The U.S. mission in the alliance is focused on the role of collective defense, and the U.S. military missions are unique and decisive. For its part, Japan's self-defense force is committed to defending Japan and the sea-lanes out to 1,000 nautical miles from the home islands. U.S. military forces based in Japan deter greater threats, as they did in March 1996 when the deployment of two U.S. aircraft carrier battle groups to the area around Taiwan convinced China that demonstrations of armed aggression against Taiwan will not go unchallenged.

In April 1996, the U.S. and Japan concluded additional defense cooperation arrangements that would marginally increase Japan's role in Asian security affairs. These steps were intended to make Japan a better partner for the U.S. in regional contingencies, not to precipitate a re-evaluation of the distinct roles played by each alliance partner.

Nonetheless, many observers dismissed these steps as cosmetic and still call for Japan to assume an even greater Asian security role in order to relieve the U.S. of some of the burden of maintaining peace and security in an uncertain and potentially unstable region. However, this view must be mitigated by the fact that, as history demonstrates, a fully remilitarized Japan with a unilateral defense policy would be destabilizing to the region. Moreover, it would do nothing to help the alliance goals of the

---

23 It also is fairly cost-effective. Japan contributes over $5 billion to the basing of U.S. troops and facilities there, by far the best cost-sharing arrangement with any U.S. ally. Although the exact figures are disputed, the Clinton Administration maintains that it would be more expensive to base the same troops back in the U.S. See Department of Defense, *U.S. Security Strategy in the East Asia-Pacific Rim Region,* February 1995, p. 24.

U.S.-Japan security treaty and could even work at odds with U.S. security strategy in the Asia-Pacific. The U.S. should not ask Japan to take over its role in deterring major power conflict in the region. Ironically, a Japanese role in that regard could precipitate precisely such a situation — major power conflict in East Asia. Instead, the U.S. should encourage the Japanese government to contribute to lesser regional missions, as it did when it contributed to the U.N. peacekeeping mission in Cambodia in 1993.

Korea. The U.S.-Korea alliance is more narrowly conceived than NATO or the U.S.-Japan alliance and serves to defend against one principal scenario: the invasion of South Korea by North Korea. Some Americans (like President Carter in 1976) question the presence of the 34,000 American troops in Korea, labeling them redundant and unnecessary. Given the large size of the South Korean defense forces, critics argue that the presence of American GIs in Korea is in keeping with the mission of collective defense but is hardly unique or decisive. However, the U.S. does not keep ground troops in Korea because South Korea physically needs another infantry division to defend itself; U.S. ground troops are in Korea as the embodiment of a unique and decisive commitment to the defense of South Korea—a cause for which the U.S. went to war and suffered some 36,000 battle deaths between 1950 and 1953.

A commitment to defend South Korea that is expressed only through long-range aircraft, fleets in the region, or the sharing of intelligence and resupply does not adequately represent the gravity of the South Korea-U.S. defense alliance. Such a transient and abstract commitment might be unique and decisive in the technical sense, but it also would cause South Korea to view the U.S. as a reckless alliance partner. This might cause South Korea to make accommodations with China and North Korea it might not make if it knew it had a full alliance partner whose vital security interests in Northeast Asia were protected by American combat forces. In an alliance such as that with South Korea, the unique and decisive military capabilities of the U.S. include a credible ground combat presence.

Coalitions of the Willing and De Facto Alliances. Coalitions of the willing and de facto alliances come into being in response to a pressing security need. These less structured arrangements are useful in critical areas of the world where a formal alliance like NATO could cause more problems than it would solve. The U.S. maintains a "coalition in waiting" in the Persian Gulf, where security agreements with Kuwait, Saudi Arabia, and other Gulf states are marked not by formal treaty, but by lower-key defense cooperation agreements. These take the form of memoranda of understanding that cover basing privileges, pre-positioned equipment, defense training and supply, and combined military exercises. Although there is no treaty requirement, it is well understood that the U.S. and its coalition allies will defend the Persian Gulf region against external and major internal aggression. In a similar way, the U.S. most likely would come to the aid of de facto alliance partners Israel and Taiwan in the event of major aggression.

This sort of need creates its own priorities, as well as a division of labor in coalitions and de facto alliances that is usually a fairly accurate reflection of different interests and capabilities. For instance, the 31-member Persian Gulf coalition of 1990–1991 took into account the different talents, resources, and capabilities that all members brought to the effort. The U.S. provided most of the combat troops and the great preponderance of the high-technology warfighting systems. Saudi Arabia and other Gulf states provided invaluable ports, bases, supplies, and key infrastructure. Germany and Japan contributed billions in financing. NATO allies and others provided air, sea, and ground assets to complement the U.S. forces. Islamic countries such as Egypt, Syria, Morocco, Afghanistan, Pakistan, and others contributed forces that were militarily irrelevant but politically vital to the diffuse coalition seeking to isolate Saddam Hussein.

When the U.S. is involved in such a coalition—one formed to protect a vital national security interest — it should always take the lead and dominate the setting of strategic objectives, military planning, and force structure. Moreover, there should never be an attempt to balance a force on paper if it does not make military sense to do so. Political correctness or too much sensitivity about delicate coalition relations should never replace such prerequisites of military success as unity of effort and a clear, responsive, and efficient chain of command. During the Gulf War, the U.S. completely dominated the military planning process despite the fact that some allied commanders with no experience in modern warfare felt they were being slighted. Conversely, after the Gulf War, the U.S. paid more heed to Saudi Arabian sensitivities than to U.S. Air Force security needs when housing American airmen at a base in Saudi Arabia. As a result, 19 American servicemen died in April 1996 during a terrorist strike in Dhahran. A coalition must have a clear leader capable of running operations with authority and diplomacy at the same time. When the U.S. is in this role, its military contributions will always be unique and decisive. When the U.S. is merely supporting a smaller coalition that is undertaking a local security task such as peacekeeping, it must measure the value of its military contribution against what regional allies should contribute.

CONCLUSION

In the ever-shifting and unpredictable post-Cold War world, the U.S. must protect an intricate web of national interests against a host of possible threats. Given that these many threats are less monolithic than those of the Cold War, the U.S. and its allies also have decided to reduce their military capabilities to a significant degree. Consequently, America is left in the position of having to defend many different interests against unpredictable threats and with a much smaller force. This condition begs for a military strategy and alliance policy that can help American policymakers decide when American military power is most needed and most effective. Such policies by themselves will not solve complex matters of international security, but they do provide a disciplined framework within which to address issues such as national interests; political and military objectives; the interests, objectives, and capabilities of allies; the relative effectiveness of the U.S. military force; and the importance of congressional and public support to the conduct of foreign affairs in a democracy.

Devising a coherent strategy requires a rigorous exercise in top-down planning. Every stage in the strategic planning process depends on the viability and credibility of the assumptions and planning that underpinned the previous stage. In the first stage, enduring goals and principles must be identified in order to derive national interests and national objectives. In turn, those interests and objectives are achieved by the identification and integration of detailed economic, social, diplomatic, political, and military objectives. In order to produce a military strategy, those military objectives must be prioritized and supported by military means that are fully funded and appropriate to the task.

A bottom-up planning process cannot be coherent in its matching of means to ends. The current Bottom-Up Review (BUR) military strategy undermines the credibility of the United States in international affairs by making it clear to allies and adversaries alike that U.S. military strategy is incoherent — undermined by a series of mismatches between defense funding, force structure, and security commitments. More important, the deleterious effects of these mismatches on readiness, morale, and preparation for the future increase geometrically every day that the military is beset by the strain of trying to accomplish a strategy for which it is both poorly structured and underfunded. Compounding this dilemma, the failure to articulate a clear role for the U.S. in global security affairs leaves a purposeful ambiguity about American military policy that encourages adversaries and confuses allies. Fixing this ambiguity and incoherence must start with a firm statement of the U.S. military's role in the post-Cold War world that explains when, where, why, and how the U.S. will use military force and specifies the role the U.S. expects its allies to play in supporting these policies.

Instituting these policies is principally a matter of presidential intent. These policies communicate very clearly to the world that America intends to remain a global leader with significant global interests. They also send the signal that the U.S. will not respond to every local and regional crisis with an American-led military effort. This sensible balance between a wasteful crusade and a rejectionist isolationism should be the philosophical underpinning of U.S. military strategy.

Chapter 16

BUILDING SUPPORT FOR MISSILE DEFENSE

Baker Spring

Defense of the homeland is the most basic purpose of any country's national security program. If any interest can be described as vital, then defending the nation's territory, air space, military capabilities, and—most important of all—its people against foreign attack is the most vital of all. Despite this fact, the United States continues to pursue a policy that purposely leaves its territory and people vulnerable to attack by the most destructive weapon man has ever invented: the nuclear-armed ballistic missile. This is historically unprecedented. The U.S. has built and maintained defenses against bombers, submarines, surface ships, artillery, tanks, and even individual terrorists. Only in the case of the ballistic missile have Americans intentionally been left vulnerable.

This policy of intentional vulnerability to nuclear attack is required by the 1972 Anti-Ballistic Missile (ABM) Treaty, which explicitly prohibits the deployment of a defense against ballistic missiles. The policy has allowed foreign countries, particularly the Soviet Union and later Russia, to exercise a veto over the capability of the U.S. to defend itself. Because of the ABM Treaty, any nuclear-armed country that opposes U.S. policy has been given the capability to threaten America with a nuclear holocaust. Even today, the Russians hint that they might threaten the West with nuclear weapons in

The author would like to thank Mark Albrecht, Ambassador Henry Cooper, Frank Gaffney, William R. Graham, Ambassador Richard N. Holwill, Fred Iklé, Sven F. Kraemer, and Senator Malcolm Wallop for their suggestions and contributions to this chapter. They do not necessarily endorse all of its views and recommendations, which are solely the responsibility of the author.

response to the enlargement of NATO. In January 1996, a Chinese official said that China might destroy the city of Los Angeles if the U.S. moved to protect Taiwan against a Chinese military assault. Even countries that do not yet possess such missiles have made their intentions known. NBC Nightly News on April 21, 1990, reported that Libyan leader Muammar Qadhafi stated that if he had possessed ballistic missiles in 1986, when U.S. war planes attacked the Libyan capital in retaliation for a terrorist attack, he would have launched them at New York. It is difficult to imagine a policy that could serve more effectively to limit U.S. foreign policy options than keeping the U.S. vulnerable to missile strikes.

The damaging impact, of course, is not limited to the conduct of foreign policy. It can be discerned in the military sphere as well. For example, because of the ABM Treaty, it is impossible for the U.S. to address the threat posed by Russian deployment of the truck-mounted SS-25 *Sickle* intercontinental ballistic missile (ICBM). No offensive systems, whether missiles or bombers, are yet capable of destroying the SS-25 before it is launched. Only a missile defense system would be capable of neutralizing the SS-25. Thus, America now lacks any military means to counter the single most threatening weapon faced by the U.S.

The threat of missile attack is growing. Russia and China already are capable of attacking U.S. territory with ballistic missiles. North Korea is developing a missile, called the *Taepo Dong 2*, that may give it the ability to attack U.S. territory by the end of the decade. Some 20 Third World countries—including such hostile regimes as Iran, Iraq, Libya, and Syria—have ballistic missile development programs. The current pattern of missile proliferation makes it clear that it is only a matter of time before these development programs allow hostile countries to threaten U.S. territory. This intentional vulnerability to missile attack must end. The most basic goal of U.S. security policy is to ensure that the nation is capable of controlling its own destiny in a dangerous and unpredictable world. This is a goal that cannot be achieved if a policy of purposeful vulnerability to missile attack is continued.

Needed: A Successful Political Strategy. Since long before President Ronald Reagan created the Strategic Defense Initiative (SDI) in March 1983, missile defense proponents have been advocating the deployment of defensive systems. They recognize that leaving America vulnerable to nuclear weapons will undermine the nation's ability to control its own destiny. Despite the concerns of these proponents and more than a decade of effort, the United States has yet to deploy a system designed to counter ballistic missiles in flight. This failure is no accident. Starting in the 1980s, opponents of missile defense successfully executed a political strategy designed to obstruct the deployment of missile defenses. The supporters of missile defense must learn important lessons from this history of their opponents' successes and their own failures.

If supporters of missile defense are to prevail, they must develop and execute a successful political strategy which identifies and eliminates the obstacles to deployment of missile defenses. This will not be an easy task. Opponents of missile defense have always had one distinct advantage: They argue in favor of the status quo. Proponents of missile defense, on the other hand, demand change. In the field of national security, it is often more difficult to change an existing policy than to defend it.

The good news for those who support missile defense, however, is that their opponents are now vulnerable. Even the Clinton Administration admits that some form of missile defense is needed. As with welfare reform and other controversial positions adopted by the Clinton Administration, Clinton's support for missile defense is disingenuous and rhetorical. But he at least is no longer arguing that missile defense is a "Star Wars fantasy," as Senator Edward Kennedy (D-MA) and other SDI opponents claimed in the 1980s. Moreover, there is a growing consensus in the defense community that a Third World missile threat is emerging; the main question is when, not whether, it will endanger the U.S. Finally, technological advances in missile defense increasingly belie the old shibboleth that missile defenses are technologically infeasible.

A second reason for hope is that conservatives control Congress. This is an advantage that should be exploited both through legislation and through the proper conduct of Congress's oversight responsibilities. Legislation can be adopted to end the policies that make the U.S. vulnerable to missile attack, and oversight hearings can spotlight the shortcomings of an Administration that is hostile to missile defense.

LESSONS LEARNED

The necessary first step in developing a successful political strategy is to set a clear and attainable goal. For a country vulnerable to missile attack, the goal must be to decide on a specific national security plan which includes a timetable for building and deploying effective global missile defense systems. One of the most consistent problems with past efforts to develop strong missile defenses has been the propensity of policymakers to focus on intermediate goals which fall short of deploying an effective system. These intermediate goals have included such elements as expanding the range of technological options for missile defense, increasing funding for specific missile defense programs, and focusing on deploying theater defenses as a first step toward a more comprehensive system later. However valuable these lesser goals may have been in their own right, focusing on them distracted proponents from achieving the far more important goal of full-scale deployment; far from unifying the various supporters, squabbles over these intermediate goals have divided the pro-missile defense community.

This focus on lesser goals allowed opponents of missile defense to advance an ever-changing and ever-growing number of obstacles and arguments. For example, some missile defense supporters believed that throwing their support behind such half-measures as theater missile defenses would be a "down payment" on full-scale deployment later. Since some missile defense critics endorsed the concept of deploying theater defense, supporters thought a consensus could be reached on theater defenses, thereby paving the way for a nationwide homeland defense later. Support for theater defenses, however, quickly turned to hostility as practical deployment plans were presented and debated in Congress. The result was that Congress became mired in a debate over theater defenses that was not supposed to occur, and the more important quest for the deployment of a global defense system was pushed beyond the horizon. A consensus over theater defenses proved to be ephemeral—yet another ruse to distract proponents from their quest for a nationwide defense against ballistic missile attack.

There is a tangible political benefit to establishing deployment as the main goal for the missile defense program. Deployment of a global missile defense system is likely to generate far greater support in the public and Congress than any of the lesser goals. This is true for two reasons. First,

LESSONS LEARNED

- Opponents of missile defense defined the requirements for a "feasible" missile defense program, making it difficult for proponents to build an effective case.

- Proponents failed to agree on a specific missile defense architecture and allowed opponents to charge that missile defenses are unaffordable.

- Proponents need to be more vigilant in preventing critics from "defining away" the threat of missile attack to America.

- An open-ended research program for missile defense has allowed the deferral of decisions to deploy missile defenses.

- By pursuing theater defenses first, proponents of a strong missile defense helped to put the deployment of a global defense system out of reach.

- Because proponents failed to demonstrate how strategic defenses encourage less reliance on offensive weapons, opponents were able to argue that missile defenses increase the nuclear threat by undermining arms control.

- By failing to make the case that the nation's vulnerability to missiles constitutes an incentive to launch a first strike, proponents allowed critics to argue that strategic defenses are destabilizing.

- By failing to repudiate the ABM Treaty, missile defense proponents failed to target the single most important obstacle to deployment.

- Advances toward deployment can be reversed unless Congress is vigilant and focused.

- Career personnel in the Department of State and the Arms Control and Disarmament Agency are obstacles to developing and implementing a missile defense program.

- Poor acquisition strategy for developing and deploying missile defenses has hindered prospects for deployment.

- The weakening of the Ballistic Missile Defense Organization has undermined missile defense in the Pentagon bureaucracy.

LESSONS (continued)

- The military services are ambivalent about missile defenses.
- Russia has been permitted veto power over U.S. missile defense programs.
- The U.S. refusal to decide on deployment has weakened allied support for missile defense.
- Because the focus has not been on the victims of missile attacks, the public remains unaware of its own vulnerability.

---

deployment of a global system will provide a tangible benefit in the form of protection to U.S. citizens and overseas troops, while the lesser goals produce only intangible or indirect benefits. In fact, the lesser goals have value only as markers for progress toward the goal of full-scale deployment.

Establishing the goal of deployment of a homeland missile defense system also imposes discipline on the political strategy. Every argument made, every obstacle identified, and every institutional reform proposed should be tied directly to the question of deployment. If a persuasive argument cannot be made as to why any proposed step is essential to deployment, it should not be made. Some will argue that taking steps short of deployment is the best approach because there is immediate political support for these steps. However, experience has shown that missile defense opponents have taken advantage of this piecemeal approach to block progress. What is sold as a clever approach is revealed not only as an excessive sensitivity to the perceived requirements of the political process, but as a recipe for political failure. The better approach is to define clearly the necessary policy and to build political support around that position.

Missile defense advocates must learn the lessons of history. For each obstacle the opponents of missile defense have constructed to block the path of deploying a missile defense system, there is a failure by proponents to overcome that obstacle. Unless lessons are learned, the goal of defending America from nuclear attack will remain elusive.

Lesson #1: Allowing opponents to define the requirements for a "feasible" defense has made it difficult for proponents to make an effective case for a missile defense system. Opponents of missile defense have often argued that missile defenses are not technically feasible. If correct, their argument removes the entire question of deployment from the realm of policy debate. No matter how desirable deploying missile defenses may be, it is not worth discussing if it is not feasible. Opponents of missile defense have made this argument with gusto, even though the facts make it clear that missile defenses are indeed feasible.

These claims about a lack of feasibility started shortly after President Reagan's March 1983 speech and have continued to the present day. In 1985, for example, Senator John Kerry (D-MA) stated on the floor of the Senate that "We never will know [whether SDI will work], because among other things we could never test the system under realistic wartime conditions ahead of time."[1] Missile defense opponents were able to get away with this line of argument because proponents dithered in defining the terms of feasibility. For Senator Kerry, the definition of feasibility was advanced testing of the system "under realistic wartime conditions ahead of time." This, of course, is a standard that has never been applied to any weapon in development. No one ever demanded that U.S. offensive nuclear missiles be tested "under realistic wartime conditions" as a precondition for their deployment. The assumption behind Senator Kerry's argument was not only absurd; it was unprecedented.

The argument against feasibility has rested also on the assumption that any missile defense system must be 100 percent effective. In 1983, former Secretary of Defense Harold Brown stated the case as follows: "If a single weapon can destroy a city of hundreds of thousands, only a perfect defense (which, moreover, works perfectly the first time) will suffice."[2] Brown never explained why the inability to save one city justified leaving countless others exposed to nuclear attack. By allowing their opponents to define feasibility in such illogical and unrealistic ways, proponents failed to counter a definition of feasibility designed to block the deployment of a missile defense system.

---

1 *Congressional Record*, December 12, 1985, p. S36302.

2 Harold Brown, "Reagan's New Idea—What About It? It May Be Plausible—And It May Be Ineffective," *The Washington Post*, March 27, 1983, p. B8.

The lesson taught by the history of the feasibility debate is that the opponents of missile defense should never be allowed to define the terms of how effective missile defenses should be. Supporters of missile defense should be arguing that a system capable of destroying "even one" ballistic missile is worth the price because it would save thousands, perhaps millions, of lives.

Lesson #2: Failing to agree on a specific missile defense architecture has allowed opponents to get away with the charge that missile defenses are unaffordable. The argument that missile defenses are unaffordable makes use of the time-tested tool of inducing "sticker shock." In the early days of the SDI program, the assertion was made that missile defenses would cost more than a $1 trillion.[3] More recently, the Congressional Budget Office estimated that a missile defense system would cost as much as $60 billion.[4] These arguments were not countered effectively because at the time there was no specific architecture, with a specific cost estimate, which could be used to demonstrate how opponents had inflated their cost estimates. A successful argument for deploying a missile defense system will require that policymakers propose a specific deployment plan with specific cost estimates that can be defended in public.

Lesson #3: Missile defense proponents need to be more vigilant in preventing critics from "defining away" the missile threat to America. Opponents of missile defense argue that there is no threat against which missile defenses can be directed. The latest example of this was the November 1995 National Intelligence Estimate (NIE), which concluded that the United States will not face a threat from ballistic missiles for 15 years. This finding boosted the arguments of those who say that no homeland defense is needed because there is no immediate threat to the U.S. This is precisely the argument used by President Clinton to justify his December 28, 1995, decision to veto the FY 1996 defense authorization bill, which would have required the deployment of a missile defense system. In a May 1996 speech announcing his opposition

---

3 Statement made by Democrat Walter Mondale during a presidential debate, 1984.

4 Congressional Budget Office estimate in a May 15, 1996, letter from Director June E. O'Neill to Representative Floyd Spence, Chairman of the House National Security Committee.

to the Defend America Act, which had been introduced by missile defense supporters in Congress on March 21, he used the same argument: "The possibility of a long-range missile attack on American soil is more than a decade away."[5]

Clinton and other missile defense opponents have been able to downplay the threat because proponents have allowed them to define the threat in unrealistic ways. For example, the Clinton Administration assessment excluded consideration of deployed Russian and Chinese missiles. It also dismissed the need to defend the territory of Alaska and Hawaii, which are closer to missiles based in China or North Korea. Some Members of Congress have gone so far as to argue that defenses against missiles are not needed because other types of nuclear threats exist. Senator Byron Dorgan (D-ND) has argued that "Far more important [than ballistic missiles], in my judgment, is the threat from a suitcase bomb somewhere; you start worrying about a nuclear device hauled in the trunk of a car and parked in New York City; you start worrying about a canister three inches high of deadly biological weapons. That is far more likely a threat to this country than a terrorist getting hold of an intercontinental ballistic missile and attempting to blackmail America."[6] Dorgan's assessment of the relative probability of a missile attack versus a suitcase bomb attack is questionable. But what is more perplexing is the absurd logic of his argument. It is akin to claiming that because a tank would be vulnerable to biological or even nuclear attack, there would be no point in building armor to protect it from artillery and machine gun fire.

Proponents of missile defense must learn from this to define the standards by which the threat will be assessed. The extreme standards used in the most recent assessment produced by the Clinton Administration, including the dismissal of the need to defend Alaska and Hawaii and the discounting of Chinese and Russian missile threats, cannot be allowed to stand uncontested.

---

5 President Clinton announced his opposition to the Defend America Act in a May 22, 1996, commencement address at the U.S. Coast Guard Academy in Connecticut.

6 Quoted in *Congressional Record*, August 3, 1995, p. S11229.

Opponents of missile defense argue that it is wise to defer deployment because tomorrow's technology will be better. Thus, if deployment is deferred, the future missile system will be better. Under Secretary of Defense Paul Kaminski used this approach during a February 16, 1996, press conference announcing the Clinton Administration's plans to postpone a deployment decision for at least three years: "it doesn't make sense for us to make a deployment decision in advance of that [three-year period], because the capability that would be achieved would be lesser [*sic*]."[7]

Once again, absurd assumptions wrapped in the language of technical plausibility serve only to counter — and to delay — deployment. Obviously, all future weapon systems will be more technologically advanced, and hence more effective, than previous ones. But that has never stopped the building of these weapons in the past. The aim of missile defense opponents now is to ensure that missile defenses are "researched to death." Further, this argument is designed to set up the charge that money is wasted because no deployment results.

Unfortunately, the proponents of missile defense have lent credibility to this argument by focusing on the intermediate goals of either increasing missile defense funding or expanding the pool of technologies. For example, the SDI program funded research into a wide variety of laser and other directed energy technologies. While advancing these technologies may be interesting, the fundamental assessment needed to decide which technology was most promising was not made. It is the application of the technology that improves defense, not merely its acquisition. There is a need to decide which technologies should be accelerated for deployment.

Lesson #5: By pursuing theater defenses first, missile defense proponents helped put the deployment of a global defense system out of reach. Some opponents of missile defense have argued that theater missile defense should proceed separately from national missile defenses for two reasons: because the threat from theater missiles is more

---

7 Department of Defense press briefing as reprinted by the Federal News Service, February 16, 1996.

immediate, and because theater defenses do not undermine the 1972 Anti-Ballistic Missile (ABM) Treaty.

In response, opponents generated a set of specific arguments against theater defenses. As a result, missile defense proponents found themselves debating theater defenses, and the two-step strategy of proceeding with theater defenses first and then moving to the deployment of a national missile defense system backfired. The lesson is that the distinction between theater defenses and national defenses is artificial. Both programs should be merged into a single global missile defense program.

Lesson #6: By failing to demonstrate how strategic defenses encourage less reliance on offensive weapons, proponents of missile defense allowed their opponents to argue that missile defenses increase the nuclear threat by undermining arms control. One of the most fiercely argued positions of missile defense opponents is that deployment of a global missile defense system will increase the nuclear threat by undermining arms control. Specifically, they argue that deploying missile defenses will result in the Russians' refusing to implement the 1991 Strategic Arms Reduction Treaty (START) and ratify the 1993 START II agreement. START would reduce the number of deliverable nuclear warheads on each side to roughly 6,000, while START II would reduce them further to 3,500. The assumption here is that the deployment of missile defenses will ignite endless rounds of incremental offensive deployments to offset deployed defenses and vice versa. As a result, missile defense opponents, who generally are advocates of arms control, see missile defenses as part of a plot to undermine arms control.

Missile defense proponents have failed to address this argument adequately. They can do so by showing how defensive systems can "cover" strategic targets (i.e., destroy enemy missiles after they are launched rather than before, which would be the case with an offense-only strategy) that otherwise would require the deployment of additional offensive forces. This failure has allowed critics to assert that defensive deployments will lead to the deployment of more offensive weapons. This need not be the case. In fact, an arms control agreement reducing offensive arms would make defenses more effective. Thus, missile defense supporters should seek an agreement with those concerned with limiting offensive weapons. As defenses help meet strategic targeting requirements, offensive arms can be reduced either unilaterally or through an arms control agreement.

Lesson #7: By failing to make the case that the nation's vulnerability to missiles constitutes an incentive to launch a first strike, missile defense proponents have allowed their critics to get away with the argument that strategic defenses are destabilizing. The claim that missile defenses are destabilizing is based on the false assumption that the deployment of missile defenses will create an incentive for either side to strike first during a crisis. The logic is as follows: Missile defenses will allow one side to strike first to weaken an opponent's retaliatory capacity; defenses then can allow the attacker to rely on his defenses to counter the weaker retaliatory strike. This logic was reflected in the adoption of a policy during the Cold War called mutual assured destruction (MAD).

Proponents have failed to make the case that executing an effective first strike against U.S. retaliatory forces will become impossible with defensive deployments. The reason is that defenses increase the survivability of retaliatory forces. The logic of MAD is wrong. Missile defense proponents can demonstrate this fact by repeatedly challenging the tortured logic of the MAD doctrine. Since the deterrent force is safer, it has more deterrent capability. This is stabilizing, not destabilizing, because the survival of retaliatory deterrence reduces the incentive of an opponent's attack in the first place.

Lesson #8: By failing to repudiate the ABM Treaty, missile defense proponents failed to target the single most important obstacle to deployment. The ABM Treaty bars the U.S. from deploying "ABM systems for a defense of the territory of its country" and imposes a host of other prohibitions against the deployment of effective defenses against missile attacks on U.S. territory. These include the 1974 Protocol that limits the U.S. to a single site of 100 fixed, ground-based interceptors and Article V's prohibition against deploying missile defense components that are "sea-based, air-based, space-based, or mobile land-based." Moreover, Article VI of the Treaty limits the ability of the U.S. to deploy the theater defense elements of a global defense system. In the view of missile defense critics, all theater defense systems so far proposed, with the exception of the *Patriot* missile, have an inherent ability to counter long-range missiles.

The ABM Treaty and the deployment of effective missile defenses are antithetical. An effective homeland defense of America is impossible as long as the United States adheres to the ABM Treaty. Proponents have been reluctant to make this point because they see honoring the nation's treaty obligations as sacrosanct. But defending the country is more vital than an international treaty which, in any event, contains provisions for legal withdrawal. Missile defense advocates must repudiate the ABM Treaty if they want to deploy a missile defense system. They must choose between the ABM Treaty and effective missile defense.

Lesson #9: Advances toward deployment can be reversed unless Congress is vigilant and focused. Important provisions of the Missile Defense Act of 1991 have been repealed because proponents in Congress lost interest in the missile defense issue. As a result, liberals were able to mount a successful campaign to weaken pro-defense legislation. Moreover, because missile defense supporters lacked confidence, they have refused to spell out exactly what they wanted. For example, the Defend America Act of 1996 mandated deployment by 2003 but recommended no specific architecture. As a result, any criticisms of missile defense deployments, including those related to cost and feasibility, were plausible. In fact, critics simply created their own costly and unrealistic scenarios: the classic "straw man" argument. Congress must be clear about what it wants and make sure the legislation it enacts is properly implemented.

Lesson #10: Career personnel in the Department of State and the Arms Control and Disarmament Agency (ACDA) are major obstacles to developing and implementing the missile defense program. The State Department and ACDA can have an enormous impact on the missile defense debate. For example, their personnel have been deeply involved in the Clinton Administration's effort to extend and broaden the restrictions of the ABM Treaty through an agreement with Russia and other republics of the former Soviet Union. They even have gone so far as to attempt to frustrate the will of Congress to deploy defenses by blocking any congressional review of such an agreement. This hostility is derived from the belief of many in State and ACDA that missile defense is incompatible with arms control. The negotiation of arms control agreements essentially defines the career interests of these officials. To remove them as an obstacle, ACDA must be abolished. Arms control lobbies inside the State Department should be abolished as well.

Lesson #11: A poor acquisition strategy for developing and deploying missile defenses has hindered the prospects for deployment. The Department of Defense can have a damaging impact on the prospects for deploying missile defenses on two levels. First, it can construct obstacles to deployment in the management of the acquisition process. For example, the Office of Program Analysis and Evaluation tried in 1992 to impose standard "go slow" acquisition rules on the Global Protection Against Limited Strikes (GPALS) deployment plan. Second, lawyers in the Department of Defense can impose strict interpretations of the ABM Treaty on missile defense development and deployment plans. Pentagon lawyers, for example, at one time prohibited the use of targeting data generated by ground-based early warning radar for ABM battle management. This strict interpretation of the ABM Treaty was dropped in 1993 when it was discovered that the Soviet Union followed a much more liberal interpretation of the ABM battle management provision.

This problem of treaty implementation is caused by a narrow and legalistic commitment to the implementation of treaties without regard to reciprocity from treaty partners. Missile defense proponents have not been mindful of these bureaucratic problems in the Department of Defense. Resolving the problems at the Department of Defense must start with establishing a streamlined management system for missile defenses and a policy of reciprocity in the implementation of arms control agreements.

Lesson #12: The weakening of the Ballistic Missile Defense Organization (BMDO) has undermined missile defense in the Pentagon bureaucracy. During the Reagan and Bush Administrations, the predecessor to BMDO, the Strategic Defense Initiative Organization (SDIO), was responsible for organizing and managing the development and ultimate deployment of missile defense systems. In May 1993, the Clinton Administration renamed SDIO and downgraded its authority by ordering the Director of BMDO to report to the Under Secretary of Defense for Acquisition instead of to the Secretary of Defense, as the Director of SDIO had done. The result has been to make BMDO too weak a player in the Pentagon bureaucracy to ensure the rapid and efficient development and procurement of a missile defense system. Stronger players, such as civilian leaders in the Office of the Secretary of Defense and military leaders in the services, now can easily override

BMDO. To strengthen BMDO inside the Pentagon bureaucracy, the head of BMDO should report directly to the Secretary of Defense.

Lesson #13: The military services are ambivalent about missile defenses. The military services place a higher priority on other missions and weapons systems. For example, the Army is more interested in ground warfare, and therefore in tanks and other ground combat systems. The Air Force has favored space systems not so much for combat operations, such as missile defense, as for peacetime activities like surveillance and monitoring. The Navy had little interest in missile defense during the 1980s, but its interest is growing because it sees missile defenses as an element of its strategy for projecting military power overseas.

Lesson #14: The Russians have been permitted a veto over U.S. missile defense programs. The Soviet Union's opposition to a missile defense deployment by the U.S. is legendary. Soviet leaders expressed their opposition mostly in the form of threats not to accede to other arms limitation agreements, including the 1987 Intermediate-Range Nuclear Forces (INF) Treaty and the 1991 START agreement. Despite these threats, the Soviets ultimately signed both treaties. The record of the post-Soviet Russian government has been mixed. The Russians put forth a cooperative deployment plan in 1992 called the Global Protection System (GPS); but the Bush Administration failed to conclude an agreement on GPS, and the Clinton Administration allowed the proposal to lapse. Since the beginning of 1993, the Russians have reverted to the Soviet stance by threatening not to ratify the 1993 START II agreement if the U.S. does not agree with Russia on missile defense.

The Soviets and Russians have been allowed to obtain this veto power by holding the arms control process hostage. As long as the U.S. treats arms control as indispensable, Russia will hold a veto over deployment. An effective policy must begin with insisting that the Russians no longer link their demands concerning offensive systems with U.S. plans for deploying missile defenses.

Lesson #15: The refusal of the U.S. to decide on deployment has weakened allied support for missile defense. With the notable exception of Israel, U.S. allies have been ambivalent about missile defense. The main cause has been the uncertainty about whether the U.S. is serious about deployment. The ambivalence of allies, in turn, has a detrimental impact on the progress of the missile defense program in the

U.S. Domestic critics can point to allied reluctance to cooperate as an indication that missile defenses will not contribute significantly to the nation's security. Thus, an endless cycle of ambivalence about missile defense ensues.

Lesson #16: By not focusing on the victims of missile attacks, missile defense proponents have allowed the public to remain unaware of its own vulnerability. The good news about public opinion toward the issue of deploying missile defenses is that there is little hostility to the idea. The bad news is that there is considerable ignorance and apathy. Public opinion polls show that a majority of Americans believe the U.S. already has deployed a missile defense system. While Americans are disturbed to discover that no such defense exists, they do not list missile defense as a high-priority concern. The ignorance and apathy quickly translate into an attitude of complacency that is very damaging to the prospects for deploying a missile defense system. The politicians are under little pressure to move forward with a deployment decision. Missile defense supporters have not done a good job of describing the missile threat in human terms which the average American can understand.

STRATEGIES FOR BUILDING SUPPORT FOR MISSILE DEFENSE

Proponents of missile defense need to learn these lessons well. They need to devise a new strategy to overcome the many obstacles to missile defense. This strategy should be broken down into concrete steps and measures that can be taken both by Congress and by executive branch officials sympathetic to missile defense.

STRATEGY #1
Congress should set a clear standard for the feasibility of a missile defense system.

Few now contest the notion that the United States is capable of fielding anti-missile weapons that can down ballistic missiles in flight. Even Secretary of Defense William Perry has acknowledged that U.S. technology is advanced enough to produce such weapons. It is only when the opponents of missile defense are allowed to set unrealistic standards

STRATEGIES FOR
BUILDING SUPPORT FOR MISSILE DEFENSE

- Congress should set a clear standard for the feasibility of a missile defense system.

- Congress should select an affordable missile defense deployment plan.

- Congress should determine the assumptions for future intelligence estimates of the missile threat.

- Congress should de-couple a missile defense deployment decision from open-ended research efforts.

- Congress should merge the existing national and theater missile defense programs into a single global defense program.

- Congress should require that the level of offensive weapons be linked to deployment of a missile defense system.

- Congress should replace mutual assured destruction with a new policy.

- Congress should demand that any agreement replacing the Soviet Union with other states as parties to the ABM Treaty be submitted to the Senate for ratification.

- Congress should craft a legislative agenda that holds individual Members of Congress accountable for their positions on missile defense.

- Congress should abolish the Arms Control and Disarmament Agency and make the State Department Legal Adviser responsible for applying the law on changes in the ABM Treaty.

- Congress should require the Department of Defense to establish a new acquisition policy for missile defense.

- Congress should strengthen the Ballistic Missile Defense Organization.

- Congress should insist that qualified proponents of missile defense are named to the new Commission to Assess the Ballistic Missile Threat to the United States.

- Congress should hold public hearings with the victims of missile attacks as witnesses.

STRATEGIES (continued)

- Members of the military services should press the case for missile defense.

- Russia should be encouraged to stop linking ratification of signed arms control agreements to U.S. positions on missile defense.

- U.S. allies should be encouraged to request demonstrations of U.S. missile defense capabilities.

---

of effectiveness that the feasibility question becomes subject to debate. This lesson should convince Congress that it should define the standards of feasibility itself.

A clear standard of feasibility was established by the Bush Administration in its GPALS proposal, a version of which Congress approved in the Missile Defense Act of 1991. The standard established then would require a missile defense system to thwart missile attacks of up to 200 warheads launched from anywhere in the world. In fact, Congress should seek to re-establish this standard. After the initial deployment, more ambitious standards of effectiveness can be debated.

STRATEGY #2
Congress should select an affordable missile defense deployment plan.

The assertions of the 1980s that a missile defense system would cost $1 trillion were, of course, wrong. But they were plausible because there was no deployment plan (architecture) against which cost estimates could be judged. In short, cost is a function of architecture. Without an architecture for a specific system, cost is anybody's guess.

This leaves Congress with the important task of determining which architecture to propose for deployment. Given the extremely tight defense budgets that have been proposed by both the Clinton Administration and Congress for the next five years, affordability is an essential consideration. Making missile defenses affordable requires three things. First, the proposed system must use existing military platforms wherever possible and thereby take advantage of the prior investments in those platforms. Second, the cost estimates should be limited to the initial deployment and should not include succeeding generations of missile defense systems. Third, the architecture must take full advantage of the ability to add space-based systems. This latter requirement will result in savings because the most cost-effective way to provide a global defense against missiles is from space.

These three criteria were at the forefront of the thinking that went into The Heritage Foundation's 1995 proposal to deploy missile defenses "first from the sea and then from space." This architecture takes advantage of the almost $50 billion investment the Navy already has made in its AEGIS ships, which can be adapted to a Navy Theater Wide (Upper Tier) defense and provide a global deployment capability. Further, it allows the sea-borne system to proceed under clearly defined budgets. Finally, the initial deployment could be augmented over time with space-based systems. The initial sea-based defense (along with space-based sensors) would cost about $440 million per year on average over the next five fiscal years, or roughly two-tenths of 1 percent of projected annual defense budgets. The cost of acquiring this initial system of 650 interceptors on 22 ships is between $2 billion and $3 billion more than what the Clinton Administration already has budgeted for the program, and it could be operational by the end of the decade. The capabilities of this inexpensive initial defense can be augmented through the adoption of upgrades, including the Navy's cooperative engagement capability, which allows the "networking" of sea-based radar, and the deployment of "Brilliant Eyes" space-based sensors. This is the architecture Congress should require the Clinton Administration to deploy.

STRATEGY #3
Congress should set the assumptions for future intelligence estimates of the missile threat.

Missile defense opponents have had considerable success in arguing that there is no missile threat to the U.S. This absurd contention is based on misleading assessments. For example, the November 1995 CIA National Intelligence Estimate assumes that there is no need to protect Alaska and Hawaii, and discounts the threat posed by the missile arsenals of China and Russia.

The following assumptions should be adopted instead for future estimates of missile threat:

- All current and projected missile arsenals (including those of China and Russia) should be considered;

- The threat should be considered on a world-wide basis (including threats to U.S. territory, U.S. forces abroad, and U.S. friends and allies);

- The rate of indigenous development of missiles in Third World countries should be based on a wide range of assumptions, including the "worst case" scenario;

- Foreign assistance should be considered as a shortcut to the development of missile arsenals in the Third World;

- The impact of the acquisition of space-launch vehicle technology on the development of missile systems should be considered;

- The prospects for the sale of missile systems to Third World countries also should be considered; and

- The possibility of accidental or unauthorized missile launches should be taken into account.

A legislative initiative can ensure that these assumptions are the basis for any future assessments of the missile threat.

Regarding the argument that other means of delivering weapons of mass destruction are more threatening to the U.S. than ballistic missiles, legislators can solve this problem easily. They can insist that missile defense is only a part of a broader policy to defend U.S. territory against attack and that, in addition to defenses against ballistic missiles, they support reasonable measures for improving air defenses, cruise missile defenses, coastal defenses, and anti-terrorist policies as well. A legislative directive could require the Secretary of Defense to report to Congress on how he is fielding defenses against all of these means of delivering weapons of mass destruction. This approach would force the Secretary to answer the question: Why would the U.S. want to continue a policy that fields defenses against every means of delivering an attack on its territory except ballistic missiles?

STRATEGY #4
Congress should de-couple a missile defense deployment decision from open-ended research efforts.

Missile defense opponents have argued against deployment by arguing that it is premature to deploy a missile defense system because better technology will be available if the Pentagon waits. This argument is really an excuse for deploying nothing. By this standard, it will always be premature to deploy any weapons system. There will always be better technology on the horizon. Proponents have been all too willing to accept this argument.

Congress can allow the Pentagon to proceed with deployment plans independent of possible future technology options. The technological requirement for deployment should be that the system meets the following performance requirement: It should be able to defeat, with a high degree of confidence, a missile attack of up to 200 warheads launched from anywhere against any target. This is not to say that the development of advanced missile defense technology should not continue. Rather, it is to say that future technological options should not be raised as an excuse to establish unrealistic performance requirements for the first phase of deployment.

STRATEGY #5
Congress should merge the existing national and theater missile defense programs into a single global defense program.

Following the Persian Gulf War, many opponents of missile defense proposed proceeding with the development and deployment of defenses against shorter-range (theater) missiles while deferring a decision on deploying defenses against long-range (strategic) missiles. This distinction was seized upon because the ABM Treaty allows the unfettered deployment of theater defenses. Accepting this approach ultimately backfired on missile defense proponents for two reasons. First, missile defense opponents used the ambiguous language in the ABM Treaty to argue that virtually all of the systems proposed fell into the limited long-range category. Second, keeping the two programs separate increased the costs and reduced the effectiveness of the systems to be deployed.

The distinctions between theater and strategic defenses are inconsistent with technological and strategic realities. The technological requirements for short-range and long-range defenses are virtually indistinguishable from one another. Moreover, the U.S. faces a threat from both theater missiles and strategic missiles. The proponents of missile defense in Congress should consider adopting legislation that directs the Pentagon to pursue a global defense capability that is effective against both theater and strategic missiles.

STRATEGY #6
Congress should require that the level of offensive weapons be linked to the deployment of a missile defense system.

Missile defense will not spark an arms race. Both the Reagan and Bush Administrations pursued missile defense options while negotiating unprecedented reductions in offensive forces through START and START II. Nevertheless, the claim that missile defenses are incompatible with arms control is still heard on Capitol Hill and elsewhere.

Those who support missile defense can end this debate once and for all by proposing a shared relationship between offensive and defensive forces at the strategic level. The substance of this new strategic bargain should be that each increment of defense deployed will be offset with a reduction in offensive forces. In other words, as offensive missiles are reduced, their strategic targeting requirements (the enemy missiles they are supposed to destroy in their silos) will be met by missile defenses (which would be responsible for destroying enemy missiles after they are launched). This proposal could be drafted into law and used to guide the U.S. strategic posture in meeting its official targeting requirements.

STRATEGY #7
Congress should replace mutual assured destruction (MAD) with a new policy.

The argument that missile defenses are "destabilizing" is fallacious. The doctrine of MAD is predicated on the assumption that the United States has only one strategic adversary and that this adversarial relationship is best managed by ensuring that both sides remain vulnerable to a nuclear missile strike. But the number of countries threatening America with nuclear missiles is sure to grow in the next ten years. Under this circumstance, the posture of vulnerability increasingly will become an incentive to strike the U.S. with nuclear weapons. The reason: As the U.S. disarms and pays little attention to shoring up deterrence in this new multipolar strategic environment, rogue states will become more convinced that nuclear threats of their own will deter U.S. military actions in the regions of the world where America has vital interests.

MAD needs to be replaced. Secretary of Defense William Perry pointed the way when he released the Pentagon's Nuclear Posture Review on September 22, 1994, and declared that the Clinton Administration sought to establish a new policy to replace MAD. This new doctrine is called mutual assured safety (MAS).[8] The problem is that no one knows exactly what it means. The doctrine could be given meaning by basing it on the assumption that continued vulnerability to attack is an outmoded and risky strategy. A new law could state that a balance of offensive and defensive strategic forces represents the best approach to protecting the peace in the complex and confusing post-Cold War era.

STRATEGY #8
The Senate should demand that any agreement replacing the Soviet Union with other states as parties to the ABM Treaty be submitted to it for ratification.

Effective missile defenses are incompatible with the ABM Treaty. Therefore, the ABM Treaty is the single most serious obstacle to the goal of deploying a comprehensive missile defense system. While there may be several paths to deployment of a global missile defense system, the problem is that they all converge at one intersection where the ABM Treaty sits. This obstacle cannot be circumvented. It must be removed altogether.

The best way to do this is to recognize that the ABM Treaty is no longer a legally valid agreement. After the Soviet Union collapsed, America lost its legally bound treaty partner. The U.S. should formally recognize the fact that there is now no treaty partner. The Clinton Administration has reached a tentative agreement to replace the Soviet

---

8 Department of Defense, "DOD Review Recommends Reduction in Nuclear Force," News Release No. 541-94 (along with supporting materials), September 22, 1994.

Union with several republics of the former Soviet Union. But such an agreement would constitute a substantive change in the ABM Treaty, and therefore would require Senate advice and consent under the Constitution and Section 232 of Public Law 103-337. The Senate could reject such an agreement. This rejection would require the U.S. to declare itself no longer bound by the ABM Treaty's provisions. The advantage of this approach is that voiding the treaty requires the support of only one-third of the Senate, not a supermajority of both houses of Congress large enough to override an expected presidential veto, which would be the case for normal legislation.

STRATEGY #9
Congress should craft a legislative agenda that holds individual Members of Congress accountable for their positions on missile defense.

Members of Congress often are loath to make difficult decisions because accountability is clear and the wrath of voters is easy to incur. Missile defense opponents, recognizing this fact, have resorted to all sorts of subterfuge to deny proponents a clear vote on the issue. In some cases, this was done by framing the debate over issues other than deployment: issues such as cost, technological options, or arms control. In other cases, this was done by exploiting Congress's own complex legislative process. For example, Senators and Representatives associated with the authorizing process which establishes defense programs in law often will try to pass the buck to the appropriators (those responsible for funding the programs) or vice versa. By shifting responsibility in this way, they ensure that nothing gets done.

Congress needs to be made accountable. Legislation can be drafted to focus on the central issue of deployment. The 1996 Defend America Act, for example, attempted to put individual Senators and Representatives on record about deployment. But the Defend America Act was never fully debated. It should be in the future.

Congress also should insist that the executive branch observe the law. The Clinton Administration has ignored provisions in the 1996 defense authorization bill regarding the management of the Theater High Altitude Area Defense (THAAD) system and the Navy Theater Wide (Upper Tier) system. Ultimately, a group of Representatives and Senators led by Representative Curt Weldon (R-PA) and Senator Jon Kyl (R-AZ) filed suit to force the Clinton Administration to comply. Unfortunately, the case was dismissed. It is ridiculous that Senators must resort to the courts to force the President to obey the law. In addition to legal remedies, Members of Congress can take such political steps as withholding consent to nominations, calling for the resignation of relevant officials, and withholding funds for other programs the President wants until the Administration agrees to obey the law.

STRATEGY #10
Congress should abolish the Arms Control and Disarmament Agency (ACDA) and make the State Department Legal Adviser responsible for applying the law on changes in the ABM Treaty.

Removing the ABM Treaty obstacle requires a legal determination that any agreement to designate states to succeed the Soviet Union should be submitted to the Senate for advice and consent. The primary defenders of the treaty are career lawyers at the State Department and ACDA who have no interest in giving the President this legal advice. These officials have sought, among other things, to replace the Soviet Union with several states as ABM Treaty partners without Senate approval.

To remove these bureaucratic obstacles to missile defense, Congress could take several steps. First, it should abolish the Arms Control and Disarmament Agency (ACDA). This should be done primarily for budgetary and management reasons, but it also will have the effect of removing ACDA lawyers from this determination process. Congress can ensure their influence is diminished by barring any lawyers who are serving now, or who have served in the past, as career employees in ACDA's Office of the General Counsel from serving in the State Department or the Defense Department after ACDA is eliminated.

Second, Congress should insist that a decision on successorship be placed in the hands of the State Department's Legal Adviser, a political appointee whose nomination is subject to Senate confirmation. Senators can insist that any incoming Legal Adviser agree to review this subject as the price of confirmation.

STRATEGY #11
Congress should require the Department of Defense to establish a new acquisition policy for missile defense.

The Department of Defense can impose obstacles to the deployment of a global missile defense system by hampering the acquisition process. This occurs at two levels. First, the standard acquisition management process is cumbersome, slow, and wasteful. Second, Pentagon lawyers impose unduly strict interpretations of the ABM Treaty on the program.

Overcoming this obstacle requires that Congress direct the Department of Defense to take the following steps. First, the Pentagon should be directed to release the missile defense program from the normal acquisition process and adopt a more streamlined process. Ambassador Henry Cooper, Director of SDIO during the Bush Administration, sought this kind of reform. He proposed removing missile defense from the purview of the Defense Acquisition Board (DAB) and putting it under the direction of a special executive committee chaired by the Deputy Secretary of Defense. Further, he envisioned the designation of the Director of SDIO (now BMDO) as acquisition executive in charge of the various missile defense programs to be integrated into a global missile defense system. This sort of acquisition process would allow the rapid and efficient development and deployment of a global missile defense system. It also could serve as a demonstration project for reforming the Pentagon's standard acquisition process.

Second, Pentagon lawyers, whose interpretations of the ABM Treaty often hamper missile defense development and deployment activities, should be directed to uphold a standard of reciprocity. Under no circumstances should the U.S. adhere to an interpretation of the ABM Treaty that is more restrictive than that of its treaty partners. This standard of reciprocity was ignored with regard to the use of early-warning radar for missile defense during the 1972–1992 period. The intelligence community should be tasked by Congress with determining the implementing standards applied by arms control treaty partners as the means for upholding this policy. Until such time as the ABM Treaty is eliminated, this reciprocity standard should be applied.

STRATEGY #12
Congress should strengthen the Ballistic Missile Defense Organization.

The Clinton Administration was wrong to downgrade SDIO/BMDO in 1993. The action reveals its opposition to the deployment of a missile defense system. The deployment of a global missile defense system will require a Director of BMDO with enough bureaucratic clout to get the entire Pentagon, including the military services, to embrace the program and to push the system through the acquisition process. When the Clinton Administration downgraded BMDO in 1993, the Director started reporting to the Under Secretary of Defense for Acquisition instead of to the Secretary of Defense. This left the Director of BMDO on a level equivalent to the Assistant Secretaries of the services in the Pentagon bureaucracy.

Upgrading BMDO means that the Director again would report directly to the Secretary of Defense. This relationship will allow the Director to appeal directly to the Secretary of Defense to resolve disputes over missile defense acquisition. Moreover, upgrading his position will provide the Director with access to the Under Secretary of Defense for Policy and provide him an audience with the Secretary of Defense in debating policy matters related to missile defense. The deployment of missile defenses is not just a question of acquisition; it is a reflection of policy. The Director of BMDO therefore needs access to the office in the Pentagon responsible for making policy. Congress can enact these institutional reforms into law.

STRATEGY #13
Congressional leaders should insist that qualified proponents of missile defense are named to the new Commission to Assess the Ballistic Missile Threat to the United States.

The National Defense Authorization Act for FY 1997, which President Clinton signed on September 23, 1996, creates a commission to review past conclusions that the missile threat to the United States is at least 15 years away. The nine members of the commission are to be appointed by the Director of Central Intelligence after consulting with the Speaker of the House on three members, the Majority Leader of the Senate on three members, and the Minority Leaders of both the House and the Senate on the three remaining members. Among those most qualified to sit on such a commission are members of The Heritage Foundation's Missile Defense Study Team (commonly referred to as "Team B"). The Speaker and the Senate Majority Leader would do well to consider Heritage Team B members for this commission.[9]

STRATEGY #14
Congress should hold public hearings with the victims of missile attacks as witnesses.

Past attempts to sway public opinion in favor of deploying missile defense systems have tended to focus on the threat. Certainly, public opinion can be swayed to some extent by explaining to the American people that menacing countries like Iran, Iraq, Libya, and North Korea may soon be able to threaten them directly with missiles. But public opinion is more likely to be swayed when the American people can empathize with people who are "just like us." As a result, more effort needs to be put into a public relations effort that relates the stories of those who have suffered from missile attacks: for example, Israelis who endured Iraqi *Scud* attacks during the Persian Gulf War or British subjects who lived through Hitler's V-2 attacks during World War II. The images should be as personal as possible. It is the realization of their own vulnerability that is most likely to convince people of the need for missile defense. Public hearings are ideal vehicles for broadcasting the message of vulnerability.

STRATEGY #15
Members of the military services should press the case for missile defense.

All the services should have an interest in fielding an effective missile defense system. As the Persian Gulf War demonstrated, missile defenses are necessary to the success of wartime operations. The Navy is coming

---

9 Among the members of Team B are Ambassador Henry Cooper, former Director of the Strategic Defense Initiative Organization; Frank Gaffney, former Acting Assistant Secretary of Defense for International Security Policy; William R. Graham, former Director of the White House Office of Science and Technology; General Charles Horner, former Commander in Chief of U.S. Space Command; and former Senator Malcolm Wallop.

to see missile defense as a necessary element of its force projection strategy; that is why it backs the Upper Tier missile defense system. For the Air Force, becoming a champion of missile defense means changing its attitude about how space-based surveillance should be exploited to support combat operations; to date, the Air Force has been more interested in using space systems for such peacetime activities as verifying arms control agreements and monitoring foreign weapons development programs. For the Army, it means proposing affordable solutions to the missile threat and getting all elements of the Army, outside the Space and Strategic Defense Command, to back these solutions. Ultimately, all three services will benefit from missile defenses in terms of their ability to perform combat missions. They can all play a positive role if they are willing.

STRATEGY #16
The U.S. should encourage the Russians to stop linking ratification of signed arms control agreements to U.S. positions on missile defense.

The Russians have reverted to Soviet-style demands that the U.S. do virtually nothing in the missile defense arena if they agree to ratify START II. The U.S. is under no obligation to do anything with respect to missile defenses and START II. However, the Russians *are* under an obligation to ratify START II, which the U.S. already is committed to ratifying.

In any event, Russian demands may be a bluff. The Soviets used this sort of bluff first by threatening not to negotiate and later by threatening not to sign the 1987 Intermediate-Range Nuclear Forces (INF) Treaty and START if the U.S. did not curtail the SDI program. Ultimately, they negotiated and signed both treaties, and SDI continued. Russians opposing the ratification of START II are not too concerned about U.S. missile defenses. They want to retain Russia's strategic arsenal and are merely looking for an excuse not to ratify the treaty. The real motive of the Russians in opposing START II is that they are having second thoughts about having to destroy their large number of multi-warhead missiles as the treaty requires. They want to keep the ABM Treaty because it keeps America vulnerable to these and other Russian nuclear missiles.

STRATEGY #17
The U.S. should encourage its allies to request demonstrations of U.S. missile defense capabilities.

The ambivalence of America's allies about missile defenses can be overcome if the U.S. demonstrates how they could provide the allies with tangible security benefits. One way to do this is to demonstrate a prototype missile defense system against an adversary's test missile. If the political circumstances are right—which should be an essential condition for any such demonstration—the U.S. could convey the seriousness of its intent both to deploy a missile defense system and to provide for allied security. For example, a future North Korean missile test designed to intimidate South Korea or Japan could be countered by a prototype of the Navy's Upper Tier system. Missile defense proponents in the bureaucracy should encourage allied officials to request such a prototype demonstration.

CONCLUSION

Since before the SDI program was launched in 1983, the proponents of missile defenses have been seduced by the prospect of achieving a political compromise with at least some opponents of missile defense. Compromise, however, has not worked. Instead, the outcome has been the proverbial one step forward and two steps backward. This certainly is what happened with the backsliding that occurred in the years following Congress's adoption of the Missile Defense Act of 1991. Many of the obstacles removed by the adoption of that act were quickly reconstructed. The supporters of deploying a missile defense system need to learn from this experience. They must eschew half-measures which fail to win over opponents and serve only to delay the necessary work of building missile defenses.

Compromises reached for reasons of expediency or obtaining a majority in Congress today can carry a steep price down the road. Reluctant supporters in 1991 proved unreliable. Building a stronger majority — one that will stand the test of time — means creating the political environment for a lasting agreement. Changing the political environment requires countering the arguments against missile defense in a systematic fashion and reducing the influence of those who remain opposed through aggressive actions. Above all, it requires absolute confidence that, sooner or later,

America will have a homeland defense against ballistic missiles. For the sake of millions of Americans, the time should be sooner.

Chapter 17

PROTECTING AMERICA'S REGIONAL INTERESTS

James Phillips

During the Cold War, American foreign policy was guided by a clear and compelling principle: containment of the Soviet Union, its satellites, and its allies. The stunning implosion of Soviet power has removed the only truly global threat to American interests. But in its place has emerged a much more complicated and threatening environment in which aggressive regional powers pose a wide variety of challenges to American interests and allies. The end of the bipolar global rivalry freed the United States from the need to engage itself in far-flung regions simply to offset Soviet actions in a global zero-sum competition. But the heightened uncertainty inherent in post–Cold War international politics and the greater unpredictability of many regional adversaries make it important for America to formulate and implement a coherent and comprehensive foreign policy strategy that focuses on key regions of the world.

During the Cold War, America's role as a global power was defined by the capability and will to defeat a global challenge from a single power. In the 21st century, it will be determined by the capability and will to defeat a myriad of threats to American interests in key regions like Europe, East Asia, the Persian Gulf, and Latin America. The U.S., as a global "regional" power, essentially must seek to create and maintain balances of power in

The author would like to thank Ariel Cohen, John Hillen, Thomas Moore, James Przystup, Baker Spring, John Sweeney, Paula Dobriansky, William Perry, Daniel Pipes, Daryl Plunk, and Bruce Weinrod for their suggestions and contributions to this chapter. The views and opinions expressed, however, are solely the responsibility of the author.

those key regions that are favorable to America's vital interests. Regional policies are now the building blocks of U.S. global foreign policy strategy rather than the subsets of a global containment strategy.

Commentators and policy analysts are fond of pointing out that the American people do not seem concerned about regional issues, or about foreign policy in general, unless it involves the loss of blood or treasure. The major controversies in the 104th Congress involved domestic and economic issues. Foreign policy and defense debates were notably absent in the 1996 presidential campaign as well. The standard argument seems to be that since America won the Cold War and now faces no significant threats, Americans can go about their daily routines without devoting much of their attention or many of their resources to foreign policy and defense issues.

Most Americans probably feel there is little they can do to affect foreign policy. They are usually content to leave foreign policy to the President, who in fact has the primary responsibility for it under the Constitution. But what happens when the President and executive branch are inept or act unwisely in carrying out this function? Mishandling of a regional crisis can have immediate, profound, and lasting consequences at home. If America cannot deter foreign aggression or prevent dominance of a key region by a hostile power, it could lose access to vital overseas markets or natural resources. This could translate into loss of prosperity and security for the average American.

For this reason, Congress and the policy community have an obligation to remain focused on foreign and defense policy. Congress obviously cannot conduct its own diplomacy — the nation cannot afford 535 Secretaries of State—and there are practical and constitutional limits to its ability to affect foreign policy. But Congress does have certain tools, under the constitutional principle of checks and balances, that it can use to shape the nation's regional policies and to mitigate the negative impact abroad of an incompetent Administration: the power to appropriate (or withhold) funds; the ability to maintain general oversight of executive branch agencies, which includes the power to investigate misconduct and bring issues to the attention of the American people through the public fora of congressional hearings; and the Senate's unique power to confirm Administration appointees—including ambassadors—and consent to ratification of treaties.

However, these powers cannot be used to their maximum effect unless Members of Congress and their allies in the policy community properly understand the regional issues facing the United States. Some general framework for a strategy is needed to achieve sound policies that will protect U.S. regional interests.

LESSONS LEARNED

Developing a long-term foreign policy framework can help to advance America's security and foreign policy interests around the world. Such a framework can avert international crises, gain a favorable resolution of crises whenever and wherever they arise, and shape U.S. policy toward both allies and adversaries. Without such a strategy, U.S. foreign policy is likely to remain a reactive ad hoc jumble of tactical maneuvers, driven by urgent short-term issues to the detriment of important long-term national security interests. A framework is extremely important if the U.S. is to be able to distinguish critical issues from secondary issues, and vital interests from less important ones.

America's most important foreign policy priority should be the management of competition and cooperation among the world's great powers: Europe, Russia, China, and Japan. These major powers have the greatest capacity to threaten American security and to challenge or help advance American foreign policy goals. Although the Soviet Union has collapsed, Russia and China remain potential great power adversaries. In addition, hostile regional powers such as Iran, Iraq, and North Korea pose substantial threats to American security interests, while dictatorships in Cuba, Libya, Syria, Sudan, and Vietnam primarily threaten American allies but may also pose military, terrorist, or revolutionary/subversive threats to American national interests.

While these regional powers lack the military muscle and strategic reach of the former Soviet Union, the worldwide diffusion of advanced military technologies, particularly missile systems and chemical, biological, and nuclear weapons of mass destruction, has enabled them to pose substantial military threats to America's military forces and allies. Since many of these countries are ruled by rogue regimes that have unleashed terrorism as an adjunct of their foreign policy, they pose a significant terrorist threat to American citizens at home and abroad. Today, hostile regional powers and even minor military powers can launch devastating military and terrorist attacks against American targets that were impractical only ten years ago.

LESSONS LEARNED

- By committing troops to Bosnia, where no U.S. vital interests are at stake, the Clinton Administration has put U.S. power and prestige in jeopardy.

- The Administration may permanently forfeit an opportunity to expand Europe's zone of peace, security, and freedom into Central Europe by not moving on enlarging NATO.

- By basing U.S.–Russian relations on the fate of one individual— President Boris Yeltsin—the Clinton Administration jeopardizes U.S. interests in the region.

- The Clinton Administration has harmed U.S.–China relations and encouraged Chinese aggressiveness in the region by failing to develop a consistent strategy.

- America's relationship with Japan, its most important Asian ally, has been jeopardized by an Administration policy that allows trade issues to overshadow strategic cooperation.

- The Clinton Administration's failure to contain and isolate hostile regimes in the Middle East jeopardizes vital U.S. interests in that region.

- The Administration's neglect of Latin America is undermining U.S. relations with its closest neighbors.

Threats posed by these regional powers have grown considerably in the recent past, yet the size of the U.S. armed forces has been shrinking because of President Clinton's ill-advised defense budget cutbacks. These cutbacks have diminished America's military margin of error to alarmingly thin proportions. The U.S. could not launch another Desert Storm–type operation without dangerously depleting its reserve forces and redeploying forces committed to other missions. This makes it all the more important for America to develop a consistent and realistic foreign policy strategy.

Challenges to U.S. interests in key regions of the world are the most important threats to America's new role as a global "regional" power. Maintaining a series of regional balances of power that are favorable to American interests—in Europe, East Asia, the Persian Gulf, and Latin America—is a daunting task for Congress and a new Administration; but all of these regions possess vast economic resources that, if mobilized against these interests, could gravely threaten U.S. security. Moreover, the economic prosperity of the U.S. is closely tied to trade with all these regions.

Because the United States is operating in an unpredictable and inchoate international arena, it is crucial that it prioritize its national interests in key regions of the world. Doing so lends coherence to American foreign policy and national security strategy. America cannot be all things to all people the world over, so it must use its power where it is most needed and most effective. Congress and the foreign policy community must heed the following lessons America has learned from the Clinton Administration's incoherent regional policy agenda.

Key Region: Europe

Europe historically has been the center of gravity for the global power struggle. The U.S. fought two world wars and the Cold War to prevent Europe from being dominated by a hostile foreign power. In addition, Europe is America's second-largest trading partner, accounting for almost $300 billion in trade in 1995: $134 billion in U.S. exports and $145 billion in U.S. imports. Roughly 50 percent of direct American investment abroad is funneled into Europe, and over 60 percent of direct foreign investment in the U.S. comes from Europe. Over 3 million Americans are employed in the U.S. by European-owned firms, and another 1.5 million American workers are supported directly by U.S. exports to Europe. The United States has an enduring interest in ensuring that Europe remains a secure, peaceful, free, and cooperative partner.

Europe currently faces no clear and present danger from any major power. As the war in the former Yugoslavia clearly indicates, the conflicts Europe will face in the near future most likely will be rooted in ethnic, regional, or religious tensions. However, these conflicts need not be regarded as urgently threatening the stability of Europe or automatically requiring U.S. military involvement. With no hegemonic power able to exploit these conflicts, Europe could be troubled by considerably more instability and even local warfare before U.S. interests are seriously threatened.

Lesson #1: By committing troops to Bosnia, a country in which the U.S. has no vital interests at stake, the Clinton Administration has put America's power and prestige in jeopardy. In his first term, President

Map 17.1

Graphic by Thomas J. Timmons, The Heritage Foundation.

Europe

Clinton deployed 20,000 troops as part of the peace implementation force (IFOR) in Bosnia and committed another 15,000 American military personnel in naval, air, and logistical support missions. Clinton first promised that these forces would return home in "about a year," but most experts doubted that the U.S. presence could make a lasting contribution to stability and genuine democratic reform in such a short period. Although the Administration has justified the operation as a move to preserve NATO, if IFOR fails NATO also could fail along with it.

The Bosnian conflict is only a secondary threat to European stability. Since no hostile outside power such as Russia is exploiting the conflict to attempt to dominate the region, America's vital interests have never been threatened, either immediately or seriously, by the war in Bosnia. The Clinton Administration should not have permitted its European allies to lead it into the Bosnian morass; instead, it should have insisted that they assume primary responsibility for this risky peacekeeping effort in their own backyard. The U.S. should not have tied its prestige, its credibility, and the lion's share of its European-based military forces to implementing a fragile peace plan in an area of peripheral strategic importance. While the U.S. can support the efforts of European allies in such missions, its singular security role in Europe must be focused on larger strategic issues.

Clinton's mistaken decision to turn a blind eye to arms smuggling from Iran to the Bosnian Muslims marginally improved the balance of power on the ground in Bosnia, but it also allowed Tehran to obtain a strategic foothold in southeastern Europe. This undermined U.S. efforts to contain Iran, eroded U.S. counterterrorism policy, damaged U.S. credibility, and exacerbated the terrorist threat to American peacekeeping troops subsequently deployed in Bosnia. Yet the Administration continued to defend this ill-conceived policy decision, oblivious to the collateral damage it inflicted even on its own declared policies.

Lesson #2: By dragging its feet on NATO enlargement, the Administration may permanently forfeit an opportunity to expand Europe's zone of peace, security, and freedom into Central Europe. The Clinton Administration agreed with NATO enlargement in principle but refused to implement any concrete policies to make it a reality. The Partnership for Peace (PFP) was instituted in 1994 as an intermediate step toward NATO membership; but while the program provides a useful framework for military cooperation between NATO and the PFP states (which include Russia and the states of the former Soviet Union), its implicit promise of NATO membership for all 27 PFP nations is not tied to any timetable. Moreover, to include all PFP members would spell the end of NATO as a cohesive and focused military alliance. There would be no reason for it to exist if Russia were a member.

Despite numerous congressional votes encouraging the Administration to offer NATO membership to Poland, the Czech Republic, Hungary, and others, President Clinton handed the Russians an implicit veto over when, where, and how NATO should expand. The longer NATO delays enlargement, the greater will be the opposition from Russia. Former communists have regained power in several countries in Eastern Europe and may soon do the same in Russia. Unless the U.S. acts soon, the opportunity to enlarge NATO may disappear.

Key Region: Russia

The only credible threat to the balance of power in Europe at this point is the potential re-emergence of an expansionist, revanchist, and revitalized Russian empire. Should Boris Yeltsin die and be replaced by an anti-American leader, Russia's new government might try to reassemble the Soviet empire. Yeltsin already has been moving to increase Russian influence in the "near abroad," establishing closer links with Belarus and forming a customs union with Kazakhstan and Belarus. Russia has imposed joint border controls on the outside perimeter of the Commonwealth of Independent States (CIS) and is integrating the bloc's air defenses. Russia also has attempted to use its economic leverage over its former client states in Eastern Europe and the former Soviet Union to maintain their dependence on Moscow.

Although Russia is economically weak and politically paralyzed, it still possesses large numbers of conventional and nuclear weapons that could destabilize Central and Eastern Europe or Central Asia if they were to fall into the hands of a hostile Russian regime. A resurgent Russia would require massive new U.S. defense spending, costing Americans hundreds of billions of dollars.

Lesson #3: By basing U.S.–Russian relations on the fate of one individual — President Boris Yeltsin — the Clinton Administration is jeopardizing America's national interests in the region. The U.S. has been perceived as uncritically supportive of the ailing Russian leader and has failed to develop ties with the democratic opposition. This perception could complicate relations with anti-Yeltsin factions should they come to power in Moscow in a post-Yeltsin era. Clinton failed to oppose Yeltsin's prosecution of the bloody war in Chechnya, which resulted in 100,000 casualties. The Clinton Administration also has been slow to recognize the importance of non-Russian former members of the Soviet Union, such as Ukraine and the oil-rich Caucasian and Central Asian states. The Administration's "Russia first" policy has turned a blind eye to Moscow's hard-line course toward its former provinces while neglecting the need to develop ties to Soviet successor states that could be important Western allies in the event a regime hostile to the U.S. comes to power in Russia in the future.

Key Region: East Asia

Asia, the home of the world's most dynamic and most rapidly growing economies, is America's foremost trading partner. America's two-way trade with Asia is approximately one-third larger than its trade with Europe. At almost $193 billion, U.S. exports to Asia in 1995 exceeded U.S. exports to

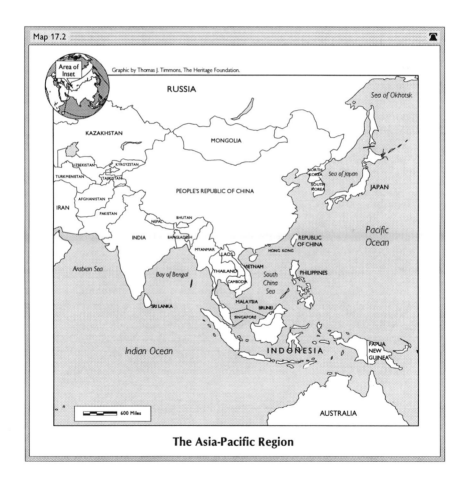

Map 17.2

The Asia-Pacific Region

Europe by more than $50 billion. These exports accounted for more than 3.8 million American jobs. U.S. imports from Asia totaled $310 billion in 1995.

Lesson #4: By failing to develop a consistent strategy toward Asia's emerging powerhouse, the Clinton Administration has harmed U.S.–China relations and encouraged Chinese aggressiveness in the region. The People's Republic of China (PRC) looms as a potentially major long-term threat to American interests in East Asia. While the PRC is not immediately powerful or expansionist, it has the potential to become both. Its authoritarian political system and hostility to Taiwan make mainland China a potential source of instability in Asia. China is building up its armed forces with weapons purchased from Russia and already possesses nuclear-armed missiles capable of reaching the U.S. As the communist ideology dies in China, the Beijing regime may resort increasingly to aggressive nationalism and international assertiveness to maintain its domestic legitimacy. China's attempts to intimidate Taiwan before Taiwan's March 1996 presidential election serve as a warning that this trend may already be in play.

After campaigning in 1992 to link China's most favored nation (MFN) trading status to its human rights record, President Clinton reversed himself in 1994 and, two months after the Chinese leadership had publicly humiliated then-Secretary of State Warren Christopher in Beijing, dropped his human rights demands and supported MFN for China. This was the correct decision, but the Administration's ill-conceived strategy forced it into a series of retreats and flip-flops that have undermined U.S. credibility throughout the region.

The most pressing short-term threat to U.S. security interests in East Asia comes from North Korea. North Korea's nuclear weapons program could lead to greater nuclear weapons proliferation or even to a military confrontation on the Korean Peninsula. If North Korea obtains nuclear weapons, South Korea and Japan could well follow suit, undermining U.S. attempts to stem nuclear proliferation. North Korea also poses a major military threat to U.S. ally South Korea and to American troops stationed there.

Lesson #5: The Clinton Administration has put America's relationship with Japan, its most important Asian ally, at risk by allowing trade issues to overshadow strategic cooperation. Simmering U.S.–Japan tensions over trade pose a secondary threat to American interests in East

Asia. The eruption of a trade war could drive a wedge between the two longtime allies and jeopardize Japanese-American strategic cooperation in the region. Clinton's policy toward Japan, which focused initially on efforts to manage trade, has been acrimonious and counterproductive. The Clinton trade team's demand that Japan accept numerical indicators to ensure that the U.S. trade deficit with Japan would be reduced has failed to produce the enforceable targets initially sought, and this has resulted in periodic flare-ups of bilateral tensions.

Key Region: The Middle East

The Persian Gulf region of the Middle East is the strategic storehouse for roughly two-thirds of the world's oil reserves and is therefore immensely important to the economic health of the U.S., the world's foremost consumer and importer of oil. Moreover, if this region were to fall under the hegemony of a hostile power such as Iran or Iraq, its vast oil wealth could be used to build military forces that could threaten the interests of the U.S. and its allies.

Lesson #6: The Clinton Administration's failure to contain and isolate hostile regimes in the Middle East jeopardizes vital U.S. interests. The chief threats to American interests in the Persian Gulf come from Iraq and Iran. Only these two countries possess the military potential and anti-Western animosity to mobilize a hegemonic threat to the Persian Gulf oil reserves on which the economic health of many Western economies depends. Both countries seek to acquire weapons of mass destruction, and both have used terrorism to attack the U.S. and its allies. Iraqi dictator Saddam Hussein shows no sign of abandoning his expansionist designs on his neighbors and will remain a threat to American interests as long as he remains in power. While Iraq poses the most immediate challenge to U.S. interests in the Middle East in the short run, Iran poses the greatest threat in the long run. Iran has replaced the Soviet Union as the chief exporter of anti-Western revolution and terrorism. Because the level of hostility from these two regimes is so high, containing them is an urgent task.

The Administration's "dual containment" policy, proclaimed in May 1993 to undermine and isolate anti-American regimes in Iran and Iraq, took a passive approach to ratcheting up pressure on these two rogue regimes. The Administration bolstered economic sanctions against Iran by banning trade with that nation in April 1995, but only under

Map 17.3

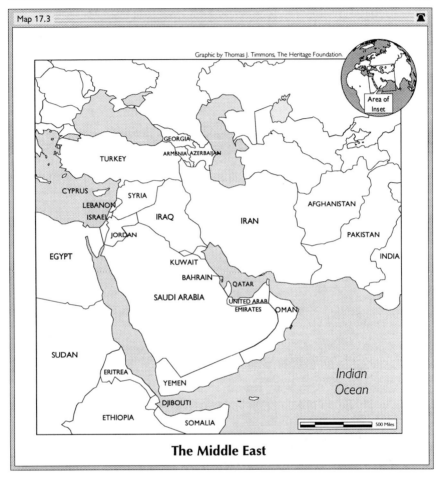

Graphic by Thomas J. Timmons, The Heritage Foundation.

The Middle East

congressional   pressure.   The   Administration   has   repeatedly
underestimated the threat posed by Iraq's Saddam Hussein and failed to
come up with an effective response to Saddam's August 1996 invasion of
the Kurdish enclave in northern Iraq. The Administration also
diplomatically wooed Syrian President Hafez al-Assad in an abortive
attempt to broker a Syrian–Israeli peace accord while neglecting to
punish Syria for its continued support of terrorism. In his two summit
meetings with Assad and the failed October 1996 Israeli–Palestinian
summit in Washington, President Clinton also mistakenly put a premium

on personal relations between the summit principals while neglecting to "pre-cook" the summits to assure positive outcomes.

Arab-Israeli tensions pose a secondary threat to American interests in the Middle East. The Arab-Israeli conflict has been muted since the 1991 U.S.-sponsored Madrid Peace Conference, the September 1993 Israel–PLO accord, and the October 1994 Israel–Jordan peace treaty. But tensions have grown because of continued anti-Israeli terrorism, Syrian and Iranian opposition to the peace negotiations, and a deadlock in the Israeli–Palestinian negotiations. A collapse of the Israeli–Palestinian negotiations could threaten Israeli security, weaken moderate Arab governments that support peace, and lead to an explosion in international terrorism.

Islamic radicalism also poses a long-term threat to American interests in the Middle East. Wherever Islamic radicals have seized power—Iran in 1979, Sudan in 1989, and Afghanistan in 1992—they have sought to export their revolution and unleash terrorism against their enemies at home and abroad. Algeria, engulfed in a civil war that has claimed 40,000 lives since 1992, currently is the state most vulnerable to a radical Islamic takeover.

Key Region: Latin America

Latin America and the Caribbean comprise the fourth-largest U.S. export market. While not as strategically important to the U.S. as the aforementioned regions, Latin America nevertheless remains critical to American foreign policy. The U.S. has a vital interest in maintaining stability along its southern border and preventing a hostile external power from dominating the region.

Lesson #7: The Clinton Administration's neglect of Latin America is undermining relations with America's closest neighbors. Latin America is not a key factor in terms of the world balance of power, but the Western Hemisphere is a critical arena for U.S. foreign policy. The economic development and political stability of Latin America and the Caribbean are of vital importance to U.S. economic and security interests. Since the end of the Cold War, however, U.S. policymakers have failed to take full advantage of the economic opportunities for U.S. business in Latin America while ignoring the proliferation of new security threats in the region. The executive branch and Congress have dropped trade

South America

expansion from their policy agenda since the collapse of the Mexican peso in December 1994 and have surrendered America's leadership in the process of hemispheric trade expansion to Brazil.

Moreover, the U.S. government has made little visible effort to modernize and restructure the Inter-American System (IAS) to deal more

Map 17.5

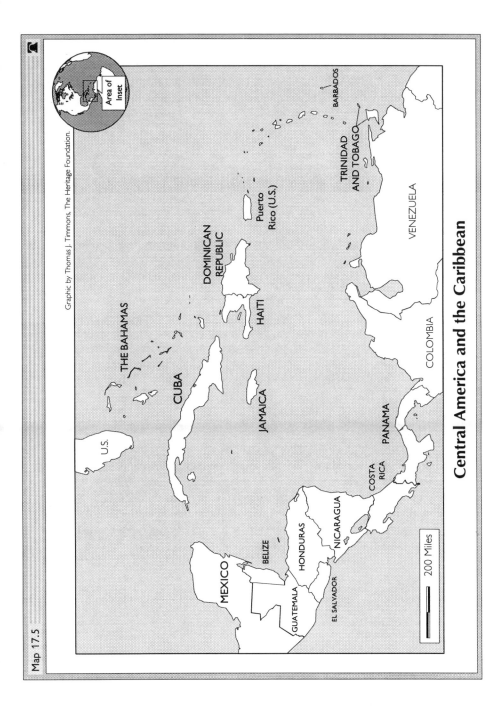

Area of
Inset

THE BAHAMAS

U.S.

CUBA

MEXICO

BELIZE

GUATEMALA

HONDURAS

EL SALVADOR

NICARAGUA

JAMAICA

COSTA
RICA

PANAMA

DOMINICAN
REPUBLIC

HAITI

Puerto
Rico (U.S.)

TRINIDAD
AND TOBAGO

BARBADOS

COLOMBIA

VENEZUELA

200 Miles

Central America and the Caribbean

effectively with new threats to regional security such as the spread of international drug trafficking and its accompanying political corruption, the growing involvement of left-wing guerrilla organizations in the drug trade, the increase in left-wing and right-wing political violence in several countries, and illegal immigration.

Mexico heads the list of U.S. priorities in Latin America. The U.S. has a vital economic, political, and diplomatic interest in supporting Mexico's transition to a fully democratic, free-market economy. Mexico is the third-largest U.S. trading partner and a valued member of the North American Free Trade Agreement (NAFTA). Political conflict or economic chaos in Mexico could create a huge influx of refugees along America's southern border and encourage the spread of organized violence, social unrest, and random crime in Mexico with potentially serious spillover consequences for the United States.

The tyranny of Fidel Castro endures in Cuba. The collapse of the Soviet Union and the growth of democracy throughout Latin America have diminished Castro's capacity to export violent revolution. However, Castro's communist regime is viscerally anti-American, has a significant military capability, and is capable of great violence, as demonstrated by the February 24, 1996, shootdown of two U.S. civilian aircraft. Yet the Clinton Administration resisted congressional efforts to impose tighter economic sanctions on Cuba and secretly negotiated an agreement with the Castro regime that requires U.S. naval forces to intercept Cuban refugees fleeing the island and return them forcibly to Cuba.

The White House has failed to follow through on Clinton's pledge at the 1994 Summit of the Americas to expand NAFTA to include Chile in 1996. This important goal was sidetracked in part because of the 1994–1995 collapse of the Mexican peso, which further derailed U.S. trade liberalization efforts in Latin America. Rather than push hard for trade liberalization and encourage economic and democratic reforms that could increase the region's political stability and reduce illegal immigration, the Administration has stressed foreign aid. It undertook a $20 billion U.S. Treasury bailout of Mexico and spent more than $3 billion on military assistance and financial aid to the regimes of Haitian President Jean-Bertrand Aristide and his successor, Rene Preval. This aid is likely to be wasted if Haiti reverts to political violence in the wake of an American military withdrawal.

STRATEGIES TO PROTECT AMERICA'S REGIONAL INTERESTS

In light of these regional issues and the lessons U.S. policymakers can learn from them, it is important to develop a set of strategies for foreign policy initiatives in each region. Congress must have a firm understanding of what steps it can take and what objectives the U.S. can and should have in each of these key international regions.

Protecting U.S. Interests in Europe

The U.S. must adopt diplomatic and security strategies that support the continued existence of a stable and free Europe composed of democratic states and strong American allies. The continued commitment of the U.S. to NATO and the collective defense of Europe is still the linchpin of this political objective. Moreover, the U.S. must ensure that the countries of Europe are committed to free trade and do not adopt protectionist policies as they pursue economic integration.

While the U.S. must formulate its European policy with the continent in mind, it should not neglect its existing relationships with such key national partners as Germany, France, and the United Kingdom. U.S. foreign policy must recognize that while some degree of political integration (perhaps even federalism) will likely emerge in Europe, the key to political stability in the near term lies in healthy relations with the continent's wealthier and more powerful states.

STRATEGY #1
The executive branch should help to refocus NATO on its collective defense mission and steer it away from peacekeeping missions.

The first step in articulating a proper U.S. security policy toward Europe is to refocus NATO, America's only institutional "bridge" to Europe, on the collective defense of Europe. This is fully consistent with America's vital political interest on the continent. Americans must know that a NATO focused on this core mission is the most authoritative, legitimate, and efficient vehicle for defending America's vital national interests in Europe. They also must know that the continued viability of NATO as an American-led alliance of collective defense is important for political, economic, and functional reasons.

STRATEGIES FOR PROTECTING U.S. INTERESTS IN EUROPE

- The executive branch should work to refocus NATO on its collective defense mission and steer it away from peacekeeping missions.
- Congress should press the Administration to expand NATO to include Poland, the Czech Republic, Hungary, and Slovakia.
- U.S. military involvement in Bosnia should be phased out.
- Congress should push for creation of a Trans-Atlantic Free Trade Area.

- **NATO** reinforces geopolitical stability in Europe and helps to make certain that Europe will not be dominated by a hostile power or bloc of powers.

- **NATO** helps to preserve general economic and political stability in Europe, which is vitally important to the U.S. economy.

- **NATO** is also an important vehicle for consolidating and spreading freedom and democracy in Europe.

For these reasons, NATO should expand immediately to include Poland, Hungary, and the Czech Republic. These Central European nations are culturally, politically, and economically part of the West; therefore, they would enhance NATO's ability to perform its core mission of collective defense. The profound geopolitical stability their entry into NATO would bring to Central Europe far outweighs any technical and financial difficulties that might be encountered. The U.S. also should press its allies to develop and implement cooperative efforts to deploy theater missile defenses.

STRATEGY #2
Congress should press the Administration to work aggressively to expand NATO to include Poland, the Czech Republic, Hungary, and Slovakia.

Congress should continue to pressure the President on NATO expansion. The GOP's Contract With America called for expanding

NATO to include Poland, Hungary, the Czech Republic, and Slovakia. Since then, both the House and Senate versions of the foreign operations bills have contained language supporting NATO expansion, but with few specifics and no concrete timetable for action. Congress should strengthen this language, mandate the expansion of NATO by 1999, and hold a vote in the Senate to show that there is a two-thirds majority in favor of NATO expansion. This is the majority that will be required to approve the changes in the NATO treaty brought on by expansion. Congress should also authorize the sale of NATO-approved weapons and military equipment by defense contractors to the identified countries.

However, NATO should keep the PFP but drop its disingenuous and ill-advised promise of eventual NATO membership for every nation in Europe. It would not be strategically credible to include those countries bordering Russia in NATO.

Enlarging NATO while reaffirming its focus on collective defense also requires a clear explanation of the U.S. military role in the alliance. The U.S. role in NATO's military operations should be determined by functional principles, not by geographic limitations or mission categories. America's European allies should take greater responsibility for their own security. The U.S., as NATO's leader, should continue to provide a nuclear and conventional force guarantee against a major power threat. In addition, the Supreme Allied Commander in Europe (SACEUR) should remain an American, as the U.S. will continue to provide the war-fighting core of NATO's forces. However, European allies must be encouraged to take decisive action to address peripheral instabilities that do not affect NATO's mission of preserving Europe's basic security condition. The Western European Union (WEU), which essentially is the European Union's (EU's) defense arm, should have the capability for crisis management, peace operations, and humanitarian missions, and the U.S. should be prepared to support these European-led efforts.

STRATEGY #3
Congress should phase out U.S. military involvement in Bosnia.

Congress should hold hearings on the Clinton Administration's lack of an exit strategy for ending American involvement in the Bosnian civil war. It should then notify the Administration that it will refuse to provide funds for American ground troops in Bosnia beyond December 31, 1997.

This would give the Administration one year to put into motion the process by which the U.S. and NATO would withdraw from the Bosnia mission and other European institutions would take over responsibility for any continued presence in Bosnia.

Painted into a corner on this issue in 1995, Congress gave the President one year and some $4 billion to implement the Dayton Peace Accords in Bosnia. Now it appears that NATO may commit troops to Bosnia for several more years for a mission that has yet to be determined. Congress must stop this pattern of committing troops first and then trying to decide what they should do and how. Congress should fund a reduced American presence in Bosnia for 1997 with the clear intention of handing off the mission to a European-led peacekeeping force by 1998. There should be no U.S. troops in the Balkans in 1998 and beyond.

STRATEGY #4
Congress should push for creation of a Trans-Atlantic Free Trade Area (TAFTA).

America's prosperity and economic stability depend in large measure on economic conditions in Europe. The U.S. must vigorously pursue policies that contribute to a European Union dedicated to free trade and a healthy growth in the new market economies of Central and Eastern Europe.

In Western Europe, the U.S. has a strong interest in preventing the EU from acting as a protectionist trading bloc. In Central and Eastern Europe, the U.S. must promote market-based reforms, investment, productivity, and economic growth. This should not be done primarily through foreign aid. Instead, the U.S. should open its borders to trade with the region and press its Western allies to open their own highly protected markets. Free trade agreements can be offered to the region, but even unilateral reduction of tariffs and other barriers would be a step in the right direction.

Both of these goals could be achieved by creating a Trans-Atlantic Free Trade Area linking the economies of Europe with the United States. Total U.S. trade with Europe in 1995 was almost $300 billion. The U.S. has a strong interest in preventing European protectionism from blocking U.S. access to the European market. The greatest danger is not from individual European states (although France is likely to remain heavily committed to protectionism), but from the European Union as a whole. In addition to seeking a TAFTA with the EU, the U.S. should use the World Trade Organization (WTO) to encourage Europe to open its markets further. For example, the U.S. should identify the most restrictive EU trade policies and file a claim against them in the WTO. The EU is likely to do the same to the U.S., which should be prepared to open its markets further to European goods and services.

In the event that the EU is unwilling to enter a free trade area with the United States, the U.S. should continue to pursue FTAs with individual Eastern and Central European countries, many of which are establishing free markets that rival those of industrial Western Europe. For example, the Czech Republic and Estonia have made great strides in establishing open economies with impressive levels of economic growth. If the U.S. had free trade agreements with these countries, it could benefit greatly from the increased export and investment opportunities presented by their economic growth.

Congress should hold hearings to educate the American people on the possible economic benefits of TAFTA. Then it should pass both a resolution expressing congressional support for liberalizing trade with Europe and fast-track negotiating authority for TAFTA.

Protecting U.S. Interests in Russia and the Former Soviet Union

Despite his communist roots, Boris Yeltsin was able to cast himself as an anti-communist during the 1996 Russian presidential campaign. However, his policies, behavior, and rhetoric bear more and more resemblance to elements of Russia's past. Over 75 percent of his administration is made up of former party *apparatchiks* or former communist industrial managers. In Chechnya, since the start of the Russian military campaign on December 12, 1994, over 80,000 people have been killed and more than 300,000—including many ethnic Russians—have become refugees. The Clinton Administration turned a characteristic blind eye to these atrocities despite protests from Russian democrats. President Clinton has bent over backwards not to offend Boris Yeltsin as Yeltsin's government has crushed the rebellion with a brutal and excessive civilian death toll.

The futility of the war effort was a major driving force behind former National Security Chief Alexander Lebed's negotiations with the Chechen rebels in the summer of 1996, which essentially postponed the decision

STRATEGIES FOR PROTECTING U.S. INTERESTS IN RUSSIA AND THE FORMER SOVIET UNION

- A new relationship with Russia and the Newly Independent States should be forged.

- U.S. policy toward Russia should emphasize the prevention of a new Russian empire from emerging in the territories of the former Soviet Union.

- Congress should increase funding for institution-building programs and exchanges with the Newly Independent States.

- Russia's increasing role in nuclear proliferation should be opposed.

- Arms control should be de-emphasized as the focal point of U.S.–Russia relations.

- Congress should demand accountability for U.S. assistance funds and introduce transparency into Nunn-Lugar funding for defense conversion and disarmament.

- Congress should allow for humanitarian and institution-building assistance to Azerbaijan.

- Congress should have hearings on the geopolitics of natural resources in Central Asia and on Russia's borrowing in international securities markets.

- Inter-parliamentary exchanges should be supported.

concerning Chechnya's status and relationship with Russia. There are disagreements over the interpretation of this agreement, and it remains to be seen whether the war really is over. Yeltsin's firing of Lebed in October 1996 increases the uncertainty about Chechnya.

If war resumes, the U.S. should denounce any new atrocities that occur in Chechnya and link Russian misbehavior to economic sanctions, such as the withholding of U.S. and multilateral aid and loans. In the past, both the Russians and the Chechens agreed to bring in impartial foreign mediators to settle the conflict. The U.S. should promote a peace process under the auspices of the OSCE, which already is active in Chechnya and would be the appropriate forum for resolving any such conflict.

STRATEGY #1
Congress and the executive branch must cooperate in forging a more reciprocal relationship with Russia and the Newly Independent States (NIS).

The period of romantic partnership between Russia and the West is over. Russia is reasserting itself as a great power, taking a path that already has led to diplomatic tensions with the West over Bosnia, NATO expansion, the supply of nuclear reactors to Iran, and the sale of modern weaponry to China. In fact, Russia is going through a period of political turbulence fraught with danger for the West. America should continue to support democracy, elections, free markets, and individual rights in Russia and to oppose anti-democratic solutions, no matter who initiates them. If Russia stays the course toward democracy and market reform, it will become more prosperous and predictable, benefiting Western security and business interests. At the same time, the U.S. must be prepared to deal with the consequences of democratic failure in Russia—and possibly even with a new Cold War. The U.S. also should develop strong relations with the NIS, such as Ukraine.

STRATEGY #2
Congress must ensure that U.S. policy toward Russia emphasizes preventing a new Russian empire from emerging as a successor to the former Soviet Union.

Moscow is attempting to re-establish its influence in neighboring regions that once were part of the Soviet Union. The Kremlin is employing a combination of economic, diplomatic, and military means to achieve a sphere of economic and military influence in what Moscow calls its "near abroad"—the Baltic States, Ukraine, and the non-Russian states of Central Asia and the Caucasus. A tightly knit union dominated by Russia would have a strong armed force and a secret police with the global reach of the former KGB. The forces behind a restoration of imperialism—the military, the security apparatus, the military-industrial complex, and certain elements of the bureaucracy — hold the most anti-American and anti-democratic positions in the Russian political spectrum. These politicians yearn for a return of East–West rivalry and the superpower status once held by the U.S.S.R. While it is impossible to predict whether the hard-liners have the will and resources to restore the old empire, the attempt itself could be devastating to the peace and stability of Eurasia and adjacent regions.

Preventing the emergence of a Russian empire in the lands of the former Soviet Union is an important Western priority. Russia cannot be an empire and a democracy at the same time. Historically, imperial Russia always posed a threat to Eastern and Central Europe. Moreover, an anti-Western policy could lead Russia to forge alliances with reactionary forces in China and radical Islamic states and movements.

Washington should make clear to Moscow that it assigns the highest priority to ensuring that Russia observes international standards in dealing with its neighbors. If Russia wants to integrate itself into the world community, it must abide by the appropriate rules of conduct, including international law and custom. Washington should make it clear that aggressive military action by Russia against its neighbors will result in international isolation and possible economic sanctions.

STRATEGY #3
Congress should increase funding for institution-building programs and exchanges with the Newly Independent States.

The U.S. must voice its commitment to the independence, sovereignty, and territorial integrity of the NIS in no uncertain terms, working with the governments of the NIS to strengthen their independence from Moscow. In short, Russia must not be granted a special sphere of influence in Europe and Central Asia.

A main concern of the West is the continuing independence, sovereignty, and territorial integrity of Ukraine and the Baltic states of Estonia, Latvia, and Lithuania. Without these vital areas, Russia cannot threaten the countries of Eastern and Central Europe. To ensure the independence of Ukraine and the Baltic states, the U.S. should develop close official contacts with these countries; boost military cooperation; provide training for security forces, commanders, and policymakers; and grant scholarships for student exchanges. As far as NATO is concerned, while these states will not be full members of NATO in the immediate future, this does not preclude closer military relationships between the

U.S. and these countries. The U.S. should also support the full integration of the Baltic states into the European Union and encourage the EU to sign an associate agreement with Ukraine. The Baltic states also should be encouraged to join the Western European Union.

Congress should increase funding for long-term training programs (from six months to a full academic degree) for government officials from the NIS. Educating a new, post-communist government elite would contribute significantly to the development of independent foreign policies in the NIS based on recognition of their own national interests. While Russia inherited the state apparatus and military power of the former Soviet Union, important NIS did not. Ukraine, Georgia, Azerbaijan, and Uzbekistan urgently need to train their current and future diplomats, civilian national security specialists, military, and police officers. Such training, in addition to advancing democratic and free-market reforms, would make the NIS less dependent on Moscow.

STRATEGY #4
The U.S. should oppose Russia's increasing role in nuclear proliferation.

Another critical issue in U.S.–Russian relations is Russia's sale of nuclear reactors to Iran and modern weaponry to China. Tehran has launched a bid to acquire nuclear weapons. It is buying two Russian-made nuclear reactors capable of producing plutonium that can be reprocessed to become weapons-grade raw material for atomic bombs. With its formidable oil and gas resources, Iran does not need nuclear power. The Clinton Administration failed to highlight this issue during the 1995–1996 Clinton–Yeltsin summits and did not offer the Russians an alternative deal that would sidetrack the reactor sale. This was a mistake. The U.S. should offer Russia cooperation in the nuclear area and in space exploration in order to stop the leakage of deadly technology to the ayatollahs in Tehran.

The U.S. should strongly oppose Russia's increasing role in nuclear proliferation. It should use every means, including covert action, to prevent Iran, Iraq, and other rogue states from gaining nuclear and chemical weapons capabilities. For example, voluntary controls on dual-use technology exports to these countries—similar to the Coordination Committee on Multilateral Export Controls (COCOM) regime used during the Cold War—should be put in place.

STRATEGY #5
Congress should de-emphasize arms control as the focal point of U.S.–Russia relations.

The U.S. Senate has ratified the START II agreement signed by Presidents Bush and Yeltsin in 1992. However, hard-line elements in Russia, including members of the Duma, object to ratifying START II. Russian recalcitrance has become an impediment to improved relations. Moreover, it is cited by the American arms control community as a reason to make further concessions to Russia on arms control, such as acceding to Russia's demands that the 1972 ABM Treaty be extended to limit certain missile defenses not covered by the original treaty. To remove arms control issues as an impediment to improved bilateral relations and reduce Russian leverage over U.S. security policy, Congress should use its legislative powers in two ways:

- **End the linkage between START II and the ABM Treaty** by declaring the ABM Treaty null and void. As discussed in Chapters 14 ("Maintaining an Effective Military in a Budget Straitjacket") and 16 ("Building Support for Missile Defense"), this strategy is within Congress's constitutional authority.

- **Use the "power of the purse"** to reduce funds available for the Arms Control and Disarmament Agency, the Defense Department's Office of Compliance, and other agencies involved in the traditional Cold War paradigm of arms control. This in turn will reduce the importance of arms control in U.S. policy.

STRATEGY #6
Congress should demand accountability for U.S. assistance funds and introduce transparency into Nunn-Lugar funding for defense conversion and disarmament.

Currently, the Russian Defense Ministry and related enterprises benefit from over $900 million a year in U.S. assistance funds for disarmament and defense conversion. Yet these organizations do not provide the U.S. government with access to accounting documents and end-use applications of funding. The U.S. Congress should make Nunn-Lugar funding conditional upon Russia's providing this access; if Russia still refuses to comply with this requirement, funding should be discontinued.

STRATEGY #7
Congress should allow for humanitarian and institution-building assistance to Azerbaijan.

Section 907 of the 1992 Freedom Support Act denies all assistance, including humanitarian aid, to Azerbaijan, an important pro-Western, secular Muslim state on the coast of the oil-rich Caspian Sea. Western access to this oil will be extremely important in the next millennium. Azerbaijan is at war with Armenia (which has occupied 20 percent of its territory) over the disputed enclave of Nagorno-Karabakh, populated mostly by Armenians. At the same time, Azerbaijan's security and stability are threatened by neighboring Russia and Iran. In order for the U.S. to maintain the balanced position of an honest broker and to counter anti-American forces in the region, Congress should amend Section 907 of the Freedom Support Act to allow for U.S. humanitarian and institution-building assistance to Azerbaijan.

STRATEGY #8
Congress should conduct hearings on the geopolitics of natural resources in Central Asia and on Russia's borrowing in international securities markets.

Given the increasing instability of the Middle East, the tremendous hydrocarbon reserves of the Caspian seabed, Azerbaijan, and Kazakhstan and the gas reserves of Turkmenistan and Uzbekistan are becoming increasingly important to Western economic development. Access to these fields is limited by Russia, which intends to control both development of the region's resources and exports of its oil and gas. The Senate Foreign Relations and Energy Committees should conduct joint hearings on securing American access to these energy resources and helping to protect secular Muslim regimes in the region from anti-Western Islamic militant movements.

Russia is one of the major debtors in global financial markets. With a national debt exceeding $130 billion, it is planning to float a $500 million Eurobond issue with a five-year maturity in November 1996, as well as an additional minimum of $1.3 billion in 1997. Gazprom, Russia's powerful gas monopoly, and the municipalities of Moscow and St. Petersburg are also planning to borrow by issuing commercial paper in Western capital markets. In addition to Russia's more than $14 billion in IMF loans, these funds may be directed to financing continuing aggression against Chechnya, fueling the ballistic missile modernization program, and financing the supply of nuclear reactors to Iran. Furthermore, the Russian tax system is in a shambles, and capital flight is approaching $20 billion per annum.

These developments make Russia's ability to repay its debts questionable at best. In short, Russia today is a bad financial risk, and Western investors who hold its paper may well be in jeopardy. Hearings in the Senate and House Banking and Commerce Committees should include testimony from the CIA, the Federal Reserve, the Securities and Exchange Commission, and the Treasury Financial Crime Division, as well as from independent experts, on the potential risks associated with Russia's access to international financial markets.

STRATEGY #9
Congress should support inter-parliamentary exchanges.

Contacts between Russian and U.S. politicians remain important in the post–Cold War era. Representative Curt Weldon (R-PA) has initiated Congress-to-Duma contacts which also are strongly supported by Duma Foreign Affairs Committee Chairman Vladimir Lukin. These contacts should receive the support of the 105th Congress.

Protecting U.S. Interests in East Asia

Over the course of this century, the United States has consistently pursued three fundamental strategic objectives toward Asia: 1) preserving freedom of the seas, 2) maintaining unimpeded access to markets, and 3) preventing the domination of the region by any single power or group of powers. These interests remain valid today; indeed, the Clinton Administration's dispatch of the aircraft carriers U.S.S. *Independence* and U.S.S. *Nimitz* to waters off Taiwan in March 1996 in response to China's threatening military exercises stands as testimony to their enduring nature. To protect these interests, the U.S. needs a comprehensive and integrated economic, political, and security strategy toward the region.

East Asia is home to the world's fastest growing economies. Since the early 1980s, the volume of imports and exports exchanged across the Pacific has exceeded U.S. two-way trade with every other region of the world. In 1995, American exports to Pacific Rim countries amounted to over $183

STRATEGIES FOR PROTECTING U.S. INTERESTS IN EAST ASIA

- The United States should seek to create the world's largest free trade area in the Asia-Pacific region.

- Congress should use its oversight functions to strengthen the alliance between the United States and the Republic of Korea (ROK), and to ensure that ROK security is not jeopardized by recent developments on the Korean Peninsula.

- The implementation of the U.S.–North Korea Nuclear Framework Accord should be reviewed to ensure that its implementation is consistent with ROK security goals.

- The United States should consult with the ROK in the conduct of U.S. diplomacy with North Korea and ensure that the U.S.–ROK relationship is not undermined.

- The United States must clearly define and prioritize its interests to be pursued in the relationship with China.

- Congress should reaffirm its commitment to the Hong Kong Policy Act.

- Congress should move to put U.S.–China trading relations on a firm foundation by exempting China from the Jackson-Vanik Amendment economic sanctions.

- Congress should demonstrate to Beijing America's commitment to the security of Taiwan and, in accordance with the terms of the Taiwan Relations Act, its determination to continue to supply Taiwan with defensive arms.

- Bilateral agreements and alliances in Asia should be strengthened.

- A cooperative policy with Japan to open markets through the Asia-Pacific Economic Cooperation forum and the World Trade Organization should be pursued.

billion and supported over 3.6 million American jobs. In today's post–Cold War world, an ever more profitable economic relationship with East Asia remains one of America's foremost strategic interests. Thus, it is imperative that Washington seek ways to expand trade with Asia.

Though booming and prosperous, Asia is also beset by a number of sensitive diplomatic and security issues whose outcome will affect fundamental U.S. interests. Foremost among them are tensions on the Korean Peninsula, relations between the United States and China, and relations between China and Taiwan.

STRATEGY #1
The U.S. should seek to create the world's largest free trade area in the Asia-Pacific region.

A large free trade area in the Asia-Pacific region would help create numerous U.S. jobs, enhance opportunities for American entrepreneurs in Asia, and offer East Asians access to U.S. markets and other markets throughout the Americas. It also would head off any Asian attempt to establish a trading bloc that excludes the U.S. The Asia-Pacific Economic Cooperation (APEC) forum, formed in 1989, is an instrument the U.S. can use to foster trade liberalization and enhance American commercial opportunities in the region.

To expand commerce between the Americas and East Asia in the long term, however, Washington needs to go beyond APEC. It should establish a forum to discuss and then implement free trade agreements spanning these two dynamic regions. Participants should include the members of NAFTA—the U.S., Canada, and Mexico—and East Asian members of APEC. Creating a trans-Pacific free trade area to underpin U.S.–Asian prosperity is perhaps the most cost-effective way to prevent conflict from arising between America and East Asia.

STRATEGY #2
Congress should use its oversight functions to strengthen the alliance between the U.S. and the Republic of Korea (ROK) and to ensure that ROK security is not jeopardized by recent political, diplomatic, and military developments on the Korean Peninsula.

The outbreak of conflict on the Korean Peninsula is the most likely large-scale security contingency facing the United States in Asia. North Korea's million-man army remains largely deployed forward along the Demilitarized Zone (DMZ) within 30 miles of Seoul, the capital of South Korea. Over the past decade, North Korea has enhanced its conventional striking power with a missile development program, in addition to chemical and biological weapons and (possibly) nuclear weapons.

Deterring the North from aggression is the central element of U.S. policy and strategy. Deterrence is sustained by the strength of the alliance between the U.S. and the Republic of Korea, the presence of 37,000 American forces on the peninsula, and forward-deployed American forces in Japan. To enhance deterrence, the U.S. should take all necessary steps to ensure that the Republic of Korea and American forces are protected by an effective missile defense system. The government of the ROK has a clear requirement to defend itself against North Korean missiles. Seoul now relies on approximately 192 Patriot missiles to protect American forces in South Korea; they are clearly insufficient to defend South Korea's forces and cities. Washington should urge Seoul to place a much higher priority on purchasing theater missile defense systems from the U.S.

STRATEGY #3
Congress should actively review the implementation of the U.S.–North Korea Nuclear Framework Accord and hold the Administration accountable to make sure its implementation is consistent with ROK security goals.

The U.S. must closely monitor Pyongyang's implementation of the 1994 U.S.–North Korea Nuclear Framework Accord. Under this agreement, the U.S. is to help finance and build two light water nuclear reactors for North Korea in exchange for North Korea's freezing of its plutonium-producing reactors. The agreement also commits the U.S. to supplying oil to North Korea while the reactors are being constructed. In return, North Korea agreed to resume substantive high-level dialogue with South Korea—which thus far it has failed to do. The U.S. must insist that North Korea live up to its obligations, in particular the resumption of substantive high-level talks with South Korea, under the Framework Accord.

Washington must be careful not to allow North Korea to foment mistrust and suspicion between the U.S. and South Korea, as Pyongyang was able to do during the negotiations leading to the nuclear agreement. Pyongyang has used its nuclear program and its threat to withdraw from the Nuclear Non-Proliferation Treaty to initiate a negotiating process with the United States. In the process, North Korea was able to achieve several of its long-standing objectives. First, Pyongyang was able to open a direct diplomatic channel to Washington. Second, in pursuing its nuclear bargain with Pyongyang, Washington marginalized the role of South Korea in the negotiating process, allowing North Korea's traditional "wedge-driving" tactics to succeed. All of these developments have unsettled the South Koreans.

A variation of this North Korean strategy is evident in Pyongyang's insistence during the first half of 1996 that the armistice that ended the Korean War must now be replaced by a peace treaty between the United States and North Korea. In response to North Korea's call for direct talks with the U.S., Washington must make clear that South Korea will be a co-equal participant in any subsequent peace agreement. At the same time, Washington must declare that Pyongyang's provocative behavior, such as sending armed troops into the DMZ in May 1996, will not be rewarded in diplomatic negotiations over the armistice.

STRATEGY #4
Congress should insist that the U.S. government consult closely with the ROK on the conduct of U.S. diplomacy with North Korea, and should monitor U.S. relations with North Korea to ensure that the U.S.–ROK relationship is not undermined.

The U.S. and its ROK ally are deeply concerned about reports of famine in North Korea because these reports raise the specter of North Korea's lashing out in a desperate military venture to solve its internal problems. But North Korea may also be using its food crisis for political ends, to manipulate the U.S. and divide the U.S. and the ROK. It is true that severe flooding in 1995 has caused North Korea to experience major food shortages, and the debate over food aid in early 1996 certainly strained the U.S.–ROK relationship. At present, both Seoul and Washington are conditioning food aid on the North's acceptance of the U.S.–ROK joint proposal, made in April 1996 by President Clinton and President Kim Young Sam, for talks involving the U.S., the ROK, North Korea, and China.

If the food shortage worsens, the U.S. should be prepared to extend food aid, but only on certain conditions. Intrusive in-country monitoring is a starting point. Washington must also insist on the resumption of serious high-level talks between Pyongyang and Seoul. Congress should make clear to the Administration that any attempt to extend economic assistance to North Korea will require a quid pro quo from North Korea, and that any economic aid is contingent on North Korea's commitment to economic reform.

Washington should be prepared to expand ties with North Korea only if the North improves ties with Seoul. Direct North–South talks are still the key to peace and stability on the peninsula, and mechanisms for direct South–North dialogue already exist. The North should avail itself of them. In the 1991 North-South political accords, the North committed itself to direct high-level dialogue with the South. In the 1994 Agreed Framework, the North again committed itself to that end. Pyongyang should live up to its commitments.

STRATEGY #5: The U.S. must clearly define and prioritize the interests it will pursue in developing its relationship with China.

China is emerging as the dominant power in Asia, in both economic and military terms. Clearly, the future of U.S. interests in the region will be determined by how well America can manage its troubled and uncertain relations with China. In seeking a sound relationship with China, the U.S. must continue to assert three fundamental concerns: 1) regional peace and stability, 2) freedom of navigation on the high seas, and 3) free access to markets. These interests promote a stable and secure world in which political and economic freedom, human rights, and democratic institutions can flourish.

The U.S. must not allow the need for a sound relationship with China to obscure the need for a strong and modern U.S. military presence in the Pacific, for greater transparency and trade liberalization through APEC and the WTO, and for Asian nations to cooperate in fighting drug trafficking, illegal immigration, and the proliferation of weapons technology. China professes to share U.S. interests in regional peace, free navigation, and market access, but greater cooperation from China will be necessary if these goals are to be achieved. The U.S.–China relationship is the axis on which the prospects for realizing these objectives in Asia, as well as in China, turn. The challenge for the United States is to keep the channels of communication and cooperation open while at the same time ensuring that China lives up to the rules and norms of the agreements to which it is a party.

Congress and the executive branch must cooperate in maintaining frequent and consistent dialogue with Chinese leaders at the highest levels. The U.S. must use each opportunity to articulate America's historic interest in Asia, to evaluate China's impact on the viability of these interests, and to describe how the U.S. intends to continue to protect these interests. Then U.S. leaders must listen carefully as China's leaders do the same, both to avoid miscalculation and to demonstrate the level of respect each side grants this developing relationship.

The U.S. must make China understand that with this respect comes added responsibility. If China wishes to maintain relations with the United States, the status of Taiwan must be resolved by peaceful means, Hong Kong must maintain its autonomy, the proliferation of nuclear and other advanced military technology must be controlled, and human rights conditions must be improved.

STRATEGY #6
Congress should reaffirm its commitment to the Hong Kong Policy Act.

The United States has a commercial interest in Hong Kong's ability to function as the world's freest economy and a political interest in Hong Kong's stability as an open, democratic society. The Hong Kong Policy Act requires the State Department to report to Congress on issues such as Hong Kong's economy, political freedoms, and human rights, all of which will affect American interests after Hong Kong reverts to PRC sovereignty. Congress should hold public hearings to review the State Department's report.

STRATEGY #7
Congress should move to put U.S.–China trading relations on a firm foundation by exempting China from Jackson-Vanik Amendment economic sanctions.

Since good trade relations are the centerpiece of a sound relationship between the U.S. and China, the U.S. must be cautious in applying economic sanctions on China like those called for in the Jackson-Vanik Amendment to the Trade Act of 1974. Jackson-Vanik was intended to increase the flow of Jewish emigrants from the Soviet Union and its East European satellites to Israel and the U.S. Each year following the 1989 Tiananmen Square massacre, Congress has threatened unsuccessfully to overturn China's Jackson-Vanik waiver to demonstrate displeasure with Chinese human rights violations which have little to do with emigration. This annual debate, usually in conjunction with the debate over China's MFN status, has been very disruptive to U.S.–PRC relations and totally ineffective in changing China's human rights policies.

The U.S. should offer to exempt China from the provisions of the Jackson-Vanik Amendment in exchange for concessions that benefit American exporters and investors. Beijing puts a high value on achieving unconditional, permanent MFN trading status. By granting the President the discretionary authority to exempt China from Jackson-Vanik, Congress would substantially increase U.S. leverage with China in WTO accession talks and other trade negotiations.

History has shown that China is far more oppressive against its people when isolated from the outside world. This was clearly the case during the Cultural Revolution of the late 1960s. Human rights and political freedom are historic American values, and Washington should continue to champion these values. At the same time, Americans must realize that advancing these values in China is a long-term process that requires both attention and patience.

STRATEGY #8
Congress should demonstrate to Beijing that the U.S. is committed to the security of Taiwan. In accordance with the terms of the Taiwan Relations Act, it also should demonstrate America's continuing determination to supply Taiwan with defensive arms.

The Republic of China on Taiwan today stands among the world's most successful new democracies. Taiwan's free-market democracy has become a model of successful economic and political development for the communist mainland. But China's willingness to use military force to intimidate Taiwan is a threat to the security of Taiwan and to the peace and stability of Asia. Use of force against Taiwan would threaten long-standing American interests in Asia. Congress should make it unequivocally clear that Taiwan is a democratic friend of the United

States even while America seeks to better its relations with the People's Republic of China.

The dispatch of the aircraft carriers U.S.S. *Independence* and U.S.S. *Nimitz* to waters off Taiwan in response to China's threatening military exercises during Taiwan's presidential election should be seen as an unambiguous statement of America's interest in the peaceful resolution of conflicts between Taipei and Beijing. In accordance with the terms of the 1979 Taiwan Relations Act, the United States should continue to supply Taiwan with arms of a defensive nature. Congress should use its legislative powers to focus on providing a missile defense system for the island that would include the new Theater High Altitude Area Defense (THAAD) system now in the testing phase of development.

Congress should hold hearings on the strategic balance in the Taiwan Straits and explore U.S. options for deterring Chinese aggression. Given China's demonstrated willingness to brandish missiles in a blatant attempt to intimidate Taiwan, America should make the selling of missile defense systems to Taiwan a top priority. At the same time, Congress should continue to demonstrate to Beijing — through hearings and resolutions — that the United States has a strong interest in peaceful resolution of issues between China and Taiwan.

The U.S. also should press for Taipei's inclusion in international economic and cultural organizations like the World Trade Organization, the World Bank, the International Monetary Fund, and the World Health Organization. Taiwan's membership in the WTO, an economic institution, should not be held hostage either to Beijing's inability to meet economic criteria for membership or to its political priority of entering before Taiwan.

STRATEGY #9
The U.S. should work to strengthen bilateral agreements and alliances in Asia.

The U.S. should focus on its ability to deal effectively with challenges in the key regions of the Korean Peninsula and China through its alliance relationships in Asia. For over four decades, the U.S. system of bilateral security alliances with Japan, the Republic of Korea, Australia, Thailand, and the Philippines has served as the foundation for regional stability and security. To protect America's economic and security interests in the

Asia-Pacific region, Washington must work to maintain and strengthen these critical alliance relationships. Without them, U.S. interests in Asia cannot be secured.

STRATEGY #10
Instead of a trade war, the U.S. should pursue a cooperative policy with Japan to open markets through the Asia-Pacific Economic Cooperation forum (APEC) and the World Trade Organization.

The U.S. government should avoid policy pronouncements or official statements that characterize Japan's economic strength as a threat to the United States. A four-year recession has undermined the myth of an invincible "Japan, Inc." The rapid rise in the value of the yen is driving down Japan's trade surplus, making Japanese exports more expensive and imports cheaper. Consequently, Japan's imports are growing twice as fast as its exports. At the consumer level, a combination of lower-cost imports and a rapid increase in the number of aggressive discount retailers is driving down domestic prices.

Under unrelenting pressure to cut costs, Japanese firms are beginning to open their tight, club-like business networks—known as *keiretsu*—to foreign suppliers and to relocate manufacturing facilities overseas. As these changes lead to further declines in Japan's trade surplus and an easing of trade friction, the U.S. should seek to engage Japan in a crafting a policy that will further liberalize trade in Asia through APEC and the WTO.

Protecting U.S. National Interests in the Middle East

Preventing the domination of the Middle East and Persian Gulf region by a hostile power has been one of the highest priorities of U.S. Middle East policy since 1947. Now that the Soviet threat has been contained and dissipated, America retains three main goals in the Middle East: 1) assuring Western access to Persian Gulf oil; 2) ensuring the security of Israel, America's foremost friend in the region; and 3) maintaining good working relations with moderate Middle Eastern states. Promoting Arab–Israeli peace is a subsidiary goal that can help the U.S. to accomplish these three main goals.

The principal U.S. foreign policy objective in the Persian Gulf has been to prevent domination of the region by a hostile power. Because of the region's enormous petroleum reserves, which are estimated to be as much as two-thirds of total world reserves, control of the region by an anti-Western regime would pose a direct economic threat to the West and the U.S. It also would give a hegemonic power enormous wealth with which to develop an advanced military capability, including weapons of mass destruction.

The principal threats to regional stability are the regimes in Iran and Iraq, both of which are committed to militantly anti-Western policies, including terrorism and attacks on Western allies. Both countries have undertaken large-scale military buildups which include chemical and biological weapons as well as attempts to acquire nuclear weapons. And despite defeats at the hands of the U.S.—Iraq in Operation Desert Storm and Iran in its various encounters with the U.S. Navy—neither has shown any sign of abandoning its goal of regional domination.

Because no other regional power is able to thwart the ambitions of these two aggressive states, the U.S. must continue to guarantee the security of Kuwait, Saudi Arabia, and the other pro-Western Arab states of the Gulf. These strategic relationships counterbalance the increasing power of both Iran and Iraq. Although the U.S. is likely to receive some assistance in this task from states in the region and from its Western allies, its principal ally may prove to be the rival ambitions and mutual distrust that exists between Iran and Iraq. Tehran and Baghdad, as archrivals, will continue to direct their energies toward undermining one another. Sufficient U.S. military power must be available to respond at short notice to any conflict to ensure that neither Iran nor Iraq (or any other power) can dominate the area.

STRATEGY #1
The U.S. must maintain a strong military presence in the Middle East.

Such a military presence would include a strong naval force backed by air and ground forces located in the U.S. and in staging areas nearer to the region, such as Turkey and Diego Garcia in the Indian Ocean. American military forces based in the region, however, should be minimized to reduce the risk of an anti-Western political backlash promoted by Iran, Iraq, or local fundamentalists hostile to the U.S. The U.S. should help the members of the Gulf Cooperation Council (Bahrain, Kuwait, Oman, Qatar, Saudi Arabia, and the United Arab Emirates) transform their loose collective security arrangement into an effective military alliance. The

STRATEGIES FOR PROTECTING
U.S. NATIONAL INTERESTS IN THE MIDDLE EAST

- A strong military presence in the Middle East must be maintained.

- Tougher U.S. and U.N. policies toward Iraq to end Iraq's ability to threaten U.S. and Western interests in the Persian Gulf region should be developed.

- Through hearings and oversight, Congress should insist on a policy toward Iran that publicizes Iran's support of terrorism and maintains a strong U.S. policy to contain Iran's efforts to dominate the Persian Gulf.

- Congress should ensure that Israel's security is protected and that the alliance between the United States and Israel remains strong.

- Congress should strengthen its oversight over the $100 million given in annual U.S. aid to the Palestinians.

- Congress should ensure that the United States is helping to maintain Israel's qualitative military superiority over possible adversaries.

- A tougher U.S. policy toward Syria should be sought.

- Close diplomatic and military ties to Turkey and to key moderate Arab states should be maintained.

U.S. can assist this process through joint military exercises and defense planning, stockpiling of military supplies, and coordinated military training programs.

In exchange for U.S. security guarantees, the Gulf monarchies should be pressed to demonstrate greater political support for American regional policy objectives. This support should include halting the flow of financial aid to Hamas and other militant Islamic movements, reducing financial support for anti-Western states such as Syria, increasing financial support for pro-Western states such as Egypt and Turkey, and maintaining unwavering diplomatic support for the Arab–Israeli peace negotiations.

STRATEGY #2
Congress should push for tougher U.S. and U.N. policies toward Iraq that will end Iraq's ability to threaten U.S. and Western interests in the Gulf region.

Iraq will continue to be a threat as long as Saddam Hussein remains in power. America's long-term objective, therefore, should be to remove him from power. The weak and divided Iraqi opposition has little prospect of attaining power by its own efforts in the near future. Nevertheless, the U.S. should provide money, arms, and training to the opposition as a way to maintain pressure on Saddam's regime. A high priority should be brokering a peace agreement between the rival Kurdish groups (the Kurdish Democratic Party and the Patriotic Union of Kurdistan) to halt the factional fighting which Baghdad exploited when it reasserted control over Kurdish areas in August 1996.

Although Iraq's fragmentation will enhance Iran's power, the U.S. has a humanitarian and strategic interest in weakening Saddam's control over the Kurds in the North and Shia Arabs in the South. The two "no-fly zones" should be maintained over northern and southern Iraq to allow these groups more independence from the Iraqi regime and to force Saddam to focus his efforts inward rather than outward toward his neighbors.

The U.S. should use its veto in the U.N. Security Council to keep the U.N.-sponsored political and economic sanctions against Iraq in place as long as Saddam Hussein is in power. Regardless of U.N. action, the U.S. should seek to undermine and constrain Iraq's ability to build or acquire weapons of mass destruction and prevent the sale or transfer to Iraq of advanced military equipment.

The Clinton Administration declared victory in the August/September 1996 crisis in Iraq when it responded with pinprick cruise missile attacks after Saddam Hussein ordered his troops to violate the Kurdish safe haven in northern Iraq. Congress should hold hearings to determine how Baghdad was able to exploit the Kurdish factional fighting to reassert its control in northern Iraq, to discover whether the Clinton Administration broke previous commitments extended to the Kurds, and to explore the long-term implications of Saddam's gains in the Kurdish enclave. Congress then should pass a resolution calling on the Administration to veto any lifting of the U.N. economic sanctions on Iraq as long as Saddam Hussein continues to threaten U.S. interests.

STRATEGY #3
Through hearings and its constitutional oversight function, Congress should publicize Iran's support of terrorism and maintain a strong U.S. policy to contain Iran's efforts to dominate the Persian Gulf.

Given its larger size and Iraq's weakened condition, Iran's relative power in the region is on the rise. With its radical anti-Western government, Iran remains a long-term political and military threat to the region. Although the U.S. should welcome moves by Iran to reestablish normal ties with the world community, it should attempt to block economic aid, foreign investment, nuclear cooperation, and sales of advanced military equipment to Iran until Tehran ends its drive for nuclear weapons and abandons its support of terrorism and revolution.

STRATEGY #4
Congress should become more involved in U.S. efforts to resolve the Arab–Israeli conflict in order to ensure that Israel's security is protected and the alliance between the U.S. and Israel remains strong.

Now that the euphoria surrounding the September 13, 1993, Israel–PLO agreement has been dispelled by repeated terrorist attacks, backsliding on security commitments by the Palestinian Authority (PA), and the September 1996 civil riots orchestrated by the PA after an archaeological tunnel was opened in Jerusalem, the risks inherent in Israel's agreement with Palestinian leader Yasser Arafat have become increasingly apparent. Israel chose to strike a deal with Arafat, regarded as the lesser of two evils, because it hoped that he could control the growing Palestinian Islamic movement. However, terrorist cells of Islamic militants have killed more Israelis since the September 1993 accord than were killed in the entire decade before that agreement.

The failure of this approach to the peace process was the main reason Israelis elected Benjamin Netanyahu as their Prime Minister. Israel's willingness to take further risks in pursuit of peace has been severely undermined by Arafat's unwillingness or inability to halt Palestinian terrorism. Arafat risks becoming irrelevant if the suicide bombings continue. The U.S. should compel Arafat to live up to his commitment to halt terrorism and press him to crack down decisively on Palestinian Islamic radicals. This would greatly help Netanyahu achieve his program of peace with security.

It is clear that the Israeli–Palestinian negotiations will be protracted and grueling. The final status talks will address many thorny issues, including the question of Palestinian statehood, the demarcation of borders, security arrangements, the status of Jerusalem, the future of Israeli settlements, the question of Palestinian refugees, and the allocation of scarce water resources. The U.S. should function as a low-key diplomatic facilitator and refrain from being drawn into the details of the negotiations unless the talks become deadlocked. Minimizing American diplomatic intervention will encourage the two sides to work things out for themselves through compromise.

Building a stable Arab–Israeli peace is an important goal that will advance American interests by helping to stem the rising tide of Islamic fundamentalism, contain terrorism, and make possible closer strategic cooperation between the U.S. and moderate Arab states. Negotiating an Arab–Israeli peace accord, however, is not a strategic goal comparable in importance to preventing hegemony by Iran, Iraq, or any other hostile power over the Persian Gulf. Nor is it as critical to America as maintaining access to Persian Gulf oil or safeguarding Israel's security. As a result, peace negotiations should not take precedence over these goals. Washington must guard against focusing obsessively on the "peace process." Overeager American attempts to force concessions from Israel may preserve the negotiations in the short run, but they damage the long-term prospects for peace by making a negotiated settlement more unacceptable to Israel.

STRATEGY #5
Congress should strengthen its oversight over the $100 million given in annual U.S. aid to the Palestinians.

In 1994, Congress passed the Middle East Peace Facilitation Act requiring the State Department to certify each year that the Palestine Liberation Organization has complied with its commitments under its peace agreements with Israel. The State Department compliance reports have been denounced by Representative Benjamin Gilman (R-NY), Chairman of the House International Relations Committee. Congress should judge for itself whether the Palestinian Authority has complied with its peace commitments. Congress should hold hearings on Palestinian compliance, including Arafat's commitment to halt terrorism, and withhold all U.S. aid if the Palestinian Authority fails to comply.

STRATEGY #6
Congress should ensure that the U.S. is helping to maintain Israel's qualitative military superiority over possible adversaries.

Congress should bolster the section in the Defense Department authorization bill that requires the U.S. to help maintain Israel's qualitative military superiority over possible adversaries. Historically, this legislative provision has amounted to little more than a statement of policy and an expression of support for the U.S.–Israeli alliance. Although the U.S. does provide considerable military aid to Israel, it is unclear whether that aid truly carries out the "qualitative edge" statute.

Congress can take steps to ensure that U.S. military aid to Israel gives that nation a qualitative military advantage over other powers in the region. First, Congress should direct the Administration to report on exactly what is being done to comply with this legislative language. Second, Congress should require the Administration to certify that the U.S. is helping Israel maintain an edge in certain key areas like missile defense, air superiority, and command and control systems.

The chief threat to Israeli security in the post–Cold War era is no longer an Arab conventional military attack, but the prospect of proliferation of weapons of mass destruction and surface-to-surface missiles. To help Israel blunt the threat of missile attack, the U.S. should continue its financial support for development of the joint U.S.–Israeli Arrow anti-tactical ballistic missile (ATBM) system. The U.S. funded approximately 70 percent of the $270 million cost of the program from 1991 to 1995. Washington also should continue its annual military assistance of $1.8 billion to help Israel maintain its qualitative military edge over potential Arab adversaries.

STRATEGY #7
Congress should push for a tougher U.S. policy toward Syria.

Syria remains a diplomatic spoiler that for tactical reasons has gone along with the U.S.-designed Arab–Israeli peace negotiations. Syria is trying to extract concessions from the U.S. and Saudi Arabia, to drive a wedge between Israel and the U.S., and to make propaganda gains at Israel's expense.

Negotiations between Syria and Israel have ground to a halt because of Syria's support of terrorism against Israel, its hard-line diplomacy, and its inflexibility in demanding the unconditional return of the Israeli-occupied Golan Heights without offering adequate security guarantees in return. Prime Minister Netanyahu has said that while he is prepared to negotiate with President Hafez al-Assad, Israel is not prepared to give back the strategically vital Golan Heights captured from Syria in the 1967 war. Only a genuinely free, democratic regime in Damascus can guarantee peace between Syria and Israel, according to Netanyahu.

Nevertheless, if the Syrian–Israeli negotiations should bear fruit, the U.S. should rule out any deployment of U.S. peacekeeping troops on the Golan Heights. Such a deployment would be a lightning rod for terrorist attack, would divert scarce active duty ground forces from other missions, would erode military preparedness, and could lead to tensions with Israel. Moreover, an American presence is unnecessary since the same peacekeeping role could be carried out by other nations. Perhaps most important, Prime Minister Netanyahu is not interested in a U.S. peacekeeping presence on the Golan Heights.

Congress should hold hearings to investigate Syria's involvement in terrorism, its opposition to Palestinian–Israeli peace negotiations, and its role in Lebanon. Congress also should press the Administration to explain how its diplomatic embrace of Syria's Assad has advanced American interests in the region, if at all. If Congress concludes that the Administration's policy has failed to produce results, it can pass legislation penalizing foreign companies that do business with Syria, which remains on the State Department's list of states that support terrorism.

STRATEGY #8

The U.S. should maintain close diplomatic and military ties to Turkey and to key moderate Arab states such as Egypt, Jordan, Kuwait, Saudi Arabia, and other Persian Gulf emirates.

Of key importance to U.S. policy toward the region is support for Turkey, whose strategic position and relationship with the U.S. make it a valuable ally. As the Islamic world's only genuine democracy with a pro-Western stance, and as a power whose influence in Central Asia and elsewhere is increasing, Turkey should be looked upon as a stabilizing influence. Because Turkey is surrounded by unfriendly states, its connection to the West is especially important, even after the demise of the Soviet Union.

The U.S. should continue its close strategic relationship with Turkey and help it to acquire more sophisticated weapons; otherwise, Turkey cannot remain competitive against the heavily armed states in the region. The U.S. also should pressure the West Europeans to accept Turkey's bid to join the European Union. If Turkey is rejected, Washington should negotiate a free trade agreement with Turkey. This could help prevent a backlash that might lead Ankara to reconsider its pro-Western foreign policy. Strong support for Turkey is needed more than ever now that the Islamic Welfare Party (Refah) is sharing power with Turkey's secular political leaders. It is vitally important that Turkey's pro-Western foreign policy orientation be maintained.

The U.S. should encourage Turkey and the moderate Arab states to undertake free-market economic reforms to assure higher economic growth rates and give their people greater opportunities for political participation. Washington also should help governments threatened by Islamic radicalism, such as those in Algeria, Bahrain, and (to a lesser extent) Tunisia, whenever possible. And the U.S. should take great pains not to undermine secular governments in the Middle East by establishing official dialogues with Islamic opposition movements. Instead, it should firmly resist the efforts of such movements to come to power through violent means.

Protecting U.S. National Interests in Latin America

While Latin America and the Caribbean region are not key factors in the world balance of power, the Western Hemisphere is a critical arena for U.S. foreign policy. The economic development and political stability of Latin America and the Caribbean are of vital importance to U.S. economic and security interests. The bases of a new post–Cold War partnership between the U.S. and Latin America were first articulated in June 1990 in the Bush Administration's Enterprise for the Americas Initiative (EAI), which pledged the U.S.-led creation of a hemispheric free trade area stretching from Alaska to Tierra del Fuego. In 1990, the Bush Administration also launched formal negotiations with Mexico and Canada to establish the NAFTA. The commercial treaty negotiations were concluded successfully before the 1992 elections. During 1993, however, the Clinton Administration delayed submitting the agreement for congressional approval as side agreements on labor and the environment were attached to the original agreement.

The U.S. Congress finally approved NAFTA in November 1993. Subsequently, at the Summit of the Americas in Miami in December 1994, President Clinton and 33 other democratically elected heads of state pledged unanimously to create a Free Trade Area of the Americas by 2005. The Miami summit was the high point of the Clinton Administration's Latin America policy. But nine days after the FTAA process was launched at the Summit of the Americas, the Mexican peso collapsed, causing a huge financial and political crisis in Mexico and surprising both the Clinton Administration and congressional leaders. The peso crisis and the Clinton Administration's subsequent $40 billion bailout of Mexico derailed the expansion of NAFTA to include Chile before the 1996 U.S. presidential elections.

The Clinton Administration's retreat from NAFTA's expansion revealed the inadequacies of its Latin American policies. With trade expansion pushed off the Administration's agenda, relations between the U.S. and Latin America quickly deteriorated. Today, the U.S. no longer leads the FTAA trade expansion process and finds itself increasingly at odds with valued Latin American trading partners like Mexico, Colombia, Venezuela, Chile, Brazil, and Argentina over a host of issues, including Cuba, drug trafficking, and illegal immigration.

Exclusively Latin American institutions like the Rio Group and Mercosur have been able to increase their hemispheric influence at the expense of U.S.

STRATEGIES FOR PROTECTING
U.S. NATIONAL INTERESTS IN LATIN AMERICA

- The Clinton Administration and Congress should work to put NAFTA expansion back on track.

- U.S. relations with Mexico should be strengthened.

- The Administration should reinvigorate and modernize the Inter-American System.

- Castro's communist regime in Cuba should be isolated.

- Congress should compel the Administration to acknowledge the failure of Operation Restore Democracy in Haiti.

---

leadership and traditional U.S.-dominated multilateral institutions like the Organization of American States (OAS). During the Cold War, the U.S. used the OAS to maintain regional support for U.S. policies designed to stop the spread of communism in Latin America. Today, however, the OAS is officially on record as opposing the Helms-Burton Act, which tightened the trade embargo against communist Cuba.

The effort from 1990 to 1994 to create a new hemispheric partnership between the U.S. and Latin America—through the EAI, NAFTA, and the FTAA process—was undertaken originally to advance U.S. economic and security interests in the Western Hemisphere. U.S. proponents of the EAI, NAFTA, and the FTAA believed that trade liberalization would:

- **Provide increased access** to Latin American markets for U.S. exports and investments, creating more U.S. jobs.

- **Encourage democratic reforms and political stability** in what historically has been an unstable region.

- **Help reduce illegal immigration** to the U.S. from Latin America by fostering greater economic growth and political stability in the region.

The original goals of the EAI, NAFTA, and the FTAA remain valid. The creation of a single, hemispheric free trade area of the Americas will help strengthen the U.S. economy, fuel economic development in Latin America and the Caribbean, and consolidate democracy throughout the Western

Hemisphere. However, the FTAA process that evolved out of the EAI and NAFTA is missing important elements, among them: 1) establishment of a new post–Cold War Inter-American Security Arrangement to replace the 1947 Inter-American Treaty of Reciprocal Assistance (also called the Rio Treaty), which provided the backbone of collective security efforts for the Western Hemisphere during the Cold War; 2) reorganization of the OAS to make it a viable multilateral organization in Latin America; and 3) expansion of NAFTA and the FTAA to incorporate the hemispheric energy sector.

STRATEGY #1
The Clinton Administration and Congress should make every effort to put NAFTA expansion back on track.

Following the collapse of the Mexican peso in December 1994, the Clinton Administration chose to retreat from the expansion of NAFTA rather than defend the trade pact's demonstrable success. As a result, the expansion of NAFTA to include Chile was delayed, and the FTAA process lost momentum and direction as the U.S. surrendered its leadership and negotiating advantage to Brazil.

To put American-led trade expansion back on track in the Western Hemisphere, the Clinton Administration and Congress should act quickly during the first six months of 1997 to renew the President's fast-track negotiating authority, expand NAFTA to include Chile, and approve a bill granting the democracies of the Caribbean and Central America trading parity with NAFTA member Mexico in terms of access to U.S. markets. In addition, Congress should hold hearings to examine the benefits generated by NAFTA from 1994 to 1996. Congress also should hold hearings to determine how a retreat from free trade is likely to affect U.S. relations with Latin America and U.S. economic and security interests in the Western Hemisphere.

STRATEGY #2
The Administration and Congress should work to strengthen U.S. relations with Mexico.

Mexico heads the list of U.S. priorities in Latin America. The U.S. has vital economic, political, and social interests in supporting Mexico's transition to a fully democratic, free-market economy. Today, Mexico is the third-largest U.S. trading partner and a valued member of NAFTA. Mexico shares a 2,000-mile border with the U.S., and two-way U.S.–Mexico trade now totals nearly $110 billion a year. Political conflict or economic chaos in Mexico could create a huge influx of refugees along America's southern border and encourage the spread of organized violence, social unrest, and random crime in Mexico with potentially serious spillover consequences for the United States.

Congress should oversee the Administration's efforts to build stronger relations with Mexico by holding hearings on the progress of NAFTA, as well as on such bilateral issues as drug trafficking, illegal immigration, and the process of political reform in Mexico. The Administration should take the lead in establishing bilateral negotiations on the thorny issues of drug trafficking and illegal immigration.

STRATEGY #3
The Administration should reinvigorate and modernize the Inter-American System (IAS).

Since the end of the Cold War, the U.S. has pressed an ambitious trade expansion agenda in the Western Hemisphere with the EAI, NAFTA, and the FTAA process. However, the U.S. has made no visible effort to modernize the multilateral Cold War–era institutions of U.S.–Latin America relations. One of these was the Rio Treaty of 1947, which established a hemispheric defense pact designed to contain the spread of communism. With the end of the Cold War, the threat of communism disappeared in Latin America; but new threats have emerged, including drug trafficking, organized crime, left-wing guerrilla violence in countries like Colombia and Mexico, and organized paramilitary political violence in other countries. Instead of attacking these problems with unilateral measures such as the decertification of Colombia on drug-related matters, the U.S. should modernize the Rio Treaty to develop a concerted hemispheric assault on drug traffickers, narco-guerrillas, and the threat of terrorism in Latin America.

The U.S. historically has paid little attention to the Organization of American States. The OAS was used to win regional support during the Cold War against communism; otherwise, however, its appropriate multilateral role in managing U.S. relations with Latin America was ignored. The U.S. should promote reorganization of the OAS so that it can become an effective multilateral agency for U.S.-Latin American relations, and Congress should support such efforts by holding hearings to explore why such reorganization is needed.

STRATEGY #4
The Administration and Congress should work to isolate Fidel Castro's communist regime in Cuba.

The tyranny of Fidel Castro endures in Cuba. The collapse of the Soviet Union and the growth of democracy throughout Latin America have diminished Castro's capacity to export violent revolution. However, Castro's communist regime is viscerally anti-American and has a significant military capability for violence, as demonstrated by the February 24, 1996, shootdown of two U.S. civilian aircraft. While his regime endures, Castro will continue to threaten American interests in the Western Hemisphere and undermine the stability of Latin America's budding capitalist democracies. America's response should be to increase the economic pressure against Castro by enforcing the Helms-Burton Act.

The Helms-Burton Act is working. Dozens of foreign companies have withdrawn from Cuba or have suspended plans to invest on the island since the law was enacted in March 1996. Critics of the Helms-Burton Act —mostly other countries doing business with Castro—complain that the bill is illegal and contrary to the rules of NAFTA and the WTO. However, the Act complies with accepted international law, as well as with NAFTA and WTO standards. Moreover, America's experience with Castro has shown that only tough measures have any effect. In addition to enforcing the Helms-Burton law, the Administration should make it clear to Castro that America will not tolerate hostile acts against American citizens or American shores, including unprovoked military attacks against innocent civilians in international waters or a new flood of raft refugees from Cuba toward Florida.

STRATEGY #5
Congress should compel the Administration to acknowledge the failure of Operation Restore Democracy in Haiti.

The expenditure of $3 billion of U.S. taxpayers' money since September 1994 has failed to establish a genuine and stable democracy in Haiti. Two years after Jean-Bertrand Aristide was restored to the Haitian presidency under the protective umbrella of 23,000 U.S. soldiers, Haiti remains a cauldron of barely contained violence. A one-party government controlled by Aristide's Lavalas party has shut out most of Haiti's genuine democrats. Economic reforms have stalled. There are no property rights. The judicial system does not function. Political killings continue. More than 6,000 armed members of rival left-wing gangs and right-wing demobilized soldiers have overwhelmed an inexperienced and weak U.S.-trained Haitian police force. Despite massive amounts of U.S. aid, about 70 percent of the Haitian people are illiterate, and 60 percent remain unemployed.

Congress should investigate whether the Clinton Administration has misled both Congress and the American people about Haiti. The House and Senate should challenge President Clinton's use of executive privilege to hide the failure of Operation Restore Democracy. They can hold hearings on Haiti and compel the appearance—as witnesses under oath—of top Administration officials involved in Haiti policy. Congress should block any further U.S. funding for the Canadian-led U.N. security mission in Haiti and compel the withdrawal of all remaining U.S. troops and other American security officials.

CONCLUSION

Unless hard and fast priorities are set, the U.S. is in danger of squandering its increasingly overtaxed defense assets and foreign policy resources on secondary concerns while neglecting crucial long-term issues that impinge on vital American interests. Without strategic priorities, the U.S. will be left rudderless in the post–Cold War era, lurching from one media-generated crisis to another and vacillating between the extremes of interventionism and isolationism. If its power is squandered, America will be too weak to respond when a real national security emergency occurs. America's security and leadership in the world depend on knowing when, and when not, to become involved in international problems.

The U.S. is a great global power and must act like one, concentrating its efforts on building solid relations with other major powers and engaging selectively in other foreign policy ventures based on calculations of national interest. The Clinton Administration has tried to be all things to all people. It is therefore no wonder that the President has failed to discriminate among vital, important, and marginal national interests. Because he has not made such distinctions, America has lost credibility abroad, squandered resources on unessential and inappropriate military interventions, and dangerously weakened its military power. This is more than a failure of strategy. It is a failure of leadership.

Chapter 18

BUILDING SUPPORT FOR FREE TRADE AND INVESTMENT

John Sweeney, Bryan T. Johnson, and Robert O'Quinn

With the end of the Cold War, the clarity of vision that sustained the historical bipartisan congressional consensus in support of free trade has been lost. It is not that American legislators and their constituents suddenly have become more protectionist and isolationist. They have not. Within Congress there still exists a significant bipartisan core of legislators who believe in free trade, and opinion polls continue to show that most Americans believe free trade is good for the United States.

Throughout the 50-year Cold War, Congress and the American people consistently supported free trade policies of successive Democratic and Republican administrations because they understood that free trade would strengthen America, undermine the communist Soviet Union, and help make the world safe for democracy. As a result, America's policymaking elites never found it necessary to launch a grassroots campaign in support of free trade. It was enough merely to tell voters that free trade would contribute to the demise of the Soviet Union and eradicate the greatest threat existing to the survival of the United States.

The authors would like to thank Edward Black, Merrick "Mac" Carey, Thomas P. Cox, Edward L. Hudgins, Harris Jordan, William Lane, and Michael G. Wilson for their contributions to this chapter. The views and opinions, however, are solely the responsibility of the authors.

Broad theoretical arguments about the macroeconomic benefits of free trade are no longer effective in the context of a post-Cold War Congress whose members place far more value on addressing the domestic problems of their constituencies than they do on trade and foreign policy. To rebuild the bipartisan congressional consensus that supported America's free trade policies throughout the Cold War, congressional leaders, policymakers, and conservative activists who support free trade must educate the 535 Members of Congress about how free trade benefits their home states, their congressional districts, and main street America.

Free Trade Is Important to America

Policymakers throughout government must continue to support free trade and investment policies for a number of reasons. First, free trade makes good economic sense. It creates jobs and maximizes personal economic liberty; it provides a larger aggressive market in which American companies can sell their products; and it enables businesses to import crucial components to manufacture products in a cost-competitive manner. American companies continue to export goods and services to other countries because of the great demand for American products, and because they can produce more than Americans want. Finally, free trade and sound investment policies have proven to be undeniably good for America and Americans, which the following facts substantiate:

- **America is the world's largest exporter of goods and services.** In 1995, America sold over $783 billion in goods and services worldwide. Total international trade accounted for 23.1 percent of the 1995 U.S. gross domestic product (GDP).

- **The value of U.S. merchandise exports has grown more than 600 percent over the last 25 years.** Since 1988, almost 70 percent of the growth in the U.S. economy was derived solely from exporting goods and services.

- **One out of every five American jobs is supported by trade.** According to the U.S. Department of Commerce, for every $1 billion earned from exports, 22,000 new jobs are created in America. In 1994, export-oriented manufacturing and service companies supported 11 million American jobs that paid an average of 13 percent more than non-export jobs. Nearly half of the manufacturing jobs created in the U.S. in recent years have been in foreign-owned companies.

- **Since 1965, unemployment has decreased every year that the U.S. trade deficit expanded** (more imports came into the U.S. than goods were exported). Conversely, unemployment increased in years in which the trade deficit shrank (fewer imports came into the U.S.). Increased exporting means more jobs for Americans, and increased importing adds to the national wealth.

- **America is as much an industrial giant today as it has been in the past.** The manufacturing base of the United States is not shrinking because of free trade, as trade protectionists contend. In fact, it is not shrinking at all. According to the U.S. Department of Commerce, manufacturing accounts for 21 percent of GDP, which is the same percentage of the economy today as in 1967. Employment in manufacturing has remained relatively stable over the last three decades. The number of Americans working in manufacturing today (about 10.5 million) is about the same as it was in the early 1960s. While that number is a smaller percentage of a growing U.S. population, it proves that Americans are still finding jobs in manufacturing.

- **The Office of the U.S. Trade Representative estimates that by 2010, trade will represent 36 percent of America's GDP.**

The benefits of free trade to a nation's economy are not new concepts to policymakers in Washington. In 1792, Thomas Paine wrote in *The Rights of Man* that "The prosperity of any commercial nation is regulated by the prosperity of the rest. If they are poor, she cannot be rich; and her condition... is an index of the height of the commercial tide in other nations." Eight years later, Thomas Jefferson wrote in a letter to Gideon Granger, dated August 13, 1800, that "The merchants will manage the better, the more they are left free to manage for themselves. Agriculture, manufactures, commerce, and navigation, the four pillars of our prosperity, are the most thriving when left most free to individual enterprise." These thoughts have been echoed in writings and speeches across the centuries.

Market Advantages. Free trade continues to make economic sense today. International trade allows countries to achieve their own "competitive advantages" since no one country can possibly produce all products the most efficiently. In order to maximize efficiency and wealth, individuals, companies, and nations trade the goods they produce best for the goods someone else produces better. Free trade also maximizes individual liberty. It is natural for individuals to want the best product, of the best possible quality, and at the best possible price—the core demand that drives competition.

Free trade also helps to keep America competitive. Free trade demands that businesses and industries maintain their competitiveness by constantly improving their manufacturing techniques and product technologies, which reduce the costs of production per unit as volume increases (a company that manufactures 1,000 widgets has a lower unit cost than one that makes only 100 widgets). When businesses achieve these higher economies of scale, they become more competitive.

Whether it comes from domestic or international markets, competition is the driving force behind innovation. When competition is limited by outside regulations, long-term economic growth and wealth stagnate. In order to compete in today's complex international economy, nations like the U.S. must maximize their potential markets for business by opening their borders to international trade.

Foreign Investment. In much the same way, investment in foreign markets provides economic benefits to both the investor's home country and the country in which the funds are invested. Above all, direct investment facilitates international trade. Firms often establish facilities in host countries in order to help market their products abroad. Direct investment enables those firms to minimize costs through cross-border production networks. A multinational company can take advantage of the different resources and skills in various countries and can situate its plants geographically to maximize production. In this way, a multinational firm can achieve a larger and more cost-efficient scale of production than if all of its plants were in its home country. For example, the North American Free Trade Agreement (NAFTA) has allowed American automakers to reduce unit production costs by diversifying component output and outsourcing across the U.S., Mexico, and Canada. As a result, the North American auto market is more competitive, and new markets have opened up in third countries for NAFTA-sourced exports of motor vehicles and auto parts.

International direct investment also accelerates a diffusion of managerial skills and advanced technology throughout the world. Firms in the host countries usually try to emulate the technology brought in by foreign competitors, and they will hire trained workers from the multinational firm to transfer the necessary skills. American firms, for example, have learned valuable just-in-time inventory management techniques from Japanese firms operating in the United States.

Finally, direct and portfolio international investment enables countries with an excess supply of savings to offer funds to countries that need investment capital. In the 1980s, such capital flows allowed the United States, with its relatively low savings rate, to sustain a higher level of private investment and to finance the government budget deficit at lower interest rates than would have been possible if it had to rely on domestic savings.

Trade Agreements. U.S. trade agreements with other countries have strengthened the American economic presence in the global economy and have defended the interests of American companies abroad and American workers at home. Trade agreements and international trade organizations do not threaten American sovereignty. None of the agreements that the United States has signed with other countries, like NAFTA and the World Trade Organization (WTO) agreement, supersede or counter American laws. In fact, these agreements contain provisions that commit foreign countries to a range of improvements in market access. These include the treatment of foreign investors, respecting intellectual property rights, better customs rules and administrative policies and procedures, improved dispute resolution procedures, and contract enforcement. Contrary to current protectionist criticism, U.S. trade agreements do not involve the cession of sovereignty to foreign powers.

Trade Deficits. In the same way, trade deficits are not harmful to the economy. If they were, America would not have become the economic powerhouse it is today, since the U.S. has run a trade deficit for most of its history. Throughout its first 100 years, the deficits were fairly large, yet growth rates were higher than they are today. A trade deficit is more a sign of strength than of weakness, for it means that Americans hold more goods than their foreign trading partners, while foreigners hold more U.S. dollars, part of which ultimately will be spent to purchase American goods. It also means America imports more than it exports because it is the wealthiest nation on earth.

Trade Quotas. Trade quotas frequently are enacted to "save jobs from foreign competition," but they often result in higher consumer prices that do more harm to the economy. For example, when trade quotas were imposed on imported cars in the early 1980s, prices for domestic and imported cars rose an average of $2,000. These quotas were intended to preserve some auto workers' jobs, but their costs were passed on to the American consumer. Instead of being able to save that $2,000 for college education, to pay down a mortgage, or to buy food and clothing, Americans have been forced to spend that money subsidizing the jobs of other Americans whose work cannot compete internationally. The economic marketplace works best when individuals, not the government, decide how much to pay for consumer goods. It is unfair to ask a school teacher making $26,000 a year to pay $2,000 more for a car just to subsidize an auto worker making $50,000 a year.

In addition, quotas can cause a net loss of American jobs. When the U.S. imposed the quotas on imported cars in the 1980s, the price of a new American-made automobile increased by an average of 41 percent from 1981 to 1984, nearly twice the average rate of increase for all consumer prices during that time. The auto industry and union leaders claim these price hikes saved up to 22,000 jobs over a period of less than five years, but they also prevented many consumers from buying new cars. U.S. consumers bought about 1 million fewer U.S. cars after the imposed import quotas, and the drop in sales forced the auto industry to lay off 50,000 workers in the late 1980s. Although 22,000 jobs were "saved," the layoffs caused by the increase in sticker prices produced a net loss of 30,000 jobs. The price increases amounted to $17 billion in higher auto prices, so in effect American consumers paid $772,727 for each one of those 22,000 jobs.[1]

Similarly, the number of retail jobs destroyed by years of import restrictions on textile and apparel products is far greater than the number of jobs created or saved in the textile manufacturing industry. According to a 1989 study by the U.S. Federal Trade Commission, Americans pay 58 percent higher prices for textile and apparel products because of U.S. trade restrictions—between $11 billion and $15 billion a year. While protectionists say these trade restrictions saved 22,390 textile and apparel jobs in the 1980s, these same jobs cost the U.S. consumer $550,916 per job. This calculation does not take into account job losses in related retail industries; when those losses are included, the cost of each job "saved" has been estimated to be well over $4 million.[2]

---

1 Robert Crandall, "The Effects of U.S. Trade Protection for Autos and Steel," *Brookings Paper on Economic Activity No. 1*, Brookings Institution, 1987.

2 David G. Tarr, *A General Equilibrium Analysis of the Welfare and Employment Effects of*

The Cost of Trade Restrictions. The Federal Reserve Bank estimated that the costs of all U.S. government protectionist policies are hefty — equivalent to a 10 percent income tax surcharge for the average American family and a whopping 23 percent for poor families.[3]

Another common misconception is that trade restrictions protect American products and demand keeps those products reasonably priced. The facts show that trade restrictions actually inflate the price American consumers must pay. In the 1970s, the U.S. steel industry sought help to cope with shrinking competitiveness, so the Nixon Administration imposed restrictions on imports for a period of three years to allow the industry to modernize. In 1971, these restraints were extended for another three years. From 1974 until 1993, the U.S. steel industry was under various forms of government protection, and wages rose from $9.90 per hour in 1970 to $17.46 per hour in 1980, an increase that was 60 percent higher than wage increases in the rest of the U.S. manufacturing sector. As a result, from 1969 to 1980, U.S. manufacturers that bought U.S. steel paid 20 percent to 25 percent more for their steel than their foreign competitors; Americans paid some $5 billion a year in higher prices.[4]

The U.S. steel industry has made a tremendous comeback, but the reason is not because of the trade restrictions. Japanese investment funds poured into the U.S. in the 1980s and gave U.S. steel companies the money needed to build new plants and adopt more advanced manufacturing techniques. Moreover, private-sector ventures between American and Japanese steel companies have taught U.S. firms how to manufacture their steel more efficiently.

America's restrictions on growing sugar cane and importing sugar keep the price of sugar in the U.S. an average of 200 percent to 300 percent higher than outside the U.S. At one point in the 1980s, the price for sugar in the U.S. was 700 percent higher than anywhere else. Several bizarre episodes have been recorded in which U.S. customs agents seized imported frozen pizzas, lemonade mix, and related items and charged the importers with

---

U.S. Quotas in Textiles, Autos, and Steel, Federal Trade Commission, February 1989.

3 Joseph E. Pattison, *Breaking Boundaries* (Princeton, N.J.: Peterson's/Pacesetter Books, 1996), p. 55.

4 Tarr, *A General Equilibrium Analysis*.

smuggling sugar because these items contained more than 1 percent sugar. These trade restrictions had their biggest impact on the candy industry, which has been forced to pay much higher prices for the sugar to manufacture its products. The sugar program has destroyed more than 16,000 jobs since it was initiated in 1982, including at least 9,000 in the candy and bakery industries. Brach Candy, for example, has moved 3,000 jobs to Canada to take advantage of Canada's free-market sugar prices.

The U.S. has often resorted to threats of trade retaliation to open foreign markets, but most of the time these threats have backfired. The principal U.S. law used to threaten countries with trade retaliation is Section 301 of the 1974 Trade Act, which gives the President the authority to impose punitive trade restrictions on imports. Of the nearly 80 Section 301 cases initiated by the U.S. since 1974, only about 15 were successful. Even in these cases, American consumers were saddled with billions of dollars in higher prices caused by higher tariffs and special duties.

Excessive government regulations stifle the competitiveness of the American economy. The U.S. Chamber of Commerce estimates that complying with federal, state, and local regulations costs American companies $600 billion a year, while the Office of Management and Budget estimates that American managers spend 5 billion hours each year completing paperwork to comply with government regulations. The Center for the Study of American Business at Washington University has estimated that at the end of the 1980s, the cost for American business to comply with all U.S. government regulations represented nearly 5 percent of GDP. This fact has not escaped foreign companies interested in establishing businesses in the United States. A 1994 study by the Canadian government entitled *Register of United States Barriers to Trade* identified 89,000 standards or regulations affecting business activities in the U.S. There are a multitude of laws that have outlived their purpose and complicate international trade, like the Jackson-Vanik Amendment to the Trade Act of 1974 and the Jones Act.

These episodes in experimenting with U.S. trade policy demonstrate the impact trade restrictions can have directly on Americans. It is important that congressional leaders and the Administration recommit to their support of free trade and investment policies and do not support reactionary policies that ultimately diminish America's leadership role in international trade and cost Americans their jobs.

The Changing Balance of Power on Trade Issues

Trade policy making in the United States is governed by the Commerce Clause of the U.S. Constitution, and by the power vested in the President to negotiate treaties with other countries. Since the birth of the American nation, the relationship between the executive branch and Congress on trade issues has always been an uneasy one. To the extent that the executive branch of government makes trade policy, it does so on authority borrowed from Congress. Historically, the Chief Executive has sought unfettered authority to negotiate trade agreements, while the intent of Congress has been to set limits on the Chief Executive's authority.

Since the enactment of the Reciprocal Trade Agreements Act in 1934, all major trade legislation has been approved and implemented in the context of executive-legislative compromise that reflected America's relative economic strength in the world and the dominance of policymakers who placed value on free trade. However, all successful trade legislation since 1934 has also incorporated trade-offs between America's prevailing free-market philosophy and the political imperatives that influence the democratic process. Thus, the desire of the executive branch for unlimited authority to negotiate and sign agreements liberalizing trade has been granted by Congress only in exchange for limits on the use of that authority.

The present "balance of power" on trade issues between Congress and the executive branch was established by the Trade Act of 1974 and the Omnibus Trade and Competitiveness Act (OTCA) of 1988. The Trade Act of 1974, signed into law by President Gerald Ford on January 3, 1975, expanded the role of Congress in negotiating and implementing trade agreements. This act also created the vehicle of five-year "fast-track" negotiating authority, expanding the scope of the Executive to negotiate and implement trade agreements beyond tariffs to include agreements on non-tariff barriers as well.

Subsequently, the OTCA of 1988 further shifted the balance of control over trade policy away from the executive branch toward Congress, and away from trade policy makers in the executive branch toward a broader group of interests represented by Congress. The OTCA was approved at a time when traditionally free-trade constituencies in manufacturing and agriculture were showing more concern with import competition and the growing trade deficit than with the development of export markets. These concerns were reflected in growing pressures to use trade measures to address issues not associated with trade, and growing support for increased unilateral activism in the pursuit of trade objectives. However, the shift in the balance of power on trade issues from the executive branch to Congress was not immediately felt in the ongoing process of trade negotiations.

The six-year period from 1989 to 1994 was marked by the greatest progress on trade issues that any U.S. Administration had experienced since the end of World War II. For example, the Asia-Pacific Economic Cooperation (APEC) forum was launched in 1989. The Bush Administration announced in June 1990 the Enterprise of the Americas Initiative (EAI), an ambitious plan to create a single free trade area of the Americas stretching from the port of Anchorage in Alaska to Tierra del Fuego at the southernmost point in South America. Also in 1990, the Bush Administration embraced a proposal by then-Mexican President Carlos Salinas de Gortari to negotiate NAFTA, the world's first free-trade agreement between an industrialized country and a developing nation. The negotiations establishing NAFTA were completed a few weeks before the 1992 U.S. presidential elections that put a Democrat in the White House but weakened the Democratic Party's control of Congress. However, the change in administrations initially did not bring about any changes in the conduct of American trade policy.

During 1993 and 1994, the Clinton Administration continued the trade initiatives undertaken during the Bush Administration. The NAFTA was ratified by Congress in November 1993, and the Uruguay Round Agreements, negotiated under the auspices of the General Agreement on Tariffs and Trade (GATT), were finally completed in 1994. During a two-month period in late 1994, Congress ratified the Uruguay Round Agreements that created the World Trade Organization (WTO), the Clinton Administration committed America to creating an APEC free trade area by 2020, and the U.S. hosted the Summit of the Americas in Miami where the leaders of the Western Hemisphere's democracies made a unanimous commitment to create a Free Trade Area of the Americas (FTAA) by 2005. Viewed in retrospect, however, this two-month period was not the beginning of a new stage in American leadership in global trade expansion, but rather the end of a 50-year era of bipartisan U.S. support for trade-oriented policies which had been an integral part of America's Cold War strategy to contain the global expansion of communism.

Two events in particular during the last two months of 1994 marked the end of America's Cold War consensus in support of free trade. The first of these events was the mid-term congressional elections on November 8, 1994, that gave the Republican Party control of both houses of Congress for the first time in 40 years. The second event was the collapse of the Mexican peso on December 20, 1994, only nine days after the Summit of the Americas concluded in Miami. Although the effect was not immediately apparent, these two unrelated events shattered the remnants of the bipartisan congressional consensus on trade left over from the Cold War.

The Republican-controlled 104th Congress was the first true post-Cold War Congress. Republicans had scored some important congressional gains in the 1992 elections that returned a Democrat to the White House, but the 1994 elections brought a sea change in the composition of Congress as 73 first-term Republican legislators won election to the House of Representatives. In all, 195 new legislators were elected to the House in the 1992 and 1994 elections, including 121 Republicans and 74 Democrats. Although mainly market oriented, the majority of these legislators lacked any experience or interest in internationalist issues such as trade and foreign policy. Moreover, many were elected with the support of voters who agreed with the protectionist and managed trade views advanced by Patrick Buchanan and H. Ross Perot.

This new generation of Republican legislators came to Washington with a strong mandate to focus on domestic issues. However, from the start of the 104th Congress, they were faced instead with the financial collapse of Mexico and with bipartisan pressures from the Clinton Administration and their own Republican leadership to bail out the Mexican government with over $40 billion in emergency financial assistance. At this time, the Republicans were following the Contract With America and were committed to reforming the federal government and ending taxpayer-financed giveaways to special-interest groups. Consequently, President Clinton invoked the authority of the Executive to bail out Mexico unilaterally with $20 billion in loans provided by the U.S. Treasury's Exchange Stabilization Fund. The top Republican leaders in the House and Senate supported President Clinton's unilateral bailout of Mexico, but most Republican legislators in the House of Representatives did not.

Two important facts became clear in the months following the Clinton Administration's bailout of Mexico in February 1995. The first was that

Republican leaders in Congress could not count on the support of their troops to advance any trade initiatives proposed by the Executive. The second fact was that the Clinton Administration was unable or unwilling to provide the strong presidential leadership needed to continue pushing trade initiatives through Congress. Without strong presidential leadership on trade issues, and without strong Republican support for trade initiatives in Congress, further expansion of free trade was highly unlikely.

In fact, during 1995, trade policy became a contentious issue between the Clinton Administration and Congress as both sides adopted inflexible positions regarding the renewal by Congress of a new fast-track negotiating authority to facilitate Chile's accession to the NAFTA. The Clinton Administration insisted that a new fast-track must include strong provisions linking future trade agreements to non-trade issues such as labor standards and environmental conservation. Republican congressional leaders were steadfast in their rejection of these linkages, arguing that fast-track must deal exclusively with tariff and non-tariff trade issues as contemplated in the Trade Act of 1974 and the Omnibus Trade and Competitiveness Act of 1988. Since neither the Clinton Administration nor Republican leaders in Congress had the necessary votes to impose their respective visions of what the proper parameters of a new fast-track negotiating authority should be, negotiations between the Executive and Congress broke down at the end of 1995 and further expansion of free trade stalled completely.

LESSONS LEARNED

Rebuilding strong bipartisan congressional support for free trade is vital to America's economic interests. However, in order to formulate effective new strategies for achieving this essential objective, congressional leaders, activists who support free trade, and American business leaders must assimilate the most important lessons of developments in U.S. trade policy since the end of the Cold War.

Lesson #1: Strong presidential leadership and fast-track negotiating authority are necessary for maintaining American leadership in the global economy. To expand America's international trade interests, strong and sustained presidential leadership is essential. If strong Executive leadership is lacking, even the wisest and best-intentioned congressional leadership will find it nearly impossible to advance America's trade interests. Similarly, fast-track negotiating authority is

---

LESSONS LEARNED

- Strong presidential leadership and fast-track negotiating authority are necessary for maintaining American leadership in the global economy.

- Support for and opposition to free trade have always been bipartisan.

- The end of the Cold War brought significant changes in Americans' views of the importance of foreign trade.

- The benefits of free trade must be balanced against constituents' concerns for domestic problems.

---

essential for the swift approval by Congress of trade agreements negotiated by the executive branch of government. Without fast-track negotiating authority, the balance of pressure from congressional constituencies with a direct interest in trade will likely shift toward a stance increasingly supportive of protective intervention. Clearly, then, the foundations for restoring a bipartisan congressional consensus in support of trade expansion are first, strong leadership from the executive branch, and second, the renewal by Congress of fast-track negotiating authority that limits the Executive's scope of action to tariff and non-tariff trade negotiations.

Lesson #2: Support for and opposition to free trade have always been bipartisan. Over the past 50 years, both support for free trade and opposition to free trade have been bipartisan. While it is true that more Republicans have favored free trade than Democrats, congressional Republicans have never mustered sufficient votes to approve trade initiatives without support from the Democrats, and congressional Democrats have never succeeded in blocking trade initiatives without the backing of Republicans.

While the Cold War was still raging, it was relatively easy to build and sustain a bipartisan congressional consensus in favor of free trade, because America's free trade policies were an integral part of the national strategy to contain Soviet expansionism. Easy access to America's vast markets provided other countries with a powerful incentive to join the global coalition against communism. Free trade made it easier for the governments of these countries to oppose internal and external pressures to join the totalitarian Soviet bloc. American goods were vastly better than Soviet goods. American markets were more receptive than Soviet markets to goods exported by other countries. Americans paid in hard cash for their foreign imports, whereas the Soviets paid in worthless rubles or inferior-quality bartered goods. Americans honored their contracts, whereas the Soviets routinely ignored or violated their contractual commitments. American exports, investment, and financial assistance helped other countries grow and achieve a better standard of living for their citizens, whereas the Soviet Union could only make poor undemocratic countries even poorer and more oppressive. America's free trade policies encouraged economic freedom around the world, whereas the Soviet Union's centrally planned policies encouraged the loss of economic freedom and the destruction of individual liberties.

With the end of the Cold War, however, the bipartisan congressional consensus that supported free trade policies has also come to an end. American legislators and their constituents have not become more protectionist and isolationist. In Congress there still exists a significant bipartisan group of free-trade supporters, while opinion polls show that most Americans still believe that free trade is beneficial for the United States. What has changed is the process of building and sustaining that bipartisan congressional support for free trade.

Lesson #3: The end of the Cold War brought significant changes to Americans' views of the importance of foreign trade. The end of the Cold War has enabled Americans to focus more attention on domestic issues and problems, which is appropriate. Many of the problems undermining America's strength and vitality are domestic in origin—big interventionist government, excessive taxation, the budget deficit, and the failed welfare state are but a few examples of domestic problems that must be resolved. Moreover, at a time when Americans harbor increasing doubts about the efficacy of a bloated federal government, it is also appropriate for them to show more interest in the trade policies that link their communities to the global economy. In this context, the curiosity and skepticism of the American electorate about free trade and other issues that affect their lives are healthy and positive.

However, the end of the Cold War has also been followed by a dramatic change in the composition of Congress. This change is partly generational and partly ideological. Older legislators who earned their spurs as lawmakers during the Cold War era, including veterans of World

War II and Baby Boomers, are being replaced by younger legislators who may be less influenced by the past and more concerned with the future of America at the portal of the 21st century. Similarly, since the 1980s American voters have become increasingly conservative about economic and social issues that affect their everyday lives. This growing American conservatism was expressed at the polls in the elections of 1992, 1994, and 1996.

Moreover, the significant turnover in legislators during the recent congressional elections was accompanied by a large turnover in legislative assistants. These incoming legislative assistants are generally young and inexperienced about trade and other issues. As a result, congressional leaders and conservative activists who support free trade are faced with the challenging task of helping these new legislators and their legislative assistants acquire sufficient knowledge to make informed judgments about the benefits that accrue to their congressional districts as a result of free trade.

Lesson #4: The benefits of free trade must be balanced against constituents' concerns for domestic problems. Decades of grassroots activism on a broad range of domestic economic and social issues built the foundations of the wave of conservatism that is reshaping the American nation in the final years of the 20th century. Similarly, if congressional leaders and conservative activists who support free trade expect to rebuild the bipartisan congressional consensus that supported America's free trade policies during the 50-year Cold War, they must provide these new post–Cold War lawmakers and their legislative assistants with concrete grassroots arguments and specific examples that demonstrate why and how free trade directly benefits their home districts. The challenge of educating a new generation of lawmakers is very great indeed. Many American lawmakers and their constituents have mistaken ideas about free trade, and it is difficult to reduce its complexities to digestible sound bites. Moreover, it is difficult to maintain a high level of bipartisan support for free trade over a long period of time. On issues related to trade, history has shown that bipartisan congressional support for trade grows in response to individual trade bills submitted for approval by the Executive or introduced by Members of Congress. However, when there are no trade bills pending, bipartisan support for trade expansion tends to diminish. Still, while the task ahead is daunting, it can—and must—be done.

STRATEGIES TO BUILD SUPPORT FOR FREE TRADE AND INVESTMENT

The 105th Congress and the Administration should seek to achieve very specific objectives. The following objectives and the strategies necessary to achieve them are perhaps the most important and immediately viable steps for America to reestablish its leadership role in the process of worldwide expansion of free trade. The general objectives policymakers should use as guidelines throughout the next presidential term are to:

- **Put** American trade expansion back on track;

- **Enlarge** and deepen the World Trade Organization;

- **Support** the Asia-Pacific Economic Cooperation (APEC) forum to make it a better vehicle for liberalizing Asian trade;

- **Improve** U.S. trade relations with China; and

- **Build** congressional and public support for free trade and investment.

Putting American Trade Expansion Back on Track

Although America's international trade priorities and commitments span the globe, the Western Hemisphere is the region where U.S. trade negotiators scored the most impressive gains during the first half of the 1990s. Therefore, the process of putting American trade expansion back on track should begin in the Western Hemisphere. Between 1980 and 1992, the Reagan and Bush Administrations forged the closest relationship with Latin America that the U.S. has enjoyed in more than a century. This new hemispheric partnership was based on both democracy and the creation of a hemispheric free trade area as established in the Enterprise for the Americas Initiative (EAI) and the NAFTA. Moreover, NAFTA was conceived as the base upon which U.S.-led trade expansion in the Western Hemisphere over the next decade would result in the creation of a Free Trade Area of the Americas (FTAA) by 2005.

Since the collapse of the Mexican peso at the end of 1994, however, NAFTA has become a political football for politicians who claim that free trade causes such domestic problems as increased drug trafficking and illegal immigration. But these critics are mistaken. NAFTA did not cause the Mexican peso crisis and is not responsible for America's social problems.

STRATEGIES FOR PUTTING AMERICAN TRADE EXPANSION BACK ON TRACK

- Congress needs to renew the Executive's fast-track negotiating authority.

- The Caribbean Basin Initiative countries should be granted trading parity with NAFTA.

- The Administration should convene a second Summit of the Americas in 1997.

Moreover, far from being a failure, NAFTA has scored some impressive trade and investment successes. During NAFTA's first two years (1994 and 1995), trade and foreign direct investment among the U.S., Mexico, and Canada increased. The average U.S. tariff on Mexican products fell from 3.5 percent to 1.5 percent, while average Mexican tariffs on U.S. products dropped from 10 percent to 4.9 percent. As a result, trade among the three NAFTA countries rose by 17 percent in 1994 to $350 billion, and bilateral U.S.-Mexico trade grew by 20.7 percent, surpassing $100 billion for the first time.

In 1995, despite the recession caused by the peso's collapse, overall U.S.-Mexico trade increased 8 percent to $108 billion, while total intra-NAFTA trade grew 10.6 percent to $380 billion. After declining by 8.9 percent in 1995 to $46.3 billion, U.S. exports to Mexico increased by 12.1 percent during the first three months of 1996 compared with the same period in 1995. More than 75 percent of all U.S. states reported a rise in exports to Mexico during the first quarter of 1996.

To put American trade expansion back on track in the Western Hemisphere and around the world, the 105th Congress and the next Administration should implement the following strategies:

STRATEGY #1
Congress needs to renew the Executive's fast-track negotiating authority.

To reverse America's retreat from free trade, the 105th Congress should grant the Executive a new fast-track negotiating authority in 1997 to facilitate Chile's accession to NAFTA. The enlargement of NAFTA to include Chile would reaffirm America's commitment to an FTAA with Latin America and the Caribbean. One of the greatest mistakes made recently by U.S. policymakers was postponing the inclusion of Chile in NAFTA until after the 1996 elections. The failure to add Chile to NAFTA weakened American leadership and influence in the FTAA process. There is no reason to delay the admission of Chile to NAFTA. Chile's total gross national product is equivalent to about 1 percent of the American economy. Chile has enjoyed positive economic growth for 14 consecutive years. Growth during the past six years under a democratic civilian government has averaged 7.5 percent annually. Chile has pre-paid a large chunk of its external public-sector debt, has no balance-of-payments problem, and has enjoyed single-digit inflation since 1994. Its investment and savings rates are approaching those of the Asian tigers. The inclusion of Chile in NAFTA would confirm America's commitment to leading the FTAA process and open a new gateway for U.S. exports to markets in South America and APEC (of which Chile is a member).

The renewal of a broad fast-track negotiating authority, without any language linking trade issues to labor standards and the environment, also would facilitate the expansion of NAFTA to other countries in Latin America and the negotiation of free trade agreements with countries in Asia. Without a fast-track negotiating authority in hand, the Administration cannot enter into serious trade negotiations with Chile or any other country. Suggestions that fast-track is not necessary to enter into trade negotiations are mistaken. No country will invest the time or resources in negotiating with the U.S. if American negotiators cannot guarantee that any agreement reached will not be mutilated beyond recognition by the U.S. Congress.

STRATEGY #2
Congress should grant the Caribbean Basin Initiative countries trading parity with NAFTA.

Congress should extend trading parity with NAFTA members to the countries of the Caribbean Basin Initiative (CBI).[5] H.R. 553, which does not require fast-track negotiating authority but has stalled in Congress since 1995, would improve market access for U.S. exports to Caribbean and Central American markets. It also would require CBI beneficiaries to strengthen rules relating to investment, labor standards, and the environment, among other improvements that strongly favor U.S. interests.

STRATEGY #3
The Administration should convene a second Summit of the Americas in 1997.

The first Summit of the Americas in Miami in December 1994 laid the foundations of a new partnership between the U.S. and the democracies of the Western Hemisphere. It also launched the FTAA process, which has lost significant momentum since the collapse of the Mexican peso on December 20, 1994. A second Summit of the Americas, plus the accession of Chile to NAFTA and the approval of a bill that grants trading parity with NAFTA to CBI countries, would reinvigorate the hemispheric FTAA process and signal America's trading partners around the world that U.S. trade policy is back on track. Moreover, a second Summit of the Americas in 1997 would facilitate the process of defining a pathway and timetable for creating the FTAA by 2005. The U.S. should urge Western Hemispheric nations to decide quickly whether the FTAA should include

---

5 The Caribbean Basin Economic Recovery Act (CBERA), better known as the Caribbean Basin Initiative (CBI), was passed by the U.S. Congress in 1983 and implemented largely during 1984. The CBI provides beneficiary countries duty-free access to the U.S. market for all products not excluded by law. The countries, territories, and successor political entities which currently receive CBI benefits include Aruba, Antigua and Barbuda, Barbados, Belize, British Virgin Islands, Costa Rica, Dominica, the Dominican Republic, El Salvador, Grenada, Guatemala, Guyana, Haiti, Honduras, Jamaica, Montserrat, the Netherlands Antilles, Nicaragua, Panama, St. Christopher-Nevis, Saint Lucia, Saint Vincent and the Grenadines, and Trinidad and Tobago.

commitments that go beyond those already made in NAFTA and the WTO or should be abandoned in favor of merely removing tariffs on goods traded within the region.

Enlarging and Deepening the World Trade Organization

The United States has long been a supporter of the General Agreement on Tariffs and Trade, an international agreement first signed by 24 countries (including the U.S.) in 1947. The first GATT trade agreement reduced barriers to trade that helped cause the global depression of the 1930s. Since 1947, there have been eight rounds of negotiations under the auspices of GATT, with each round liberalizing trade a little more. The most recent, called the Uruguay Round, was signed into U.S. law in 1994 and created a new body called the World Trade Organization (WTO).

There are now 124 members of the WTO, which provides these countries with a means to resolve trade disputes without resorting to trade protectionism. The WTO establishes the rules of international trade by which all members of the WTO must abide. These rules govern business contracts, the liability for not fulfilling a contract, and the resolution of disputes over interpretation of a contract's terms. Without agreement on these rules, any nation could conduct business arbitrarily according to its own domestic laws, which often are contrary to laws in other countries. However, the Clinton Administration has not utilized the WTO effectively to avoid trade disputes with America's trading partners. Instead, it has tried to bypass the WTO and has used unilateral trade measures, like Section 301 of the 1974 Trade Act, to settle trade differences with other countries.

Instead of resorting to unilateral trade measures, the U.S. Administration should seek more actively to expand and deepen the WTO by implementing these strategies:

STRATEGY #1
The Administration should implement the Uruguay Round Agreements.

The U.S. should make sure that all members of the WTO fully and faithfully implement their trade liberalization commitments in accordance with established timetables and deadlines for compliance. The U.S. also should ensure that tariff barriers phased out by WTO members are not replaced by regulatory barriers. This means that, instead of bypassing the WTO to manage trade differences unilaterally, the U.S.

STRATEGIES FOR ENLARGING AND DEEPENING THE WTO

- The Administration should implement the Uruguay Round Agreements.

- The Administration should urge the WTO to hold a new negotiating round with the goal of achieving global free trade and investment by 2010.

- The Administration should promote accelerated implementation of the Trade-Related Aspects of Intellectual Property Rights Agreement.

- The Administration should negotiate a Multilateral Agreement on Competition Policy.

- The Administration should negotiate a Multilateral Agreement on Investment Policy.

should make full use of the WTO's multilateral dispute resolution rules to go after regulatory barriers that undermine American exports and foreign investment. In addition, the U.S. should complete in 1997 the sectoral agreements to liberalize trade in financial services and basic telecommunications. The completion of these multilateral agreements was deferred until 1997 as a result of the Clinton Administration's refusal to sign the agreements before the 1996 U.S presidential elections.

STRATEGY #2
The Administration should urge other members of the WTO to hold a new negotiating round with the goal of achieving global free trade and investment by 2010.

The President should exercise bold leadership and press other WTO members to convene a new round of global trade liberalization talks by 1998. The new WTO round should subsume APEC's goal of free trade and investment by 2010 as its own. This policy should encourage APEC to accelerate the liberalization of trade and investment in Asia. It would not be the first time that trade liberalization in one set of negotiations spurred liberalization in another. For example, the creation of APEC helped bring the Uruguay Round negotiations to a successful conclusion in the early 1990s.

STRATEGY #3

The Administration should promote the accelerated implementation of the Trade-Related Aspects of Intellectual Property Rights (TRIPS) Agreement.

Strong protection of intellectual property rights benefits both developed and developing countries. Weak intellectual property protection deters the foreign investment that helps fuel economic development. The Uruguay Round Agreements, which took effect in 1995, represented a significant advance for the protection of intellectual property. The Trade-Related Aspects of Intellectual Property Rights (TRIPS) Agreement, which also took effect in 1995, formally codifies substantive standards for the protection of all forms of intellectual property and includes administrative and judicial procedures, civil and criminal penalties and procedures, and customs regulations designed to uphold these standards. However, the American business community considers the TRIPS agreement only minimally acceptable. It is U.S. policy to encourage other countries to adopt intellectual property protection standards more stringent than TRIPS. For example, the NAFTA standards for intellectual property protection are more rigorous than TRIPS. These standards should not be lowered for any country — such as Chile, Argentina, Australia, New Zealand, or Singapore — that wishes to accede to NAFTA.

STRATEGY #4

The Administration should negotiate a Multilateral Agreement on Competition Policy.

Because there is no international agreement governing competition policy, the U.S. and other governments have been tempted to act unilaterally to resolve what are, in reality, competition policy problems. Such unilateralism increases global trade friction and undermines confidence in the recently established WTO dispute settlement mechanism. The U.S. government should seek to negotiate a Multilateral Agreement on Competition Policy. The most promising route for such negotiations is the Organization for Economic Cooperation and Development (OECD). While the WTO ultimately is the proper forum for negotiating a worldwide agreement, developing WTO rules on competition policy would be a very lengthy and difficult process because of the diverse development levels and legal traditions among WTO members. Consequently, the developed countries, which share similar interests, are more likely to reach a workable competition policy agreement through the OECD in a reasonable time. The Multilateral Agreement on Competition Policy should incorporate competitive conduct rules, separation of commercial and regulatory activities, and privatization and competitive neutrality principles. A Multilateral Agreement on Competition Policy based on these principles would force most signatory countries to reform or abolish their existing antitrust or antimonopoly laws.[6] In addition, such an agreement would foster economic deregulation and significantly alleviate trade friction arising from competition policy differences, reducing the likelihood of disruptive unilateral trade actions.

STRATEGY #5
The Administration should negotiate a Multilateral Agreement on Investment Policy.

The Uruguay Round Agreements established the first global rules for liberalizing international investment with the Agreement on Trade-Related Investment Measures. As a result, the U.S. now has three major sets of rules for investment liberalization: the WTO Agreement on Trade-Related Investment Measures, the NAFTA, and the APEC Investment Principles. The U.S. is also negotiating a fourth agreement: the Multilateral Agreement on Investment (MAI). Dissatisfied with the limited scope of the WTO Agreement on Trade-Related Investment Measures and the non-binding nature and deficiencies of the APEC Investment Principles, the U.S. and other developed countries launched negotiations through the OECD in May 1995 to draft a comprehensive, binding MAI. The finance ministers from the OECD member countries directed their negotiators to have the MAI treaty ready for signing before May 1997. The U.S. should not seek exceptions for itself to the rules for

---

6 Regardless of the existence of a multilateral agreement on competition policy or the lack of one, the U.S. should not hesitate to abolish its antiquated antitrust laws immediately and unilaterally. These laws burden America's business with outdated regulations that prevent them from engaging in joint ventures with other domestic and foreign firms. Moreover, these laws are often misused by the U.S. government to persecute and harass productive and successful U.S. companies like the Microsoft Corporation.

investment liberalization, and should press other OECD members to make as few exceptions as possible.

Supporting the APEC Forum as a Better Vehicle for Liberalizing Asian Trade

East Asia is the home of the world's fastest growing economies. Since the early 1980s, the volume of imports and exports exchanged across the Pacific has exceeded U.S. two-way trade with every other region of the world. In 1995 American exports to Pacific Rim countries totaled over $183 billion and supported over 3.6 million American jobs. In today's post-Cold War world, an ever more profitable economic relationship with East Asia remains one of America's foremost strategic interests. Thus, it is imperative that Washington seek ways to expand trade with Asia. To accomplish this goal, the U.S. should seek to create the world's largest free trade area in the Asia-Pacific region. The Asia-Pacific Economic Cooperation (APEC) forum, formed in 1989, is an instrument the U.S. can use to foster trade liberalization and enhance American commercial opportunities in the region. To make APEC a better vehicle for liberalizing Asian trade, the U.S. should execute several strategies:

STRATEGY #1
The Administration should harmonize and merge NAFTA and the Australia and New Zealand Closer Economic Relations (CER) agreements.

The governments of these important U.S. trading partners have expressed strong interest in a faster process of trade liberalization than that which was agreed upon during APEC's November 1994 meeting in Bogor, Indonesia. By merging the NAFTA and CER agreements, the U.S. could promote American economic and strategic interests in several areas. For example, since trading disciplines currently contained within the NAFTA and CER are more rigorous than those established by the WTO, the merger of the NAFTA and CER agreements would place increased pressure on other U.S. trading partners to upgrade their own trade standards and regulations. Similarly, the convergence of the NAFTA and CER agreements would provide a powerful inducement for other APEC countries—such as China, Japan, and South Korea—to speed up APEC's timetable for trade liberalization. Such trade agreements also would energize the sluggish FTAA process in the Western Hemisphere,

---

STRATEGIES FOR SUPPORTING APEC

- The Administration should harmonize and merge NAFTA and the Australia and New Zealand Closer Economic Relations (CER) agreements.

- The Administration should strengthen APEC's Investment Principles into a binding agreement.

- The U.S. should support concerted unilateralism in the Asia–Pacific region.

- The U.S. should support the Australian initiative to harmonize and merge NAFTA, the Association of South-East Asian Nations (ASEAN) free trade area, and the 1983 Closer Economic Relations (CER) agreement between Australia and New Zealand.

---

contribute to restoring American leadership to that process, and generate momentum for the eventual merger of the FTAA and APEC into a single free trade area encompassing more than half of the world's population.

STRATEGY #2
The Administration should strengthen APEC's Investment Principles into a binding agreement.

At the Leaders' Meeting held in Bogor, Indonesia, in November 1994, APEC adopted a set of non-binding Investment Principles. While these principles represent an important step toward a more comprehensive accord than the WTO's Agreement on Trade-Related Investment Measures, five of the ten principles are inadequate and should be strengthened. These inadequate principles cover the transfer of funds, capital movements, national treatment of foreign investors, performance requirements, and investment incentives. At future APEC meetings, the U.S. should press other member countries to establish an unfettered right to move funds across international borders, eliminate any restrictions on cross-border investment flows, eliminate all exceptions to national treatment, prohibit all trade-related investment performance requirements, and prohibit any special government grants and tax subsidies to attract investment that are not generally available to all potential domestic and foreign competitors. Once these voluntary investment guidelines have been improved, the U.S. should press for the conversion of APEC's Investment Principles into a legal agreement that binds all APEC members.

STRATEGY #3
The U.S. should support concerted unilateralism in the Asia-Pacific region.

This building block approach to trade liberalization acknowledges the great diversity in economic development of APEC's members and is a necessary stage in the process of building the confidence required to undertake more comprehensive trade negotiations after the year 2000. Under "concerted unilateralism," each APEC member would be responsible for presenting its own individual action plan for meeting APEC's broad trade liberalization objectives. These plans would be subject to peer review and peer pressure by other members.

STRATEGY #4
The U.S. should support the Australian initiative to harmonize and merge NAFTA, the Association of South-East Asian Nations (ASEAN) free trade area, and the 1983 Closer Economic Relations (CER) agreement between Australia and New Zealand.

APEC members are not located only in the Asia-Pacific region, but in the Americas as well. Current Western Hemisphere countries that form part of APEC include the U.S., Canada, Mexico, and Chile. Currently there is some disagreement among Asian members of APEC regarding the admission of new members. For example, ASEAN is opposed to admitting any new members, especially India, that might diminish the trading advantages enjoyed by ASEAN countries. The U.S. should press APEC to admit new members, particularly from Latin America where governments generally are more supportive of rapid trade liberalization.

Improving Trade Relations with China

China is indisputably one of the most important challenges facing American policymakers. China's emergence as a great power will be among the defining events of the next century. This will be true not only for Asia, but for the international system as well. How China integrates into the international system, and whether it accepts or rejects existing international

---

STRATEGIES FOR
IMPROVING TRADE RELATIONS WITH CHINA

- The U.S. should support the accession of China to the WTO as a developed country.

- Congress should reform the Jackson-Vanik Amendment to the Trade Act of 1974.

- Congress should encourage the Administration to negotiate a bilateral intellectual property protection pact with China.

---

economic, political, and legal norms, will define the very nature of that system. The U.S. should not try to isolate China in the international community. Instead, U.S. policy should seek to open and expose China to the outside world. Washington should work to expand the economic freedoms which international commerce and China's own modernization have engendered. International trade will continue to open China's economy, furthering economic reform, economic freedom, and, ultimately, greater political openness. To achieve these goals, the U.S. government should pursue several strategies:

STRATEGY #1
The U.S. should support the accession of China to the WTO as a developed country.

The accession of China to the WTO would give China an enhanced stake in the stability of the global trading system and in the peace and prosperity of the Asia-Pacific region. By integrating China into the WTO, the ability of U.S. policymakers to persuade China to respect the rules of the international trading system would increase significantly. Moreover, the conditions under which China joins the WTO will establish a precedent for about 30 other countries that also want to join the world trade body.

If the conditions for entry are too rigid, China may be discouraged from joining the WTO and choose instead to remain outside the global trading system, exporting its goods to other countries (including the U.S.) without being subject to the same trading rules observed by its trade partners. However, if the conditions established for China's entry into the WTO are too lax, other countries waiting in line to join the WTO certainly will seek similar conditions. The U.S. should encourage China's accession to the WTO as a developed country, allowing some flexibility in terms of the deadlines for China's compliance with the standards applicable to developed countries. However, purely political considerations—such as Beijing's insistence that it enter the WTO before Taiwan—should not be a factor.

STRATEGY #2
Congress should reform the Jackson-Vanik Amendment to the Trade Act of 1974.

The U.S. should not apply to China the economic sanctions called for in the Jackson-Vanik Amendment to the Trade Act of 1974. Jackson-Vanik was intended to increase the flow of Jewish emigrants from the former Soviet Union and its Eastern European satellites to Israel and the U.S. The amendment forbids the U.S. from granting permanent, unconditional most favored nation (MFN) trading status to any country (except Poland and Yugoslavia) that had a communist government (legally defined as a non-market economy) as of January 3, 1975. Under Jackson-Vanik, however, the U.S. may grant conditional MFN trading status to such countries if they allow free emigration. If countries do not allow fully free emigration but the President certifies that such countries are making progress toward allowing free emigration, then the President may grant such countries conditional MFN trading status for 12 months. Congress may overturn the President's certification by passing a joint resolution.

Each year since the Tiananmen massacre in 1989, Congress has threatened to overturn China's Jackson-Vanik waiver to demonstrate displeasure with Chinese human rights violations that had little to do with emigration. In fact, it is American immigration law—not Chinese emigration policy—that restricts the flow of Chinese emigrants. Deng Xiaoping offered to send as many as 10 million Chinese emigrants per year to America. However, U.S. law limits the annual number of immigrant visas that may be granted to natives of any country to 20,000. Moreover, Jackson-Vanik needlessly complicates negotiations to bring China into the WTO. Under Jackson-Vanik, the U.S. cannot grant China the unconditional, permanent MFN status it must grant a new WTO member. The U.S. would be forced to invoke an exception to WTO rules and negotiate a separate but parallel trade agreement with China.

Jackson-Vanik's threat of withdrawing MFN status is ineffective at best and more likely counterproductive. MFN tariffs are not a special privilege but instead are the standard rates that the U.S. extends to all but a handful of small countries. Withdrawing MFN would compel the U.S. to apply Smoot-Hawley tariffs on Chinese exports. After the inevitable Chinese retaliation against American exports, there would be a virtual cessation of China-U.S. trade. Maintaining MFN is so clearly in America's economic interests that everyone knows threats to withdraw it are hollow.

STRATEGY #3
Congress should encourage the Administration to negotiate a bilateral intellectual property protection pact with China.

As a *quid pro quo* for reforming Jackson-Vanik and supporting China's accession to the WTO, the U.S. government should press China to negotiate a bilateral agreement on intellectual property protection based on NAFTA standards rather than the WTO's TRIPS agreement. The objective of such an agreement should be to apply the rule of law across the entire country, instead of the current unwieldy and inefficient process whereby China's progress in this area is based on a quota system that quantifies the number of factories closed for violating intellectual property rights.

Building Support for Free Trade and Investment

During the Cold War, a bipartisan congressional alliance supported free trade policies. However, with the end of the Cold War that bipartisan consensus dissolved, in part because Congress has been more focused on pressing domestic problems and in part because the composition of Congress has changed dramatically. The 104th Congress was the first true post-Cold War Congress, and the new generation of lawmakers is well-grounded in the free-market philosophy that made America the world's greatest nation. But many lack internationalist experience and do not necessarily share the global outlook of their older colleagues and predecessors whose congressional careers unfolded against the background of America's 50-year struggle to win the Cold War.

STRATEGIES FOR BUILDING
SUPPORT FOR FREE TRADE AND INVESTMENT

- Members of Congress should create a bipartisan coalition to promote and defend America's free trade interests.

- The committees and subcommittees that have jurisdiction or legitimate interest in trade-related issues should be encouraged to hold hearings.

- Members of Congress should develop outreach programs to put new lawmakers in contact with activists, business leaders, and government officials who support free trade.

- Members of Congress should work with businesses and activists to develop educational outreach and support programs for legislative assistants responsible for trade issues in the House of Representatives and the Senate.

- Congressional and executive branch agencies responsible for trade issues should be tasked with producing detailed studies on the benefits of free trade.

- Free trade supporters in Congress should re-establish the bipartisan trade caucus.

- Congressional leaders should take steps to inform the American people of the benefits of free trade.

- Congress should consider restructuring the executive branch to minimize duplication of efforts and the influence of special interests, and to maximize development of a coherent trade policy.

Energizing broad-based enthusiasm for major trade initiatives will require sustained grassroots efforts to show the Members of Congress and the voters who elected them how free trade benefits their states. Congress and the American people need fewer theoretical arguments about why free trade is good for the United States and more clearly defined specific reasons about why they should support free trade, backed with concrete examples of benefits realized from free trade in their home states or congressional districts. To build congressional and public support for free trade and investment, congressional leaders, conservative activists, and policymakers who support free trade should implement these strategies:

STRATEGY #1
Members of Congress who support free trade should create a bipartisan coalition to promote and defend America's free trade interests.

The principal responsibility and jurisdiction for all major trade bills rests with the House Committee on Ways and Means and the Senate Finance Committee. Most of the nuts and bolts work on trade bills is done by the House Committee on Ways and Means. Traditionally, the lawmakers who chair congressional committees and subcommittees have been jealous guardians of their respective areas of authority and responsibility. These committees and subcommittees also include many lawmakers ranked by seniority. For example, during the 104th Congress, the House Committee on Ways and Means was comprised of 21 Republican legislators and 15 Democrats, while the Trade Subcommittee was made up of nine Republican legislators and six Democrats — all supported and advised by their respective legislative assistants and the committee professional staff. Of course, not all of these individuals support free trade; some are managed traders or outright protectionists. However, by identifying the free trade supporters in their midst, congressional leaders can develop strategies to build bridges between these lawmakers and the groups that support unfettered trade expansion.

STRATEGY #2
Committees and subcommittees that have jurisdiction or legitimate interests in trade-related issues should be encouraged to hold hearings.

One of the great disappointments of the 104th Congress was the paucity of hearings on trade issues, which is all the more surprising given the large number of subjects that Congress ought to be looking at on a regular basis. In 1997 the 105th Congress should be encouraged to hold hearings on the following topics:

- The renewal of fast-track negotiating authority on the accession of Chile to NAFTA;

- The demonstrable success of NAFTA in boosting North American trade flows significantly between 1994 and 1996;

- The importance of granting the CBI countries trading parity with NAFTA members;

- The success to date of the WTO's dispute resolution efforts;

- The status of WTO negotiations on multilateral agreements relating to basic telecommunications and trade in financial services;

- U.S. efforts within the OECD to negotiate multilateral agreements on competition policy and investment policy;

- The negotiation of free trade agreements with Australia, New Zealand, and Singapore;

- Intellectual property rights issues involving China, Brazil, Argentina, Mexico, Chile, and many other countries;

- The status of the APEC;

- The harm caused to American competitiveness by U.S. antitrust and tax laws;

- The costs to American consumers of the growing use of anti-dumping and countervailing duty laws;

- The harm caused to U.S. economic interests by the unilateral use of trade sanctions in American foreign policy.

In preparation for these hearings, Congress should ask firms involved in joint ventures and strategic alliances with firms overseas to provide a list of those ventures, the products produced as a result of those ventures, the revenues gained from those products, and the jobs supported by sales of those products. There are hundreds of joint ventures and strategic alliances between U.S. companies and companies from abroad. Unfortunately, many policymakers are completely unaware of the existence of these alliances. These businesses should become more active when the International Trade Commission and the Commerce Department solicit advice and information, and when Congress holds public hearings on new laws which may restrict importing and change the regulatory environment.

The House Ways and Means Committee and the Senate Finance Committee are the only two committees in Congress with the legal mandate and authority to craft trade bills and submit bills to a floor vote.

Ways and Means has a Subcommittee on Trade, and the Finance Committee has a Subcommittee on International Trade, both of which held frequent hearings on trade issues during the 104th Congress. However, there are many other committees and subcommittees, in both the House and the Senate, whose areas of responsibility and authority include trade issues. These committees and subcommittees and their respective chairmen should be encouraged to hold frequent hearings on trade issues that fall within their purviews. For example, the Senate Foreign Relations Committee has three subcommittees that should be encouraged to hold hearings on trade issues: the Subcommittee on International Economic Policy, Export, and Trade Promotion; the Subcommittee on East Asian and Pacific Affairs; and the Subcommittee on Western Hemisphere and Peace Corps Affairs.

In addition, the Senate Committee on Banking, Housing and Urban Affairs has a Subcommittee on International Finance that should be encouraged, for example, to hold hearings on the pending WTO Multilateral Agreement on Trade in Financial Services. The Senate Energy and Natural Resources Committee has a Subcommittee on Energy Production and Regulation that should be encouraged to hold hearings on the possible negotiation of international energy agreements between the U.S. and such trusted American friends and oil suppliers as Venezuela and Saudi Arabia. And the Senate Judiciary Committee has a Subcommittee on Antitrust, Business Rights, and Competition that should be encouraged to hold hearings on the proposed Multilateral Agreement on Competition Policy that the U.S. is negotiating within the OECD, as well as hearings on how U.S. antitrust laws are undermining the international competitiveness of American business.

In the House of Representatives, the Small Business Committee has a Subcommittee on Procurement, Exports, and Business Opportunity that should hold hearings on the advantages and disadvantages faced by small business in global markets. The House Judiciary Committee has a Subcommittee on Courts and Intellectual Property that should hold hearings on intellectual property issues involving the WTO's TRIPS agreement and problems U.S. firms are having in China, Mexico, Brazil, and Argentina. The House Committee on International Relations has Subcommittees on International Economic Policy and Trade, Asia and the Pacific, and the Western Hemisphere. These subcommittees should hold frequent hearings on NAFTA, the FTAA process, APEC, and U.S.

relations with key trading partners such as Chile, Brazil, and Argentina in South America and China, Japan, Australia, New Zealand, and Singapore in Asia. The House Committee on Banking and Financial Services has a Subcommittee on Domestic and International Economic Policy that could hold hearings on issues relating to NAFTA, the WTO, and APEC. Moreover, the House Appropriations Committee has a Subcommittee on Foreign Operations, Export Financing, and Related Programs that should hold hearings on the tariff revenue effects of trade agreements.

The point of encouraging so many different committees and subcommittees to hold frequent hearings on trade issues is to focus increased congressional and public levels of attention on trade. Potential witnesses for such hearings should include congressional leaders, conservative activists, academics, and business leaders who support free trade. If possible, the invited witnesses should include individuals from the home states or congressional districts of the lawmakers who comprise these committees and subcommittees, as well as experts with substantial personal experience in global, regional, and country-specific trade.

STRATEGY #3
Members of Congress who support free trade should develop outreach programs to put new lawmakers in frequent contact with activists, business leaders, and government officials who support free trade.

Congressional hearings are an important means both for attracting more congressional and public attention to trade-related issues and for providing less experienced lawmakers with the information input they need to form realistic and balanced judgments about the benefits of free trade. However, it is vitally important that newer lawmakers also should build personal bridges to constituencies that support free trade, including conservative activists, academics, and business leaders. Public policy institutes and private business associations should join forces to develop congressional outreach programs to put lawmakers in personal contact with high-level conservative activists and business leaders who support free trade.

STRATEGY #4

Members of Congress who support free trade should work with businesses and activists to develop educational outreach and support programs for the House and Senate legislative assistants responsible for trade issues.

The typical legislative assistant is young (under 26 years of age), inexperienced, and generally burdened with the need to know literally thousands of details about trade. Providing these congressional staffers with timely and accurate information on how free trade benefits their home states and districts would aid them in performing their legislative tasks with greater accuracy, efficiency, and success.

Public policy institutes and private business associations should be encouraged to develop, separately and jointly, educational outreach and support programs for all legislative assistants responsible for trade issues. Examples of such programs include the organization of seminars for these legislative assistants conducted by congressional leaders, conservative activists, academics, and business leaders who support free trade. One of the key goals of such programs should be to provide these legislative assistants with grassroots arguments and examples in dollars and jobs of why free trade benefits their particular home states and districts.

Similarly, these legislative assistants should be provided with tightly summarized arguments (one-page memoranda or even index cards) on every important trade issue they are responsible for tracking. Congressional staffers should develop strong relationships with businesses engaging in international trade and utilize them for casework and information on the effects of trade policies on business.

STRATEGY #5

Congressional and executive branch agencies responsible for trade issues should be tasked with producing detailed studies on the benefits of free trade.

Congress has access to many different congressional and executive branch agencies with the expertise to perform in-depth studies on macro and micro trade issues, including the International Trade Commission (ITC), the General Accounting Office (GAO), and the Congressional Research Service (CRS) at the Library of Congress. In addition, Congress should request studies from the Executive's own watchdog agencies on the tangible benefits or disadvantages of current trade policy.

Congress also should task the Joint Economic Committee with reporting on the tangible benefits of such trade agreements as the Uruguay Round Agreements and NAFTA, and also with providing information broken down by congressional district on the jobs and exports supported by free trade and investment. For example, in southern textile manufacturing states like North Carolina, vanishing low-wage textile jobs have been offset by high-wage jobs created by foreign investors such as German automakers BMW and Mercedes-Benz and Swiss pharmaceutical producer Ciba.

Other tasks that Congress should authorize for the Joint Economic Committee include a series of studies on the realistic benefits of extending NAFTA to include all of Latin America and the Caribbean; on the extension of NAFTA membership to APEC members like Australia, New Zealand, and Singapore; on the creation of an APEC free trade area by 2010 or earlier; on the convergence into a single free trade area of APEC, NAFTA, and Latin America; on the accession of China, Taiwan, and other countries to the WTO; and on the negotiation by NAFTA and the European Union (EU) of a Trans-Atlantic Free Trade Area (TAFTA).

The GAO should be instructed by Congress to conduct an annual study identifying areas of the U.S. economy that are dependent on overseas markets as well as on imported raw materials and components. The study should break down the information for national, state, and local levels. The study should identify the number of Americans employed as a result of U.S. exports and imports, the industry sectors where those jobs exist, and a list of countries buying these American goods or selling goods to American companies that manufacture finished products for domestic consumption and final assembly export.

Currently, a host of executive branch departments provide weekly, monthly, quarterly, and yearly data on international trade: the Department of Commerce, the Census Bureau, the International Trade Administration, and the U.S. Trade Representative's Office, among others. The Departments of State, Treasury, and Justice also work on the development and enforcement of trade policy. To reduce overlap and waste, agencies and offices tasked with keeping statistics relating to trade should provide the following to Congress regularly: information on service exports and imports; data on the number of jobs created from U.S. exports on a state and local basis; specific U.S. industries experiencing increasing exports and employment trends in those industries; the types of raw materials American businesses import, and from which countries; and a comparison of the cost of these imports by weight and the domestic costs for comparable raw materials.

STRATEGY #6
Free trade supporters in Congress should re-establish the bipartisan trade caucus.

Trade has not been a popular issue in Congress since the collapse of the Mexican peso in December 1994. Congressional Republicans and Democrats who support free trade consequently have failed to present a strong bipartisan case for free trade. Instead, they have allowed protectionists on the Left and the Right to dominate the national debate on trade. If congressional free traders decline to defend free trade, the American news media will not report their remarks in defense of free trade. Since the peso crisis, protectionists and economic nationalists have been waging a relentless campaign of sound bites against free trade, while supporters of free trade in Congress and the private sector have said little to set the record straight.

Restoring the bipartisan consensus for free trade requires aggressive bipartisan leadership. Strong executive branch leadership is required to negotiate trade agreements with other countries and to push trade bills through Congress. However, strong congressional leadership is required to nurture and sustain the bipartisan congressional consensus to support these agreements. Republican and Democratic congressional leaders who support free trade should join forces in order to rebuild the congressional consensus on the benefits of free trade and put American trade expansion back on track.

STRATEGY #7
Congressional leaders should take steps to inform the American people of the benefits of free trade.

Few Americans seem to understand how trade restrictions on apparel and textiles threaten the jobs of those who work in the retail sector, or how regulations that affect one industry directly affect others with which those in that industry do business. Congressional leaders, government agencies, and conservative activists can work together to increase the exposure of free trade issues in the media—a powerful tool in educating, influencing, and changing public opinion and public policy. Large gaps in the information the public needs to know have been allowed to pass unfilled; for example, little has been written in the mainstream press about the positive benefits like jobs that have resulted from both NAFTA and WTO agreements.

Congress should take the lead in getting this information out with effective use of hearings and press conferences. Organizations like the National Association of Manufacturers, the National Foreign Trade Council, and the U.S. Chamber of Commerce can be called upon to assemble CEOs of small and medium-sized businesses who could testify before Congress on how trade restrictions have affected their businesses. Frequently, the media report such testimony.

STRATEGY #8
Congress should consider restructuring the executive branch to minimize duplication of efforts and the influence of special-interest groups, and to maximize development of a coherent trade strategy.

A major obstacle to developing a consistent international trade policy based on the benefits of free trade and investment is the fragmented structure of agencies charged with developing such policies. There are many overlapping, duplicative, and often contradictory agencies, bureaus, and departments developing their own agendas on international trade. Such a process leads to inconsistent and often contradictory policy initiatives. It impedes proper decisionmaking and encourages the capture of small, low-profile agencies by special interests. This is particularly true with regard to anti-dumping and countervailing duties law enforcement. In order for the executive branch to develop and enforce a sound international trade policy, its structure must be reformed.

For example, Congress could abolish the U.S. Department of Commerce and consolidate its international trade and investment functions with the International Trade Commission into the Customs Bureau of the Department of the Treasury. The enforcement of existing trade laws is scattered among the Export and Import Administrations of the Department of Commerce, the International Trade Commission, and the Customs Bureau of the Department of the Treasury. The consolidated agency could be placed under the Department of the Treasury.

The executive branch also could abolish the office of U.S. Trade Representative and move its functions into the State Department. Negotiating trade agreements, and monitoring their implementation, are service delivery functions that should be placed within a separate office in the Department of State. This is more consistent with the monitoring and implementation of other U.S. treaties and international agreements.

The executive branch could restructure the Council of Economic Advisers into a Department of Economic Policy. Developing trade policy and evaluating the performance of other federal agencies handling trade issues are policy advice functions that would best be handled by a separate department within the executive branch. This new agency would subsume the functions of the current Council of Economic Advisers. By not having regulatory or service delivery responsibility, the Department of Economic Policy could be far more objective in providing economic and trade policy advice to the President and far less likely to be tilted toward any single special interest since the department's mandate would cover all economic issues. These changes would streamline the policymaking process within the executive branch and remove much of the conflicting and overlapping decisionmaking that exists within the various departments and agencies today.

CONCLUSION

America has always benefited from free trade and investment. Whenever Washington has erected protectionist walls around America, it has paid the price with lost jobs, higher consumer costs, lower competitiveness, and infringements on individual economic liberty. To ensure America's economic growth and stability in the future, America's leaders, especially in Congress, must rededicate their efforts to support free trade and investment. They must make the opponents of free trade, the media, and the general public understand how much of their economic well-being depends on their freedom to buy and sell goods from whomever they choose.

American leadership has consistently pushed the world toward democracy and economic freedom. As America approaches the 21st century, it must become increasingly more competitive in a global economy. No country has ever prospered by closing its domestic markets to foreign trade or investment. In order for the U.S. to maintain the highest living standards in the world, it has to face the challenges of the global market and lead the world in strategies for overcoming them. The restoration of public and political support for free trade requires strong leadership with a commitment to free trade principles and a willingness to take immediate action. To continue to straddle the free trade fence will condemn America to economic stagnation and allow other countries to lay claim to the title of Land of the Free.

Chapter 19

RESTRUCTURING AND REFORMING THE FOREIGN AID PROGRAMS

Bryan T. Johnson and Brett D. Schaefer

Amerⁱcan taxpayers have spent over $2 trillion on foreign aid since 1945,[1] and the Clinton Administration—despite congressional cuts in these programs—continues to call for increased aid spending. Foreign aid, however, does not work. Most countries receiving economic assistance today are the same ones that depended on it 35 years ago. If America fails to reform its foreign aid program, less-developed countries will continue to be harmed and U.S. taxpayers will be forced to continue to underwrite one of the most poorly run and ineffective government agencies in existence: the U.S. Agency for International Development (AID), which bears the primary responsibility for handing out the bulk of America's $12 billion foreign aid budget.

When President John F. Kennedy established AID in the early 1960s, he called it a "temporary agency." Today, it is one of the most solidly entrenched of all federal bureaucracies. U.S. foreign aid bureaucrats have

The authors would like to thank James Przystup and Thomas P. Sheehy for their suggestions and contributions to this chapter. The opinions and views expressed, however, are solely the responsibility of the authors.

1 Total budget outlays for economic development aid since 1945 are about $500 billion. But since most of this money was borrowed by the government, accrued interest and inflation increase this amount to about $2 trillion. These figures are based on *Foreign Relations Revitalization Act of 1995*, Report of the Committee on Foreign Relations, U.S. Senate, June 9, 1995, p. 13.

long argued that foreign assistance is vital to the economic well-being of less-developed countries. Perhaps the most breathtaking manifestation of this view is AID Administrator J. Brian Atwood's claim, in remarks to the Center for National Policy in December 1994, that the overall economic prosperity of the post–World War II era can be attributed largely to the Marshall Plan and successive foreign aid efforts. This assertion grossly exaggerates the benefits of development aid while ignoring its many harmful effects. Not only has the U.S. foreign aid program failed to promote economic growth in less-developed countries, but many recipient countries are in fact worse off economically because of it.

Efforts to abolish development aid are portrayed by its advocates as heartless and draconian. They argue that abolishing development aid will condemn lesser-developed countries to perpetual poverty. Nothing could be more inaccurate. There is no conclusive evidence that foreign aid encourages economic development. There is, however, more than enough evidence to suggest that development aid is at best ineffective and at worst downright harmful.

America's Foreign Aid Program

Foreign aid is composed of several different facets: humanitarian aid and disaster relief, military and security assistance, and development aid. Together, these projects receive some $12 billion a year in federal funding. Of this $12 billion, only 38 percent goes to humanitarian assistance, disaster relief, military aid, and security assistance (see Chart 19.1); fully 53 percent of the entire foreign aid budget is dedicated to development and economic aid, either bilaterally or through multilateral institutions, that has been of little benefit to developing nations — the intended beneficiaries of these programs. An additional 5 percent is parceled out as corporate welfare through various export promotion programs. Another 4 percent goes to support AID, the U.S. bureaucracy whose primary responsibility is to manage the country's ineffective development and bilateral economic aid.

The future of AID and America's foreign aid program has been in question for some time. The 1989 Hamilton-Gilman Task Force Report by Representatives Lee Hamilton (D-IN) and Benjamin Gilman (R-NY) found that the U.S. foreign aid program lacks focus and is overburdened with too many overlapping objectives. In the early 1990s, the State Department, under the direction of then-Secretary of State James A. Baker III, commissioned a study of the existing foreign policy structure. The result of

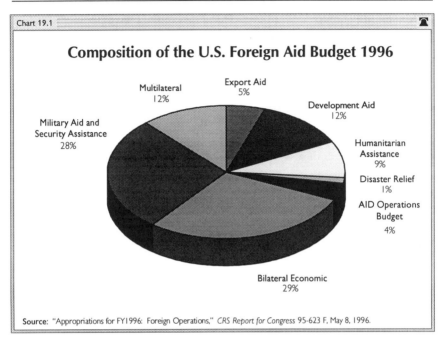

Chart 19.1

Composition of the U.S. Foreign Aid Budget 1996

Multilateral
12%

Export Aid
5%

Development Aid
12%

Military Aid and
Security Assistance
28%

Humanitarian
Assistance
9%

Disaster Relief
1%

AID Operations
Budget
4%

Bilateral Economic
29%

Source: "Appropriations for FY1996: Foreign Operations," *CRS Report for Congress* 95-623 F, May 8, 1996.

that study, *State 2000, A New Model for Managing Foreign Affairs*, was published in December 1992. This study argued that the current foreign policy apparatus is overburdened with overlapping and conflicting agencies and bureaus. Its recommendation: Merge AID into the State Department.

In 1993, Vice President Albert Gore spearheaded the Clinton Administration's "Reinventing Government" initiative, which recognized that AID needed serious reform. One result of this initiative was the Administration's Peace, Prosperity and Democracy Act, proposed in Congress in 1994. It failed to generate much support, however, and failed to pass. At about the same time, Secretary of State Warren Christopher submitted proposals to the White House that called for the integration of AID and other agencies into the State Department.

In 1995, the Republican-led Congress tried to reorganize the U.S. foreign aid bureaucracy. In June, the House of Representatives passed the American Overseas Interests Act (H.R. 1561), which provided for the dismantling of several executive branch agencies, including AID, and the consolidation of their activities within the State Department. This bill was vetoed by the

President, and conservatives in the House were unable to gather the votes necessary to override the veto.

Senator Mitch McConnell (R-KY) introduced legislation to abolish AID and condition economic aid on how well a recipient country scores on an index like The Heritage Foundation's *Index of Economic Freedom*. But since Senator McConnell sits on the Appropriations Committee, not the Foreign Relations Committee where such legislation usually originates, his bill was never brought up for a vote.

However, the Foreign Relations Revitalization Act (S. 908) was voted out of the Senate Foreign Relations Committee. The goal of this bill, the brainchild of Senator Jesse Helms (R-NC), was to abolish AID and other agencies and move some of their functions into the State and Defense Departments. Faced with opposition from the Clinton Administration and filibuster threats by Senate Democrats, Senator Helms was unable to bring his bill to the Senate floor for a vote.

Senator Helms also drafted the Foreign Aid Reduction Act of 1995, which substantially would have altered the way the U.S. spends its foreign aid dollars. Originally, the Helms legislation would have required the President to certify 1) that money spent on military and security aid, as well as development aid, is spent in the U.S. national interest; 2) that countries receiving development aid have sufficient levels of economic freedom, based on the findings of a study like the *Index*; and 3) that a sunset provision for funding is included in all foreign aid projects. These certification requirements eventually were weakened. Like the State Department reorganization bill, the foreign aid bill fell victim to threats of a Senate filibuster and a presidential veto. Though it was approved by the Senate Foreign Relations Committee in 1995, this bill never was voted on by the full Senate. Consequently, as in every year since 1985, Congress appropriated funds for a foreign aid program without authorizing legislation.

Scrambling to pass the various appropriations bills as quickly as possible so Members could concentrate on the upcoming elections, and anxious to avoid another government shutdown, Congress in 1996 packaged the majority of the appropriations bills into an omnibus appropriations bill. This passed the House on September 28, 1996, and the Senate on October 3, 1996. Again, there was no attempt to pass authorizing legislation for foreign aid. The House version of the bill called for appropriations of $11.9 billion for foreign aid, a $460 million reduction from the 1996 level and $1 billion less than the President requested. The Senate called for $12.2 billion in foreign aid, $299 million more than the House version but $162 million less than the previous year and $707 million less than the President's request.

The Case Against Foreign Aid

Many policymakers remain convinced that America's foreign aid program is effective in helping the poor around the world. It is not. While supporters of foreign aid may be able to point to a specific program that has helped a particular country in a particular instance, the evidence clearly demonstrates both the futility of giving foreign aid and the damage such aid has done to less-developed countries.

A Failure to Help Developing Countries. Foreign aid does not help countries develop economically, and in most cases does not support America's national interests. Using the most quantifiable measure of development — the average wealth of a country's citizens — *The Index of Economic Freedom* examined the figures on gross domestic product (GDP) per capita for the 67 long-term development aid recipients over 29 years, from 1965 to 1994.[2] Of these 67 countries, 37 had achieved average per capita GDP growth rates of less than 1 percent. Most economists agree that this rate of growth is low. Moreover, fully half of these 37 abysmal performers, such as Haiti, Ethiopia, or Guyana (see Table 19.1), are worse off than they were 29 years ago. These countries managed to make their citizens poorer despite the foreign aid they received. This evidence clearly demonstrates AID's ineffectiveness as a force for economic development.

Development Aid. Foreign aid also has a poor record in promoting American interests. While aid for political or military purposes can serve the national interest, economic development aid does not. For example, two out of every three recipients of U.S. foreign aid voted against the U.S. a majority of the time in the United Nations General Assembly in 1995.[3]

---

2 1994 is the most recent year for which reliable figures could be found for most countries. These figures are included in the *1996 Index of Economic Freedom* (Washington, D.C.: The Heritage Foundation, 1996).

3 See Bryan T. Johnson, "Foreign Aid Wins Few Friends at the United Nations," Heritage Foundation *F.Y.I.* No. 101, May 13, 1996.

Table 19.1

Long-Term Recipients of U.S. Foreign Aid and Their Economic Perfomance: 1965-1994

	GDP per Capita 1965, Constant 1987 US$	GDP per Capita 1994, Constant 1987 US$	Increase in GDP per Capita 1965-1994	Years Receiving Aid
Bolivia	$682	$780	14%	52
Chile	1236	2359	91	52
Colombia	690	1326	92	52
Costa Rica	1128	1905	69	52
Ecuador	626	1237	97	52
El Salvador	913	1022	12	52
Guatemala	690	907	31	52
Haiti	360	225	-37	52
Honduras	746	939	26	52
Panama	1371	2379	74	52
Peru	1126	1103	-2	52
Philippines	464	623	34	52
India	217	399	84	51
Indonesia	189	628	233	51
Mexico	1136	1857	63	51
Turkey	834	1758	111	51
Uruguay	434	626	44	51
Liberia ††	627	486	-22	50
Ethiopia **	187	154	-18	49
Nicaragua	1752	801	-54	49
Lebanon	—	—	—	48
Thailand	366	1680	358	48
Israel	4654	**9887**	112	47
Jordan **	2253	1559	-31	47
Morocco	500	934	87	46
Nepal	151	198	31	46
Dominican Republic	372	832	123	45
Egypt	300	712	138	45
Tunisia	638	1428	124	45
Guyana	479	519	8	44
Kenya	221	372	68	44
Afghanistan	—	—	—	43
Sierra Leone	137	139	1	43
Sri Lanka	213	510	139	43

Note: Shaded countries experienced less than 1% annual economic growth. Figures in **Bold** are from 1993.
   * First GDP/capita from 1986.   ** First GDP/capita from 1983.   ‡ Second GDP/capita from 1990.
   † Second GDP/capita from 1992.   †† Second GDP/capita from 1987.
Sources: *World Data 1995 CD-ROM*, The World Bank, 1996; *Foreign Aid Reduction Act of 1995*, Committee on Foreign Relations.

| Table 19.1 (Con't) | | | | ☎ |

Long-Term Recipients of U.S. Foreign Aid and Their Economic Perfomance: 1965-1994

	GDP per Capita 1965, Constant 1987 US$	GDP per Capita 1994, Constant 1987 US$	Increase in GDP per Capita 1965-1994	Years Receiving Aid
Zaire †	282	153	-46	43
Belize	830	2133	157	42
Jamaica	1272	1588	25	42
Malawi	113	116	3	42
Somalia ‡	111	111	0	41
Uganda **	452	514	14	41
Gambia	225	276	23	40
Ghana	501	405	-19	40
Portugal	1849	**5048**	173	40
Sudan	806	**806**	0	40
Tanzania	134	135	0	40
Benin	346	367	6	39
Guinea *	386	413	7	39
Madagascar	320	212	-34	39
Togo	366	314	-14	39
Zambia	478	253	-47	39
Cameroon	618	668	8	38
Gabon	2798	3689	32	38
Mauritania	516	490	-5	38
Mauritius	968	2372	145	38
Myanmar/Burma	210	267	27	38
Burkina Faso	180	**242**	35	37
Burundi	124	181	46	37
Central African Rep.	408	338	-17	37
Lesotho	126	319	152	37
Mali	227	247	9	37
Niger	617	272	-56	37
Nigeria	335	352	5	37
Senegal	752	627	-17	37
Seychelles	1918	4847	153	37
Swaziland	478	752	57	37
Chad	202	176	-13	36
Rwanda	229	**280**	22	36

Note: Shaded courtries experienced less than 1% annual economic growth. Figures in **Bold** are from 1993.
    * First GDP/capita from 1986.   ** First GDP/capita from 1983.   ‡ Second GDP/capita from 1990.
    † Second GDP/capita from 1992.   †† Second GDP/capita from 1987.
Sources: *World Data 1995 CD-ROM,* The World Bank, 1996; *Foreign Aid Reduction Act of 1995,* Committee on
    Foreign Relations.

Moreover:

- **India,** the fifth-largest recipient of American foreign aid, received some $157 million in U.S. foreign aid in 1996 and voted against the United States 83 percent of the time. That is as often as Cuba and more often than Iran.

- **Egypt,** the second-largest recipient of American foreign aid, voted against the U.S. 67 percent of the time. This is worse than in 1994, when Egypt voted against the U.S. 65 percent of the time. Egypt received some $2.2 billion in U.S. foreign aid in FY 1996.

- **Haiti,** which benefited from President Clinton's decision to send American troops to restore deposed President Jean-Bertrand Aristide, voted against the U.S. 60 percent of the time in the U.N. 1996 session. Despite this, the U.S. sent some $124 million in foreign aid to Haiti in FY 1996.

- **Mexico,** which will benefit from President Clinton's $40 billion international economic bailout at the expense of U.S. taxpayers, voted against the U.S. 58 percent of the time. Aside from the $40 billion economic bailout plan, the Clinton Administration endorsed an additional $25 million in foreign aid for Mexico.

- **The top ten** countries that voted against the U.S. the most often received about $212 million in foreign aid in FY 1996 (see Table 19.2).

- **Seven of the ten largest** recipients of U.S. foreign aid also voted against the U.S. a majority of the time (see Table 19.3).

- **Nine of the ten** countries that voted with the U.S. the most often are former Soviet bloc countries (see Table 19.4).

There may be many reasons why a country votes with or against the U.S. at the United Nations, but it is clear from the data that U.S. generosity in foreign aid does not buy friends abroad. Clearly, the U.S. foreign aid program in general and the Clinton Administration in particular have done little to convince the American public that their tax dollars are being used wisely by America's foreign aid bureaucracy. President Clinton has defended two of his biggest foreign policy and economic initiatives — restoring Aristide to power in Haiti and bailing out the economy of Mexico — as being in the U.S. national interest. Yet these countries seem to care

Table 19.2		☎

Top Ten Countries Voting Against The U.S.
at the U.N. and Total Foreign Aid for FY 1996

		FY '96 U.S. Aid	Voting Against U.S. in the U.N.: 1995
1.	India	$156,650,000	83 %
2.	China, People's Rep. of	604,000	78
3.	Seychelles	240,000	75
4.	Lebanon	8,475,000	74
5.	Laos	2,000,000	73
6.	Pakistan	2,500,000	72
7.	Nigeria	26,827,000	69
8.	Sierra Leone	869,000	69
9.	Djibouti	250,000	68
10.	Burkina Faso	13,386,000	67
	Total Aid	$211,801,000	

Source: *Voting Practices in the United Nations, 1995,* U.S. Department of State, March 31, 1996.

Table 19.3		☎

Many of Largest Recipients of U.S. Foreign Aid
Vote Against the U.S. in the U.N.

		FY '96 U.S. Aid	Voting Against U.S. in the U.N.: 1995
1.	Israel	$3,000,000,000	3%
2.	Egypt	2,116,000,000	67
3.	Russia	264,241,000	27
4.	Ukraine	162,389,000	40
5.	India	156,650,000	83
6.	South Africa	132,378,000	53
7.	Peru	124,377,000	53
8.	Haiti	123,385,000	60
9.	Bolivia	121,489,000	54
10.	Ethiopia	109,125,000	54
	Total Aid	$6,310,034,000	

Source: *Voting Practices in the United Nations, 1995,* U.S. Department of State, March 31, 1996.

Table 19.4

Israel, Former Soviet Bloc Countries are Least Likely to Vote Against the U.S.

		FY '96 U.S. Aid	Voting Against U.S. in the U.N.: 1995
1.	Israel	$ 3,000,000,000	3%
2.	Tajikistan	7,000,000	9
3.	Latvia	7,835,000	13
4.	Georgia	21,250,000	14
5.	Uzbekistan	12,424,000	14
6.	Hungary	30,242,000	17
7.	Estonia	385,000	18
8.	Lithuania	13,074,000	19
9.	Slovenia	4,595,000	21
10.	TFYR Macedonia	16,974,000	22
	Total Aid	**$3,113,779,000**	

Source: *Voting Practices in the United Nations, 1995*, U.S. Department of State, March 31, 1996.

little about America's interests when it comes to supporting the U.S. position in the U.N. General Assembly.

Food Aid. Food aid improves neither the agriculture nor the nourishment of less-developed countries on a long-term basis. The United States currently has several programs (known collectively as P.L. 480 programs) that focus on food aid. They are divided into three titles. Title I programs provide credit that foreign countries can use only to purchase U.S. agricultural products; Title II programs provide emergency food relief to foreign countries; Title III programs distribute direct grants to foreign countries for the express purpose of purchasing U.S. agricultural products.

Title I and Title III programs provide no incentive for economic development; rather, they retard development of the agricultural sector in the recipient country. U.S. food aid funds are offered to countries that have large numbers of undernourished people. These countries, which often are strapped for money as well, feel an obligation to feed their people through government programs; they frequently accomplish this task by purchasing food and distributing it at subsidized prices, or else by regulating the prices in the official market. The result: Domestic farmers are discouraged from producing or are forced into the black market.

Less-developed countries often seize on U.S. food aid money as a quick answer to their problems. They take U.S. food aid and use it to support their subsidized food distribution. However, since the U.S. funds are tied, they can be used only to purchase U.S. agricultural products. This has an even more detrimental effect than normal government food programs, because the government no longer buys food produced domestically. Thus, local farmers cannot sell their goods on the legal market and cannot even sell their products to the government at below-market rates. These programs are maintained because they are indirect subsidies to American farmers, not for their value to less-developed countries. They should be eliminated.

The World Bank. Multilateral development banks (MDBs) like the World Bank have failed to help the economies of supposed beneficiaries, even after 20 years of aid. The largest of the government-supported international financial institutions is the World Bank, created after World War II to help rebuild the war-torn economies of Europe and Japan. Because many policymakers in Europe and the U.S. feared that private banks would not lend money to rebuild Europe and Japan, they decided to create state-backed lending institutions that would provide loans to rebuild roads, schools, hospitals, and telecommunications networks.

The World Bank's original mission was to help rebuild Europe and Japan, but by the late 1950s, this mission had been substantially fulfilled. The economies of Europe and Japan had recovered from the war and were growing rapidly. Faced with the choice between shutting its doors or evolving into a new organization, the World Bank chose the latter course. Its new mission became one of fostering economic growth in the less-developed countries.

Thus, the World Bank began to create new organizations and institutions which were geared not toward helping the world's advanced economies and democracies rebuild after the destruction of war, but toward bringing economic development to countries that have never experienced it. By the mid-1960s, the World Bank was heavily involved in providing subsidized loans to many poor countries. This lending—about $1 billion in 1968—grew to over $12 billion by 1981.

The amount of money lent by the World Bank to the developing world has been substantial, but the results have been far from successful. Indeed, the World Bank's record overall has been one of failure. After decades of subsidized loans, most of the world's less-developed countries are no better off economically today than they were before. In fact, many are worse off (see Table 19.5).[4]

- Of the 66 less-developed countries receiving money from the World Bank for more than 25 years (many for more than 30 years), 37 are no better off today than they were before receiving such loans.

- Of these 37 countries, 20 are poorer today then they were before receiving aid from the Bank.

- Of these 20, eight have economies that have shrunk by at least 20 percent since their first World Bank loan.

Thus, there is no evidence that the World Bank has helped poor countries develop. If anything, the evidence shows that recipients of World Bank loans generally are worse off economically today than before receiving such aid.

The International Monetary Fund (IMF). Created after World War II, the IMF was established to stabilize international exchange rates. Following years of war and depression, many of the world's currencies were in disarray. For example, some countries would not allow their currencies to be traded in international financial markets. This made it difficult for those who wanted to trade with foreign countries, because they could be paid only in foreign currencies or had to purchase imports with foreign currencies. Moreover, many countries had artificially inflated the value of their currencies with other currencies.

The IMF's main mission was to help countries make their currencies convertible with other currencies. It also supervised the international exchange rate system, which was based in the beginning mainly on the gold standard. Thus, all the world's major currencies were pegged at a certain value to a specific weight in gold. If a country allowed its currency to weaken substantially— meaning its established value to a weight in gold

---

4 These figures were derived by including all countries with a change in their per capita GDP of 25 percent or less from the year in which they first received a World Bank loan to 1992. The 25 percent change represents less than 1 percent annual growth in per capita GDP for that period.

Table 19.5							☎

Economic Growth Rates of Recipients of World Bank Loans

	First Year Receiving Loans	Total World Bank Loans Through 6/30/95 Millions US$	Total World Bank Loans per Capita Through 6/30/95	GDP per Capita, First Year Receiving Loans 1987 US$	GDP per Capita, 1992 1987 US$	Change in GDP per Capita, First Year-1992 1987 US$	Change in GDP per Capita, First Year-1992
Algeria	1965	$4,891.5	$186	$1843	$2735	$893	48%
Argentina	1965	10,166.8	307	2931	3583	652	22%
Benin	1969	610.1	121	362	331	-31	-9%
Bolivia	1965	1,342.1	178	665	681	16	2%
Botswana	1967	296.5	218	260	1822	1,562	601%
Brazil	1965	22,241.7	145	884	1869	985	111%
Burundi	1967	698.8	120	114	236	122	107%
Cameroon	1967	1,809.4	148	551	743	192	35%
Central African Rep.	1969	403.5	127	440	337	-103	-24%
Chad	1969	511.5	86	198	181	-17	-9%
Chile	1965	3,429.4	252	1237	2164	927	75%
Colombia	1965	8,129.1	243	690	1291	601	87%
Congo	1967	391.3	161	526	928	402	76%
Costa Rica	1965	894.4	280	1128	1765	637	56%
Ivory Coast	1968	3,713.5	288	927	763	-164	-18%
Dominican Republic	1970	616.9	84	494	734	240	49%
Ecuador	1965	2,261.8	205	624	1182	558	89%
El Salvador	1965	511.2	95	913	946	33	4%
Ethiopia	1965	2,111.4	39	116	94	-22	-19%
Gabon	1965	212.0	177	2798	3499	701	25%
Gambia	1970	160.2	162	241	279	38	16%
Ghana	1965	3,000.7	190	501	400	-101	-20%
Guatemala	1965	734.5	75	690	879	189	27%
Guinea	1966	995.2	163	452	421	-31	-7%
Guyana	1969	349.9	434	543	444	-99	-18%
Haiti	1965	545.6	81	356	282	-74	-21%
Honduras	1965	1,222.9	226	730	900	170	23%
India	1965	45,185.8	51	220	377	157	71%
Indonesia	1970	22,760.5	124	227	568	341	150%
Israel	1965	284.5	56	4654	9727	5,073	109%
Jamaica	1965	1,228.1	513	1356	1440	84	6%
Kenya	1965	3,467.6	135	221	366	145	66%
Lesotho	1967	334.2	180	134	272	138	103%

Notes: This table lists all countries receiving World Bank loans between 1965 and 1970. This time window was chosen for several reasons: 1. To exclude the European countries who used the loans for reconstruction. 2. To ensure that the developing countries received their loans after independence, and 3. To allow a large enough time frame for development loans to influence the countries' development. All OECD countries were excluded from this list. In addition, this table does not include the following loan recipients: China, Cyprus, Iran, Jordan, Liberia, Syria, and Uganda because reliable GDP data from 1965 to 1970 was unavailable. **Total World Bank** loans includes all loans distributed to the listed countries by the International Bank for Reconstruction and Development and the International Development Association since the Bank's founding. **Total World Bank Loans per Capita:** The per capita figures are understated. Total World Bank Loans were divided by the 1992 population of the recipient countries, while most of the countries received the bulk of their loans in the 1960s and 1970s when their populations were smaller.
Sources: *World Data 1994* on CD-ROM and *World Tables 1987, 1995*, The World Bank.

Table 19.5 (con't)   ☎

Economic Growth Rates of Recipients of World Bank Loans

	First Year Receiving Loans	Total World Bank Loans Through 6/30/95 Millions US$	Total World Bank Loans per Capita Through 6/30/95	GDP per Capita, First Year Receiving Loans 1987 US$	GDP per Capita, 1992 1987 US$	Change in GDP per Capita, First Year-1992 1987 US$	Change in GDP per Capita, First Year-1992
Madagascar	1967	$1,270.8	$103	$333	$217	-$116	-35%
Malawi	1967	1,533.9	169	133	145	12	9%
Malaysia	1965	3,446.6	185	846	2600	1,754	207%
Mali	1968	979.9	109	202	246	44	22%
Mauritania	1965	539.0	259	516	476	-40	-8%
Morocco	1965	7,198.1	275	500	854	354	71%
Myanmar	1965	837.4	19	210	250	40	19%
Nepal	1970	1,394.1	70	143	178	35	25%
Nicaragua	1965	637.3	164	1752	875	-876	-50%
Niger	1965	589.3	72	605	280	-325	-54%
Nigeria	1965	7,151.1	70	351	360	9	3%
Pakistan	1965	10,289.8	86	183	375	192	105%
Panama	1965	901.3	358	1345	2231	886	66%
Papua New Guinea	1969	655.2	162	810	916	106	13%
Paraguay	1965	767.1	170	560	1000	439	78%
Peru	1965	3,884.1	174	1141	953	-188	-16%
Philippines	1965	9,363.1	146	464	594	131	28%
Rwanda	1970	694.4	95	299	300	1	0%
Senegal	1967	1,436.0	183	725	668	-57	-8%
Sierra Leone	1965	367.0	84	137	138	0	0%
Somalia	1965	492.1	59	124	114	-10	-8%
South Africa	1965	241.8	6	2079	2104	25	1%
Sri Lanka	1965	2,111.7	121	213	474	260	122%
Sudan	1965	1,518.9	57	806	695	-111	-14%
Swaziland	1965	112.6	131	486	845	360	74%
Tanzania	1965	3,022.2	116	137	178	41	30%
Thailand	1965	5,372.3	93	354	1396	1,042	294%
Togo	1969	592.3	152	414	321	-93	-23%
Trinidad and Tobago	1967	247.8	195	3157	3779	622	20%
Tunisia	1965	3,742.1	445	638	1435	797	125%
Uruguay	1965	1,247.2	398	1910	2635	724	38%
Venezuela	1965	3,132.7	155	3205	2894	-311	-10%
Zambia	1967	2,106.3	255	421	250	-171	-41%

Notes: See previous page.
Sources: *World Data 1994* on CD-ROM and *World Tables 1987, 1995,* The World Bank.

decreased (known as devaluation)—the IMF would move quickly to infuse capital into that country, either to bring the value of the weakening currency back up to the established weight in gold or, at a minimum, to slow the level of devaluation. Another method the IMF employed was to remove the weakening currency from circulation by purchasing it in foreign currency markets.

The gold standard was abolished in 1973, and the world's currencies were allowed to fluctuate freely. Such a floating exchange rate system removed the main mission of the IMF. Thus, faced with possible extinction, like the World Bank, the IMF transformed itself beyond the visions of its creators into an entirely new institution. By the mid-1970s, the IMF had become a new economic development institution instead of an international currency stabilization institution. It became more involved in the development policies of the world's poorest nations. In order to address this new challenge, the IMF began to allow countries to borrow money at below-market rates to support the value of their currencies.

As a requirement for these subsidized loans, the IMF often imposed conditions on the recipient country. However, the IMF often ignored the economic policies that created the currency devaluation in the first place. In most cases, for example, a country's currency loses its value because of poor economic management. In many less-developed countries, the government often spends too much money on unprofitable state-owned businesses, inefficient and corrupt government bureaucracies, and similar wasteful and costly government programs. Since many of these countries could not raise enough revenue by increasing taxes, they simply printed more money.

As the government prints more money, there is more of the currency in circulation, and the value of that money decreases as the supply increases. The conditions the IMF imposes on countries receiving loans do not deal adequately with this problem. Instead, the IMF focuses on broad economic solutions like reducing the budget deficit. While this may be good economic policy, many less-developed countries seek to reduce their budget deficits by such counterproductive means as increasing taxes and raising tariffs.

In fact, most recipients of IMF loans are no better off today than they were before receiving such assistance. For example, Benin received its first loan from the IMF in 1978. Since then, it has received over $60 million in IMF loans. Yet its per capita income shrank from $334 in 1978 to $330 in 1992. Ghana received its first IMF loan in 1979. Since then, it has received some $480 million in IMF loans. Yet its per capita wealth shrank from $441 in 1979 to $400 in 1992. Madagascar has received some $90 million in IMF loans since 1978. Yet its per capita wealth fell from $296 in 1978 to $217 in 1992. The results are repeated for most of the recipients of IMF loans.

The main result of IMF assistance in less-developed countries has been to enable poor countries to maintain counterproductive economic policies that cause lagging economic development. Meanwhile, countries like Hong Kong, Singapore, Taiwan, and South Korea have moved from the less-developed world to the developed world over the last 30 years. None of these countries received aid from the IMF. In fact, these countries adopted economic policies on their own to stabilize their currencies. In some cases, as in Hong Kong, the local legal tender is tied to foreign currencies like the U.S. dollar through a currency board. This makes it harder for the government to manipulate the value of the currency simply by printing more money. In Singapore and Taiwan, the governments use lower taxes, limited government spending, and other sound monetary policies to maintain the value of their money. These examples of sound monetary policies implemented without the aid of the IMF raise two questions: Why is the IMF needed, and why should the U.S. continue to fund its operations?

Other Multilateral Development Banks. There also are several other MDBs, including the Asian Development Bank, the African Development Bank, and the Inter-American Development Bank. Most of these work closely with the World Bank to coordinate loans tailored to their respective regions, and their approach to development is no different from that of the World Bank: providing subsidized loans to less-developed countries. Each of these MDBs functions like the World Bank but is tailored to a specific geographic area (Asia, Africa, or Latin America). Yet there is no evidence that any one of these institutions has helped countries in these regions grow economically.

Government Investment Programs. U.S. government investment and export programs have failed to aid less-developed countries. Programs that give subsidies to businesses are intended to help build U.S. exports by giving U.S. businesses an advantage in overseas markets. They also are regarded as a method of development. In reality, they are nothing but the corporate side of government welfare. Proponents claim that corporate welfare, such as the Overseas Private Investment Corporation (OPIC) and the Export-Import (Ex-Im) Bank, are necessary for developing countries to attract investment. This is simply untrue. Developing countries need to adopt the correct economic policies to attract investment. These programs are merely subsidized loans, insurance, and other benefits. Ultimately, U.S. taxpayers and other businesses must pay higher taxes to support these subsidies. Additionally, for some of these organizations, such as OPIC, the potential loss to U.S. taxpayers can be much greater than expected. Despite their proponents' claims, these programs do not promote U.S. exports, U.S. jobs, or economic growth—either at home or abroad—effectively.

LESSONS LEARNED

While there is general recognition within the Clinton Administration and among many Members of Congress that much of America's foreign aid program should be eliminated and the rest reformed, policymakers so far have been unable to do so. Why? A review of the recent attempts by the 104th Congress to eliminate and reform AID and foreign aid activity reveals several crucial lessons.

Lesson #1: Direct frontal assaults to reform AID as an institution and foreign aid as a program are likely to fail. The original Helms bill would have eliminated AID and other agencies, but Democratic opposition prevented the bill from coming to a vote on the floor of the Senate. To overcome Democratic obstruction, the Senate Foreign Relations Committee accepted an amendment by Senator John Kerry (D-MA) that did not require the Administration to abolish the agencies but did mandate $1.7 billion in budget savings. Ultimately, the legislation approved by the House–Senate conference mandated the abolition of one agency. The President vetoed the bill, and the House was unable to override his veto.

Such a frontal assault failed because the Clinton Administration was determined to oppose any legislative initiative to eliminate AID and cut foreign aid. This determination was so strong politically that the White House overruled the plan advanced by the Administration's own Secretary of State to eliminate AID and consolidate its functions within the State Department. The most telling statement of the Administration's determination is found in the words of an internal AID memorandum leaked to the newspapers, in which a "top official" made it clear that the Administration's strategy was to "delay, postpone, obfuscate, derail" in

---

LESSONS LEARNED

- Direct frontal assaults to reform the Agency for International Development (AID) as an institution and foreign aid as a program can fail.

- Domestic institutions and organizations that benefit from foreign aid can be powerful obstacles to reform.

- The 104th Congress failed to follow through on its plans to eliminate and reform foreign aid.

- Congress allowed proponents of foreign aid to categorize its attempts to eliminate AID and reform foreign aid programs as "isolationist" and "cold-hearted."

- Congress failed to counter public opinion polls that mistakenly suggested a majority of Americans support foreign aid.

- Congress failed to provide strict guidelines for the AID report on economic freedom.

---

order to kill such a merger.[5] The reality is that without the numerical strength in the Senate to invoke cloture, and in both Houses to override a presidential veto if necessary, it is impossible to abolish AID simply through legislation.

Lesson #2: Domestic institutions and organizations that benefit from foreign aid are powerful obstacles to reform. Surprisingly, the largest supporters of America's foreign aid program often are not the foreign countries that receive aid, but American businesses, consultants, and contractors that each year siphon off some 80 percent of the entire foreign aid budget. Out of every foreign aid dollar the U.S. designates to help the poor overseas, 70 cents to 80 cents stays in the United States.

AID Administrator J. Brian Atwood takes great pride in pointing out how important America's foreign aid program is to American business: "[W]e certainly have a strong constituency, made up of some of the

---

5 Robert Pear, "Imperiled Agencies Mount Life-Saving Efforts," *The New York Times*, May 20, 1995, p. A26.

largest businesses in this country."[6] He also admits that business seriously influences the budget process: "In just the last year, a coalition of over 1000 businesses has called for the foreign aid budget to be increased to $18 billion a year.... I think these constituencies have really come together because of the deep cuts that were taken in the fiscal 1996 budget."[7] One such group which came to the defense of America's foreign aid program recently is the Business Alliance for International Economic Development. In a report distributed to Congress in June 1996, the Alliance proudly declares: "A vital factor linking all the components of our foreign assistance budget is that most of the money is spent right here in the United States."[8]

This process has created a powerful lobby in America that obstructs cuts and reforms in the foreign aid program. Many businesses support the program not because they want to help the poor, but because they benefit from it. According to Larry Byrne, Assistant Administrator for Management at AID, "Ninety-five percent of [AID's] procurement went to a few firms that only did business with AID. They were inside-the-beltway firms that employed former AID staffers."[9] These businesses are a powerful obstacle to abolishing AID and reforming the foreign aid program.

Lesson #3: The 104th Congress failed to follow through on its plans to eliminate and reform foreign aid. When the 104th Congress convened, it set out to evaluate all the federal aid programs across the board and to consider which programs should be kept, cut, or abolished. Congress undertook this agenda as part of its overall strategy to reach a balanced budget for the first time in decades. One of its initial findings was that America's foreign aid program was indeed wasteful, redundant, and harmful to less-developed countries. But Congress allowed this issue to be politicized by the Clinton Administration and ultimately caved in to

---

6 "Reassessing Foreign Aid," *CQ Researcher*, Congressional Quarterly, Washington, D.C., September 27, 1996, p. 852.

7 *Ibid.*

8 "Foreign Assistance: What's in It for Americans?," Business Alliance for International Economic Development, Washington, D.C., June 1996, p. 2.

9 Ben Barber, "Foreign-aid agency's staff cites fear, chaos amid cuts," *The Washington Times*, August 19, 1996, p. A8.

pressure from the Administration not to eliminate or cut most of the foreign aid program.

Lesson #4: Congress allowed proponents of foreign aid to categorize its attempts to eliminate and reform AID and the foreign aid program as "isolationist" and "cold-hearted." When congressional opponents of foreign aid first began to consider ways to abolish wasteful aid programs, there was an immediate backlash from the foreign aid community. One tactic used by supporters of these programs was to categorize attempts to eliminate and reform foreign aid and AID as "isolationist." Referring to the new Republican Congress's attempts to cut foreign aid, Atwood warned darkly that "The recent election seems to have unleashed market libertarianism and neo-isolationism."[10]

Supporters of such initiatives did little to counter the charge by focusing on the merits of their proposals. Proponents of abolishing AID and most of its functions failed to anticipate the effect the "isolationist" charge would have on many undecided policymakers. In the end, this accusation proved to be very effective in convincing undecided Members of Congress not to support either the elimination of AID or additional cuts in foreign aid.

Another tactic used by proponents of foreign aid was to argue that reducing foreign aid spending was "cold-hearted." Many policymakers were unwilling to challenge these assertions. The major reason proponents of foreign aid were so successful in this regard is that they were able to portray all attempts to abolish AID and eliminate development assistance as attempts to cut back such things as disaster relief and humanitarian aid. This allowed proponents to equate any attempt to eliminate wasteful programs like development assistance with causing mass starvation and forcing babies to die. Faced with such demagoguery, some policymakers may have determined that foreign aid reform was not worth the political heat.

---

10 Remarks of J. Brian Atwood before the Center for National Policy, Washington, D.C., December 14, 1994.

Lesson #5: Congress failed to counter a series of public opinion polls that mistakenly suggested a vast majority of Americans support foreign aid. During the congressional debate on foreign aid in the 104th Congress, development aid advocates consistently pointed to polls and studies that seemingly concluded that a majority of Americans support foreign aid. These studies claimed that when most Americans were informed about the actual size of the foreign aid budget, they would generally support current spending levels and oppose cuts. Armed with these studies, supporters of foreign aid felt confidant of great constituent support.

The most recent of these polls is the "Foreign Policy and the Public" poll conducted by the Center for International and Security Studies at the University of Maryland.[11] This study is used by supporters of foreign aid to influence congressional budget decisions. One of the study's conclusions is that a strong majority of Americans believe the U.S. is spending too much on foreign aid. But supporters of foreign aid say the reason for this result — which the study also tries to prove — is that the American public overestimates the level of U.S. foreign aid expenditures. When respondents were asked, for example, to state an amount they believe the U.S. gives in foreign aid for every $1,000 of gross national product (GNP), they estimated $100 per every $1,000 of GNP. When asked how much the U.S. *should* give, the average answer was $25 per $1,000 of GNP. However, if this were the case, the U.S. foreign aid budget would balloon to approximately $150 billion, given America's $6 trillion economy. Informed of this fact, few Americans would support a foreign aid program of this size.

Thus, proponents of foreign aid argue that if the American public actually knew the U.S. spent $12 billion on foreign aid, they would be more likely to support increased funding. However, the pollsters fail to tell policymakers that when the respondents were asked "What if you heard that the U.S. gives say a dollar and a half for every $1,000 of GNP? Would you feel this is too much, too little, or about right?" almost 65 percent said that this amount was "too much" or "about right."

---

11 "Project on Foreign Policy and the Public: Poll on America's Role in the World," University of Maryland, College Park, Md., June 1996.

In fact, there is no substantial public support for increased foreign aid spending. The problem is that those who sought cuts in foreign aid funding failed to provide more accurate polling data to countermand the University of Maryland study. They also failed to point out the inconsistencies in the study itself. This allowed the opponents of cuts in foreign aid to mislead policymakers about the polling results.

Lesson #6: Congress failed to provide strict guidelines for AID's report on economic freedom. The appropriations bill for foreign operations—passed in November 1995 and signed into law by President Clinton in February 1996—requires AID to "submit to the appropriate congressional committees an annual report providing a concise overview of the prospects for economic and social growth.... For each country, the report shall discuss the laws, policies and practices of that country that most contribute to or detract from the achievement of this kind of growth."

The purpose of this requirement is to force AID to recognize the importance of economic freedom in helping countries develop. It also was intended to give Congress information by which to judge AID's programs. But AID failed to meet the congressional requirements. When AID finally submitted a report in the fall of 1996, it provided neither a "concise overview of the prospects for economic and social growth" nor a discussion of "the laws, policies, and practices" that most contribute to economic growth in countries receiving U.S. foreign aid. AID was able to ignore Congress's request because the original language requiring AID to submit a report was watered down before the bill passed.

STRATEGIES TO REFORM FOREIGN AID

Even though Congress has worked to eliminate and reform AID, it has had only limited success. Congress should continue to seek elimination of the foreign aid programs. The strategies it employs should focus on the following:

STRATEGY #1
Congress should use the appropriations process to eliminate AID and most of its functions; it should not rely on authorizing legislation.

The U.S. foreign aid program has not been authorized by Congress since 1985. Congress therefore must rely on the annual appropriations

---

STRATEGIES FOR
REFORMING THE FOREIGN AID PROGRAM

- The appropriations process should be used to eliminate AID and most of its functions. Congress should not rely on authorizing legislation.

- Congress should limit the influence of special-interest groups in the process of funding foreign aid.

- The charges of "isolationist" and "cold-hearted" can be countered by hearings on the detrimental effects foreign aid has had on the economies of recipient countries.

- The General Accounting Office should be instructed to conduct a study of the existence, reliability, and findings of available polling data on foreign aid.

- Congress should be more specific in directives that require AID to report on economic freedom.

process to keep AID and its programs running. If the last few years demonstrate anything, it is the extreme opposition within the White House to abolishing AID. Congress should use its constitutional powers to restructure the foreign policy apparatus despite opposition from President Clinton and bureaucrats within the State Department and AID. It can do so through its oversight jurisdiction and by exercising the power of the purse.

While Congress generally has left the organization of the administrative branch of government to the Executive, it retains the legislative power to create and abolish bureaucratic agencies. However, for Congress to do so against the wishes of the Executive requires that its leaders have a veto-proof majority. The legislative history and political fate of Senator Helms's plan to reorganize and revitalize America's foreign policy institutions suggests that in the absence of a veto-proof majority, an incremental and indirect legislative approach offers the best promise of success. In the Senate, 21 Democrats supported the Helms-Kerry compromise mandating agency budget savings but not termination. Yet the Senate vote on the Senate-House conference report mandating termination of one agency was along straight party lines:

52–44, with three Democrats and one Republican not voting. In the House, only 12 Democrats supported the conference report.

With these realities in mind, Congress should use its budget authorization and appropriation authority in a coordinated fashion to pare back funding in order to force personnel and organization choices on the Administration. Congress, for example, could cut the international operations budget by 50 percent in the next appropriations process. This would force the Administration to begin moving in the desired direction since it would be faced with having to decide which programs survived and which ones did not. In addition to being smart politically, forcing the Administration to make the hard choices on which foreign aid programs should be abolished, cut, or reformed, also makes budgetary sense: Such a program would save about $6 billion in the first year.

AID, however, should be only part of the strategy. There are specific programs, such as economic and development aid, that Congress could abolish through the appropriations process. In order to do this, Congress also will need to identify which foreign aid programs to abolish and which ones to keep. The best solution would be to eliminate all development and economic aid programs and all of their funding. Even for humanitarian aid, disaster relief, and military and security aid, Congress should require the executive branch to certify that each program directly supports the national interests of the United States.

While Congress's use of the appropriations process would be effective in abolishing AID and much of America's foreign aid program, it also would be effective in eliminating America's role in related programs. For example, Congress should eliminate funding for multilateral development banks like the World Bank and the IMF during the next appropriations process. If the U.S. withdrew its financial support, these institutions would be forced to do one of three things:

- **Privatize** and operate as private financial institutions;

- **Liquidate** and absolve themselves of the responsibility to provide more loans; or

- **Operate** on a more modest scale with their remaining funding.

Congress also should refuse to provide funding for development assistance-related programs, including family planning, food aid, population control, and export financing (such as the OPIC and the Ex-Im Bank). Funding should be withheld from such programs as the Commission for the Preservation of America's Heritage Abroad, the East–West Center, the Japan–United States Friendship Commission, the North–South Center, and the United States Institute of Peace.

STRATEGY #2
Congress should limit the influence of special-interest groups on the foreign aid funding process.

The pressure to defeat attempts to eliminate AID comes mainly from the many U.S. companies, contractors, and consultants that feed from the foreign aid trough. In order to make progress in the future, opponents of the current foreign aid bureaucracy will have to overcome this obstacle. To accomplish this goal:

- **Congress should require an annual audit of foreign aid contracts.** This audit should examine which U.S. and foreign companies receive contracts from AID, what the projects were, and what the economic benefit to the countries or regions from those projects has been. Armed with such information, Congress could determine which U.S. contractors and consultants are on the foreign aid bandwagon and force programs to eliminate funding for those companies that are abusing them for their own financial gain.

- **Congress should require foreign aid organizations that receive U.S. funding (AID, the World Bank, the IMF) to list all the organizations to which they grant funding or contracts in annual presentations to Congress.** This would serve a purpose similar to that of the Foreign Agents Registration Act of 1938, as amended, which requires foreign agents to register with the U.S. government the names of the countries they represent. When individuals from the foreign aid industry lobby Congress and the White House, elected officials often are not aware of their level of involvement in the foreign aid industry. This would add a level of transparency to a process that currently has little.

- **Congress should lower the level of funding that can be granted to Non-Governmental Organizations (NGOs) and Private Voluntary Organizations (PVOs).** Congress should reform the current law and restrict NGOs and PVOs from receiving more than 49 percent of their total funding from the government. This will help prevent a repeat of the current situation, in which certain organizations in the development field depend on the government for nearly all of their funding. By reducing the percentage of funding these groups can receive from the government, Congress could ensure that the majority of their funding comes from the private sector. In essence, since these organizations would have to show demonstrable results to engender private support, the ones that were not effective would disappear. They could no longer survive on government largesse while producing few results.

- **Congress should require "truth in testimony" from those appearing before Congress.** Witnesses testifying on behalf of foreign aid should be required to report whether they or their organizations receive any government funding. If they do, the total amount of direct and indirect[12] government funding received should be reported, as should the percentage of their budgets that these funds represent.

STRATEGY #3
Congress can counter the "isolationist" and "cold-hearted" charge by holding a series of hearings on the detrimental effects of foreign aid on the economies of recipient countries.

Congress plays an important role in educating not only its own policymaking members, but bureaucrats who administer federal programs as well. One way this happens is through congressional hearings. Such hearings allow experts to testify on the effectiveness of government programs. The problem is that Congress often has not done

---

12 Direct funding involves an outright transfer of funds from the U.S. government to an organization or individual. Indirect funding involves the transfer of government grants or loans to an organization or individual, which then redistributes those funds. Indirect funding allows an organization to be funded by the government without possessing a direct link to the actual government grant or loan. In this way, an organization that receives the majority of its funding from the government can present an appearance of independence from government funding.

enough to bring in experts to testify on the failings of foreign aid. Many congressional hearings on foreign aid in the 104th Congress included the same individuals who testified on such subjects when the Democrats controlled the previous Congress. Committee staffs should work harder to identify expert witnesses who can counter the perception that efforts to abolish AID and cut foreign aid spending represent "neo-isolationism."

Specifically, these hearings should focus not just on the budget savings derived from abolishing AID and cutting foreign aid, but on a variety of currently neglected issues. For example, rather than focus on how much aid is given to the world's poor, they should reinforce the idea that America's global leadership should be measured instead by the extent to which America supports democratic military alliances like NATO, promotes international stability and the rule of law, and encourages global free trade. In addition, these hearings should highlight the level of money American citizens donate to private charities that directly aid the poor in less-developed countries. AID estimated in 1989—the last time it has publicly done so—that individual Americans contributed some $12 billion a year in private donations to aid the poor around the globe. This money comes from local churches, international relief agencies like the Red Cross, and organizations like Feed the Children. It is probable that this level of funding has increased since 1989.

Another focus should be the stories of countries that refuse to accept, or that discourage the use of, U.S. foreign aid. One of the most compelling arguments for foreign aid has been that it is needed by less-developed countries for both economic and social development. Having prominent individuals of aid-recipient countries denounce foreign aid's effectiveness and laud the success of economic freedom will undermine this claim. For example, several countries have come forward recently to announce both their opposition to foreign aid and their recognition of the harmful dependency it fosters.

- **Eritrea.** Last year, the President of Eritrea, a country that holds the dubious honor of receiving more foreign aid per capita than any other African nation, stated, "Aid is used and abused, so why not cut it? If we here have faith in foreign aid as the maker and breaker of

Eritrea, then that is the end of Eritrea. The effective use of aid is to free society from any dependence on outside sources."[13]

- **Uganda.** While not publicly opposed to foreign aid, Uganda also provides evidence that commitment to economic reform is unlikely to accompany foreign aid. Uganda has been a recipient of foreign aid for 41 years, but this aid has failed to promote economic growth. From 1965 to 1989, the average growth rate in Uganda was -2.8 percent.[14] Faced with the possibility of reduced U.S. development aid, Uganda began to liberalize its economy. Not so coincidentally, Uganda's economy responded. Annual economic growth rates were 10 percent in 1994 and 1995, with similar results expected for this year.[15] It was not until foreign aid was threatened that Uganda felt compelled to initiate economic reforms.

- **Israel.** In his address before a joint session of Congress last July, Prime Minister Benjamin Netanyahu declared that Israel no longer needed all of the foreign aid given annually by the U.S. This is concurrent with the views of many economists and politicians in both America and Israel who believe that reducing and eventually eliminating this annual $1.2 billion in economic assistance is necessary if Israel is to reform its inefficient, state-dominated economy.

- **Chile.** In 1970, Chile was one of the world's largest recipients of foreign aid on a per capita basis, yet it was stagnating economically. The government controlled an estimated 75 percent of the economy. After President Augusto Pinochet assumed control, Chile was denied foreign aid and was forced to liberalize its economy. Under Pinochet's privatization program, the government controlled only 25 percent of the economy. As a result of economic liberalization, Chile's economy has doubled, from $1,236 per capita GDP in 1965 to $2,359 in 1994.[16]

---

13 Statement by Senator Rod Grams, quoting the President of Eritrea, before the Senate Foreign Relations Committee, September 19, 1996.

14 World Bank, *World Development Report 1991.*

15 Growth data from Economics Department, Embassy of Uganda, 1996.

16 GDP data from *World Data 1995: World Bank Indicators on CD-ROM*, World Bank, Washington, D.C., 1996.

Representatives of these countries should seek (and be encouraged) to testify before Congress and meet with individual Members to share their stories.

STRATEGY #4

Congress should instruct the General Accounting Office (GAO) to conduct a study of the existence, reliability, and findings of available polling data on foreign aid.

The GAO often provides Congress and other policymakers with in-depth studies on a variety of topics, usually at the request of Members of Congress. Congress should instruct the GAO to conduct a study of the existence of polling data on foreign aid. Such a study should include a description of the major findings of these polls and some analysis as to which ones are the most scientifically accurate. Americans have been skeptical of the U.S. foreign aid program, and it is doubtful the University of Maryland study is the most comprehensive poll on this subject. Armed with more accurate information provided by other polls, policymakers would gain a better understanding of what Americans really think about foreign aid.

STRATEGY #5

Congress should be more specific in its directives requiring AID to report on economic freedom.

Congress's reporting requirement in the FY 1996 foreign operations appropriations was too weak. It allowed AID to ignore the issue of economic freedom altogether. To prevent the Administration from circumventing the will of Congress, more specific criteria should be required in AID's economic freedom report. Specifically, Congress should include a list of specific items which AID must include in its annual Congressional Presentation Report. These items should address the following questions:

- **Trade:** What is the average tariff rate? Are there any significant non-tariff barriers? Is there corruption in the customs service?

- **Taxation:** What is the top income tax rate? What tax rate applies to the average income level? What is the top corporate tax rate? What other taxes exist?

- **Government Intervention in the Economy:** What is the government consumption level as a percentage of the economy? To what extent does the government own businesses and industries? How much of the economy's output is produced by the government?

- **Monetary Policy:** What was the average inflation rate from 1985 to 1994? What is the average inflation rate for 1995?

- **Capital Flows and Foreign Investment:** Does the country have an investment code? Does it provide for 100 percent foreign ownership? Are there restrictions on foreign investment in specific industries and companies? Are there restrictions and performance requirements on foreign companies? Can foreigners own land? Are foreign and domestic companies treated the same under the law? Does the country allow foreign companies to repatriate their earnings? Can foreign companies receive local financing?

- **Banking:** Does the government own any banks? Can foreign banks open branches and subsidiaries? Does the government influence the allocation of credit? Are banks free to operate without government regulations such as deposit insurance? Are banks free to offer all types of financial services like the buying and selling of real estate, securities, and insurance policies?

- **Wage and Price Controls:** Does the government have a minimum wage? Are businesses free to set their own prices without government interference? Does the government set prices for any products? If so, to what extent? Does the government provide subsidies to businesses to affect prices?

- **Property Rights:** Is the legal system free from government influence? Is there a commercial code defining contracts? Does the country allow foreign arbitration of contract disputes? Can property be expropriated by the government? Is there corruption within the judiciary? Are there major delays in receiving judicial decisions? Is private property legally granted and protected?

- **Regulation:** Is a license required to operate a business? Is it easy to obtain a business license? Is there corruption within the bureaucracy? Does the government force businesses to subscribe to established work weeks, paid vacations, maternity leave, and similar requirements? Does the government force businesses to subscribe to strict environmental, consumer safety, and worker health regulations? Are regulations on businesses burdensome? If so, to what extent?

- **The Black Market:** Is a significant level of the country's labor supplied by the black market? Are significant levels of the country's transportation, service, agricultural production, and manufacturing supplied by the black market? Is there a significant level of piracy of intellectual property? Is there a significant level of smuggling?

Armed with the information on these factors for each recipient of U.S. foreign aid, Congress will be better able to determine the level of economic freedom that exists in countries receiving U.S. aid.

CONCLUSION

The 105th Congress can restructure and reform the way America aids other countries. Moreover, the level of influence currently held by many U.S. companies and non-governmental organizations that benefit from U.S. aid can be curtailed. Congress should abolish the ineffective and poorly run Agency for International Development and most foreign aid programs by significantly cutting funding. Such changes would force the Administration to make difficult choices regarding which individual programs to eliminate, cut, or reform.

Not only has the federal government wasted some $2 trillion in U.S. taxpayers' money on its failed approach to promoting international economic growth, but its economic aid program has actually damaged the economies of the developing world. The U.S. no longer can ignore the basic lessons of history: Only economic freedom can provide countries with the best chance for economic growth and equip them with the best tools to achieve development. If this truth is ignored, American taxpayers will be forced to throw even more of their hard-earned money at this failed program. Even worse, much of the dependent developing world will continue to remain impoverished.

Chapter 20

REFORMING AND WORKING WITH THE UNITED NATIONS

Brett D. Schaefer and Thomas P. Sheehy

The United Nations was founded to maintain international peace, promote economic prosperity, and advance fundamental human rights. These goals are far from modest; but in the aftermath of World War II, many believed that the countries of the world had a responsibility to their citizens to work toward these ideals, and the U.S. supported the organization wholeheartedly. Indeed, the U.S. was the driving force in its creation. After 51 years of funding and effort, however, it is evident that the U.N. has not wholly achieved even one of these goals. The U.N. has taken on a life of its own, increasing its size and branching out into areas unforeseen by its creators. If the U.N. is not open to reform, and is no longer capable of serving America's interests, then it is time for the U.S. to reassess how the U.N. can best serve America—or whether it can do so at all.

Even if the United Nations were a marvel of efficiency and influence, there would be no justification for maintaining U.S. membership if it did not advance America's national interests and foreign policy goals. By the same token, if America's national interests are being served by membership in the

The authors would like to thank Ambassador Charles Lichenstein, Pedro Sanjuan, and James Lucier for their suggestions and contributions to this chapter. The views and opinions expressed herein, however, are solely the responsibility of the authors. Thomas Sheehy's contributions were made prior to his taking a position as Legislative Director for Representative Edward Royce (R-CA).

U.N., some tolerance of the organization's faults is acceptable, unless those faults outweigh the benefits.

The question of whether America should continue to participate in the United Nations is a very broad one. It involves five key issues:

- **Should** the United States withdraw from the United Nations?

- **What** role should the United States play in the United Nations?

- **What** role should the United States play in U.N. peacekeeping efforts?

- **What** stance should Congress take on the commitment of funds to the United Nations?

- **How** should the United States encourage the U.N. to reform?

Key Issue #1: Should the United States withdraw from the United Nations? A debate has arisen in America over the future of the United Nations and the role America should play in it. The choice: Should the United States withdraw from the organization because it is hopelessly inept, corrupt, wasteful, and detrimental to U.S. foreign policy goals, or should the U.S. remain in the U.N. and encourage reform?

The Clinton Administration has argued for continued membership, insisting that without the U.N., the U.S. would be forced to "act alone or not at all." In contrast, Representative Joe Scarborough (R-FL) has led the call to withdraw from the United Nations. His proposed United Nations Withdrawal Act of 1995 would require America to withdraw from the U.N. by the year 2000, retaining its membership only in the U.N.'s independent and specialized agencies. Scarborough contends that the U.S. receives little or nothing in return for membership in the U.N.

In reality, the truth lies somewhere between these two positions. The Clinton Administration position demonstrates selective memory at best. The U.S. generally has acted unilaterally or in concert with its allies over the last 50 years. In most instances, cooperation with the U.N. has been an afterthought or has been limited to a facilitating or supporting role. Indeed, two of the U.N.'s greatest claims to success—the Korean War and the Persian Gulf War—involved U.S. initiatives that likely would have been undertaken without U.N. approval or participation. While the U.N. does not contribute a great deal to promoting America's national interests, however, it does afford some limited benefits. For example, it is a forum for political discussions and diplomatic overtures with allies and adversaries alike. Under the right circumstances, it can also be a venue and means for the U.S. to mobilize international political support, as was the case during the Persian Gulf War.

Another benefit of membership is that it can help promote America's leadership role in international politics. This largely perceptual feature, however, has a downside. It means there would be consequences from a unilateral U.S. withdrawal from the U.N. In the post-Cold War era, isolationist and protectionist elements have been undermining America's commitment to international involvement. Even long-standing international covenants such as the North Atlantic Treaty Organization (NATO) are being called into question. Unilateral withdrawal from the U.N. would likely fuel American sentiment to withdraw from other international spheres of engagement, with unfortunate consequences.

For example, if the U.S. were to withdraw from the U.N., it would be more difficult for the President to make the case to the American people that U.S. troops stationed on the Korean Peninsula are essential to avert North Korean aggression and nuclear war. Likewise, because of the implied reduction of commitment to vital interests abroad, it would be difficult for a President to convince the American people of the necessity of fighting another Persian Gulf War. Though conservatives may not agree, most Americans view the U.N. as an important symbol of America's commitment to an international presence. Destroy that symbol, and this important commitment is weakened.

Rightly or wrongly, rogue states such as Iraq and Libya view the U.N. as a tool of American diplomacy. A U.S. withdrawal from the United Nations would send dangerous signals to enemies and rivals of the United States. Beijing might well reassess the strength of the U.S. commitment to Taiwan. So, too, might the North Koreans be led to reassess the U.S. commitment to South Korea. Pyongyang would not view America's divorce from the U.N. as anything other than a sign of weakness.

International perceptions of America's will and resolve do matter in the realm of foreign policy. The U.S. participation in the U.N. should be understood in this light. Over 40 years ago, University of Chicago Professor Hans Morgenthau, the father of realism in American foreign policy, recognized prestige as a component of power. Whether or not Americans think much of the U.N., other nations assign it great prestige.

That is why Japan, Germany, India, and Brazil are eager to gain a permanent Security Council seat. While much of the U.N. is objectionable, the U.S. should remain involved in it to advance American interests throughout the world.

Key Issue #2: What role should the United States play in the U.N.? The correct U.S. role in the U.N. is determined by the original U.N. charter. Currently, the U.S. has one vote among 185 in the General Assembly, but it also possesses veto power in the Security Council. Historically, the U.S. has played a relatively passive role in the U.N., allowing the organization to be guided for the most part by the majority of its member states. This policy has been influenced heavily by the Wilsonian concept of equality among nations. The assumption is that the U.N. acts in the best interests of all its member states.

The reality, however, is entirely different. The U.N. is merely a collection of nations acting in their own self-interest. They may cooperate on any number of issues, but they do so because it is mutually beneficial, not because they believe there is some transcendent international ideal to which they all aspire.

The U.S. should recognize that the U.N. is a vehicle for advancing American foreign policy and security interests. The U.S. should use the U.N. whenever possible to build diplomatic support and address international problems, as in the case of the Gulf War, but it should never let U.N. bureaucrats impose their agenda on U.S. policy, as happened in 1994 when Secretary General Boutros Boutros-Ghali vetoed a contemplated American air strike against Serbian targets in Bosnia.

Key Issue #3: What role should the United States play in U.N. peacekeeping efforts? Under the guidance of Secretary General Boutros-Ghali, and with the acquiescence of the Bush Administration and the active support of the Clinton Administration, U.N. peacekeeping has undergone a profound transformation. Traditional peacekeeping operations involved small numbers of lightly armed troops whose mission was to monitor a peace settlement. A general requirement for traditional peacekeeping was that all factions of the conflict sought peace, had agreed to conduct negotiations, and had requested the presence of U.N. "policemen." Peacekeepers were simply to facilitate the peace efforts of the parties in dispute; they would refrain from combat except in truces, policing cease-fires, and acting as buffers between combatants—

restrictions which ensured that peacekeeping involved minimal cost and missions with a high potential for success.

Peacekeeping under Boutros-Ghali has run roughshod over the restrictions placed on earlier missions. Boutros-Ghali's missions centered on intervention and nation-building. They often involved the use of force, even the waging of war. However, the most radical change was one of environment: While traditional peacekeeping missions required a pre-existing peace settlement between belligerents, these more dangerous and ambitious peacekeeping missions did not. They often involved inserting peacekeepers into civil wars. This change in mission focus involved a massive increase in the number of missions, the number of troops involved, and the risk of failure. It is this expansion of U.N. peacekeeping missions that produced the expensive disasters in Somalia and Bosnia.

Though U.N. peacekeeping efforts have been reduced considerably from the "great expectations" of 1993 and 1994, they are still more extensive, more expensive, and more ambitious than during the Cold War years. The U.S. can expect frequent calls for direct and indirect participation in U.N. peacekeeping operations. While U.N. peacekeeping occasionally can be a useful tool for solving some problems of international security, the U.S. should continue to play only a limited role in U.N. peacekeeping operations. Its role should be determined according to the following four criteria:

- U.S. involvement in peacekeeping efforts must be restricted to situations that have a direct impact on America's security interests.

- The U.S. should mandate only those peace operations that have clearly defined and attainable objectives that are consistent with traditional peacekeeping efforts.

- The U.S. should not commit any ground troops to U.N. peacekeeping missions.

- The U.S. should not participate in any U.N.-managed peace enforcement operations.

Key Issue #4: What stance should Congress take on the commitment of funds to the United Nations? Much of the congressional debate about the U.N. involves the U.S. contribution to the U.N. budget. Even though the U.S. pays 25 percent of the U.N.'s general administrative budget and is assessed 31.7 percent of the peacekeeping budget, it has only one vote among 185 in determining the size and allocation of the budget. Most nations pay virtually nothing for their membership. The minimum payment for the poorest of the member countries is 0.01 percent of the U.N. budget; over 90 countries are assessed dues at or near this amount. Therefore, a majority of the U.N. General Assembly pays only 1 percent of its expenses, while 14 members contribute over 80 percent of the budget. The U.S. is understandably frustrated by not having a voting weight commensurate with its contribution.

The problem is inadequate accountability in the U.N. budget. In short, the majority of countries deciding the U.N. budget are spending someone else's money. As a result, the U.N. has become bloated and very expensive. For example, the general administrative budget, which was only $20 million in 1945, has expanded to $10 billion today.[1] The U.N. peacekeeping budget in 1990 was less than $700 million per year; by the end of 1993, it was over $3.5 billion per year. As the largest single contributor to the U.N., the U.S. has paid most heavily for this expansion. Though there is no comprehensive U.S. account, it has been estimated that annual U.S. expenditures on the U.N. have approached $4 billion.[2] Members of Congress are rightly appalled and wish to curtail this expense.

Congress should take action to restrain spiraling U.S. expenditures for what is essentially an inefficient organization rife with waste, abuse, fraud, and red tape.

---

1 "The United Nations Is Out of Control," *Readers Digest*, November 1995, pp. 149-154.

2 Charles M. Lichenstein, "We Aren't the World: An Exit Strategy from U.N. Peacekeeping," *Policy Review*, No. 72 (Spring 1995), pp. 62-67. The $4 billion total includes the U.S. portion (25 percent) of the general administrative budget, the U.S. share (31.7 percent) of the peacekeeping budget, voluntary U.S. contributions to U.N. specialized agencies, and the services and goods the U.S. voluntarily contributes to U.N. peacekeeping missions in particular.

Key Issue #5: How should the United States encourage the U.N. to reform? Successive U.S. administrations, at least as far back as the Reagan Administration, have tried to bring about management reform at the United Nations, but these efforts have been undermined by diplomatic concerns, such as advancing specific policies and minimizing friction within the organization. Congressional efforts like the 1984 Kassebaum-Solomon amendment, which sought to force the U.N. to adopt methods of fiscal discipline, or Representative Scarborough's bill have met significant resistance. Thus, efforts at reform so far have met with only limited success.

The few times when reform efforts have experienced some results have occurred when the U.S. has withheld or threatened to withhold funding. The Kassebaum-Solomon amendment forced the U.N. to adopt a pro-reform stance toward weighted voting and established the consensus requirement in the Advisory Committee on Administrative and Budgetary Questions (ACABQ), commonly referred to as the Fifth Committee, for the U.N. budget. The legislation introduced by Senator Larry Pressler (R-SD) in 1994 was instrumental in establishing the first inspector general's office at the U.N. Though neither of these attempts culminated in substantial reform, they were more effective than other efforts because they were tied to U.S. funds.

LESSONS LEARNED

Experience has shown that the U.S. has limited power to promote U.N. reform. Although it is the most influential country at the U.N., it still has only one voice among many. In 1996, U.N. Ambassador Madeleine Albright noted: "I have often compared [the U.N.] to a business with 185 members of the board; each from a different culture; each with a different philosophy of management; each with unshakable confidence in his or her opinions; and each with a brother-in-law who is unemployed."[3] American efforts to reform the U.N. have been weakened further because the other major powers have demonstrated considerably less interest in rooting out waste, fraud, and abuse.

---

3 U.S. Ambassador to the U.N. Madeleine Albright, in a speech to the North Carolina Community Foundation, Raleigh, North Carolina, March 4, 1996.

LESSONS LEARNED

- The United States can realize the best results from its membership in the United Nations when it is clear and determined about its objectives.

- Attempts to reform the U.N. by working through the "system" and cajoling other member nations and U.N. bureaucrats to work to improve its management have been fruitless.

- Reform of the U.N. organization must be fundamental.

- Proponents of U.N. reform must present a comprehensive blueprint for change.

- Congress can influence the U.N. by exercising its "power of the purse."

Repeated Failure of Past Efforts. Much has been learned over the years as successive U.S. administrations have launched campaigns to reform the U.N. Unfortunately, most of these lessons have been gained from efforts that failed, from a lack of initiative, and from insufficient U.S. determination to provoke reform. Nevertheless, understanding these past mistakes provides fertile soil for new ideas.

Many Washington administrations recognized the problems at the U.N. and expressed the desire to bring about management reform. There is every reason to believe that they were sincere. Nevertheless, notwithstanding these good intentions, past efforts at reform have produced few tangible results.

The Clinton Administration has claimed an interest in reforming the U.N. bureaucracy. Then-Secretary of State Warren Christopher, in a September 1995 address to the U.N. General Assembly, proposed a "concrete agenda" for U.N. reform which included ending programs that achieved their purpose, consolidating overlapping programs, and downsizing regional economic commissions. Yet it is unlikely that the second Clinton Administration will make much progress. It has brought about few improvements in the three years since former Under Secretary General for Administration and Management Richard Thornburgh reported that "The United Nations presently is almost totally lacking in effective means to deal with fraud, waste and abuse by staff members."[4] While an inspector general's office — the Office of Internal Oversight Services — has been established, its powers are limited. Senator Nancy Kassebaum (R-KS) and Representative Lee Hamilton (D-IN), two long-time advocates of an inspector general's office, have described it as a "disappointment" in need of strengthening.[5] A high-level U.S. official at the U.N. has recognized that the inspector general's office is too small for its tasks.[6] Moreover, the office is tasked merely with increasing efficiency.

In fact, the lack of progress in reform is the prime reason the Clinton Administration has opposed a second term for Secretary General Boutros Boutros-Ghali. One senior Clinton Administration official, referring to Boutros-Ghali, has noted that "Every time we asked for some bureaucratic change, asked him to rethink some expenditure or the way something was done, it was hand-to-hand and inch-to-inch."[7]

Obstacles to Congressional Reform Efforts. One of the first reform attempts was initiated under a Republican-controlled Senate. The Kassebaum-Solomon amendment to the congressional appropriation for the U.S. assessment of the U.N.'s general budget, passed in 1984, was an attempt to force the organization to impose fiscal discipline on itself and change the system of voting in the General Assembly to a weighted system dependent upon financial contribution. Unfortunately, the Kassebaum-Solomon reform effort largely failed. A last-minute veto by the Soviet Union halted any action. The only tangible effect was to restrict the U.N. budget to zero growth over the next two years and establish the consensus requirement for the U.N. budget; no substantial changes were made, either to halt waste, fraud, and mismanagement or to encourage reform.

---

4 Richard Thornburgh, "Report to the Secretary-General of the United Nations, 1 March 1993," p. 29.

5 "Fix the U.N.," *The Washington Post*, June 25, 1995, p. C7.

6 Ambassador David E. Birenbaum, U.S. Representative to the U.N. for U.N. Management Reform, U.S. Mission to the U.N. Press Release No. 31-(96), March 12, 1996.

7 Thomas W. Lippman and John M. Goshko, "Opposition to Boutros-Ghali Cuts Both Ways for Clinton," *The Washington Post*, June 21, 1996, p. A25.

Another attempt to reform the U.N. was made by Senator Larry Pressler in 1994. This effort tied U.S. funding to the President's certification that an independent U.N. office of inspector general had been established. The inspector general's office, whose job it would be to root out and reveal inefficiency and corruption, was considered one of the keys to enacting future reforms. This was spurred by Under Secretary General Thornburgh's 1993 report, which concluded that the office of the inspector general was necessary for any meaningful reform of the U.N. Under threat of restricted funding, an inspector general's office was created in 1995. However, the office was weakened when it was subordinated to the authority of the Secretary General and was refused an independent budget. The inspector general also was forbidden to correct any faults found or to initiate criminal proceedings against offenders.

Efforts by the 104th Congress. In 1995, frustrated with this lack of success and believing that the U.N. does not aid America's national interests, Representative Joe Scarborough (R-FL) introduced his United Nations Withdrawal Act, which would require the U.S. to withdraw from the U.N. by the year 2000 and retain membership only in selected independent and specialized agencies. This drastic measure caught the attention of the U.N. community. Realizing the seriousness of the initiative and fearing the loss of its greatest source of revenue, the U.N. began to proclaim its dedication to reform and to trumpet what few reforms had been implemented.

Senator Jesse Helms (R-NC) subsequently stepped forward with a more moderate position. While Senator Helms insists that the U.N. must initiate structural, financial, and managerial reforms, he believes that the U.S. should reserve the option to withdraw from the U.N. if these reforms do not materialize within a reasonable time frame.

Other recent congressional actions regarding the U.N. include:

- Legislation enacting a unilateral reduction in U.S. appropriations to the U.N. peacekeeping budget, capping the U.S. contribution at 25 percent of the total budget (of which the U.S. is assessed 31.7 percent by the U.N.), was included in the State Department Authorization Act for FY 1994, which passed in April 1995 as P.L. 103-236. It went into effect in 1995.

- A measure passed with the 1997 Omnibus Appropriations Bill[8] withholds the U.S. payment of arrears, contingent upon reforms. To secure the arrears payments outlined in the Omnibus Appropriations Bill, the U.N. must meet two of three specific requirements: 1) the U.N. general administration budget for 1998–1999 must fall below the $2.6 billion 1996–1997 budget; 2) a 10 percent reduction in staff at the U.N. Secretariat, based on the January 1996 level, must be realized; and 3) a $100 million savings from budget cuts in related agencies such as the United Nations Conference on Trade and Development (UNCTAD), the Department of Public Information, and the Department of Conference Services must occur.

This general overview of past attempts by Congress and members of the Administration to reform the U.N. reveals a number of lessons which can provide congressional leaders with a good framework for discussing future strategies for reform.

Lesson #1: The U.S. can get the best results in the U.N. when it is clear and determined about its objectives. The U.N. can be only as harmful to the U.S. as a President permits. It cannot impose its will on America unless the President agrees. Therefore, the risk posed to American interests by U.N. membership is only as great as the President's lack of resolve and sagacity in foreign policy matters.

A striking illustration of this fact is the radical difference between America's approach to the organization during the 1970s and its approach during the 1980s. During the Carter years, the U.S. was reluctant to use its power to influence the U.N., and the organization acted against American interests on many occasions. U.S. policies and actions were attacked routinely as the organization advanced socialist policies such as the "New International Economic Order." America's allies also were vulnerable, as was obvious in the 1975 General Assembly resolution that equated Zionism with racism—an outright attack on Israel and America.

However, in the 1980s, once the Reagan Administration quickly asserted U.S. priorities, this situation changed radically. President Ronald

---

8 Facing the possibility of another government shutdown and eager to recess in order to campaign for the upcoming elections, Congress combined a number of appropriations in an omnibus appropriations bill.

Reagan withdrew the U.S. from the United Nations Educational, Scientific, and Cultural Organization (UNESCO), which was renowned for its waste, fraud, and opposition to the free flow of ideas in global communications. The U.S. also began to challenge the anti-American proclamations of the U.N. organization by highlighting their hypocrisy. For example, the U.S. criticized the human rights record of Cuba, China, and other communist nations.[9] This determination helped halt many objectionable practices and actually helped bend the U.N. to the will of the U.S. This more muscular approach culminated in the use of the U.N. to prosecute the Gulf War during the Bush Administration.

The lesson should be clear: Insofar as U.S. representatives to the U.N. adhere to their agenda and understand the limits of the institution, the U.S. can block any unwanted action by the U.N. As a last resort, the U.S. always possesses the veto, the mere threat of which is often enough to counter undesired policies. Since the U.N. depends on the U.S. for financial support, it can be influenced by U.S. policy. The threat of fiscal retaliation is an effective deterrent to misguided policies and an impetus for reform.

Another lesson surely is that the U.S. must use threats and influence with great care. Confrontations with the U.N. over reforms and criticism of the organization must be undertaken knowledgeably and without idle threats. The benefits of this approach are exemplified by Ambassador Jeane Kirkpatrick's tenure at the U.N. during the Reagan Administration. Highlights of this period include the first warning of U.S. withdrawal from UNESCO, withholding funding for the International Atomic Energy Agency (IAEA) and the United Nations Relief and Works Agency (UNRWA) in retaliation for discriminatory policy toward Israel, and voting against the U.N. general budget. Threats were carried out after open objections and clear listing of consequences, and U.S. interests were protected.

As a contrast, the Kassebaum-Solomon amendment insisted on specific reforms under threat of withholding contributions. Instead of holding

---

9 John R. Bolton, "The Creation, Fall, Rise, and Fall of the United Nations," paper presented at a Cato Institute conference on "The United Nations and Global Intervention," October 22, 1996.

firm as opposition mounted, the U.S. caved in. As a result, no substantial reforms were realized, and the U.S. was left paying lip service to U.N. reform.

Lesson #2: Attempts to reform the U.N. by working through the "system" — cajoling other member nations and U.N. bureaucrats to work to improve its management — are fruitless. One of the most influential changes in the U.N. since its founding was the emergence of about 100 new nations as the old colonial empires expired. As these countries became incorporated into the U.N., they brought along their own agendas and interests. For the most part, these nations regard the U.N. as an avenue for expanding their power and influence in the world. Consequently, they are firmly opposed to restraining the U.N. In fact, they regard such efforts as attacks on their power base.

Perhaps inevitably, this attitude has become deeply ingrained in the U.N. management structure. Even its most ardent supporters recognize that the U.N. lacks a "management culture." Management decisions, including personnel decisions, are motivated by political considerations that are shared by all the smaller members. One way these countries measure their influence is by securing positions for their citizens; therefore, efforts to trim the bureaucracy are treated as attacks on national prestige.

This mentality has contributed to the growth of the United Nations and is one of the strongest sources of resistance to reform. The U.N. Secretariat, located in New York, and all the affiliated specialized agencies and commissions based throughout the world constitute a massive bureaucracy. The New York bureaucracy alone employs over 10,000 people to guide a labyrinth of agencies, offices, and committees that are commonly irrelevant, ineffective, and duplicative. Many of the U.N.'s employees perform no discernible function except to resist reform and protect the status quo.

The overwhelming support shown by member nations and U.N. bureaucrats for Secretary General Boutros Boutros-Ghali, a bulwark of the status quo, in his battle to win a second term demonstrates that the constituency for meaningful U.N. reform is weak — perhaps even nonexistent. Thus, the U.S. needs to be willing to take a unilateral approach to reform, deciding which U.N. activities to support regardless of its funding obligations to the United Nations.

Lesson #3: Reform of the U.N. organization must be fundamental. The U.N. has fallen prey to the dysfunction of big institutions everywhere, including bureaucratization, the imperatives of self-preservation and perpetuation, and a loss of focus. Reforms over the last several years have been only marginal, despite the fact that the Clinton Administration has made reform the *leitmotif* of its U.N. policy and has pushed some reforms in earnest.

The U.N. system is a massive bureaucracy. U.S. Ambassador to the U.N. Madeleine Albright has described this bureaucracy as "elephantine." The entire U.N. system comprises over 70 agencies and programs and employs over 50,000 personnel. Many of the activities undertaken by U.N. agencies and programs are of little value. The large, expensive conferences, such as the International Conference on Population and Development (ICPD) in Cairo and the U.N. Conference on the Environment and Development (UNCED) in Rio, do little to resolve the problems they are supposed to address. Additionally, U.N. agencies turn out mountains of paperwork and reports that have no discernible impact. These activities are examples of U.N. waste; numerous others exist. America should not support them.

Past reform efforts, by focusing on the symptoms of dysfunction, have failed to address the U.N.'s fundamental problems. Reform must go beyond trimming around the edges to increase efficiency. The hard fact is that many U.N. activities simply are not worth the trouble. For example, the U.N. Development Program (UNDP) has spent billions of dollars advocating counterproductive policies while claiming to aid developing nations. Programs and agencies like the UNDP should be hauled out for transparent review and, in many cases, simply abolished.

Instead of limiting itself to working for reform within the system, the U.S. should present the U.N. with its own terms of participation. Specifically, the U.S. should support the U.N. with an annual appropriation, but at a drastically reduced level of America's own choosing, and should target this support to assist the work of worthwhile agencies and eliminate such particularly egregious agencies and programs as the UNDP, UNESCO, and UNCTAD.

Lesson #4: Proponents of U.N. reform must do more than criticize the U.N.'s waste, fraud, and abuse; they must present a comprehensive blueprint for change. Conservatives have become accustomed to pointing out egregious cases of waste, fraud, and abuse at the United Nations. Nevertheless, pointing out these shortcomings will seem a bit petty if no constructive solutions are proposed. Such horror stories can be a useful weapon in the reformer's arsenal, but they are not sufficient by themselves.

Policymakers need to have in hand a comprehensive blueprint for a revamped U.N. that is significantly reduced in size and scope, and they need to express their willingness to support such a revised structure financially. Defenders of the status quo typically justify the entire U.N. system by pointing to one or two functions that the organization performs. Reformers should acknowledge the few legitimate U.N. functions which warrant American support, but they should also insist that most aspects of the U.N. either need to be reformed or are irrelevant and should be eliminated. Examples of the U.N.'s constructive functions are its ability to serve as a diplomatic forum, as a tool for the advancement of U.S. foreign policy goals, and as a structure for a few useful agencies like the International Civil Aviation Organization (ICAO). Reformers should isolate these aspects of the U.N. for support on a case-by-case basis.

Lesson #5: Congress can influence the U.N. by exercising its "power of the purse." The U.N. is strapped for cash, but this problem is caused by skyrocketing budgets, not by America's failure to pay its dues. Withholding funding has proven to be the most effective way to get the U.N.'s attention and encourage reform. Until the specific reforms desired by the U.S. are completed and implemented, no back dues owed by the U.S. should be paid.

However, Congress should not rely on withholding U.S. arrears as its sole financial weapon. Though the U.N. has felt the strain of reduced funding in the past and desires the liquidity that paid arrears would lend it, paying the current annual U.S. assessment would merely allow it to continue with business as usual. Thus, withholding arrears has little effect on current operations. To have a sustained effect, financial pressure must be applied on an ongoing basis. The U.S. should unilaterally lower its payments to the U.N. below its assessed levels.

This action is particularly important since the U.S. has been voted off of the Fifth Committee, the Advisory Committee on Administrative and Budgetary Questions (ACABQ) which formulates U.N. budgets. The ability of the U.S. to influence U.N. budgetary reform is therefore severely restricted, leaving the congressional appropriations process as the primary avenue through which the U.S. can express its financial concerns and press for reform.

STRATEGIES FOR REFORMING THE U.N.

The U.S. should deal with the United Nations on radically new terms. While this change may be politically difficult to bring about, it will be well worth the effort. The alternatives are an unacceptable status quo or a costly withdrawal from the U.N. There will be no better time for reformers to act: The U.S. relationship with the U.N. is at a crossroads. The U.S. is "in debt" to the U.N. for back dues amounting to some $1.2 billion. The Clinton Administration would like to make good on these arrears and alleviate the U.N.'s financial crisis by paying the back dues over a five-year period in exchange for minor U.N. reforms. The selection of the next Secretary General also is on the 1997 agenda.[10] The Clinton Administration can be counted on to argue that it is essential for the U.S. to be in good financial standing with the U.N. if it wishes to influence this decision. Without a sound reform strategy, the United Nations is sure to be successful in resisting reform.

STRATEGY #1
Congress should require the establishment of a truly independent inspector general's office to conduct an independent audit and review and to oversee U.N. affairs.

The first step toward reform must be an independent audit and review of all U.N. agencies and functions. The U.N.'s many problems can hardly be addressed unless their extent is known in detail. This can be accomplished best by a truly independent inspector general with a staff that is both competent and not subject to the authority of the Secretary

---

10 As this book was going to press, the U.N. chose Kofi Annan of Ghana as the next Secretary General.

STRATEGIES FOR
REFORMING THE UNITED NATIONS

- Congress should require the establishment of a truly independent inspector general's office to conduct an independent audit and review and to oversee U.N. affairs.

- Reform efforts should be focused on reducing the size and scope of the U.N.

- Congress should enforce its constitutional powers to restrict the U.S. role in U.N. peacekeeping.

- Congress should insist that the United States adopt a policy of selective participation in the U.N.

- The focus of the debate should be shifted from waste, fraud, and abuse to the fact that many U.N. efforts have proven to be largely irrelevant.

- The United States should ensure that the next Secretary General is committed to a reform agenda, not to expanding the power of the U.N.

- Congress should focus its attention on the "power of the purse," its most effective weapon in encouraging reform.

- Congressional reformers should refute the "isolationist" label.

- Congress should guide appointments to the U.N. as far as possible.

General and a budget that, once set at a fixed and adequate amount, cannot be manipulated by the Secretary General or even by the General Assembly. The U.N. system has demonstrated considerable resourcefulness in resisting past reform efforts and will not refrain from using budget blackmail to manipulate the inspector general's office.

It is also imperative that the inspector general's office have complete access to all U.N. and related agency records to conduct its review. A primary goal of this audit should be not only to identify corruption, waste, fraud, and abuse, but also to identify which among the U.N.'s 70-plus programs are worth continuing, which should be eliminated, and which tasks should be relegated to other organizations that can perform them better. It is imperative that this audit be completed soon and publicly released.

STRATEGY #2
The U.S. should focus its reform efforts on reducing the size and scope of the United Nations.

The U.N. Secretariat could be scaled down to less than half its current size. This reduction in the overall size of the U.N. bureaucracy would serve a double purpose:

- U.S. taxpayers would save a considerable amount of money. Contrary to U.N. claims, the U.N. and its related agencies do not dedicate the majority of their resources to addressing global problems, such as disease and famine. Instead, the U.N. spends most of this money on bureaucracy. The organization has grown from 1,500 employees and a $20 million budget in 1945 to over 50,000 full-time employees and a $10 billion budget in 1995.[11] The U.N. spends over 70 percent of this huge budget on salaries and related expenses, not on its professed goals.[12]

- Waste, fraud, and abuse would be reduced by restricting the U.N. budget, thereby reducing both the level of the organization's employment and the scope of its activities. If the U.N. were forced to cut manpower, it would be forced to concentrate its efforts more effectively. The U.N. system is currently composed of a haphazard maze of useful and useless organizations, replete with duplication and rife with paralyzing turf fights. For instance, the U.N. has hundreds of agencies, departments, and offices dedicated to agricultural policy. Many organizations seem to do little more than sponsor a never-ending stream of papers and conferences. In 1993, U.S. Ambassador Madeleine Albright detailed a 1991 situation where the U.N. spent $2.5 million to produce a report on the Chernobyl disaster. Not only did the report never appear, but another $2.5 million was requested

---

11 "The United Nations Is Out of Control," *op. cit.*

12 "Is the U.N. Beyond Rescue?," *U.S. News and World Report,* June 5, 1995, p. 42.

to produce a second report explaining why the first report was not produced.[13]

Two scandalous examples of waste during the recent famine in Ethiopia highlight the misplaced priorities of the U.N. While thousands died from a lack of suitable water, U.N. bureaucrats and a well contractor argued for months over the construction details of a well that ultimately took only two days to build. At the same time millions in Ethiopia were malnourished, the General Assembly authorized $73.5 million to construct a U.N. conference center in Addis Ababa that is not expected ever to be fully utilized.[14]

The U.N. has shown a disturbing tendency toward mismanagement and misplaced priorities. The most effective way to reform the U.N.'s management system is to trim the fat from the budget and force the U.N. to rank its functions for funding. However, this is not enough. The U.S. must take an active role in the budget process to help ensure that worthwhile programs are not cut in favor of unworthy efforts; it also must monitor the process on a daily basis, or at least ensure that the inspector general does so.

Reduced funding will minimize the scope of the U.N. but not its influence. The functions that actually lend the U.N. its credibility and good reputation will remain intact if the process is carried out correctly. Additionally, the U.S. role in the U.N. will remain undiminished. The U.S. will still possess its veto and will still be able to use the Security Council for its own purposes, such as mobilizing a political coalition against an enemy as it did in the Gulf War.

STRATEGY #3
Congress should enforce its constitutional powers and restrict the U.S. role in U.N. peacekeeping.

Conservatives in Congress have been uneasy about the expansion of U.N. peacekeeping efforts. Involvement in these efforts has been expensive and has distracted the U.S. military from its prime mission—

---

13 "Some Work Hard, Others Hardly Work at the U.N.," *Chicago Tribune*, September 15, 1993.

14 "The United Nations Is Out of Control," *op. cit.*

defending America and its principal security interests—by dragging the U.S. into conflicts in countries like Somalia and Bosnia that involve no vital American national interest.

Congress has the authority to restrict U.S. participation in U.N. peacekeeping missions. The Constitution grants Congress the sole power to declare war and to authorize the employment of the military or naval forces of the United States. This authority is further supported in Section 6 of the U.N. Participation Act of 1945, which requires that any agreements of the Security Council involving the deployment of U.S. troops, beyond an aggregate total of 1,000 in "support" roles, "shall be subject to the approval of the Congress by appropriate Act or joint resolution."[15]

Congress should restrict U.S. participation in U.N. military operations to the following:

- **The U.S. should support U.N. observation and traditional peacekeeping missions that meet the preconditions for successful peacekeeping.** These preconditions include the existence of a previously concluded peace agreement, the cooperation of the local factions, and the absolute impartiality of the U.N. force. When the U.N. Security Council (and the U.S.) mandate the creation of such an observation or traditional peacekeeping mission, the U.S. should be prepared to support that mission. Such support would include:

  Airlift to move U.S. peacekeeping troops to their areas of operation, as well as other air and naval support that might be needed.

  Equipment from the excess in the U.S. inventory that might be needed by the U.N. mission.

  Logistical support in the form of resupply, staging areas, and base storage facilities.

  Intelligence gathered in the normal course of U.S. global operations.

---

15 From "U.S. Participation in UN Military Actions: Is Advance Congressional Approval Needed?," *CRS Report for Congress,* 95-480 S, April 12, 1995.

Funding of the U.S. share of the peacekeeping budget, which should be reduced to between 15 percent and 20 percent of the total peacekeeping budget.

- **The U.S. should not commit any ground troops to a U.N. peacekeeping mission.** U.N. peacekeeping forces succeed when they are small, lightly armed, and operating passively with the consent of local factions. They perform best when undertaking simple military operations in supportive political environments. There is no need for the U.S. to contribute ground troops to these missions; many other countries are better suited to providing a few impartial peacekeepers. The presence of U.S. ground troops could compromise the neutrality of the U.N. force and undermine its legitimacy.

- **The U.S. should not participate in or mandate U.N.-managed peace enforcement operations.** On occasion, the U.S. may become involved in a peace enforcement operation if it serves the national interest and has clearly defined and attainable military objectives. However, it should work these missions through rehearsed military alliances such as NATO or through an American-led coalition. The United Nations does not have the political legitimacy, military authority, or institutional mechanisms and procedures with which to manage large and complex military operations. Peace enforcement operations often require combat, and combat operations require military forces that are trained to a common standard and operate under an authoritative and responsive command and control structure. The U.N., a voluntary and disparate collection of 185 member states, cannot provide that framework.

Congress also should enforce its constitutional power of the purse. For example, the Clinton Administration has improperly used Department of Defense funds—money earmarked for specific purposes such as training, maintenance, or the stockpiling of goods—to support U.S. participation in numerous peacekeeping operations. The Department of Defense obviously must pay some of the costs of U.S. involvement in peacekeeping missions—missions which, by their very nature, are largely unanticipated. Instead of approaching Congress for supplementary funds to support these missions, however, the Administration has drawn on money already appropriated for other purposes. As a consequence, the original purposes for which those funds were supposed to be used have suffered. Congress should require that the President request additional and separate funding for peacekeeping missions. If the President violates this requirement, Congress should hold hearings on such illegal action.

STRATEGY #4
Congress must insist that the U.S. adopt a policy of selective participation in the United Nations.

Congress must identify which U.N. activities are worthy of support and which are not, and adopt an *à la carte* approach to participating in U.N.-affiliated agencies, commissions, and organizations. Reformers need to be able to identify which U.N. organizations deserve American support. To aid its efforts, Congress must conduct studies of the U.N. system to determine which agencies the U.S. does and does not wish to support. The executive branch has experience in evaluating American participation in U.N. agencies, but Congress needs its own sources of information and analysis in order to reach fully informed and independent judgments.

The list of U.N. organizations that fail to warrant American support includes, but is not restricted to:

- **The United Nations Educational, Scientific, and Cultural Organization (UNESCO).** The United States withdrew from the United Nations Educational, Scientific, and Cultural Organization in 1984 because of the organization's radical politics. Today, the activities of this poorly focused organization are duplicated by several other U.N. organizations, including the World Health Organization (WHO). In 1990, the U.S. Department of State reported that confusion about UNESCO's mission had resulted in "a work program of astounding breadth, with resources spread so thinly that it has often been difficult to discern any measurable impact."[16] Nevertheless, the Clinton Administration has expressed its desire to rejoin the Paris-based organization. The U.S. should not rejoin UNESCO.

16 Thomas P. Sheehy, "Stay Out of UNESCO," Heritage Foundation *Executive Memorandum* No. 403, January 27, 1995.

- **The United Nations Conference on Trade and Development (UNCTAD).** The U.S. should withdraw from the United Nations Conference on Trade and Development, an organization focused on trade, particularly as it concerns the developing world. Throughout its 30 years, UNCTAD has demonstrated its hostility to the private sector, particularly multinational corporations. According to the U.S. Department of State, "[UNCTAD's] ability to play a meaningful and effective role in international economic policy has been extremely limited." The State Department also recognizes that the organization has serious management problems.[17] The few useful activities undertaken by UNCTAD, such as technical analysis of trade issues, should be handled by the World Trade Organization.

- **The United Nations Development Program (UNDP).** The U.S. should eliminate funding (currently $50 million a year) for the United Nations Development Program, the largest of several U.N. development organizations. The UNDP has spent billions of dollars over the years attempting to promote development in the Third World. It can claim few successes. In fact, the very notion that such aid promotes economic development is a fallacy. The Heritage Foundation's *Index of Economic Freedom* examines foreign aid and economic development and concludes that the countries which have lifted themselves out of poverty, such as Chile, Taiwan, South Korea, and Hong Kong, have done so largely because they were deprived of development aid, which often subsidizes statist, anti-growth economic policies. Countries frequently make the necessary free-market reforms, including privatization and trade liberalization, only when they are denied development aid. This was the case in Chile. Washington should withdraw its support for the UNDP.

There are, however, some U.N. organizations that deserve U.S. support. Most of these were established before the United Nations itself. The International Civil Aviation Organization (ICAO) provides the essential service of setting standards for international civil aviation. The World Intellectual Protection Organization (WIPO) provides developing

---

17 "U.S. Views on Reform Measures Necessary for Strengthening the United Nations System," Bureau of International Organization Affairs, February 20, 1996, p. 9.

countries with technical assistance on intellectual property systems and laws. The International Postal Union (IPU) and the International Telecommunications Union (ITU) both provide a service by establishing standards for and coordinating inter-country communications.

Once it identifies which U.N. activities merit continued support, Congress should adopt an à la carte approach to funding. The U.S. should stay in the General Assembly and the Security Council. With respect to the U.N.'s many specialized agencies, however, it should continue to support those which provide valuable services and withdraw from the others. This approach would save the U.S. millions of dollars in annual assessments and contributions. In addition, faced with the possible loss of their largest source of support, these agencies finally might be forced to improve their operations significantly. In other words, at least some U.N. organizations would have to pass a basic market test: They would have to prove their worth to maintain their financial support.

STRATEGY #5

Policymakers seeking U.N. reform need to shift the focus of their message from emphasizing waste, fraud, and abuse to emphasizing how irrelevant much of the work of the U.N. has been.

The message of reformers today is to expose the fraud, abuse, and waste of the U.N. This is not enough. The noble intentions embodied in the United Nations elicit support from the American people.[18] Even though they have heard about the U.N. printing office churning out useless documents ten years after the fact, as well as the U.N.'s shameless featherbedding and incompetent management,[19] Americans remain favorably disposed toward the world body.

---

18 A poll conducted by the United Nations Association of America in April 1996 found 49 percent of those Americans polled believed the U.N. was doing a good job and 64 percent believed the U.S. should always pay its dues.

19 See, for example, "Once Created, Agencies Refuse to Just Fade Away" and "Costly Publications Raise Concerns About Red Ink," *The Washington Post*, September 20, 1992, p. A27; Lichenstein, "We Aren't the World: An Exit Strategy from U.N. Peacekeeping"; "Draining the Swamp," *Time*, October 23, 1995, pp. 74-76.

To convince the American people of the need for substantial reform of the United Nations, reformers need to explain why the U.N. is poorly managed. Until this is done successfully and the American people and moderates in Congress understand the true nature and extent of the problem, they will remain susceptible to the philosophy that adding a few more competent managers to the U.N. staff is all that is needed. However, the U.N.'s problems are far too substantial to be dealt with by a few well-placed managers.

Reformers should emphasize that the U.N. has become so destructively politicized that much of its work is irrelevant. Many U.N. agencies claim an agenda that they cannot hope to effect. For example, few believe that the UNDP "contributes to the sustainable expansion of the world economy," or that the United Nations Industrial Development Organization (UNIDO) does very much to promote industrial development. Many U.N. agencies still promote development aid and redistribution of income as the road to economic development.

The U.N. stands in stark contrast with organizations like the World Trade Organization, whose member states put a premium on competence. The reason: In the WTO, the stakes — decisions on trade disputes involving potentially billions of dollars — are real, and member nations must insist on effective policy and action. The WTO will suffer the consequences of errors, inefficiency, and bad policy. The U.N. does not; no matter how bad its policy, errors, and inefficiency are, its funding and employment continue. This is because member states have allowed the U.N. to be politicized and no longer expect any real results from it.

It is no coincidence that the few specialized agencies providing valuable technical services, such as the International Civil Aviation Organization and the World Intellectual Protection Organization, are the least political and best managed organizations within the U.N. system.

STRATEGY #6
The U.S. should ensure that the next Secretary General is committed to a reform agenda and not to expanding the power of the U.N.

The confrontation between the United States and U.N. Secretary General Boutros Boutros-Ghali over whether he will serve a second term will be the focus of the American relationship with the U.N. until the next Secretary General is selected. In June 1996, the Clinton Administration made public its desire to see a new Secretary General in 1997, citing Boutros-Ghali's lack of commitment to reform. At the same time, Boutros-Ghali announced his intention to challenge the U.S. and its veto power over the Secretary General's post by seeking a second five-year term. This dispute provides a valuable opportunity for reformers to press their agenda.

The Senate Foreign Relations Committee, currently chaired by Senator Jesse Helms (R-NC), should be encouraged to hold "confirmation hearings" for the position of Secretary General. Administration officials, including Ambassador Madeleine Albright, and outside experts on the United Nations should be called to testify concerning the desirability of Boutros-Ghali's serving a second five-year term. These would be mock hearings designed to emphasize the need to oppose Boutros-Ghali, but they also should examine why he is undesirable and what qualities should be sought in a U.S.-backed candidate for Secretary General.

Such "confirmation" hearings on Boutros-Ghali's bid to serve another five years as Secretary General should examine the following issues:

- **Boutros-Ghali's support in 1996 for international taxes to give the U.N. a "minimum of independence from member nations."**

- **Boutros-Ghali's lack of progress in bringing about U.N. reform.** The Clinton Administration over the last several years has made the case that the U.S. should pay the $1.2 billion it owes the U.N. because the U.N. has made significant progress with reform. However, the Administration's opposition to Boutros-Ghali is an acknowledgment that these touted reforms have been insignificant.

- **Boutros-Ghali's forgotten pledge to serve only one five-year term.** At the time of his appointment, Boutros-Ghali stated that not having to campaign for reappointment would free him to bring truly significant reform to the United Nations.

- **Boutros-Ghali's advocacy of U.N. nation-building operations, such as the Somalia peacekeeping operation.** The Secretary General's position was articulated in his 1993 *Agenda for Peace*.

- **Boutros-Ghali's resistance to the creation of a truly independent inspector general's office.**

- **Boutros-Ghali's alleged suppression of the 1993 Thornburgh report on U.N. reform.**

Boutros-Ghali has shown no real interest in his primary responsibility: managing the United Nations. Instead, he has spent the bulk of his time as world diplomat and peacekeeper. The Secretary General is constantly away from the New York bureaucracy, often to campaign for a second term, which reveals his disinterest in managing the world body. Boutros-Ghali's fundamental misunderstanding of his position fuels the unhealthy notion that the U.N. represents more than the sum of its parts: the member states.

While these hearings should be focused on Boutros-Ghali and the Secretary General's office, they also could become an excellent forum for reform-minded policymakers to unveil a new vision for the United Nations. Boutros-Ghali embodies what is wrong with the United Nations. His faults bolster the case for radical reform. Given the likely high drama of this dispute, any congressional hearings would attract a great deal of media attention.

The Clinton Administration may hold firm in its opposition to Boutros-Ghali. It has committed itself publicly to seeing a new Secretary General put in place in 1997. However, Boutros-Ghali enjoys the support of at least three of the five permanent Security Council members: China, France, and Russia. It is not inconceivable that the Administration eventually will back down from a showdown with these and other countries which support Boutros-Ghali. The fact that the Administration has not put forth an alternative Secretary General candidate makes this more likely.

Whether or not the Clinton Administration continues its opposition to Boutros-Ghali's bid for a second term, reformers should be very cautious in proposing an alternative Secretary General. The ideal candidate would be one with management abilities and an understanding that the U.N. serves best as a forum for political discussion. The new Secretary General should not strive to build peace or reconstruct economies.

The U.N. does not need a "world class statesman," as some lawmakers have suggested. In any event, none of the commonly discussed alternatives to Boutros-Ghali fits this description. Some, including Norwegian Prime Minister Gro Brundtland, are socialists and would likely be even more objectionable than Boutros-Ghali. In putting forth a radical reform agenda, conservatives in Congress should not feel compelled to act "constructively" by proposing an alternative candidate; it is the Administration's burden to do this if it so chooses.

STRATEGY #7
Congress should focus its attention on the "power of the purse," its most effective weapon in encouraging reform.

The ability of the U.S. to reform the 185-member United Nations is limited. To the extent that Washington does have leverage, it comes primarily from the fact that the U.S. currently pays 25 percent of the organization's administrative bills (some $313 million in 1996); underwrites 25 percent of the peacekeeping budget ($270 million in 1996, out of a total U.S. assessment of 31.7 percent); and voluntarily contributes as much as $1.5 billion in funds, equipment, and supplies to U.N. peacekeeping missions. Congress must impose fiscal authority, given an Administration that is both sympathetic to the U.N. and limited in its ability to influence the organization's budget.

There are two options in reducing the amount the U.S. is assessed to support the U.N. First, the U.N. budget process is a biennial affair. U.N. budgets are determined in the Fifth Committee and traditionally are not submitted to the General Assembly for vote and approval unless consensus is reached in the Fifth Committee. America had been a member of this committee since its founding but was recently voted out, leaving it effectively marginalized insofar as U.N. budget decisions are concerned. The U.S. is merely one voice among 185 in the General Assembly, which must pass the U.N.'s budget by a majority vote. Thus, the U.S. contributes far more to the U.N. budget than any other member nation but is able to exercise only negligible influence on U.N. budget decisions.

The U.S. representative to the U.N. should make regaining a position on the Fifth Committee a primary goal. Membership on this committee can be used to state clearly the position America will take on a proposed budget while enforcing U.S. fiscal priorities.

The U.S. should attempt to reform the funding process, changing it to the voluntary funding scenario described above in Strategy #4. The U.S. should refuse to vote for any U.N. budget that is unacceptable in size, structure, or priorities. Finally, the Administration should declare that the U.S. is unwilling to fund the U.N. at the current allocation schedule and that it will supply up to a certain set dollar amount or percentage of the administrative and peacekeeping budgets, whichever is less. An appropriate alternative assessment might be a maximum of 20 percent or 15 percent of the entire budget. The General Assembly would still possess the option to fund programs as it wishes; it simply could not demand that the U.S. supply the funding for its wasteful and irrelevant functions.

Because this option relies on the willingness and determination of the U.S. ambassador to the U.N. and U.S. mission staff, it is highly dependent on the Administration for action. No Administration has stated its position on the U.N. budget in the above manner, though recent Administrations have claimed to have set budgetary priorities. This option is very unlikely under a second Clinton Administration. The Clinton Administration prefers to work through the U.N. to advance its foreign policy objectives, and the resentment created by budget demands probably would not be deemed acceptable. Additionally, the Administration's ability to influence the budget is restricted by the lack of U.S. representation on the Fifth Committee.

Thus, a second and more effective capability to reduce the U.S. assessment exists in the authority of the U.S. Congress, which can refuse to pay for objectionable programs and expenses in the U.N. budget assessment. An example of this congressional power over the U.N. budget is the current law which caps the U.S. contribution to the U.N. peacekeeping budget at 25 percent of the total, despite the U.N. assessment of 31.7 percent. This congressional approach could be applied to the U.N.'s general budget as well, or used to further reduce peacekeeping expenditures.

Since 1984, as a consequence of the Kassebaum-Solomon amendment, the U.S. has been in arrears on its U.N. dues. While close to half of the other member states also are in arrears, the U.S. leads the pack by owing the U.N. $1.2 billion, according to U.S. State Department figures (the U.N. disputes this figure, claiming the U.S. is $1.7 billion behind in its payments). However, the U.S. has not linked its arrears with an expressed dissatisfaction over particular U.N. activities. In other words, the U.S. has failed to meet its voluntary commitment (assumed with the signing of the U.N. charter in 1945) to help pay for U.N. expenses while offering no principled rationale for its delinquency.

A truly reform-minded Administration or Congress would explain exactly why it is blocking the U.N. budget. If it became clear that the U.S. was very much alone in its tactics, as would likely be the case, it could then calculate its own contribution based on the activities it deemed worthy of support.[20] In this case, the U.S. would still fall into arrears but at least would have presented a principled rationale for doing so. The U.N. would be forced to make do with what it received from the U.S., with other member states free to make up the financial shortfall.

Driving the U.N. into fiscal disarray is a blunt reform instrument. It is guaranteed to generate hostile press, both at home and abroad. Since the Clinton Administration has expressed its desire to pay America's back dues, the responsibility for U.S. reform efforts falls largely on Congress.

STRATEGY #8
Congressional reformers must refute the "isolationist" label.

Those who would reform the U.N. at the margins and support the status quo, including the Clinton Administration, can be counted on to attack radical reformers as "isolationists." This charge has arisen repeatedly over the last several years as the Administration and the Republican-controlled Congress have dueled over U.N. arrears, foreign aid budgets, Bosnia, and other peacekeeping operations. The establishment media will join in the attack. In responding to these charges, reformers should point out that opposition to a corrupt and fundamentally flawed bureaucracy in New York is anything but isolationism. Rather, it is essential if the U.N. is to pursue its legitimate functions in a proper and effective manner.

Reformers should present an alternative type of internationalism: They should highlight their support for American engagement, including an

---

20 The U.N. assessment table is based on national GDP. It was last reconfigured in 1971 and should be re-examined. It is not healthy for the U.N. to be dependent on one nation for 25 percent of its funding.

endorsement of free trade and a strong American military presence around the world and within security alliances such as NATO. These principles will help blunt the isolationist charge. Reform-minded congressional policymakers must be cautious in dealing with those who call for immediate U.S. withdrawal from the United Nations without giving the U.N. at least a limited amount of time to implement reform.

STRATEGY #9
Insofar as it is able, Congress should guide appointments to the United Nations.

In the past, Congress has been reluctant to express its will with respect to U.N. appointments, and the President typically expects to appoint whomever he wishes. However, given the anticipated importance of the U.N. issue over the next several years, congressional oversight of these appointments is appropriate. If Congress wishes to guarantee that its reform agenda will be advanced, it must supervise the staffing of the U.S. mission to the U.N. to ensure that it is staffed with people who are motivated to advance the interests of the U.S. The Kirkpatrick team, arguably one of the most effective in recent decades, for the most part was not staffed with people possessing extensive knowledge of the U.N., but they did possess the correct attitude and were determined to protect the interests of the U.S. first and foremost.

In the Senate confirmation hearings, proponents of reform must require appointees to state their position on U.N. reform. The Administration must be required to list specific reform and funding goals. If the Administration fails to follow through on its goals, Congress should hold hearings on why reform has not been pursued. Statements from the confirmation process can serve as the basis for these hearings, providing evidence and political ammunition for congressional reformers.

CONCLUSION

America must remain engaged in political and economic affairs worldwide to ensure that its interests are protected. Influencing world opinion and events through international organizations such as the United Nations is important to this objective. However, after 51 years of membership in the U.N., it is time to reassess the efficacy of this organization. The U.N. was founded to maintain international peace, promote economic prosperity, and advance fundamental human rights. Instead, it stands as a monument to inefficiency, waste, fraud, abuse, and bureaucratic paralysis. The time for reform has come. In an era of budgetary crises and nebulous foreign policies, reform is not a luxury, but a necessity.

The U.S. must decide what its new role in the United Nations will be. The U.S. should present to the U.N. a listing of its terms of participation. And while the U.S. should continue to support the U.N. with an annual appropriation, the amount should be of America's own choosing. The only way to bring about a fundamental "reinvention" of the United Nations is through such a strong statement of U.S. leadership predicated on the power of the purse.

The U.S. should follow a policy of selective participation in the U.N., utilizing the organization's functions and world presence only when doing so helps to build support for U.S. diplomatic initiatives, foreign policy objectives, and military interventions. Through selective participation, the U.S. can participate diplomatically in the U.N.'s attempts to address global concerns and in its social, economic, and humanitarian activities on a case-by-case basis. America must always pursue its own agenda; it must never allow its vision to be superseded or altered by the concerns of international bureaucrats whose interests often conflict directly with those of the United States. Participation in the United Nations can benefit America only if the U.N. undergoes reform and only if it is on terms the United States itself has established.

INDEX

The following is provided as a general reference guide to primary individuals, issues, actions, occurrences, and organizations presented by the authors in *Mandate for Leadership IV*. Cross references have been included to aid in finding related information.

Churchill, Winston, and leadership of, 506
Civil Rights Act (1991), 328
civil service, 199-243
  appointments approach under Clinton, 207, 214-15
  appointments approach under Reagan, 213
  and careering-in abuses, 209
  and chart of current structure of, 226
  and merit pay, 219, 221-23
    building support for, 236-38
  muddying of functions under Clinton Administration, 207-08
  and opposition to reform from the permanent government, 199
  as part of permanent government, 199
  and federal employees performance appraisal system, 220
  and reductions-in-force (RIF) procedures, 220-21
  reductions under Bush, 227-28
  reductions under Reagan, 225-29
  reductions under Reagan, Bush, Clinton, compared, 213-15, 225-29
  reform of
    benefits, 223
    career and non-career functions, 206, 216, 218, 240
    and commissions, 205, 231-32
    and duplication of federal programs, 233
    Hatch Act weakened under Clinton Administration, 201, 209
    and Iron Triangle, 201
    and National Performance Review, 213, 220
    and 104th Congress, 200
    and payment system, 238
    and political appointments, 210-12
    and retirement programs, 229-31, 234-35
  and role of Office of Presidential Personnel (OPP), 216
  and theories of government, 203-04, 213-15, 218, 235-36
  and "core-spoke-rim" model, 235-36
  and use of labor-management councils, 217-19, 238, 242
Civil Service Reform Act (CSRA) (1978), 202, 216, 219
  and use of in improving management and accountability, 219, 238
Clean Air Act Amendment. *See* regulation, Clean Air Act Amendments (1990)
Clean Water Act (1977), compliance with, 98
Clinton Administration, 402, 405
  and adoption, 195
  and AmeriCorps, 194-95
  and Anti-Ballistic Missile (ABM) Treaty, 402
  approach to achieving an agenda, 7
  approach to civil service reform, 204, 213
    and career and non-career functions of civil service, 209
    and civil service reform, 219
    and muddying of civil service functions, 207
    and reductions in civil service, 227, 228
    and use of labor-management councils, 217-19, 238, 242
    and "reinventing" the civil service, 212-13
  attitude to abortion, 195
  and Bosnia, 581
  and Bottom-Up Review (BUR), 512
  and Chechnya, 597
  and China, 586
  compared to Reagan Administration, 7
  and democracy, 398-99
  and Cuba
    response to downing of U.S. civilian aircraft, 592
    U.S. embargo of, 402